ALSO BY BRADLEY K. HAYNES

HOW YOU CAN GROW RICH THROUGH
RURAL LAND - Starting From Scratch

THE IdealESTATE MAN: A novel

How I Turned $50 into $5 million in Country Property –Part Time

And How You Can Do the Same

B.K. Haynes

How I Turned $50 into $5 Million
in Country Property–Part Time
And How You Can Do the Same

For information contact: Greatland Publishing Company
501 South Royal Ave, Front Royal, VA 22630.

FIRST EDITION
Designed by Charles Thorne Graphics

Library of Congress Cataloging-in-Publication has been applied for.
ISBN 0-932586-03-1

Acknowledgments

In early January of 2003, I entered the fortieth year of my experience with country properties. These years have taught me much more than I have learned from books; yet experience teaches us much too slowly, allowing age to consume our bodies and minds. So we turn to books as we grow in life to deliver us from the sin of ignorance and to help cultivate our thoughts.

The sure sign of knowledge comes quickly down to us in the written page. Knowledge, of course, if focused properly and not diffused, can also lead to power and the ability to achieve your goals in life. It is my feeling that knowledge, in the general sense of the word, exists only to be shared. With this thought in mind, I decided to write down what I learned in the field of country properties and to pass it on. In January, 2004, while recovering from hip surgery, I completed this work.

The following people helped me to pull this book together: My son, Bradley K. Haynes, Jr., CCIM; my assistant, Leah Williams; Charlie Thorne of Charles Thorne Graphics; Marc Adams, editor; and my brother Wally, who furnished historical family background.

CONTENTS

Effective Resources

Introduction

I was twenty-seven, married, and two years out of George Washington University with a degree in Business Administration. But I never attended my graduation exercises, and you won't find me in the yearbook. The fact is, I had never planned to go to college, never aspired to receive superior grades, and have never formally graduated from any elementary, middle, or high school, or any other public or private school, other than Leadership School in the U.S. Army – a cadre for training troops. I suspected this was a school for misfits, and the Army no doubt sent me there because I was active in organizing variety shows for the troops, where I sang and acted as master of ceremonies. I did this in my late teens at military bases and hospitals all over the Washington, D.C. area during the Korean War. So it was that I both entertained *and* trained the troops. I thank the Army for my college education under the G.I. Bill, and in which I reached the lofty rank of PFC.

I boarded a bus for the Army with my guitar, few close friends, and no girl to write home to, or from whom I would receive mail. Mail call, in a family of soldiers, can deliver the deadly pierce of loneliness.

During college, after appearing in an amateur production of a musical, *The Boy Friend*, all of the cast went to New York to meet back stage with professional actors performing the same play off-Broadway. I married after college and never went back to New York because I didn't think my wife could take the stress of living in a tenement with a struggling entertainer. So I began writing songs, singing, and playing guitar around the D.C. area and getting nowhere. Now here I was, two years after college, still bumbling aimlessly around, rejected for both graduate and law school, writing radio and television commercials, selling hot nuts in vending machines – a dead-broke loser, half living on my wife's salary as a bank bookkeeper. But I never lost hope and, as strange as it may seem, throughout my life I have enjoyed the good fortune of being generally underestimated by my foes and competitors and of being blessed by recurring failure.

The perceived misfortune of failure often comes from the lack of energy, not from empty pockets or formal education, the latter of which can largely be a waste of time to entrepreneurs and may even breed a degree of inferiority. My masters degree came from peddling peanuts and mucking out horse stalls, my doctorate from writing books and hustling country properties.

In 1963, I shelled out fifty bucks on a riverfront lot, thinking against reality that I would start a boys' camp. A few months later I traded the lot for a shell cabin on five acres and opened a riding stable. In 2004 – forty-one years later – that fifty dollars has turned into five million. After launching a large corporation and becoming a millionaire by 1969, I traveled around the world with my wife, young son, and a maid. I then downsized myself into semi-retirement following the recession of 1970. Throughout the seventies, I spent most of my time writing, traveling, helping to raise my son, and enjoying life, only to seriously return to work when I felt I needed the cash.

Along the way, I started a publishing company in the eighties, taught a college course on land development, rebuilt my development company, downsized it again after the recession of 1990, and returned to a life of relative leisure.

Now, semi-retired again on my farm, I work when I want to, with lots of time to read, write books and a screenplay, play the piano, ride horses, travel, and fly my super cub airplane from my private airstrip. How did I do it? I have always freely given information to those venturing into country real estate, either as a career field, investment goal, or simply with the objective of buying the right land or property. I have observed over the years that most of those who have followed my advice have profited significantly, and a great many careers have been launched, or jump-started, through the advice given in my book, *HOW*

YOU CAN GROW RICH THROUGH RURAL LAND–Starting from Scratch. Some of you may say, "That was then; this is now. Times have changed, and the same opportunities are fewer now." To a certain extent, and for the avowed pessimist, this sentiment could ring true. However, for the optimist and positive thinker, I suggest that opportunities come to all, but many simply fail to recognize them.

I am not writing this book because I feel the world needs another "short-cut" book about making money; nor is this a complicated instructional manual, or a treatise on my memoirs. Knowledge is your ultimate good, and it should be imparted, not hoarded. The art of teaching it is another thing, and what I have learned is not mine to keep but what I can hand down to you for your gain. The world does not care how talented or how smart you are. To succeed in life you must go boldly forth and present your case; otherwise you will be left behind.

As a fifteen-year-old, pedaling off with a dog in my bicycle basket to a shadowy future, and abandoning a broken home and thoughts of further education, I knew *who* I was but not by any means *what* I was to become. And along the road I encountered very few genuine and beneficent mentors, along with a host of losers. Life's highways are littered with angry losers for whom there appears to be little sympathy, while the winners can appear to do no wrong.

If you think that life has let you down, I suggest to you that there is a divinity in life that shapes our ends. This does not mean that our destiny is preordained. It simply means that we must not nourish such negative feelings as failure and discontent. Faith, hope, love, and charity are all fundamental Christian principles, with faith being the primary force in life. We must have faith in ourselves of course, but we must also believe in an eminently higher power, lest we fall in love with ourselves and become consumed by the fires of egotism. Faith is the fuel of accomplishment. Without faith, you are running on fumes and you will soon burn out. Hope is the mother of faith, a comforting principle that embodies the expectation that we will succeed. Both virtues –faith and hope–are unleashed through the acknowledged power of positive thinking. Love beats hate and anger hands down. It is simply no contest. Hatred, however, is unmistakedly self-punishment.

And intemperate anger strikes at only ourselves and loved ones. Hatred, discrimination, and intense dislike of your fellow man are like misguided arrows shot back into your own heart.

Love is ethereal and volatile. It can be *perverted* through unrighteous anger, envy and pride. It can be rendered *defective* by sloth and greed, and its delicate nature can be *despoiled* by gluttony and lust.

It is said that in the perfect Christian family, the virtues of mothers are equal to those of the father, with the children forming a common bond of love and care. I say that, in my family, the mother was superior in virtues, this because of her indomitable spirit to keep our family together as best she could in the face of an errant and irresponsible father. Though I honor them both, her influence and affection did much to form my destiny.

My mother was born on April 22, 1909 on a farm near a small town in northern Virginia called The Plains. The farm was nestled in a valley at the base of Bull Run Mountain to the west of Washington, D.C. A wide stream called Broad Run rippled, and often roared, through the cow pasture. She was the second child in a family of six. Her mother died after giving birth to the youngest child, Johnny; this when my mother was about eight years old. The family was poor, and my mother had to care for the younger children. Her father, John Hitaffer, ran the farm for a wealthy lawyer in Washington, D.C.–a man of many wives, one of whom was a Zeigfeld Follies dancer. John, at age 31, married Lilly Soper, a young lass of about half his age.

The family moved to Beltsville, Maryland some time after Lilly died, bequething maternal guardianship of the family to Lucy, then nine. Their home was the old McCoy's Tavern building on Vansville Hill by the Baltimore-Washington Turnpike. George Washington sometimes stopped at the tavern in the late 1700's on his way to Philadelphia and New York. John worked as a farrier at his shop in the historic tavern. In his labor as a blacksmith, John invented a new plow blade that was adopted by many farmers in the area.

When she was young, my mother was socially isolated from children, other than companionship from her brothers and sisters. She lived in poverty on the Virginia farm and at the shop in Beltsville where she had to tend the younger children after school. Classmates at school taunted her, in part because of the plain and tattered clothing that she wore, dresses often crudely tailored from potato sacks. The classmates sang to the Hitaffer girls, "Ching ching Chinaman sitting on a fence, trying to make a dollar out of fifteen cents." Despite the harassment and mockery, Lucy was a good student. Her seventh-grade report card showed all A's in health, behavior, and scholarship, even though she was absent from class 24 days during that year.

My grandfather, John Hitaffer, was a brutal man with an angry disposition. Around 1920, John married Hattie D. His choice for a stepmother to his children was more appropriate to the selection of a prison guard. Hattie worked as a matron in a youth correctional institute. The two of them made life miserable for the children. John beat my mother's older brother so severely that one day he borrowed a friend's bicycle and ran away to Virginia. The young boy was taken in by a doctor who treated his injuries and raised him as one of his own children, this after reporting the cruelty to local authorities. My mother and the older children were subsequently removed from the abusive home and placed in foster care around 1921 or 1922. The youngest child, Johnny, then about five years old, was left with his father and stepmother when the family was broken up.

Lucy, my mother, a pubescent 12-year-old at the time, was assigned to the family of Irving Miller, an insurance executive. The Millers treated her with kindness. She shared her new home with the five Miller children and was eventually given her own room and spending money in return for household work. The 1930 census lists her as a servant with housework duties. Although the Miller children were enrolled at the private Sidwell Friends School in Washington, D.C., my mother attended Hyattsville High School. When she was about 15 years old and a member of the *Washington Post* Junior Writer's club, the *Post* held a contest for essays and poems about "The Flag and What It Means to Me." My mother won a prize for her composition. She was presented with an award on June 14, 1924 at the Metropolitan Theater in Washington, D.C.

As a teenager, my mother and a younger sister managed to make their way across the Potomac River into northern Virginia to search for relatives living there. At dusk, they came upon the house where one of the grandmothers was living. It was a run-down shack in the Virginia countryside. The old woman who lived there, my mother's maternal grandmother, appeared at their knock on the door like an apparition. Before them, in the shadow of a setting sun and candle light, hovered a disheveled-looking hag. The witch was not happy to see the frightened young girls, but she reluctantly led them into the shack, stoked the fire beneath a kettle, and quickly vanished into the night. Neighbors told my mother that the withered crone made a living brewing moonshine.

Those were the days of Prohibition, and the demand for alcohol was strong enough to support the hasty construction of illegal stills throughout the back woods of rural Virginia. There was no food in the house, so the two girls trudged through the fields in the dim light of dusk to the nearest store where they could buy something to eat. They then hurried back to the shack to spend the night. At the glimmer of dawn, the old woman was yet only an apparition. The girls returned to Maryland and never established a relationship with their long-lost family.

After high school graduation, my mother attended the University of Maryland for about a year. There she met a gentleman whose father owned a grocery and clothing store. Years later, after managing the store, he inherited the business from his father. Clifford was the first real boyfriend in my mother's life. Lucy was a pretty and shapely girl with a quiet and gentle personality. She was also intelligent, hardworking, and had modeled at the National Gallery of Art for nude paintings. Clifford asked her to marry him, and she consented. While she was shopping for a wedding dress in Washington, D.C., she stopped at a cafe for lunch. There she met a young man who was waiting tables. To everyone's astonishment, especially Clifford's, Lucy fell for the smooth-talking waiter and turned her back on Clifford. Two days later she married my father.

Sins of our Fathers

My Dad, Lawrence (Larry) Haynes, was the first born in a family that had settled in Erie, Pennsylvania. He was about five years old when the family moved to Iowa. Larry's father, Lynford, attended college in Ames, Iowa to study agriculture journalism. Lynford later went to work in Des Moines, Iowa as an editor for Henry Wallace, Sr., who published *Wallace's Farmer*, an agricultural magazine. Wallace became United States Secretary of Agriculture in 1921.

When Larry was about 11 years old, he moved with his family to Maryland. Larry's father, Lynford, had been invited to work for Henry Wallace, Sr. at the Department of Agriculture in Washington, D.C. Lynford progressed rapidly in his job, eventually becoming personal assistant to Secretary Wallace. After Wallace died in 1924, Lynford continued in his job until 1929, when, for some reason, he was reprimanded, demoted, and ordered to submit to a physical examination. Shortly afterward, Larry's father left the government to devote full time to his own business, a printing and mailing establishment called Standard Business Services. It was during the Great Depression, and Lynford struggled to keep his fledgling business alive to support his family. Lynford's wife died in 1931, leaving the family of two boys and four girls without a mother.

Larry Haynes, a handsome young man who knew how to charm women and take their money, was twenty years old in 1930 and was expected to take care of himself. Sometimes he took money from other people. Once he arranged to provide the entertainment for a church function. The church sold tickets to its members. Haynes family members also sold and bought tickets to the event. The money was turned over to my father so he could pay the entertainers.

The only entertainment provided for the festivity was the disappearing act that my father did with the money. The congregation was not amused.

My father dreamed about having his own family. His favorite song was "My Blue Heaven," and he made the older children sing the words ". . .a turn to the right. . .a little white light. . .will lead you to my blue heaven. Just Molly and me. . .and baby makes three. . ."

He realized that dream when he met and married my mother. She was happy for the first year or two, but by the time I was born she realized that something was wrong with my father. He was unable or unwilling to support the family. He was seldom home, often beat her, and was often in jail for one reason or another. The Salvation Army stepped in and arranged for the family to move to a row house near Union Station in Washington D.C. They also furnished the house and supplied clothing and household goods. My mother said that she should have stopped having babies after I was born in 1934. From that year on the family was on a slow decline to eventual destruction.

Larry was pleasant and cheerful when he wasn't drinking, but as time went on he was seldom without a bottle of rye whiskey in his hip pocket. Sometimes he would disappear for days, weeks, months, without telling my mother he was leaving or where he was. Sometimes he was in the clink for fighting in neighborhood streets and back alleys, and on numerous occasions he was seen drunk when staggering on or off buses or trolleys.

And he frequently embarrassed my mother and caused dissension in the family by being discovered in compromising situations with other women. My mother usually got pregnant when my father returned from his tomcatting and drunken binges. He would then shape up, finesse his way into a job, and con his boss with some slick ideas to get his hands on big money. His passion for easy money reached ridiculous heights when he applied for and was actually given the job of a security guard in a Brinks armored car. My mother, fed up with his errant behavior and philandering, decided she would have to support the family without him. So she took to the streets looking for full-time work.

World War II had begun, and employment opportunities for women suddenly opened up. My mother's first steady job was at the Bureau of Engraving and Printing in Washington, D.C. Her main task was to feed the paper during the process of printing money and certificates. As a seven-year-old kid, I thought it was an important job because she told me they always searched employees when they entered or left the pressroom. One day my father showed up at her workplace and tried to get inside so he could talk the payroll clerk into giving him her paycheck. The guards knew what he was up to and threw him out.

My father was not called to military service during the war because he was supposed to be supporting a family of eight. My mother, watching Dad drain the family of its resources and contributing very little money toward its existence, went to the draft board and told them about her husband's consistent irresponsibility. The board soon drafted Daddy into the Army, and Mom began receiving regular allotment checks from his military pay. He was eventually assigned to recruitment duty, and despite some disciplinary actions he worked his way up to staff sergeant.

I remember Mom once listening to the song, "The Old Lamplighter." She started to cry, and I asked her why she was crying. She told me that it reminded her of the time she was in love with Daddy. When she first met him, he worked occasionally as an assistant to the park lamplighter. Even though I was very young, I understood the heartbreak she felt, because her dreams had vanished, and the love had died with his drinking, philandering, and physical abuse.

Around 1948, my father went to work for Jacque, a restaurateur and lawyer from New York who owned a restaurant in Washington, D.C.

Dad dreamed up an office catering operation for the restaurant that flopped. But one plan that my father presented to Jacque was truly brilliant.

He persuaded him to hire my mother. Most of Jacque's employees were heavy drinkers and unreliable. Jacque quickly discovered that my father had the same faults. My mother proved to be different. She was a nondrinking good worker, and she was reliable. When Jacque got to know her and learned about her family, he began to understand the difficult situation that confronted her. He admired her for her work ethic and strong desire to take care of her family. Jacque came to depend on my mother to help manage the restaurant, and, because of her reliability and dedication to her job, he was able to open a second restaurant.

At that time, in the early 50s, some of our family lived in a rooming house near Dupont circle in Washington, D.C. An alleyway behind the restaurant led from the house to the restaurant, so it was just a short walk for my mother to get to and from work. Jacque had fired my father, but Daddy occasionally showed up at the house. One day, while my mother was at work, someone told her that my father had a woman with him in the house where we were living. My mother left the restaurant and found my father in bed with the woman. Deeply upset and in tears, she told him to get out and never come back.

The friendship that my mother developed with Jacque became fondness and perhaps more than that. They spent lengthy periods with each other away from work, taking short trips to places like Ocean City in Maryland. They were going to get married, but Jacque died suddenly of a heart attack. The emotional blow devastated my mother, leaving her depressed for a considerable amount of time.

My mother was 58 years old before she learned to drive a car. She got a job driving for two elderly couples who wanted to tour the U.S. But it was not a pleasant experience for her.

So she quit the job and moved to Albuquerque, New Mexico, to be near my sister and her family. All of my family but myself and a younger brother had since relocated to the western states. Mom lived alone for a while in Albuquerque. She learned to make Ojo's (pronounced Oho's), the Indian name for a craft item that represents the eye of God. The Ojo's she crafted were of good design and quality. Those that she sold had a card attached to them noting that they were made by "Luci," the native American name she adopted for her craft work. She also learned to paint western scenes in watercolors and oils.

The Path to God

While she was living alone, my mother fell and hit the back of her head on the bathtub. She was stunned and temporarily blinded. At that moment, the phone suddenly started ringing. She crawled to the telephone by following the sound of the ring. It was my brother, Jim, calling to check on her. She might have died right there because of the bleeding and damage to her brain if Jim had not gotten immediate medical attention for her.

Over the next several years, my mother continued to suffer additional bleeding and consequential damage to her brain. Most of the time she seemed rational and coherent, but occasionally she became disoriented and confused. When her condition worsened, she was taken to a convalescent center in Santa Fe, New Mexico, where she shared a room with another patient. The nursing staff helped my mother with her daily clothing, bathing, eating, and wheelchair movement.

But the environment was clearly not to her liking. Although her body continued to be in reasonably good health, my mother's mental condition and paralysis were getting worse. She was spending most of her time in bed. Her ability to speak coherently was gone. But she seemed to be aware of events occurring around her, and she still had a glimmer of remembrance. On a visit to her in Albequerque, I walked into the room and over to her bedside. Her eyes lit up and she said to me, "Hello, son." And then her mind resumed its child-like state, reacting to me as if I were not even there. My mother died on the 14th of August, 1991 in Santa Fe. I loved her deeply.

Love, in a material world, can be likened to our frame of mind after tasting prosperity. Once richly blessed, we have a tendency to become fat and happy (a general oxymoron–but our shortcomings seem infinitely more beautiful when we're in love) or we may feel we have stumbled upon the goose that laid the golden egg. Indeed, viewed through the tearily infatuated eyes of the suddenly prosperous, the fair goose appears to possess the wings of an angel.

Yet when the golden eggs have become too burdensome for us to carry, we curse the ugly creature that has deceived us, only to seek salvation for our lost and misguided souls through our penance to charity.

With these thoughts in mind, we can get down to business with a brief recounting of Napoleon Hill's fundamental success principles uncovered from the tombs and times of the world's richest men. These essential guidelines have driven and motivated achievers throughout the ages and have played a crucial role in the construction of my career. You may want to bring them to mind and work positively on those mental qualities in which you may find yourself deficient:

(1) Develop the savings habit
(2) Build self-confidence
(3) Strive for self-control
(4) Sharpen your concentration
(5) Tune up your cooperation with others
(6) Follow the golden rule
(7) Develop imagination
(8) Mold a pleasing personality
(9) Cultivate patience and tolerance
(10) Learn to profit from past failures
(11) Rehearse for leadership
(12) Pursue a definite chief aim in life
(13) Think accurately
(14) Go the extra mile; do more for the money
(15) Practice enthusiasm.

As I have begun to write this book at the end of 2002, my net worth is about four million dollars. I don't consider this fact to be significant, other than to prove a point, because the pursuit of wealth for the sake of riches has never been a particular goal of mine. But I know enough about goal-setting and positive thinking to know that by the time this book is published in 2004, I will have reached the five million mark. I could have multiplied that figure five times over if I had worked full time at making money. The point I make is revealed in a simple mantra repeated over and over in the minds of positive thinkers and successful entrepreneurs throughout history: *"Whatever the human mind can conceive can be achieved."*

Thought Forms

To gear up your mind for your grand ideas and goals in life, it can be helpful to develop the habit of examining your thoughts before you act, this to determine whether or not you are on the right track: I have identified eleven of these basic thought forms:

1. **GOOD -** *Do unto others*

2. **BAD -** *Kill your neighbor*

3. **ERRONEOUS -** *Half truthful*

4. **LOGICAL -** *Does it work?*

5. **EMOTIONAL -** *Think before you act*

6. **EGOCENTRIC -** *In love with yourself*

7. **FANCIFUL-** *Escape from reality*

8. **CONSTRUCTIVE -** *Positive thinking*

9. **CONTEMPLATIVE -** *Thinking without acting*

10. **JUDGMENTAL -** *Speaking without hearing*

11. **PASSIVE** - *The mind's trash*

Before rushing into a decision, it is beneficial and advisable to identify the thought or thoughts that are compelling you to act. You will realize that many of your decisions require multiple thoughts. For example, a most dangerous and counterproductive combination would be a mind-poisoning mixture of erroneous, egocentric and emotional thoughts. Once this compound is identified, you should attempt to immediately retract your line of thinking. A beneficial thought pattern would obviously be a model of good, logical, and constructive characteristics.

It should be apparent to most readers who must work for a living that the accumulation of riches in life is not an easy task. The fabric of your life is woven thread by thread. The habit of identifying your thoughts on a regular and persistent basis has a tendency to sharpen your mind and can help you to (1) make better decisions and (2) correct your mistakes and give you more power to reach your goals. This process, if used in combination with your development of the aforementioned fifteen success principles, will allow you to outdistance your competitors and to overcome the obstacles that may have held you back.

PART ONE

Little or No Money Down

If you had a sailboat, empty pockets, and grand ideas about crossing the ocean, you would certainly need wind in your sails. But, of more importance, you would need someone with deep pockets to finance your voyage. The winds of chance blow for us all. In successfully undertaking a voyage to financial independence, it is the lack of adequate provisions that could hold you back. By the sweat of the brow, we spend precious time on the docks of time, sacrificing opportunity for mere survival.

Simply put, we miss out on the grand voyages of our lives because we spend most of our time making money, merely to survive on the corrosive docks of the world. Our investments are often short-sighted and meager. The rich, in general terms, sacrifice neither wealth nor sweat, because they can afford to live off of the sweat of others, this primarily in the form of interest on their investments. When those of modest means borrow money from other people to pursue and acquire perishable and pleasurable things in life, they often discover themselves aground on a sandbar of debt. The debt-laden person, if emboldened with grand ideas and great expectations, could find his trip to riches cancelled or indefinitely postponed.

Your journey to riches begins with money from other peoples' pockets, unbridled initiative, and innovative thinking. Think about the monster wave of 77 million baby boomers now approaching retirement, many of whom see themselves at home in the countryside. This tsunami is surging beyond the cities into outlying areas and eroding all manner of containment by social engineers. Massive Social Security and Medicare obligations will soon be cast ashore, inflating the economy, and watering down the value of the dollar. Riding this wave are the second careerists, who can work from their homes, and who are seeking a more laid-back lifestyle. Lurking in the storm clouds behind this wave of change is an insidious armada of terrorists, indoctrinated with hatred of western civilization, and bent on destroying our cities and industries and changing our culture through violence. More and more people will seek economic security and family safety in the countryside and small towns. Market forces are swallowing up country properties today at a pace and financial thrust that dwarf the giant recreational boom of the sixties. You can start off in a small way, as I did with $50 – say $500 or $1,000 in this day and age–and invest in pleasurable and enduring country property in a multitude of ways.

I routinely make million-dollar deals with no money down. Later on in this book I will show you how to locate country properties for investment or development and how to accurately score them for potential worth. Wise investments in country properties can catapult you from the dock of failure and frustration to the deck of your ship embarked toward your destination of financial independence. If you're big on ambition and short on funds–as I was when I started–you may ask: "How do I get on board the money boat if I don't have the fare?" I can think of at least fifty proven ways.

Refinance 100% of the Acquisition Cost

This method is possible even when the property appraises lower than the selling price. Assuming you buy a fixer-upper in the country with a little land and divide it into two or more lots before closing, your small subdivision can be worth more than your purchase price for the property as a whole. And even though your lender may have a policy of loaning, say, only 80% of the appraised value, he may lend you all you need on the basis of a possible pre-sold contract(s) on the divided parcels. Of course, you would support the value of your subdivision with an appraisal of the subdivided lots. Experienced developers often finance 100% or more of the land, plus improvements costs, based on values established through legitimate appraisals.

Pre-Sell Improvements to Raise the Down Payment

Assume you can't raise enough cash for the down payment on a 100-acre farm, but you have a buyer for the house and five acres. If your credit is good, your lender may accept the assignment of a purchase contract, or possibly a letter of intent, from this sale as your down payment. After your closing on the farm, or through a simultaneous closing (your buyer closes along with your purchase of the farm) the lender agrees to release the house parcel from the first lien. The lender credits the sale of the house parcel to your loan and–depending on the appraised value of the remainder–the lender can possibly provide you with additional cash to further develop the farm.

Refinance with Seller Taking Back a Second Mortgage

You've been ogling a quaint old country house on three acres with a running stream. The sellers have advertised the place for $125,000. They still owe $100,000. You know enough about property values in that area to figure the house and land are worth around $150,000, maybe more. You offer $120,000, and the owners accept; but they want to close right away and move to a retirement village in Florida. You have good credit and can qualify for a loan through your bank.

The problem is you have a light wallet, and a hefty down payment is required to lift the deal.

You discuss your situation with the sellers and bring up the possibility of the sellers taking advantage of declining interest rates on their other investments and refinancing their $100,000 loan while rates are low.

If they are in a hurry to sell, they can pick up a bundle of cash and loan you $12,000 at an attractive rate for the down payment (questionable if the lender asks for the source of your down payment). Your qualification for the new loan amount effectively takes them off the mortgage hook. They can then head south with a second mortgage in their portfolio, this securing their loan to you. The sellers could likely get a significantly higher yield on this second trust than they would derive from the stock market if they had completely cashed out and reinvested a portion of the proceeds. You hold the property for a short period of time, possibly make a few cosmetic improvements, obtain an appraisal that reflects the true worth of the property, and then sell at a handsome profit.

Use a Note for the Down Payment

In troubled economic times, you will often nestle up to a buyers' market in real estate, and sellers will be more inclined to make a deal to move the wheel. In this version of the "no money down" deal, you offer a promissory note for the down payment on your investment and then follow through with owner or bank financing. Both you and the seller realize that cash is king, but times are tough, and kings are under siege. You pledge your good faith note for entry into the deal, possibly producing your end of the closing costs. The seller secures the note with a first or second mortgage against the property. If, after closing, you default on a secured note, the seller can, of course, foreclose and, if necessary and deemed advisable, seek a judgment against you for any monetary deficiency as the result of a foreclosure auction. Also, keep in mind the fact that some lenders will require written disclosure from you as to the source of your down payment.

Use Your Home for the Down Payment or Full Amount

For the right deal, it may make sense to use your home as a source of acquisition money, or as collateral for a loan to buy country property. You may also consider refinancing, or taking on a second mortgage to raise investment capital. But remember, until you are firmly established as a successful investor, it is generally not wise to risk core real estate assets, such as your home, for speculative projects, particularly if you are cash poor. I recall an attractive riverfront project, where I, along with my partners, were required by the bank on a foreclosure sale to pledge our homes as additional collateral for a no-money-down loan in excess of a million dollars. For me, as an experienced developer and investor, the deal was risk-free, since I had developed a great many riverfront projects over the years. Experience has taught me that profits are at the front end of a development project.

If your expectation is that profits are shipped to you with the last lot sold, you may only see the stern lights of your money boat.

Provide Services for the Down Payment or for the Property

Lawyers, doctors, building tradespeople, surveyors, engineers, accountants, etc. all have services they can offer sellers in lieu of a down payment on country property. A soils scientist made a pile of money from me by trading services for a couple of rural lots on the outskirts of a growing town. Within a year, the value of the lots more than doubled. A handyman agreed to remodel an old home in return for acreage sold from an estate. Surveyors routinely accept subdivided lots in return for their work. What do you have to offer?

Use a Real Estate Commission as Your Down Payment

If you are a licensed real estate agent, you can, of course, with proper disclosure and broker's consent, transfer your commission from a sale as all or part of the down payment on a country property deal. If you only get a slice of the commission pie, and you need an extra helping to fill up the deal, you can offer the other agent(s) an interest-bearing note for their share. Real estate brokers often wheel and deal with their commissions when negotiating for country property they intend to buy from their clients and then sell at higher prices for their own account.

Real Estate Broker Loans You the Down Payment

The real estate arena features a multiple of bulls eating into commissions. If you're a reliable salesperson, and you're on to a hot property, your broker–faced with sharing his commission with another agency on a co-brokerage arrangement–may loan you the money you need for the down payment, this if he is confident of your ability to secure his loan and return to him a fair profit.

Use Installment Plan for the Down Payment

You've found a sleepy little farm with subdivision potential and an anxious seller. You can qualify for a mortgage loan, but you're cash poor. You may convince the seller to take the down payment over a period of months so that you can close on the property. The seller can secure these payments through a purchase money second mortgage on the property and can agree to release specified acreage from the second lien when all or part of the down payment is paid. The seller could, under certain circumstances, agree to take back an unsecured personal note for the balance of the down payment. If the property is listed with a real estate agency, the selling broker may agree to co-sign this unsecured note to solidify his commission.

Use Multiple Notes for the Down Payment

For months now, you've seen the faded "For Sale by Owner" sign on the board fence of that run-down farm near the town dump. From the hand-painted phone number, you pick up the scent of an out-of-state owner. Maybe the owner has a hang-up against real estate agents –doesn't want to fork over a commission; or maybe some ossified agency had buried the listing in its files because it was on the wrong side of the dump, and now the owner is sniffing out buyers on his own. Doesn't matter, really. The place may stink as a listing, but you can smell green, as in paper dollars. The deal to too big for you. And you and your cash-starved buddies no longer swoon over mail for new credit cards because you're choked with debt.

Finally, just short of dancing on his grave, you yank a decent price out of the artful dodger and shoot him a contract; then you, et. al., sign individual notes payable to a lender who will finance the deal. Each note secures a portion of the down payment with a lien against valuable real estate, such as your precious shotgun homes.

As an alternative, the seller may agree to finance the entire deal, or in the event of third-party financing, allow these junk notes to be secured with a second mortgage on the land. Of course, a default by any one of you on any of these notes could place your whole conniving gang in default. The right to cure any default by a partner should be given to the buyers at large.

Exchange Real Estate for All or Part of the Property

Laws affecting tax-free exchanges can be amended from time to time. And your seller may only be interested in a tax-free exchange. If you don't have suitable, or qualified, property for an exchange, and you want to stay in the game, you may try to structure an exchange deal to gain control of the property. Following are questions and answers on this complicated subject:

What type of transaction qualifies for a 1031 Tax Deferred Exchange?

Answer: You must exchange real estate for real estate. Here are some samples: (1) house for land; (2) farm for home; (3) shopping center for marina; (4) apartment complex for cattle ranch; (5) oceanfront lot for condo; (6) office building for apple orchard; (7) city lot for country acreage.

How much time is allowed to complete the 1031 exchange?

Answer: You have 45 days to identify the replacement property, or properties, and 180 days (or the due date of your tax return, whichever occurs first) to consummate the exchange.

Who can handle the exchange?

Answer: An exchange intermediary–generally an attorney, accountant, or title or escrow officer. Try to locate a professional practitioner to act as an intermediary, such as a tax attorney or certified public accountant (CPA). Ask if the proposed intermediary is familiar with tax deferred exchanges and current tax laws.

What is a Starker Exchange?

Answer: This is an exchange in which the proceeds from the sale of real estate stay, in theory, on the intermediary's table until the _**seller**_ finds suitable property for the exchange. It is like the exchange is held "in suspension" by the intermediary. No money or deeds actually change hands between the buyer and seller in the initial stages of the exchange. Under the "Starker" ruling, you may have theoretically sold your home, but you cannot be taxed on your "theoretical" profits if you identify a potential replacement property within 45 days, and if you *fail* to complete the exchange within 180 days.

How do I identify properties to be exchanged under the 1031 provision?

Answer: Provide the intermediary with a _**legal**_ description of the properties to be exchanged, including addresses.

How do I identify property to be exchanged under the Starker ruling?

Answer: Provide the intermediary with a legal description of the property you are selling, and a *general* description of the property for which you would like to exchange. If you've got a buyer for your home at, say, three hundred thousand, and you want to exchange it for a farm; and your buyer cannot provide a farm at the time of sale, you sell your home "on paper" to the buyer through the Intermediary. When the farm is identified, the buyer (1) produces the three hundred thousand dollars; (2) tells the intermediary to buy the farm and; (3) exchanges your home for the farm. This type of transaction is, in effect, a three-way exchange between (1) You, the seller of the home; (2) The buyer of your home and; (3) the seller of the farm. Three deeds are involved:

(1) Farm owner sells and deeds the farm to your buyer

(2) Your buyer buys the farm and deeds it to you

(3) You deed your home to your buyer

How many properties can be identified in an exchange?

Answer: The following guidelines apply to the 1031 rule:

(1) If you plan to exchange your real estate for up to three properties, you can do so, providing you end up buying one or more of them.

(2) If you plan to exchange your real estate for more than three, and up to ten properties, the total value of the identified properties cannot exceed twice the value of the real estate you are giving up in the exchange.

(3) If the value of the identified properties (up to three) totals more than the established value of the real estate you are relinquishing, you must buy 95% or more of the properties you have identified as exchangeable within the process. Value is usually set by certified appraisals.

Any excess in value received by an exchange participant as the result of a 1031 or Starker exchange is considered "boot" by the IRS and can be taxable under current capital gains guidelines, However, excess value, or "boot," received in the form of an installment note, and transferred through a qualified intermediary, ***may not*** trigger capital gains and could act to further defer the payment of taxes. This is because such excess value is _**not considered to have been received**_ by the transferee until the installment note has been paid in full, i.e. until the exchange has been fully completed.

This ruling is invalidated when the installment note is secured by cash or a cash equivalent, such as a certificate of deposit. Finally, you must factor the transaction fees into the exchange: brokerage commissions, attorney closing costs, recording fees, etc. These charges are not tax deductible as gains; therefore the tax deferment amount can be altered. So check with your tax advisor.

What if the Buyer refuses to participate in the exchange?

You may have a sale for your home and plan to trade it for a farm, but the buyer of your home refuses to participate (_sign the appropriate papers for the exchange_), potentially washing out your tax deferment.

Answer: Acting under an exchange agreement, you, the seller, may consider transferring your home to a friend, who will act as an intermediary. The friend can then transfer your home to your buyer who, in turn, transfers (sells) your home (the exchange property) to your buyer. The friend (through you) then locates a suitable farm for you to complete the exchange, enabling you to qualify for tax-deferred treatment. An installment note, transferred as "boot" in this diversionary type of transaction is, however, taxed at face value – as if the note were payment in full for your home by the buyer. Appraisals are usually required to determine relative values associated with exchange transactions.

I want to exchange my rental property for raw land. What should I do first?

Answer: Insert language in the sales contract stating the fact that the transaction is part of a 1031 or Starker exchange. Consult with an intermediary and/or a qualified tax attorney to establish the transaction's conformity with current tax laws and to mark a paper trail for the IRS.

Tie Your Option to Prime Rate or Consumer Price Index

You've placed an ad in the paper looking for country property to buy. Some sharpie hick calls you up wanting to unload some junk land he's got in the mountains. He has cut off all of the big timber, doubling his money on the turkey; now he wants to hustle the scraps. He plays the option game out in the sticks all the time, knows his way around – gets up early, goes out and options timberland from out-of-state owners, determines from a timber cruise how much the trees are worth, borrows against his contracts to close, then cuts the timber, pays for the land and sells the leftovers dirt cheap to some poor sap like you who can pay for the land by the month thinking you're getting a dandy deal. He tells you they ain't making any more land. Inflation, he says, is eating up the dollar.

You're hungry and figure you can make a few bucks dividing up the land. You need a three-month option to buy while you "study" the deal, i.e. obtain commitments to buy your subdivided parcels. He sniffs at your conventional option, musing he could lose money while the land is off the market. But his eyes light up when you feed him the line about tying your option money to the prime lending rate. If you fail to buy the land, you won't walk from the deal and leave him holding the bag for any loss caused by a rise in rates while you hijacked his land.

Give Real Estate as an Option or as a Down Payment

A prospective land buyer came to me with a proposition. His parents had died, and he had inherited a lot in some Godforsaken swamp down in sunny Florida. He didn't get down that way much, although he described the place as almost heaven. Who wouldn't want to own a part of the sunshine state? Must be worth a pile of money, that land. He offered the lot free and clear as a down payment on twenty acres I had for sale in the boonies. Maybe the deal looked sweet to him, but I wasn't smelling roses. Real estate, given in trade for cash, is only good if you've sniffed out the trade-in property first. Some lots are virtually worthless because, for one reason or another, they cannot be built on or even used for camping. Junk lots often act like a swamp, sucking up your hard-earned cash through the pull of taxes. Each year, thousands of lot owners across the country stop paying real estate taxes on unusable lots that produce no value. But if you own property with established and verifiable worth, it could open the doors to a profitable deal.

Use Effort Equity as Your Share of the Deal

A friend comes to you with a "can't lose" deal on a fixer-upper on fifteen acres out in the country. He's got a buyer for the house and five acres that will pay for the place. He could sell off the other ten acres in two lots and be sailing down to Florida before the snow flies. He's out to sea on credit and offers you the opportunity to float him a loan. He asks you to think it over. He'll even pay two points over prime. You process the thought in a microsecond and tell him you're not a bank. You do, however, have access to the vaults though your credit line, and you may throw him a lifeline if the plan checks out. You suggest a fifty-fifty split, with you fronting for the financing. This form of effort equity could be extended to larger development ventures where your talents could support the show in arenas other than financing.

Private Loans Can Get You Started

When I first got wet in this business, I had partners – often two, sometimes three or more. I remember one riverfront project of considerable acreage that washed up a hidden treasure for everyone on board, including every buyer who later sold. None of the partners had any play money in those days, so we raised the fifty-thousand-dollar down payment by floating five $10,000 loans from high-interest consumer credit companies, with each of the partners lashed to the dotted line.

Hook into Your Credit Line on the Web

With the advent and proliferation of credit cards, the same floating shell game can be played, with each partner surfacing to the limit of his credit line. Sometimes an investor(s) can be hooked to a deal through an advertisement in the financial section of a major metropolitan newspaper; or an offer cast out on the Internet could lure an investor(s) looking for a juicier return on his money. Such an investor(s) will probably not want ownership involvement. A straight loan, properly secured, and not in violation of securities laws, may be the way to catch your next country property deal.

Get Start-Up Money from Family or Friends

A solid and well-timed country property purchase can be the safest investment around, especially for those close to you who are confident of your abilities. One of my out-of-state buyers informed his brother-in-law about some riverfront acreage that he had just purchased at a good price. The buyer told his relative about a deal on a fixer-upper cottage that had just fallen through. The relative, a whiz-kid home repair guy, had just lost a bundle in the stock market and had no ready cash. So he panhandles a loan from his sister's husband and locks onto a deal that could net him a high five-figure profit if he decides to sell while real estate is hot.

Use Your Credit Union for Down Payment Money

You can't give credit to credit unions for making mortgage loans and financing raw land. But they can be blessed saviors for the quick buck needed to nail down a deal. A buyer heard about an old home with a stream and a few acres that was on the auction block. The flyer said a $5,000 deposit was needed up front. The hopeful investor successfully auditioned for a personal loan, won first place at the auction, secured a 100% mortgage loan before closing to pay for the place, took a bow, and closed the curtain on a big profit.

Soften the Deal with Interest-Only Payments

If the seller won't budge on price, he may bend on terms. An aspiring investor had his eye on a lakefront cottage in a high-growth area that was awash with speculators. Prices on waterfront properties were rising more than 50% a year. The price was firm and elevated to a steep six-figure threshold, slightly beyond current appraisal figures. All previous low-ball offers had been rejected. The investor offered the seller full price, with seller holding 50% of the purchase price in a second mortgage, interest-only for the first year. By closing time, the appraisal figure surfaced to the threshold price level, and the investor smoothly sailed into a 95% loan, almost doubling the acquisition figure when he resold a year later.

Borrow on Your Insurance Policy

Don't overlook this low-cost source for keeping your investments afloat. If you've built up cash value in a life insurance policy, you'll often find it can be put to more productive use as ballast for the right investment venture, or as cash flow for your current investments. A hot-shot speculator in country properties needed to carry his heavy mortgage load through the throes of winter. Facing a blizzard of bills and with little comfort from a lean purse, he didn't want to seek refuge in the banks, lest they suspect the wolves might have his scent. He built a comfort zone with fifty grand from his policy and kept the wolves from his door until spring. His investments then thawed into a lake of liquidity and nurtured bountiful profits.

Borrow on Mortgage Notes for Venture Capital

Why not turn your depreciating investments into seed money for appreciating equity investments? A lender may loan you 50% or more on the value of any mortgage notes or trust deeds you hold. Even land sales contracts can be used as collateral for loans to buy into solid and potentially profitable country properties. Usually, the payments on this paper are used to amortize the loan. If you're just starting out and people are paying you by the month on land and properties you have sold to them, you may have overriding mortgages (your paper notes may be second in line to first liens) and cannot, in most cases, be legitimately sold to raise funds. Many lenders, however, reaching for the sky on rates, may look on your paper as manna from heaven.

Sell Paper at a Discount to Raise Acquisition Funds

If the deal is too good to pass up, and you can afford to trigger taxable income, it may make dollars and cents to sacrifice some of your mortgage notes or trust deeds for potentially greater profits. Keep in mind, however, that, when discounting your mortgage notes, you may also suffer a tax bite on these transactions; so the loss in potential profits is compounded. In the dawn of an upside real estate or stock market trend, profit margins on investment capital may grow exponentially before contracting. And potential gains from reinvested proceeds from discounted notes securing real estate may exceed their current value and future yield, thus providing stimulus for the sale of these notes. In the early years, when banks suspected I was playing a shell game, I would often sell selected notes at a discount when I needed down payment money on owner-financed properties. Over time, the banks, seeking Shylock-yield loans, began to solicit and buy many of these high-interest notes, albeit usually below face value and with my personal endorsement (See Appendix VI for more information).

Acquire Ownership by Turning Bad Deals Around

Does the owner/seller have a dodo bird property that won't fly? Maybe you have the talents or skills, such as sales and marketing savvy, to spread the wings on a loser. For example, some people love railroad tracks; others hate the sound of trains. The seller of a small farm can't sell his land because people think trains are bad news. The disheartening news in the media is that ominous events overseas are threatening security in the cities. You option the farm and reposition the advertising to those who fear the worst. The railroad can be a lifeline to goods and services when the highways are clogged with vehicles fleeing the cities. Bingo! You sell the farm at a profit.

Another example: A bank is stuck with a foreclosure on a flooded riverfront cottage. Nobody wants to touch the place. You snatch it for a song with no money down and divide the parcel into two lots, both waterfront; but with one lot on higher ground. You patch up the cottage into a basic shell and sell it as a weekend camp to pay off the mortgage; then you unload the high and dry lot as a premium riverfront homesite yielding you a prime profit. Inside every negative deal there is a positive seed. Your objective is to find the seed, cultivate it, and grow profits.

Use Tax Credits to Reduce Your Down Payment

In some states, when you acquire property at year's end, most of the tax obligation for the year usually belongs to the seller. At closing, you may receive funds earmarked for taxes as a credit. Until the tax bills are actually due, you will have use of these funds. This stash of money could feed a profitable real estate deal. Say you're a new investor in country properties and you've just wrapped up a real lulu in November, with five grand in tax credits buried in the package. Along comes January and you're onto a hot foreclosure, but you spent your cash wad on Christmas and your credit line is so tight it's starting to sing. If you could get your hands on about five grand for a down payment, you could double, even triple, your money on a quick flip. You decide to delay the tax payment and accept an interest penalty.

Avoid Risking Your Gains with an Effort Option

Often a winning deal requires extensive development plans and approvals by various government agencies and authorities. While these people are fiddling with your deal, your acquisition and development capital may be burning up through interest charges. To keep your gains on ice, try for a no-cash option period, during which you will draw up development plans and seek the required approvals. If the politicos and bureaucrats yank your chain too hard, you slip out of the noose and walk away with no further obligation. The seller either benefits from your work, or he gains by discovering the limitations of the property for specified ventures.

Seller Takes Back a First and Second; Cashes in First

You find the proverbial mansion on the hill, but the access road to your occupancy is strewn with cash potholes. You live in the world of vassals, so few are they who knock on the door of your thatched hut. You see new industry moving in, with pricey executives looking for opulent digs. Hell, the place could double in value in a few short years. So you boldly venture forth and offer the seller a $10,000 buyers premium – meaning you will pay an extra ten grand for the manor house and the surrounding grounds, with the seller holding an inflated first and a generously yielding second for half the purchase price.

"To what do I owe such generosity?" the seller asks. You reply that your offer is contingent on your paying no money down and unloading the first mortgage at a discount before closing, this requiring that he willingly participates in the arrangement. You point out (1) you will have no difficulty selling the first; (2) auctioneers often add buyers premiums to the price of properties sold at auction, so the deal enjoys legal cover and; (3) no exposure to him on the second due to your good credit and reputation. Of course, this type of transaction is not recommended for licensed real estate brokers and agents who may run afoul of disclosure laws.

Assume First Mortgage–
Seller Takes Equity on Second

You find a horse farm for sale where the sellers want to move back to their home in town. They have reached retirement age and are thirsting for an income stream, rather than cash up front. They have offered the place for sale with owner financing. Their one hang-up is the first mortgage on the farm. It pricks them like a burr under the saddle bothers a horse. They would feel more comfortable if this debt were gone; hence you need to feed them about fifty grand to get moving. You want to develop the farm, but you're short on cash and available credit. If the sellers are convinced that their farm is valuable enough to support both mortgages, they may let you assume the first mortgage for, say, the first year. In return you may spur up the interest on the second to put the deal at the starting gate. During the first year you (1) secure contracts to pay off both loans, and (2) obtain releases from the lender(s). You finish the year with trophy profits.

Buy with No Cash–
Seller Keeps Improvements

A real estate broker has this farm for sale, but the sellers would prefer to keep the home, barn, and about ten acres. The well has run dry on potential buyers, this since the improvements are seen as the main source of value. Your first move is to determine the fair market value of the land without the improvements. You offer a slightly higher price for the land on a no-money-down mortgage deal, with generous monthly payments at a bountiful interest rate. And the real estate broker accepts a second-mortgage-secured note from you for his commission. A variation of this tactic is to buy on a land sales contract that could shield the sellers from a possible capital gains tax bite. Of course, you will want release provisions in the paperwork, allowing you to sell off acreage to third parties in return for curtailments on your mortgage notes or contract.

Subdivide into Lots or Parcels
Before Purchase

Developers have woven this tactic into the fabric of rural land. They buy or option a tract of raw land, cut it up in lots and obtain purchase contracts before closing; then they use the proceeds to simultaneously close with their sellers. Often this approach is done with little or no money down. This methodology requires release provisions in the first mortgage documents and a cooperative and understanding seller. Your lot buyers should also fully understand and concur with the simultaneous closing process.

Buy or Option Land with Income-Producing Paper

I once drifted into a profitable riverfront project on some deed of trust notes secured by properties I had developed and sold. The seller accepted these notes as payment in full for the land when I responded to an advertisement offering land for sale with no money down. You can also try the note approach if you don't have cold cash to put down on a hot deal. An offshoot of this tactic is to agree to redeem the paper at the end of a prescribed period of time, say within a year, during which you develop and sell the property, effectively cashing out the seller. When used as collateral for an option to buy, you may agree to forfeit the paper if you don't buy during the option period, this because the amount of monthly payments received by the seller from the notes may not cover the cost of holding the land off the market without the firm possibility of a sale.

Help Yourself While Helping Seller Avoid a Tax Bite

In your search for a sweetheart deal, you find an anxious seller who would rather die than pay taxes. He agrees to marry you to a million-dollar deal on a contract for deed, an arrangement wherein he is taxed only as the money is received, and not as if he had completed the sale to you through the conveyance of a deed. But he wants a $30,000 "good faith" dowry, and you have a meager $10,000 in your tattered purse. On your way to the church, you encounter a shark lender and disgruntled ex-suitor for the deal who will lend you $20,000 on your contract for deed. You are overjoyed and begin popping the corks on future profits, this mindless of the fact that, if you default, the shark, with seller's blessing, goes home with the sweetheart deal and your ten grand.

The Letter of Credit as a Form of Option

You may find a hot property that requires investigation before you can act. Why play with your own cash when you've got a stand-in? Offer a letter of credit from your bank as a substitute for the cash deposit needed to open the deal. If the deal gets a good review and you fail to perform, the seller can collect on the letter; otherwise the letter is voided when you finish your act. The letter of credit can also stand-in for cash when government agencies demand bond money to ensure performance on development plays such as road construction.

Buy Property Using Collateral Security

A hunt club shot me a contract on a piece of land I had for sale. When the loan application hit the bank, the deal was almost dead on arrival due to a weak down payment. I set up a meeting with the honchos on both sides, and we revived the deal by pumping in a second trust on a gas station owned by one of the hunt club officers. With proper appraisals, city or country real estate alone can often substitute for the down payment or option money when buying country property. You can even lay down a second trust on property you own if you've got a hot deal in hand. But don't keep the bet open-ended. You will want the pledged real estate released from the first mortgage when you have stacked up enough equity chips to satisfy the lender.

A Wraparound Contract Could Keep Your Deal Warm

You may have a peachy deal ready to bloom, but the cold reality of seller's tax problems has settled in. Say he's on ice because his mortgage exceeds his adjusted basis, and he will be pounded by heavy capital gains. He wants installment sale treatment, but he can't afford to take any more payments on the mortgage without being hit by taxes on the entire amount of his gain. You, of course, have your own reasons for wanting to keep the deal ripe. A cure can be found if the deal is kept warm with a wraparound real estate contract, subject to the existing first. This treatment effectively gives the seller immunity from any taxable income during the current tax year. If you close using this practice, remember that you have to escrow your sales of any subdivided parcels until the tax year has passed. Have a real estate attorney draw up the contract.

Option Property Using Increased Payments

This is a gutsy way for the aggressive newcomer to attack the deal. I often used this technique when I was first thrown to the bulls of real estate. Let's say you're face to face with a killer deal. If you have little cash cover and you're nimble enough to get in and out fast, try dodging a first lunge at the deal until you can gain confidence through sales and improvements. On an option to purchase, offer, say, $500 the first round, $1,000 the second, and $2,000 the third. During this bolero, you may have sales contracts, options, or letters of intent to buy some or all of the property. You can use proceeds from the first sale(s) as the balance of the down payment and activate a simultaneous closing with your seller.

Consider Borrowing Against a Trust

You hear about a lake that is under construction to generate electric power and are shocked. . . shocked, by the current of land speculation surging through the surrounding countryside. Too bad your funds are all tied up in your yacht and car collection. You could really make some money in land. Then you remember that your grandma, bless her heart, has set up a trust for you. It's true that money is not immediately forthcoming; nor are the dwindling funds being doled out to you in small amounts.

But you can smell the cabbage, even taste the bubbly when you finally pop the cork on the old girl's generosity. Boy, what you would give if only the trust were liquid. Liquid . . . almost rhymes with loan, you think. Your mind leaps to the reality that the paper stocks in the fund's portfolio are being scorched by the down market. You had better hotfoot it down to the bank and get a loan on the trust, and make that killing in land.

Incentive Financing May Work When All Else Fails

Nobody finds good deals like you, nobody. They just fall right into your lap. Trouble is you sit at a desk all day fretting about your bills. Take that Smith place up on the mountain. The homefolks are getting old and want to sell the land and keep the house and a few acres. And you can pick up the land el cheapo. All you need is a fix of a hundred grand. You've been talking up the deal around the water cooler, down at the bar, and people tell you they feel your pain, but they'd still like to get a few acres up there because of the view. Joe, the loan shark down at the bar, threatens you for double his money. You beat him off and feed him a deal where he gets fifty percent of the profits. Feed the shark. Save the deal.

The Compensating Balance Trick

Often a lender will not scratch your back unless you scratch his. If you scratch long and hard enough, he may joyfully lend you all you need to do your deal and go sailing. Bankers need to make loans to stay in business. So you'll see them busily stocking their shelves with cash to sell to the needy and greedy, this within a certain ratio of deposits. If you can heap plump deposits on their scales, you'll see consistent smiles and handshakes behind the counter instead of cold shoulders. And if you're short on deposits, but long on friends and relatives with plenty of dough, you can have them dump their lump on the bank scales to balance your loan. Of course, in fickle times these steadfast stewards of the community are often well-supplied with cheap, fresh bread from a liberal Federal Reserve stocking up the bank stores for ominous events, such as those dreadful wintry recessions, and your deposits during these cash banquets, though welcome, may smell a bit moldy.

The Land Sales Contract-Refinance Route

A seller was trapped between a rock and a hard place. He needed someone to throw him a rope of cash to escape from the trap. The rock was his vacation farm in the mountains; the hard place was the whopping tax bite he would suffer from the sale. Here it was the Ides of March, and the seller wanted to leap off the civilized world into an ashram in the Himalayas. I tossed him a refinancing line, intertwined with a land sales contract, with me holding ownership rights to the farm. He willingly grabbed the refinancing, pulled himself out of the farm without being cut up by taxes and secured passage to the Far East with money from the loan. The following year, the seller returned with a shaven head, qualified for generous tax treatment under an install-ment sale, and agreed to officially sell the farm to me with a deed. We cancelled the land sales contract; I then assumed the existing first mortgage and gave back a second trust to the seller. A variation of this strategy can occur when the seller finances you into part of the prop-erty, this while selling you the balance on a land sales contract.

The Land Sales Contract as a Quick Out for the Seller

Another seller wanted to get out of Dodge and head for Alaska to fish for salmon. He had a cottage on a small fishing lake in the moun-tains. I was new to the business and not familiar with all of the lures and angles. I told him I liked the place but I needed to unload a few lots around the lake before I could buy the place. This didn't seem to shake him. He seemed more interested in skipping town than getting ready cash. He offered to sell me the lakefront cottage on a one-year, interest-only land sales contract. The deal was around $60,000 at 10% interest. So I could drop up to $6,000, or $500 a month, if the deal sunk. I was probably in over my head, but I knew lakefront properties were scarce and going up in value. Six months later and $3,000 in the hole on the deal, all of the lakefront lots were history. I then closed on the cottage and sold it for about $90,000.

The Contract for Deed as a Quick In for the Buyer

Economic storm clouds are looming, and maybe you've got a boat-load of acquisitions that you're trying to dump. Suddenly the catch of a lifetime surfaces, begging to be hooked. Rather than head for shore and bore your financial backers with fish stories, you try to chance the storm and reel in the deal using a contract for deed, baited with a token down payment. If the seller bites, make sure you can assume any mortgages when and if you're ready to develop the property.

Promise Him Anything . . .

Say you don't have the down payment on a can't-lose deal. Maybe you've got 10% and collateral other than real estate, such as stocks, bonds, livestock, or personal property. If the deal is grounded by lack of security, an assignment of these assets could help the deal take off. One cash-poor investor traded a farmer a motor home for a riverfont lot. Within three years, the motor home had lost value, while the riverfront acreage had risen in worth by 50%. Many times I have substituted deed-of-trust notes, secured by land, in place of the down payment on other country properties. Bank stock doesn't often rapidly increase in value; yet to the farmer who has money in that bank, the stock might beef up your down payment on a piece of his turf.

Giving the Seller a Life Estate

A farmer wanted to sell his farm, but he was glued to the old home place and wanted to squat on the farmhouse and ten acres. Any sharpie developer scouting the deal would surely focus on the profits buried in the home lot and improvements. Mr. Whizbang could chomp his cigar, shove the contract in the codger's face, sell off all the land, and still get stiffed when he pulled up his development tent. Those windfall profits, it might seem, would have to wait for the sun to set on the old guy, or until he moved on. I have learned from experience that life estates have grades of established and verifiable worth, depending on standards set within the state. In other words, you can view the mortgage behind a life estate as a marketable asset that can be sold at face value, discounted, or used as collateral for a loan. Sentiment does not have to be sacrificed for financial reward. A life estate can often turn out to be a compassionate blending of the two.

Transfer the Mortgage to Gain Land Free and Clear

As a general rule, lenders are more enamored of improved property than vacant land. Say you're feuding with a wheeler-dealer mortgagee who won't release from the blanket mortgage those subdivided parcels you have hustled off of his land. You were stupid enough not to provide for such releases in your purchase contract. Now this bigshot wants to nail you to the cross and watch you suffer. One way to get off the hook is to have the lien transplanted to other property you may have in town, such as a home, building, or improved commercial land, even if you have to infect these assets with a second trust. The basic economics of the deal may make those cost spikes a minor sufferance for you in the end.

Sell Natural Resources to Cover Your Down Payment

Years ago, with a small deposit, I bought a million-dollar slice of land topped with more than three hundred grand in hardwood timber and doubled my money in a year. The timber company paid me for the big trees up front at settlement on an 80% loan. I grossed out at the closing table with a hundred grand in my pocket and a mortgage on the land. Sure, there was some detraction from the land value, but the name of the game is *no money down, and then some.* You do the math on this deal. Gas, oil, coal, gold, and other minerals are all obvious sources of value when found on the land you may be buying. Other familiar, yet often overlooked, natural resources that can be sold are sand and gravel deposits. A lender, of course, may want a share in the spoils.

Give on the Interest to Gain on Price and Terms

The seller who is financing the deal may be hung up on high returns for his money. Assuming he's got his price emblazoned on his forehead, why not offer him a sky-high interest rate if he'll come down to earth on the required down payment. If you're developing a tract of country land, you'll find buyers swinging with more jive to higher rates for your subdivided parcels than they would for the property as a whole. Your competitors for the acquisition, plugging the cost of money into their analysis, may decline to turn up the volume on interest rates, especially if they plan to relax on any sales promotion for a few years. The rate jump could make your day.

A Rental-Option May Be the Way to Go

No fooling. This game is played by land speculators all over the boonies. It's not for me, but some crafty hustlers say the hokum pays off for them. You're all decked out in your boots and overalls, moseying around the back roads, looking to set a spell at some country store and pick up what's goin' on in them thar parts. Say you get wind of a good ole' boy who's about to lose his horse spread. "Now that Junior Jones's got the mad cow since his daddy died. Drinkin' and horse flesh. Both'll kill you. Neither one'll make you a dime. Fields are shot, fences gone to pot, stock runnin' the roads. Offered him a good price. Said he's gonna lay that ole paint off on some slicker and keep the place." You shift your ear, jot down this malcontent's name and slink out of the store to the post office. "I'm lookin' for Junior Jones" you say. "Got any idear where he lives?"

The feller in the post office points up the holler, tells you to turn right at the creek. "Look for a trailer," he says. Minutes later, your knuckles are denting the door of the manor house and you're touting an offer the lord of the manor can't refuse. You'll rent his land for beer money, tend his fields, fix his fences – hell, even feed his horses now and then when he's sloshed. All you want is the first option to buy the place when it comes up for sale. Just sign here. Happy Trails.

Use Growing Crops to Offset
Down Payment and Taxes

You're focused on a farm with corn as high as an elephant's eye. The farmer gives you a selling price with or without the crop. You like the looks of the crop and tell him you'll buy the whole show. But you want to close after the harvest. The income you reap could offset all of your down payment and maybe cover the real estate taxes; plus you can deduct from your current year's income that amount of money you spend for the crops.

Lender Buys Land and Leases It to You

Maybe you've found some hot land that you want to put on the back burner. You're sweltering with acquisitions, but this deal is giving you land fever. The seller, however, wants a quick shotgun marriage – a firm deal. You track down your father-in-law who agrees to buy the property and lease it to you like you said. He asks you how much you want for your fee. You tell him no, he doesn't understand. It's your deal. You just want a loan. You'll pay two points above prime. He says he's not a bank. So you end up paying through the nose for the lease to get the deal, but the end result could be a stack of chips in your favor.

Offer to Buy with Gold

If you believe in throwing the dice, it's probably a good idea to throw them away when buying land and country properties. My experience has been that money is usually made when you are giving an equivalent for what you buy. So the following technique is suggested only for the inveterate gambler. Assume you're buying land, and the closing will not occur for six months. If you're convinced that gold will rise dramatically within that period, then offer to escrow the entire down payment in the form of gold coins. Should the value of gold rise as you predict, the seller can agree to credit the increase in value to your down payment. If gold drops in price, you agree to offset the loss by paying more for the land, though your down payment can remain the same.

Seven Deadly Sins

Once you have mastered the art of the deal and have become a developer of sorts you should be aware of the tablet of sins that can cause you to stumble and fail in your endeavors:

    1. You positively have to have that deal.

    2. You have inadequate cash flow to sustain development.

    3. Your concept of development is flawed.

    4. You believe your profits are at the rear end.

    5. You fail to do your homework.

    6. You have faulty associates.

    7. You are in love with the land.

For example, you may need dirt for your land-hustler salesmen to peddle, and you blunder foolishly into a project to sustain your operations. You may overbid for properties at an auction to the sacrifice of your bottom line. Or you may wistfully feel you are contributing to the betterment of mankind by making an acquisition to save the planet.

You may see yourself as Donald Trump's greatest nightmare and recklessly buy trophy castles in the air without the cash flow to pay for them.

You could sponsor grand ideas in your mind of creating a utopia in the countryside that will marry the practical needs of mankind to the faulty idealism of bureaucratic land planners, only to preside over a field of broken dreams.

Your conventional belief in just rewards for diligent work performed could have you waiting for your pot of gold at the end of your development rainbow, only to find that your figures were all wrong.

You think you know it all and can do no wrong, only to observe your million-dollar investment sinking into the quicksand of bureaucratic red tape and public opposition.

You return from a trip around the world and discover your charlatan partner has built a pyramid of duplicity and you are under indictment for criminal fraud and tax evasion.

You absolutely cherish the ground you are walking on and would not defile it for a million bucks, so you take your good old sweet time swooning over a pile of dirt, only to watch the no-growth environmental zealots zone you out of the development game.

Yes, Virginia, there are devils along the development road, and it's best to detour away from them whenever you see signs of these seven deadly sins.

PART TWO

Small Beginnings

Washington D.C.
JAPS ATTACK PEARL HARBOR – December 7, 1941 –
Frank Sinatra

War clouds–the stinking Japs. A seven-year-old knickered street urchin is tossing a knife into a half-divided square in the dirt of a tree box in front of a run-down row house. The name of the game is "Land." The boy carves out a slice of ground, and the perimeter has changed. The boy has gained land, and his opponent has lost terrain. To the victor belongs the spoils of territory.

I had nothing in my pockets but marbles as a kid, and "relief" trucks dropped off food supplies in front of our house, but I didn't know I was poor. "Land" was the game I loved to play. My waterfalls were the fountains at Union Station where I dived for passenger coins, much to the exasperation of the cops; and my tunnel to freedom was the congressional subway on Capitol Hill where I stole rides with the country's bigshots, not knowing or caring who they were.

Washington, D.C. outskirts
FRENCH BOMB HANOI IN LOOMING WAR – Christmas, 1946 –
Hank Williams

The Cold War–Asia falling to Commies. A twelve-year-old malcontent sulks about a Christmas stocking stuffed thin with an I.O.U
from his errant dad. Armed with a .22-caliber rifle in snowy woods on
a dark December night, I shot out a street light my neighborhood cluster of frame shanties. The whites in the shotgun homes enjoyed higher
terrain than the Negroes in the brick apartment complex below. There
was talk around the project of a race war, but the whites held the high
ground. The Negroes always got better than the whites. That's what I
heard. But it didn't matter, because everybody seemed to have better
things than my family anyway. Growing up, I traded white bread for
Italian bread from my pals. We lived next door to shanty Irish royalty.
My father borrowed money from the filthy rich Chinese, the debt lingering like an incurable disease. The hillbillies (country folk) in my
white ghetto got the first TV and, after taking their good ole' time,
they finally invited me to set a spell and watch the noble sport of wrestling.

But that was life. It seemed almost natural to take a back seat to the
immigrants.

I liked to go down in the woods and build rickety log cabins with
the Negroes until I was told by neighbors to keep my place. When my
home was broken up by divorce, I quit school, gave up my paper route
and refused to leave the run-down abandoned house, existing on candle-
light and canned beans and listening at night to hillbilly songs on an
old wind-up Victrola, this until the coal bin was empty and I realized
that things were as they were, not what I wished them to be.

One morning I picked up my puppy and meager belongings, stuffed
them in the basket of my trusty old bicycle that I had practically built
from scratch and pedaled off to an uncertain life on the city streets of
Washington, D.C., where I found half of my family of eight had been
packed off to a Methodist home for children.

Bethesda, MD
SUBURBAN HOUSING BOOM HITS U.S. – Spring, 1956 –
Elvis Presley

Security, fresh air and sunshine for the sprouting baby boomers. A twenty-two-year old college student, robbed of sleep, totals an unusually high stack of food and bar bills at a ritzy suburban country club – a golfing Mecca for men of fortune and political friendship. Congress has just passed legislation financing the interstate highway system. Champagne corks are popping at power restaurants all over town. Soon huge tracts of rural land will come under seige from real estate investors and speculators.

The stage was set for a new wave of settlers to move inland and to discover the countryside. Thousands of them would find the luxury of sleep in Holiday Inns. Still, to me, the soft bed of luxury remained only a dream.

PART THREE

The Sixties

Arlington, VA
CUBA CRISIS THREATENS NUCLEAR WAR–Oct., 1962 –
The Four Seasons

The flames of fear. President Kennedy orders a boycott of Cuba over Soviet missiles, and he pledges fallout shelters for Americans. A 27-year-old college-educated peanut vendor listens to news reports of the crisis while counting his coins in the basement storage area of his apartment complex. Why worry? The tyrant has yet to kiss him.

I was stuck in a crummy apartment at ground zero and felt I had nothing else to lose. Fear, of course, can be noiseless, as when experienced in a wide wilderness. Thousands of city dwellers whistled to themselves and struck out for the countryside. This was the first spark of the sixties' land boom and migration to the countryside. Hell, even *I* had scraped up enough coins to buy a lot in the country. I used to remark to friends that "I'm going up to the land."

Washington D.C.
200,000 MARCH ON WASHINGTON–August, 1963–
Peter, Paul & Mary

I was still living in the apartment when Martin Luther King led the civil rights charge on the nation's capital with Lincoln's creed that all men are created equal. The fifties had come and gone, and the newly affluent and war-weary bourgeoisie in the suburbs were busily shuttling their blossoming cargos of baby-boomers to soccer games and dancing lessons. Great strides had been made in race relations, but much more had to be done. Among other acknowledged and justifiable concerns, blacks, largely ghettoed in the cities, were busting the gates for greener pastures in which to play and build their civil rights agenda. Though not widely reported in the media, an invasion of suburbia by the colored underclass lay hidden in the bogs of discontent and injustice.

Compounding this unrest were the fear of impending violence lurking in Whitey's monstrous mind, and his insatiable need for more territory on which to play. The white hordes in suburbia then began staking claims to the outlying playing fields of the lords. This thrust for the redistribution of land holdings in the rural countryside spurred a nationwide partitioning of the sparsely inhabited regions beyond the suburbs into smaller and more equitable sizes. Like a rocket booster, the March on Washington–aside from its powerful impact on the nation's psyche–served to ignite the excess monetary fuel burning in the pockets of the middle class and helped to launch the nascent recreational land-boom rocket of the sixties, this dramatically expanding the fencing of America.

Rural Virginia
KENNEDY SHOT DEAD IN DALLAS–Nov. 22, 1963 –
Bobby Vinton

President Kennedy is assassinated. The eagle has fallen. I had traded my river lot for a shell cabin on five acres. Now here I was–a twenty-nine year old maverick in a cowboy hat, essentially a frozen fish in a pond. After stomping the snow from my boots, I plodded into the cabin, tossed away my hat and dropped exhausted on the bunk. I had been the only prey on a failed hunting trip, so I focused on the beat-up rabbit-eared TV, the first step to something better. The snowy screen evolved into a fuzzy account of Lee Harvey Oswald's foul deed in Texas. I sat glued to the set. It took a while for the event to take hold in my mind. Kennedy. . . gunned down. I had, just moments before, rested my surplus British Enfield rifle from a similar attempt on one of God's creatures, and for reasons I can't explain, I never hunted again.

I had weaseled my way into the manor born the previous spring with $50 down and was paying for my initiation into land ownership by the month. And I even tried to beat myself out of this first bit of good fortune. Back in the 1962 winter of my discontent I foolishly brooded over how I was going to pay for the land, so I called the developer and said I wanted out of the deal. He came to my apartment one evening and politely explained to me that the contract called for me to close, or I could possibly face legal action. Not wanting to lose what I never had, I cracked a crooked smile and stuck around. I never forgot this good turn, and I am thankful to the developer.

Now I was running a stable of cheap horses on a farm down the road. City dudes and local lot owners would rent my menagerie of skinny-looking nags for trail rides in the mountains, over the river, and through the woods. My steed was a fatally fast thoroughbred named Cousin Buddy that I had rescued from the meat man at a local horse auction for about a hundred bucks, this thanks to my wife who had bankrolled the snatch as a birthday present. The rejected racer had been hopelessly in love with the starting gates on the Charles Town, W.VA. track. But once on the trail, this steed could corral any dude's nag that figured it had a mind of its own and started to wing it back to the barn. And if he stumbled while racing across a field, leaving me tumbling head over heels from the saddle, he never left me without a ride back home.

Of course, no one falls feebly from a horse, and the older I get the more respect I have for such hazards. One time, while leading a line of horses, I was dragged up a road to the edge of death by a outlaw roan, this when the horse bolted and my foot became entangled in the lead line when I fell. Luckily the rope broke while being taken in tow at full speed up the road, leaving me battered and bruised as if I had been chained to the back of a fast-moving pickup truck.

My muddled thoughts of Kennedy, though fixed with compassion for a fallen leader, somehow drifted to the nearby Middleburg hunt country and the noted Kennedy estate. I had dragged my rent-a-wreck horse trailer, with its divergent pairs of flea-bitten nags, countless times through that bastion of inherited horsey wealth and never imagined I would ever jump the formidable financial gap separating the rich and poor, much less find myself hurtling over cultural rock fences in a silly scarlet suit, straddling a pampered seventeen-hand beast and chasing some hapless fox to its gruesome demise in the bucolic country-side. (I say this with no rancor toward the controversial sport of fox hunting; but this was my frame of mind at the time.)

The silliest suit I ever wore in my stable days was a white sheet. One summer night I connived to play a trick on the crowd at the community swimming pool. My brother-in-law and I slipped down to the barn and saddled up Cousin Buddy and another nag and trotted back to the pool in our white-sheeted garb, the outfit complete with appropriate tie-downs and eye holes. In those days I had no clear conception of the Klu Klux Klan and its devilish ways. In fact, when the name was first brought up in a high school class discussion, I don't even recall associating the organization to Whitey's terrorism of blacks.

After racing past the pool, sheets flowing on top of a fearful yell, we turned tail, galloped back to the barn, stabled the horses, and stashed the sheets in the hayloft. We then sped back to my house where we were accosted by a few property owners who had surmised that the night was thick with horse thieves in white sheets who were riding the roads and scaring the hell out of people. Right away I cut loose for the barn in my beat-up station wagon, the property owners in hot pursuit. Sure enough, there were the stolen horses in the stalls, still dropping sweat from the terror ride. A quick investigation turned up the white sheets. I thanked the concerned property owners for their quick thinking and told a story that I would report the incident to the sheriff.

End of story.

If this trick was a permitted vice, it betrayed an underlying virtue of wanting to be free from worldly convention. We know that a rider in a white sheet is likely to receive less respect than a uniformed officer. Man's outward appearance, however, often masks another self. We must wear the mask through life's light-hearted victories, lest we succumb to the stronger troops of our principles. I often thought I should have been born and raised out west, and I have worn a cowboy hat most of my life. I recall being in Europe on a tour. People would come up to me and ask where I was from. At first I told them, "Virginia." When the only recognition I received was a querulous look or a frown, I began telling people I was from a trivial western outpost called Texas. That's when their faces lit up. Now, in parts of Old Europe, it could be High Noon for Texans, since the U.S., under President Bush, rescued

Iraq from the bad guys without checking his guns at the bar.

The often tragic desire to throw off the mask and express oneself beyond the human comedy is reflected in a movie of that day, *Lonely are the Brave,* starring Kirk Douglas. Here an aging cowboy refuses to accept the convention of fenced fields, vehicular mobility, and structured identity. He cuts fences at will to ride freely through the plains and mountains. For personal transportation he chooses his horse, Whiskey, over a truck or car. And he disavows any form of personal identification, such as a driver's license, claiming that he already knows who he is.

His mind is painted black with a feeling that he must be true to himself, and this judgment leads him and his mount through a fugitive's life to a tragic demise when crossing a rain-soaked highway in the path of a fast-moving eighteen-wheeler hauling plumbing supplies.

True happiness in life, of course, does not spring from this type of unbridled thought. A calm horse generally makes a better all-around mount than a spirited one. And a healthy horse holds a saddle better than an overfed steed. Moderation, it would seem, is the tonic for a charmed life, though some would suggest that you spike this drink with principle. Seems like wherever I rode in those days, some nameless devil was fencing the mountains, the valleys, the fields; and all across the countryside blew the winds of change.

Snowfalls were particularly heavy in the sixties, and sometimes I found horseback as my only reliable means of transportation. In warm weather, I often took to riding wherever I pleased, often audaciously and recklessly spiriting a gang of dudes across the river, dropping a trail of horse manure on the estates of political bigwigs and often trampling through the sacred mountain hideouts of Washington's media elite. In August of 1964, gunfire in the Tonkin Gulf ignited the Vietnam War, and in December of that year grown-up educators at Berkeley surrendered to the California university's recalcitrant children.

The year 1965 opened to an orgy of urban strife . . . Malcolm X gunned down in New York, Martin Luther King and his demonstrators greeted by night sticks, tear gas, and death as they marched into Selma and Montgomery, Alabama. The world was going bonkers. By December, 170,000 U.S. troops were in Vietnam, and a disgruntled herd of city dwellers was being stampeded by land developers to the safety and reward of a so-called good life in the country. I noticed that many of these Nervous Nellies showed up at my stable in brand new cowboy hats to ride my old nags. I herded many of these dudes to comforting salespeople in the development and never asked for any form of compensation when the dudes ponied up for a lot. Money was a necessity to me of course, but the primary shining metal in my mind at the time were new horse shoes.

What does a peanut-vending saddle bum know about making money anyway? I never had any, never aspired to have wealth. So there was nothing to lose. I had my freedom. That was enough. Sensing this imminent stampede of humanity in 1964, I had casually mentioned to a real estate friend that I wanted to lay claim to some land next to the Shenandoah National Park where I could retreat from the marauding exodus. He later located a suitable farm, and I had become butt boy on a three-man partnership to develop the property.

Rural Virginia
RACE RIOTS TORCH LOS ANGELES – August, 1965 –
Rolling Stones

I was saddling up for a trail ride in the mountains when a dude told me the National Guard had been called to attention by a bloody carnival in Los Angeles–an imploding cradle of crime called Watts. The city was in flames. That same day, I burned the bridges behind me and hit the trail for my adventures in country properties. The salesman on our development next to the Shenandoah National Park was suddenly unavailable. Paying customers were breaking down the doors in response to my first ad. And I was called out to sell land. I had never aspired to be a land salesman. Customers had often been referred to as "pigeons," as if they were caged for imminent release to a barrage of high-pressure sales talk.

After college, I wrote radio and television commercials for an ad agency. So I had a feel for brevity in advertising. My first thought was to avoid positioning the property as a recreational development. I lived in one and recognized the inherent limitations on freedom of movement within communities. So I began advertising individual parcels of affordable land.

VALLEY VIEW FARMS
NEAR SKYLINE DRIVE

Excellent stone house on 10 acres in secluded hollow
surrounded by Shenandoah Nat'l Park. Trout fishing,
year round stream, fantastic views, plenty of turkey and
deer. 90 min. D.C. $9500. $500 down.
To inspect call collect. Boyce, VA 310.

When I first started in the land development business, the ratio of gross returns was about six or seven to one – meaning for every dollar of acquisition capital, the retail price would be multiplied by six or seven. Land purchased for a hundred dollars an acre could be retailed out in the form of residential lots at six or seven hundred dollars per acre, this after survey and improvements, such as roads. Other ratios still apply, and continue to vary, particularly in highly infrastructured developments where property owners enjoy the common use of facilities such as lakes, pools, tennis courts, ski slopes, lodges, country clubs and golf courses. Properties adjoining usable government land, such as national and state parks and forests, and land on rivers and lakes, can generally be considered improved properties (though not by lenders) by virtue of the already established recreational amenities inherent within their natural geographical features. In the development of country properties without a large-scale infrastructure, acquisition land cost is usually the value established after the sale of any buildings.

Joins Shenandoah Nat'l Park
Below the Skyline Drive

Enjoy 50 mi. view. Watch your own leaves turn this fall. 300 sq.
miles of scenic mountain country in your back yard. Riding trails
and trout streams. 5 secluded acres. Pasture and woods. 90 min.
D.C. $3200. $32 dn. $32 mo. Call Owner collect. Boyce, Va 310.

Valley View Farms was one of those country property deals within the six-to-seven to one ratio. For example: The land cost us about $100 per acre. In those days we were able to sell five acres for a little over $3,000. Most of the sales were owner-financed transactions, and the

notes were often traded (with or without personal guarantee) for services such as road construction and survey work. Cash purchases were
rare and often induced through the offer of a price discount on the
property. Available cash was used to pay expenses.

In most cases, notes were discounted to bank lenders to pay off any
mortgage. Keep in mind that mortgages were generally low in the sixties. It was fairly easy for young people, just starting out, to own a
home. For example, a local contractor built for me a two bedroom
home at that time for under $10,000, even though this debt was my
worst poverty. I recall hiding in the basement on one occasion to avoid
an anxious creditor.

Often, the sellers, from whom we purchased property for development, held all or part of their first lien mortgage in the form of these
installment notes. Profits were distributed to the partners in the form
of notes secured by country real estate. I once traded thirty thousand
dollars in such notes for a 1965 Cessna airplane that I kept for almost
thirty years. My financial portfolio was born through the accumulation of installment notes. Of course, some customers defaulted on their
notes; but because prices were steadily rising on well-located country
properties, such as those at Valley View Farms, I quickly and easily
sold the property again.

I sold off the two farmhouses and assorted lots in this development
from horseback, whipping out a plat from my back pocket when the
customer drove up. I was herding people onto land so fast that some
investors flipped their choice lots for profits before closing. One investor, observing this frenzy for lots, smelled gold in them thar hills.
He bought a lot, hightailed it down to the courthouse, discovered what
we paid for the land, and hired me to set up his shop to sell lots. He
subsequently panned for gold for many years before retiring to sunny
Florida on the wind of his land sales.

Valley View Farms joins the 300-square-mile Shenandoah National
Park and offers scenic views of the Shenandoah Valley. It would be
fair to say that, since 1965, and as of the publication of this book, I
have sold and developed more land over four states – Virginia, West
Virginia, Maryland, and Pennsylvania – than the land area within the
broad expanses of this park.

Land of Opportunity

It can be like pushing a mule when dealing with many government land planners. Their education has often been kicked into them at the shrines of social idealism by academic mullahs intoxicated with the aroma of communal living, and who instruct their disciples to take no prisoners when battling it out with developers. Yet millions of land-seekers have been given the opportunity to own country property through the efforts of legitimate, ethical and conscientious developers. Figures from the National Association of Realtors (NAR) reveal that 6% of all homes sold in the U.S. in 2001 were second homes and that 80% of these homeowners use their homes for vacations. For the past forty years, I have watched prices on country properties – at a minimum – double every decade as city and suburban dwellers doubled their share of home ownership. Thousands upon thousands of people have taken swift advantage of the hour to buy country real estate; and their property, when resold, usually gained them significant profits.

Some gate-closing "come heres" from the cities may feel threatened by this so-called democratization of the countryside, and the threat exposes a basic hypocrisy: "I've got mine. Now let's close the gates." The very mention of such a radical concept as democracy in land ownership may grate like chalk on a blackboard to those bleating social engineers who wail like banshees at the exaggerated threat to precious open space and who hope to foist on the United States the landed gentry pattern of jolly old England and "old" Europe. Untold millions of Americans would not own homes or land if opportunities were curtailed to the extent desired by overzealous regulators and socialist-minded planners out to "preserve" the countryside.

I owe a debt to the many public servants and property owners who have helped and supported myself and others out of a fellow-feeling. But in every village and town in America there are miscreants who claim they represent the will of the people but whose concerns are either primarily for their own comfort, or they represent the promulgation of misdirected ideas about who should own land and how much.

To investors, the significance of the Valley View Farms development is the fact that it enjoys a common boundary with a national park; hence the property enjoys inherent value beyond your ordinary rural landscape. Nothing attracts buyers and builds value faster than land with scenic natural attractions and the use of free land adjoining your own.

My pleasant memories of this project are tempered with a particularly unpleasant incident. I remember being called to the development one day, only to be suddenly ambushed by a veritable posse of park rangers. The incident was provoked when I asked the selling farmer to clear away brush from an old park trail so that the new land owners could find their way to Skyline Drive without getting lost in the woods. It seems the farmer and his neighbor exhibited irrational exuberance in carrying out their mission by cutting and marking trees along an old hunting trail that was blazed by trappers before the land was condemned by the park in the thirties–this when the feds ran the mountaineers off of their homesteads. I was told by the rangers that anything I said could be used against me in a court of law. After my day of judgment, and with a savvy lawyer beside me, I was scolded by His Honor for not babysitting the farmers, and I was ordered to direct the farmers back to patch up Mother Nature.

Investing in properties next to government land can be profitable. But you should keep in mind the fact that rangers and their environmental sidekicks are, as a rule, in love with Mother Nature. So don't go stepping on her grass skirt or start to disrobe her in any way.

Rural Virginia
U.S. BOMBS HANOI AND HAIPHONG – June, 1966 –
Simon & Garfunkel

U.S. planes were bombing cities in North Vietnam, and opposition to the war erupted on campuses throughout America. And Buddhists in Vietnam were setting themselves ablaze in fiery suicides. I had returned from Richmond, Virginia, believing I had bombed on my real estate test for a brokers license, yet hoping otherwise. But self-confidence is no way akin to hope. Here I was, this dumb, educated flop, flipping country properties like pancakes, eating cake and drinking vintage champagne–and sometimes even foolishly brokering deals without a license, and often not receiving a dime for my efforts. One creep refused to pay me for selling his land because my broker's license was dated after I made the sales. The jerk later fell out of a tree and broke both of his legs. The Bible says that whoso diggeth a pit shall fall therein.

I dug such a pit for myself when, under the aegis of a broker friend and mentor, I foolishly and illegitimately sold a home without a license, giving the deposit to the seller. When the misdeed was uncovered, it could have caused the Virginia real estate commission to feast upon his license. Fortunately, the only hit I got was a thump on the back by a figurative old shoe as I slunk away from the scene.

During the winter of 1965-66, I sat through a real estate course and persuaded the powers-that-be in Richmond that I needed to skip the bootcamp for salesmen. My argument was that I needed to hire sales-men–*so please let me be a broker right away.* I had wasted too much time trying to find out what I wanted to do when I grew up. I had to aim for the top.

This was a wild shot at policy, but my letters to the commissioners hit the mark, and I was allowed to sit for the exam. Bombs were falling in Vietnam, race riots were breaking out across the country, thousands of civil rights marchers had descended on Mississippi, and peaceniks were planting angry signs in the swamps of Washington, D.C. About that time I planted a real estate broker's sign on my modest home in the woods, applied for my American Express card, and took up flying. My partners and I bought an Aeronca Champ taildragger that some pilot later crashed when he hit a power line. I then bought a Cessna 172 in which I was flying the friendly skies of the Shenandoah Valley when my son was born in October, 1966, this two months after my second major venture into country properties.

Turtle Rock Farm–August, 1966

People are always asking me how I dream up names on the properties I develop and sell. It's very simple. I look for natural features in the landscape and try to bring the name into focus. In the case of this riverfront piece, I spotted a large turtle sunning itself on a huge rock in the Shenandoah River. Bingo: "Turtle Rock Farm."

After reaping my financial harvest on a number of properties, I breezed into a local real estate office and asked what they had for sale. The agent handed me a sheet of paper with some listings. I asked about the Turtle Rock property and was given directions to look on my own. After checking out the land, I quickly sketched out a development plan and went to the seller with a $500 option deal. If I didn't bite within 60 days he could eat my money. Lucky me. He was a compassionate entrepreneur who probably saw a bit of himself in my hubris.

After nailing down the deal, I contacted a road builder and surveyor and began developing the land into lots, this recklessly without permission. The seller could have closed me down, but he let me proceed with bulldozing a road and surveying lots–work I paid for on the cuff. How did I know if I could sell the lots? How was I to get the whole show financed? Good questions. I never searched for the answers. I just plunged ahead. Seven basic entrepreneurial principles come to mind here:

1. SET HIGH GOALS
2. MOVE AHEAD FAST
3. DON'T WAIT FOR COMPLETION
4. FINISH WHAT YOU START
5. SOLVE PROBLEMS
6. TAKE RISKS
7. VISUALIZE RESULTS

Other success-related principles may also have been be in play, such as (1) playing it straight; (2) thinking accurately; (3) building consensus and; (4) maintaining control.

I tested the waters by running some newspaper ads on credit while the road was being built. Within a month, I had most of the lots under contract and figured I would rope a couple of my college frat bothers into the deal so I could wrap up financing for the land and improvements.

Until the late sixties, there were few, if any, disclosure requirements regarding interest rates. Generally we were getting six to eight percent on owner-financed country property sales, and note buyers were paying close to face value for the notes. An investor bought most of the notes from this deal at a small discount and cashed us out. Here is one of the *Washington Post* ads.

SHENANDOAH RIVER FARM
W/ HOME AND FIVE ACRES

Restored 3 BR homeplace. Excellent shape. Oil heat & all utilities. Scenic views of two mountain ranges. Shade trees. Garden. Lakesite. Right-of-way to river. Fenced for horses and cattle. 90 min. D.C. Priced to sell. $11,500. $1500 dn. Call Boyce VA 218.

If this place were for sale in, say, 2003, it would bring more than twelve times that price. "Location, Location, Location" has long been the shopworn mantra of real estate people trying to hawk properties. Folks, if it's acreage on or near the water, they're not lying to you.

White Oak Lake–September, 1964

My wife's family owned a fifty-acre farm in Madison County, VA. on the east side of the Blue Ridge Mountains. Nothing fancy. Just an old tenant house adjacent to the grounds of a prep school for rich kids. I used to slip down there in my college days to take in the country and forget my troubles. But, trouble, like babies, grows larger by nursing. Not being rich, I felt for the poor, and in my junior year in Business Administration at George Washington University I took a job supervising a church community center in downtown D.C. When the older black kids learned I was studying business, I sensed a hidden wailing that they felt only whites could become executives. After college, and a self-imposed seven-month sentence with General Electric, I managed to file down the mental bars of what I perceived to be a corporate prison. A few days later, when I finally reached a mountain cabin to hole up with my wife and guitar, I felt I was no longer a bird in a cage.

I have never worked for anybody other than myself since I split the corporate world and started my nickel-and-dime vending machine operation. In those days I would head south with bags of coins and count the loot next to the wood stove of that old tenant house in Madison County, Virginia. When the stacks of coins got higher than I could reach, I started sniffing around the boonies, snooping for land where I could bury some cash and watch it grow. That's how I found my cabin in the woods for a sack of quarters. Anyway, I snatched knowledge of the region by steering my trusty 1959 Volkswagen down to the old homeplace on weekends before I started my riding stable.

After acing a few deals in the Valley, I was dealt a hand on some land for sale on a new lake under construction as a state-controlled water conservation measure. By then I had enough experience to float the acquisition, but not enough financial wind behind me. So I tacked into the deal with my two partners from the Valley View development.

NEW MOUNTAIN LAKE
Waterfront just $30 dn. $30 mo.

Crystal clear lake 1 hr. 40 min. D.C. Wooded setting in Blue Ridge near Shenandoah National Park. Private, non-commercial. Quiet, secluded. 60 ac. stocked with a wide variety of fish. No noise. Sailboats & elec. motors. First offer. Quick sellout expected. No safer place for your money than waterfront. 1 full acre from $29,500. Call collect: Madison, VA 948-4135.

For investors, the lesson learned here is the importance of lakefront property in the human psyche. It seems that nobody ever owned land on a lake that somebody didn't want to buy. The size of the lake really doesn't matter, because people prefer their lakes in various sizes for a myriad of reasons. Some people seek big lakes on which to sail and venture out; others prefer smaller lakes where their passion is fishing. Still others are quite content with a small pond where their chocolate labs can spash around and chase ducks. White Oak Lake is about sixty acres in size. True to form, almost all of the lakefront lots were spoken for before closing. As you may know, one acre of lakefront in this day and age can easily sell today far in excess of $100,000.

A tragic reminder of this development was the loss of two young boys, both of whom drowned when one tried to save the other. One lot owner–a young mother with the pioneer spirit–had left her brood in a lakefront encampment in the care of an older sister. While the sister was away, or preoccupied, the younger of the two brothers had some-how fallen in the lake and did not know how to swim. The older boy, in a vain attempt to rescue him, was pulled under, and he lost his life as well. Sleep they may, so that dreams may come.

Wide River Farms–October, 1966

Wealth is like a river. If it floods the banks today, it could run dry tomorrow. The *motivation* for building wealth is another matter. Obviously, the successful pursuit of monetary gain is likely to bring tempo-rary access to power, leisure, and freedom from human drudgery. There is, however, one constant in the purchase of riverfront. It tends to cost you more every year.

Investors have long realized that riverfront property is, as a commodity, essentially a package of too little land wanted by too many. The foundation of my financial portfolio has always been the solid returns from the investment in, and brokerage of, riverfront properties. As a broker, the riverfront I sell at one price today is sure to rise in price tomorrow, creating additional income for me through commissions.

That's why there are no dams of discontent when a riverfront opportunity flows my way. My commissions on brokerage activities have generally run the financial gamut from ten to thirty percent, often exceeding the net gains from my own developments. Here's an ad from a sideline deal I handled between investments on my own account. The developer of this property no doubt found a veritable Aladdin's lamp through this and other riverfront investments. As for me–getting paid big for what you love to do is, without question, the discovery of unrepented pleasure.

FIRST OFFER OF PRIME
RIVERFRONT NEAR D.C.

Only 40 mi. from Beltway. Limited number of one-acre estates on the wide Shenandoah below Harpers Ferry National Park. First to come get first choice. Level, open and wooded. Build, camp, fish, swim. Canoeing, power boating. Sound investment. $3,950. Min. $40 down $40 per month. Call 948-4135.

In February, 1966, I flew down to the Bahamas with one of my partners in my Cessna 172 for a week-long break. Our wives flew commercial. Time shares were beginning to take off at that time, and land hustlers were working the streets in Miami and Nassau. My mind has never turned in the direction of time shares. Share the wealth, but not the real estate.

Madison, VA
HIPPIE TRIBES GATHER IN SAN FRANCISCO – January, 1967
– The Monkees

While thousands of cars inched toward the San Francisco "Human Be-In," A Jeep wagon in rural Virginia stopped along a muddy road, and a real estate agent began nailing a "For Sale" sign on the fence of an old mountain farm. I happened to be driving by, so I stopped and inquired about the place. He waved his arms and pointed toward some white-capped hills before directing me down a one-lane path leading to a hidden valley with a stream.

Lost Valley

When I arrived in the valley, the old farm appeared to have no redeeming or outstanding features other than a lakesite and its remoteness for hunters. The decrepit farmhouse was leaning on its last legs in a frosting of snow. Brown grass waving through a blanket of white told me that weeds had claimed the pasture, and an accumulation of household junk and rusting hulks of cars attested to the landowner's deep and abiding respect for the environment. But the place was cheap, so I bought it. While developing this property, I received an angry letter from an adjoining property owner stating that he did not want the old farm cut up into lots because the added traffic would interfere with his privacy. He was prepared to deny any road improvements on the 12-ft. right-of-way, and he would not sign utility easements for the extension of electric and telephone lines over his land.

I ended up having to buy the man out at higher than market value, and he moved on to greener pastures. Better than house and land is the lesson that you must do your homework when buying country property, this whether you are purchasing it for your own enjoyment, or buying it for investment or development. The lucky horseshoe I picked up in this acquisition was the unforeseen value gained through the state's establishment of a public wildlife area next to my land. Diligent homework on my part would have nailed this good luck charm on the door to the deal.

Cheap Hunting Camp at Fishing Lake $1800

Madison, VA–3 ac. joining 8,000 ac. Govt. Wildlife Area. For cabin, tent or trailer. Stone's throw from small lake to fish, swim. Herds of deer. Mountain views. Secluded, Easy to own. Just $25 dn. $25 mo. Call Owner collect at 635-8637.

W. VA

10,000 HIPPIES RALLY IN NEW YORK–April, 1967 –
The Beatles

A swarm of hippies descended on New York's Polo Field for a "Be-In" to promote free love, world peace, and to share acid. The gathering was modeled after the tribal blast in San Francisco in January where dropouts from a new generation hallucinated for a mythic oneness within humanity and hoped-for personal identity.

An investor hopeful called me on the phone with a washed-out riverfront deal he had stumbled into. He said he had been eyeballing my ads and hinted that he wanted to be a player, but that he was in the bush leagues for loot. I liked the color green in waterfront property, so I hustled him to the county courthouse and showed him how to pull a plat and deed from the records.

A quick scan of this information revealed that the sellers had divided up some land and now wanted to dump the project. By looking at the required tax stamps on the deed, I determined what the sellers had paid for the land and compared that figure with the asking price. In those days, Internal Revenue documentary tax stamps were placed on deeds when land was transferred and subsequently recorded. Today, the federal government is no longer involved in taxing land, and most states impose their own taxes on land under similar ratios. For example, 50 cents in revenue stamps may be required for each $500, or fraction thereof the sales price. Based on the asking price for the land, the potential sales numbers looked good. Back then, I was all over a two-state map running the show out of my basement, with my wife hired on as bookkeeper. So I promoted this hopeful investor to limited partner, arranged financing, and we ribboned the deal.

Two months later he was giving away rowboats and breaking sales records on the shores of the Cacapon river, this in the company of his rug-selling friends and relatives. This project, along with other wise investments in country properties, provided him with a magic carpet to a very prosperous career.

NEW RIVERFRONT
in the nearby mountains

Close to Cacapon State Park. 2 acres on the clean and clear Cacapon
River. Wooded, level. Very picturesque. Enjoy lazy summer days
along the river. **FREE BOAT INCLUDED!** Just $1,950. Can
take $19 dn.$19 mo. Less for cash. Call Owner collect at Baltimore, MD 1-424-3042.

In 2002, I sold two acres on the Cacapon River for $35,000. I also
sold many twenty-acre parcels for close to $100,000 in that same year.
What will they be worth in 30 years? You will note that the customers
in 1968 got far more than a free boat. At $19 down and $19 per month,
the entire deal was practically free. If you're short of funds and friends,
carefully chosen owner-financed properties–particularly waterfront–
could yield you twice the value if you play your cards right.

Woodstock, VA
ISRAEL INVADES ARAB NATIONS –June 5, 1967–Young Rascals

Black Bear Crossing

While Israeli tanks, troops, and planes swept with great dispatch
over the deserts of the U.A.R., Syria, and Jordan, the land boom descended on Virginia's Shenandoah Valley with monstrous force and
amazing speed. Local governments were ill-prepared for the flood of
city people overflowing into the region and laying claim to land and
country property.

One of the first objectives seized by this army of land seekers was a
park-like peninsula that forms a part of the George Washington National
Forest and is surrounded on three sides by the crystal clear North Fork of
the Shenandoah River. The pastoral river and mountain scenery is unex-
celled. The farm has great historic and archeological significance

Indians camped here centuries ago and many relics of this civilization can still be found in the fields and along the river banks. The
Massanutten Mountains soar to a height of 1800 feet above the seven
bends of the river as it winds serpent-like through the Shenandoah
Valley. Spoils of purchase include hunting, fishing, swimming, canoe-

ing, mountain climbing, and artifact searching–an all-in-one setting for the family seeking an ideal vacation and weekend retreat.

ON RIVER JOINING NAT'L FOREST FIRST OFFER!

Where mountains meet the sky. Eagle's nest. See 3 river bends. 3 ac. with 220 ft. on Shenandoah and 400 ft. on the Forest. Hunt million ac. in your back yard, and canoe, fish, swim in front. At road's end for privacy. Old Indian campground. Discover wealth of artifacts. Unusual vacation and weekend spot for cabin, home, or camp. All woods with trail leading into Nat'l Forest for hiking and mountain climbing. Less than 2 hrs. D.C. area. $2,950. Min. terms: $40 dn, $40 mo. Call Owner collect at 1-635-5789

UNUSUAL OFFER OF RIVERFRONT FARM

Historic 3 BR, 3 BA brick and frame home on 15 fertile acres. Circa 1780. Now remodelled. 36X18 LR with two fireplaces. Spacious DR with fireplace. Breakfast nook and study next to kitchen. Shaded by centuries-old elm trees. Sound brick barn constructed as fort for protection from hostile Indians. Could be a real showcase. Fishing, canoeing, swimming in your front yard. Hunt in adj. National Forest. Now occupied. Steal for $3,000 below appraisal. $24,500! Sale by Owner. Call 1-535-5789

In re-reading the no-growth alarmist propaganda of the day, you would think that the Valley had been under assault by a task force of fast-buck, fly-by-night land hustlers and a rag-tag army of squatters who were littering the landscape with shacks, old school buses, and broken-down trailers. Folks, this scenario never happened on my watch. Admitting no particular altruistic motivation on my part, Black Bear Crossing turned out to be a profitable project for the three developers, of which I was one. It was a well-timed acquisition, purchased with the theory in mind that "If you build it, they will come." Bold investors and developers have followed this timeless mantra to great fortunes and blessed failures.

The lesson harvested here is one of fortune blossoming out of the fruits of past experience and boldness. The lots were bound with sensible building restrictions, and the project has yielded enduring and enjoyable benefits to the county and all who have lived there. Yearly price hikes on riverfront within Black Bear Crossing are as predictable as the rising river level in spring.

Since 1963, when I gambled $50 on my first riverfront lot, I have watched waterfront prices rise consistently at a minimum rate of 10-15% per year. The same is true for soundly purchased country properties as a whole. Of course, many investors and successful developers are realizing far greater returns, albeit at added risk. But effective entrepreneurs realize that constant exposure to opportunity has a tendency to sharpen the eye and make one wary of second-hand opinions from others, such as agents with their own agendas. So risk has its own reward.

How do smart investors and successful developers locate the right properties? Some of God's creatures have the right instincts and the required motivation. A bull will plunge forward, but will not attempt to fly. Others will blunder through life using the trial-and-error method, all the while gaining wisdom from failure. For those players just starting out in the country properties game, I have developed a scoring system shown later in this book that will bring the gods of chance to your service. With practice, you may soon discard this system and rely on your own good judgment to discover those diamonds and pearls hidden in the countryside. But before venturing further, you should be aware of some potentially harmful forces lurking in the shadows of your proposed discoveries.

Endangered Species Act

No-growth environmentalists often unleash this law to eat up the value of country property and to make it immune from any consideration for development. For example, if a certain type of woodpecker was spotted drilling holes in those woods you envisioned for your cabin, you could be forced by the U.S. government to give up your proposed habitat to the woodpecker without compensation.

This type of land control is clearly for the birds. Or suppose you saw a protected species of rat gnawing a door into your abode above the river. You could be forced by the feds to allow the rats to occupy your surrounding territory, rendering the remainder of your land useless for further human habitation and creating a firetrap of grassland that cannot be cut or disturbed while the rats are sleeping and building their families. The least we know is that some enraged and devious "come here" or environmental whacko could plant a lazy endangered snail in the creek on your land and alert the federal snail catchers, this forcing you to put a shell on your proposed subdivision. And be lynx-eyed toward the endangered eagle that lands anywhere near your proposed profit center in the country. That bird can make the day for environmental land grabbers. Your investment could sink 90% or more when the eagle lands on your property and is granted his own domain.

Salamander Granted 43,000-Acre Kingdom

Twenty years after the Endangered Species Act was introduced, an agreement was reached between the U.S. Fish and Wildlife Service and the G.W. National Forest to protect the Cow Nob salamander from the alleged threat of mankind. The move made the salamander one of the largest landholders in the states of Virginia and West Virginia. This sacrifice to the gods of the environment occurred on public land and supposedly stabilized the species so that it would not have to be placed on the endangered list.

Humans Keep Out

The official explanation for this showcase conciliatory approach is that it would save the taxpayers millions of dollars by heading off future environmental controversies, such as the flap over the Spotted Owl. This time they were giving license to public land to the insect community. But beware the Ides of March. Encroaching government environmental policies offer little consolation to private landowners facing economic ruin when caught "red-handed" with an "endangered" species on their property.

Endangered Humans

Washington would soon discover that small farmers of the human kind were more of an endangered species than flies and lizards and that it may be wiser to offer legislation expanding existing programs for the productive use of suitable public land by allowing those who qualify to undertake, with compensation to the government, such legitimate activities as farming, grazing, and logging, all of which make a meaningful and measurable contribution to the advancement of mankind's standard of living and overall happiness in this world.

Of course it's disconcerting for some of us to see our government force a choice between the worth of the human condition and the inestimable value of a lizard. But an agency of this government that would throw human comfort into a spittoon in favor of a creature that "eats insects and hides under rocks and logs" would make anyone nervous about the wisdom and insight of our bureaucrats and political leaders.

Playing God

In the continuing saga of man's relentless pursuit to play God, we witness time and again the spectacle of overzealous federal agencies literally prostrating themselves before rats, birds, and insects and granting them vast kingdoms, while restricting legitimate human activity on both public and private lands. Far-flung habitats that rival the holdings of the world's richest rulers have been set aside for creatures of questionable value, because tenured government bureaucrats and well-healed environmental zealots, in all of their flawed, self-granted wisdom, have determined that these species are critical to the survival of mankind, this while the citizenry of the nation is frequently suffering through unprecedented economic turmoil, terrorist threats, and natural disasters of the worst kind.

Mad Scientists

Scientists say that plants and animals should be protected from extinction because they form important links in natural systems and because they may yield yet-undiscovered products.

By the year 1994, approximately 820 protected species were on the scientists' wish list, with only 4,100 more to go. With science having to consistently revise its handle on the "facts" about life, one need not wonder how the human species endured these millions of years without the help of scientists, as lesser species died out. If such creatures as the dinosaur and the wooly mammoth were meant to still roam the earth, God assuredly would have restricted man's dominion over the earth's creatures and provided him with a more heavenly authorized endangered list than the one dreamed up by man's often feeble mind.

The Great Snail Retreat

A 1994 article in the *Wall Street Journal* reported that a federal judge removed Idaho's Bruneau Hot Springs Snail from the endangered list. This is the tiny mollusk that threatened to shut down the economy of Idaho's Bruneau Valley. Judge Harold Ryan criticized the U.S. Fish and Wildlife Service for withholding scientific data from the public and said its behavior "represented self-serving and superficial responses from an agency that had already made up its mind."

Babbitt Backs Off

Also in 1994, President Clinton's Interior Secretary, Bruce Babbitt, said the issue of the endangered snail was essentially a hollow shell. In response to a group of 100 or so ranchers, he remarked, "There's a lot less here than meets the eye." Angry landowners in the valley used the government's environmental retreat as evidence that the Endangered Species Act was being used by extremists to halt unwanted development and to restrict private property rights.

Live facts show that not all environmentalists are crafty land-grabbers and that all developers are not greedy and insensitive toward the environment. Clever real estate investors realize that appraisals are generally required by lenders and that, in most cases, appraisal standards call for the identification of any known endangered species, wetlands, floodplain areas, and coastal zone concerns on the subject property. If you don't want to be painted as foolish on your investment, be aware that these legalized elements – introduced into the real estate picture by the environmental movement and the ESA – are potentially harmful to you, this when they are used against you with blind prejudice and partiality. It is through the widespread misuse of laws such as the Endangered Species Act by radical environmentalists, that these human frailties can kill your investment plans while being passed off to the public as the flaming spirit of enlightenment.

Mousetrap Laws

Other laws, such as those dealing with historic preservation, could also have a negative impact on your investments in country property, particularly when public hearings are required before local governmental bodies. For example, following the discovery of a real or imagined Indian civilization along a river on your property, hostile environmentalists and angry no-growth chanters could belt out a war cry to burn your development plans at the stake.

In today's sociopolitical environment, riverfront developments such as Black Bear Crossing could not be pulled off due to the enforcement of these mousetrap laws. I would have to dream up another concept if this land were to be developed in this day and age. Dreams, of course, must work their way through the mind on their way to reality, or they will always be dreams and nothing more.

As mentioned earlier, I created a scoring system, explained in later pages, to help investors determine whether to make an acquisition. Keep in mind that none of these mousetrap laws were set out during my early years in this business, though I was not safe from lawsuits. Certainly, you will want to avoid those investments that can snare you in a prolonged lawsuit. Unwanted litigation can entrap your mental prowess, cause ill health, and dissipate your investment.

Woodstock, VA
CHE GUEVARA SHOT. REBELS STORM PENTAGON–Oct. 1967
– The Box Tops

The true revolutionary lay still in the blood-stained furrows of Bolivia while his shadow, the anti-war Armies of the Night, polished their plans to march on the military palace overlooking the Potomac. In the Shenandoah Valley, a small-time operator approached me with an offer to sell his remaining lots inside the G.W. National Forest. I ran the numbers and took him up on the deal, bringing in two partners with whom I had worked before.

The unique feature of the sales promotion was the arming of buyers with brand new Winchester rifles. Needless to say, this stirred up the anti-gun lobby. Alarmist letters were sent to local newspapers about the insensitivity of such a thing, especially in view of President Kennedy's assassination by a high-powered rifle several years before. The *Washington Post* even chimed in that I had to retune the promotion if they were to continue accepting my advertising. I guess it was okay for hunters to have guns, but to give them away, well, that's another thing. There's too many whackos out there with guns already. What if they got in the hands of the blacks?

In 1967, it was widely known that it was not okay for blacks to own land in the Shenandoah Valley, or almost anywhere else in the rural south for that matter. In fact, to paraphrase Shakespeare, we were prepared to talk to them, walk with them, sell merchandise to them, and so following; but not eat with them, drink with them, pray with them, or sell them land or guns.

Of course I was concerned about in-grown local objections to blacks establishing a beachhead in the Valley, but I was not going to deny anyone the opportunity to own land because of his or her color. In the spirit of the slain leader, Martin Luther King, activists for integration had organized squads of counterfeit buyers to test real estate agents on their willingness to sell to blacks.

I remember a situation in which a salesman, who had participated in the 1963 Civil Rights March on Washington, balked at dealing with a black couple. The salesman had a good heart, but he was not good at morally confronting the circumstances in which he found himself. I greeted the couple, showed them around, and they left without buying. I don't recall if any blacks bought land in the development called Hidden Pass at the time of this promotion; but if they did they got their guns.

UNUSUAL OPPORTUNITY TO BUY A SMALL TRACT OF LAND IN NAT'L FOREST

FREE!–NEW WINCHESTER LEVER ACTION HUNTING RIFLE TO BUYERS OF EACH LOT

OWNER SELLING BALANCE OF PRIVATE LAND HELD BACK FROM FOREST SERVICE. ONLY 2 HOURS FROM D.C. USE FISH POND, SWIMMING LAKE

(1) Attractive wooded camping site of 2/3 ac. with mountain view. Nice place for cabin $495. Min. terms: $25 down. $25 per month. 6% int. on unpaid balance. (2) Nearly 2 acres with excellent road access and long frontage on Nat'l Forest line. Wooded. Great views. $1450. $25 down. $25 per month. Less for cash deal. (3) Over 3 ac. joining Forest for about 550 ft. Good road frontage $2250. A-1 investment. Involves 3 lots. To inspect, call Owner collect at BOYCE, VA 218.

After we had armed scores of lot buyers, a high U.S. government official warned county fathers about the imminent threat to their way of life. "It is hard to raise taxes on something that will fit on a half-acre lot," he said. "Twenty-five dollars down gets the buyer a free hunting rifle and guarantees him a front porch seat in a rural slum, where old school buses come to die." I will give equal measure to this viewpoint, since all apple barrels contain some rotten fruit. But for the record, all of my developments have restrictions against junk cars and old school buses. As for the reference to slums, a visual audit would show that most purchasers of country property do not foster slum conditions; nor are they steeped in poverty.

The words, FREE GIFT, are redundant when used in a sales promotion. Gifts are obviously given for the giver to get paid. I have given away a multitude of inducements, including guns, meals, tents, boats, picnic tables, fireplaces, books, tractors, cars, ATV's, gas, motor homes, camping trailers, amphibious vehicles, coins, and even drilled wells. In most cases the giveaways proved fruitful. The one flop I recall was the offer of free motorcycles to land buyers. The promotion was doomed because it didn't make good sense. How many customers ride motorcycles? How many scorpions have crawled all over me through customer complaints? I have no excuse for my faults. I leave them where they lay before more monstrous ones.

The worst con game I can recall in past years was the lure of a FREE VACATION to consumers, just for sticking their nose under a lot sales tent. High-pressure dirt peddlers would then whip so-called "ups" with a heavy sales pitch and pack them off to Florida (on their dime) where they would bed them down in some Third World hotel and torture them for hours on end, hitting them again with a sales pitch for some newly drained swampland paradise with mosquitoes so big they can carry off your dog. A Florida land hustler once told me "If they ever stop us from givin' things away, we're outta business."

In 1969, the feds locked onto the scams and passed legislation to protect consumers from their own gullibility, and some con men were thrown in the slammer. Under assault by the feds, the land industry fought back by attempting to assemble and mingle the dirty crooks and the good-guy developers into some kind of defensive lobbying organization with headquarters in Washington D.C. and to pin badges of credibility on the group's members. When the feds attacked by requiring intensive and detailed disclosures, the unredeemed Devil's Brigade within this band of developers began to brazenly pitch these disclosures as prima facie evidence that the feds had endorsed their scams. The fed chief, observing these tactics in print, then went ballistic and promptly overkilled the developers with further disclosures that haunted them with suspicion. This move resulted in the bankruptcy of some good guys, while driving gangs of land hustlers into less regulated scams.

My first two years in this business had been quite a ride. I sometimes made foolish mistakes, but I was able to laugh at them because the experiences were not enough to make me sad. Roaring into 1968 was like entering a world gone amok. U.S. combat deaths in Vietnam had almost reached 20,000. The Black Panthers were on the march, student protests were rampant, and Martin Luther King's assassination had left a legacy of violence in the cities.

L.A., California
ROBERT KENNEDY ASSASSINATED – June 6, 1968 –
Simon & Garfunkel

Kennedy, the presidency of the U.S. just beyond his grasp after claiming victory in the California primary, was gunned down in the kitchen of the Ambassador Hotel as he exited from a speaking engagement. Sirhan Sirhan, a young Arab, was indicted the following day on a charge of first-degree murder. He had gone to the hotel with the intention of assassinating Kennedy.

Deer Rapids

Late in 1967, I had gone to look at a 500-acre riverfront farm with a real estate agent, and he got lost trying to find the property. But fortunately the end result surpassed the beginning.

Eventually we found the place, and I, along with two partners, purchased it for $110,000 cash. The real estate salesman, in a twist of fate, ended up working for me. The farm was located in a distant bucolic county then considered safe from an undue infiltration of city people, much less an invasion by an overwhelming horde. Each of the partners ponied up a thousand dollars as a deposit, and the rest of the down payment was raised through loans from three small loan companies. Our fortunes in those days were based on ever-increasing stacks of promissory notes from land buyers, so we were always short of cash. We were winging it on the balance of the purchase price, because we had no financing lined up and no contingency option in the contract, this to strengthen the offer and make it immune from competitive bids.

Meanwhile, hysteria and xenophobia raced through the county court-houses, into newspaper print, and out into the villages and small towns. The county fathers worked with lawyers far into the night preparing paper barriers to protect the citizenry from the infectious outsiders. "SURBURBIA TO COME TO THIS COUNTY?" blared the headline of a local newspaper. "Sooner or later, these people are going to take possession of these mail-order lots," went the story. "That's gonna place a terrible burden on the county. It's our watershed they're talk-ing about." Pictures were shown by the ex-mayor to the commission-ers of a wild kid in a leather jacket displaying obscene statements. The teen-ager was arrested in a local shopping center for petty larceny and displaying obscene writing. He had been camping in the National For-est with his parents the weekend the arrest was made. The barbarians were inside the gates.

NOW YOU HAVE THE CHANCE TO OWN A PLACE ON THE RIVER
First Offer! Adjoining the G.W. Nat'l Forest
On the Shenandoah, where the mountains meet the sky. Nearly 2.5 ac. with 200 ft. on the river. Spring water. Perfect for fishing and get-a-way. Camp in the mountains. Lovely level and shaded meadow now alive with wild flowers. Water so clear you can see the bottom. Ideal for camping trailer, tent, or cabin. Swim, fish, take canoeing adventures from your private shoreline. Build a dock. Hunt and fish in adj. Nat'l Forest. $3,750. Min. terms: $50 dn. $50 per mo. Cash discount. B.K. HAYNES REAL ESTATE - On cor-ner of Rts. 55 and 340 "At the turn to Skyline Drive" Call for appointment any day 9-5.

By the time this development started stirring up dirt and gossip, I had purchased a small building in Front Royal and set up a real estate office with a large sign showing a running deer.

The building would soon become a landmark for locating rural prop-erties in the Shenandoah Valley. To kick off the Deer Rapids promo-tion, I offered, in my display advertising, a free lunch or dinner (up to $5.00, which was the going fare back then) at several local restaurants to lookers and buyers alike. I took some local flak from a few developers–presumably more brainy than me–that I was insulting the intelligence of the general public. We got paid for the free gifts through record sales. The cost of a riverfront lot in this development would hit the $70-$80,000 mark by 2004.

Strasburg, VA
½ MILLION U.S. TROOPS NOW IN VIETNAM – July, 1968 –
Herb Alpert

The U.S. sank deeper into the Vietnamese quagmire with the build-up of troops. A Gallup poll found half of Americans opposing the Vietnam War. Disillusioned military personnel formed a protest group, Vietnamese Veterans Against the War. Ron Kovic, the Marine sergeant who volunteered to go back for a second tour, and who wrote *Born on the 4th of July*, was hit by enemy gunfire in an assault on a Vietnamese village. Paralyzed, and never able to regain use of his legs, he later joined the dissenting veteran group.

Recovering Investments Through Rentals

When sinking your money into country properties you can often recoup your down payment and offset your monthly mortgage payments by selling off or renting out any homes on the property. Almost all of my riverfront developments had money-making homes that usually recouped my down payment when sold off. And although I never rented out properties, I frequently sold to customers who, in turn, recovered all or part of their mortgage payments through rentals.

UNUSUAL OFFER OF OLD RIVERFRONT FARM

Owner selling out. 5 BR stone charmer and fixer-upper for up to two families. Circa 1830. Oil heat. One Bath. Quality barn. Sturdy outbldgs. Sweeping mtn.views. Fields and trees, on sparkling Shenandoah River. Steal this gem for weekends, vacations, or rental income. Just $25,000.

Today's real estate prices exceed any overstated testimonial as to the appreciation rate on this type of property. Following are other examples of country properties that investors–assuming they had the money–could have purchased in July, 1968. Buying and selling this kind of property has helped me to amass a considerable pile of green over the years. If you're a beginner, it may take you a little time to become acquainted with property values in your region of interest.

Obtaining a real estate license could probably help you along, but a license is not necessary. It is more important that you recognize and act upon the opportunities that are out there before your very eyes. The process of building wealth through country property differs little from the well-documented activities of smart city investors who have accumulated riches through the purchase, improvement, and resale of urban real estate.

Chicago, Illinois
CONVENTION RIOTS IN THE STREETS – August, 1968 –
The Doors

Protests over the Vietnamese war turned into a riot as the Democrats assembled to choose Hubert Humphrey for their presidential candidate. The violence resulted in blood and tear gas when policemen with nightsticks charged into organizers leading a march to the convention center. Amid the melee, more than 100 were injured, including children, elderly people, and reporters.

In August, I was on the horn with Bob, a recently retired sergeant and radio operator on the flying White House, now known as Air Force One. Bob had landed in the real estate business and wanted me to look at a development property on the Maryland shoreline of the Chesapeake Bay. I figured he was representing the owner of the property, and the pitch was a troubled development needing a fix of some kind. I had been splashing expensive display ads all over the Washington and Baltimore areas, and Bob suspected I had a few talents that might help his client. Over lunch and a couple of drinks we jawed about life in the fast skies.

I asked him who his favorite commander-in-chief was during his tour (Eisenhower). And we relived his 25 missions over Germany in a B-17. The next morning we cranked up my plane and flew over Washington and the Potomac River. In the distance I could see Fort Myer where I often burned up the streets of D.C. piloting an ambulance as an army medic. My thoughts turned to Foundry Methodist Church, just blocks from the White House, the whole vicinity restricted from overflights. As a lost soul of eighteen, I had wandered aimlessly into the church one day and found good friends and a spiritual anchor. Then, after moving to the mountains, I had lost touch with these true friends; but throughout all of my travels, religious studies, and disillusionment with a few preachers, I have never lost my faith in Christianity and its guiding principle of having friends for the sake of giving rather than receiving, and for offering me the power of prayer.

Oft remembered are the times I have found my words flying up to reach my thoughts only to discover another prayer fulfilled. Soon we were over the Chesapeake Bay and on final approach to a grass strip at the client's weekend and vacation farm.

The owner was fumbling with the idea of dividing the land into lots and needed a savvy development partner and advice. After several flights to check the wings of the deal and to meet with all the players, we came to a partnership agreement, and I met with Bob and the owner at the owner's office in downtown D.C. to ink the deal. It was convenient for me because I was booking suites at the newly-constructed Watergate complex and using the hotel as my in-town hangout.

I used to be a flunky messenger boy for an airline lobbying organization, and I remember seeing an official, for whom I performed many errands, chatting over the phone in a booth. He was a nice guy and then-new president of a major airline. I thought of the days when I had delivered bottles of booze to Capitol Hill at Christmas for the company. Now here I was ordering vintage wines and getting massaged in the same salons as the big-time executives and politicians.

When I hit it big in the country I often split for the city to conduct business and dine with fine wine. I could have picked up a condo at the Watergate for about $70,000 before the locks were worth picking.

No, I don't want to know what it would cost me now. The joy would come too cheap.

I worked with the owner's surveyor and contractor to design a development acceptable to the county fathers and regulatory cops. One of the peculiar concepts of the day along parts of the world's largest estuary dealt with sewage disposal. The theory was that sewage could be pumped down into the high water table and that the subsurface infiltration of Chesapeake Bay waters would act as a flushing mechanism and purification process, performing the same task as a septic system installed in sand and porous soils. It would appear that this controversial process could lead to groundwater defilement, contaminated wells, and the potential pollution of Bay waters. I believe that this process was approved by health authorities at that time; although it has probably been modified or is no longer permitted.

Another activity that developers freely practiced in the fifties and sixties was the dredging of canals to create waterfront properties and the subsequent filling in of wetlands. Now both activities are heavily regulated and, in many areas of the country, not permitted at all. Permits for development activities were much easier to obtain in the late sixties than they are today. And almost all new large-scale land developments now require federal regulatory disclosures that further delay the introduction of new country and waterfront properties on the market and add costs to the developers' bottom line.

Within a month of my first meeting with Bob, and while some permits and the required approvals were still gathering dust on some public servant's desk, lot stakes were in the ground, canals were being dredged, and the Swan Harbor project was launched.

It seems certain that waterfront prices will never be this low again. However, successful people make more opportunities than they find. That said, I feel you can find profitable real estate opportunities by looking for legitimate waterfront offers and getting there first. Of course, there are frequent times when you may not be in a financial position to invest.

Nevertheless, a wise first investment in the right waterfront property can yield significant returns and compound itself as you re-invest your profits in other sound properties. The reasoning behind a concentrated effort toward waterfront investment is obvious. A rising tide floats all boats. The price tide rises faster and more fully at the water's edge. As a new development builds out, the push for waterfront expands exponentially. Demand tends to outdistance supply. But you lose much of your touted investment edge when you buy from speculators and buyers who outraced you to the water.

LIMITED BAYFRONT OPPORTUNITY!

BOAT OWNERS, DUCK HUNTERS, OUTDOORSMEN
Need investors with $500 down, $55 per month for waterfront on the Eastern Shore prior to completion of channel dredging. Tremendous resale potential. Wooded land fronting on Chesapeake Bay and deep inland waterways with boat slips. Steal 1 to 5 acres with 200 ft. or more waterfront on each parcel. Airfield, club house. Adjacent to government wildlife area. Only 55 air miles from D.C. $4,950 NOW. BUT NEVER AGAIN. Proposed new Chesapeake Bay bridge below property. Get in on ground floor. Call Owner.

Money was pouring in from projects in three states and from my brokerage operation. One day at Swan Harbor I was introduced to a slick character who claimed to have been the financial manager for Rocky Graziano, the famous prize fighter. He was pitching a grand scheme to promote a Shopper's Passport credit card entitling consumers to receive cash rebates for purchases from selected merchants. This was the precursor of the Discover Card. Sensing a need to diversify my business operations, I cleansed myself of excess cash and became a player with control of international franchise rights. I remember the brains of the operation–a computer that filled an entire room and that performed tasks now accomplished with a desktop PC.

At the time, my brother-in-law was working for a bank on the West Coast, helping to kick off the new Mastercard. I hastily imported him and his family to the D.C. area, mantled him with a vice presidency, and charged him with authority to help build up this house of cards. Within a year, he was back on the Coast, disillusioned with the whole escapade. I should have seen the bats among the birds when the passport promotor said he needed a few grand to fly down to St. Vincent for a pow-wow with some monied CEOs. I said I would like to go along for the ride. For reasons I can't remember, he said he didn't think it was a good idea. The whole scheme eventually collapsed into a fraud investigation, and I had to fight a bloody audit when I claimed legitimate losses to lessen the considerable tax bite on my gains in 1968.

Rural W. VA
MORE BOMBS FALL ON NAM THAN IN WWII – Sept. 1968 –
The Beatles

In the fall of 1968, I was dropping into land sales offices in three states–Virginia, Maryland, and West Virginia. In the Mountaineer State we had ransomed a king-sized forest from some greedy landowners. And in these nearby ridges and hollows, my partners and I were building lakes and vacation cabins to accommodate hordes of woeful city dwellers seeking refuge in the mountains outside of D.C. and Baltimore. Guns and butter were plentiful as the Vietnam War dragged on, and discord over the war and discretionary income were at record levels. Racial tension was palpable, and more and more whites retreated west to trade their dollars for the hills and hollows.

FOUR-STATE VIEW

Own the sky! Approx. two acres joining 25,000 acre state forest. See W. VA. VA. MD. and Penna. Soft green meadow under shade of massive oaks. Ideal for chalet. Build or camp. Hunt and hike in king-sized forest bordering your land. Deer in your fields on most nights. Swim, fish, canoe in ½ mi-long lake. $1,950 $50 dn. $50 mo. Less for cash. Call Owner.

BEST FALL BUYS IN MOUNTAIN PROPERTY!

Sky high A-Frame–New shell home joins 25,000 acre state forest just 90 minutes from D.C. 30-mile-view. Swim, fish in ½ mile-long lake. Hunt, hike in sprawling wilderness in your back yard. A-frame includes fireplace, loft, and large deck.1 ac. Just $5700.

Avoid crowded campgrounds–4-acre forest kingdom for camp or cabin joins vast state forest. Top of the world views. See 3 mountain ranges. Big woods. For camp, cabin. Lake nearby. Just $1950. $40 dn. $30 per mo. Call Owner.

As you might suspect, these low-end offers, while legitimate, are teasers to encourage large numbers of prospective customers. Generally speaking, high sales numbers are built on crowds of people. When a customer feels all alone, he has no competition for the offer and is less inclined to make a decision to buy. I look back on the days of my early teens when I sold magazines, and later in my early twenties when I sold pots and pans door to door. These products were among the hardest items to sell under the worst possible conditions–cold canvassing, one on one. Urgency is the lifeblood of a sales pitch.

Generally there was always some gimmick in the pitch that tried to bring forth a sale. In magazine sales it might be " working your way through college", or in pots and pans it was "sacrificing your samples below cost." In high-pressure land sales it was largely the pitch that "they ain't making any more land." When there were large numbers of people milling about, you were expected to believe that the last of the earth's surface was about to fall into the hands of the next guy in line. Some land hustlers even slunk to a two-way radio gimmick to call in a phony offer when another sales hero was hosing down his customer to confess his love for the same lot.

I have never encouraged high-pressure tactics when selling real estate because the technique is based on a false premise–that customers at large are either totally uninformed about the product or too stupid to think for themselves. Uneducated customers need to be brought up to speed by the sales person and weak-willed persons should not be preyed upon by aggressive commission seekers. A legitimate sales presentation based on facts is a far better approach and results in more satisfied customers. Consistently selling somebody something the customer doesn't want or need can lead to a very shallow life for the conscientious salesperson.

Madison, VA
U.S. STOPS BOMBING VIETNAM – October, 1968 –
The Supremes

Cynics called President Johnson's suspension of further bombing an attempt to bolster Vice President Hubert Humphrey's election chances. Johnson hoped the move would lead to progress in the Paris peace talks. In exchange for the bombing halt, Hanoi agreed to allow South Vietnamese participation in the peace discussions.

With thousands of acres under contract east of the Blue Ridge, I began bombarding the D.C. area with large full-page color display ads in the *Washington Post* touting an amazing offer.

The ads went on to describe properties so unique that I have never
seen their like again outside of the National Parks. Here are a couple
of samples:

E. Blue Ridge Mtns. 90 min. 495
Own Your Own Trout Stream Adjoining State Hunting Land

Look for sites like this only in the Nat'l Parks. High country camp beside 200 ft on roaring, cascading stream with leaping trout. 2 ½ acres of soaring timber with scenery displaying every color of the spectrum. 8,000 acres of hunting land in your back yard bordering the 300-sq.-mi. Shenandoah National Park for privacy and unlimited hiking. Trails, waterfalls, scenic vistas. Swimming lake below. $1,950. $30 dn. $30 mo. or $1650 cash. B.K. HAYNES REAL ESTATE

In a great many cases, I was dealing with the remnants of a mountain civilization that existed before the park snatched the old settlers' land for pennies on the dollar. These abandoned homesteads were on the fringes of the park boundary and, in some situations, they had not been occupied for more than thirty years, this when the mountain people packed up thinking they, too, were to become victims of a voracious land-grabbing federal bureaucracy.

ABANDONED MOUNTAIN FARM ON TROUT STREAM

Old run-down mountaineer's homestead back in hill country joining Shenandoah National Park. Postcard scenery. Galloping white-capped trout stream along eastern border of this 6-acre farm. Ageless run-down shack with rock chimney left to die in overgrown fields. 2 huge spruce trees guard the state road entrance to this ghost of the past. $6,750. Min. 10% dn. $70 mo. Or steal for cash price, $5,500. B.K. HAYNES REAL ESTATE

Washington, D.C.
NIXON BEATS HUMPHREY– November, 1968 – Marvin Gaye

Richard Nixon, in a remarkable comeback, edged out Hubert Humphrey by 500,000 votes to claim the presidency of the U.S. In 1962, Nixon had lost the race for governor of California. And in 1960, then-Vice President Nixon was defeated in a run for president by John F. Kennedy. Nixon waited six years in the wings of the Republican party gathering support for his victory.

Fools Rush In

A short Jimmy Hoffa-type guy in an army sweater, one year shy of 60, sits in the lobby of the Watergate Hotel waiting for his son. The character needs a shave and looks totally out of place, as if he had wandered in from the street to get warm. Having come upstairs in the world, I had, in the company of my two brothers, set out on a foolish quest to find my long-lost father who had abandoned his family and who had mentored me on how *not* to get ahead in the world.

A couple of days before, my morning coffee had been sweetened by word that my old man was holed up in a hovel behind a barber shop on the white-stepped streets of Baltimore, a city that I remember once had a saloon on every corner. In his heyday he wore dark shirts and white ties and sang like Crosby. Now he was dressed like a rummy in Salvation Army clothes and actually seemed proud of his frugality.

After finding him reveling in the lap of poverty, I invited him to meet me in Washington and toast my success with a bottle of champagne. He much appreciated the gesture and welcomed the opportunity to bond once again with his offspring; but he said he was on the wagon and would never again imbibe. But I managed to quiet my fears about my father at the expense of hope. Didn't he run PDQ Duplicating, a one-mimeograph enterprise that was, in the fanciful world of my dad, the precursor to IBM? When the venture failed, didn't we flee a rooming house in the dead of night and leave a little old lady screaming that we were beating her out of her well-earned rent money? Birth trumped wisdom, and I failed to judge a man by his deeds. I needed a trusted and talented confidant to handle advertising and to set up a direct mailing system for a burgeoning list of prospects.

Of course, his activites with me could be nothing but legit. He lasted about a week at my house before my wife forced me to throw him out, this with the primary interest of my son at heart. He packed up and moved into town where he kicked off a credible and effective direct mail operation that produced monthly bulletins of country properties for sale. Of course, a decent car and salary, additional personnel, and all sorts of duplicating machines and racks of metal plates were required to sustain operations. Today, a full-scale, efficiently run direct mail operation can be done through the Internet by one person using a single-unit computer, scanner, and printer.

After an uncomfortable champagne and coffee lunch, we laid out plans for the old con man and promoter of half-baked schemes to visit me in Virginia where–as I pointed out earlier–I would regrettably drag him into the life of my wife and son. Perhaps he could even be of value to me in my business, since he had a gift for words and could convince old ladies and such to part with their fat purses. The bubbly lunch at the Watergate occurred years before the bungled heist by Nixon's men, but hazy thoughts of my boyhood drifted though my mind, such as memories of newspaper headlines where Daddy et al. were nabbed inside a government building trying to lift a civil service mailing list for grandpa's direct mail operation. Then Daddy was away for a spell in the slammer. I recall being pinched as a kid for trying to break into a theater to see a movie. When the manager asked me where my father was, I cried when I confessed he was in jail. He was a wise guy whose attitude could leave him beat up and bloodied in some alley by young punks or plastered by brass knuckles when he felt some clown was flirting with his wife.

Daddy lasted about a year promoting small-town dreams and, after marrying a local widow for her money, he skipped town with her plump purse, slipped back on the bottle, and later died alone in his beloved city of Balitmore. Years later I went to a memorial service for him and have since learned from the experience to take seriously the commandment that we must honor our mothers and fathers, and show respect for our elders, this regardless of their faults. The truth about life is that it never ends and that it is bonded with love and the possibility of redemption.

Shenandoah River Lodge

A local real estate agent noticed that the sun had never set long on the bulk of my properties, so he came to my office with a deal I could not refuse. He had just listed a small riverfront resort, including a lodge and cabins, all overlooking the water. I snapped it up for redistribution to users before some altruistic soul could salt it away for himself as an historic preservation tax dodge. Please understand that I am in favor of historic preservation, this as long as it does not become a religion. And when investing in country property deals, keep in mind the fact that the rubbish of the past can bring the highest prices.

Sale of Riverfront Cabins
in Famous Mountain Resort

Fish from your front porch. 2 quality cottages for the price of 1.
Beautiful furnished rustic pine design. Unique setting under mammoth hemlock trees along the sparkling Shenandoah River. Rent
one to pay for both. Clear, clean canoeing waters. Long-range
mountain views into G.W. Nat'l Forest. Each unit has large rm,
BA, closet, stone fireplace. Tax break on rental units. Swim in
pool just steps away. All utilities incl. sewer, water. Most scenic
and restful location on the Shenandoah River. I know because I'm
keeping a unit for myself. Only 90 min. out. Just $9,950 to $11,950.
Also a few riverfront lots with central water & pool privileges
$3,500. Hurry before sellout. B.K. HAYNES REAL ESTATE

A Life of Leisure

I spent much of the winter in 1968-69 traveling to the Hawaiian
Islands, Acapulco, Mexico, the Bahamas, and other relaxing destinations. Vietnam peace talks had broken down in Paris, and the Viet Cong
were pushing toward Saigon. Back in the states, my staff and various
partners were keeping a lid on operations and preparing for the spring
push into the countryside by restless city dwellers.

Investors in country properties do not need to maintain a staff to
handle sales and development. Many of these activites can easily be
farmed out to qualified people. It is not generally advisable to use
urban real estate brokers to sell land in the country. The travel time
getting to and from your properties would eat up the agents' time, and
you would probably get lame and impotent results and inefficient service. When dealing with real estate agents, your best friend on a listing contract is a clause that gives you a 30-day right to cancel the
contract if you become dissatisfied with the services provided. If you
have hired the right broker, such a clause would not be necessary; but
expectation often fails in its promises, and you have to move on. You
cannot afford to wait, and wait, and wait for your properties to be sold.
And don't haggle over the commission, unless you've got a property
that people are literally begging to buy. Weaseling the broker down on
his commission is a sure way to ridicule agents' enthusiasm for selling
your listings.

Madison, VA
U.S. LOSSES IN NAM EXCEED KOREA – March, 1969 –
Beatles' White Album

Since 1961, when President Kennedy first sent military advisors into Vietnam, 33,641 Americans had died in combat. What had originally been a "cat and mouse" game of catching Viet Cong guerillas infiltrating through Laos into South Vietnam had evolved into a major war effort for the U.S., with eight consecutive years of military operations.

I had been playing country property monopoly for about four years, long enough to get a degree in the game. My customer base had been mainly the Washington, D.C. area, with Baltimore a close second. But I had reached as far north as Philadelphia for customers, and now I was on track for Richmond, Virginia, close to 3 hours south of the northern Shenandoah Valley.

A property hit my desk that fronted on a small fishing river and joined state hunting lands. Hunt and fish are words that go together like love and marriage.

A large market segment is always scouring the countryside for hunting and fishing land. When scouting for country properties you will want to keep this fact in mind. Some land is made for hunting; other parcels lend themselves more to fishing. The combination is dynamite for consumer response. So I hopped in my Skylane and flew down to Orange, Virginia, where my brother-in-law picked me up for an inspection trip to the subject property, a tract located in a rural county about an hour south of the airport. I had enlisted my brother-in-law into my growing cadre of limited partners, and I would want him to handle sales and field operations.

The development of rural land can be time-intensive, so it is best to have experienced people on site if you are spread out too thin, or if your primary occupation soaks up the bulk of your time. To handle necessary development tasks I have, over the years, contracted out the work so that I could have more time to write, travel, and enjoy life. Investors in country properties, as opposed to developers, may have neither the time, talent, or inclination to subdivide their land. This property was on a state road and required no road construction. Beyond the sales and promotion concept, our main development concerns were boundary and lot surveys, health permits, and compliance with subdivision regulations.

LAZY HUNT–FISH CAMP

Toss line in river from shaded bank on your own four acres joining state hunting lands on small, scenic river. Hook bass, blue gill, cat-fish, crappie, and other fresh water fish. Shoot deer and turkey across stream from your campsite. Bring tent, camper, build a small cabin. Hunt, hike trails deep in state forest to fishing, boating lakes. On state road for all-year access and only 1 hr. west of Richmond. $1,750. Min. terms: $50 dn. $25 per month. Call Owner for appointment.

Many customers for country property are looking for small farms, but these gems are hard to find. Often a large tract of land will come on the market with a high price tag and with large acreage, both far beyond the customer's comfort level. When you have armed yourself with financial clout, you can take a swing at the high-end deals out there. Here is a small farm created from a much larger parcel in a no-growth county back in the late sixties. The balance of the farm was probably sold off in strictly controlled minimum sizes of 25 to 50 acres. In a thriving economy, with creeping inflation, wisely purchased places like this can jump in value by hundreds of thousands of dollars within only a few years, this due to their historical significance.

HISTORIC SOUTHERN PLANTATION
FOR $75,000

Built by craftsmen in 1780 from bricks made on farm. Colonial beauty is right out of history books. Located in Valley setting with sweeping mountain views. 70 acres of rich bottom land and hill-side along creek fenced for horses and cattle. Huge barn, work-shop and other outbuildings. Beautifully landscaped along 1 mile of state road. Long black-top driveway with white board fencing. Completely restored 4 BR home has foyer, parlor, open staircase, and family room. Kitchen with fireplace, hearth, beamed ceiling, built-in appls. Rec. Room, 2 ½ baths. Oil-fired hot-water base-board heat. Porches up and down, all around. You must see to appreciate. Financed by owner with excellent terms. Shown by appt. only. B.K. HAYNES REAL ESTATE

Another valuable real estate commodity that has gained favor in the country property resale market is the once-common riverfront camping lot. Economic pressures on the general population have contributed to an explosion in the camping market. Riverside campsites are often overbooked and unavailable when vacationers check into crowded campgrounds. And fewer campgrounds and campsites are being created across the country due to strict new subdivision and environmental laws. Choice waterfront lots that sold for $2,000 in 1969 were bringing up to 10 times that price in 1999. People just like to camp by the river on their own place. A campsite on the river can often be likened to a silken bed, while others can resemble a sack of leaves.

RIVERFRONT FOR SALE

100 ft. on Shenandoah River. 3/4 acre on hard road next to Nat'l Park. South of Luray. Fish, swim, canoe. Ideal for camper trailer. Dock permitted. $2,000. Call Owner.

It very seldom happens that a man's business is his pleasure. But after you've been thrashed to the point of exhaustion by media personalities telling you how happy they are married to their profession–and that they would gladly do it for nothing–I won't perpetuate this myth. Almost every media or business personality is in it for the money. You need look no further than the ritualistic angst over the size of their next contract. I will admit to enjoying my work in country properties, but I could not do it full time because my life is full of things I want to do that are left wanting. All of our possessions amount to nothing, and all of our resources are spent, this if we have fulfilled our desires, yet are still dissatisfied with our lives.

One of my greatest pleasures has been in discovering and bringing back to life the vestiges of a vanished civilization in the Blue Ridge. At one time this region was so remote and backward that missionaries, seeking to keep Christianity alive, established schools so high up in hollows that the primitive mountain folk were often left buried in clouds. On occasion, these self-reliant settlers would drift down from their oblivion to a back-country outpost for staples and provisions that they could not produce or manufacture themselves. The following ads describe a culture of herbs and weeds and what was left behind when the herbs were watered by cultural fountains of the twentieth century.

E. Blue Ridge Mtns. 90 min. 495
Old Mountain Schoolhouse

Abandoned 1 room schoolhouse on 5 open and wooded acres back
in Blue Ridge Mtns. Antique structure, once alive with sound of
childrens' laughter now creaking and sagging under strain of time.
Giant hemlock tree guards this ghost of yesteryear and shelters
childrens' shortcut on their path to school. Aging books, organ,
and hand-hewn school desks tell story of self-sufficient mountain
community cast aside when the boys and girls were ransomed to
another culture. From the school you can see the ageless mountains and hollows of their heritage. Now, most of the old homesteads have been claimed by the Shenandoah National Park. 2
swimming lakes close by. $4,800. $200 dn. $55 mo. or $4,100
cash. Call Owner collect.

E. Blue Ridge Mtns. 90 min. I-95
OLD MOUNTAIN STORE

Historic 5 ac. open and wooded tract on trout stream at site of old
mountain community, long abandoned. Creaky store bldg. with
shelves and counters. Antique radios and remnants of World War
II still survive in musty building. Collapsing, ageless barn in back
used as shelter for livestock. Forgotten relic faces endless mountains of Virginia Game Commission & Shenandoah Nat'l Park.
Beautiful scenery all around with fields for livestock. At country
crossroads in center of ghost town. Several families live nearby.
Just $4,950, $200 down $55 per month. Call Owner.

San Francisco
BERKELEY POLICE FIRE AT STUDENTS – May, 1969 –
5th Dimension

The United States was at war on two fronts–Vietnam and at home.
Turmoil in the cities continued to fuel an exodus of urban and subur-
banites into outlying regions of imagined peace and tranquility. People
were fleeing to the countryside in all directions. In the D.C.-Baltimore
area, we were aggressively selling hundreds of country properties a
month–east along the Chesapeake Bay, north and west into West Virginia, and south and west in Virginia. Thousands of acres were under

contract and planned for development in rural areas north, west and south of my base of operations in Front Royal, VA.

In 1969, I had purchased a large stone mansion and about 30 acres at the best corner in town and was planning a move from my little building of incubation across the intersection. The mansion belonged to the relatives of a brother-and-sister Hollywood pair then enjoying stardom in a series of separate blockbuster films. The male star has returned to his old stomping grounds on a number of occasions. I happened to be in the office on his last visit and had the pleasure of meeting him and his new wife, an actress, and their family. They were holed up in the nearby countryside at one of the world's best inns–an establishment whose prices betray its commitment to patrons with money, royal birth, political clout, and beauty–located in a ritzy baronial county with xenophobic barriers against intrusion like the Great Wall of China.

The great flood of city dwellers that had been released on the countryside by consumer anxieties and recreational needs soon overran hastily enacted legislative dams that had been designed by the various counties to restrict growth. New settlers pressed local legislators to close the gates, now that they, the "come heres," had staked claim to their own sections of land. Rural land sizes kept growing exponentially with each surge of newcomers, and the larger parcels resulted in proportionally more lost countryside. Dreamy-eyed planners came up with screwball ideas of herding the newcomers into clusters, or rural ghettos, where everyone could own a half acre or so, and the rest would be communally owned–sort of like a country condo, with each buyer assigned a unit of land. Aside from this idea having almost zero appeal to land buyers, and being a guaranteed recipe for failure, many idealistic local and regional land planners obviously had little or no concept of the market forces at work in the land boom of the sixties.

The Closers

Into this flood of country property seekers swam a swarm of predators called *closers*.These sharks preyed on gullible consumers who, in garnering information on resorts and country property from media spiels, took the bait of free gifts and other seemingly generous rewards. Customers lured in by these offers were, in a manner of speaking, considered less than human–merely "units" to be manipulated onto small overpriced lots at the will of the closer who would not take no for an answer. A "unit" was a man and wife. Single persons, and those without a partner, were characterized as "one-legged ups" and treated with contempt because these wimps would usually dodge the bullet by saying they had to talk with the proverbial "little woman."

And while you sweated through the wait for your audience or indoctrination with the *closer*, you were hustled, like a captive slave, to a "holding pen." If this were not a free country, the process might have resembled your introduction to a prison or concentration camp.

At this time, I was at work developing several thousand acres of mountain land into smaller sizes to meet consumer demand. We were dealing with remote rural land, thought by many locals during that period as too far away from the cities to cause concern or alarm around the country store barrel stove or the county courthouse.

One of my concerns at the time was the callousness and greed of some developers–including those affiliated with a few nationally known companies–inherent in the treatment of their consumers. CEOs of major corporations listed on the New York Stock Exchange seemingly looked the other way while their subsidiaries unleashed Gestapo-type sales organizations to ride roughshod over naive and gullible consumers to protect the corporate bottom line.

There is worth in any questionable activity to raise a few words of caution, so I decided to write a couple of informative booklets that I hoped would help consumers who were beginning their search for country properties. I mention this here, not because these booklets are of any particular significance as a writing effort, but only to acquaint you with the tone of the times. These ads were placed in the classified country property sections of area newspapers, and respondents were sent the booklet and placed on our mailing list.

BE SAFE, NOT SORRY- FREE LAND BUYERS GUIDE. Write to: B.K. Haynes Real Estate Rts. 55/ 340 at turn to Skyline Drive. Front Royal, VA

LAND TRAP? Will your land dream be a nightmare? Send for a FREE booklet. **"Tips on Buying Recreation Land"**. Be safe, not sorry. B.K. Haynes Real Estate, Front Royal, VA

Madison, VA
ARMSTRONG LANDS ON THE MOON – July 20, 1969 –
Blood, Sweat & Tears

In one of history's most dramatic moments, Neil Armstrong, followed by Edwin Aldrin, Jr., stepped from the Apollo lunar module onto the surface of the moon. Armstrong described the ground as "fine and powdery," saying that his boots sank in "only a fraction of an inch."

Hundreds of millions of people–an estimated one-fifth of the world's population–watched the momentous event on television.

A group of salesmen sat in front of a snowy television screen in an old farmhouse and watched the scroll of prophecy unfold. Few customers were roaming the hills looking for land in the Greene and Dogwood Valley projects. These two developments are located along the back roads and hollows adjoining the Shenandoah National Park on the eastern side of the Blue Ridge Mountains. In the 1930's, President Hoover established a trout fishing camp on the Rapidan River in this vicinity and later donated the camp to the National Park.

Land for the two adjoining projects was assembled over a couple of years through real estate agents, direct sale from owners, and at real estate auctions. As a rule, I generally co-brokered my acquisitions, resulting in lower commissions for me. But on occasion I will forgo the commission when the deal has multiple bidders. Licensed real estate salespeople must disclose their agency relationships and the fact that they are representing either the buyer, seller, or both.

Dealing with Agents

If you find a desirable property, and you want to cut to the chase, ask the agent what he thinks the seller will take. The usual answer, if the agent represents the seller, is that the seller will take the asking price, but you can make an offer. You can retort by asking the agent whether he and the owner would be comfortable if he, the agent, represented both of you. (Keep in mind the fact that agents owe their first allegiance to the commission.) This will in all probability lead you to the owner who will, in turn, give you some hint as to what he might take. Of course, the seller might stand firm on his price, so you will have to make a decision based on your observations.

If there are other players in the game, you may have to pay full price, but maybe you can get some concession on the terms and inject into the contract some contingencies or safeguards beyond those printed in the contract. But what if the seller won't budge from the listed price and terms?

If you've run your numbers, and the deal looks solid, you will want to submit the cleanest contract you can, or you could lose the game to rival players.

Dealing with Owners

When dealing with owners, don't sit down with characters who will not give you a price for their property. You don't want to play this cat-and-mouse game. The seller will say something ridiculous like, "What will you gimme for it?" Under no circumstances would you want to take this bait. If the seller does not know what he wants for his property you would be well-advised to suggest that he have it appraised. In the majority of cases, the seller has grandiose ideas of what his property is worth and you only magnify his delusions by suggesting a purchase price. I can't recall a single time when I was reeled in by the line "What will you gimme for it?" Any seller who asks that question is probably too parsimonious to pay for a legitimate appraisal anyway. So you better just swim quickly away, and don't look back.

Playing the Auction Game

Auctions are another card game. All sorts of tricks are played on you here, including salting the crowd with confederate bidders to run up the price and selling unsurveyed land at a per acre price and not providing for an adjustment in price after survey. Other pitfalls include absent or faulty disclosures and insurmountable title problems requiring prolonged negotiations and additional money beyond the successful bid price. However, I have found that the majority of auctions are legitimately run by certified auctioneers who know their business, and I have played many winning hands in the auction game. The strongest competitive hand is usually held by an adjoining property owner who will have a tendency to overbid. However, a solid development plan or viable resale strategy could mute this factor. And since real estate auctions are a prime source of acquisitions, you should subscribe to local newspapers in your areas of operation and have your name placed on the mailing lists of auctioneers handling country properties.

Absolutely Almost Absolute

Confused about auction terminology? Writing in the trade paper, *Auction World*, George Richard, an industry commentator, shed some light on the subject of "absolute" auctions. He said that many people have remarked to him that they have stopped reading the auction brochure or ad the moment they see an asterisk in the heading that could dilute the term "absolute."

Richards remarks, "Auctions conducted subject to a reserve price, or subject to seller confirmation, have a place in our industry. Some sellers are not able to sell at absolute auction; or they may have substantial mortgages or other encumbrances against the property, making the 'absolute' form of auction out of the question. Potential buyers should not be misled by the word, 'absolute', if the property is sold subject to something . . . Buyers appreciate honesty and will come to auctions prepared to purchase when there is a perception of integrity and a truly motivated seller. It is more important to convey the idea that the seller is interested in selling."

The Selling of the Shenandoah National Park

This 300-square-mile refuge from humanity acts as a great eastern wall of Virginia's Shenandoah Valley, a land mass wrested from Indian tribes by German and Scotch-Irish settlers who first appeared in the late 1600's. In the 1930's, the feds kicked out the ancestors of these settlers and created the park, primarily for the enjoyment of city folk. Since that time, there has been a lingering, though dissipating, hostility toward the feds by ancestors of these refugees.

My first job in country properties was to sell the concept of gaining access to a large amount of free territory that consumers could use and not have to pay taxes on. After all, who can afford 300,000 square miles of land? And even if you could afford it, why suffer the perils of paying taxes on this much land when you can use it for free? This said, I concentrated many of my early acquisitions on land adjoining the park.

During the Great Depression of the early thirties, the Civilian Conservation Corps carved out of the Blue Ridge mountains the famous Skyline Drive, a 105-mile-long scenic roadway below the crest of the mountain range, now about 90 minutes west of Washington D.C. On both sides of this range exists an adventuresome world of startling beauty, teeming with deer and abundant wildlife. It is a lost world of waterfalls and hiking trails, birds and bears, remote trout streams, and decaying remnants of a civilization, gone, as they say, with the proverbial wind.

Over the years, I have sold thousands of acres in almost all of the counties bordering the park. I have discovered that it is increasingly hard to find land for sale abutting the park, since most of such properties coming up for sale are generally sold to adjoiners, or transferred by word of mouth. The inevitable consequence of scarcity is value. In 2003, the following farms, if they were available and sold "as is," would have brought more than ten times as much as their price in 1969.

HAWKSBILL MOUNTAIN FARM JOINS THE PARK

Best farm investment listed. Borders Shenandoah National Park. Small and bright 3 BR farmhouse on 80 acres of tall timber and pasture. Hawksbill Creek traverses land. 2,000 ft. along paved state road. Several springs and 3 cattle ponds. Fruit and walnut trees. No plumbing in house. Small barn and outbuildings. Magnificent views of valley and mountains. Just $16,750. Bank financing.

B.K. HAYNES REAL ESTATE

PRE-CIVIL WAR FARM BORDERS NAT'L PARK

Elkton, VA. 2 hrs. out. Ghostly, run-down 3 BR house with no bath. Ten acres on a cool, fast-moving stream. Located in Blue Ridge next to Shenandoah National Park. 1,000 feet on state road. Alpine meadow and woods, $6500.

B.K. HAYNES REAL ESTATE

L.A., California
MANSON "HELTER-SKELTER" SLAUGHTER – Aug. 1969 –
The Beatles

The second half of 1969 was particularly brutal for the country. Charlie Manson and a few of his cult followers from middle-class backgrounds protested the cultural and financial gap between the rich and the poor by butchering a pregnant actress, three guests, and a pass-erby in a Hollywood neighborhood, and, while on the run that same evening, murdering a couple elsewhere in Los Angeles. From that night on, the year grew darker.

In the east, 400,000 aliens from the far-out Woodstock Nation made a pilgrimage to their new Mecca–a 600-acre farm in upstate New York for two days and nights of marijuana smoking, acid trips, rock music, idle sex, and free-flowing palaver about peace. Among the musical icons in attendance at the time were Jefferson Airplane, Janis Joplin, Jimi Hendrix, Joan Baez, and The Who.

In November, drug-beleaguered soldiers and sisters of the Woodstock counterculture were dispatched to Washington, D.C. to participate in a massive anti-war rally consisting of a quarter million "peaceniks" who, led by Senators Eugene McCarthy and George McGovern, marched from the Capitol to the Washington Monument. I was then living in a recreational development with my wife and three-year-old son. The small home I had built was buried in the woods on five acres behind my small shell cabin, where one of my younger brothers then lived. Washington, D.C. was a hotbed of violence and agitation in those days, and I carried a small handgun that I hid under the seat of my car. I remember firing a few shots in the air to test the gun, and then sped off for the city. My beloved brother, who chose to die before his time, was a hippie, counter-culture type, who had been stationed in France during the Vietnam War. He heard the shots, saw me depart in a cloud of dust, and later remarked with a cynical smile that he thought I was enlisting in Nixon's crusade against the peaceniks.

President Nixon appeared in the dark of night before this assem-blage with a few "wind-chime" remarks about how we, as Americans, should seek peace on earth and goodwill toward men. Back in the safety of the White House, the President loaded up his secret weapon, Vice President Spiro Agnew, whom he then proceeded to launch against the anti-war media. Agnew was hurled that autumn across the nation in a flame of rhetoric about "impudent snobs" and "nattering nabobs of negativism."

From Vietnam, it was revealed to the American public that Task Force Barker of the U.S. Army had massacred 450 villagers, mainly old men, women, and children, this while sexually assaulting many of the victims. The task force commander, believing the village of My Lai was infested with Vietcong and their sympathizers, ordered his men to burn and completely destroy the rural hamlet.

The year ended on a sour note at the Altamont festival in California where Woodstock new-age believers were entertained by the Hells' Angels' fatal stabbing of a fan who approached the stage while the Rolling Stones were blasting off. It was learned that the Angels performed their security work for free beer. Also assaulting the ears of the stoned crowd of 300,000 that evening were the Jefferson Airplane and the Grateful Dead.

At year's end, I was president of B.K. Haynes Corporation, with a construction company, regional vice presidents, a financial officer, office staff, and branch offices, with operations in Virginia, West Virginia, and Maryland. Now living in town in a fancy house on one acre along a leafy and quiet street, I was worth about a million dollars, but I was about to get a first-rate education on the subject of cash flow. I had a bundle of notes, but the proceeds amounted to no more than a dribble when writing out checks for the payroll and operational expenses. More and more of my real estate ads offered a considerable discount for cash. Notes were being sold at steep reductions to sustain operations. Profits began to vanish like water poured into sand.

A recession was looming, and I was holed up in New York at an economic conference listening to a prominent economist mouth off, "There ain't gonna be a recession." Other speakers believed just the opposite. I came back with no clear-cut vision. We were top-heavy with chiefs and short on Indians, so I ordered the officers into the field on weekends to handle sales. Some sought refuge in the privileges of rank and brooded that their mounts were being taken away. Customer response dried up due to the rapidly advancing downturn. And troublesome war cries could be heard across the nation. Interest rates soared to new highs. Scavengers appeared like Simon Legree, offering fifty cents on the dollar for real estate and on notes secured by real estate.

Banks cut off their spigots of cash and shook hands only with those who did not need money. Loan officers caught the smell of too many dying developers, and they noticed that many investors were financially dehydrated from the lack of cash reserves. Death, it would seem, was at their doors, too. I came down the stairs of my home one morning and decided I would dissolve the corporation as it stood. A couple of days later, with all of the officers present, I offered a fair price for their stock and let them go. Office staff was cut to the bone, and eventually the cash hemorrhage abated.

The dissolution of my corporate structure was a basic lesson in form, and this lesson has been taught consistently at the turn of the century in the business world. Aristotle's theory of form as it relates to the corporate business model can be explained briefly as follows:

1. *What is this form made of?* Answer: material assets, human beings.

2. *What makes it efficient?* Answer: computers, machines.

3. *What gives it shape?* Answer: people with ideas, money

4. *Why was it created?* Answer: to make money

When a corporation acquires a form that it had not originally possessed, then change is inevitable. The bloom of many business mergers in recent years soon wilted away in the midst of falling stock prices, the losses largely attributed to failures in cross-pollenating old cultures within the new corporate frameworks.

Consider point *one* of the business model above: *What is this corporate form made of?* My attempt to merge the varied partners into one organization was misguided and doomed to failure. Each partner was committed to acting out his own life and could not work in sufficient harmony for the ultimate benefit of all. Of course, I did not recognize this flaw in the basic form of the corporation at the time. Point *four* above: *Why was the corporation created?* You might think that most business corporations are created to make money for the stockholders. Here again there was a critical flaw in my thought processes. The primary goal was actually to harmonize effort, this while building efficiency and strength. If I had focused on the primary objective of making money, the corporate form would not have been fatally scratched by my fanciful attempt to harmonize egos.

Change, of course, is not always bad, and it is often the remedy for success. The point is this: We must understand the theory of form to have a comprehensive grasp on our lives. It is a crucial element of success that we have a ***definite chief aim*** in life. This aim, or defined goal, takes on a form over time through our thoughts and actions. We can nourish that form and see it fulfilled, or we can neglect it, hide it, or simply let it wither away into nothingness. This said, I entered the seventies as an aspiring writer and a failed corporate leader, and I had only the vaguest of notions about where I was going and what form my life would take.

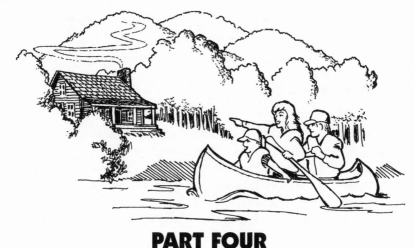

PART FOUR

The Seventies

Three factors were evident in the reason for rapid population growth in rural areas during this decade: (1) a generally healthy economy, as the country skipped over one crisis after another; (2) the completion of the interstate highway system and; (3) the "Back-to-the-Land" movement.

Kent State, Ohio
FOUR KILLED BY GUARDSMEN – May, 4, 1970 –
Jackson Five

Dissent over the U.S. invasion of Cambodia turned bloody as National Guardsmen fired at student demonstrators on the campus of Kent State University in Ohio. When the students refused an order to disperse, the gathering was sprayed with tear gas. Students responded by throwing rocks, and a shot was heard. Tired and edgy guardsmen then fired into the crowd about 25 yards in front of them. Four in the throng were killed, and ten were wounded.

In 1970, the world's wounds were ripped open by tragedy, instability and chaos. Anti-war protesters burned down a bank in California, venting their rage with shouts of "burn, baby, burn" and "death to corporations." U.S. and Vietnamese cavalry and paratroop units invaded Cambodia. Student anti-war strikes closed down or curtailed activities at 451 colleges across the nation.

Havana, Cuba
SKYJACKERS KILLED AFTER BLASTING CASINO–June, 1970
The Beatles

"Eight U.S. Nationals, including one small child, were killed when attempting to land at Havana's Jose Marti International airport in a thunderstorm. There were reports that the victims were members of a revolutionary group seeking political asylum in Cuba. U.S informants stated that the group led the destructive raid against Great Springs Casino in Nevada as a protest against the exploitation of the masses by capitalistic imperialism.

It was reported in the U.S. how this group discovered evidence of widespread heroin and cocaine smuggling by a billionaire casino owner prior to their raid and the appropriation of a Twin Beech aircraft used in their escape. Cuban authorities released the names of the victims, including the pilot, who was forced by the revolutionaries to fly his plane into Cuban airspace and to land in Havana."

The above news report is a fake. It is taken from a screenplay that I wrote to dramatize events of the late sixties and early seventies as they related to greed and excess in the land industry and to the dangers of an emerging form of radical environmentalism. (See Appendix for Environmental Acts passed by Congress.) This exposition is introduced here in dialogue form to highlight the tension and tempo of the times.

One night, after attending a real estate seminar in Las Vegas I had a disturbing dream.

I was in the process of writing a screenplay at the time and, while half asleep, drifting from fantasy to realism, I forced myself to write down smidgets of the dream and tidbits of the characters I could vaguely recall, this while creating dialogue. And it is truly amazing how many characters can emerge from a single dream. In the dream, I was involved in a plot to blow up a casino owned by Howard Hughes who, at one time, owned half of Las Vegas. Here is how the dream was incorporated into the screenplay.

The issue was the building of a dam in the west, with the resultant destruction of natural habitat by a wealthy casino owner, and the overreaction to this event by an idealistic hippie tribe.

While not condoning violence as a method of protest, I take no position one way or the other on the controversial subject of dam construction, though invariably the creation of lakes generally leads to home building, and the very thought of human beings displacing flora and fauna drives some environmental zealots up the wall. I leave this sensitive issue in the hands of elected and appointed officials. *Any similarity to persons living or dead in this dramatization is purely fictional.*

In 1969, Steve Black, a disillusioned real estate developer in Nevada, organizes the raid on the casino and the subsequent hijacking of the airplane used in the ill-fated escape to Cuba. Bankrupt and resentful, his marriage a hopeless charade, Black had left Great Springs and the land development business, abandoning his hopes, dreams, and material possessions and, at age twenty-eight, lived briefly as a castaway in San Francisco, only to return in the spring of 1970 as an embittered revolutionary outcast from society.

Steve and his buddy, Jason, are standing in front of a large wall map of Great Springs Lake, a fictional location. Their plan is to blow up the casino at Great Springs Lake in the High Sierras, this during a performance by Elvis Presley and after calling for an evacuation to save lives. An elaborate escape attempt by the perpetrators involves the hijacking of a plane to Cuba.

Sipping joints and beer are Hannah, Jenny, Jason, Janice, Big Larry, four hippie cats, and a well-stacked chick named Marcia–a damsel with raven-colored hair wearing a faded U.S. Army fatigue jacket. She is curled up on a couch nibbling from a cluster of green grapes. The others are decked out in assorted types of handout dress, sitting on chairs, the floor, leaning against the wall, while Jason–eye bruised, cheek cut, bandage on his chin from an altercation with John Law– ushers Steve around, introducing him to the group. Imagine, if you will, the following scene while listening to the clandestine recording of this fictional conversation delivered to the FBI after the casino bombing: Jason speaks up, "Steve, first we've got to get organized. We've still got some weak links. Some think it's a bad trip to blow up the casino." Pointing to the dark-haired girl, he says, "This is Marcia . . . our resident Communist . . . born in Cuba."

Marcia holds up a grape, pops it in Steve's mouth.

Jason continues with the introductions, "Randy Hill . . . escaped from Camarillo State Hospital ... Harold Parkins ... broke probation

for stomping a pig . . . Don Scarritt, did two years for dealing pot . . .
Robbie Goodman . . . burned down his draft board . . . and here's our
refugee, Roland 'Dynamite' Brown, Bible student . . . and deserter from
the establishment war in Vietnam."

Brown is short, black, with a prominent afro haircut.

They all give a clenched-fist salute, followed by scattered laughter.

Steve has been observing the undisciplined crew with concern–a
communist, a psycho, couple of felons, a draft dodger, and a Bible-
toting deserter. After a moment, his grim face relaxes. It's war.

Steve smiles at the deserter, "Roland, if you're as awesome as your
name, we'll have a real blast."

They then share a revolutionary handshake.

Brown speaks up. "Lend me your ears, brothers and sisters . . .I'm
ready to send the whole ....' system to China. I got a half-assed
slave name and a ......- shootin' war I wanna forget. You know what
I'm sayin?"

Jason replies, "Roland was a demolition expert in the army. He believes Jesus was the first hippie, says the system is Satan."

Brown spins around, arms spread out like an evangelist, "And what
did Jesus say? Love your enemies. And who's our enemy? The ......'
system. The system is Satan. Pure evil. The only way we gonna love
evil is to blow it up."

Everyone giggles and ad lib conversations spread throughout the
room.

"Okay, okay," says Steve. "Let's cool it. They'll have all the tender
love they need without us. Elvis is on stage when the shit comes down."

Robbie leaps to his feet, "Elvis? Man, we can't jam to that fifties
shit. We'll have to pop a few redbirds. Like we'll be blastin' through to
the other side, man."

They all laugh, but there is an underlying uneasiness, and the laughter subsides.

"Intermission, man. I don't want anybody on speed before this gig,"
says Steve.

He stops in mid-sentence, laughing quietly. He is trying to compose
himself, but he cannot.

"What? Let us in on it, Steve," says Big Larry.

Steve replies (breaking up) "Elvis. He might be singin' soprano when he gets goosed by the blast."

Steve is laughing convulsively. The others fall apart.

Steve (impersonating Elvis) "I'm all shook up. . ."

Laughter gets wild before the talk again turns serious

"Nobody paid no mind to Elvis till he goosed up Black soul," says Brown. "They may not pay their dues to us neither."

An uncomfortable silence settles in; they look to Steve.

"This won't mess up their minds. . . when they hear there's a bomb inside . . ."

Apache Joe cuts in, a morose look on his face, "Now wait a minute, Steve. I guess I'm gettin' the roarin' shits or somethin.' Like if we pin the snout on the pig–for the rest of our lives, what's gonna happen?"

Randy, shirtless, long hair, bandana headband, is cradling a black cat, petting it like some sort of pacifier. "It's outta sight, man. I bet there's a million dollars in that casino."

Harold pipes up with another banality. "Groovy! .... this revolutionary shit. Why don't we take the money and run?"

Before Steve composes an answer about their destiny, Jason wraps himself in a discourse on all the establishment elements from which they must split. " Like the man wants to flood the canyon for profit. My grandad homesteaded up there. But they forced him off to die in the city, where they control people."

The group hones in to Jason like radar.

"Harold asked about the money. Well, if its nothing but money, then we're no better than the financial and political elite. Listen, are we gonna let 'em kill our home? Kill the river?

Kill us. . . like they killed the clean air in the cities. . . the wolves. . . the mountain lions. . .?"

Scarritt's eyes ignite. Randy's facial expression intensifies into anger.

Jason continues, "Like there's no place in nature for transmission lines and concrete. When man kills nature that way, it's bad karma, like his ego is killing a part of himself. We owe a loyalty to the earth.

Every living thing is sacred. Are we going to deny that God is in all of nature?"

Many faces rejoin in this emerging New Age truth as Jason proceeds with his discourse. "Like if we don't protest now. . .what will we do when the man comes to program us? Roll over? Go to a detention camp? Or walk into the ovens? The Nazis tattooed the Jews. In Rome, they forced the slaves to carry a tessera stone for identification. Do we want to be refugees in our own country?"

Heads wag *no*. IDs are obviously a very bad idea.

Jason continues, "I remember being told once that in a past life I was a Carthaginian general . . . Like the Creator could be using us to put the Romans on a cross."

Roland and a few others jump to their feet. A chorus of outcries rings out in agreement as Steve and Jason feed into each other.

Steve calls out for calm, "Whoa. . . Let's cool it."

Once he has their attention, the noise subsides, and he proceeds, "Let's talk about the future. . .Most of us feel this is not an ego trip. A whole generation of kids are bein' crucified by the system. Maybe it's good karma to shock the hell out of it. All I can say is that life in Cuba may not be any better than what we have now. But all we've got left now is hope. . .And that's not a threat to us."

Apache Joe speaks up, "I don't know shit about karma. All I know is that my ego's been on a gypsy wander anyway. . . I'm in."

Steve replies, "But I wanna lay it on you straight. Things could get messed up. We don't want anybody's lights put out. . .And I want the girls to stay parked."

Don still doesn't get it. "Yeah, I figure I'll park myself on a Cuban beach for a while. You sure we can't take the money?"

"No way," says Steve. "We need to put a shock to the system. Listen, Che Guevara wrote the script for what's goin' on up here. He spent his whole life struggling and making choices. And he died a good man, without any guilt. I sat here one night reading his diaries, and it blew my mind. Hannah asked 'What's the matter?' I said, 'This is just so absolutely beautiful.' He gave up his minister's post, his rank–everything, to go and fight in somebody else's jungle. . ."

Jason interrupts him. "The CIA had him assassinated. The Man's paranoid about Cuba."

Hannah interjects, "I wanted to go to Cuba–I really did. I didn't know why. I just wanted to be part of it."

Jenny enters the conversation. "Somebody tell me I just wandered into Crazyland. A buncha peacies blowin' up a casino and splittin' for Cuba? You guys wanna get hosed down by bullets? The pigs are executin' college freaks, you know. I think this whole thing sucks."

Big Larry pipes up. "If the chick doesn't think the gig's worth doin', what's she doin' here?"

Jenney responds with anger, " Now look, weedhead."

Hannah calms her down. "Easy, Jenny, easy. He's just on edge."

Big Larry lays a hand on her shoulder, says. "Hey, why get uptight? Let's get on with the plan. You know this gig is so far out . . . it just might work."

Hannah speaks directly to Steve. "Steve, Jenny doesn't think it's possible. She'll stay with us until we leave for Cuba. Is that all right?"

Steve responds, "You're gonna split up?"

"We all have our own agendas," said Hannah. "But she goes her own way, like always."

"Okay, back to the plan" said Steve. "Any of you got a name for this operation?"

Faces wag at one another; then Jason pipes up. "This could all be a dream. And I don't know if we're on a trip or just waking up. Let's call it Operation Dawn."

His words gain momentum. " Boys and girls, this is our moment to *arise*."

Steve turns fast, begins acting. "To *arise*. . . as the preacher said when entering the widow's house. . ."

Steve cracks up; the others catch on with laughter.

Of course, during the second half of 1970, events turned out to be less than humorous in the real world as we shall see.

Front Royal, Virginia
JUMBO JET WITH 379 HIJACKED TO CUBA–August, 1970–
The Carpenters

During a New York-to-San Juan flight, a beret-clad passenger broke his way into the cockpit of a 747 and forced the pilot to land in Cuba.

The plane, the largest to land in that communist country, was greeted by Fidel Castro, who walked around and admired the aircraft. No one was injured, and some passengers slept through the incident. Castro was in a pleasant mood, asking the pilot about the plane's speed and capacity; and the pilot was happy to respond.

In New York City and Washington D.C., a small army of women and their supporters paraded for equal treatment with men in the workplace. An estimated crowd of 50,000 protesters marched down Fifth Avenue in New York and converged on the Capitol in Washington D.C., demanding fair pay and benefits under an Equal Rights Amendment to the Constitution.

Front Royal, VA
ARABS HIJACK 5 PLANES. 3 BLOWN UP IN DESERT–Fall 1970
–Diana Ross

In September, worldwide tension heightened as terrorists blew up three planes in the Jordanian desert, this after a Palestinian splinter group hijacked the planes of three nations, while failing in a fourth attempt. On Saturday, passengers in Europe boarding a TWA Boeing 747, a Swissair DC-8, and a British Overseas Airways DC-10, found themselves landing in the sweltering heat of a Middle East desert at the invitation of gunmen belonging to the Popular Front for the Liberation of Palestine.

More than 50 airline passengers from the United States, Israel, Britain, Switzerland, and West Germany were held hostage for a week as the terrorists pressed for the release of prisoners held by Israel, Great Britain, Switzerland, and West Germany. The terrorist attack began the week before in Cairo with the blowing up of a Pan Am 747 Jumbo Jet on a flight from Beriut. Another hijacking was thwarted by Israeli guards when terrorists attempted to take over an El Al 707 on a flight from Amsterdam. Two Palestinian commandos were seized on board, one of whom was killed.

In September, drugs finished rock star Jimi Hendrix. And in October, soulful singer Janis Joplin died from drug overdoses. The bear market in the U.S. touched bottom, and a presidential panel advised Nixon that he must solve a political crisis that "has no parallel in the history of the nation." Commenting on widespread racial dissension in the nation, a Nixon aide was quoted as saying the Negro problem would solve itself through a policy of "benign neglect," a statement that sent the Black Panthers and Black Muslims into rhetorical orbit. I thought then that it was about time to leave town.

I called a travel agent and booked a private two-month trip around the world for myself, my wife and five-year-old son, and our maid. The adventure, beginning after Christmas and continuing through February, 1971, would take us to San Francisco, Australia, Fiji, New Zealand, Singapore, New Delhi, Karachi, Bahrain, Athens, Madrid, London, New York, and finally back to Dulles Airport near Washington in a fierce late-night thunderstorm. In Sydney, Australia I purchased a portable typewriter and, without any journalistic training, literary background, or knowledge of how to begin, I started a novel that took me almost ten years to complete.

Colorado
McGOVERN CAMPAIGN PLEDGES END OF WAR–Jan., 1971
– Neil Diamond

Senator George McGovern opened his campaign for the presidency by stating that he would withdraw all American troops from Vietnam. Critics saw the statement of withdrawal before victory as a continuation of flawed U.S. war policy since the end of World War II.

They feared any stalemate in war by America, or withdrawal of its forces from military conflict, could lead to future attacks on the U.S. and its interests throughout the world, this while opening the door to terrorism by hostile forces who would view the U.S. as a paper tiger.

Shortly after my 37th birthday, I withdrew from the country properties scene and left on a jet plane from Dulles Airport. We took off in damp gray skies–me with a sad, empty feeling about leaving my business rudderless. In Colorado to visit my brother, the mountains reminded me of the Shenandoah Valley. A day later I was still drugged by the thought of leaving my business affairs. And my eyes were yet plagued by dull gray skies, only this time they were gifted with hope by sharp, snow-covered mountains. I remember musing that some good would come from tomorrow.

Clear skies and unlimited visibility greeted me the next day as we flew over New Mexico to check on my long-lost sisters in Albuquerque. Below me was a carpet of open rangeland deceptively close to the mountains, a hundred or more miles away. Compared to the often visible smog and haze that characteristically provide the Blue Ridge with its definition, the clarity of the landscape below was almost unbelievable. What a place to fly an airplane!

While in Albuquerque, we took a tramway to the top of Sandia Peak at 10,000 feet. At the time, a television episode was being filmed, featuring a couple of big-time film stars. I made friends with one of the cast members, and later I happened upon one of the movie stars, who was glancing through a book in a gift shop. Dumb me, I asked the star if I could take his picture–certainly not a request without precedent. After all, while at dinner in the Bahamas in 1967, my wife had asked Bob Hope if she could take his picture, and he smiled back a polite "yes."

This exalted luminary, his head in the firmament, glared at me as if I were interrupting the moment of his life. I took the picture and moved on, ever the wiser that I would never again disturb a movie star at work or play. In his defense, the figure was no doubt absorbed in his role, and I should never have bothered him; nevertheless, to this day I try to avoid watching his movies. My son was too young to be impressed with media personalities and continued to draw attention wherever we went, evidently feeling that he was, in fact, the real star of the trip. On to the City of Angels–Los Angeles. Does anybody know my name in this town?

Success in business back east was not enough. I had dumped a singing and songwriting career. But there was still the piano. When are you going to start practicing again? Maybe I could be a writer. I seldom read novels. I knew ziltch about structure, plots, editing, journalism, you name it. But I could write a mean ad. My musings drifted to flying again. I still needed to get my instrument rating. And what about acrobatics? When are you going to get with it? These thoughts took wing as I took in the jumbo magic of Disneyland, this after one week into a two-month trip around the world. So much to see, so little time.

However happy the beginning of the trip may have been, it all came to a stop at the Los Angeles airport. First of all, we arrived late at the airport only to find that we had overpacked.

Our travel agent had failed to tell us about the limitations on luggage in tourist class. From the look of the Quantas ticket agent, you might have thought that our prodigious amount of luggage could well destabilize the aircraft. I have never been known to travel light and, after shuffling what we could into carry-on bags, I lightened my wallet and shipped the load on board for a direct flight to Auckland, New Zealand, while we stopped in Honolulu and Fiji. The last time I had visited Honolulu was in 1968. Hawaii had become a state in 1959, the year I graduated from college. And after observing the rapid growth coming in on the wings of jumbo jets, I thought seriously about buying real estate in the Islands, but I never fulfilled that aspiration until 1989.

We crossed the equator at 5:00 P.M. and were given a signed certificate from *King Neptune by Order of Equatorial Air Voyages*, that we had crossed between the hemispheres in a Quantas 707 V-Jet. At the airport in Nandi, Fiji, we received our first indoctrination in exchange rates. Prices were comparatively low, and I picked up the first of many gold charms–one from every country we visited–for my wife's bracelet. The country looked relatively undeveloped, yet loaded with tourists from Australia and New Zealand, and my mind grew fruitful with thoughts of hustling tropical lots for sale. Away from business, and far outside my territory, my mind was steadily searching for more practical things to do, so I channeled my creative energy into composing a new melody for a song I had written, "The Battle of Gettysburg."

We landed in Auckland on a sunny morning after passing over green plains and forests and sparkling white beaches. Memories came back to me of a paper I had written as an art student in a high school geography class about New Zealand. The teacher, an intelligent football coach, was compelled to ask me where the country was located. *But, hey, it was a vocational school.* Most of the automobiles looked like relics. The country appeared to be at least 20 years behind the U.S. in cultural development.

Food was cheap but hard to take, with the smell of mutton wafting up to us throughout most of the meals. But the wine was good, and the movie houses were full. One keenly enjoyable visit was a trip to spectacular thermal fields at Rotorua, where we soaked ourselves in warm mineral pools and watched steam being harvested as it rose in geysers from the bowels of the earth. I carried a pocketfull of B.K. Haynes Corporation *"Land Treasures"* promotional coins *(worth 5 gallons of gas or $50 in trade on land)* that I smuggled in for name recognition around the world. Before we left the region, I tossed a couple of coins on the ground, this to fulfill an objective of depositing at least one coin in every country we visited.

One of the funniest episodes of our New Zealand trip was the incident involving "Maimie's Coke." It seemed that we were all very hot and thirsty and having trouble finding a vending machine that dispensed Coca Cola, my son's drink of choice at the time. He was simply going to die if he didn't get a Coke. After purchasing two bottles of this precious commodity at a grocery store–one for our son, Brett, the other for our maid, Maimie – Brett upended his bottle and gulped down a swallow, much satisfied with the taste. As we approached the hotel, he happened to stumble, dropping his bottle on the ground and spilling out the remains. He then promptly reached for the bottle in his mother's hand, exclaiming " Oh dear, I just dropped Maimie's coke." Of course, we all had a big chuckle out of a five-year-old's concept of possession. For what another has in his hand, one can take for his own without discomfort.

In 1971, about half of the land area on the North and South Islands comprising the country of New Zealand was used for agriculture, with the average farmer owning between 100 and 200 acres. Two thirds of the people lived in city areas and one third in farming regions, about the same ratio as Virginia–a state two-thirds as large.

The flight to Mt. Cook was awesome. Snow-covered peaks came into view as we approached a small valley nestled between two mountains of incredible grandeur. From the window of our commuter-type plane I could see people, cars, buildings, all dwarfed into pebble and matchbox sizes by the surrounding peaks. A highlight of the visit was a turbulent skiplane trip, above mountains poking through the clouds, to a smooth landing in blazing sunlight on a glacier.

In Virginia and West Virginia, I have handled properties that were so isolated by rivers and mountainous terrain that they were extremely difficult, and sometimes impossible, to reach by 4WD vehicles, this during prolonged snow, ice, and flood conditions. While in New Zealand we visited a sheep station on the South Island that was isolated from the world by a serpentine clear and clean mountain lake, the longest in the country.

Though the ranch was located on a large land mass–the South Island–the residents might just as well have been living beyond the sea. And while the ranch may have boasted a small airstrip, the primary means of transporting supplies, mail and livestock was by coal-fired steamboat from the village of Queenstown across the lake. During a tour of the ranch, the leather-faced owner carefully shepherded my maid, Maimie–a convivial and attentive black woman–away from the group, while engaging her in close conversation.

Living in an isolated environment and largely culturally detached, except for sporadic visits from tourists, it is likely that he had encountered few Americans of color, possibly few or none in the capacity of a maid. The light-skinned Maoris, a warlike indigenous tribe of Polynesians, had settled mainly along the coastline of the North Island, leaving settlement of the interior of the South Island throughout the 1800's to whites, many of whom were descendants of escaped convicts from Australia, deserters from whale and seal-hunting ships, and adventurers.

On February 3, 1971, we boarded an old flying war horse, the DC 3, and leaped over the Southern Alps mountains to a bumpy landing on a dirt strip at a remote village near the east coast, where we were hustled into a bus. Sixty miles of dirt roads, and three hours later, we shook the dust from our clothes and lunched at a tourist lodge beside a strikingly beautiful fiord called Milford Sound. A boat tour down the narrow cliff-shrouded inlet to the ocean offered the best scenery I had seen in New Zealand. Again, the inspiration hit me to write a novel, and I looked forward to reaching Australia where I would try to master that art form.

February 5 was a busy travel day on four types of aircraft before our jet swept down on the tarmac at Sydney, Australia. The weather was warm and humid, and the people we met all seemed to greet us as friends. After bucolic New Zealand, it was a pleasant change to be back in a large city again. Sydney, with its abundant white sand beaches and fantastic harbor, appeared, in my view, to have the ideal climate for enjoying waterfront activities. I was particularly impressed with the vast amount of park land, open space, and waterfront available for the public to use.

This observation switched my mind onto real estate again, so I rented a car and we drove on an overcast day toward the nearby Blue Mountains, where I compared prices on country properties with those in the U.S. and discussed potential investments with a local real estate broker.

Checking into our hotel on February 9, the first amenity I noticed was the television set. I don't recall having television in our New Zealand rooms. A day later, I remember watching news of the Los Angeles-area earthquake that killed more than 50 people and injured almost a thousand, this on the day I had bought a portable typewriter and started to write my first novel, *The IdealESTATE MAN*.

Our son enjoyed the trip to Phillips Island to see the popular koala bears and a ritual of nature called the Penguins' March, where these flightless birds, acting on an internally prescribed schedule, tramp en masse down to the sea. The next day we flew to Adelaide on the south coast and then on to Alice Springs in the geographical center of the country and in the heart of the desolate "Outback." To understand the vastness of this continent, you can consider the fact that, in 1972, Australia offered one square mile of living space for every 4 persons, compared to 57 in the United States–a ratio of more than 14 to 1.

My first impression of Alice Springs was that of a dusty frontier cattle town in the American southwest. Located in very rugged desert countryside, it offered, in 1971, little in the way of comfort to tourists. It seemed to me at the time that the future of the Northern Territory depended on the government's ability and desire to entice settlement in habitable regions of the territory through some sort of subsidized land grant program aimed at aggressive pioneers and to encourage investment through inducements to responsible developers.

I learned later that the Australian government, until 1981, had a program to lure British settlers. One facet of the program involved free land and heavily subsidized fares from Britain to Australia. In 1971, the country was somewhat xenophobic and considered itself an Anglo-Saxon society, though its immigration policy had always been fairly liberal, particularly after World War II, when "bloody reffos," or refugees, poured in from a ravaged Europe.

On February 15, we flew for a tedious two hours over the desolate Outback in a twin-engined Cesssa to one of the world's most famous phenomenons, Ayers Rock–a monolith towering 1,000 feet above flat, dry desert. With the temperature above 100 degrees, the guide seemed somewhat indifferent toward conducting a tour. At the time, our petty vexations centered around our general discomfort, the pervasive flies, and the inconvenience of it all. And it wasn't until we reached Brisbane, a city on the east coast, that reality overtook my annoyances. While observing the abundance of land for sale nearby, I was suddenly stunned by the rugged desolation of the Australian Outback, a land of kangaroos, wild camels, and Aborigines, some camped with scant clothing beside dry river beds, and others working as stockmen and dressed like cowboys of the American west. It takes a rugged man to live out there.

When we left Australia for Singapore I remember telling my son that we were beginning our trip back home. We had been gone for more than a month and had traveled almost half way around the world. After settling into a luxurious hotel, we met our private guide and honked our way through a mass of humanity to the straits where, in World War II, Japanese army forces waded across from the Malaysian peninsula in a surprise attack on the island from behind. The British, with their heavy artillery guns facing the sea, were forced to surrender without much of a defense.

Two days later we boarded a flight to Bangkok, with a stop in Kuala Lumpur, the capital of Malaysia, arriving in 95-degree heat and high humidity. Unfortunately, my wife was sick from drinking unbottled water in Singapore, and she was bedridden at the hotel and under medical attention during our stay in Thailand. It was our good fortune to be traveling with a maid who could stay with her while she recovered.

This was our first experience in a non-English-speaking country, and I took charge of my son who spent much of his time at the pool while I pecked away at my novel. The highlight of the trip was a tour by water taxi on the rivers and canals that serve as roadways thoughout the country. People utilize motorized boats much as Americans use automobiles, and many Thai live in houseboats. Thatch-roofed homes and commercial establishments are built on stilts along the riverbanks and canals. Thailand is a mineral-rich country containing treasures of gemstones and gold, with many of these resources yet to be discovered. As we slowly navigated through traffic on these outboard waterways, I was struck by one of the most unusual sights I had ever seen–displays of gold leaf dangling ostentatiously in wide strips from racks at open-air thatch-roofed jewelry shops. The majority of Thais practice the Buddhist faith and are, by nature, generally peaceful and tolerant. Many steps of knowledge later, I would find myself, in 2002, selling a large tract of riverfront land to Korean Buddhists in the United States for use as a regional monastery in West Virginia near Washington, D.C.

From Thailand it was on to India. My wife was still sick as we touched down in Dacca, Pakistan (now Bangladesh), where, due to a recurring clash of religions and cultures between Hindus and Moslems, the airport was ringed with artillery batteries, and we were not allowed to leave the plane. Arriving in New Delhi, I found the crowded streets steeped in poverty and the soft bed of luxury at our hotel.

Then it was up at 4:00 A.M. for a flight to Agra and one of the great wonders of the world, the Taj Mahal, a white marble tomb built by an Indian ruler for his favorite wife. The famous mausoleum stands in a garden above elongated pools reflecting its image. That morning, it was hard to fill my eyes with this perfect form of beauty in the midst of incredible hardship, this as a scattering of villagers loped slowly into the fields to rid their bodies of human waste.

On February 26, 1971, under tight security, we boarded a Lufthansa jet for a long and tiring trip to Athens, stopping in Bahrain to refuel. Intensive security greeted us as we landed in Greece, where airport inspectors rifled through all our luggage. Among other historic areas, we visited the Acropolis, the ancient part of Athens, site of the marble temple ruins known as the Parthenon, and the prehistoric city of Corinth, where Saint Paul founded a Christian church in A.D. 51. I was impressed with the cleanliness of the Grecian countryside but, because of the extraordinary security measures and omnipresent overcoated characters in sunglasses lurking about at every stop, I felt like we were touring a police state.

The Ides of March were approaching as we landed in Rome. Almost two months had passed since we left the States; now, having left the fountain of knowledge in Greece and upon settling into a plush hotel, I remember the elegance of Rome drawing me closer to my own culture. The next day, our guide picked us up for an extensive tour of the Vatican Palace where we were visually stopped in our tracks by the powerful art of Leonardo da Vinci and Raphael.

And in the Sistine Chapel, we were literally awestruck before the divine perfection of Michelangelo's paintings on the walls and ceiling. We visited the Colosseum, a half-ruined amphitheater, where gladiators once fought to the death before crowds of cheering spectators and where persecuted Christians were mercilessly fed to the lions for the crowd's amusement. Next it was on to the catacombs. From the period 100 A.D. to the early 400's, the early Christians dug these underground hiding places to avoid persecution. The rooms and passages were also used as tombs and chapels, and the walls and ceilings are decorated with paintings and Christian symbols.

For the first time since 1965, it began to snow in Rome. We shopped for shoes and discovered the magic of Italian bootmaking–boots and shoes appeared to be made for wide feet. This suited me and my son just fine, since both of us feel constrained with narrow sizes. One pair of boots I purchased in Rome slipped on my feet like a pair of gloves, and I wore them for many years until I retired them to my attic. My son became ill for the first time on the trip, and my diary notes tell me that, for some reason, I began to feel as if my real estate activities in the States were relatively insignificant. Our time in Rome was short, and when we left for Spain, Italy was the only country on the tour that I wanted to visit again.

It was still snowing when we landed in Madrid. While waiting for our guide, I tuned in to BBC on my portable radio and heard that 1,000 U.S. planes had bombed Laos and Cambodia. Checking into the Ritz Hotel we found the place swarming with servants and bellboys and the level of service befitting that of European royalty. The tour company, however, seemed more prepared for the butler and his staff.

An indifferent guide showed up in a small car with barely enough room for four including driver, so our son was plopped on my wife's lap throughout the tour. However, a visit to Toledo saved the day, this when I regained some knowledge of Spanish history. Among the numerous conquerors were the Carthaginians from North Africa, Germanic tribes, the Romans, and the Moors in the early 700's, when the country was brought under Moslem rule. Spain remained largely a Moslem nation until the late 1100's and early 1200's when the legendary conqueror, El Cid, drove the Moors from power.

At the time, I was relatively ignorant of world religions, so the fact that the sword of Islam had yielded to the cross of Christianity was like finishing half of a puzzle. Not until the aftermath of militant Islam's attack on the twin towers in New York and the ensuing flames of conflict with Iraq that this puzzle of knowledge was complete.

I knew then that a great power, submissively functioning under a progressively egalitarian and geopolitically correct agenda, could be conquered from within by a foreign power and essentially have its culture and traditions transformed. A nation has no power if it fails to use its power for the protection of its citizenry in time of need. Many feel that divided loyalties and further erosion of faith are sure to follow unrestrained immigration and a declining birth rate in the United States. Proof of this imminent danger can be found in Europe where rapid Caucasian depopulation and accelerated immigration from Third World countries has produced a contagion of anti-Americanism while seriously threatening western civilization.

In 1480, Ferdinand and Isabella spurred the Spanish Inquisition, an intolerant religious movement that persecuted and imprisoned Jews, Moslems, and others who did not believe in Roman Catholicism. Of course, this same king and queen sponsored the voyage of Christopher Columbus who, in effect, discovered America. Spain's decline as a major world power began in 1588 with the defeat of the Spanish Armada, a fleet of 130 warships that set sail from Spain in a futile attempt to conquer England.

On March 10, 1971, we left Spain on a flight to London, and that old arbiter, time, would soon bring our tour to its end after a pending three days in England. My lineage happens to be English and German and, while cast adrift on the unknown seas of my feelings, I have often viewed the British as snobbish and the Germans as arrogant, though this is not necessarily my conviction since such feelings may be reciprocal toward Americans. Of course, cultural pretentiousness and toleration of wickedness and immorality can be viewed as equal forms of snobbery, and those who were once proud and mighty risk the inheritance of arrogance when they have lost their crown. It is when men are most arrogant that they make the most mistakes..

My immediate gut feelings about the English was that of efficiency in performing their duties and a pronounced regard for human rights. In 1972, England had a population of about 47 million people–about one fourth the populace of the United States–all crowded on a land mass smaller than the state of Alabama, and this dispersion has taken place with 80% of the inhabitants living in cities and towns. Population density figures at the time showed 933 persons per square mile, compared with just 57 in the United States.

We wined and dined at a grand hotel, shopped 'till we dropped, were treated to the show *Oh, Calcutta,* and then, on the following day, we were given an enlightening tour of London.

Of particular interest to me was the Tower of London on the East End, where a ghostly array of famous persons was held prisoner in damp, dark cells, after which many of those imprisoned in these dungeons were beheaded. Shakespeare said, "Uneasy is the head that wears the crown."

In this same tower of terrors, tourists can ogle the "royal jewels" – crowns, scepters, and other glittering treasures of the English royalty. We understood at the time that some young people in the country objected to the fairy-tale monarchy with all its pageantry, yet most of these dissenters seemed to believe that the tradition must endure as a link to the nation's history.

That said, and with all due respect to the British royal family, I have never understood why media hounds and talking heads in the United States reference some of our families as being "American royalty" and why they froth so fervently over various prominent figures in their vacuous search for the next American "Prince" or "Princess," this with history's revelation that such grandiose titles–ill-begotten or bequeathed–often mask an allied lineage to the likes of scoundrels, thieves, or worse.

On March 13, we said goodbye to jolly old England and boarded a 747 for New York and Dulles Airport, landing in Virginia during a late-night thunderstorm. Once at home, all was well. But rather than a finale, the trip was actually the beginning of many overseas adventures throughout my career in real estate.

Washington, D.C.
ANTI-WAR PROTESTS THREATEN D.C.–May 3, 1971–
Three Dog Night

A thirty-something, mustachioed character in a leather jacket checks into the Hay-Adams Hotel across from the White House in Washington D.C. He has invited himself to a pseudo-war party aimed at closing down the capital of the United States. A partisan army of 7,000 counter-culturists has assembled in Arlington, Virginia, on the shores of the Potomac, this prior to taking the Memorial Bridge and cutting off entry to the capital. The character in the leather jacket seems almost lost in time with the young radicals organizing the operation and with their proposed symbolistic assault on the capitol grounds. *(The protestors probably thought I was a fed spy and infiltrator.)*

This character had fallen in this Army of the Night because of his disenchantment with the establishment and their policies. Though born in poverty, nourished on the welfare state, and taught that Franklin D. Roosevelt was the savior of the world, I had never bought that line, and from age thirteen, when, while the world was asleep, I started reading the newspapers I served, I had generally supported the Republicans. I was there, at this protest rally aimed at closing down the government of the United States, to garner material for my great American novel.

My presence at this meeting of unhappy campers at the Memorial Bridge in Arlington, Virginia could be attributed to my gradual skid into the vice of extremity. From history, we understand that mankind's never-ending search for happiness often leads to extreme behavior, from which we must eventually escape to a midway point of thought and behavior. Thus an abrupt decline from materialistic thinking to idealistic thought can be likened to falling off a cliff, rather than climbing down to the nearest knoll–in effect reaching the middle ground, or summit of reality.

Similarly, the midway point between, say, self-indulgence and stinginess would be a level of generosity. A rapid slide from foolish behavior into cowardice can he halted by a foothold in courage. An inferiority complex would best be raised to a reasonable level of self respect, rather than taking a wild leap toward vanity. And arrogance–the ultimate obstruction to wisdom–is often beaten down by personal ruin, driving the defeated person into shyness and disgrace when he could have found refuge in modest behavior.

On October 1, 1971, Walt Disney World opened in Orlando, Florida, capping an unprecedented run-up in land prices around Orlando. A similar wave of land speculation ripped through the Virginia countryside in the early nineties when the Disney organization optioned a site for an historic theme park outside of Washington D.C. After considerable local dissension and political maneuvering, the concept became a Disney fable to be discussed later in this book. In August, the U.S. military assigned all further ground operations in Vietnam to the South Vietnamese.

Throughout the balance of 1971 and until 1973 I was writing, traveling, skiing, flying, and frequenting Disney World with my wife and son, and occupied only part-time in the country properties game. While writing an investigative report on misdeeds and fraudulent activities in the land development industry, I traveled to Florida to check out the high-pressure land sales racket.

Jack Katcher was a hotshot land promoter from New York who had migrated to the sunshine state where dollar bills (he was told by a buddy in land sales) grew on trees like oranges.

His wife was happy with her tan. And they were in the money. A hell of a lot better off than sweatin' through life in that shabby apartment in the Bronx –Jack selling suits to the junkies.

In Miami they belonged to the country club. "You should see the money we're making down here," she told her mother over the phone. "Jack's in for a piece of the action. Yeah, everybody wants a piece of Florida."

Jack had smiled at her then. Beats the shit outta hustlin' rags. Him knockin' himself out in the garment district fittin' out workin' stiffs when guys like Rascalli and Romanoff were makin' a killin' selling swampland by mail. What a set-up! His buddy advised him to kiss the rat race goodbye and help sell what's left of Florida. His friend was really raking in the bucks: junk lots, apartments, condos. A hundred dollars a day. Double what he made in the Bronx.

"Come on down," he told his buddy, Jack. "A sales hawk like you don't need a license. I'll vouch for you over at Cape Rainbow. And I'll fix it so you can draw against commissions. You can go straight with a license later if you want. Right now it's a hassle."

His father was a huckster who had told him, "An honest man can't make a livin' if the doors are closed." And Jack had profited from that advice. "Above all," his dad said, 'Make everybody think you're their friend. That makes you a bigger man.' That way you got 'em by the balls, cause they figger they gotta go along with you. And when you got control, you make the sale."

Katcher senior was proud that his son graduated from CCNY. The son studied business. When the neighborhood went bad, the father took his loot and retired to Sun City, Arizona.

Jack was in Florida selling land when his father died. And Jack always remembered what his mentor had told him "You got your whole life to do good, but you might have only one chance to make a killing. Go to Florida. Sure you got your sheepskin. But underneath, you gotta remember you're still a wolf. The customer asks for dirt. You make like it's gold. Land they ain't makin' anymore."

Jack was a great land salesman, one of the best. He was knocking down close to a hundred grand a year in commissions and was promoted to sales manager, working for Romanoff, a cosmetics tycoon who owned handsome chunks of Florida, Nevada, and a mysterious island in the Bahamas. After the crackdown on sales abuses by the Florida Land Sales Control Board, Jack dumped some of the "land whores" who had drifted into the business from used car and magazine sales. He upgraded the quality of his sales force, directing his men not to sell lots to losers who could not afford the payments. And when lot owners from New York, Minnesota, or Michigan, blew into town from the blizzards up north and found their lots switched on them, Jack would move them to a better lot or refund their money on the spot.

And the customers who kept their lots thought well of him. His morality and integrity were shown through his works. They left much-satisfied with their slice of Heaven and went home to the snow, the blizzards, the sooted slush, knowing that Mr. Katcher was right. Some day they would share in the wealth and hope that was Florida. Jack worked closely with the cabal of Florida land developers, for he knew that divisiveness and dissension meant death for all of them.

"For God's sake," he told a pack of them, "don't kill the goose that laid the golden egg. There's plenty to go around down here. We're fighting for our lives right now. Let's get organized or we'll all be driving Hondas."

Paradise Island, Bahamas
HOWARD HUGHES BOOK A "HOAX" – February, 1972 –
Don McLean

Howard Hughes, the eccentric billionaire, reportedly in bad health, had fled his Las Vegas lair and was holed up in the Britannia Beach Hotel. To dilute the tax consequences of his $500 million profit from the sale of TWA airlines, Hughes had plowed 300 million dollars into Las Vegas real estate, casinos, aviation, and mining ventures. Con-man author, Clifford Irving, after bilking the McGraw-Hill publishing company out of $750,000, was charged with fraud by helping to write and promote a phony autobiography of the famous recluse. Multiple criminal offenses committed by Irving during this episode eventually led to his indictment and a jail cell.

I was staying at the adjacent Paradise Beach Hotel with my wife and son while doing research for a novel. Hughes was once a big topic at a gathering of the land industry in Florida.

Curious thing about Hughes said those in the land industry. Nobody in the business cares a good shit about the bastard. AT ALL! But the sonafabitch sure as hell owns dirt.

"Did you hear about Hughes buying up Vegas?"

"The bastard's got millions."

"Where's Hughes now?"

"On some private island, I read. He owns half the Bahamas."

"Shit, you say."

"No shit. There's a new book out about him."

"I heard it's a fake"

"The writer swears it's true"

" I can look you in the eye any day in the week if I want your wallet."

Even in his early twenties, Jack Katcher, then 35, thought of himself as a reasonable man. He, like Howard Hughes in his youth, espoused a business creed that he should, in addition to making money, keep others gainfully employed and have a good time.

He told his buddy, "You have to share. There's plenty for everybody"

And then Jack would laugh, "Except land. They ain't makin' it anymore."

Jack always wanted to meet Howard Hughes.

"We would make a good team," he said. "With his money and my talent we could lock up the state."

He tried a few times to contact Hughes, by telephone, by letter, but the "queer nut" wouldn't respond. Sure, there were other wealthy benefactors–big land developers around in Florida . . . Nevada–men of vision; greedy men, but reasonable men, who saw how tough it was to develop land. These men would listen to reason; if not to him, Katcher, then to Hughes, the billionaire. The Hughes-Katcher partnership would explain to these men why they should become organized like General Motors. This they would do with great patience and detail. The Hughes-Katcher offices would be theirs, for meetings, to get things started. With Howard Hughes, Katcher saw himself on the wings of an eagle. Then Hughes died.

In February 1972, President Nixon landed in China on a breakthrough diplomatic mission, thus solidifying another four-year lease on the White House grounds. In September, the U.S. Senate approved a pact with the Soviet Union to halt future production of offensive nuclear weapons. Finally, in December of 1972, the U.S. called off all bombing of North Vietnam.

The left hand of the nation was still at war on both the domestic and foreign fronts, yet the right hand appeared to carry a gentle peace.

Washington, D.C.
NIXON'S TOP AIDES QUIT – April, 1973 –
Tony Orlando and Dawn

In 1973, the swift and troublesome wave of Watergate swept over the nation, engulfing Nixon in the scandal, even as the Vietnam War and the draft were ending. The brooms and shovels that swept away the troubles of 1972 were back at work on new potholes in the road to peace, harmony, and prosperity in the nation. It seems that the socio-economic soil of every decade in the 20th century has been seeded under a cloud of calamity, such as a war, recession, oil crisis, or stock market crash–conditions that stunt economic growth and stability. History has shown that each decade then usually blossoms into economic sunshine around the middle of the 10-year cycle.

As previously discussed, beginning in the late sixties, I had assembled 5,000 acres, consisting of the two adjoining developments–Dogwood and Greene Valleys–in the Blue Ridge Mountains west of Washington D.C. To understand my development technique for such a large amount of land, we need to return to my previous discussion of forms. Whether you are planning a sculpture or a land development, the same principles of organized thought apply. Let us compare the two:

1. *What is it made of?*

    A. Sculpture = rock

    B. Land Development = land, water

2. *What makes it efficient?*

    A. Sculpture = hammer, chisel

    B. Land Development = heavy equipment, survey work

3. *What gives it shape?*

    A. Sculpture = sculptor

    B. Land Development = Developer, Surveyor, Planner

4. *Why was it created?*

    A. Sculpture = To make a likeness of a person. object, etc.

    B. Land Development = money? ego? jobs?

A sculptor takes a slab of rock and forms it into a man, using a hammer and chisel.

A developer forms a development out of a tract of land using bulldozers, front-end loaders, backhoes, graders, pans, and other types of heavy equipment. The sculptor has possibly been commissioned to create a stone image, or perhaps the sculpture has taken form for his own pleasure and enjoyment. The developer, aside from wanting to make a profit, may have personal reasons for formulating his development, such as job creation for his employees, or to leave his signature on the landscape. With these points in mind, we can move on to a discussion of how land developments are conceptualized.

The first step is to break the project down into marketable elements. The nation is literally junked up with unusable grids of lots that represent the efforts and stumbling blocks of developers who moved with speed and cunning, but who lacked dispatch and skill. Mountainsides and marshes have been hastily surveyed into cookie-cutter lots and passed off by promotional geeks to the public as pieces of paradise. The following headline concept describes an offer of affordable and usable one-to-three-acre tracts in a desirable region of rapidly rising prices that provides a host of natural recreational amenities. As attractive as this concept might be, it does not lend itself, in this enlightened age, to developing 5,000 acres into cookie-cutter lots.

From the Land of Lakes and Streams
AN ANNOUNCEMENT
OF UNUSUAL IMPORTANCE
Spacious vacation estates on hard road
from $29 down and $29 monthly

In 1973, prices began at $2229 for land alone and $6989 for land and a shell cabin. The concept was appealing to the camper market and to buyers looking for low-cost homesites. Each tract carried a three-day money-back guarantee on the deposit, and the customers had full use of the land during the trial period to determine whether the land was of benefit to them.

These developments adjoin the Shenandoah National Park and State Fish and Game lands and offer access to trout fishing streams and man-made lakes. Part of the region was conceptualized as small affordable forests of three to eleven acres.

Ten Small Forests You Can Buy in the Shenandoah Valley
for as low as $2939–Some Joining
Shenandoah Nat'l Park
"Yesterday is ashes, tomorrow wood.
Only today does the fire burn brightly" - Old Indian proverb
Own Your Own Forest for just $5979
and be richer by 10,000 trees!

These "little forests" of three to ten acres were called *forestettes* and were located in a primary recreational region spread over three counties. The promotional premise at the time was that five or six thousand dollars might buy you a recreational lot in some densely populated subdivision. Now, here was the opportunity to gain–for the same money–up to 10,000 trees at a time when lumber prices were inching up faster than grass on the consumer's lawn. The limited promotion also offered the consumer a choice of land and cabin, with model cabins on site.

Tracts of pasture land were promoted as *ranchettes* rather than ordinary lots. Illustrated display ads showed cattle grazing in Alpine pasture, with a happy couple gazing in awe at the world below from the deck of a nearby chalet.

Alarmist "saviors of the earth" at the time predicted that by the year 2000, an area the size of Virginia and Maryland would be lost forever to urban sprawl. The agony of more people owning their own land reached a crescendo with the whining prediction by some research outfit that more than one million acres of rural land would disappear into the hands of citizens who might build houses on their land.

To believe this skewed prophecy you would have to choke down the hogwash that 30 million acres of rural land had been contaminated by urban sprawl over the thirty-year period of 1973 to 2003. If true, the entire east coast of the U.S. should by now be nothing but a congested cluster of cities and bedroom communities. You need take nothing but an airplane flight to see the millions of acres of open space still in existence outside of the cities.

Often we tend to believe that of which we know the least. The author of a national magazine article investigated land use issues of the day and reported that "B.K. Haynes offered a three-acre forestette with tumbling, talking creek, bountiful trees, and a 480 sq. ft. shell cabin with entertainment deck for $6989 –$89 down. Haynes has sold hundreds of parcels and built some 200 cabins in a rustic stream-laced region that joins the Shenandoah National Park and the Rapidan Wildlife Area." Of course, this region is far removed from the cities, and a development there could not possibly be a contribution to "urban sprawl."

As for rural land-use policies, the dominant and more legitimate issue that should confront a democratic nation as large as the United States is one of more people having the opportunity to own land, rather than the creation and perpetuation of a feudal society in which the wealthy upper class and vested land holders own most of the land, while the middle and lower classes are denied similar opportunities and are essentially reduced to a form of serfdom in collective villages throughout the countryside.

A tried and true marketing device is the concept of giving dimension to your product. In the land development business, you can look at a piece of land and call it a lot, and the person who is selling the land is, in effect, selling lots. You could ask him what he does for a living and he could well reply: "I sell lots." In the paper products industry, you might as well say you are selling paper, when, in reality, you are selling a diversity of imaginative products to enhance your lifestyle. The successful marketing of any product requires creative thinking, and this process almost always includes adding dimension to the product to give it life. The concept headline below shows how an ordinary lot can be transformed into a forestette and further transfigured into an entire forest.

These $49-per-month FORESTS give you nearly twice the land of our $39-per-month Forestettes
plus 5,000 valuable trees growing for your future
**– A PRIVATE FOREST SO BIG A SQUIRREL
COULD TRAVEL THROUGH
YOUR TREES MORE THAN 5 CITY BLOCKS
WITHOUT TOUCHING GROUND**

The full-page ad showed a squirrel leaping from a tree limb above a happy couple and their two children on the deck of their cabin in the woods. To those living in a crowded suburb, an ordinary five-acre lot could take on the image of an entire forest, this if the property, through conceptual advertising, were given dimension, factual content and presented with creativity.

Here are a seven of the talking points built into this ad promoting the concept of

FORESTLANDS:
1. Our forests are vanishing
2. Prices are going up; land sizes are going down
3. Up to 10 times as much land for your money
4. As few as three acres can be called a tree farm
5. Hunt, fish, hike, swim, ski, ride horses, play golf, all nearby
6. No risk, money-back guarantee
7. Money-saving Shenandoah Valley guidebook free with appointment

Kennedy Airport, New York
SOVIET SST EXPLODES OVER PARIS – June, 1973 –
Paul McCartney and Wings

The Soviet's first commercial supersonic airliner exploded during a flight at the Paris air show, killing the crew of six. The crash delivered a devastating blow to Soviet aviation.

In June of 1973, on a hot, muggy morning, I flew the coop with my wife, seven-year old son, and my godson for a month's tour of Africa. Out of New York, we boarded an uncrowded 747 to Lisbon; then on to Casablanca, arriving about 7:30 A.M., with the temperature in the 60's.

After being shuffled to a somewhat arrogant English tour guide, our group of about twelve, all half asleep, was rounded up for a welcoming cocktail party. I remember the Moroccans as being excessively proud of their independence from France and Spain, achieved in 1956.

The next day, following a tiring and dusty bus trip, we pulled into Marrakech, a desert city at the base of the Atlas Mountains, where we were quickly herded like goats through narrow streets of pink clay buildings and imperious mosques into an open-air market lined with crowded stalls of merchants selling fly-infested food, clothing, jewelry, and tourist trinkets. Here, in the midst of a maddening crowd, and while watching a decidedly unfriendly scrap between a mongoose and a snake, some unfriendly little Berber conveniently relieved me of my wallet containing my full inventory of travelers checks, cash, and credit cards. Compounding this misfortune was my difficulty in communicating the problem to the natives, even with my limited vocabulary of junior high school and college French.

In the early morning, I remember ducking into a hotel getaway van under a barrage of expletives from an outraged desk clerk, this when I questioned the bill and complained about the lack of hospitality I had received in the marketplace. I decided that the enjoyment of a good vacation begins with patience, so I would attempt to rebuild that quality in myself, while not succumbing to the evil of intolerance.

When our Alitalia jet landed in Rome, the touchdown was greeted with a resounding roar of applause from the passengers, registering, no doubt, a feeling of relief that we had escaped a militant threat. In Rome I made an expensive $70 call to the states to report the stolen credit cards and to order a fresh supply of cash. Meanwhile, we would have to wing it with my wife's credit cards and thin wallet.

For reasons I can't remember, we left Rome for Nairobi in the darkness of midnight. What a mass of humanity the world contains, I thought–everyone shuffling off of airplanes, into terminals, going places, speaking a multitude of languages. Soon after bedding down in Nairobi, we outfitted ourselves with safari suits and were assigned a personal Land Rover, complete with native driver, for a somewhat civilized excursion into the Heart of Darkness. The trip to Tanzania was long, each hour filled with the expectation of adventures in a foreign world. Hordes of gnus (large African antelopes) and zebra thundered across our path in their annual migration from the north. We passed through Masai country where seven-foot-tall black warriors lumbered into view carrying spears and striking the party with a feeling of awe and a lingering measure of discomfort.

At dusk, the caravan of Land Rovers and Volkswagen buses halted at Lobo Lodge, a watering hole for well-to-do tourists, and an incredible piece of architecture, with views across the Serengeti Plain. Indigenous rock outcroppings were retained inside the lodge and I thought at the time it would make an impressive retreat on about a hundred acres in the Shenandoah Valley.

(Years later, in 1996, I would find a thousand acres of uspoiled land along the Shenandoah River that mirrored this part of Africa. I developed the area into large luxury estates of twenty to thirty acres–property that doubled in value within five years after the sale.)

On June 8, 1973, in a cloud of dust, the caravan sped south across the Serengeti Plain toward the ancient Ngorongoro Crater, site of early man. Our Land Rover slowed its pace in the game preserves and we aimed our cameras at huge lions stalking their next meal of zebra and gnu, focused our binoculars on leopards in trees about to lunge at six-inch-thick coiled snakes, and chased swift cheetahs overtaking small gazelles and seizing them with clamp-like jaws for their next feast.

Our trip conveniently excluded a visit to Uganda. In July, Israeli commandos launched a successful raid on the airport at Entebbe to free 105 hostages held by pro-Palestinian hijackers.

The 400-mile round trip through the game preserves was broken up with a stop in Nairobi to pick up laundry. Afterwards, the caravan hit the trail for an overnight stop at the Mt. Kenya Safari Club, arriving about 7 P.M. for drinks at the bar. The English guide reminded me that the American actor, William Holden, was the guiding genius behind the Lodge and that he, the guide, was bloody sick and tired of seeing the arrogant chap strutting around the bar, spouting off about his adventures in the movies. I thought at the time that Holden must be a great guy, seeing as we were assigned to a fabulous private bungalow. At dinner that night with the tour members I hosted a champagne and cake birthday celebration for my godson, Curtis, who had turned seven.

On the road again, we stopped at the equator for lunch and gifts at an elaborate country club. Under the influence of too much fine wine, we were then transferred to a bus for an overnight visit to the Ark, a wildlife observation lodge where tourists, from the indoor comfort of the lodge, can gaze at night through picture windows at wild buffalo, rhinos, elephants, giraffes, and an ark of nature's creatures, all watering themselves under outdoor lights.

After a comfortable night in cell-like rooms, we returned to Nairobi, and a strange, almost overpowering desire grasped me, a feeling that I must buy a farm when I returned to the states. The picture of this farm took on varied forms in my mind, and thoughout the trip I was so haunted by this compelling aspiration to the point where it became the pulse of my soul. It is hard to explain, but there I was enjoying the fruits of Africa, yet thirsting desperately for a farm in the United States. Soon after my return to the states, I found the farm. And far outpacing a passing thought, it was the strikingly clear image of the farm I had dreamed of in Africa. This is a classic example of proven success principles at work, where a *definite chief aim* is brought into reality through *concentrated visualization* and *persistent thought*.

On June 15, we flew south to Salisbury in Rhodesia, where we were met by a pleasant German girl and transferred to a hotel that seemed twenty years back in time. We dined that evening in a creepy old hotel dining room that gave me an eerie feeling of being back in the Cairo Hotel, in Washington, D.C.–a musty 1950's establishment in which I, at fifteen, was lured into a questionable magazine sales job through a promise of a round-trip adventure to the sunny Rio Grande Valley, when in actuality I found myself knocking on doors in the sooted coal field towns of Pennsylvania.

The next morning we boarded a light plane and flew over the "smoke that roars" from one of the Seven Wonders of the World–Victoria Falls, on the Zambezi River between Rhodesia and Zambia, where the thunderous mist and spray can be seen for ten miles. Quite a contrast, I thought, from the relatively petty, yet beautiful falls of the Shenandoah Valley. Waterfalls have life in them, and their sounds and colors speak to you where words may fail. Many a customer has asked me to find them a waterfall to own, but seldom have I located one for sale. Most appear to be locked away in the bosoms of our nation's parks and forests.

The next day we took off from Salisbury for Johannesburg, the largest city in South Africa. My first impression upon landing was that we were in a high-security country, this evidently due to racial tensions aggravated by the primitive, tribal living conditions of many nonwhites.

Another personal observation was the efficiency of company employees, both at the airport and the hotel. On a dull rainy Sunday, during a tour of the city and a quickie sideline trip to the diamond mines at Pretoria, I sensed a strong feeling among the white populace that the races must be separated; this I gathered through random conversations and from perceived attitudes of the Caucasians I met along the way.

Looking back on my notes at the time, I see where I was getting more and more concerned about finding the farm that seemed to be always on my mind. Another concern that bugged me was frustration over the lack of funds since the day my wallet had been lifted in Morocco.

A day later, the English guide anointed me the leader of a small group making a side trip to Cape Town. After a friendly flight on a 707, we landed in a clean, fresh, and hospitable city somewhat resembling San Francisco. I recall taking a cable car up to Table Mountain, a great flat-topped peak, with fantastic views. I also remember checking the mid-1973 price of gold on the Capetown market and finding it out of sight. Good for the land market, I thought–people fleeing the dollar for more tangible assets. But my finest recollection was news that much-needed funds from the states were on their way to Johannesburg, this after two weeks into our journey. Back in Johannesburg the next day, I hustled down to the American Express office and picked up the loot.

In the morning, we flew north to Nairobi for an overnight stay before boarding, on the following day, a BOAC 747 for a comfortable flight to Addis Ababa in Ethiopia. After checking into a Hilton-style hotel, the first thing I noticed from the window was a large gathering of nomads with tents and camels encamped in front of the emperor's palace. Out of curiosity I asked the bellhop what was going on. He said they had come to pay homage to his majesty, the king.

Of course, I was skeptical, since I knew that such a gathering of the unscrubbed in front of the White House would clearly be a sign of unhappy campers with axes to grind. I later heard that most of the population were farmers who raised crops on small plots of land in the cool windswept highlands. If, in fact, they were allowed to own their own land, perhaps there was more democracy in land ownership than I would have imagined in this kindly country with an emperor on the throne of power.

The city reminded me of a previous visit to India—women carrying bundles on their heads, donkeys in the streets, cows and goats on city lawns, although these people walked in a very distinctive and digni- fied manner, this no doubt being a reflection of a unified pride in their 2,000-year-old independence from colonialism. In the marketplace we were besieged by vendors.

I bought a goat rug that never saw a floor in my house, a few rings, pendants, and old silver crosses. The two seven-year-old boys in my party, bargaining for trinkets, gained experience that they would later put to good use in Egypt. In the hotel that night, during an emotional farewell dinner party, the adults in the tour group ended up getting smashed. Our party of four would split two days later for Egypt. Our departure from cordial Ethiopia was, however, a little unpleasant: ex- cessive check-out procedures, overweight charges for luggage, bad food on the plane. But despite the down side, nature appeared to have taught the Ethiopians to regard us as friends.

On June 24, 1973 we landed in Cairo, the largest city in Africa, and disembarked from the Ethiopian Airlines 747. Intense heat sweltered up from the tarmac, and tanks were positioned near the terminal. On the way to the Hilton, we passed through Old Cairo on the eastern side of town, with its narrow, crowded streets and bazaars. Towering out of this jumbled mass of humanity were a multitude of slender towers or *minarets* topping off the prolific mosques, these holy structures seem- ingly on every corner. Crowds milled about in long, flowing robes mixing freely with those in western dress and often causing our slow- moving driver to honk his horn or come to a complete halt.

The temperature was 96 degrees when we reached the bridge over the Nile, where we caught a small breeze and finally pulled up at the Hilton on the less populated west bank. The next day, besieged by local vendors, we made our way with a tour guide to the ancient Pyramids and the venerable Sphinx, to which I would later return in the late eighties.

A day later, we were stuffed into a small twin-engined plane for a flight down the Nile to Luxor. A capable tour guide led us in stifling heat through the magical Valley of the Kings, where my wife fell ill, probably from a lack of water. My notes from the trip revealed that we were allowing the children to drink beer to avoid dehydration. No doubt this is why my son was feeling dizzy after visiting King Tut's tomb. That evening, too late to cash any travelers checks for tips and gifts, we were hurriedly driven in a horse-drawn wagon to the railroad station for a train trip down the Nile to the Aswan Dam. Fond memories of the trip included those of being well-pampered on the train by an attendant who served us a delicious spaghetti dinner and who kept me well supplied with beer and ice.

At the Aswan High Dam, we crossed the cool, wide Nile in a flat-bottomed sailboat called a *felucca* to take in the ancient temples of Abu Simbel. In the mid-sixties, the temples were cut into 20-to-30 ton blocks and moved from lower ground destined to be flooded to form Lake Nasser. I remember my wife and son getting sick from the heat and resting that afternoon at the tour guide's home while my godson and I poked around the temples. The next morning we flew back to Cairo, and on to Rome where we were happy to settle into the relative luxury of a 747, this time to Paris, and then New York. After a quick and turbulent flight to the Washington area, we touched down again to the crescendo of thunder and lightning at Dulles Airport, where we bunked overnight at the Marriott –all happy to be home.

Madison, VA
NIXON'S OFFICIAL DISCUSSIONS ON TAPE – July, 1973 – Jim Croce

President Nixon's aide, H.R. Haldeman, claimed in testimony before a Senate committee that tapes of White House discussions failed to show that neither he, or the President, knew about the Watergate break-in. Two weeks earlier it was disclosed that presidential discussions were routinely taped in the Oval Office. Critics of the administration considered the tapes to be of considerable value in prosecuting the President and calling for his impeachment.

The Secret of Subdivesting

Establishing value in country properties is often the bailiwick of appraisers; however, appraisers generally depend on comparable sales to determine worth. Throughout my career, I have been called upon to price properties where few, if any, comparables were on record, this because I was constantly breaking new ground with many of my promotions. Experience, of course, is achieved and perfected by the process of being tried and tutored in the real world, a domain that exists beyond the rules of theorists.

In my book, *HOW YOU CAN GROW RICH THROUGH RURAL LAND–Starting From Scratch,* I elaborate on an investment technique I call "Subdivesting", which can be defined as: *Making maximum profits from the development and quick sale of subdivided rural land which, in turn, can be resold at a profit.*

Without a legitimate appraisal, sellers have a natural tendency to price property at high levels for maximum gain; whereas buyers tend to devalue a property's worth for similar self-serving reasons. Once a property has been subdivided, the value of each divided lot is subsequently altered. Let's assume you owned a home on ten acres and you divided the property into (1) a home on five acres, and (2) a five-acre lot. Based on a recent appraisal, the home would generally be worth less as one lot than it would be if sold on two parcels; however, the five-acre lot *without the home* may be legitimately and significantly worth *more* than the theoretical loss of land within the parcel as a whole.

Time and again I have been informed by appraisers that property I had for sale was overpriced; yet the appraisers would return later to establish comparables for new sales from the very properties they had characterized before as being overvalued. To establish value where no legitimate comparables are readily available, it can be helpful from a promotional point of view to relate the offer to known components. Following is an example of establishing conceptual value on newly created five-acre lots:

NOW, JUST $39 PER MONTH BUYS YOU A VALUABLE 5,000-TREE FORESTETTE – so big a deer could dash the length of 5 football fields to pass through your forest.

I could make this claim based on documented facts regarding (1) average number of trees per acre in a typical Blue Ridge forest; (2) characteristics of a Shenandoah white-tailed deer and; (3) the length of a football field. Worth enhancements in the ad copy also included reference to the five-acre lots as "forestettes," "small forests," and "valuable woods."

Other ad headlines I have used to create value and opportunity include:

More Land for Less Dollars–Over 5 City Blocks
Rich Man's Riverfront Tract at Poor Boy's Price
$89 Down Buys a Little Italy–1/2 mi. Waterfront
10,000 Tree Forest Joins Trout Stream, Nat'l Park

Madison, VA
U.S. STOPS BOMBING CAMBODIA – August, 1973 –
Diana Ross

Immersed in the Watergate scandal, the Nixon administration called off its controversial decision to bomb Cambodian supply lines into Vietnam from the north. From Phnom Penh, the Cambodian capital, it was reported that Communist-led rebels had effectively cut off supply routes from South Vietnam to the besieged country, then in the throes of a civil war. The country is rich in rice and rubber, but otherwise dependent on foreign aid to survive as a neutral republic.

If you ask someone if he or she would like to be rich, you can usually count on an affirmative answer. Obviously the accumulation of riches will not guarantee contentment, but wealth will certainly exclude you from the inconvenience of poverty. Through the purchase of certain homes and automobiles we find we can often project the *image* of being rich without actually possessing wealth. During the sixties, in a turnabout to this approach, Volkswagen embarked on an advertising campaign to encourage the consumer to **THINK small** (read smart and thrifty). So the image technique can be used to encourage you to be either wise and thrifty or smart and rich.

In the summer of 1973, I created an advertising campaign for the sale of affordable mountain chalets that was designed to brighten the consumer's image in the eyes of his neighbor–in other words, make his friends think that he had hit it big and was moving up to first class.

The quarter-page ad showed a Swiss alpine chalet, with a smiling couple, their son and a dog on the deck, gazing at the mountains all around:

It Makes You Look Rich! $6,989
on Over One Full Acre
(OTHER CHALETS TO $7,995 ON 1-3 ACRES)
Down payment to suit. Bank-rate financing up to 10 years

The on-target ad told the story of how the consumer may have suffered through inconvenience, noise, and misery on a recent camping trip, while the more privileged vacationers were enjoying the comfort and privacy of their second home in the mountains. It went on to describe how the consumer could own a shell home and land for about the same price as other people were paying for just a small lot in many recreational communities. Since I was dealing with a 5,000-acre region joining the Shenandoah National Park and state game lands, I could offer these chalets in high forestland, on alpine hillsides, and along creeks in the lush foothills, all with access to nearby trout streams, golf, riding stables, and swimming lakes.

As an inducement for early response I offered a FREE VACATION (with no strings attached) at one of three area mountain lodges. The all-expense-paid trip was for 3 days and 2 nights (2 people) and included meals, tennis, swimming, horseback riding, trout fishing, hiking, nature talks, and movies–all free with any purchase of a chalet during a particular week.

Front Royal, VA
ARAB ATTACK SURPRISES ISRAEL – October, 1973 –
Rolling Stones

In October of 1973, Egypt and Syria, supported by Iraq and Jordan, attacked Israel in the middle of Yom Kippur, the Jewish religious holiday. In response to U.S. support for Israel, and on the eve of a swift

Arab defeat, a coalition of oil-producing Persian gulf nations embargoed all shipments of oil to the U.S., this resulting in gas rationing thoughout the country. As a direct result of the embargo, people drove their cars mainly out of necessity, and the market for outlying country properties was as dry as many gasoline tanks. I spent most of the winter traveling and writing. My real estate activities slowed to a crawl.

Front Royal, VA
OIL EMBARGO LIFTED–PRICES STILL HIGH – March, 1974
– John Denver

One night while I was working on my novel, a real estate broker who knew what I was looking for called me about a farm for sale. I had been checking out a number of small farms since I had returned from our African safari. But none suited my needs. The next day I took one look at the place and–as strange as it seems–I knew that this farm was written on my forehead in Africa. Without further thought I made an offer and wrapped up the deal.

The farm enjoys a significant historical background, and only three previous owners have lived here. A local writer, Lucy Burnett, wrote a brief essay on the property. One of the first settlers in the Shenandoah Valley was an immigrant from Germany named Jost Hite, previously known as Hans Jost Heydt. He was an adventurer, skillful at buying and developing land, and possessed of strong leadership characteristics, the latter of which earned him the complimentary title of "Baron."

Hite first settled with his family in parts of New York and Pennsylvania, and in 1717 he helped colonize the community of Germantown, Pennsylvania. In 1729, the Baron heard about a new country being carved out of the wilderness west of the Blue Ridge Mountains in the Virginia colonies. Dissatisfied with his limited reign, Hite purchased a land grant and set out with a contingent of settlers for a new foreign world in what is now known as the Shenandoah Valley. The party included his three daughters and their husbands and his five sons: John, Jacob, Isaac, Abraham, and Joseph.

The settlers dispersed on homesteads in the northern region of the Valley throughout the period 1734-38, with Isaac, the third son, and still of minor age, being given the premier estate called Long Meadows. Issac had five children and remained at Long Meadows until he died.

Isaac's only son and last child, Isaac, Jr., rose to the rank of major in the Revolutionary War as an aide to General Muhlenburg, a statesman and Lutheran minister. Major Hite was chosen by organizers of the Phi Beta Kappa Society to be the group's first member in 1777, and it was around this time frame that the original brick home on the farm was constructed as a hunting lodge near Middletown, Virginia. He named this section of land "The Forest."

The region was, at that time, a trackless forest, largely unexplored by white men, and teeming with wild game. Shooting matches were often held on the property, and the woods surrounding the home remained a game preserve for many years, though some land was cleared for farming.

It has long been said that old ways are the safest and surest ways. For those readers interested in the ruins of the past and the restoration of country properties, here is a brief description of how colonial homes were constructed in the 1700's.

Walls on this four-story lodge are four bricks thick from the basement to the attic. Not built as a manor house, the center hall is short, with a staircase flanked by a room on each side of the two main stories. Each room on the main floors is eighteen feet square and eleven feet high. The attic was divided into two rooms and used in later years, it has been told, as slave quarters. Hand-carved woodwork similar to that found in historic mansions of the colonial era adorns the staircase and fireplaces. In fact, paneling thoughout the lodge resembles the craftsmanship shown within the halls of Mount Vernon, George Washington's home on the Potomac River. The doors and windows are all forty-eight inches wide and the windows are set low and hand-carved.

When we first moved to the farm, the height of the basement was too short for most people to stand erect, perhaps reflecting the smaller stature of humans in colonial times. So we hand-dug another foot of dirt from the basement floor and uncovered several artifacts, including a rare coin. In those days, the basement contained the kitchen and storeroom. The walls were built of pure hard wood, and the logs, doting with age, looked verdant and smooth, measuring two to three feet in diameter.

The roof of the original structure is covered with block tin–old, yes, but so shiny when viewed from the inside that it looks like new. It has yet to leak and remains unchanged in two centuries, well beyond remembrance of the builder's name. Major Hite's main home was at Belle Grove, an historic mansion outside of Middletown, VA. His first wife was Nellie Conrad Madison, a sister of President James Madison.

In 1839, the hunting lodge and six hundred acres of surrounding land were purchased by P.S. Davison, a congressman, who was also a law-practicing squire and physician. The Davison family were Southerners who, at one time, owned more than a hundred slaves. They named their plantation "Forest Farm." The main road to the farm, called "Plantation Road," was once lined with shanties in which history has faded into fable. Nature has now cunningly covered the slave burial grounds with grass and morning dew, and their epitaphs are written in the dust.

In pre-Civil War days, Forest Farm, along with Belle Grove and Long Meadows, was a center of heightened social activity for the region. Lines of carriages would deliver the local gentry for parties, marriages, and community sings in the front parlor. And two one-room school houses, doubling as churches and Sunday schools, were located on the plantation, with one place of learning named Forest School was situated near the house. The schoolmaster or schoolmarm was allowed to board at the brick lodge.

Civil War lit the skies above Viginia in 1861, and President Lincoln called for a blockade of the South. The bloody conflict raged for four years until General Lee surrendered to General Grant at Appomattox, VA on April 9, 1865. The Davisons at times felt they were in occupied territory as soldiers dressed in blue roamed over the farm looking for food. Meat and other edibles were cooked, then hurriedly rushed to the attic to be safe from raids.

A major battle at Cedar Creek at nearby Middletown soon raged over the farm, and in later years bullets were found embedded in the frame addition to the main structure. We have built a third addition to the place, now called Greatland Farm, and considerable remodeling and restoration have taken place. During the years we have owned the farm, hidden artifacts such as bullets, arrowheads, and coins are still surfacing when the hallowed earth is disturbed by tools or machines.

In the dim mist of history, the shadow of Squire Davison secretly burying a cache of treasure on the grounds can be seen, though no buried treasure has been actively sought out or found, including an old cannon that was allegedly sunk in one of the many ponds and springs on the farm. General Sheridan rode into the Valley to burn barns, homes, food supplies, all of which gave comfort and support to Confederate soldiers and sympathizers. Great mansions were destroyed by gun powder, and fields of yellow corn turned black by torches, yet Forest Farm and Belle Grove were somehow spared.

In 1898, Forest Farm was sold to friends of the Davisons, the Hensell family. Previous divisions to numerous sons had reduced the parent parcel to 245 acres, and the farm became known as the Hensell Place. The soul of the plantation house then shuttled into the shadow of life as a simple farm home before awakening with electricity in 1948.

The Rental of Farms and Agricultural Land

When building wealth, there is an element of civilized virtue in the acquisition and holding of an old farm; whereas profits made from the quick sale of newly developed land must grow old, lest your gains come like the snow and blow away into drifts, this through bad judgment, profligate spending, excessive taxes and the like. In the case of old farms and historic estates–and assuming you do not plan to immediately occupy the premises–you may wish to rent out your property for tax purposes while it appreciates in value. You can, of course, reside on your farm or estate and rent out the land. Aside from the rental price, here are some considerations you should include in your lease. Some are from my own experiences; others are derived from government publications dealing with farm and agricultural operations:

1. **Farming:** What practices are allowed? What is the rate per grazing animal? Who tends the fields? Are pesticides allowed? How is winter feeding performed? How is manure handled?

2. **Fences:** Who maintains them? Who pays for new fencing? What type of fencing is permitted?

3. **Fields and forests:** Is spraying and cutting allowed? What type of spraying is not permitted? What are the limitations on wood cutting?

4. **Soils:** Who pays for fertilization? How often will the soils be tested?

5. **Government programs:** Who is responsible for compliance with regulations? Who receives any benefit checks?

6. **Taxes and Insurance:** Who pays what? How is liability covered? Are you a retiree and eligible for any tax breaks that may allow you to exclude rental income from your taxable gross?

7. **Landlord and tenants rights:** What are the lease terms? When can the owner inspect the property? How many occupants are allowed permanent residence during the lease? Is subletting permitted? How and when can the lease be terminated in emergencies, resale, death, forced relocation, foreclosure, etc?

8. **Improvements:** What improvements will the owner permit the tenant to make?

9. **Repairs:** Who pays for general repairs, such as plumbing, electric, roads, etc?

10. **Hunting rights:** Is hunting allowed? Who can hunt? What? When? Where?

11. **Environmental concerns:** What practices are not permitted, such as the storage of junk, hazardous materials, old cars, tires, etc.? How is trash removal handled?

12. **Legal matters:** Have an attorney draft the lease. Isolate yourself from the tenant by legal document to avoid any form of complicity that could involve you in his personal activities, this so you will not be perceived as a partner. Tenants could conduct illegal enterprises and acts that may harm and endanger others beyond your knowledge or control, yet still expose you to liability.

Madison, VA
INDIA SETS OFF ATOMIC BOMB – May, 1974 –
Elton John

The oil embargo was over, and a fundamental change in housing was sweeping across America. In some metropolitan areas, almost 50% of dwelling units under construction were condominiums. These "condos" were less costly than detached homes and provided affordable housing close to the workplace in the cities for the burgeoning crop of young people born after World War II. Appealing features included tax-deductible mortgage payments and joint ownership of amenities such as tennis courts and swimming pools. Major complaints about condominiums at the time were tacky construction, high maintenance fees, and outdated consumer protection after the sale.

Now that the oil embargo had been lifted, older Americans turned their attention once again to the countryside. Distances, though, were often characterized to consumers in terms of how many tanks of gas it took for a trip to and from their destination. Many developers, myself included, would frequently include free gasoline to prospective buyers visiting outlying projects.

The Legend of Flattop Mountain

From our Madison, Virginia office, far off in the distance loomed a great mountain lost in the clouds. I had often speculated about the mountain and wondered if it could be purchased and developed into a mountain resort. After expressing my interest to a local real estate broker, he investigated this possibility and returned a week or so later with a listing agreement. Thereafter, I entered into negotiations that eventually led to my purchase of the five hundred acres known as Flattop Mountain. Realizing the uniqueness of the mountain, I conceived it literally as being a gift from God. Only in Biblical terms could I describe its magnificence.

The highest reaches in the Blue Ridge had already been incorporated into the Shenandoah National Park, yet here was a lofty pasture in the sky higher than the parklands and from which you could actually peer down on mortals driving their tiny earth-made machines along the famous Skyline Drive–a ribbon-like, winding roadway carved into the Blue Ridge during the Great Depression of the thirties. During the French and Indian Wars, a trading post was established on the mountain from which the eastern Piedmont of Virginia and the western reaches of the Shenandoah Valley can be viewed. A prominent member of President Reagan's cabinet purchased the section on which the original log cabin from this trading post still stands.

I decided that the mountain would have widespread appeal throughout the mid-Atlantic region, so I prepared a half-page advertisement for newspapers in Washington D.C., Baltimore, MD, and Richmond and Tidewater Virginia. The ad showed a couple, with a small child on the man's shoulder, standing in a cloud-swept field and literally gazing down on the east coast of the United States. In fact, at over 3,000 feet in the sky, this family was viewing the multicolored world below from a site higher than the customary cruising altitude of many light planes. Carved into the mountain, and at the feet of this family, were block letters chiseled in stone that said:

ETERNITY

Following is the text from this ad that brought in the bulk of our sales. The first two paragraphs, overlaid on the sky, were displayed in a letter face that resembled a Biblical-type script.

It is written, you shall not buy the gift of immortality. But you may be among the few to see far and forever, and have visual dominion over fish and fowl and over the five millions of people whose lands stretch to the sea.

In this way you shall be privileged on the Mountain, for none will be higher, nor see farther than the prudent few who claim their places on this great height.

Let it be written: Trade your paper money for the richness of these green pastures in the sky. Preserve the miracle of the human body by giving it clean air and clean thought.

These are the facts:

The mountain is called a Miracle because great springs flow from its heart and streams meander through its forests, and grasses and wild flowers are spread over her slopes and meadows and through her vales. Yet she claims more sky than earth, for she ascends to higher than three thousand feet above the level of the sea.

And the views are among the finest that fall from the sky, and you will know this to be true if you have traveled in foreign lands, or if you have tried to buy elevated lands from your own people.

There were, among those governments of our people, men who would acquire and protect for the people of the nation all those nearby lands in the sky above three thousand feet, and this quest was successful, but for this lone Mountain.

And so it is true that this Mountain is of higher elevation than the great Skyline Drive, and those who take land here will be favored with grand views, more striking and sweeping than those known to all the people.

And your back will be toward a great Wilderness, on a great three-hundred-square-mile National Park, where deer and quail and other wild creatures are protected. And you can walk in the great Park, or take to the back of a horse, or to skis, and your land may join this Wilderness.

Now Flattop Mountain has been lost to the multitudes of people for many generations, and as the farm people and the shepherds moved down from the Mountain to the cities and towns, the wandering roads and lanes grew thick with weeds, and rocks and rubble and all manner of wild growth covered them.

Then, in the year Nineteen Hundred and Seventy Three, in the months of the painted leaves, a road was made, leading to the summit. Yet even now does this land appear strange and lost as before. And the president of the company that owns the land and that built the roads, saw that the land was unique in his time, and he took ground on the Mountain for his own family, for he knew its richness, and it was rare among all the lands he had worked for more than a decade.

In that time, new laws came to protect the people, because there was abuse by the land merchants and defilement of the earth. So the people were told to move down from the mountain tops and to keep back from the rivers and streams, so that these places would be kept free from further defilement.

And thus it is true that Flattop Mountain is counted among the last summits on which land can be taken by the people. Therefore, future generations will be offered none here at the summit, except that you give up your own.

(from $49 PER MONTH (PAPER MONEY)

Among the foresighted people who saw beyond their feet and took ground on Flattop Mountain was a sailor once stationed on a carrier that, at the Battle of Midway, helped drive the Japanese 3,000 miles back to their coastline and their ultimate defeat during the Second World War. And the contemplation by a war-wearied, carrier-based seaman of being stationed on a flattop in the sky was evidently given a powerful tug. Land on Flattop Mountain was sold in sizes ranging from 3 to 13 acres at prices scaled from $3,749 to $15,000. A swimming pool and tennis court were provided as amenities for landowners.

Madison, VA
INFLATION REPLACES ENERGY AS CONCERN – July, 1974 –
John Denver

In the early 70's, most Americans looked out on the economic horizon and saw the high cost of living approaching like a gathering storm. Coming in behind this front was an ominous attack on their pocketbooks by the foreign oil producers. Now, a Gallup poll showed that 48% of Americans were running for cover in reaction more to a more immediate threat–the winds of inflation, a much-feared terror that ripped hard-earned dollars from their hands.

The bear market that began ravaging the nation in 1973 was still a threat to the economic health and security of most Americans. Advertising and marketing people across the nation began adjusting their promotions more to value-oriented concepts. If the dollar was worth less than before, then the product would have to deliver more for the money, this if the advertiser was to move out his goods. Following are some successful headlines of the day that I used to move out thousands of acres during this transitional period.

Old homeplace on mountain has Old-fashioned price - $4250

Cheap Alpine farmette has rushing stream and blushing price - $2900

Depression price on land for campers on hard-top road at lake - $995

Twice the woods for your money at swimming hole - just $59 per month

Steal this forest for 99 cents per day to regain your lost inflation dollars

Before the advent of "stagflation" in the late 70's, there existed a "Camelot" of opportunity for investors, this as smart consumers–even those with a small degree of liquidity–moved their increasingly devalued paper money into undervalued real estate. The economic situation found a parallel at the turn of the twentieth century as deteriorating stock values forced investors into creating a new real estate bubble.

Here are a couple of classic buys in country properties from the buyer's market in 1974:

FARM BUY OF THE YEAR

Rockingham Co.–37 ac. mountain farm with several streams and springs. Joins Shenandoah National Park on 2 sides. 75 ac. open, balance in hardwoods. A steal at $310 per acre with owner financing.

B.K. HAYNES REAL ESTATE

VALUABLE OLD MILL

Madison, VA - Historic 4-story Wolftown mill and antique shop. Property incl. 3 BR trailer (now rented) and all mill machinery. Over 315 ft. road frontage, creek, 1 1/3 acre. Water rights to Rapidan River. Sacrifice. $49,500. Bank financing avail.

B.K. HAYNES REAL ESTATE

How to Get Financing on Country Properties

In most cases, country properties are acquired for second-home use, and financing standards established by lenders are generally more strict than when buying primary homes. Purchasers of the two properties shown above would find willing lenders at local banks familiar with the areas. A mortgage application would require (1) contract showing down payment; (2) recent appraisal; (3) certification of water and sewer source (well, septic); (4) possibly a new survey; (5) home inspection for habitable dwelling(s); (6) insurance binder on buildings; (7) credit application.

When using third-party lenders (not owner financing) you can go directly to the lender or obtain the services of a mortgage broker, whose fee is usually paid by the lender. If you have credit problems or any past bankruptcy, you will not find a hospitable reception if you go directly to a conventional lender such as a local or regional bank. You will have a better chance of obtaining a loan if you retain a mortgage broker who will, in many instances, be familiar with any lender(s) willing to work with you. If you are working with (1) a real estate agent; (2) directly with the lender or; (3) through a mortgage broker, you will need to bring the following information along with your contract: (1) tax forms (W-2's) showing taxes paid over, say, 2-3 years and recent corporate returns (if any); (2) bank statements showing financial assets and data on stocks, IRA's, 401(k's), precious metal holdings, etc.; (3) recent paystubs showing income from borrower(s); (4) explanation of credit problems including any bankruptcy and discharges.

Credit problems can often be smoothed over by plausible explanations and sizable down payments. And substantial equity in your primary home can be (1) adequate collateral for the loan amount or; (2) a source of the down payment or of the entire purchase price. Another advantage of a home equity loan is the tax write-off provision for the interest, not generally allowed on raw land and on those second homes not in compliance with certain rental and use provisions.

Owners of vacation homes can deduct mortgage interest and property taxes on federal tax returns if they use their property (1) at least 15 days each year or (2) more than 10% of the days under rental at fair market prices. To avoid reporting rental income (while not claiming expense deductions), owners are restricted to use periods up to 14 days per year. Rental property owners seeking favored tax treatment must use their property no more than 14 days a year, or 10% of the days that the property is rented at fair market prices. Mortgage interest, property taxes, and expenses connected to the rental period can be used to offset rental income and to create tax losses. Further tax advantages can be gained through property depreciation. See your tax advisor.

Charlottesville, VA
U.S. WARNS OF WORLD DEPRESSION – Sept. 1974 –
Olivia Newton-John

Alarmed by escalating oil prices, President Ford and Secretary of State Henry Kissinger told the United Nations that a world depression was at hand. Speaking at a World Energy Conference in Detroit, the President said that the world was heading toward "the breakdown of world order and safety." Kissinger later warned the gathering that *"the early signs of a major economic crisis are evident. Rates of inflation unprecedented in the past quarter century are staggering under the most massive movements of reserves in history. And profound questions have arisen about meeting man's fundamental needs for energy and food."*

Meanwhile, agricultural scientists at the International Maize and Wheat Improvement Center in Mexico were busily producing several new plant varieties that could enable farmers to fill the gap between food production and demand around the world. Talk of a coming worldwide famine was rampant, this largely due to an exploding global population. Scientists at the Center were hoping to increase wheat yields by 50-60 bushels per acre through the use of better seed and fertilizer. Their goal was to beat starvation by doubling food yields and training developing countries in the new techniques before the world was engulfed by famine and deprivation.

Many consumers, assaulted by bad news, concerned about the safety and welfare of their families, and stripped of hope, looked to the countryside for salvation. "Back-to-the land" became the mantra of many city dwellers. Following are some of the headlines of the day:

Dirt cheap mini-farm in Walton Country for fun, food, and profit - $4950!

Po'Boy's farmstead yours for beer money $49 mo.

EZ-to-own mini-farm has creek, views, fields, woods cropland for just $55 mo!

A display ad I placed in the *Washington Post* announced this remarkable array of bargains for consumers heading back to the land. In those days, anyone who was willing to cut back on his daily beverage allowance at the local pub could have bankrolled his retirement account.

Even if your credit was marginal you could have been on the road to wealth if you had held onto your land. Our owner-financed transactions that went to foreclosure were always sold at higher and higher prices. So almost nobody was turned down if they wanted to own land.

ANNOUNCEMENT OF FORECLOSURE SALE ON VALUABLE COUNTRY PROPERTY AND SALE OF PROFITABLE SURPLUS LANDS
Little required down. Payments as low as a dollar a day.
Absolute sale, with price cut by $200 per week until sold

9 ACRES ON TROUT STREAM, DEPRESSION PRICED TO DOUBLE YOUR MONEY- $5,450

FOR ½ THE PRICE OF A CAR PAYMENT, USE 193,000 AC. & OWN 10 AC. FOR JUST $74 MO.

19 ACRES INCL. 6 LOTS ON TROUT STREAM PRICED TO DOUBLE YOUR MONEY - $9950!

LESS THAN A DOLLAR A DAY BUYS 5 AC. AND 5,000 TREES GROWING FOR YOUR FUTURE

Charlottesville, VA
ALI REGAINS WORLD HEAVYWEIGHT TITLE – Oct. 1974 –
Stevie Wonder

While Muhammad Ali floored George Foreman at the so-called "Rumble in the Jungle" in Zaire, Africa, a knockout relief deal was delivered to long-suffering losers from the staggering rate of inflation. Here was a country property offer that was not only too good to refuse, but, based on what it would be worth today, turned out to be a financial windfall to anyone who took a dive for it. This was part of a government-subsidized low-cost home program that we married to a limited number of agriculturally designed rural lots that were quickly sold.

Attention: Inflation sufferers

Steal this small farm at less cost than a city apartment to regain lost dollars and beat the food crisis. Just $29,500!

Charlottesville, VA (area). Area recommended by AARP. New 3 BR home on 4 ac. green farmland. Fenced grounds, paved state road. Well water for livestock. Home has carpeting , A/C, LR, DR, BA, all appliances, Elec. Heat. Small barn, woodlot, hayfield, meadow, ½ ac. garden plot. Minutes from village, school. No noise. River close by. 30 min. Charlottesville and U. VA. Not a gimmick. Just dirt cheap. Hurry to avoid waiting list. Bring $500. $2450 in 30-60 days. Own for rent money: $222.85 per month, 30 years, 9.5% apr. $193 per month with more down.

HAYNES-ANDERSON ASSOCIATES

Madison, VA
AUTO MAKERS OFFER REBATES TO BUYERS – Jan., 1975 –
Barry Manilow

The big three U.S. auto makers, caught in the worst slump since World War II, looked at the dark winter skies and saw nothing but economic gloom. Perhaps, during the first month of the year, they should give penance to the gods of wealth. They would sacrifice a portion of their profits–a ghoulish thought that they had long banished from their minds. They would call it a "rebate." It could amount to, say, up to $500. And it would be enticing to customers, luring them into the showrooms to take the growing backlog of unsold cars off their hands. It was a classic buyers' market. Everybody had something to sell, especially cars and real estate, and they wanted it sold, even if they had to take a loss or give it up. Those with spare bucks in their pockets, a spark of luck, and perhaps an acute sense of timing, were walking away with incredible bargains and whistling a happy tune. Look at the country properties that some people picked up for a song:

Make $ on Foreclosures
Owners of valuable rural land lose thousands due to recession. Their loss, your gain. Steal property with no money down, take over pmts. Samples: Shenandoah, VA CABIN ON RIVER $6989, $89 dn. 10 AC. FARMETTE w/ creek $4950, $50 dn. Madison, VA CABIN on 3 ac. $6995, 5 ACRE RUN-DOWN FARM $4975, 3 AC. WOODS 0% dn. Write for FREE LIST. People stealing bargains every week. Or call for speedy appointment. Not a gimmick to sell land. Values are real. Contact: B.K. Haynes Corp.

Let's say you are the kind of person who likes to get lost in your own woods–one who could spend fruitful hours just following the course of lively, talking streams, perhaps even on horseback. Maybe you would like to see your timber grow, and in later years clear some land for farming and sell off some of the mature trees, or subdivide for profit. You may want to put a mobile home on the property for weekend and vacation use. Maybe do a little hunting or shooting now and then.

In the winter of 1974-75, you could have picked up 50 acres close to the James River near Charlottesville and the University of Virginia at a figure below the lowest auction price around, and 25% below the listed price. For just $390 per acre you could have stolen the whole show. And look at the dream terms: $550 down, $975 in 30 days, $975 at closing; then payments of $199.51 per month, 144 months at 9.65% apr. If you had your own financing and could pay cash, the price would have been scraping bottom. Great fortunes have been made by those who were prepared to buy when the poor had little bread and the rich were losing their shirts.

Charlottesville, VA
COMMUNIST ARMY IN RANGE OF SAIGON – March, 1975 –
The Eagles

As the North Vietnamese forces closed in on Saigon, local governments near Washington D.C. seemed less concerned about the Viet-

nam war than the army of refugees fleeing American cities in search
of peace in the countryside and out to get their cut of the American
dream. County after county began implementing strict new controls
on the subdivision of land to restrain what they called "uncontrolled
growth," arguably the shopworn euphemism for "close the gates." One
of the handy methods used by local legislators to allocate land to the
unneedy was to thrash this hungry army of land seekers with a lengthy
whip of restrictions on subdivisions not located on state-maintained
roads.

Meanwhile, legislators ensconced on Capitol Hill were under assault by their constituents about the pressing need for affordable housing. Various government programs were put in place to subsidize this
noble effort. Of course, developers in these outlying fiefdoms of the
rich and ennobled subsequently proceeded to litter the bucolic road-
sides with low-cost housing units, this blighting the gemstone homes
and estates of the power elite and setting off a firestorm of "not in my
backyard" rhetoric, this accompanied by a chorus of environmental
zealots whining tirelessly about urban sprawl. Preservation councils,
endowed by wealthy landowners, began organizing and barraging the
media with alarming propaganda about the loss of open space and
farmland, as if these elitist organizations were arbiters of who should
own land and how much land could be allocated to the masses. Prod-
ded by xenophobic fears, many county officials acted in lockstep to
solve this perceived sociocultural problem by imbedding politically
correct solutions into subdivision regulations restricting the size and
number of lots allowed in certain "districts," thus driving a stake into
the bottom line of many rural developers building low-cost housing.

The Construction of Country Homes

My partner and I toyed briefly with one of the government programs before abandoning the effort because of the high overhead, administrative intensity, and management headaches associated with
home construction. The homes we built in the country on two or more
acres of land laid down a foundation of wealth for those of meager
incomes who managed to hold onto their properties. If you've found
your slice of paradise in the country and you decide to build a home
there, you can find a veritable library of plans on the Internet. Try:
www.homeplans.com and **www.DreamHomeSource.com.** Mean-

while, you should be aware of the typical home construction process. Keep in mind the fact that you must apply for a building permit when constructing a home and major improvements, such as barns, decks, additions, etc.

1. Obtain an up-to-date health permit for sewage disposal from the seller.
2. Confirm the water quality and approximate depths of local wells.
3. Determine the type and size of the home based on your budget.
4. Establish a possible source of financing.
5. Locate a reputable builder and view the homes he has built.
6. Seek references from the builder's home buyers.
7. Obtain a building permit from the county.
8. Builder begins excavation and concrete pouring for footings.
9. County inspects footings.
10. Builder excavates basement and constructs foundation on footings.
11. County inspects foundation, waterproofing, drain tiles.
12. Garage layout is inspected before concrete slab is laid.
13. County inspects all work so far.
14. Garage slab is laid.
15. More inspections, backfill, termite treatment.
16. House is framed; doors, windows, roofing installed.
17. Home exterior and roofing shingles are installed.
18. Plumbing, electric wiring, heat, air conditoning, installed and inspected.
19. Framing and insulation inspected.
20. Builder begins drywall and joint filling.
21. Cabinets, bathroom fixtures, trim installed.
22. Painting, drywall finishing begins.
23. Final flooring, carpeting, appliances, electrical, plumbing fixtures installed.
24. Vents and returns installed for heating, AC, and appliances.
25. Grading and landscaping occurs.

26. Outdoor lights, sidewalks, driveway installed.
27. Builder and buyer do "walk through."
28. Finishing touches noted and completed.
29. Builder obtains occupancy permit.
30. Final payment to builder and closing with lender.

Following is the text of a display ad that sold out an entire project of homes and land:

McConnelsburg, PA
SUEZ CANAL OPEN AFTER 8 YEARS – June, 1975 –
Captain & Tennile

The Suez Canal, closed since the Arab-Israel War in 1967, was re-opened by Egyptian President Anwar Sadat as a gesture of peace. And as convoys of ships passed through the strategic waterway, my partner and I were moving out a boatload of land in Pennsylvania, where the original "World War" began. Let me explain. In May, 1754, a force of soldiers was sent by Virginia Governor Dinwiddie to expel the French from that country's trading intrusions into the Virginia colony, then a British territory extending into what is now Pennsylvania. Second in command of this military unit was a 22-year-old officer, Lt. Col. George Washington.

Washington's force, including a complement of Indians, caught the French napping and a fight ensued, during which the French were over-whelmed and decimated, leaving many dead and wounded strewn about the encampment. During the surrender, the wounded French com-mander handed Washington a note from the French king demanding British withdrawal from the territory, and while Washington was dis-tracted by the translation process, the Indians killed the French com-mander. In the resulting melee, all but one of those Frenchmen still alive were brutally slaughtered and scalped. The lone escapee ran 60 miles on his bare feet to report the incident at Fort Duquesne, now called Pittsburgh.

Following the encounter, Washington learned that the senior officer of his unit had died, leaving him in command. He quickly withdrew to a defensive position and erected a makeshift outpost called Fort Ne-cessity. There he prepared for a French retaliatory attack. The assault came shortly thereafter, and the battle reached a stalemate, finally re-sulting in a truce. Washington's expeditionary force then withdrew, abandoning any plans to attack the French at Fort Duquesne.

In 1755, a British band of rag-tag regulars, with Colonel Washing-ton as second in charge, attacked the French at Pittsburgh, losing the battle, along with their pompous commander, General Braddock, in a firefight. Again Washington withdrew, this time assuming responsi-bility for building forts throughout the frontier region for Virginia's defense against the French and those Indians hostile to the British.

The French and Indian War, ignited in Pennsylvania, burned for two years, spreading north and west from the Virginia Colony into Canada and flaring up into the "Seven Years War" as Britain, France, and Spain fought over their territorial possessions in North America and the Caribbean. The war ended when the Treaty of Paris was signed in 1763.

Today, western Pennsylvania is still being invaded, this time by an army of city people looking for affordable country properties. Back in the summer of 1975, smart investors along the east coast from Washington D.C. to New York City were out in force trading inflated dollars for rich Pennsylvania farmland. Take a look at these giveaways:

Bargain farm paradise near 8300 acre lake at cost of city lot $9900!

Raystown Lake, PA–Valuable 10 acres just minutes from 27-mile-long mountain lake. Pasture, fields, woods, spring-fed stream. ½ mi. frontage on 2 township roads. Keep some. Sell off part to help pay for your farm. Money-making farmstead will outpace inflation and give you a survival place in the country. Low price on this farmstead is already history. Look for high 5-figure price next year. Some of the most beautiful land you will ever see. Bring $100. $400 at closing; $119 mo. 120 mos. 9% apr. Less for cash.

Haynes-Anderson Associates

Less than 2 hours by interstate
Cheap farm helps you profit from hard times and inflation $39,500!

McConnelsburg, PA - Own for less than cost of a shotgun home. Use weekends now. Retire here later. 6 large BR, BA, full w/o bsmt & attic, storm doors, windows, elec. heat. Old home in broom-clean shape. Floors redone; farmhouse, outbuildings just painted. A fortune in spring water from overflowing spring house, yours for the bottling. Built-to-last outbuildings include storage shed or barn. Clear pond for swimming, fishing. Stream through pasture. Rich green fields and cropland, shade trees, mountain views. All this on 10 sprawling acres with 1/5 mi. on 2 township roads. Farm will show and sell itself. No need for appointment to drive by. Adj. 30 acres available if you inspect before sold.

Haynes-Anderson Associates.

Finding Country Properties

One of my primary concerns when locating potential country property investments is their general proximity (1-3 hours) from metropolitan areas in which the bulk of potential customers for rural real estate customarily reside. The Census Bureau classifies these more heavily populated regions of the U.S. as Standard Metropolitan Statistical Areas (SMSAs). There are roughly a quarter of a million socioeconomic regions throughout the nation, each containing at least one city with a minimum of 50,000 inhabitants and encompassing contiguous towns and counties, all designated as an integral part of any SMSA.

Country properties usually abound within the SMSA regions, though the prices for such real estate can decline as people move exponentially from the heart of the region. Drive longer, pay less, is a general rule for city dwellers. Of course, outlying residents may save money on their real estate purchases, but asking prices on such properties are based primarily on economic factors and can be relatively neutral as to where you live. A listed price may be the same for the property no matter how far you have to travel within some regions beyond the suburbs. City dwellers, presumably those with a higher pay scale and traveling farther to reach their place in the country, can find their economic edge chipped by the loss of time and dulled by transportation expenses.

Beyond my concern about the characteristics of the real estate itself and its market history, the mode of financing, and distance from population centers, I also have some fundamental concerns when scouting for country properties. For example, I try to get answers to the following questions:

1. What is the current tax rate?
2. Is there a shortage of homes and building sites in the area?
3. Do people want to go there?
4. How close is shopping, a hospital, fire department?
5. What are the employment opportunities?
6. Are there any natural attractions for outdoor recreation?
7. What does the surrounding neighborhood look like?
8. How good is the educational system?
9. How strict are local government regulations on development?
10. Are there any adverse detractions or environmental problems?

11. Is there an unusually high rate of crime and violence?

12. How far is the nearest municipal airport?

13. What are the general climate characteristics in the region?

14. Where is the nearest public library and college or university?

15. How fast is real estate moving in the area?

16. In what ways, if any, is the neighborhood changing?

Charlottesville, VA
FORD SAYS ALASKA'S OIL LIBERATES U.S.– Nov., 1975 –
Elton John

> *"Great abundance of riches cannot be gathered*
> *and kept by any man without sin"*
>
> –Erasmus

The OPEC oil embargo was a disease that spread over the industrialized world like a plague. Earthly privileges of the black gold were hoarded by devilish men, and their punishment was yet to be purchased. President Ford, touring the Alaska pipeline, proclaimed the nation on the way to independence from foreign oil sources. He said construction of the pipeline "has proven to be an outstanding example of how ecology can be preserved while energy needs are met."

In 1975, the majority of Americans, far from overflowing with wealth like the oil titans, were simply trying to cut living costs down to size, this while making modest investments in their future. Following is a sample of how investment and environmental concerns were merged while meeting the need for affordable housing.

After a suitable property was located, the task was accomplished through landscaping, land planning, and effective advertising. Similar bargain-priced properties can be purchased today at foreclosure sales, through print media ads, real estate agencies, and from Internet searches; or you can buy them directly from owners, who place signs in the yard or on bulletin boards.

CORNUCOPIA FARM

Easy-to-buy country living near Charlottesville, VA. Worry less about food and crime. Cut living costs down to size. Large almost new 3 BR all elec. home (1294 sq. ft.) w/ cedar shake siding, carpeting, picture window, spacious panelled kitchen and dining area. Includes all appliances. Copper wiring throughout. Inside storage area. Walk-in closets. Storm doors and windows. Owners giving up dream place. Cannot be reconstructed at anywhere near the asking price. Completely land-planned as a 4.3 acre farmstead with fencing and entrance gate. New detailed survey shows 1/3 woods, 2-acre pasture and garden area; balance in orchard with fruit trees in place. On paved state road around cnr. from elementary school. 30 min. U. VA. $32,950. 95% financing over 30 years.

HAYNES-ANDERSON ASSOCIATES

Opportunities like this are more abundant for investors when higher interest rates tend to devalue real estate and squeeze out greedy speculators, overextended developers, and illiquid homeowners. Keep your eye on any political mischief that could dry up the money supply and set fire to interest rates. Only in the misfortune of the times can you see what you should avoid.

Central Virginia
SUNBELT LEADS IN POPULATION GROWTH – Feb. 1976 –
Barry Manilow

The year 1970 had given birth to an inherently callow recession that was still trying to draw horns on a bear, speak the word "bull" and spell the word "growth." Huge numbers of frustrated and disillusioned people had abandoned the countryside for opportunities in the big cities and their suburbs. Now, the Census Bureau had reported that the metropolitan areas of the South and Southwest were the only regions showing significant population growth since the decade was hatched. Flashback to the beginning of a generation.

Since 1946, millions of Americans had traded the sight of muddy barnyards and dusty roads for the drudgery of manicured backyards and city pavement. Now the noiseless foot of time was at their butt, and sharper than the sword was their hunger for land. They were off for a piece of small-town America, a slice of the fruited plains, or a chunk of the purple mountain majesties. Across the nation, only the metropolitan regions of the South and Southwest, along with parts of Colorado, had gained population over rural areas. Here are a few headlines from the lean days of 1976 when land was cheap.

Pick up this troubled farm for peanuts–$95 Down

The dollar a day you fritter away can buy you a river

Own 1/4 sq. mi. of forest for less than a car payment

Go back to 300 sq. mi. for $3.00 a day–Joins Park

If you can't buy a mountain, settle for the top $40 mo.

Front Royal, VA
CARTER ELECTED PRESIDENT–November, 1976–Bee Gees

The art of seizing opportunities can be developed and nurtured over time, but the habit of neglecting opportunities is pervasive in our nature. This habit haunts our bodies like a sickness. When given a dose of opportunity we often take the medicine too late or don't take it at all. Thus we remain in a kind of economic sick bay, wishing we were in better health financially.

A classic example of people snatching nuggets of gold from the stream of life, rather than clutching grains of sand, is reflected in the following opportunity offered to prospective buyers in the Washington D.C. area. My partner and I had purchased a large tract of land from the note holder on a failed planned-unit development along the Shenandoah River.

This was my first major venture into the sale of distressed country properties owned or lost by developers, a dissolution trend that gained momentum and lasted for at least ten years, from 1976 until the latent Reagan economic recovery in the mid-eighties. A large display ad in the *Washington Post* delivered a relentless mob of buyers who literally overran my small real estate office in Front Royal. By 2002, some properties purchased during this sale had risen in value by eight to ten times their original sales price.

Distressed Property Sale! Dissolution of planned-unit development on the Shenandoah River

COMMUTE TO YOUR OWN AFFORDABLE COUNTRY PLACE AT FRONT ROYAL, VA
5 ACRES IN THE COUNTRY from $5900
RIVERFRONT FARMS FROM $9950

An illustrated cut in the ad showed a plot of land with a small home, barn, garden with fresh vegetables, berry bushes, a strawberry patch, flower garden, a vineyard, chicken house for fresh eggs, hog pen for ham and fresh pork, pen for goats and rabbits, a fruit orchard, woodlot, and bee hives for honey. Prices for five-acre parcels in other local areas were shown crossed out with an X. The dissolution offer was priced up to four times lower than comparable prices shown.

The ad described how the new I-66 was under construction and almost completed from Washington to Front Royal and how land prices would soon rise dramatically. Acheological digs were in progress on the property, and the ad explained how remains of prehistoric Indian settlements were being uncovered along the riverbank. A high Carter administration official, alerted by archeologists and the environmental police, called to express concern about preservation issues to which I had no objection. A preservation zone was established and designated on the plat and embedded in the protective covenants providing the archeologists with legal authority to continue their "digs" within the specified area. Inducements for quick response included a free amphibious "Duck" ride across the river to a museum established by the archeologists.

The ad utilized effective graphics, informative copy, and was crawling with a multitude of fact-based elements calling for immediate action:

1. Quick access to the D.C. area on Route 66, then under construction
2. Buying distressed property is the cheapest way to own land
3. Possibility of discovering valuable artifacts on your land
4. Up to 20 times more land for your money than in planned-unit communities

5. Offer not available at this low price through local Realtors
6. Priced 50% or more below other offers
7. Scarcity of affordable land for burgeoning D.C.-area population
8. Present the ad for $200 discount this week only
9. 5% discount for cash
10. Any reasonable offer considered
11. Just $50 down can tie up a five-acre homestead
12. Payments just $73 a month in inflated dollars
13. Property deeded to buyer at closing
14. Money-back guarantee after closing
15. Free overnight camping along river while you select your land parcel
16. Free Visitor's Kit including: Shenandoah Valley history book, admission to local Confederate Museum, 2 tickets to Skyline Caverns, maps, brochures, and credit slip for free hamburger and coke (so you won't go away hungry)

The ad was a classic example of an advertisement demanding quick response. Successful radio and television spots and direct mail offers often attempt to include the following elements:

1. Stop the viewer, listener, or reader and get his attention
2. Hold his attention with effective copy, sounds, and visual devices
3. Involve the consumer through empathetic attraction (shared emotions, feelings)
4. Back up the offer with facts
5. Substantiate the bargain with comparables
6. Remove risk from the offer through a guarantee
7. Reward the consumer with benefits for acting NOW!

Aside from this being a dynamic offer of lasting value–and an eventual financial windfall for purchasers–consumers, in their reaction to the ad promotion, were (1) stopped by the headline and display of the homestead, a graphic that invited him to (2) focus his attention on the graphic of how he could effectively utilize the land which, in turn, (3) involved him in the ad. The ad was (4) loaded with facts, and (5) comparables were discussed and displayed. (6) A money-back guarantee was included in the ad and (7) the ad was rampant with inducements for acting NOW! Side elements were: (1) graphics that moved the consumer's eye step by step through the four columns of copy, (2) an unspoken urgency in the copy that convinced the consumer that he could lose out big time (be penalized in the pocketbook) for inaction, and (3) the use of a real estate land trust to convey the property, allowing us to conduct the sale with the official sanctity of HAYNES-ANDERSON, Trustees, the latter word a legal euphemism in some cases for "developers."

Nags Head, N.C.
ELVIS PRESLEY DEAD IN MEMPHIS – August, 19, 1977 –
Andy Gibb

I was on working on my first real estate book in a motel on the sand dunes of the Outer Banks when the idol fell. Though I was not a huge Elvis fan, I admired his musical talent and was impressed with his reticence about wearing a crown of gold and of politically pontificating to the world as if he were a great prophet, this in a society where singers and movie stars are often transformed by fame into cultural attack dogs who feel they have feasted on the *Book of Life* and now wish to share their perverted wisdom with all mankind.

I first heard about Elvis in 1954 when I was in the Army and rock and roll was in its cradle. A year or so later, during my first year in college, I ran into Roy Clark, the country music star with whom I had gone to high school. We sat next to each other in art class and played football on the school team that seemed to lose almost every game. He was yet undiscovered and on his way to Las Vegas, the new mecca for entertainers, and I asked him what he thought about Elvis. He told me the kid was going to be a great star. Here was a poor kid who grew up on the wrong side of the tracks in a shotgun shack and who was given a spark of talent and the breath of popular applause that catapulted him almost overnight to incredible fame and fortune.

Now, in 1977, just 20 years after Elvis plunked $10,000 down on his $102,500, 18-acre Memphis estate called Graceland, the crown of life had come to him. To many people in this life, the influence of a homeplace, or base of operations, is critical to their existence. When a person has a few acres of land, maybe a farm or ranch–and our past presidents prove the point of needing a place to come home to–he can claim to be part of the land itself; in other words, he is *from* someplace. Growing up in and around D.C.–then a voteless nowhere–and never having owned land, I always remember referring to my frequent departures to my property with the provincial remark of "I'm going up to the land." In 1974, twelve years after I purchased my first piece of land, I bought my farm, or base of operations. It is my strong feeling that everyone should be given the opportunity to own land, and I have tried to make this dream come true for thousands of people throughout my career in real estate.

Madison, VA
FIRST TEST-TUBE BABY BORN IN LONDON – June, 1978 –
Grease

The birth of artificial insemination, though without relevance to the creation of land product, marked the death knell for one of the dreamy-eyed concepts of avant-garde land planners and idealistic environmentalists.

Farm Colony

This sociocultural nightmare, reeking with distorted communist notions, was conceived to assemble a colony of progressive people on a communal farm, sell each of them a couple of acres at an exorbitant price and expect this conglomerate to share the rest of the farm, hoping, it might seem, that they would emerge as witnesses to the second coming of the earth goddess, Gaea.

Politicians magically appeared on the scene and sprinkled the farm with holy rhetoric. Articles and commentary in newspapers and magazines liberally praised the insane concept as the saving grace of American agriculture and the final solution to urban sprawl. Television reporters were encouraged to spread the gospel of this new age form of agriculture and communal living. The bizarre scene was blared out to the general public with such fervor that you would have thought the fiascoes of the hippie communes of the sixties and early seventies had been unreported or falsely maligned by conservative theorists as failures, this without any apparent regard for the concept's economic feasibility and marketability.

Sure enough the project went down the tubes, and I bought the distressed farm at public auction, restructured the survey, added a few road improvements and subsequently sold out the offer in a couple of weeks.

Distressed Property Sale! Dissolution of Planned-unit development. *Unusual opportunity to*

SAVE UP TO 50% ON PRIME
FARM & ESTATE LAND NEAR MADISON, VA
FIRST OFFER! 5 ACRES OF PRIME VIRGINIA
FARMLAND Only $100 DOWN
For lasting farmettes similar to $30,000 estates around Middleburg
and Warrenton, VA. Foreclosure priced from just $7900

The half-page display ad in the *Washington Post* showed a photograph of an elegant entrance and the cut of a five-acre farmette with home, barn, garden, berry bushes, grape arbor, chicken house, hog pen, woods, fields for horses and cows, and an orchard. Figures from the U.S. Dept. of Agriculture revealed in the ad showed that the average price of farmland had tripled in the ten years between 1967 and 1977. Reference was made to the alarming fact that 30% of all foreign investment in this country was allocated to the purchase of farmland and that inflation's bite on the dollar was expected to double in size by 1979.

It was explained in the ad that this was distressed property, the cheapest way the consumer could obtain usable land. And despite the failed concept, the land was the best that money could buy, because it was chosen for purchase by the upper class and was close to Charlottesville and the University of Virginia. The reader was shown comparable cost figures for similar acreage around favorite local locations for country property. It was clear that the consumer could save up to 50% and still get upscale land.

Reference was made to Middleburg, a favorite haunt of the rich and famous, where, at the time, you might have been fortunate enough to fall into a place near the county dump for thirty grand (make it three hundred grand in this day and age). The spiraling cost of food was also referenced as a possible reason to grow your own, and the property was conveyed with the right to subdivide for potential profit.

The general public was invited to put roots down on affordable land outside the D.C. metropolitan area adjacent to territory owned by the privileged elite. The ad referred to a recent television broadcast predicting that, because of the current land boom, the prices for five to ten acres in the nearby countryside would soon double. Proof of this boom was to be found in a recent B.K. Haynes sale in Front Royal that was sold out in two weeks.

Time, indeed, was running out for those who expected the price of land to come down. Ten consumer goals were cited for buying land: (1) build a home; (2) keep horses; (3) beat inflation; (4) getting back to the land; (5) relocation; (6) recreation; (7) organic gardening; (8) a place for the kids; (9) investment; (10) subdivision. For those with these goals slumbering in their minds, it was wake-up time. A 28% population gain was expected in the Washington D.C., Richmond and Tidewater regions between 1973-1985. Almost 1/3 more people would have to be compressed into townhouses, apartments, and condominiums, this because local "controlled growth" measures and the consequential high cost of area land was putting single-family housing out of reach for many.

A 40% increase in the number of households would soon put an end to privacy. Only the criminal would covet such an environment.

The land was described as rolling green fields and clean park-like woodland where buyers could enjoy bridle paths, cow pastures, cropland, and (on some acreage) a lazy brook or fishing stream. Property owners could see mountains looming on the horizon, and expensive homes stood at the entrance to these country estates. White board fencing, such as you would find on a thoroughbred farm, lined the roads leading to their land. And a quiet, safe, and cultured university city was only minutes away.

One might have thought such magnificent land would cost a small fortune, yet a meager $100 deposit, $100 at closing, and $99 per month was all that was needed to enter the land of the rich and ennobled. And no reasonable cash offer would be refused. A small price indeed for an estate worthy of the wealthiest families. The offer came with a money-back guarantee prior to settlement. Bonus features for acting quickly included a (1) $200 price reduction; (2) free Land Buyer's Guide; (3) free 20-page full color Home Planning Kit and; (4) a $5.00 gasoline allowance.

Rural Virginia
IRAN SEIZES U.S. EMBASSY – November 26, 1979 – Styx

A revolutionary movement in Iran, led by the fundamental Islamic cleric, Ayatollah Khomeini, had forced the pro-U.S. Shah to flee the country, and he was seriously ill in Mexico. President Carter's decision to allow the Shah entry to the U.S. for hospitalization unleashed the fury of Iranian Shiite students who, with the support of Khomeini, stormed the U.S. embassy, burned the American flag, and took 49 hostages, this in the shadow of an impending U.S. recession, spiraling gas prices, rising interest rates, and stampeding inflation, all of which ignited an economic firestorm that hit the nation with a double-whammy monetary shockwave, then uniquely termed "stagflation."

An heroic CIA figure, to whom I later sold land, and who had become a close friend, was caught up in this geopolitical maelestrom. His cloak-and-dagger activities have literally snatched him from the edge of death and torture on numerous occasions, including once in the Iranian desert during the almost suicidal rescue attempt of American hostages. Highly decorated and assigned to run the U.S. clandestine war effort that eventually defeated the Russians in Afghanistan, he has since become a true "Lawrence of Arabia" legend.

At the time, I was occupied with my writing and publishing activities and had temporarily withdrawn from aggressive acquisitions of country property; still I sensed (1) that raw land prices had peaked due to the land boom and excessive real estate speculation, and (2) the pending recession and energy crisis were dampening consumer response. Land financing was hard to find, with interest rates rising to 15-16%. It was not a comfortable economic climate in which to do business. The real action, as it turned out, was in the disposal of distressed properties, where sellers could get some cash and buyers could pick up solid deals.

I remember selling five-acre tracts of country property within 50 miles of Richmond, VA, for as low as $4750 on terms, and even less for cash. This figure, at the time, would have reflected a developer's acquisition cost of about $300 per acre! The property was near a large lake and just off of an interstate highway, and the headline on one of my ads in October of 1979 announced:

COMMUTE TO YOUR OWN AFFORDABLE COUNTRY PLACE AT A BREAKTHROUGH PRICE–5 AC. $4950!

The ad cited facts about the current economic situation, including figures from the U.S. Dept. of Agriculture estimating an increase in land prices of 14-15% for the year 1979, followed by a factual statement: *"Because this was distressed property, we have acquired the land for about half the cost of raw land in the area; consequently, we are able to pass along significant savings to you, the consumer."*

An appeal was made in the ad to investors regarding the new fuel boom: firewood. Because of the rising cost of oil and gas, the price of cordwood in New England had doubled over the year. In fact, this very land was being considered for acquisition by a timber company for growing pulpwood. It had to be cheap. And productive.

In troubled times, product sales are generally motivated by perceived value. So it is important for sellers to establish and substantiate value. The ad promoted the sale of land, so any component of the land product was fair game for discussion. Soil and terrain features were addressed. The property consisted of highly productive soil for growing food. Abundant surface water flowed through the land in the form of streams. And there were absolutely no problems with percolation for the construction of homes, or for the placement of approved mobile homes.

The shrinking supply of private land was discussed in the ad. Figures at the time from *U.S. News and World Report* revealed that state and local governments across the nation were buying up land at the rate of a million acres a year. In just 15 years, from 1959 to 1974, a total of 17 million acres (the size of Delaware, Rhode Island, and West Virginia combined) was transferred from private to public ownership, mostly to state and local governments. More and more homeowners in the future would have to be compressed into tightly clustered housing.

The general public was reminded that no miracles were available to cure the scarcity of affordable privately owned land. In fact, during the previous decade, U.S. Dept. Of Agriculture figures showed rising land prices outdistancing the inflation rate. Millions of landowners are still confronted with this fact every year by local governments when they open envelopes containing tax assessments showing ever-increasing real estate values.

To prove value, I asked the reader to draw an imaginary circle 50 miles around Richmond. This band, given the worsening gas crisis, was a suggested outer limit for commuters and country property seekers. I advised commuters, who were scouting for country property, to check prices on real estate that was (1) within that circle, (2) near an interstate freeway for quick access, (3) located near a small town offering all municipal services, (4) close to a large body of water for recreation, and (5) in a county with a low tax rate. Then the readers were told to compare the price of such country real estate with the property advertised, this to make sure they were getting full value for their money. Of course, it was expected that few potential buyers would actually take this test. But if they had, they would have either (1) lost out on the offer because they were too late, or (2) proven the value hands down.

PART FIVE

The Eighties

As the result of a prolonged farm crisis, record numbers of rural Americans fled their farms and home towns, reversing a general countrywide population trend of people moving from cities to rural areas and dampening land values in outlying regions beyond commuting distance.

Edinburg, VA
710 FAMILIES TO LEAVE LOVE CANAL – May, 1980 –
Robert Palmer

Government officials, concerned about health hazards, ordered 710 families to evacuate their homes in the Love Canal area of Niagara Falls, New York. The homes were built near an old chemical dump, and scientists said they had detected chromosome damage in 11 of 36 residents.

Bad news seemed to follow bad news as the year progressed. Money was tight all over, and interest rates continued to skyrocket in the peculiar inflationary recession. Home construction was at a standstill, and mortgage rates were out of sight. Homes and commercial buildings that had been planned for construction in 1980 were indefinitely postponed. Thousands of builders were going broke. Millions of people were out of work. The cities were hit particularly hard by the economic downturn. Investment gurus advised clients to channel some of their available money into America's future–country properties near small growing towns.

In early 1980, I had published the book *"HOW YOU CAN GROW RICH THROUGH RURAL LAND–Starting from Scratch* that I sold primarily by mail order as a home-study course, with audio tape and study guide. The book and attendant publicity generated a wealth of opportunities for me in country properties. One of many troubled properties I handled during the eighties was offered to me by a bank:

Building slump in scenic Shenandoah Valley lets you
**STEAL YOUR NEXT HOMESITE IN NEARBY
SMALL TOWN AMERICA**
–and enjoy 10 times more land for the money
3 acres with town water from $6,950. Less for cash

Edinburg, VA is a charming, small Shenandoah Valley town surrounded by mountains. The air is clean and healthy. You can get there nonstop from the Washington D.C. beltway in less than 80 minutes. Half-acre homesites in the town with central water were then selling for around $10,000 in this small community, an area somewhat reminiscent of the Scottish Highlands.

Then, because of the building slump, these sites were being sacrificed; and only six were available.

The sites are within walking distance of quaint main-street shops, gourmet restaurants, doctors, banks, and Interstate 81. Residents can enjoy skiing just 20 minutes from their doors, and even closer are the million-acre George Washington National Forest for hunting, and the South Fork of the Shenandoah River, where the public can fish and canoe. Obviously, given the harsh economic climate of the times, the offer was pitched mainly to investors, who, up until 1986, could write off interest charges on consumer debt. The ad explained that:

(1) When interest rates went down, homes would be built on these and other lots within the town, with some lots as small as 1/3 acre.

(2) There was only so much land available within the town.

(3) No reasonable cash offer would be refused.

Considering the fact that this was a sale of "in-town" property, the offer provided the investor with a relatively large amount of usable and marketable residential land for a comparatively small amount of money. The land is open and wooded; some enjoy small ponds. All have mountain views and town water.

Advertised interest rates for those buyers with minimum down payments had reached 14.51%, and rates were on the fast track to go higher. The usual money-back guarantee before closing was provided, and it was mentioned that on past cancellations at previous distress sales, the land in question sold at higher prices the second time around. Soaring gas prices were still a major concern of consumers in 1980, so six gallons of free gasoline were given, along with other discounts and inducements, this for quick response by anyone bringing the ad to inspect the land.

As my book became known, I began to pick up scattered real estate deals over a broad region. I had leased my larger stone building to another Realtor, and I was conducting brokerage and development operations out of my smaller original office across the street. HUD watchdogs, suspecting that I might have been violating a federal rule requiring registration of certain combined subdivisions in advertising campaigns, later requested my presence in Washington to explain suggested misdoings. I had to hire a knowledgeable D.C. attorney to lead me through that bureaucratic maze. During the same time frame, I was fighting a local subdivision ordinance, and my office was well-stocked with young ladies to cope with the political work. One harmless lecher, from whom I had purchased a stagnant subdivision, remarked, "You seem to have a lot of women in stock." He was convinced he would bed at least one of them. Unregulated and wild indulgences of the mind, of course, have their consequences.

Front Royal, VA
REAGAN IS 40th PRESIDENT – November, 1980 –
Kenny Rogers

President Reagan was elected in a landslide and immediately promised to "put America back to work again." Indeed it is our work that determines our value, and millions of Americans–knocked down and disillusioned by hard times, business failures, botched military action to free the hostages in Iran, and wimpish diplomatic behavior–wanted to get back on their feet, throw their shoulders back, and get on with their lives. Because, unless a man works, he loses pride in himself and cannot find out what he wants to do. And the country was wrestling with problems of the dejected unemployed and dealing with those countless lost souls seeking other careers and avenues of opportunity within our economy.

Now along comes this character in a cowboy hat promoting a book about investing in rural land and talking about how you can become a millionaire. He says that because real estate ownership plays a big part in millionaire density, individuals who own a great deal of land, particularly in some of the farming states, become millionaires because of the large increases in land values. He was even planning to teach a course on what he calls "subdivesting" at a local community college. Come one. Come all.

Of course, the purpose of many career-based books is to define oneself. In life, if you fail to clarify yourself and to clearly state your objectives, someone else will handle these tasks for you. If you don't know who you are or where you're going, you're not going anywhere.

Public invited

FREE LECTURE

"How to Profitably Invest in Rural Land"

*–the secret of **Subdivesting***

The ad said "Mr. Haynes's popular course, *HOW YOU CAN GROW RICH THROUGH RURAL LAND - Starting from Scratch,* has been ordered by people from every state and from many countries overseas. *Real Estate Agent* magazine has just published an article on the author's unique rating system for eliminating speculation from rural land investment. They say the course may be the first and only one yet written on profiting from rural land transactions."

Those attending the lecture obtained some valuable advice including:

1. Why many people fail in rural land, and how you can succeed
2. Common land speculation mistakes and how to avoid them
3. How to achieve financial independence through rural land investments
4. Where the seed money is for your investments and how to get it
5. How to choose the right partners for your ventures
6. How to buy land with no money down
7. What you should know about Location, Location, Location
8. How to find the beauty in an ugly piece of land
9. Why some ads succeed and others fail
10. What you should know about real estate brokers

The book you are reading, of course, examines in detail all of these concerns and provides a great deal more information about utilizing the land around you–information that some people would spin as counterproductive to their own peculiar socioeconomic cultures and would rather not have brought it to mind. In fact, after teaching a course on rural land investment at the local community college where I had given this lecture, a few alarmed elitists with influence on the board of directors felt I was giving away their precious store of the bucolic countryside by promoting ideas that their idyllic environment could be broken down into smaller and more equitable pieces for others to enjoy.

An empathetic educator at the institution alerted me to the long knives at work behind my back, and after the conclusion of my well-received course on land investment, the daggers struck in the form of a tart letter from the president of the college telling me not to refer to their college in my book promotion and real estate advertising. Education, it would seem, can be as thin as the blade of ignorance that punctures the back of new ideas.

Middletown, VA
IRAN RELEASES HOSTAGES – January, 1981 –
Kool & the Gang

Fifty-two American hostages were flown to freedom after a 444-day ordeal at the hands of militant Islam. They left on an Algerian 727 to the chilling chant of "God is great, Death to America." The purchase of freedom had been costly and humiliating.

The Purchase of Country Land

"I've often wished that I had clear,
For life, six hundred pounds a year
A handsome house to lodge a friend
A river at my garden's end,
A terrace walk, and half a rood
Of land, set out to plant a wood"
– Swift

This was the time of my life when, at the beginning of the year, I wrote down on a 3X5 card my goals or wishes for the future, giving each a deadline for accomplishment. If these goals had been accomplished during the previous year, or the wishes fulfilled, I crossed them out and replaced them with others. Each morning and evening I would attempt to repeat these aspirations and desires to myself like a mantra. "By (such and such a date) I will have a farm, motor home, airplane, etc. Generally, I got what I wished for. Of course, if all of our wishes were granted, life's pleasures would consequently be withdrawn.

It was necessary that the goal or wish be as specific as possible and realistic. For example, when striving for monetary gain, I would write down a net worth figure to which I aspired, while someone else may have written down a specific amount of money that they wanted to have in the bank. One specific material reward that I sought at the time was to own a Piper Super Cub airplane.

I vividly recall reading an ad in a local newspaper offering riverfront land for sale with generous owner financing. I responded to the ad, inspected the farm, liked what I saw, and offered a bundle of notes–secured by land and with my personal endorsement–in exchange for the land. After wrapping up the deal, the seller mentioned that he also had an airplane for sale under similar terms. Strange as it may seem, I knew intuitively that plane was a Piper Super Cub. When I asked him what kind of plane he was selling, he validated my intuition. So I upped the ante of notes, and within a month or so he landed the plane on the riverfront pasture where I took a test flight and subsequent delivery.

This was an unusual, though not infrequent, way that I have acquired land throughout my career. Somehow I have always known whether I want to acquire or reject a piece of land after first looking at it, and in most acquisition cases it was imperative that I act quickly or lose the deal.

Impulsive acts can carry a penalty, because you are disregarding certain prescribed safeguards. But, to the entrepreneur, security can sometimes be your worst enemy. Over the years I have developed a *Land Acquisition Checklist* that I find helpful, and I often try to include a clause in the purchase contract calling for a study period. The general length of these study stages can vary from, say, 30 to 90 days, depending on the requirements and proclivities of both buyer(s) and seller(s). A standard Realtor's contract should contain safeguards for both parties, including the study period option, delivery of free and clear title, and a provision for price adjustments when acreage is gained or lost after a new survey.

Developer's-Investor's Land Acquisition Check List
(See example pages 430-437 and Appendix I)

1. Is there a recent survey? After personally inspecting the land, and in the absence of a survey with geographical overlay, try to position the property on a topographical map to analyze terrain features, a process generally and more efficiently done with the assistance of a surveyor, who will refer to the deed calls and possibly do the survey. In most of my transactions the buyer pays for the survey, although the cost is often split between the buyer(s) and seller(s). Occasionally the seller will agree to pick up the tab.

2. Is the quality of the soils suitable for home sewage disposal systems? This factor is usually determined through tests performed by a health department-qualified analyst or a certified soils scientist.

3. Is any of the land floodable or subject to frequent natural disasters, such as earthquakes, tornadoes, landslides, mudslides, hurricanes, or avalanches? If so, how will this affect the price structure and the bottom line of the homesite(s) or development.

4. Are there easements or encroachments on the property, such as power and gas lines, rights-of-way, etc? Are they serious enough to affect consumer usage, response and sales?

5. Will there be any zoning problems? If so, is the contract subject to obtaining approvals?

6. Are there any adverse influences present in the area that could affect sales and property values, such as high-tension power lines, smoke-spewing and noisy factories, contaminated waterways, landfills, butchering plants, and foul-smelling farms?

7. Are utilities available? If not, will there be any problems or additional expenses involved with bringing in electric and telephone services? How will this affect the bottom line?

8. Who maintains the road to the property? If not the state, then who is responsible for maintenance? If you are responsible, then do you have enough of a right-of-way to adequately service the property under existing state and county regulations?

9. Do you have the required sight distance(s) for your entrance(s) to obtain the necessary permits from the department of highways for your development?

10. Can you see or foresee any evidence of adverse possession (squatters)? Do the adjoining property owners agree with the survey? If there is no survey, have there been any known disagreements with neighbors over existing boundaries and fence lines?

11. Is your financing lined up? Are terms and conditions spelled out clearly? If the owner/seller is holding your note, can the obligation be prepaid?

12. Are there any defects in the title? If so, can they be cleared up before closing? Can you obtain title insurance if the title has an unsolvable minor problem(s)? If not, will your lender agree to a lawyer's opinion that the title is essentially clear? If closing is extended, what effect will this have on your plans?

13. Will you and your buyers control the water, timber and mineral rights? Is this spelled out in the contract and deed?

14. Do you have full riparian rights (unobstructed use and enjoyment of your waterfront)? Can you obtain, and do you need, flood insurance?

15. What is the general well depth and degree of water quality in the area? Have any wells in the vicinity recently gone dry? Will the well water require a softener? Have there been any reports of contaminated wells in the area? Check out these questions with the local health department.

16. Is the land near enough to a town or city to avoid unusual buyer concern? Shopping? Doctors? Hospital? Schools? Fire protection? How much will distance affect sales?

17. Will there be any restrictions on what you can do with the property? If so, can you live with them? How will your customers react to such restrictions?

18. Is *specific performance* written into the contract so the seller cannot renege? Do you have a loophole or two built into the contract so you can walk away from the deal if necessary and without penalty?

19. Is the contract subject to obtaining approvals from local, state, and federal government bodies, agencies, and departments? If so, have you allowed enough time in the contract and in your plans to get through the red tape?

20. If you are developing the property, have you tried for an interest-only period at the beginning your mortgage to help with cash flow? Have you allowed enough time to pay back the loan?

21. Are release provisions built into the contract allowing you to sell off parcels by paying specified amounts toward the remaining principal balance on the loan? Lenders will usually require you to pay them a specified per-acre figure, or a minimum of 70% of the selling price on any out-parcel sales. Premium properties, such as waterfront, can require higher figures or percentages when sold off; or releases of the best lots can be restricted in some way until a certain percentage of less desirable land has been sold.

22. Will the seller subordinate (generally referring to an owner/seller agreeing to hold a second trust or mortgage in deference to a lender requiring first position when financing a home or building on the property)? If so, for what consideration?

23. Were you able to build an exculpatory clause in the contract to avoid personal liability? (In the event of a default, the lien holder considers only the land as security against the debt.)

24. Does the contract specify that all release payments are to be applied against the next principal payments due? This is a safeguard for your cash flow when developing land.

25. Have you protected yourself against prepayment penalties?

26. Have you deducted from the total acreage any land tied up in easements and encroachments that adversely affect, in a material way,

the value of the land and requested an adjustment in the purchase price?

27. When using owner financing, will the seller suspend payments during any unforseen delay in the development process caused by governmental authority? Only in rare cases would a bank or commercial lender agree to suspend payments.

28. Are the closing costs apportioned in accordance with legal standards? Realtor contracts generally spell out the obligations of both buyer(s) and seller(s).

29. Will the seller allow you to name the trustee in the deed of trust or mortgage securing the property? You will want (1) quick delivery on the deeds of partial release when you sell off lots, and (2) proper preparation of the deed of dedication (your protective covenants, etc.) easements, and rights-of-way. A friendly lawyer can grease the slide for you.

30. Have you provided easements on your plat and in your protective covenants for the installation of utilities, this so the utility companies can operate without undue delays and obstructions from any property owners from whom signatures may be required. Will you need easements from adjoining landowners to provide utilities?

31. Will any highway entrance permits be required? If so, how many? How will the number of permits affect your bottom line?

32. Will any permits be required for soil and erosion control and wetlands disturbance?

The Importance of Concept

Before buying country property for development, I try to have a concept fixed in my mind. Successful concepts, as opposed to ideas, are generally measured by time, whereas pure thought perceives both ends of the idea at the same time. You can have an idea of what you would like to do with a piece of land, but that is a cannon's shot away from pulling it off. By the time your army of thoughts reaches the cannon, you may have lost the battle, whether it be a desired land acquisition or a fruitful development. It is primarily through the discovery of marketable concepts that great victories in commerce are brought home. Through the dark hours of the recession, my extensive advertising promoted the catchline: **"For every city dweller, his own country homestead,"** and the idea had evolved into a concept beyond the lights and shadows of the consumer's dream into a much sought-after commodity in those troubled times. You might call this catch-line phrase the discovery of a waking concept.

With regard to the riverfront property that I acquired through the exchange of notes, I named the project NORTH FORK HOMESTEADS and developed a display ad showing my little homestead graphic in a setting beside the rolling Shenandoah River.

OPPORTUNITY SEEKERS WANTED
There is a beautiful nearby valley that still lives in the "good old days"... minimal government ... low crime ... fair taxes ... stable community and is a genuine haven of health and happiness
On the Shenandoah River.

Homestead Riot!
3 acre homestead at river from $5950
3 acres of prime riverfront from $9950

The ad described a consumer revolt. The price per acre on these riverview and riverfront homesteads was the same as we had offered in 1968. And back then people stood in line to buy. In those days, said the ad, you could have purchased a one-acre riverview lot on the same river for $2,000. Now, county subdivision laws had raised the minimum lot size on private roads to three acres. But the ad said you could see from the figures shown that the basic price *per acre* for riverview homesteads was about the same as 12 years before. The pretention of truth in an advertisement must be supported by a degree of faith in the product to fulfill the consumer's needs while living up to the buyer's expectations.

The ad pointed out that all of our previous offers of homesites on the Shenandoah River had been quickly snapped up and that they carried a built-in price appreciation as good as gold. That statement is as true today as it was in 1981. Five-acre riverfront farms around Front Royal were selling then for about $15-20,000. In 1977, four years before, the selling price had been closer to $10,000 The ad continued to hammer down valid selling points:

(1) Then, as today, we have always had to turn people away when we have offered riverfront homesteads for sale.

(2) Demand has always exceeded supply.

(3) Seldom do any resales come on the market.

(4) People love to be on the Shenandoah, not only because of its excellent canoeing, fishing, and swimming, but because it is one of America's cleanest rivers.

(5) All homesteads were above flood plain

(6) Ideal land for raising food and livestock

(7) Access into G.W. National Forest for hunting

(8) On navigable water that never runs dry

(9) All homesteads face south for potential solar heat

(10) All have mountain views.

**Location, Location, Location**, the real estate mantra, was stressed in the ad. The consumer could reach his homestead nonstop on interstate highways from the D.C. beltway. Some landowners were already commuting. The historic town of Woodstock is only three miles away for shopping and all municipal services, including a large, fully staffed hospital.

Shakespeare said that "Present fears are less than horrible imaginings." Yet many consumers waxed their minds with desperate imagination–personal survival in the event of a major economic collapse and widespread social disorders in the cities, leaving criminal elements marauding the countryside. The ad said that all vehicles entering the homestead area from existing public roads on the west must pass through a single gate and that the parallel eastern boundary was secured by the river and Massanutten Mountain range.

Here it was the dead of winter, and I was encouraging people to leave the comfort of their homes, get in their cars, and spend precious gasoline money to venture out into the cold and possible snow to look at land during the worst recession in recent history. I referenced our recent liquidations–many sold out within a week–and quoted prominent investment gurus who advised clients that the purchase of country property in a diversified agricultural environment was the safest investment move they could make, both monetarily and for their own well-being.

The price for three acres was lower than the prices some people had recently paid for half-acre lots in nearby recreational communities.

And the payments were less than $100 per month. The offer included a ticket for seven gallons of free gasoline and a host of other freebies.

As usual, the offer carried a no-obligation, money-back guarantee of the deposit.

The Subdivision of Country Land

Shortly after I completed the aforementioned project, two local Realtors approached me about a riverfront farm that they had just listed on the North Fork of the Shenandoah. The farm belonged to the estate of a deceased recluse, and the heirs were anxious to sell. I looked at the place, decided it had development potential and submitted a contract that, after some negotiation, was accepted. At the time, county minimum requirements for lot sizes on private roads was three acres, so I had the soils tested and subsequently constructed private roads throughout a three-acre subdivision, using the "Homestead Riot!" promotional theme.

I appealed to the readers' sense of adventure and told them they could rummage through the ghostly old farmhouse that was for sale and stumble over a hoard of worthless antiques, this while viewing a way of life gone with the wind:

DEATH ON THE SHENANDOAH

Strasburg, VA area–Antique farmhouse gasps for life beside Shenandoah River. Grim relic hides valuable log construction under aged board siding. 10 rambling rooms with irreplaceable plank flooring. Sagging home now abandoned to bats and tormenting winds. A real rarity for weekend fix-up buff. Creaky back stairwell offers quick escape from questionable shapes. Ghostly dwelling of deceased recluse now cluttered with antique junk and memorabilia. Grim outbuildings almost beyond hope. A treasure of authentic Americana dying for restoration. Generous 3 ½ ac. grounds fronting 254 feet along legendary river. All framed by a fortress of magnificent mountains in G.W. Nat'l Forest. Reduced to $27,500 for quick sale this weekend. Discount for cash.

B.K. HAYNES CORP.
"For every city dweller, his own rural homestead"

A form of fright for most people when they think about owning land is the price. So I asked the reader, "Why should only the wealthy own land?" There's something about owning a few acres at the water that sets you apart from everyone else. There were only 27 river access homesteads and a smaller number of homesteads on the river. Each one was easily affordable and would give its owner, his family and friends, many years of pleasure and peace of mind.

Following is a checklist of information generally required for salespeople when handling subdivided parcels of country property. Pertinent consumer information can be made available to the general public on a website.

1. Plat of the subdivision prepared by a licensed surveyor; a map showing the specific location within the county and, if practical, a topographical (topo) map of the parcel(s) or project.

2. Advertising and promotional materials related to the project.

3. A list of restrictive covenants, if any, that are recorded with the plat and deed, and usually prepared in consultation with an attorney.

4. Approximate amount of annual real estate taxes and costs of utility hookups, if any, along with names, addresses and phone numbers of the utility companies.

5. Fact sheet describing points of interest near the project. If the property is located near a town having a chamber of commerce, this information is readily available, along with a list of schools, churches, shopping areas, public transportation, hospitals, fire depts. etc.

6. Financing sheet, showing the price of each parcel and sources of financing.

7. Salesperson's information sheet showing commission breakdown and outlining exactly what duties are expected of each salesperson handling your properties. When using the services of a real estate agency this data is usually jointly prepared.

8. List of any environmental requirements or other restrictions on the property that are outside of the landowners' control. For example, use of the property may be restricted by a scenic or coastal zone easement, participation in an agricultural district; or land use may be impaired through reservations for water, timber, and mineral rights.

9. Color photographs of the land offered for sale.

10. Written directions to the property (if advisable).

11. Complete legal information about the project, including copy of seller's title opinion and (if available) title insurance policy, and the

type of deed to be conveyed. The following questions should be addressed and answers readily available within the project's files:

    a. What are the average closing costs, including title opinion, and title insurance?

    b. Are there any flaws on the title?

    c. Is there a blanket mortgage on the property?

    d. How much are the release fees?

    e. Where will settlement take place? When?

12. Official health reports on each parcel determining the type of sewage disposal system.

13. Costs for installing various home sewage disposal systems, along with names and phone numbers of local installers and building contractors.

14. Copies of any highway entrance or soils disturbance permits required for the project.

15. Copies of the sales contract to be used.

16. Checklist of items needed along with the contract, such as credit application, deposit, disclosure forms, disclaimers, indemnification agreements, rezoning requests, etc.

Luray, VA

RACIAL MINORITIES INCREASE IN SUBURBS – June, 1981 – Juice Newton

Sociologists once described the exodus of white Americans from the inner city to the suburbs as "white flight." Now it was catch-up time for blacks and Hispanics. Census Bureau figures showed a sharp rise from 1970 in the numbers of minorities fleeing the cities in search of the "good life" further out. This injection of newcomers into the ranks of the middle class acted like a shot of adrenaline to many of the more prosperous in the middle class, who then began to swell exponentially in their quest for the pathless woods and lonely shores of the countryside.

A real estate agent brought me a newly acquired listing of a farm and campground on the Shenandoah River near Front Royal. I looked at the property, recognized its potential, and immediately made a contract offer, which we hastily took to the sellers. After a little negotiation we came to terms, and I walked out with a contract on one of the best country properties I have ever owned. Several people called me up and wanted to buy it at a handsome price over what I was prepared to pay. However, this was not a farm to be flipped for a quick profit. It was begging to be developed. Its popularity and desirability are proven by the fact that riverfront parcels in this development seldom come up for sale to the general public.

The economy was picking up. People were spending more, and they still were not giving up their precious vacations. I figured the vacation angle was a good prop for my promotion.

After all, when your sojourn is over, you've spent a lot of money, and all you've got is a memory.

When your vacation is just a memory, you can still commute to your own affordable homestead at the river!

You can't spend it. An adventure upon it can be hazardous. You'll spend long hours in slavish devotion to it. Yet for the first to come, the Shenandoah River offers you self-sufficiency, recognition, and future financial reward. Liquidation of historic farm and campground along the Shenandoah River near Front Royal, VA. All property must be sold. Most join the river and G.W. Nat'l Forest.

3 acre river access homesteads from $7950
3-5 acre riverfront homesteads from $14,950

The ad showed a cut of a three-acre homestead spread out along the banks of the Shenandoah River. A tag on the homestead contained testimonials from previous campers, one of which said... *"Our favorite overnight camping area. We plan to be first in line."*

It's hard to believe. You'll come over the hill to see the countryside fall away before a long relentless river whispering in a green valley. An almost impenetrable mountain range walls off the western horizon. Another range looms in the sky to the east. You can't own land here for love nor money, except for this limited offering along a bend of the river that has escaped government ownership.

The ad also showed an illustration of man, woman, and child in a canoe. The man, who is paddling the canoe, is wondering, *"Whose woods are these?"* And the woman is asking, *"Are they for sale?"* The text goes on to discuss the urgency of quick action, based on fast sales in the previous year's riverfront liquidation sale on the Shenandoah, where many customers had missed the boat and where land values had since increased by 25% to 40%. Other compelling reasons to act now were: (1) the Forest Service's active bidding for river access land, and (2) pending new laws restricting the subdivision of land.

Other selling points in the ad addressed current concerns of consumers and suggested that a homestead on the river could help to alleviate these concerns:

1. Personal survival from disorder in the cities
2. Safety from crime elements
3. Southern exposure for solar heat during energy crisis
4. Food source for growing your own
5. Fish from the river, deer meat from the forest
6. Some sites suitable for in-ground homes to save on fuel costs
7. All tracts have homesites above the flood plain
8. All homesteads are guaranteed to perk

Concluding paragraphs in the ad explained why we could sell land so cheaply and offered a no-obligation, money-back guarantee of the deposit before closing. A $200 discount was given to all buyers that week, and five gallons of free gasoline and a value-packed Visitor's Kit were thrown in for all parties attending the sale.

REASONS FOR LOW PRICES

We have built our reputation on liquidating farms and estates very, very quickly in smaller acreage tracts. We also use our own road building equipment to keep costs down. Further, we deal with banks who specialize in financing raw land. We will profit from giving you this unique opportunity, and we expect you to profit as well. You can get the lowest price by making an acceptable cash offer. Or you can own with a minimum of $150 deposit and $250 at closing, with payments of $122.49 mo., 120 mos. at 15.86% apr. Slash rate with minimum of 10% down.

Strasburg, VA
SADAT SHOT DEAD IN EGYPT – October, 1981 –
Rolling Stones

Moslem fundamentalist soldiers, opposed to President Sadat's peace treaty with Israel, assassinated the Egyptian leader in a hail of automatic gunfire during a military parade in Cairo.

Troubled conditions and wars in the Middle East between Israel and its Moslem neighbors, including the Israeli aerial attack in June on Iraq's nuclear reactor, continued to disconcert Americans while still holding them hostage to high oil prices.

Cheaper energy production became an obsession with the government and consumers all across the country. Many homeowners were finding some financial relief on their monthly fuel bills by using solar heat and firewood. In the early fall, a financially strapped developer came to me with a tract of woodland that he wanted to unload. Searching for a development concept, I asked myself: Where is the money trail leading today? My thoughts whirled like a potter's wheel and produced the image of a bank and a forest.

The first entity has money, the second image consists of trees, a potential fuel source. Hence the concept "Tree Bank" was created. Private three-to-ten-acre banks of trees–a renewable energy source for consumers that would help pay for the land itself through savings on firewood. Banks of 3,000 to 10,000 trees for sale at distressed prices, with up to 500 trees per acre in a mature growth stage–a land product that should be selling for up to twice as much in normal times.

Some people may look at a growth of trees and call it a wooded lot or a patch of woods.

The term "tree bank," while theoretically applicable to the same area of tree growth as a "lot" or "patch," is a concept requiring definition in the public's eye, and therefore the concept could not take the centerpiece of any initial promotional effort without creating widespread confusion. The headline, "Tree Banks for Sale" could draw attention, but the "big idea" behind the promotion of a new product is to make sales, not to baffle the consumer. Reducing the concept to its elements, I determined that what I was basically selling was cheap woods that could be characterized as wooded lots, hardly a breakthrough offer.

The promotional banner through which this product was sold was quite simple:

Commute to the D.C. area on I- 66
Buy below auction and brokers prices
CHEAP WOODS!
Near Front Royal and Strasburg, VA
3-5-10 ACRE PRIVATE "TREE BANKS"
Tie up for as low as **$150 down**
SAVE UP TO 40% from original prices from **$5950**

The quarter-page ad was embellished with an illustration of a happy family and dog approaching a chalet in the woods. Another graphic showed a rounded homestead within the bark of a tree. Other cuts showed a hunter, a home, a log cabin, a hiker, and a travel trailer.

Rural Virginia
REAGAN GRAVELY WOUNDED BY ASSASSIN – March, 1981
John Lennon

On March 30, after giving a speech at the Washington Hilton Hotel, President Reagan, his press secretary, James Brady, and two law officers were gunned down by John Hinckley, Jr. At the hospital, the President continued to act out the game of life by musing to his wife, "Honey, I forgot to duck." He obviously did not enjoy being shot, and up until he was hit by gunfire he had played his cards well, and, like most of us, he wanted to stick around to the end of the game.

The country property game at this time was becoming harder to play, and it was facilitated mainly by the minds of investors and speculators. Price was always trumped by cash, and opportunity fed on easy terms and quality offers. During the spring months I put together the best close-in buys in country property I could find, both from my listings and the inventory of land that I had purchased with little or no money down, and at interest rates of 15% or more–rates that I would have to pass on to the consumer. When selling my own property in those days, many consumer notes were sold to banks, which, in turn, escrowed up to 10% of the proceeds for reimbursement of loan funds in case of default. I personally endorsed the notes. At first they paid no interest on these escrow funds, but later they reversed this policy to remain competitive with other lenders.

The Selling of the Chesapeake Bay

White Stone, VA
REAGAN WANTS $180 BILLION FOR ARMS – November, 1981
– Hall & Oates

Reagan had been president for almost a year and was in the process of exchanging a demoralized U.S. military for a superior fighting force to win the Cold War. In October, one of my ex-partners came to me with an exchange deal. His client, a builder and developer, was in the process of wrapping up a 1031 exchange agreement that left him with some waterfront lots just off the Chesapeake Bay, the world's largest estuary. The client needed to dump these lots super pronto as part of the agreement. I agreed to do the deal for a healthy slice of the gross, with me taking the hit for advertising and sales promotion.

The participants in the exchange, along with my ex-partner, picked me up at the Winchester, VA airport in a twin, and we flew down to an airfield where we were loaded into a Mercedes and driven to a nearby bayfront resort called Windmill Point. The lots were located on an inlet off of Chesapeake Bay, and all were waterfront properties adjacent to the resort. I sized up the situation, gathered some facts, formulated a rough promotional plan aimed at investors, and we flew back to Winchester.

After my ad campaign had been polished, I selected the hottest sales guns whom I had on staff, and a few talented salespeople who had worked for me, and I explained the promotion to them in detail. We had to be in and out of the campaign within two weeks, three at the most.

I put them up at the Windmill Point resort, conducted the necessary lot inspection and briefings, and everybody retired to the bar.

The half-page ads broke on Friday in the *Washington Post*, Friday and Saturday in the *Richmond Times Dispatch*, and Saturday and Sunday in the Tidewater newspapers in Norfolk, Hampton, and Newport News. A light rain was falling on our resort office Saturday morning when a dribbling of customers turned into a mob by noon, when the skies had cleared.

The whole sold-out promotion is explained in the following ad. Needless to say, buyers of this property literally struck gold, this despite the extraordinarily high interest charges, which were tax deductible at the time. Successful investors in country properties tend to get there first when they smell true value and are usually financially prepared to snap up bargains in troubled times, even if this means leveraging their way into the deal with little or no money down.

Unheard of
WATERFRONT OPPORTUNITY
Land bust prices on valuable deep water estates adjacent
to Chesapeake Bay and the Intracoastal Waterway
Save up to 40% from original prices

2+ ACRE WATERFRONT ESTATES
with quick access to the Atlantic Ocean
from $19,500 to $34,500

Remember the great Florida waterfront bust of the twenties? Smart investors made millions by sopping up inflated resort waterfront at depressed prices.

But ground floor opportunities like that are rare. By the time everybody knows about a troubled Miami Beach, the time for rapid price appreciation is over. Opportunities at newer waterfront resorts, such as Hilton Head Island, are even more rare. Most people end up missing the boat on waterfront. So they settle for back lots. Or they go away disappointed. At Windmill Point you cannot buy a "back lot." All property is on the water. You can't even buy a lot. Period. All property is estate-sized, at two acres or more. All are depression priced to reflect these troubled times. All are located at a new and exciting marine resort and destination point yet to be "discovered."

Where is Windmill Point?

If you lived in historic Williamsburg, you might pop over to the Yacht Club for lunch. This is the Colonial Area, the cradle of our nation. You're at the Intracoastal Waterway, where the Rappahannock River meets the 40-mile-wide Chesapeake Bay. You don't have to fight the Bay Bridge or Tunnel, yet you're at the last marine resort before reaching the Atlantic Ocean from the north. Only the size of your boat keeps the world from your dock. You're about 2½ hours from Washington D.C.; 1½ hours from Richmond; 1¼ hours from Newport News/Norfolk; and about 45 minutes from Williamsburg, Busch Gardens, and Jamestown.

You're on uncrowded sandy beaches. You're in the land of Pleasant Living, without exhaust fumes and the carnival atmosphere of high-density waterfront resorts. There are three nearby towns to serve you: White Stone, Irvington, and Kilmarnock, with its fully-staffed hospital. The famous Tides Inn, an airport with rental cars, and several golf courses are also close by.

Why Windmill Point?

Your primary motivation may be to tie up waterfront acreage at gone-with-the-wind prices. Even more important is the quality of your destination resort. How many people want to go there? What does it have to offer? Owning a two-acre waterfront estate at Windmill Point in 1981 could be like buying an oceanfront lot at Nags Head ten years ago. Few people can afford one today. But what about tomorrow? The trick is to find a uniquely located resort, yet to explode as a destination point. Then check the quality of housing. Are people with money buying there? And look over the resort facilities. Are they in place, or merely planned? Finally, check the weather. At Windmill Point, there are no hot and cold extremes because you're on water.

The average annual temperature is close to 60 degrees. Winds are cooler in summer and warmer in winter by 20-30 degrees. Plus, you'll enjoy all four seasons without the snow.

On the Beach

But these considerations are dwarfed by a larger and more vital concern–your security and personal survival. You may not be a survivalist, but you have your safety and your family to think of. Windmill Point is on a peninsula at land's end, surrounded on three sides by water, ideally suited for private wind-powered generators, and away from through streets and highways. You will not be subjected to the hazards of bridge and tunnel traffic and an influx of crime.

And you need not be isolated and cut off by man-made bridges, tunnels, and conventional power sources. What better place to be during hard times than along the East Coast's major sea lane?

How Big a Value?

At Brightwater–a planned residential community on Windmill Point–the first two-acre waterfront sites were sold in the early seventies for up to $55,000. Today, developers would consider two-acre waterfront estates an economic waste of land, due to the enormous cost of installing roads, amenities and utilities. That's why few are being created. The first houses in the Brightwater community sold for $150,000 to $175,000. Want to try to buy one today? Today, waterfront lots *without* resort facilities are selling for $30,000 to $50,000 in Lancaster County. We know, because we checked with local brokers. Townhouses are now being constructed and sold at Windmill Point Marine Resort for $125,000.

At Windmill Point, you can walk, jog, or bike from your waterfront estate to a large salt-water pool, three tennis courts, white sand beaches, gourmet restaurant, and a lounge with live entertainment. The Yacht Club offers open and covered slips and overnight accommodations in the lodge or in beachfront rooms and apartments. Complete facilities are also available at the resort for conventions, meetings, and banquets.

Still More Value

Most waterfont lots in planned communities are only about a quarter-acre in size. At Brightwater, you get up to eight times more land, and waterfrontage averaging 200 feet along a protected Bay inlet. You're right at the Bay–where you want to be–and not miles and hours away. You can also choose between property on a dredged boat basin or on a sandy Rappahannock River beach. Some property even offers double frontage on a back bay beach and on a lagoon. Here you can harvest crabs, clams, oysters, trout, sea bass, rockfish, blues, and flounder. You can sail, waterski, harbor a 16-ft. boat at your own private dock, or keep larger deep-water craft at the yacht basin next door. There are slips for more than 100 yachts.

Make no mistake about it. Windmill Point is the Cadillac of stops along the Intracoastal Waterway. It's the place to be if you're into boating and a carefree life. If you're planning for retirement, or if you've been priced out of other waterfront communities, this may be your last chance to locate on the water. It's a fact that inflation has been known to double values on some scarce properties within a few short years. And remember, you're paying a deflated price on this waterfront to begin with. Here, too, you get central water to your property, underground utilities, plus a guaranteed septic system permit. And taxes are 1/10th those in urban areas because of the rural character of the county.

Why the Low Prices?

The market for high-priced property is depressed due to a flat economy and high interest rates. Few houses are being built. Still, creative financing and exchange agreements keep property moving. In a recent exchange agreement, the builder/developer of Brightwater gave up future construction plans and sold his remaining land. The terms of the agreement call for immediate liquidation of the remaining waterfront estates. Since we are the area's most experienced and successful liquidators of small acreage rural properties, we were consulted. Right away we asked for and were given authority to slash prices by as much as 40%. We insisted on offering speculator's terms, so you could easily leverage your way into the property.

As you know, price reductions on some distressed properties are not unusual. What you may not have noticed, however, is that such devaluations on prime waterfront are unheard of, barring a repeat of 1929. This is the first time you've seen this offer. Why, then, buy from speculators when you can be an original owner? And if you come this weekend you will get first choice.

Serious Words of Advice

You won't find this kind of opportunity in the hands of local brokers and developers. Sure, you can settle for land on an upper estuary. But you don't want to spend hours on your boat getting to the Bay and back. And you certainly won't settle for tidal marshland.

These are the last two-acre estates for sale on the Windmill Point peninsula. Have you priced the resale market on places like Cape Cod and Martha's Vineyard? And if you've tried to buy waterfront here, at the Chesapeake Bay, you would have run into tiny lots, severe erosion, and outrageous prices. You missed the boat at Ocean City and the Outer Banks. Myrtle Beach took off without you. You missed out on Sea Pines. Obviously you won't want to be late at Windmill Point. Only once or twice in your lifetime will an opportunity like this come along where you won't be caught napping.

Bring This Ad and Save

Drive out to Windmill Point this weekend and reserve two acres on deep water before it's all gone. You'll get a general warranty deed and new survey with your purchase. You do not have to pay off the mortgage for the land to be yours.

But don't pay what others pay who buy from cooperating brokers. Simply bring this ad and get $200 off the already low price, plus a full year's membership in the Windmill Point Marine Resort (total $500 value). Pay cash, buy more acreage, or make larger down payments, and get further discounts and lower interest rates. There are only 16 waterfront estates available. Because this is a liquidation sale, they must be sold quickly. Sorry, to avoid excessive speculation, you must close on your property prior to any resale.

Tie Up Waterfront for $500

You can get the lowest price by making an acceptable cash offer. If you're in a high tax bracket and need the interest write-off, then buy with inflated dollars. Here's a sample: You buy a two-acre waterfront estate for $19,500. Deduct your $200 for acting this week ($500 if you do not want resort privileges). Tie up for $500. Pay $1500 at closing. Then $288.32 mo., 120 mos @ 15.86% apr. Slash this rate with larger down payment. For even lower monthly payments, ask about our 20-year balloon financing.

No Sales Pressure–Look on Your Own

If you would rather not have a salesperson accompany you, simply take the plat map and select any two acres of your choice that may still be available. The property has just been re-surveyed and will go very quickly. Our personnel will be on site this weekend to answer questions and to assist you in any way we can.

Lunch or Dinner on Us

It's well worth your while to make an appointment this weekend. We'll pick up your luncheon or dinner check (for two) at our gourmet restaurant if you'll help with our scheduling.

Obviously we don't know the extent of the crowd, so we would prefer to work by appointment.

If you would like a beachfront room for the night, please let us know, and we will arrange a special rate, which will include a hunt breakfast. Fall is a spectacular time of the year to visit the Bay and the Colonial Area. Since you're only a short drive from Williamsburg and Busch Gardens, you may want to make your trip a combined visit. If you're flying in, please let us know, and we'll pick you up at the airport close by. You are under no obligation to buy property when you call.

The ad contained photographs of the beach and yacht harbor, along with an illustrated cut of a waterfront estate with home, dock and horse stable. Comparable waterfront prices at local beach areas were also shown, with the high figures running up to $150,000, all numbers crossed out. Directions were included from Washington D.C., Richmond, and the Tidewater cities.

Tidewater, Virginia
HOUSING UP 25% IN NEWPORT NEWS – March, 1982 –
Journey

One largely underreported trend in Virginia during the recession of the early eighties was the fact that home sales were booming in Tidewater, this despite the troubled economy. And since many Americans owe most of their wealth to their rising home values, we can learn a great deal from the following discussion of a successful promotion in Tidewater. Figures from the Virginia Real Estate Research Center at the time showed home sales up a whopping 25% in Newport News-Hampton and up 9% in Norfolk-Portsmouth.

The Southeastern Virginia Planning District Commission predicted a housing shortage during the period 1982-89 for the Hampton Roads-Tidewater area. Data from the Tidewater Builders Association showed yearly housing starts would have to triple to meet demand.

But even though sales of existing homes had risen, there were few new starts due to the unusually high interest rates. Many builders were going bankrupt. Still, the Virginia Employment Commission reported the Tidewater jobless rate about the lowest in the U.S. Federal jobs, and the deficit kept growing under the new Reagan adminstration. Military pay was up. Local planners expected the pending influx of new workers, retirees, and personnel and dependents from the planned Reagan military buildup to increase the area's population by 23% through 1989.

The Pentagon was asking for two new carriers to be built at Newport News. The area was looking at the potential economic stimulus of up to 15 new ships and a small city of additional military people. The region hosts the largest naval complex in the world. A dozen military bases and stations were headquartered in the Tidewater vicinity.

I was not aware of these facts until I went down to Tidewater at the invitation of a troubled builder and investor in rental properties. He had attended one of my lectures to a local real estate exchange group, and he subsequently sent me a letter with a $50 check if I would pay him a visit to see if I could unload his building lots in the Tidewater town of Smithfield. After considerable research, I determined that the area was on the verge of a major economic boom, this to be fueled largely by years of pent-up demand for housing caused by high interest rates.

If the past was any guide, I knew that investors and speculators would soon drive up homesite prices in the Hampton Roads-Tidewater area. The more desirable and accessible the location, such as Smithfield, the higher the prices. The longer people waited to buy their homesites, the more it would soon cost them. This is an undisputed fact in residential areas abutting harbors.

All of this aside, I still faced a formidable obstacle in convincing consumers to act on this offer–the abnormally high interest rates. This said, it then became imperative that the consumer examine the facts to determine whether the value was really there. In direct response advertising, the successful establishment of truth or certainty in any offer depends on the customer's digestion of facts, real or imagined. In half-page display ads throughout the region, I nudged readers off the couch with the point that if they waited five years hoping interest rates would go down, they would need about $14,000 to buy an in-town homesite that they could steal then for $7,950, this fact being based on *Personal Finance* inflation tables.

The Art of Establishing Value

The general public is aware of the fact that all is not gold that shines. No matter how bright the picture, there is usually a shadow of doubt. That's why I try to go the extra mile to establish value, whether in an advertisement or a sales presentation. In the Smithfield situation, I piled it on. Town water was available on site, with tap-on fees already paid. Telephone and electric lines had been installed, and all sites enjoyed paved roads. Highlighted in this discussion are excerpts from the promotion that paint the offer with value:

Location, Location, Location

Smithfield and Isle of Wight County are just across the James River Bridge from Newport News. The sign says five miles to the county line. Both the town and the county were, at that time, on the urban fringe of the Hampton Roads-Hampton Metropolitan Area. The country in those days was largely agricultural (less so now over the span of twenty-odd years).

I needed to convince the customer that the demand for homesites was set to explode on the south side of the bridge and in the Smithfield port vicinity. A dead giveaway of exploding growth and rising home values could be seen in the recent construction of townhouses over-looking the harbor. Units costing $150,000 were then in place.

The Case for Smithfield

The port town of Smithfield was laid out in 1750. Historic restoration and new housing exist side by side. The buyers would live in a quaint waterfront town of about 5,000. The South Hampton Roads cities would be their cultural neighbors. Williamsburg, Busch Gardens, Jamestown, and Yorktown are close enough for lunch. I explained to the readers that if they were newcomers, they would enjoy winter temperatures in the fifties. And cool sea breezes keep the weather mild in summer.

How to Write a Direct Response Real Estate Ad

The ad was busy with graphics and photographs to show movement and to substantiate facts. Illustrated cuts showed the Newport News Shipyard and the Smithfield Packing Plant.

A 4-picture montage showed a sailboat, a fishing craft, and people swimming and playing tennis. One illustration showed part of a Monopoly board with two homes sitting between some vacant lots, with these words labeled on the street: LAST CHANCE! 20 SITES SOLD IN 20 HOURS.

Other graphics included a map showing the close proximity of Smithfield to the neighboring cities.

The coming Tidewater boom and how you can profit from recession homesite bargains in historic Smithfield, Virginia

Unusual opportunity to steal a ½ to 5 acre in-town homesite just 15 minutes from Hampton Roads Harbor and the shipyards. Some creekfront and waterfront sites. Why you should hurry.

Save up to 40% from original prices

½ to ¾ acre port town homesites
adjacent to Virginia's major metropolitan area
from $7950–a few 5 acre sites $14,950

Why were these lots being sold at such low prices? The finger was pointed at high interest rates and the plight of builders who could not start new homes. But Tidewater had a sleeping housing market that was about to wake up. I laid out the simple fact that builders and developers could not start from scratch and create large in-town lots at these prices.

I stressed the fact that the region encompassing Smithfield and the south side of the bridge represented the final link in the Hampton Roads development chain. Investors in city real estate were advised that their financial future was to be found in the metropolitan fringe area. There was simply no place left in the region to find an inexpensive homesite. I invited readers to check the local classified ads to prove this fact. In the ad, I compared Isle of Wight County with Fairfax County, outside of Washington D.C.–then one of the fastest-growing counties in America–where such an offer as this would have caused an uncontrollable stampede.

The promotional approach to selling in-town lots differs, of course, from the sale of country properties where low density, peace, tranquility, and the laid-back lifestyle are emphasized. Customers for suburban lots are looking for convenient access to schools, transportation, shopping, hospitals, and varied degrees of recreation and culture. I explained to readers that, if they owned a homesite in Smithfield, they could be out boating and fishing in one of the world's finest harbors faster than from most waterfront communities.

Swimming? Tennis? Right where you live. Just join the club. Shopping? Right next door–adjacent to the community. And newcomers will also benefit from seven beaches, five coliseums, five fishing piers, a fleet of charter boats–the largest in Virginia, 30 theaters, 40 libraries, five colleges and universities, 28 hospitals, and two international airports for quick flights to anywhere in the world.

A battery of questions was asked in the ad. Can you find a cheap suburban homesite like this in metropolitan Florida? In California? Near a major city anywhere in the western world? What would you pay for such a homesite on the metropolitan fringe of Washington D.C. or New York City? You may not want to live there. Maybe you won't want to live here, either. The point is you got here before the next guy, who will pay you good money for what you own.

How Big a Value?

I explained how buyers could get more potential value out of a Smithfield homesite in one year than they could with an ordinary house lot in five. And the cost would be about half that of the plain lot. In 1981, *Land Review* newsletter reported the average cost of a building lot in the U.S. was $14,593. Most in-town lots are about 1/4 acre–half the size of the smallest that I was offering for sale in Smithfield. Some are 3/4 acre. A few are five acres. And industry predictions were for smaller houses on smaller lots to keep costs down.

In Moonefield Estates, where these sites are located, the homes were priced from $75,000 to $150,000. Most sites had houses on them. The community was 10 years old at the time and had been annexed to Smithfield. The average retail price for half-acre homesites was $12,680.

The five-acre farmettes, which fronted on Morris Creek, were average priced at $20,000.

Most had been sold. During this liquidation sale, buyers could literally steal the remainder of the Moonefield sites at up to 40% below these prices. That left a lot of room for future profits.

But there were only 30 sites left at the start of this sale. That's why I advised readers to act fast.

Times were tight. And people were financially stressed to the point where many could not trust their own minds. And when questions dealing with money were left on the doorstep you could be sure that doubt would slip in through the window. So I walked the reader through the financing phase step by step:

1. *How much down and a month*? Depends on the deal. But here's a sample. You steal a $12,500 homesite for $7950. Write a check for $300 to bind the deal. Bring $500 more to closing. You then get a clear deed. The bank collects $122.13 per month until you resell or rebuild. The term is 120 months at 16.53% annual percentage rate, and remember that consumer interest charges are tax deductible. *(Later tax reforms eliminated this deduction on raw land.)*

2. *Can I buy with no money down?* Yes, if you've got at least $800 equity in your home, we can arrange a second trust.

3. *Must I pay off the bank before I resell?* No. In most cases your buyer can assume your loan.

4. *Must I wait for credit approval to tie up the property?* No. Most applications can be approved on the spot.

5. *Can I split mortgages if I tie up more than one homesite?* Yes. You can buy and sell separately.

6. *May I get my own loan?* Yes. You may be able to get a lower rate.

7. *Is there a discount for cash?* Yes. The amount depends on the deal. Ask us about it.

8. *Can I buy more than one homesite if someone defaults?* Yes. The bank does not want to hold property. Often they will let you assume the note.

Hamming It Up

The Smithfield Packing Company had emerged from the smoke of a country kitchen to become world famous for its hams. Queen Victoria and other heads of state had ordered these culinary delights for very fussy guests. To waft the fumes of the offer in the minds of customers and to build a crowd, I ordered a hundred hams as gifts to visitors for just showing up.

FREE SMITHFIELD HAM TO FIRST WHO CALL – NO STRINGS

The customer was advised to call ahead so we could better gauge the crowd. There was absolutely no obligation to buy. We only had a hundred hams. No lines to wait in. No strings. Just call early, the readers were told, to have a free ham set aside in their names. The offer was quickly sold out to a fortunate few who later feasted on their profits.

The Death of the Countryside

As the restless mass of humanity along the East Coast continued to break down suburban gates and trample over the countryside seeking to establish themselves on outlying land, a deepening fear stuck like a knife in the hearts of socioenvironmental elitists and socialist-oriented planning officials who whined and wailed about the spreading tumor in their gut that has been diagnosed by antigrowth witch doctors as "urban sprawl." There are tyrants in every community in the country who allegedly speak for "the people" but who, in fact, would deny them the opportunity to own land.

In their unrelenting moaning about the perceived ailment of urban sprawl, no-growth advocates formed self-serving support groups and sopped up the largesse of wealthy landed-gentry benefactors to lobby against the right of average Americans to own land. They squawked like wounded parrots to the media and to elected officials, this while repeating the ridiculous rubric of hard-sell land hustlers that "There ain't gonna be any more land."

To "save the land," these faceless patriots continued to feast themselves on a banquet of regulations mandating larger and larger land parcels for the super rich, reaching obscene dietary portions in later years of one home per fifty acres in one county outside of Washington D.C.

An article in the *Washington Post* in March of 2003 stated that "No other U.S. region of comparable size has protected so much land this way, according to a survey of urban planners."

Branding this type of exclusionary zoning as "smart growth," the proponents of these misdeeds literally rode roughshod over property rights, reducing land values, and essentially seizing private property in violation of constitutional safeguards. The end result of such misguided planning was a dramatic surge in housing costs due to the arbitrary rationing of building sites. Opponents of exclusionary zoning practices (an inclination often characterized as "snob zoning") took the position that governmental bodies pushing measures to preserve "open space" should find ways to buy the land or safeguard it by encouraging, through tax credits, grants of conservation easements from overtaxed and idealistic landowners.

Another favorite device of elitist-leaning local officials and landowners to discourage riff-raff interlopers from settling on their turf was the use of transfer development rights (TDRs), an antigrowth noose that slowly strangled land ownership opportunities through the arbitrary rationing of subdivided parcels based on hypothetical fair market values. In theory, these rights assigned to land parcels in low-density areas could be transferred at artificial financial figures for rights to develop property where local politicos may condescend to sprinkle a potion of growth. Reduced to its essence, these TDRs are, in many cases, "takedown rights" because they reduce the landowners' rights to subdivide their land based on rigged, politically motivated master plans.

Under the recipe for these plans, a smattering of "smart growth" is simmered in a stew pot and out comes a magic potion of fairly distributed division rights assigned to each land parcel, rights that are, in many cases, flavored to keep low-density areas (farms and estates) in limbo, while offering an impotent jolt of development to areas of greater density. In reality, the theoretical sale of development rights from low-density areas to growth regions within a particular county is an exercise in unreality, because such transactions seldom occur, this partially because of the arbitrary manipulation of land values by the county or a fiduciary entity. Essentially, any antigrowth county cooking up a batch of TDR's as a palliative planning cure for its xenophobic ailments is still drugged up with its no-growth identity.

The Fall of Urban Sprawl

In the mid-Atlantic region, and in other population centers of the U.S., opponents of so-called "urban sprawl" found great joy in declaring immense swaths of the countryside "off limits" to developers through the enactment of increasingly severe zoning and subdivision measures.

A case in point is the Washington D.C. Metropolitan Area. Instead of controlling population density in nearby exurban counties, some self-proclaimed social engineers have fostered a malignant growth pattern that spread exponentially like a cancer far outside the city, this as developers hopped over the privileged estates of the wealthy in their search for less expensive land in counties with fewer growth controls.

The devastating results were self-evident. Fields, forests, and farmland were gobbled up at alarming speed by castle-building contractors catering, in many cases, to the nouveau rich, wannabe royalists, and a smattering of idealistic tree-hugging vassals, some of whom feasted on fine wine and cheese, yet who complained vociferously about the restless and impertinent serfs in the villages and cities who wanted to shanty-up the precious fiefdoms of their lords. The radicals in this vassal group were the mildest mannered that ever cut the throat of a patriot, or who would let a terrorist off the hook for blowing up a building. With such classy virtues to their credit, you certainly could never have known their true thoughts.

Some county fathers, viewing the world through the murky prism of taxes, often considered the construction of affordable homes in their countryside as an unwelcome burden, preferring instead the plutocratic establishment of a landed-gentry class that required no additional schools or municipal services. Exclusive private schools were, of course, most welcome, and the rich could go there. In those metropolitan areas where the politics of urban sprawl had taken hold, the middle economic classes, unable to find affordable homes and homesites in the de facto fiefdoms of the rich, simply moved farther out and endured longer commutes. A few lucky ones found homes they could afford and settled down in a foggy vassal status, forever dependent for privacy on the preservation of the rich man's fields and forests by self-perpetuating ruling oligarchies. Often these political oddities were the result of unholy alliances between smug conservatives and hypocritical liberals whose never-ending chatter about "smart growth" was intellectually shallow and more akin to a parrot constantly squawking "keep out."

The lower economic classes, including many professionals, are relegated to a form of serfdom by exclusionary and antiquated no-growth laws. Turn-of-the-century figures published in *Realtor* magazine revealed that a teacher's salary could not buy an average-priced home in 60% of our country's housing markets. It was estimated that 14 million Americans were spending more than half of their paycheck on housing. In rural areas, these poor souls mulled about the countryside in a perpetual daze searching for almost-extinct rental homes, with most of these habitat seekers eventually settling into small-town apartments and run-down dwellings in village ghettos.

Outsiders and tourists venturing out for a Sunday drive along the bucolic country roads in these no-growth counties frequently imagined themselves living the good life behind the fancy stone and rail fencing, this until the price tag turned their hopes into sickening pangs. The strange paradox of it all is that the general public yearns for freedom from congestion, yet, through naivete, lack of knowledge, and media brainwashing by the backward-leaning preservation lobby, they appear to support many antigrowth measures that deny them the very freedoms associated with land ownership that they so desperately and futilely seek in their search for country properties.

As a conscience pacifier to whining and often hypocritical figures who live in their own bastions of luxury, the government threw in the sop of a low-income tax credit to confine the underclass to urban ghettos and communal housing on the other side of the railroad tracks in small-town America. This provision gave investors a dollar-for-dollar reduction in taxes in return for investing in low-income dwelling units, most of which were hastily constructed tenement-like apartments that sprouted up like weeds and perpetuated the pervasive "have" and "have not" reality that is choking the nation. Attempts by tax reformers to eliminate the taxation of stock dividends was considered by many liberals to be a threat to this compassionate caging of the lower economic classes. Investors, they feared, would simply move from tax-exempt government bonds to dividend-paying stocks and undermine the whole socialistic scheme.

More freedom for the masses through tax credits for home ownership and the curtailment of exclusionary zoning laws to halt the widening division of social classes seemed to be alternatives beyond the vision of politicians who preferred to buy votes through class warfare and immortalize their careers as preservers of the underprivileged. In rural enclaves around the cities, the farmers of old had traded their agricultural base for horsey manicured estates and hobby farms, plowing into ridicule, it would seem, any argument that productive farmland was being preserved through new subdivision and zoning controls. Whenever a modicum of development was allowed, it was often too little too late to alleviate the crisis of affordable housing for the lower and middle classes seeking to build a better life for themselves in the countryside. Simple supply and demand factors tended to dictate higher and higher prices on any new homes built in no-growth counties. Thus the "urban sprawl" syndrome was projected sixty to a hundred miles beyond many cities, this when more reasonable and sensible land-use measures, if they had been enacted, could have contained this ill-adapted trend.

The policy of strangling growth did nothing to solve the problem of affordable housing at the turn of the century. Beyond the suburbs of Washington D.C. and Baltimore, MD, residential developers were forced to scour the countrysides of Pennsylvania and Delaware looking for feasible projects, thus accelerating the difficulty of commuting, while driving up the price of rural land. Figures cited in a 2003

Washington Post article showed population growth in the D.C. metropolitan area rising 15% between 1990 to 2000, this while the number of miles traveled (to and from work) increased 27%. The article quoted figures revealing land consumption in the developed areas of suburban Washington D.C. growing at three times the population rate in Virginia, and twice as fast in nearby Maryland.

And in recreational and retirement hotspots across the country the problem of affordable housing seemed stuck on the horizon like an impenetrable mountain range, with home and land prices reaching ethereal heights. One letter writer to an Oregon newspaper described the local situation as "overpriced, overrun, and overrated," terminology that could well apply to the highly touted redoubts of the leisure class and culture-conscious retirees with fat wallets. An article in the *Wall Street Journal* reported thrilling 65% returns to many investors surfing this wave of rising prices over the period 1998-2003. Needless to say, local workers were priced out of the market and many remain, to this day, refugees in their own surroundings.

It is an irrefutable fact that the United States has more that enough territory outside of government control for the majority of its citizens to qualify for land and home ownership.

Yet affordable real estate is becoming more and more difficult to find. The *Wall Street Journal* reported in an April, 2003 article that affordable property around Las Vegas–a barren, but a habitable wasteland beyond the city–is "as scarce as a royal flush." Developers are rolling the dice on multimillion dollar patches of scorched earth on which to shoehorn working people into desert abodes as small as 1,000 square feet, this in one of the nation's fastest-growing cities.

The shutout of affordable homes and land to the average family is particularly acute in the Northeast and in Southern California. To live in the countryside in many parts of the nation you must either be rich or have tails or talons. Rats and owls have been afforded more freedom of habitation than many humans. A 2003 Associated Press article highlighted the issue in the American west where discrimination against private land ownership had reached obscene proportions. In Oregon, for example, zoning officials launched a preemptive attack on landseeking refugees from the cities by mandating 80-acre lot sizes in the Cascade foothills. And it was reported that, on the prairies of a sparsely populated Wyoming county, urban sprawl was contained by requiring you to settle on one square mile of land, this to provide a comfort zone for four-legged critters with horns. The menagerie of antigrowth interests who fiddle with, and fume about, the fundamental economics of broad-based real estate ownership run the risk of burning down huge segments of the free enterprise system and choking average Americans who are forced to pay through the nose for homes and land. And history has shown that what goes up must eventually come down.

A house-of-cards real estate market–built under the aegis of misguided politicians, idealistic planners, environmental pressure groups, and landed elitists–can come crashing down in a recession and wipe out multitudes of investors and wobbly homeowners. The *Wall Street Journal* article quoted a respected California economics professor who attributed 15% of a 2002 home price rise in that state to land-use restraints, this pulling the shades on many young families hoping to have a glimpse of the American dream.

The U.S. Government practically owns the entire state of Nevada, likewise Alaska. Federal land holdings are enormous, and this excess continues to grow as more and more territory is removed from the market for public parks, forests, monuments, and wilderness areas, the latter of which are often treated as sacred ground for fauna and are practically off-limits to humans.

Environmental protection aside, the wisdom of government bodies unjustly removing land from the market that is needed for human habitation and settlement is open to legitimate questioning by the citizenry. Some may view the idea of land ownership by the masses as insupportable and that land must be doled out by the government based on some grand socialistic scheme. Land-hungry consumers and the real estate industry, of course, view the world in a different light.

This nation was founded on principles of free enterprise, where incentives for achievement were readily available and followed, presumably, by adequate reward. Land was available for settlement, often without financial cost. Reward blossomed through the fruits of labor.

Excessive government intervention in people's lives and oppressive rule in the form of dictatorships tend to stifle initiative and act as deterrents to the exercise of free enterprise. People's lives, in those countries where these forms of government exist, are, in effect, monitored and controlled almost day to day by higher secular authority, and many people have little control over their destinies. When this higher secular power becomes overbearing or ruthless to the point where (1) class divisions are clearly evident between the "haves" and "have nots," (2) where the middle-class, if any, has been beaten back or blurred to the point of extinction, and (3) when the upper-class persona appears hedonistic and self-serving, the authority is eventually overthrown by the electorate, war, or revolution; and political structures beyond simple party change could occur, resulting in the emergence of such ruling forms as anarchy, communism, dictatorship, and liberal socialism, the latter of which, in my view, poses the greatest domestic threat to the United States beyond terror. All are committed enemies of democracy and free enterprise.

The unspoken agenda of liberal socialists is to: (1) keep 'em fed, (2) keep 'em clothed, (3) keep 'em sheltered, (4) keep 'em medicated, (5) keep 'em poor, and (6) keep 'em indebted.

In changing socioeconomic times, it is important to observe the role of those who overtly affiliate themselves with either (1) those in power, or (2) those opposed to those in power.

Clearly, abusive issues are rampant–economic, racial, environmental, terror, etc. We live in an imperfect world, and neither those in or out of power are blessed with all the answers; nor is either group "anointed" as saviors of the nation. You know them by their actions.

The Case for Clusters

An elderly land planner pulled me aside when I first started in this business and offered me some advice. He said that the future of the countryside could be summed up in one word. Curious as to how a plain-wrapper planning official had distilled this conundrum to its essence, and always thirsty for a taste of wisdom, I encouraged him to bend my ear. "B.K.," he said in the whispery and worldly manner of a father addressing his son, "the word, my boy, is 'clusters.'" My experience up until this secret word was divulged to me–and continuing to this day–was that people looking for country property did not want to be clustered and caged. They wanted to be free from containment so they could pursue their own things on their own places away from the city.

This said, as a solution to the problem of affordable housing in reasonable-growth counties within, say, fifty or sixty miles of a major city, the idea of clusters does hold some merit, though the concept holds no discernible allure for country property seekers. No-growth county planners and officials in some outlying regions–had they been blessed with a degree of foresight, compassion, and realistic planning, and weaned of exclusionary political concerns–could have contained this widening circle of growth, saved thousands upon thousands of acres in open space, and reduced the cost of rural housing by allowing a mixture of smaller lot sizes and clustered residential developments within their jurisdictions, this without forcing developers to leapfrog over obscenely large and expensive estates and hobby farms.

These enclaves for the rich remain the legacy of misguided planners and county officials pushing either (1) a quick fix to perceived growth problems or (2) a political fix for deep-pocketed land owners and their fellow travelers. This "dumb-growth" concept of large-lot zoning has become shopworn beyond any point of credibility and has effectively been hijacked by entrenched elitists as a device to preserve the status quo, this while they busily erect roadblocks to legitimate developers of clustered communities.

Planners like to characterize clustered housing communities and PUD's (Planned Unit Developments) as "smart growth" concepts. Carried to their extreme, these idealistic projects in exurban areas can emerge from their incubation periods as satellite towns and villages, offering a harmless placebo to restless city and suburban dwellers seeking renewed fresh air and open space in the countryside. It is true that a multitude of farms, and thousands of acres, may be saved by cramming thousands of people into the perimeters of a single farm, while still maintaining a measure of fields and forests for the communal inhabitants to watch birds and romp around.

Equally true is the fact that a combined utility and road infrastructure can lead to: (1) less costly housing, (2) future new schools and shopping convenience, and (3) potential access to medical and professional services. This said in support of a "smart growth" concept, the process of people settling down in such a milieu can be likened to your entering a revolving door, wherein you leave one crowded environment and exit into a large human cage or environmental bubble, albeit with more greenery, possibly a murky lake, and a yellow brick road for jogging.

When your sentence in this man-made "Pleasantville" is over, you'll no doubt still yearn for your own place in the country. But don't believe for a moment that your servitude in a PUD is penance for protecting the countryside. Outside the gates you'll still hear the barking and carping of the self-appointed "country police" who complain about clusters cluttering up the countryside.

For the investor in country properties, the enactment of severe and arbitrary antigrowth measures can mean financial loss and the devaluation of your property. Just as ruthless and pecuniary stock manipulators and corrupt CEOs have savaged the portfolios of many investors at the turn of the century, those lobbyists and politicos who play with the value of rural real estate through the use of over-the-hill antigrowth schemes are a clear and present danger to small farmers and their families, land investors, and seekers of country property. In one Virginia county outside of Washington D.C., more than 200 lawsuits were filed in February 2003 by disgruntled landowners, builders, and developers in protest over the county's antigrowth land-use policies. And the fight for the protection and preservation of private property rights has just begun.

Country Properties Versus Stocks

In recent years, the price of homes and land in exurban regions has skyrocketed, this largely because an army of baby-boomers are out cooking up their retirement pies. Toss into the filling a retreat from stocks and an element of fear about terrorism in the cities; then frost the pie with growth controls, and you have hungry buyers standing in line, sellers licking their chops, and a feast for wise investors in country properties. Owners of multiple properties have found their net worth running wild and their return on investment leaving puny stock market yields in the dust.

The situation mirrors a joyous chorus of happy homeowners cashing in the bountiful equity on their primary dwellings. Of course, homeowners could be singing the blues when the next real estate bubble bursts and they find their equity watered down by devaluation.

Figures from Fannie Mae show that homeowners who made a $10,000 down payment on an $80,000 home at the end of 1989 would have grossed a $53,427 payoff on the money invested if they sold their property in 2002– an approximate 15% return over a twelve-year hold on the property. The Nasdaq index fund yields on ten grand planted in the market over the same time frame produced a stunted $19,000 or 5.5% growth, and the S&P 500 index fund returned a paltry $15,000 and change on the same investment, for a 3.5% yield. The Fannie Mae study makes the following caveat: *Housing gain is tax free; stock fund gains are pretax. Housing gain does not include mortgage costs, agent fees and other costs involved in selling the property, which can reduce the gain by up to 10 percent. Comparison assumed that the two investors in stock funds would pay about the same in rent as the housing investor did in monthly mortgage payments.*

In 2003, the National Association of Realtors reported that, over the previous three years, investors in second homes along the Atlantic coast had almost doubled their money. Ground rules for tax breaks require that such homes be rented out for an aggregate of six months or more every year, this while the owner enjoys occasional use. The changing investment landscape at the turn of the century showed that owners of second homes in resort locations were less prone to rent out their properties for tax benefits because the phenomenal increase in the value of vacation homes far exceeded any returns from their stock investments.

Of almost equal concern is the promise of security and a laid-back lifestyle that a second home offers to baby-boomers approaching retirement. The NAR expects the tsunami of pending retirees to sweep out, in each foreseeable year, much of their stock portfolios for the relative safety of 150,000 new vacation homes.

Tax considerations aside, my files show even greater gross returns to investors in select country property investments than the yields enjoyed by sellers of primary homes over the same period. Keep in mind, however, that (1) economic woes can deflate values, (2) interest on raw land is not currently deductible, (3) dealers and developers are generally given the same tax treatment as business owners and corporations, and (4) interest write-offs and other tax deductions allowed to owners of second homes, and applicable to the rental of these homes, can vary depending on use factors. Itemized deductions are permitted. Net proceeds from sales of second homes are now taxed at the lower 15% rate, though this figure could change in coming years.

Obvious advantages to investors purchasing second homes for later retirement are the federal capital gains exclusions for resale profits of primary residences, not generally available for owners selling second homes. But moving from your first home to your second home as your primary residence for at least 24 months can result in up to $500,000 in tax-free capital gains for a married couple and up to $250,000 for a single seller. The same tax-free benefits apply when you sell your first home, if you occupied the home for at least 24 out of 60 months. This process of moving between homes every 24 months and enjoying capital gains treatment can be repeated over and over if you comply with the rules. Check with your tax advisor.

Heathsville, VA
KNOXVILLE, TENN. HOST TO WORLD'S FAIR – May, 1982 – Vangelis

The energy crisis was still with us as the southeast U.S. hosted the first World's Fair ever in that region. President and Mrs. Reagan attended an opening ceremony, along with thousands of tourists. Nearly two million advance tickets were sold as the world went *down country* U.S.A. Real estate prices in the Knoxville countryside took off like a rocket.

In rural Virginia, one of my customers bought a fix-up home on five acres at the Chesapeake Bay for $12,950 with $1,000 down. Assuming he made $14,000 in improvements the first year, and given a 20-25% yearly increase in rural home values in the Bay area, the property would have been worth about $145,000 twelve years later in 2002. Using the same analysis of return on investment cited in the previous Fannie Mae example, the $15,000 investment would have yielded this investor, if he had sold, a gross return of about 21 percent.

Fix-up Buffs! Run-down Home on 5 Acres at the Chesapeake Bay $12,950

Heathsville, VA - Affordable project for weekend restoration handyman. Bleak frame farmhouse at navigable creek just off Bay. Wind-weathered siding. 3 chimneys. Used as a duck hunter's, waterman's shelter. Walk to protected anchorage. Oysters and crabs for the taking. Lots of antique sea-goers memorabilia for your rec. room. Rich farmland grazed by deer. Storage shed, smokehouse. Drafty 9 room relic may be a century old. Bring min. $500; $500 at closing; then $198.81 mo. 120 mos. at 16.5% apr, or best cash offer. **B.K. Haynes Real Estate.** If we've got it listed, it must be a bargain.

The Evaluation of "Fixer-Upper" Country Homes

"THIS OLD HOUSE"

How old am I? What is my exterior made of? What kind of a foundation do I have? What are my walls, floors, ceiling, roof made of? Do I have any additions? Alterations? How are my windows? Stairs? Porches? Have you looked at my attic? My cellar? Ask about my plumbing, my electricity, my water source. Look at my fixtures. How am I heated? What keeps me cool? I may look bad now. But I'm twice the young child I used to be. *Just a good old home looking for a new person to patch me up.*

Many country dwellings have aged beyond the point where extensive evaluation is practical and therefore are sold "as is." Old-time construction techniques and electrical systems do not, in most cases, meet contemporary standards and requirements. Be sure to consult with a licensed electrician before using a gasoline-powered generator as an auxiliary power source for a home with an antiquated electrical system. Buyers of old homes who are unfamiliar with the construction process are advised to: (1) retain the services of a home inspector to pinpoint any problems and deficiencies, and (2) to hire a professional remodeler or contractor to correct any problems to bring the home in conformity with livable standards. In addition, you will want (1) a termite inspection, (2) a thorough check on the quality of the water source, and (3) an investigation into the condition of the septic system, all often handled by a single specialist.

The home inspector will focus on the following major areas of concern: (1) structure, (2) exterior, (3) roof and related aspects, (3) plumbing, (4) electrical, (5) heat and air conditioning, (6) interior, (7) miscellaneous.

Structure

Examples of problem areas could be: (1) excessive beam span to carry structural members, (2) columns loose or not plumb, (3) weakened footings in crawl space and under porch, (4) makeshift supports under the house, (5) interior cracks, (6) door jams not square, (7) uneven and unlevel floors, (8) rot in crawl space, (9) untreated wood, too close to earth.

Exterior

Limitations could include: (1) lack of guard rails on porch, (2) weakened hand rails, (3) deteriorating brick or masonry, (3) doors not locking. (4) siding rotting and too close to earth, (5) space difference in step risers, (6) insufficient caulking, (7) poor drainage, (8) leaking underground oil storage tanks, either in use or abandoned.

Roof and Related Aspects

Areas of concern could be: (1) inadequate and leaking flashing, (2) loose gutters, (3) missing shingles, (4) stained sheathing (inner covering) on roof, (5) downspouts too close to house, (6) insufficient slope on porch to carry water, (7) rotting on porch.

Plumbing

Indications of potential trouble include: (1) cross connections of hot and cold water faucets, (2) improper drainage from tub and shower, (3) gray water drainage into soil; soggy earth, indicating a failing septic system, (4) inadequate support under floor for tub/shower, (5) lack of proper insulation for exposed pipes, (6) visible stains on subfloor, (7) trapped water in tub or whirlpool.

Electrical

A home inspector could find deficiencies such as: (1) restricted access to disconnect box, (2) exposed wiring, (3) non-functioning GFI's (ground fault indicators that turn off the voltage when someone with a ground gets shocked by touching a faulty appliance), (4) insufficient GRI's for appliances, (5) missing light fixtures and receptacle cover plates, (6) broken switches, (7) dead receptacles.

Heat and Air Conditioning

Troublesome factors could include: (1) inadequate heating capacity for some rooms, (2) lack of heat in certain rooms, (3) insufficient chimney extension above roof line, (4) no return-air duct, (5) fireplace chimney needs cleaning, (6) furnace filter missing, (7) air conditioning source not provided for some habitable rooms.

Interior

An inspection could uncover the following problems: (1) cracks in ceilings, walls (2) drywall, trim incomplete, (3) rooms without doors, locks, (4) weak hand rails, creaky floors, (5) trip hazards on stair risers, (6) stains on ceilings, (7) inoperable windows, (7) damaged cabinetry, loose tiles.

Miscellaneous

Limitations during an examination might reveal: (1) dirty and inoperative appliances, (2) poor quality cabinetry, (3) missing or exposed insulation, (4) lack of proper vents, (5) excess condensation/humidity concerns, (6) fire hazards, (7) cracked/split vinyl cover.

The Lowdown on Country Fixer-Uppers

How to Buy Them at the Right Price

Let's say you want to be a player in the real estate game, and you've decided to buy old homes, fix them up and sell them for a profit. You've been ogling an old log and frame dwelling that has seen more than two centuries go by, the historic structure piquing your interest through a folksy legend of George Washington having spent a night on the premises. The asking price is $300,000.

Your first order of business is to determine the cost of repairs, followed by an analysis of your costs of holding onto the treasured possession. The major carrying costs are: (1) closing expenses when you buy and sell, including a real estate commission, (2) property taxes, (3) interest on your mortgage, and (4) insurance on the property. Of course, there will be utility bills, but we will not include minor charges in this analysis.

Next, you must have some idea of the amount of profit you are shooting for. Let's assume you are not greedy and would only like to double, maybe triple, your money in a year. You will be puttering around the place, ennobling it with "sweat equity," and your contractor tells you he will need fifty grand to make it new again. You run some numbers in your head and figure you could put it back on the market in less than a year at **$450,000**, *if you paid the asking price*.

To begin with, you deduct the estimated **$50,000** cost of repairs from your projected sales price, throwing in your "sweat equity" for the love of the game. The revised valuation figure in determining an offering price for this restoration project is subsequently decreased from $450,000 to **$400,000**. But this figure does not reflect the expenses of holding the property during the remodeling period. After totaling up closing costs, anticipated taxes, and insurance for the year, you come up with a round number of **$15,000**. You're now at **$385,000**, *if there are no cost overruns beyond the contractor's estimate.*

You know you can get a 95% variable interest rate loan at 5.95% APR to swing the deal.

Your investment equity (down payment) would be **$15,000** at the asking price; plus you would be paying out about **$17,000** in interest over the year ($285,000 X 5.95%). That raises your cash outlay to **$32,000.** You could have $32,000 invested in the place, plus $65,000 or more in remodeling and holding costs ($50,000 + $15,000)–totaling a 21% stake at your proposed selling price. You have already deducted the remodeling and holding costs, so you are down to a valuation of **$353,000** ($385,000 minus $32,000). You worry about these financial termites eating into the deal.

If any more costs creep into the analysis, your proposed selling price may not hold up.

If your target selling price of $450,000 is about to crumble, at what figure will you sell this relic of the past that you would soon make new again? Before bolstering your potentially bearish price in the bullish real estate market, or scrapping the deal, you return to your revised starting point for determining property value of $353,000 and suddenly remember you will need to make a further deduction for a real estate commission when you sell.

Let's say you choose to stick with your original plan–to list these reconstructed ruins at an agency for $450,000, with a 6% Realtor's fee, and then your moulded piece of antiquity finds its destiny on the National Register of Historic Places. Without considering the benefit of possible tax breaks for restoration, you may still be out a real estate commission of **$27,000**, this assuming you get full price. You then reach a price evaluation depth of **$326,000** ($353,000 minus $27,000). *Remember, you are trying to arrive at a price you can offer for the property–not what you will sell it for.* Some investment theorists will take the position that an analysis of your offering price should exclude your down payment, but, having a "no money down" mentality, I always factor in any cash outlay as a cost of doing business. Total expenses amount to about **$124,000**. ($50,000+$15,000 +$15,000+$17,000 +$27,000).

Your head is drowning with numbers, but you somehow recall that you're in the game to make a decent profit. You want to–at a minimum–double your money in a year. Your jumping-off point for making an offer on the property is to find a *break-even price*. You surmise this figure must be the projected sales price of the property, less the aforementioned expenses ($450,000 - $124,000). **The break-even price, you figure, is therefore $326,000.**

If you paid the full price of $300,000, you would need to deduct your calculated expenses of $124,000 before adding a profit figure. Subtracting the $300,000 from your proposed selling price of $450,000 leaves you with a pie-in-the-sky $150,000 gross profit. Now deduct your expenses of $124,000. That leaves a crummy profit of $26,000. And that could be eaten up by some greedy speculator with a low-ball offer on your year's worth of hard work. Your expectation of big money has dwindled to a presumption that you could lose your shirt. There's no way you can offer full price for that eyesore, aka "treasured possession," property.

You return to the break-even price and check your numbers. You'll have $124,000 in a project that you expect to gross out at $450,000. You need to at least double your money.

So you proceed with your elementary math, deducting your expected gross profits ($150,000) from the projected sales price after restoration ($450,000). That's funny. After deducting the expenses of $124,000, you're back at the lean net profit of $26,000–a bone of contention that is red meat for some grizzly low-baller. You'll have to (1) scratch the deal, (2) raise your selling price, (3) cut expenses, (4) steal the deal with a laughable offer, or (5) combine these tactics.

You figure you're on a roll–flipping properties, patching up rundown shacks in villages and naming your price, so you perform a quick down-and-dirty analysis, aiming at three times your money actually invested in the property; this before you incur any expenses ($15,000 down payment X 3 = $45,000). You deduct this figure from your break-even price to see how the result may influence your offering price ($326,000 - $45,000 = $281,000). The deal then takes on a more appetizing look. Obviously you cannot pay full price.

You could upset the seller with a low-end slice of $275,000; however, if you were to pay more than, say, $285,000 for the property, you would have to cut costs or sell at a higher price to reach your profit objectives. Of course, profits could be dramatically increased through cost reductions, a fast turnover, and the co-brokering, or elimination of, a real estate commission, this through a sale of the property by an owner/agent or owner/developer.

MARKET VALUE before remodeling $300,000
MARKET VALUE after remodeling $450,000
Less cost for repairs and remodeling $50,000
Preliminary valuation $400,000
Less carrying costs and down payment $47,000
Revised property evaluation price $353,000
Less real estate commission $27,000
Break-even price $326,000
Less profit expectations $45,000
Reasonable offering price **$281,000**

The projected selling price of $450,000 yields a proposed profit of $45,000, if the property can be purchased at $281,000. This profit figure is based on a ratio of three times money actually invested before expenses. An analysis of this transaction, without adding in the down payment, would have resulted in a break-even price of $341,000 ($326,000 + $15,000) and a quadrupling of profit expectations, this assuming the property was purchased for $281,000. When flipping properties, and on fast turnarounds, where the cost of money may be of little consequence, your analysis could exclude the down payment as a factor when programing profit expectations into your proposed offering price. No two purchases of country properties are the same, and there can be wide fluctuations in projected profits due to the dynamics of the deal.

To validate your proposed offering price, you may wish to buy subject to having the property appraised (usually a buyer's expense). A review of the county's tax assessment value on the home and land would also be helpful, though these numbers may not reflect *fair market value.*

For example, there may be more demand for fixer-upper country homes than there are homes available on the market. This means you may have to pay the asking price if you desperately want the property. The county's tax assessment may be outdated. If the property has been on the market for a considerable length of time, this may or may not give you a bargaining edge.

Some sellers will hold out for the asking price until values reach their level of profit expectations; however, *length of time on the market* is definitely a reason to offer a lower price, this providing there is no serious defect in the property that cannot be corrected or ameliorated.

For example, a home in the path of a proposed major interstate highway may cause buyers to steer clear of the deal because of the uncertainty of the home's very existence. On the other hand, the home may hold extremely high potential value in future negotiations for its sale to the state. A home may have been on the market for a long time because the surrounding soil has been contaminated by illegal dumping of waste from a local manufacturing plant. This factor may permanently plague the home as a potential investment.

With All Due Respect

I dislike dealing with customers who come armed with complaints about the deficiencies in what I have to sell, because I feel I have priced the property fairly for the buyer to make a sound and profitable investment. Of course, as a licensed real estate broker, I would normally be aware of any deficiencies and would ethically be required to readily disclose them to potential buyers.

Obviously, when I am buying property I do not anticipate that the seller will make these same disclosures, this unless he or she is represented by a Realtor, licensed agent, or a reputable broker or attorney. An exception to the disclosure practice is generally allowed when property is sold "as is," particularly at auction sales. Licensed agents, selling listed property "as is," are bound by a code of ethics to reveal all known deficiencies when asked about them by potential buyers.

When purchasing fixer-upper country homes I prefer to buy "as is," rather than to pay a higher price and have the seller make improvements. I feel I have better control over the outcome and can earn more profits at the front end through price negotiations. I make it a practice not to downgrade a seller's property as part of the negotiation process, this because sellers of country property are often proud of their homes and land and take offense at aggressive purchasing tactics. I feel they already know about their property's deficiences, even though they may not readily disclose this information. Usually you can get to the facts about a place through the process of politely asking questions without giving offense. Your offer does not have to be primarily based on what both buyer and seller know from honest discussion. And any needed safeguards can usually be inserted in the purchase contract, this if consumer protections are required beyond the standard provisions in the contract. *Remember–to be legally binding and enforceable, all real estate contracts must be in writing.*

When dealing directly with sellers, you can often work out better deals on your own than when a real estate agent is representing the seller. Some sellers are interested in quick cash-outs and will drop the price for a solid cash offer, this if few strings are attached; other sellers will be concerned about getting a better-than-bank-rate return on their money and will offer owner financing if you pay full price. You can run the numbers based on your financial situation and time frame for home improvements to see which alternative could produce more profits.

A seller's real estate agent may negatively influence the amount of any cash discount that you can negotiate on your own, and the agent's involvement and need for a commission could interfere with a little-or no-money-down, owner-financed deal.

Country property auctions and foreclosure sales advertised in county newspapers are excellent sources for potential deals. Tax sales are usually less productive, due to the leniency of many state governments in allowing delinquent taxpayers generous time frames for reclaiming their property through restitution of past due taxes.

Dealing with Handymen and Contractors

Your first order of business should be to determine if your specialist has a license (if required) and experience for the job(s) you need accomplished. Older homes may have structural damage requiring the services of a professional engineer, and potentially hazardous improvement work may have been performed by unlicensed amateurs such as jerry-rigged electrical service upgrades, makeshift repairs, and unstable home additions. The county building inspector's office can give you license requirements. To determine structural integrity and foundation stability, you can first consult with an experienced builder, and in some cases you may want the foundation analyzed by a landscape architect.

When hiring general contractors, builders, or remodelers, be sure to ask for references and check them out. You will also want assurance that their work is bonded and that they carry liability insurance. A call to the local Better Business Bureau can tell you whether any unresolved complaints are on file against the firm or individual performing the work. It is advisable to obtain several bids, if possible, to obtain the lowest price. But do not let price be your only guide, since you may end up with inferior workmanship and a delayed or unfinished job.

As a general rule, you will be presented with a contract with specifications as to (1) what work is to be performed, (2) what permits and materials are required, and who is to pay for them, (3) how payments for the work are to be made and in what increments, (4) when the work will begin, and when it will be completed. The type and quality of materials may also be specified in the contract. You will also need assurance that all subcontractors and suppliers have been paid so that there will be no "mechanics' liens" placed on your property after the work is over. A signed document to this effect–along with affidavits from subcontractors and tradespeople–can be given to you after the final payment and job completion.

On big construction projects, such as complete home restoration or home-building, it is advisable to have your attorney review the contract and to check for potential liability while the job is in progress, and when it is finished. A reputable handyman, remodeler or contractor will usually give you a written warranty on his work, generally a guarantee for at least a year.

Timing Your Investment

The best time to invest in country properties is at the end of a recession and after any real estate bubble has already burst. Timing, of course, is a key element in any investment strategy.

In 1982, the country was at the threshold of recovery from the economic ailment of "stagflation" and intolerable interest rates, but the door to opportunity was still closed for many developers.

Some had financial difficulties and desperately needed to move their land; others required professional assistance in creating workable projects. Since I had just written a book on the subject of developing and selling rural land, a number of them turned to me for advice.

I was at the Hyatt Hotel in Richmond when I received a call from a new developer who had read my book and wanted advice about a proposed development he had in mind. After a brief discussion I told him

I would dispatch an associate to look over his project and report back to me. After getting a grasp on the development, I flew down to a grass airstrip on Virginia's Northern Neck, a rural peninsula south of Washington D.C., and Baltimore, MD.

The project was also west of Richmond, VA, and north of the Tidewater Virginia cities of Norfolk, Newport News, and Hampton, all potential markets for the property. I quickly came up with a workable concept, negotiated a sizable sales and marketing commission for a fast in-and-out deal, and gave him the outline for a viable development. Working within county regulations, he retained a surveyor and road builder and soon delivered the project to me for promotion and sales.

As a general rule, lot prices, by the year 1982, within rural property developments lacking expensive infrastructure and amenities, were scaled down to yield net returns to the developer of at least twice his acquisition price, this assuming his "hold," or interest-bearing period on borrowed money was relatively short. Competitive pressures and other economic factors can also significantly influence the pricing structure.

This necessity for "quick sales" was–and still is–critical to the bottom line of many land developers, since the cost of money can quickly erode profits. With this factor in mind, I had been intrigued and somewhat consumed with the prospect of marrying direct marketing concepts with the land development process. Understand that I am not talking about high-pressure sales and marketing techniques, but the establishment of value through factual advertising and credible promotional concepts. Therefore, in venturing into any land development project, I was concerned about how to promote the product, rather than how to boost the profile of the development.

Returning to a variation of Aristotle's theory of forms, you might ask, *"What is the product I am trying to sell?"* An institutional-type ad may attempt to sell you on the merits of the development and the lifestyle it provides. A bland headline may ask the prospect to "Come to Paradise Acres," this followed by eloquent text touting the appeal of the virgin countryside and suggesting that you will indeed find heaven on earth if you come. There is, of course, no specific urgency in this approach; nor is there any particular originality in its conceptual form. Moving on to the second element of Aristole's theory: *"What makes it work?"* The institutional advertiser may hammer away at the planned infrastructure and mold the merits of the development into full-page color spreads and glossy magazine ads.

Again, this approach instills no sense of immediacy in the mind of the consumer. "Who *makes it work?"* is the next question. Obviously this factor depends of the level and magnitude of the product being created. At the very least, the sale of country properties requires a buyer and a seller; and in the case of a development, you would need the services of a surveyor, road builder, salespeople, an attorney, government officials, and possibly a land planner.

Finally, the marketer is confronted with the question of, *"Why was this product created?"* The institutional advertiser of a country property development may be inclined to extol the virtues of the project's ultimate benefit to the community and to mankind's search for the chalice containing the "Good Life" and fulfillment of the "American Dream," this while ribboning the product with endorsements, both real and fictional.

This marketing approach is beauty in its best estate to large corporations with overflowing coffers of stockholder's money to play with. To the small investor, however, time is money, and prolonged development activity could lead to the quiet haven of financial ruin. With these considerations in mind, we can proceed to a discussion of direct marketing concepts as they are applicable to the sales and promotion of country properties.

First let us relate a piece of property to a consumer product such as, say, a walkie-talkie. During the CB craze, Joe Sugarman, a direct marketing wizard, educator, and acquaintance of mine, combined the relatively new broadcast medium with the hand-held communication device and called the product a "Pocket CB" selling untold thousands of the units through television spots and hard-hitting magazine ads. "Or your money back" still remains the closing mantra of direct marketers in all media forms–print, radio, direct mail, or television.

Return, now, to my work for the successful new developer who wanted advice and for whom I marketed several profitable projects. Let's call the project Paradise Cove, although we are not concerned about promoting any development structure by name. A five-acre waterfront lot within the development would be the product we are selling, and the *lot* would become, say, in direct marketing terminology, a *family compound* at the Bay." An advertisement for the product might go something like this:

WATERFRONT COMPOUND
5 AC. JUST $9950. $500 DN.

Recession land bargain. On navigable creek off of Chesapeake Bay. Woodsy, camp-like setting with approx. 400 ft.on deep water for canoes and outboards. Explore 15 miles of tidal creek shoreline charted to the Bay and Atlantic Ocean. Just 3 miles to Potomac River at mouth of Bay. Harvest crabs, oysters by the bushel. Paradise for ducks, Blue Heron, other waterfowl. Quiet and secluded. At end of private road. Ideal for a family retreat, tax shelter, retirement home, fishing camp, survival site for self-sufficiency. Great place for kids to grow up and enjoy their summers. Tall woods overrun with deer and other wildlife. $500 due at closing. $148.54 mo., 120 mos @ 15.75% apr. Cut rate with more down.Make cash offer. Hurry! Early bird gets the worm. B.K. HAYNES REAL ESTATE *"Rural land bargains since 1966"*

Capon Bridge, W. VA
REAGAN GETS $98 BILLION TAX HIKE – Aug. 1982 –
Fleetwood Mac

In a broad-based political attempt to trim the deficit and restore economic health to the nation, Congress and President Reagan agreed to increase taxes–mainly in the business sector–and to cut federal outlays by $17.5 billion. But this token payment to fiscal responsibility would still not exempt the country from its recessionary ills.

Reporting on the real estate market, *Landowner* newsletter stated that the industry was in worse shape in 1982 than in the 1930's. And it was widely known that high interest rates had all but destroyed the construction business. In West Virginia's panhandle near Washington D.C. and Baltimore–one of the fastest-growing areas in the mid-Atlantic region–the situation had evolved into a buyer's market. The National Association of Realtors complained that the real estate industry had reached the bottom, this after the group's figures revealed a devaluation of 25% in home and homesite prices–a more severe drop than during the Great Depression of the 30's. But history has shown that most real estate fortunes are born in such troughs.

The main question in the minds of consumers was "How long will this downturn last?" Most economists at the time predicted an end to the recession by the last quarter of 1982 or early in 1983. As a harbinger of good times ahead for West Virginia in the 80's, the National Planners Association predicted a growth rate of 28%. This placed West Virginia in the top quarter of the fifty states in projected growth. Energy, it appeared, was the reason for the expected boom.

The Mountain State was awash in gas, oil, and coal. Other boosters to the state's economy were (1) the abundance of outdoor recreation, (2) cheap labor, and (3) a more relaxed quality of life for harried city dwellers and retirees.

In early August of 1982, I was packing up for a trip with my wife, son, and friends to the Outer Banks of North Carolina. Usually I take a number of books and research materials because I frequently do a prodigious amount of writing. On this occasion I had taken on the assignment of writing a promotional campaign for the sale of some mountain property in West Virginia–a campaign that was to be launched for a developer over the Labor Day weekend.

I remember this campaign quite vividly because the offer was essentially sold out in about three days. We were so swamped with customers that we were compelled to turn people away.

Hardscrabble real estate depression hits nearby
Wild and Wonderful West VA and hands you this
WEST VIRGINIA LAND AND VACATION HOME OPPORTUNITY!
At Capon Bridge–Base camp for whitewater expeditions
on the wild, scenic Cacapon River
2-5 Acre Homesteads from **$2950** to $14,950
2-5 acres with starter home
or mobile home $9950 to $14,950

To build urgency into the offer, I explained to the public that by the time most people "discover" a thriving West Virginia, the time for rapid price appreciation in real estate will have passed. And I quite candidly advised them that there was no guarantee that they would make any money from the opportunity. This said, I expressed my opinion that missed chances on real estate opportunities in the booming sunbelt and mountain states almost numbered the population in those states. Most people, it seems to me, end up being priced out of the vacation home market because they act too late. So they spend hard-earned money renting somebody else's place. Or they settle for a time share or tiny overpriced lot.

The summer of 1982 was an excellent time to buy land and vacation homes. We were in the bowels of a recession, and I, myself, could have made a pile of money by investing in waterfront property on the Outer Banks of North Carolina. But my plate was full in other territory closer to home. At Capon Bridge, investors could not have been priced out of the market if they had acted on the opportunity offered to them at the time.

Where else could they have added two city blocks (2 acres) of land to their estates for about a dollar a day? Where else could they have entered the rich man's second-home world on a working man's budget? Sure, they would gain through "sweat equity"–fixing up a shell home into something better. But it would take a modest-income consumer a long time to save up money to buy and qualify for a finished vacation home at three times the cost of an entry-level shell.

And a projected double-digit inflation rate was destined to drive up prices even more.

In 1982, this opportunity allowed the consumer to pay for a vacation home in a very short time by fixing it up himself. And consider the tax savings angle alone, where interest payments were deductible, along with faster depreciation on investment property permitted during the period to encourage positive economic activity. Travel expenses, too, could be deducted if the owner was renting out the dwelling under required tax rules. To the consumer considering relocation or retirement, the offer provided a potentially cheaper lifestyle in the country than what would have been available in most cities. And think of the money the average family could save by retreating to their own vacation home, rather than fighting the costs of crowded campgrounds and expensive resorts.

Why Capon Bridge?

From nearby Winchester, VA., this is the first town the traveler hits when crossing the state line into West Virginia. I pitched the offer as about as close to "Almost Heaven" as the consumer could get if he was looking for a dirt-cheap real estate bargain in the West Virginia hills. I described the entry into the region. "You'll come over the mountain to see a wild, untamed river snaking through a long green valley. If you're into whitewater rafting, the spring flow on the river will test your courage as you're tossed through forests and farmland and funneled into lost and almost inaccessible canyons." Twenty years later I would return to this to town for an amazing waterfront offer to be discussed later in this book.

The Cacapon River is beautiful enough to qualify for federal designation as a Wild and Scenic River. Local landowners, however, voted down the honor to hold back an expected flood of city folks. The vicinity was, at the time, designated as a "Host Area" for metropolitan D.C. evacuees in the event of a real or threatened nuclear attack. The Cold War buildup had spawned an army of survivalists who may have considered the region as the closest area with the lowest risk to their families. At every turn you'll see mountains. And morning fog hangs in the hollows.

You're seldom out of sight of public hunting and fishing lands. Some of the hills have changed little since George Washington fought Indians at Capon Bridge, located just 17 miles west of his historic office in the fast-growing city of Winchester, Virginia.

The region was settled mostly by homesteaders of English and German descent who began migrating down from Pennsylvania around 1730 into a five-million-acre land grant–an area then commonly known as the Virginia territories and owned by the crown loyalist, Lord Fairfax.

The sizes of these homesteads varied from 250 to 400 acres, many of which were first surveyed during the period 1748 to 1752 by George Washington, a friend of Lord Fairfax.

After a stint at Mount Vernon–an estate on the Potomac inherited from his brother–and following his promotion to Lieutenant Colonel in the Virginia militia–Washington was dispatched from Williamsburg, Virginia to Capon Bridge to forcefully confront the French about their trading excursions into English territory and their inflammatory flirtations with hostile Indians–infractions that threatened British-backed settlement and growth patterns. This was Washington's second attempt to oust the French intruders by diplomacy, the first having been summarily rejected. Enroute to the encounter, a military incident occurred in the vicinity of western Pennsylvania that ignited the long-flaming French and Indian War, a conflagration mentioned earlier in this book, and often referred to in Europe as The Seven Years War.

Cabin at Capon Bridge

Cabin at Capon Bridge was a conceptual advertising promotion offering a finish-it-yourself 20' X 24' vacation home shell and 19-20 ft. mobile homes on 2 to 5 acres of land in a planned-unit community. Each parcel came with well and septic installed. These homes were originally priced at up to $20,000, but now prices were cut to the bone. Homesites were given price tags of around $2200 per acre. The community is laced with greenbelt conservation zones for hiking and horseback riding. You can roam over 480 acres without trespassing on your neighbor. You can walk into a private hunting preserve. The area is an outdoor paradise–overrun with wildlife. Views drift off to infinity over sleepy green mountains. And the community is located near popular West Virginia ski areas. A minimum set of restrictions allows you to do your own thing, this while still protecting property values. Homes and mobile homes enjoy separate, privately imposed zoning.

Homesite prices had nosedived due to high interest rates and the prolonged recession. And builders, like other merchants, must sometimes sacrifice inventories to survive. Since we were, at the time, the East Coast's most successful liquidators of small rural acreage, we were asked to step in and quickly move this property. Right away I asked for and was given permission to slash homesite prices by up to 40%.

Projected profit figures went out the window. I insisted on cutting the price of the starter homes by up to 50%. How? Construction costs were axed. Homes were made smaller. Basic wiring, well water, and plumbing became optional. Any and all options could be added to the price and financed on the spot. I also insisted on offering speculator's terms, so the consumer could leverage his way into the property.

The consumer realizes that price reductions on some distressed properties are not unusual. I made readers aware of the fact that the scale of devaluations on this promotion were virtually unheard of. Ten years before we had offered a land and starter home package similar to this for $8,000. I said in the ad, "I look back now and wonder how we could again be offering this opportunity in almost 1972 dollars. And what will the 1982 dollar buy you tomorrow?" I asked. "The trick is to buy now in a buyer's market and sell in a seller's market."

For readers interested in advertising, you may have noticed that this print message is following a prescribed and proven trajectory for gaining maximum reader attention and response:

1. Stop the reader (headline).

2. Hold his attention (graphics, copy).

3. Involve him in the action (graphics, copy).

4. Build belief in the offer (facts).

5. Establish value (more facts).

6. Move to the close (overcome objections).

7. Reward quick action (stress urgency of response).

So far this advertising message has reached steps six and seven where the effective direct marketer must strike down any shadow of doubt regarding the offer and present the carrot.

Following are closing excerpts from the display ad.

Move to the Close

You won't find this kind of offer in the hands of local brokers and developers. Those who have survived this far into the recession can afford to wait for their price. Many of those who cannot wait call us. And we throw the price out the window. All of our liquidation sales have been complete sellouts. So it's best to be early and get first choice.

But don't pay what others pay who haven't seen this ad. Bring it with you this weekend, and the owner will slice $200 off the liquidation price. This is a legitimate discount. But you must ask for it. If you'd rather not have a salesperson accompany you, or if we're facing a crowd, look on your own if you like. You can take the plat map and select the homestead, mobile homesite, or starter home of your choice. Six starter homes are up for your inspection. Two styles of mobile homes are on site and for sale.

Come up and camp free this weekend. Water and toilet facilities are available. Or just bring the family for a cool and pleasant day in the mountains.

Reward Quick Action

FREE GAS AND VISITOR'S KIT. The owner has an attractive bribe for you.The catch? Just call and let us know you're coming. We'll set aside the following values in your name. It's your reward for calling and letting us gauge the crowd. No strings. No need to take a tour or buy property. Simply call for an appointment. (1) Six gallons of free gasoline (2) Two free tickets to George Washington's Office-Museum (3) Illustrated 250-page history book of the area (4) $5.00 discount on Cacapon River canoe or raft trip (5) Two free drinks at the restored Stagecoach Inn in Capon Bridge (6) Credit slip for free hamburger and coke in Winchester (7) Up to $100 in discounts good at area restaurants, shops, and attractions (8) Plus, if you call for a morning appointment this weekend: Free lunch at Fort Edwards Inn in Capon Bridge (up to $10),

Support Advertising

The unfolding of an advertising campaign is like the opening of a show. You want to focus as many media spotlights as you can on the production. Often I would splash little spot ads throughout the newspaper calling attention to a larger ad, a display usually placed in the financial section, this if I am promoting distressed properties or investment real estate.

Grand Rush for nearby
WEST VA REAL ESTATE
Land $39 mo.–Starter Home $148 mo.
See Financial Section "West Virginia Land"

Further support was often provided through one-minute radio and television spots calling attention to the display ads in various city papers. These spots usually were presented on weekends to correspond with ad publication in the print media.

Kilmarnock, VA
ECONOMY AT LOWEST LEVEL IN 34 YEARS – October, 1982
– John Cougar

In the fall of 1982, we were almost a year and a half into the recession, and a third of the country's industrial capacity was at rest. Never had more people stood in unemployment lines since the Great Depression. And record deficits continued to smother the economy. On Virginia's Northern Neck, with its extensive waterfront and exposure to the Chesapeake Bay, about a third of the area's economic vitality depended on tourism and real estate transactions. As more and more developers eyed the economic storm clouds overhead, and observed the perilous market forces working against them, they looked for ways to unload their cargo of land.

Many sailed into my port of call. At first I operated out of a Winnebago with a wild group of salespeople. Away from their home in the Valley, they took to playing practical jokes to let off steam. One time while I was in an outhouse, they hooked a rope to it and a jeep and hauled me away pants down. Another time they knocked on the door of a motel room with a car bumper, jacking up my bill for the night. Lest I be accused of operating a dog and pony show, I later established respectable offices in Heathsville and then in Kilmarnock–at the time a sleepy Bay-area village–to consolidate the offers of several developers into large-scale regional promotions:

FIRST OFFER! Attention: Opportunity Seekers.
Depressed housing market on lower Chesapeake Bay
hands you this unprecedented

LOWER BAY LAND BUST!

In the Northern Neck hotspot: Kilmarnock,
Irvington, Tides Inn area.
Why you should act now–while
Chesapeake Bay property is devalued.

1-3 acre estates at charted water from **$59** to **$99** per mo. (**$3950-$6950**)
Preferred estates with more acreage or state road front **$7950**-$9950

1-5 acre waterfront estates $8950-$39,500

Most people act too late on land devaluations. They wait until the crisis is over and pay inflated prices. Ideally you should buy at the bottom, and sell at the top. But how do you know when prices have hit bottom? Obviously you don't know for sure. You may see interest rates falling across the board. You may observe housing starts on the rise. And you may have a gut feeling that a buyer's market for homes may be ending. Savvy investors in country properties stay ahead of the curve and anticipate where people are planning to build in the future.

In tracing country property transactions in the lower Chesapeake Bay area over the 20-year period, 1982-2002, you'll find a classic example of the real estate market landscape that investors hope to discover. With an aging U.S. population, retirement centers like the Kilmarnock-Irvington, Virginia area have gained considerably more residents. This fact is evident by observing the mushrooming shopping centers, home construction boom, and skyrocketing real estate prices. In 1982, the region ranked third in the state for residents aged 65 and older.

It would have been a sucker bet to sell short on this figure climbing year by year. U.S. government figures from the early eighties showed more people moving to rural areas than into the cities and suburbs. A major reason—somewhat reinforced in recent years by the threat of terrorism—was a vital concern for security and personal survival in light of the intensified Cold War during those days. The government, at the time, had drawn up plans to evacuate city people into rural areas in the event of a real or threatened nuclear attack. I repeated selling points from previous ads.

The Kilmarnock-Irvington area is on the mainland near land's end. Substantial waterfront isolation is provided by Indian Creek, the Chesapeake Bay, and the Rappahannock and Corrotoman Rivers.

Heightened security and personal safety are largely measured by the degree of exposure to main roadways and busy transportation corridors. Waterfront and water access properties are usually away from through streets, and you can easily reach other waterfront communities by boat if necessary. In extreme national emergencies, such as widespread street riots, and chemical, biological, or nuclear attack, residents of country properties in the lower Bay region are not readily subjected to the hazards of bridge and tunnel traffic and an influx of crime. What better place to be during hard times than in deep-water anchorage off the Intra-Coastal waterway?

Location, Location, Location

My research in 1982 showed that the Kilmarnock-Irvington-White Stone, Virginia area was one of the premier destinations for retirees and those seeking the advantages of leisurely small-town living.

Population density in Lancaster County, VA, was estimated by local planners to be one person for every ten acres. Single-family homes had jumped 35.5% for the period 1970-77. And the local comprehensive plan expected the majority of new homes to be built around Kilmarnock, Irvington, and White Stone, the county population centers–exactly where we were selling these greatly devalued properties. But I was quick to remind buyers that the offer could not be repeated because the county comprehensive plan called for containing population sprawl by imposing further restrictions against the ownership of land in the countryside.

How Big a Value?

Prices on properties assembled for this sale were slashed by 25-40% due to the depressed housing market. At nearby Deltaville, we had just sold 69 Bay Country homesites for an average price of $15,000. And all were snapped up in just four weekends. Normally this would have been the going price for two improved acres at the water around pricey Kilmarnock. But these were not normal times. Yet, despite the recession, we were getting $35-40,000 for five acres on the nearby Piankatank River. So the offer was, at face value, extremely affordable and extraordinarily profitable in the long run for investors.

Feed 'em with Facts

In the mind's digestion of information, facts can be considered the food of health and wisdom. Advertising hyperbole and overexaggeration are not assimilated well in the consumer's mind and are often refuted, just as the human body would reject bespoiled fruit. That's why I like to back up my claims and fortify them with facts. Obviously I cannot guarantee price appreciation of every parcel sold. In these liquidation sales, the customer has to make up his own mind about how much devaluation has occurred and whether an economic upturn is in the cards. I can, however, provide comparable price figures and certain disclosure information so that the consumer is not deliberately misled.

In the "Land Bust" promotion, I published, up front, factual data that answered many questions possibly lingering in the consumer's mind: (1) Local homeowners were drawing water from shallow wells at depths of 60-80 feet. (2) Individual septic systems were used for sewage disposal systems, and all parcels were guaranteed to perk by the sellers. (3) All roads were level-to-moderate in grade, gravel-based, and maintained by property owners' associations, this where state maintenance was not provided. (4) Electricity and telephone were available to every homesite. (5) Taxes were about the lowest in Virginia–at $208 per year for an $80,000 home. (6) Permits were required by appropriate state agencies for the construction of private docks. (7) Limited shell-fishing privileges were granted to waterfront landowners. (8) Owners of off-water property were given deeded access to the water within walking distance of their land.

Front Royal, VA
LEONID BREZHNEV DEAD AT 75 – November, 1982 –
Lionel Richie

Leonid Brezhnev, the leader of the Soviet Union for 18 years, lies in a sea of red roses and revolutionary flags, dead from lingering heart and lung problems. And while President Reagan contemplates attending the funeral of his communist adversary, an official announcement from the Soviet press agency, TASS, states that communism will live forever.

From my office in Front Royal I contemplated the enormous task of simultaneously resuscitating dead and dying developments in the mountains of West Virginia, the lush Shenandoah Valley, and the rolling Piedmont region of Virginia. Times were tough in the Mountain State. Builders faced bankruptcy in record numbers. It was a classic buyer's market. But why would anyone want to own land in West Virginia? The state has some of the most rugged terrain in the U.S. There are no large areas of level ground. Mountain chains cover the eastern section. To the west there are steep hills and narrow valleys. Wild, whitewater rivers rip and roar through awesome canyons threatening precious tillable ground, property, and human life.

Sure, you may want to own land on a navigable mountain river. But the price could scare you off, or you may be afraid of possible flooding. Nevertheless, demand for this type of waterfront exceeds supply. And subdivision and environmental restrictions continue to aggravate this imbalance against private ownership.

WEST VIRGINIA WHITEWATER AND CABIN OPPORTUNITY

at historic Berkeley Springs–probably our last offer of affordable land on the Cacapon River because of coming new subdivision restrictions

2-3 acres on the river - $14,950 to $18,950

2-5 acre riverview homesteads $6500 to $11,500

CABIN ON RIVER BELOW COST - $5500

The developer had paid a high price for the land–too high to sustain long-range development plans in a high-interest economy. Five-figure prices on waterfront were sliced to four. Prices on high meadow sites above the river were dropped by a third. And profits on starter homes were axed by cutting back sizes and making basic utilities and wiring optional. We also arranged speculator's terms so investors could easily leverage their way into the property.

This was our first offer of land on the Cacapon River since 1966. Millions of visitors come to West Virginia every year for the beautiful scenery and recreational opportunities. Few will have a chance to own land on the Cacapon. The vast majority of people who read my ads arrive too late to take advantage of the opportunities. At Berkeley Springs I only had 30 waterfront farmettes for sale. More people were turned away losers than winners. These were the last truly affordable riverfront parcels available at the time along the Cacapon River before it enters the mighty Potomac. (A little over twenty years later, most riverfront lot sizes on the Cacapon would jump to 20-acre minimums, with price tags approaching the six-figure range.) Towering cliffs dominate the opposite bank. Tourists and history buffs make pilgrimages to these rocks. Canoeists appear to worship this scenic stretch of the river because of the quick run to the Potomac.

Why Berkeley Springs?

Long before the first Europeans discovered the warm waters of Berkeley Springs, it was already a famous health resort attracting Indians from Canada to the Carolinas. George Washington's fascination with the resort made it popular among the colonial elite. You can stay there today and enjoy live entertainment at the quaint Country Inn. Nine miles south is the incredibly beautiful Cacapon State Park. The Park's boundaries extend across the state from Virginia to a point near Maryland's border. Hiking and bridle trails climb 1400 feet into misty blue mountains. Horses and rustic cabins are available for you to rent and enjoy.

You'll appreciate an uncrowded 18-hole championship golf course–often labeled the most beautiful in the East. Cacapon Lake offers your family and friends a white-sand swimming beach, paddle boats, and fishing. Picnic areas, playgrounds, marshmallow roasts, and camp-fires are maintained and sponsored by Park naturalists. Beautiful Cacapon Lodge overlooks the golf course. You can stay in luxurious air conditioned rooms with private TV, enjoy fine dining, while your children amuse themselves in the game room.

What would you pay for two riverfront acres in a resort area of Colorado or Arizona that offered proximity to such amenities? In 1982 I speculated that the price might be $25-50,000, with that estimation reaching well into the six-figure range at the turn of the century.

A Shenandoah Valley Story

The president of a local bank contacted me about some defaulted land that the bank wanted to purge from its books. A developer had called it quits and walked away from the loan. The bank attempted to auction off the land, but the highest bid did not cover the amount owed. So the bank offered me a no-money-down deal and subsequent financing for lot buyers, this to take the bank off the hook. I jumped at the opportunity because it was waterfront property within commuting distance to the Washington D.C. area.

Distressed property! Bank orders immediate liquidation of valuable waterfront property at distress prices

Now you can commute to your own 20 ac. farm on a whitewater canoeing creek

$19,500 to $24,500

Route I-66 had recently been completed to the Shenandoah Valley from the Washington D.C. beltway, reducing the commuting time, in many cases, to about an hour. And because of the severe recession, even productive farmland had suffered a devaluation. Waterfront farms, though, were scarce. This promotion was a breakup of a larger grazing farm into six smaller farms, and the fortunate few who picked up these deals saved up to 50% over what they would have paid had they waited for the recession to be over. I would have priced such properties as these in 2002 at around $140-$150,000.

The farms are off the beaten path in an area of extreme beauty. The land, at the time, was mostly open, with generous stands of trees to shade homes and livestock. In the spring and late fall, Cedar Creek becomes a wild, cascading river of no return. If you launch a canoe or kayak in this region you should be prepared for a Grand Canyon-type experience, as rip-roaring white water propels you past awesome cliffs and plunges you into the Shenandoah downstream.

In early spring you can pull trout from deep pools that offer pleasant swimming in summertime. Mountains grace the horizon almost everywhere you turn. This is the kind of land that the government likes to set aside in national and state parks.

I have talked to hundreds of people over the years who wanted to kick themselves for not buying a waterfront farm when they could have picked one up this cheap.

Lumber Company Cuts Losses

Bowlers Mill Lake was built as a reservoir for the town of Gordonsville, VA. In 1982, the lake had been sold to Louisa County. At the time, the lake was somewhat remote and had escaped development. Because of the building slump, a lumber company was forced to liquidate its holdings on the lake. Planned rich man's estates costing $25-50,000, and located on paved roads, would not be offered. Now almost anybody with $200 could tie up a place at the lake. Since the county owned the shoreline, it was not legal "waterfront" property, though common access was permitted all around the lake. Boats with gasoline motors were not permitted.

This was a breakthrough offer aimed at the general public, rather than to investors at large. It was a waste of time for the average family to search for nearby lakefront property. The price would have been prohibitive. Lake construction does not come cheap, and developers are faced with enormous infrastructure and amenity costs.

The lake was back in the woods. Few cabins and homes dotted the shoreline. I encouraged readers to act on this offer immediately so they could be among the first to establish a presence at the lake. And I reminded them that some of the nation's most prominent families were once first-time settlers and land speculators.

All estates are wooded. Most have streams. Many have mountain views. Landowners can camp in their own woods overlooking the lake and leave a camper or mobile home as long as they liked. They could build a small home or cabin in the woods, cut all the firewood they needed and even clear off land for growing food and grazing livestock.

Life on the Lake

If the landowner liked to fish, he would never want for a meal. The lake at the time was relatively undiscovered. These were dark days for the average family, and few could boast that they were going away for the weekend to their place at the lake. For those concerned about culture and convenience, the University of Virginia in Charlottesville is only 15 miles away, and the town of Gordonsville is a five-minute drive. Property owners could benefit by vacationing at the lake, rather than spending their hard-earned money at crowded campgrounds and resorts.

The rich can send their kids away to summer camp. Here was an opportunity for the average family to teach their kids to sail from their very own summer place. Think of the canoe adventures they could take into hidden coves. And there was ice skating in the winter.

Other concerns on the consumer's mind were crime, crowds, and the threat of war. Now that land prices had crashed, there was never a better time for getting away to the lake.

Irvington, VA
AMA CALLS FOR BAN ON BOXING – January 13, 1983 –
Men at Work

In light of Muhammad Ali's deteriorating condition, and in consideration of the brain damage to other boxers, the American Medical Association called for a banning of the sport. Meanwhile, the nation's economy remained on the mat. Investors, still in the ring at the time, were punch drunk with values.

The Kendall Hall Story

It seems that the more you're talked about, the more you have to lose. This is why I have never courted notoriety. You need to look no further than the entertainment industry to see that anyone given fame and fortune can be hailed as a prophet audaciously wise enough to critique the President and his men. But whenever we observe a successful person in any profession who may serve our needs, we have a tendency to seek him out. Those who had country properties to sell and wanted them sold often came to me. Few knew that I was born–as were countless others–in a cellar and, forswearing a useless life, I, like them, came upstairs primarily through initiative and hard work– even, as a teenager, making signs for a haberdasher in exchange for clothing to wear to school.

A lady called me on the phone after observing my successful advertising and promotional campaigns in Virginia's Northern Neck. She and her husband owned one of the historic waterfront mansions in the area and needed to sell quickly so they could move on with their lives. It was her opinion that I was the man for the job. I scheduled a trip, made a thorough inspection of the house and grounds, conceptualized the offer, and negotiated a listing agreement. Shortly thereafter, the following ad, complete with photo, appeared in the financial sections of the *Washington Post* and Tidewater newspapers:

Set in Florida or California at the time, this waterfront estate would probably have been offered at twice the price and is obviously worth well over a million dollars today. The ad drew considerable response, including prominent political figures, luminaries, authors, and media personalities. After a few months the property remained unsold. So I decided to buy it myself, along with all of the antiques. I held onto the property for about a year, and when my wife became terminally ill, I decided to sell, packaging Kendall Hall with an adjoining seven-acre estate called the "Bell Tower." This offer added a 12-room, five-bath mansion, guest cottage, and boat house on a total of 1,000 feet along Carter Creek.

My promotional brochure conceptualized the 12-acre offer as a "SPANISH STEAL." Believe it or not, the whole complex could have been purchased for about $800,000 in 1983.

Today, this figure could amount to little more than a down payment on this complex that, if it were offered for sale, would comfortably bed down a corporate sultan or fulfill the hedonistic lifestyle of an aging rock star.

Property on Carter Creek does not come cheap. The tributary, named for Robert "King" Carter, a seventeenth century planter and one of the largest landowners in the Virginia colony, is a tributary of the Chesapeake Bay and has become the preferred playwaters for yachting and sailing enthusiasts in the mid-Atlantic area. Myriad coves and branches for anchoring out, and fine resorts with country-club atmosphere abound in the region. The eastern branch is dotted with stakes and traps, but is widely traveled by cruising boats. There are several marinas along the shoreline, a posh inn with golf courses, and an abundance of edifices to established and newly acquired wealth. You might consider the lifestyle here as being that of the *rich and famous*.

The "Chesapeake Bay Lifestyle" is a societal commodity fiercely protected by those who have arrived, and often coveted by those on the way up. Surrounded by natural waterways and laced with creeks and inlets, the area is a boating and fishing paradise. Wherever you go, you're never far from a marina or boat landing. Sail the Bay and the rivers, spend a day cruising in a powerboat, paddle a canoe on quiet ponds and creeks, or engage one of the friendly charter boat captains for a day of saltwater excitement. And you won't want to miss the daily guided cruises to historic Tangier and Smith Islands.

At the end of a day on the water, there's nothing better than a seafood feast. You'll find fresh fish, crabs, and oysters served, along with hush puppies and fresh vegetables, at restaurants in quaint villages and towns throughout your travels in the region.

Ghosts of the Northern Neck

Kendall Hall was offered complete with resident ghost, allegedly the apparition of the woman who commissioned the construction of the mansion. Doors were mysteriously opened or coffee cups toppled by some unknown force. The sound of footsteps could be heard when no one was there. Sometimes a scream would haunt the halls and drive away sleep. A window that you had latched down in a thunderstorm would fly open, allowing torrents of the rain to rip into your bedroom through 18-inch-thick concrete and plaster walls. In the dead of night, pans and dishes that had been meticulously put away in their cabinets would rattle and move about as if an unknown guest was preparing a midnight snack. The ghost was, however, friendly and harmed no one. The sellers had no fear of the apparition and had learned to live with the spirit.

Spirits, like dreams, are not finely touched, so when I owned the estate, and until I could get a grasp on how I would use the place, I decided to embed a temporary caretaker. Now that Kendall Hall was for sale again, a tenant appeared on the scene with an offer I could not refuse. Months later, when I sent my farm manager back to clean up after this character, he spent the night alone in the mansion and returned with a bleached face and a bizzare tale of strange noises, doors slamming shut and blood in the kitchen sink when he awoke.

The tenant was in the area for the summer and needed a large home on deep water that could dock an ocean-going sailing vessel. His objective was privacy and spacious waterfront grounds for the entertainment of his many prominent guests. This somehow did not make any sense because he was calling undue attention to the whole show by insisting on paying the rent in cash dollars–$5,000 a month, with four months rent to be paid in advance. I met with him at a local Realtor's office where he produced $20,000 in crisp new $100 bills from a briefcase in the trunk of his red Mercedes coupe, advising me that it was foolhardy to deposit the money in a bank, since the paper transaction would then have feet. Only an idiot would allow the IRS to chase them down and gobble up a third of such a windfall. After counting the loot, I immediately proceeded to the bank and made the deposit.

Returning to the mansion to wrap things up, I perceived–in conversation and in observation of the character and his girlfriend–that they gave vague answers to questions and appeared circumspect and slightly evasive. They paid particular attention to a hidden tunnel that led from the mansion to the basement furnace room. On subsequent visits to the mansion, and having become addicted to champagne at the time, I noticed with particular curiosity that the trash cans seemed to burp with empty bottles of the finest $100 vintage. The final cork on this story was pulled over a year later in a spurt of calamity and intrigue. But we'll devour the rest of the story later in this book.

Front Royal, VA
REDSKINS BEAT DOLPHINS IN SUPERBOWL – Jan. 30, 1983
– Marvin Gaye

While riotous Washington Redskins fans toasted this rare victory in the streets and bars of Georgetown, others, with little or no concern for the sport of American football, were striking their chins and sipping tea in misery over their deteriorating real estate portfolios. Two British clients approached me with their compelling need to liquidate real estate holdings in Virginia's Shenandoah Valley by yesterday. One property–a lodge on the Shenandoah–was of particular interest to me because I had handled a previous sale when it had transitioned from a folded boy's camp into a hippie colony and redoubt for cultural "dropouts," some of whom became prominent Hollywood personalities.

Only 1 hour to Beltway on I-66
OLD LODGE ON SHENANDOAH
PRICE SLASHED $30,000

FRONT ROYAL, VA–Foreign owners liquidating U.S. holdings. Want sale this week. Skymont Lodge was the crown of an upscale boy's camp on the Shenandoah River. 2-story relic haunts cliffs above turbulent white water below. Mountains shroud the horizon. Ghostly lodge measures 52' X 42' on the main floor. Double this space on 2nd. Historic compound once alive with boys' laughter now begs for new life. Huge central dining room with stone fireplace. Wide-pine board floors. Dormitory sleeping room. Run-down kitchen, toilet and shower areas. Old concrete swimming pool. Oil-fired hot-air furnace in sad shape. Central water lines need repair. 6 gutted cabins and garage hover in shadows under aging hemlock trees. Cliffside cottage and old bath house, now crumbling piece by piece into swirling waters below. ½ mile river frontage accessible by hiking trail and private road. 12 AC. GROUNDS INCL. 4 RENTAL HOMES EASY TO REPAIR FOR TAX CREDITS. One of the world's most impressive settings available for private ownership. River site alone worth the price. Was $120,000. Now $89,900.

B.K. HAYNES REAL ESTATE
"Nearby Land Bargains Since 1966"

As incredible as it may seem, just 20 years later a single waterfront acre without improvements in this setting could easily command a price of $100,000. For investors in country properties, the lodge offer stresses the importance of timing. Obviously we, as individuals, have scant control over the country's economic circumstances. However, it is not beyond reason that, to a certain extent, we can control our own *personal* economic circumstances to take advantage of opportunities when they arise. If you are out to make a fortune, you could trade an MBA degree from the Wharton School for the insight of a prudent investor who has liquidity in hard times and who spends his money wisely.

Northern Neck, VA
REAL ESTATE GAME DECLARED UNFAIR – February, 1983 – Michael Jackson

The Supreme Court halted the game company, Parker Brothers, from passing Go when the originators of the board game, Monopoly, tried to stop a competitor from marketing a game called Anti-Monopoly, this on the basis of possible copyright infringement. Monopoly cannot be "monopolized," said the court. Success, it appears, can often cost more than it is worth.

Many successful developers had played the *real* real estate game with so much success that they were sandbagged by the IRS for enormous chunks of change. Some recreational land developers, over their heads in debt, simply asked me to dump their inventories at the best price I could get. A few hot-shot commercial operators shuffled through their assets and handed me stacks of personally owned country properties from the Virginia coastal plains to the West Virginia mountains. All of these developers needed to trade their land for cash.

As I have previously discussed, prices on waterfront and off-water in the Chesapeake Bay region had been torpedoed by the recession. But at the lowest ebb is the turn of the tide. And for those beleaguered consumers with some spare change in their pockets, the hope and safety of prosperity was within sight, just like a rescue ship on the horizon. In the past, they may have thought of themselves as sick in the world's regard–too "poor," perhaps, to own land. Now comes along an opportunity to own their own property at the beach and escape from the beach crowd. For as low as $25 per month they could own a nearby waterview homesite.

MUST LIQUIDATE at below list prices
WATERFRONT PRICE WRECK!
Northumberland County, Virginia
Water view homesites from **$25 per month** for 1/3 to 10 acres
$1950 to $12,950 **Waterfront from $8950** to $19,950
1/3 to 5 ac. on deep water to $29,900

I had opened an office in the Northern Neck to handle these liquidations and often flew down to a nearby airstrip. We were offering land bargains on the following tributaries just three to ten miles from the Bay: (1) the Great Wicomico River, with deep water relatively close to the shoreline; (2) the Little Wicomico, a beautiful estuary just off the Bay and; (3) the Coan River, which, at the time, appeared just as it did a half-century before.

Unlike other waterfront areas in the mid-Atlantic region, the Northern Neck was not "discovered" until bridges were built across the Rappahannock River in 1927 and 1958. With the influx of more and more people came rising land prices. To buy a good waterfront homesite charted to the Atlantic Ocean you might have expected, in those days, to spend, say, $45-50,000.

The devastating effect of high interest rates and the recession had temporarily devalued waterfront properties by 25-40%. Someone buying a $30,000 deep-water homesite in 1984 during one of these liquidation sales could have tripled his money by 2003. Over this 20-year period, variable interest rates on raw-land loans had plunged by more than 40% from about 14.75% apr to as low as 5.75% apr in 2003. And, no matter what the price, good waterfront was still a commodity in high demand and short supply.

Waterfront, combined with the magic of **location, location, location,** makes a powerful attraction for investors and boaters. The Chesapeake Bay area is arguably the finest cruising area in the world. It is 195 miles long, with 150 rivers, creeks, and branches containing 6,000 miles of shoreline. The Chesapeake Bay is the largest bay in the U.S. It is teeming with shellfish. If you're into fishing and a self-sufficient lifestyle, you can take a bushel each of crabs and oysters, and up to 250 clams per day for your own use (1983 figures). Fish catches are largely unlimited. Ducks, geese, and swan share the quiet shoreline. For recreation enthusiasts, activities such as weekend sailing, power boating, and waterskiing, are always close at hand.

Shenandoah Valley, VA
OPEC AGREES TO CUT OIL PRICES – March, 1983 –
Michael Jackson

For the first time in its 25-year history, the Organization of Petroleum Exporting Countries, responding to competition from non-cartel oil exporters, dropped its price to an average of $29 per barrel. Prices had spiraled from $5 in 1974 to $35 before the recent cut.

Gas prices at the pump began to fall, along with interest rates, and some glimmer of hope began to pierce the iron curtain of economic gloom that hung over the country. For the depressed real estate market, however, it would take at least another year for a significant turn-around and a stabilization of prices, this spiked by an end to the recession and a return to realistic interest rates.

To intelligent real estate investors with money to spend, the cut in oil prices and the drop in interest rates were clear signals that all sparkling moments of opportunity soon come to an end. Nothing is more dangerous to the investors' minds than the thought of lost treasure. They must take swift advantage of the hour. Only a fool could believe that you can keep cutting real estate prices without reaching a bottom sooner or later.

If money can be considered the lifeblood of our nation, then cash, mixed with liquidity, in the spring of 1983 was the required tonic of many newly born real estate millionaires. Even millionaires, of course, have their ups and downs, and they realize their economic health is dependent upon sufficient doses of cash mixed with a degree of liquidity. Following is one of best investments I handled at the time. It was sacrificed by a millionaire and sold to a person of modest means. By 2003, this property would have been worth at least four times its acquisition cost.

HORSE FARM ON RIVER
PRICE CUT $10,000

Woodstock, VA - Millionaire owner liquidating possessions. Kids grown. Wants simple life. 11 ac. grazing farm on Shenandoah. At river bend with 1/4 mi. on white water. Sturdy home-sized 6-stall barn with feed, tack rooms. Loft for hay storage. Old chicken house. Rich, level ground for crops and livestock. Room for light plane airstrip. Duck pond. Homesite in woods out of flood plain and overlooking river. Great survival farm, buried in valley, shrouded by mountains. Quick escape from Metro area in just over 1 hour by interstate. Unique possession. Owner only acquired the best. Was $39,500. Now $29,500. 10 adj. ac. on river also avail. 90% fin. possible.

B.K. HAYNES REAL ESTATE

Northern Neck, VA
U.S. EMBASSY BOMBED IN LEBANON 40 killed – April, 1983 –
Styx

Islamic terrorists were blamed for the car suicide bombing that killed
at least sixteen Americans. The Middle East was in flames, with U.S.
Marines patrolling the streets on a peacekeeping mission. International
relations were in a state of disaster. In England, antinuclear protesters
formed a human chain 14 miles long. The Soviet Union was labeled
the "Evil Empire" by President Reagan. China was up in arms over the
defection of its premier tennis star to the U.S. Ties with South America
were unraveling as the Americans prepared to set up a training base
for Nicaraguan rebels in Honduras. And the U.S. had ousted three Soviet
diplomats as spies.

These events, compounded by the recession, joblessness, and high
interest rates made uncertainty the order of the day. And Heaven itself
will not help a man if he does not act.

Wreck and ruin await the seaman who cannot choose between the
storm clouds and the catch. A vicious hurricane had devastated the
Outer Banks of North Carolina, leveling homes and crashing many of
them into the sea. The devastating storm had swept into the Northern
Neck of Virginia, swamping pleasure boats, overturning planes and
bringing havoc to the whole waterfront region.

Mother Nature had brought even more anguish to an already distressed state of affairs. How could things get any worse? The vast
majority of consumers were inclined to wait until things blew over
before they made major decisions about buying big ticket items.

To blow away this fog of indecision in the minds of consumers,
marketers were faced with the enormous task of creating urgency when
urgency, in the midst of current events, was thinner than air. It seemed
to me at the time that (1) the consumer had a number of basic concerns
on his mind; (2) these concerns were not being fully addressed; (3) the
concerns were being compounded by events and; (4) I had to bring
them together and offer legitimate solutions as best I could into my
advertising, this if I were to keep up the momentum of my liquidation
campaigns. Following are the **nine basic consumer concerns:**

1. **VALUE–Desire to get more for the money**
2. **SECURITY–Need of material satisfaction for self and family**
3. **SAFETY–Instinct to protect self and family from harm**

4. **PLEASURE**–The pursuit of fun for self and family
5. **OPPORTUNITY**–Drive to get ahead and increase income
6. **PRESTIGE** - Necessity to build image and self esteem
7. **COMFORT** - Quest for a better lifestyle
8. **CONVENIENCE** - Effort to make life easier
9. **SATISFACTION** - Contentment with the offer

For months I scoured the Northern Neck assembling an all-waterfront offer that would have broad-based appeal to consumers in all income brackets beyond the level of poverty. Anyone responding to the offer would not be shown any property that was not on navigable water.

Unprecedented Chesapeake Bay
WATERFRONT OPPORTUNITY
First known in-depth search for distressed waterfront properties, developers' waterfront close-outs, & *overlooked waterfront bargains– now offered up to*
50% BELOW ORIGINAL LIST PRICES
NO INTEREST - SEE BELOW
Original list prices $13,950-$69,950
1/3 to 2 acre estates on charted water $8950 to $18,950
2-5 ac. on deeper water $19,950 - $29,950
½ to 7 ac. Bayfront estates $19,950 - $39,950

Conceptualized retail sales are somewhat analogous to orchards. The sale blossoms forth attracting the eye and bearing a fruitful product. Dampened response, due to constant weathered promotions, can leave the fruit useless and wasted. The feelings and attitudes of consumers must be deepened into decisions to pick the fruit, or the crop may be entirely dissipated by delay.

Attention to this offer was accentuated by 3" X 3" spot ads showing a beachfront home crashing into the sea from a recent hurricane and entitled **"WATERFRONT PRICE CRASH."**

These "attention-getters' were placed in varied sections of area newspapers calling attention to the main display ad which usually was positioned in the financial or business section. Pleasure, satisfaction, and prestige were all enhanced within the ad by small illustrated caricatures of (1) a nice home, (2) a log cabin, (3) waterskiing, (4) tennis, (5) swimming, (6) sailing, (7) fishing, (8) camping. But rather than reproducing any verbatim advertising, we can begin with a synopsis of the key elements within the widely published 1/3-page print ad showing how the nine basic consumer concerns were addressed during this campaign. From such an analysis, the writer can develop suitable ad copy.

First we'll begin with an appropriate quote from the Bard of Avon:

> "There is a tide in the affairs of men, which
> taken at the flood, leads on to fortune;
> Omitted, all the voyage of their life
> is bound in shallows and in miseries; and
> we must take the current when it serves,
> or lose our ventures."
>
> *—Shakespeare*

Value, Opportunity

It is often as hard as crab claws for us to make decisions. The same metaphor can be applied to the creation of affordable new waterfront parcels. Costly regulations. Limited shoreline. Strong demand. High raw land prices. All of these factors tend to price people off of the water and force them onto backland parcels.

The objective in this campaign was to produce an offer that would make waterfront affordable to the average consumer and not just available to those in the higher income brackets.

The product would need to be depression priced, buildable, and located on navigable waters.

Prestige, Pleasure, Comfort

By owning waterfront, the average consumer can start at the top. No more dreaming about trading up later in life. No wishful thinking about what might have been. No second-rate treatment at public boat landings. The ad tried to show that the consumer could theoretically (1) launch his boat from his own dock, (2) swim from his own shoreline, (3) waterski with the kids within sight of his home, (4) harvest crabs and oysters from his own beach, and (5) set off for points of call along 6,000 miles of Chesapeake Bay shoreline. And why would anyone throw away money on vacations in hard times when he could vacation from home? It would seem reasonable that the owner of waterfront property would still have his place on the water long after he had blown the family vacation at a crowded campground or resort.

Value, Convenience, Pleasure

There is always a market for usable waterfront property. Most of the offers in this promotion were located in rural recreational developments with few, if any, amenities. Not all were perfect. The development may have a swimming pool or tennis court–that's all. All are close to marinas and boat landings. But the sound of silence is more prevalent than the roar of motors and the explosive noise of the beach crowd.

Most of the time you can only hear the honking of geese and the splashing of surf on lonely beaches. On the cheaper parcels there will not be the depth of water needed for large power craft and sailboats. Shallow draft boats, such as pontoon craft, dinghies, skiffs, and dorys can reach the shoreline of any parcel.

Pleasure, Opportunity, Comfort

In good times and in bad, consumers are generally concerned about their future lifestyles.

Recreation? Retirement? With an aging U.S. population, the expected surge of permanent residents into outlying regions beyond the cities has become a reality. And despite the so-called "baby bust" throughout the world, United Nations population control figures show that the U.S. population is growing dramatically, this primarily because of increased immigration. Almost everybody wants a place on the water. The Chesapeake Bay area lifestyle, with its mild climate, salt air, and sea breezes, is the main reason people build there.

Value, Convenience, Opportunity

For people building homes in 1983, the taxes were low–about 42 cents per $100 in assessed valuation. The towns of Burgess and Heathsville are close by. And you're just 15-20 minutes from Kilmarnock. This friendly town has a hospital and shops that carry everything you can buy in Richmond, VA. The famous Tides Inn is no more than 20 miles from most parcels. Some people may complain about the time it takes to get there: about 2-2 ½ hours from the D.C. and Baltimore, Md., areas, 1 to 1½ hours from Richmond and Williamsburg, and 1 to 1½ hours from Tidewater. But consider the low price and potential. Natural shoreline is limited. No more can be created by man. In the ad, I asked readers this question: Does this mean you will pay more if you wait? I pointed out that most economists agreed that the recession was ending. Obviously, if the reader agreed, then the buyer's market in waterfront was about over.

Safety, Security, Comfort

But the previous advantages paled beside a more vital concern–personal and family survival. "Ground Zero" was more than an unwelcome shadow. The government felt we would have at least three days warning and had plans to relocate people to "host" areas in rural counties.

I don't know if these plans are still on the shelf. But even if the reader was a critic of the government evacuation plans, or of survivalists in general, he still had his family's safety and comfort to think of. I asked this question in the ad: Do you want your family treated like refugees in these communities? Many people, concerned about their families' ultimate safety and security, sought out a place in the country to which they could retreat.

Value, Opportunity, Prestige

It's a fact. In 1983, you did not have to be rich to give your family the safety, security, and prestige of a waterfront retreat. Government economic policy at the time had driven interest rates through the roof and caused a temporary devaluation in most types of real estate. Investors and developers who wanted to bail out were willing to take a loss, or less of a profit than expected.

Navigable waterfront parcels that went for $20,000 in the early 70's were up for grabs at 45-50% below original prices.

Some inlet homesites that listed for $15,000 went for half price. Scarce bayfront listed at $30,000 were on the block for 20-25% below what others paid. Five-to-seven-acre waterfront estates just off the Bay were priced at $69,500. Some investors saved up to $30,000. And many buyers later subdivided their land for additional profits. The Northern Neck was a disaster area of undervalued waterfront.

Opportunity, Prestige, Satisfaction

This kind of opportunity was not in the ready hands of local brokers and developers. These were the last bargain-priced waterfront parcels I could find in the lower Northern Neck.

So the offer could not be considered an exaggeration, I had local newspaper ads showing comparable prices when prospects arrived. Many buyers had missed the boat on other waterfront offers: Ocean City, MD., The Outer Banks, N.C., Hilton Head Island, S.C. Their children had watched neighbors leave for their vacation homes at the beach, and they felt left out. Obviously they didn't want to be left behind anymore. Some knew from experience that only once or twice in a lifetime will truly lucrative opportunities come along where they would not be caught napping.

Satisfaction, Satisfaction, Satisfaction,

The ad presented pertinent facts that the reader would need to know before they came.

Local planning officials reveal homeowners drawing water from shallow wells at depths of 60-80 feet. About half the parcels have central water. Individual septic systems are used for sewage disposal. Most parcels are on hard-surfaced roads. Most parcels are in the state road system or were in the process of being accepted. All roads are level to moderate in grade. Some are maintained by private property owners associations. Electricity and telephone are available to every parcel.

Most estates are wooded. Some have open land for gardening. Permits for private docks must be obtained from appropriate state agencies. Limited shell fishing is granted to waterfront land owners. Buyers received a general warranty deed and a new survey. They did not have to pay off the mortgage for the land to be theirs.

Satisfaction, Value, Pleasure, Opportunity

I pointed out to readers that they obviously can't believe everything they read in the papers, and that fortunately the offer was close enough for them to check out. We were expecting a sizable crowd. So if they would help with our scheduling, we rewarded prospective buyers for calling ahead. When they called for an appointment, we set aside a credit slip for five gallons of free gasoline. They also received a free copy of the popular book, *Understanding the Chesapeake*. Plus, if they called for a morning appointment when we were less busy, we reserved two free cruise tickets for them to visit either Smith or Tangier Island in the Chesapeake Bay.

The boat leaves from Reedville, VA, the "#1 Fishing Port in the U.S."– just 5-10 miles from most parcels. Customers did not have to take a property tour to gain these benefits. If they thought they knew what they wanted, they could look on their own.

Value, Opportunity, Satisfaction

The ad told readers not to pay what others pay who buy through cooperating brokers.

Customers were advised to bring the ad and get $200 off the liquidation price. This was a legitimate discount. But the customer was advised to ask for it. All of our liquidation sales had been sellouts. The primary reason was that we handled only those properties that could be sold far below market value. So it was best for the customer to be early for the best choice. Theoretically, it was possible to flip properties for a quick profit, and the practice is still widespread in markets with scarce real estate. Nevertheless, I emphasized to buyers that they must close on their property prior to resale, this to avoid excessive speculation.

"Here's how to become a waterfront property owner at the Chesapeake Bay. Liquidation price (after discount) $8750. Bring min. $300; $575 at closing (plus closing costs); then $124.67 per month, 120 months @14.5% annual percentage rate. NO INTEREST CHARGES IF PAID WITHIN 90 DAYS. Lower rate with more down and/or shorter term. Most owners give a discount for cash."

The Financing of Land Transactions

Despite the difficulty of borrowing money, the majority of sales during this promotion were financed by local banks at face value without discount, though some notes may have required owner endorsements. Banks ordinarily try to gain at least a three-point spread above the rate they pay to the Federal Reserve to borrow money. To stimulate the economy, the "Fed" could drop its rate to as low as, say, 1%, and the "spread" to the bank could expand, this theoretically increasing profits and encouraging lending. To fight inflation and curtail the money supply, the Fed could raise its rates in tactical attempts to balance the economy. Business activity and consumer borrowing generally react positively or negatively to the Fed rate strategy.

When the Fed rates go up and inflation still rises, we have, as we have previously discussed, the economic nightmare called "stagflation," the gloomy situation experienced in the late seventies and early eighties.

The financial world establishes and publishes in the *Wall Street Journal* a so-called "prime rate" at which it will loan money to preferred customers, this figure being keyed largely to the Fed rate adjustments. As you may have noticed from the high interest rates offered to consumers during these liquidation sales, the cost to banks of borrowing money from the Federal Reserve was far beyond the norm in the early eighties, hence the phrase "tight money." Many buyers paid cash. Prospective buyers with bad credit were usually rejected.

Our commission rates were considerably higher than normal brokerage fees due to heavy expenditures for advertising and sales and promotion. On some brokerage sales I would infrequently accept owner-financed notes for part of the commission. When selling my own property, I would readily finance consumers with marginal credit and either (1) sell these notes to a bank with my endorsement, (2) discount the notes to a third-party lender, or (3) hold the notes for personal and corporate income.

Northern Neck, VA
U.S.-COMMIE WAR HEATS UP IN CARIBBEAN – July, 1983 –
The Police

The Caribbean, once an American Lake, had been transformed into a sea of troubles. President Reagan stepped up military movements in Honduras and threatened a blockade of Nicaragua in an attempt to halt the Russian-backed Sandinista rebels from expanding their revolution throughout Central America.

In the U.S., interest rates had dropped slightly, and the gas crisis was beginning to ebb.

A developer had cleared off an overgrown waterfront farm on a river leading to the Chesapeake Bay and needed some marketing advice. He had observed my liquidation campaigns throughout the region and asked me to conceive a development plan and launch a sales promotion. We came to terms, signed a contract, and I went to work.

The first order of business was to come up with a concept to dispose of the off-water property, since most customers are looking for waterfront. One way was to graphically tie the back land directly to some object of value, utility, and pleasure on the water. Following is the newspaper headline I used over the drawing of an oceanliner. This transference of attributes from one object to another is critical to conceptual thought. And inventive thinking evolves around concepts. Above the headline was an illustration of a family looking down on a nice home in an agricultural setting, with sailboats on the horizon.

Now, just $50 per month gives your family a valuable Chesapeake Bay Farmland Estate larger than an oceanliner and as lasting as the earth

2-15 ac. Farmland Estates $3950 to $15,950

Most with streams, woods, cropland

All with access to river and Chesapeake Bay

2-6 acre Waterfront Estates from $13,950

Key selling points in this successful promotion were:

(1) Use your vacation money to own something of lasting value.
(2) Own more usable space than on the deck of an ocean liner.
(3) Valuable, productive farmland will serve you well in hard times.
(4) Buy land adjacent to a large body of water for more pleasure.
(5) Save money by vacationing in camping trailer at the Bay.
(6) Retire to nearby safe environment with low taxes.
(7) Build a small cabin or economical modular home.
(8) Buy at distressed price, sell for profit in the future.
(9) Provide your family with security and togetherness.
(10) Get your children out in the country away from city vices.
(11) Accomplish all this for just $50 per month.

In another effective promotion at the time to dispose of Northern Neck land, I packaged eight properties into a quarter-page ad that ran in the *Washington Post:*

Even when you've quit work someday, your land on the Northern Neck will not quit working for you.

In a crowded world, it's the man with the land who stands out from the crowd.

Within the Chesapeake Bay region is an unspoiled country of hills, valleys, rivers & creeks known as "Ye Northerne Neck."

The text of the ad started out with the words: **"He owns land"**–To natives of the Northern Neck, this expression meant security. If a man did not have wealth, he still had land and social position. An illustration in the ad showed a man, wife, and child smiling at a sailboat in the background. Properties described were cut by up to 40% from their original prices due to the recession and building slump. Twenty years later they had quadrupled in price.

Northern Neck, VA
$7.5 BILLION LOAN TO SAVE ILLINOIS BANK – May, 1984 – Madonna

Drowning in debt, the Continental Illinois Bank and Trust Company appealed to the "lender of last resort"–the Federal Reserve–for a $7.5 billion life raft. This was the largest loan package ever granted to a private bank by the federal government. The economic shipwreck in the private sector had also left many sellers swamped with debt, and buyers with ready cash were salvaging incredible deals. Look at these treasures:

---

30 AC. WATERFRONT FARM
on the Rappahannock River cut to $79,900!

Tappahannock, VA - Why settle for a waterfront lot when you can own a 30 ac. farm on a 7-mile-wide river? Only 25 mi.from Chesapeake Bay. Clean beach cottage to fix up. Stables or barn. Old log slave cabin. Garage, storage shed. Pasture fields, cropland. Woods laced with bold stream. Dream homesite on wooded bluff above seagull-filled coastline. Windlashed waves on beach below. Horizon active with ships. Deep water for dock and pier.

Distress Sale!
Home on Deep Water Cut $25,000

Wicomico Church, VA - Debt-plagued owners must take loss. Custombuilt rambling rancher on 3 ac. grassy knoll looking out to sea. Built 8 years ago by a retired general. Early colonial vessel haunts an aquatic grave off pier and dock. Wonder world for divers. Fishing, crabbing, oystering from 235 ft. shoreline. Sailboat waters. Just 5 mi. from Chesapeake Bay. 4 BR, 3 BA dream home, attached "in-law" apt., DR, LR, garage enters to kit. Screened porch overlooking water. Sunny Florida room, heat pump, B.I. appliances. Cannot be duplicated at this price. Site alone with sunken ship is said to be priceless. Below appraisal at $125,000. 90% financing.
B.K. HAYNES REAL ESTATE

False Treasures

But golden opportunities are not always what they seem. And deceit can be found on sandy shores beneath waving palms and soaring pines. A real estate broker tipped me off on a development for sale in North Carolina–a real smooth deal with potentially deep profits. I hit the road in my new Cadillac to link up with the hotshot owner of some swampland that was being dredged into canals to create waterfront lots.

The seller was an 83-year-old con man who told me he once was a big-time real estate operator in New York. He said he used to front for an upscale international firm–one of those brokerage outfits that sniff at any deal below seven figures. (You'll find their glossy catalogs on coffee tables in the parlors of the rich and famous.) Now this old gray fox was bypassing his fat profits on these lots to snatch the lamb of retirement.

After inspecting his work-in-progress and a luncheon engagement at a local barbecue take-out, we entered into negotiations. He said the local health department had approved his plans, and I had nothing to worry about. He even produced a vaguely written letter from some official regarding the issue. I asked him a simple question about the price. He dissimulated the question into a statement that he was practically donating the lots to me because he wanted time to smell the roses. But, he exclaimed, I (me) would have to make up my mind fast before the deal was history. Now, the surest way of being fooled is to let your victim suppose you are the victim, and I had, in the past, never suspected old age of trickery. Of course, I am still respectful of that tyrant. It shadows all of us. But over the years I have earned the right to be suspicious.

We signed a contract; I left a $5,000 deposit, and my assistant subsequently contacted the health department regarding the proposed development of the property. "Can't be done," was the reply. Start fooling around with the King's wetlands, and all officialdom will have your head on a platter. I called the scoundrel and told him the bad news. His high-powered lawyers and handlers sent me a letter that said, in essense, "Tough luck. You signed a contract. Feed our horse his due, or he'll trample you in court." I hired a sharp defense attorney who sent them a terse letter stating that I had been sold a blind horse, and they backed off. Of course I lost the five grand. Experience is the teacher of fools, and no amount of gold can buy it.

The Rest of the Story . . .

Earlier in the book–January, 1983 was the timeline–I had begun the story of Kendall Hall, the ghost-inhabited mansion on Carter Creek and my shady tenant who ordered $100 bottles of Dom Perignon by the case and who swilled it down it like a kid drinking soda pop. His booze bills were probably hitting a couple of grand a week.

A later criminal investigation showed the character had a rap sheet and multiple identities, with a pattern of using monikers having two first names, such as Charles Gregory, aka, Gregory Charles; or Edward Michael, alias Michael Edwards. Or he might have checked into a hotel using the name, Dick Richards. Shortly after renting the elaborate home, Slick Dick slid into the bucket seat of his Mercedes and lead-footed it for the trendy Commonwealth Park Hotel in Richmond, Virginia, where he coughed up cash in advance and gave a phony name and California address. The next morning a chauffeured limousine arrived at the hotel and Richard Dick slipped into the back seat, uncorked a chilled bottle of Dom Perignon, and the limo headed for Byrd International Airport where he picked up a Polynesian-looking woman who had just arrived from the Hawaiian Islands. The limo then returned to the hotel.

One month later, a pickup truck with camper bed and an Ohio registration showed up at the Kendall Hall boat ramp towing a speed boat. A balding, full-bearded man in his late twenties got out and docked the boat. He then strolled out on the pier to check the water depth. Weeks went by, and the speedboat was often seen churning water down the creek from Kendall Hall toward the Chesapeake Bay.

In early May, a 46-foot, double-masted sailboat called the "Daddy Warbucks" was observed at the Kendall Hall dock. Several men disembarked, one of whom was the bearded character with the speed boat. All three trudged up to the house, later returning for their sea bags. While the vessel was tied up at the dock, my assistant was on the pier showing the property to prospective buyers, totally unaware that men with submachine guns were crouching in the cabin.

Slick Dick made numerous trips down the stairs from the mansion grounds and through the ornamental iron gate to the boat dock. He walked the length of the pier like a bird beating its wings, yelling at my assistant to keep away from the vessel and scanning the creek for any boating activity. Darkness fell upon the scene. Men then scrambled from the hull of the boat and began unloading large bales, all tightly wrapped in black plastic. White tape strips marked the stairway from the dock to the mansion grounds as the men toted 5 ½ tons of marijuana into the mansion and stored it in the hidden tunnel.

It was the night before payoff, and the clatter of a helicopter rousted the gang from their beds. No doubt visions of iron bars then raced through their heads. The sheriff and four state troopers quickly sealed the grounds, jailing six drug smugglers and confiscating the sailing vessel, two speedboats, and several vehicles including the Mercedes. Unknown to me, the mansion had been under surveillance by a coalition of law enforcement officers from the day Slick Dick handed over the twenty grand in rent money. The street value of the marijuana, picked up from the Virgin Islands, was estimated at $10 million dollars.

Weeks later I sold the property, describing the estate as a Great Gatsby-style waterfront mansion that rented for $5,000 a month and had been the site of a recent international drug bust. Get this! The local "D.A." tried to confiscate the twenty grand rent money, claiming I sold the mansion because of the drug bust. I hired a good attorney who thought the long arm of the law had reached too far and was now picking the pockets of honest citizens. And the judge agreed.

Shenandoah Valley, VA
ALLIED LEADERS MARK D-DAY ANNIVERSARY – June, 1984
– Prince

While President and Nancy Reagan visited Omaha Beach at Normandy, leaders of the other six industrial democracies, then meeting in London to commemorate the D-Day invasion of Europe, seemed more concerned about the mounting U.S. deficit than the rows of crosses in Normandy marking the enormous toll of the dead from the assault on June 6, 1944. European participants said the debt contributed to historically high interest rates, slowing the recovery.

The situation was worsened by a looming debt crisis in the Third World. The foreign leaders asked the U.S. to focus attention on the gloomy economic picture.

History is little else than a picture

of human crimes and misfortunes

−Voltaire

The Shenandoah Valley of Virginia is steeped in history. Human crimes of the past have taken on great names like the Civil War and the French and Indian War. And misfortunes of times gone by have their dignity and redeeming power. All this is evident in the old homeplaces and log cabins scattered throughout the Valley−vestiges of yesteryear that have grown so old that they are becoming new. May of 1984 was a busy time for me. I was juggling several projects in the Valley, orchestrating a promotion in the Northern Neck, and disposing of distressed properties in nearby West Virginia. Small contingents of salespeople were stationed at each project. Headquarters in each area was usually a trusty, timeworn Winnebago, a rented office or trailer, a cabin, or an old home.

In the spring of 1984, I had purchased an historic farm at auction and had set up my sales headquarters in an old home in the Shenandoah Valley that had seen its share of war and misfortune. Generally, the first order of business in my projects was to sell off the improvements to reduce the effective cost of the land. This particular farm was rich with the spoils of time as reflected in the following ads of ghostly structures that−at the advertised price−look like giveaways in this day and age. Over time, the improvement and restoration of these old homes and cabins has become a religion.

GRAY GHOST!
on 30 ac. Joining Nat'l Forest
Distress Price $39,000

Mt. Jackson, VA -Farmer forced out by auction. Early settler's home left to die beside lively stream. 3 room antique has known Indians and the agony of war. Priceless battle-scarred logs and aging plank floors. Wood stove. Elec. No bath. Spring water. Farmer says home is worth $10K if moved. 1,000 feet on rushing stream beneath mountain peak. Some pre-finished pasture in cutover state. Joins million-acre G.W. Nat'l Forest. Bring $500; $1400 at closing; $262.19 mo.120 mos. at 13.75% apr. Less for cash. Commute via I-81-66. B.K. HAYNES REAL ESTATE

GONE WITH THE WIND
DISTRESS FARM $39,000
Mt. Jackson, VA–Farmer forced out by hard times. Crippled farmhouse of yesteryear left to guard fallow ground seeded with Civil War bullets. 20-mile-views across Shenandoah Valley and New Market battlefield. Ghostly relic of war, depression, and hardship is now partially remodeled. Classic restoration project. Kitchen, BA, study, LR, DR, 3 BR, woodstove, refrig., gas stove, wide plank floors, antique siding. Rich 10 ac. grounds include large barn, stables, silo, poultry house, storage shed, well, cistern. Farm shadowed by mountain peaks in Nat'l Forest. Walk or ride horseback into million ac. of back country. See nearby ski slopes from windows of farmhouse. Generous terms same as Gray Ghost.

B.K. HAYNES REAL ESTATE

Lost City, W. VA
AVERAGE HOME PRICE NOW OVER $100K – June, 1984 –
Bruce Springsteen

The failed U.S. economy was making a nightmare of the American dream. Inflation was driving up the price of homes, and high interest rates were preventing more and more people from owning a home. The housing boom that began after World War II was now a confirmed bust. And 4% interest rates that preceded the seventies were like castles in the air. Wishes, at least, are the easy pleasures of the poor. They are both inexpensive and nontaxable. But wishing can often be a stretch, outdistancing reality and leading to disillusionment and failure.

Anatomy of a Failure

I was preparing a promotion for some W. VA properties that joined the G.W. National Forest. The ad I developed showed a man sitting at a campfire with his son. The headline read:

"Here's a million acres, son –we own <u>real</u> land now!"

A brief explanation of the headline followed in text:

A father took his son camping inside the George Washington forest. The campground was crowded. He said to the ranger on duty, "I'll take anything available in the forest." The ranger asked why he insisted on camping in the forest when there were private campgrounds close by. The man answered, "Here you have a million acres. I wish I could afford a spread this large." The ranger told him, "If you owned land adjoining the forest your wish would practically be granted."

The man found a small plot of land bordering the George Washington National Forest and gave his son the use of a million acres for the price of a few. It was inexpensive and he paid taxes on just the few.

The ad copy continued on with an explanation of the offer. Salespeople raved about the ad, expecting a big crowd. But it was a party to which few people came. The ad failed, purely and simply, because it violated my basic rules of direct response advertising. At first glance, it could have been an advertisement for insurance, camping gear, stock investment, whatever. Plus, the concept was too much of a stretch. Who can afford a million acres?

When the ad concept was transformed into dollars and cents for this or that, and given an affordable pitch, the promotion took off. The winning ad showed a man, wife, and child on a hill overlooking a vast forested region. Here was the headline:

1/2 cents an acre and only 1/4 tank away

The headline was preceeded by an introductory line that read:
Amazing West Virginia Land Find

Once the ambiguity of the headline was eliminated, the reader could be encouraged to read the text and subsequently be led through an explanation of the offer.

How the Civil War Killed an Ad Campaign

It has been said that experience is the only teacher in war and peace. And you would think that, having been wounded by the previous ad failure, that I would be a fool to write another off-target storybook ad. And this in the same month!

I was liquidating the rural land assets of a successful commercial developer, and the project in question was a farm adjoining a Civil War battlefield. I figured I would juice up the ad with a little history. Wrong. In the swift course of a few weeks, here I was injecting a story line into a headline and diluting the message. The ad failed. And to make matters worse, I got stung by some historical hornet who claimed I was pillaging history for commercial gain. The ad showed a grainy photograph of a young Confederate soldier set between illustrations of a furious Civil War battle, the scene complete with charging infantry and smoking artillery. We won't go into the ad text, but you might as well see the headline and read the beginning of the story:

How this boy helped stop an army and how $65 per month gets you a farmette next to the battlefield

---

On May 15, 1864, this boy was one of 250 cadets from the Virginia Military Institute who bowed their heads and charged into an iron cloud of Union fire at New Market. Ten were killed and 47 wounded. It was the only battle in U.S. history in which schoolboy cadets fought as a unit under fire. They bayoneted Union soldiers, took prisoners, and turned captured artillery down enemy lines. The victory saved General Lee's Shenandoah Valley supply line and made it possible for the Confederate army to threaten Washington D.C. later in the Civil War.

The land around New Market contains some of the most fertile soil in the Shenandoah Valley. In Civil War days, the town was a central point for marketing farm products. But in the summer of 1984, due to the economic downturn, the product was land, not fruits and vegetables.

To turn the this project around, I went back to basics and quickly sold it out using a simple on-target headline and promotion:

New Market, VA–Just off I-81
QUIT FARMING LAND SALE!

The ad featured (1) a 3-acre river homesite with barn for $13,950, (2) a 3-acre mini-farm with stables and silo for $6950, (3) a 17-acre farm with pond for $10,950, (4) a cheap 3-acre homesite overlooking the river for $3950, and (5) a 3-acre low-cost riverfront homesite for $8950.

Flooding and Flood Insurance

When buying and selling riverfront property consumers should be aware of the flood plain areas, generally labeled as the *frequent* flood plain and the *100-year* flood plain, the latter of which is a buildable region in many counties. The *frequent* flood plain is sometimes characterized as "annual" due to yearly water levels over the banks. Flood insurance is readily available from many insurance companies and is subsidized by the federal government. It covers periodic damage to homes and dwellings in flood-prone areas.

Construction standards in 100-year flood plain areas usually require elevated foundations similar to those of homes and cottages built along low-lying oceanfront beaches. In recent years the government has gone overboard in preparing their flood-plain maps, often delineating land in the mountains as flood-prone, when throughout recorded history the nearest body of free-flowing water has never touched the area. Surveyors have protested, as have property owners and local governmental authorities who know the land. Imagine, if you will, having to obtain flood insurance on a ski area described in the following ad. Such mapping errors abound on flood-plain designation maps. Proving the government wrong and getting them to change their maps is anything but fun.

Washington, VA
REPUBLICANS NOMINATE REAGAN & BUSH – August, 1984
– Prince

Many people don't know that there is a Washington, VA, as well as Washington, D.C., the latter of which which is located on the east side of the Potomac River across from Virginia and adjoining the state of Maryland. The west side of the river, once the site of large plantations such as Mount Vernon, George Washington's home, was removed from consideration as part of the nations's capital by the Continental Congress in the late 1700's. The U.S. Capitol was located on the high ground beyond a once swampy area now called Foggy Bottom, site of the Kennedy Center for the Performing Arts and the noted hub of political intrigue–the Watergate Hotel. Once the decision was made to locate the Capitol on the high ground, land speculators flooded into the region, and land prices reached exorbitant levels. Congress then decided to buy up the marshy ground to the west for the remainder of its buildings.

Throughout its history, the D.C. metropolitan area grew exponentially into both Maryland and Virginia, creating suburban Washington D.C., this until it reached a moat of non-growth to the west, beyond which great wealth had established a new plutocracy. This multicounty kingdom of foxes and hounds and golden roofs has endured for generations, forswearing a grave with headstones of ticky-tacky houses. One of the world's ten best inns is located there in the hamlet of Washington, Virginia. Prominent political figures, powerful CEO's, and movie stars often arrive by helicopter. Land prices in the region are so high they can now be characterized as obscene.

In the summer of 1984, I was asked to liquidate a ski area in this self-perceived Camelot.

At the time, the county fathers of the round table declared that subjects residing in the countryside within this realm of privilege would be required to own a minimum of 25 acres (presumably to prevent the rain from falling before sundown). For $35,000 you could have become a vassal in this virtual kingdom, residing on a 25-acre wooded estate with a rushing trout river. By 2003, the price for similar acreage in the realm was close to three hundred thousand in princely dollars.

Nearby ski area goes bust Just 55 miles from Beltway
Commuters! Steal 25 ac. on Rush River in nearby Rappahannock County, VA

Waynesboro, VA
BEIRUT CAR BOMB KILLS 23 AT U.S. EMBASSY – Sept., 1984
– Tina Turner

The terrorist bombing was the second assault on the American Embassy in Lebanon, the first having occurred in April, 1983. The incident was far removed from the United States, and the fog of Islamic terrorism had yet to reach our shores. On an overcast day, I drove down to Waynesboro, north of VMI (Virginia Military Institute) to check out some foreclosure property then held by a local bank.

The day was so foggy that I got only as far as the entrance to the property. All I knew at the time was (1) that the land was mountainous; (2) that it bordered the Shenandoah National Park and; (3) that it was abandoned manganese mining property, with several small lakes and a trout stream.

Manganese is primarily used in the production of steel, and a reliable source of water is critical for "gravity" washing of the ore. The process leaves open cuts in the earth from shallow mines. But mines in the U.S. do not produce enough manganese for the country's steel industry, and all of such mines in the Shenandoah Valley have long since been abandoned. In the midst of the recession, some previous owner had defaulted on the mortgage, and the bank repossessed the land. Now the bank wanted to get it off of the books.

I usually don't buy property sight unseen, but this time I took a gamble that paid off big.

I drove down to Roanoke, Virginia, the bank headquarters, drafted a contract and submitted it to the person in charge of the bank's real estate holdings. The deal was accepted, and I went to work on a promotion that made the buyers–mostly local folks–the biggest winners:

Distress Sale of
LOST MINES
& Wilderness Lake Property joining the 300-sq.-mi. Shenandoah Nat'l Park
20-40 acres from $447 per acre

Those buyers who struck it rich at Crimora Mines found land on small deep lakes and a native trout stream. Others staked claims to remote land joining the park with views that rivaled the best of those offered to the general public from world-famous Skyline Drive. One tract enjoyed a rare and beautiful waterfall. Many properties had spring water on them. The only disappointed people in the whole deal were the off-roaders, trappers, and hunters, who no longer had free access to roam the land.

Rural W. VA
CANADIAN RIVER DROWNS OVER 7,000 CARIBOU– Oct.1984
– Stevie Wonder

In what was called "a major environmental catastrophe," Canadian biologists counted 7,100 carcasses of migrating caribou that had tried to cross two swollen rivers in northern Quebec province. Wildlife authorities in the region estimated that the actual number of the killed "reindeer-like" animals was over 20,000. The tragedy was blamed on officials of a hydroelectric utility company who issued a controversial order to release water from a nearby dam during a period of heavy rainfall. Eskimos and homesteaders in the area were up in arms.

A client of mine owned a hunting camp deep in the mountains of West Virginia along an old stagecoach route to the great American west. He had remodeled the main structure at the old rest stop into a hunting lodge, and now he wanted to sell. I had advised him on how to partition the land and was then in the process of selling it out. At one time, caribou, elk, and buffalo had roamed this rangeland. Now it was a habitat for white-tailed deer and cows.

I called the area "Buffalo Ridge" and aimed the promotion at homesteaders and hunters.

A few shell cabins were constructed to stimulate activity. The "big idea" was to create an affordable product for the maximum number of potential buyers–in essence, a low-end offer.

This type of offer lends itself to relativism when establishing the product's value. Here are a couple of concepts from the promotion:

Pasture = cows = one cow per acre = **12-COW FARM FOR LESS THAN $12,000**

The ad described a small cattle ranch back in the mountains along an old stagecoach route.

The place was an ideal homesteader farm with deer in the fields every night–ideal for farming, home, trailer, hunting cabin, or target-shooting camp.

Apt. rent = $4.50 per day = payment on cabin = **HUNTER'S CABIN FOR ABOUT A DAY'S RENT.**

The offer was a 480-square-foot stucco cabin on three wooded acres that adjoined a "no man's land" for $9950. You could shoot deer from your front porch. The place was a handyman's dream, with well water, electricity, refrigerator, stove, woodstove, sink, bunks, furniture, and an outdoor john. It was easy to fix up and could be rented out when not in use.

During the promotion, we had a number of affordable shell cabins constructed for the average working person with limited income. This was the featured cabin offer:

YOUR CABIN IN THE FOREST
from $6950 erected on 2-10 ac. $96 mo.

My favorite headline from the promotion was right out of the old west:

Starter Ranch on Old Stagecoach
Trail - A Holdup at $69 per mo!

Here are a few other catchy headlines from the fall of 1984, all aimed at "Po' Boy" buyers.

6-Cow Farm For Less Than a Round of Cheese

Estate on River for a 6-Pack of Beer

3-Cow Ranch for Less Than a Gallon of Milk

Northern Neck, VA
FAILED FARM FILMS LOSE TO ACTION FLICKS – Fall, 1984 – Prince

Hollywood's romance with the drama of failed farms ended when box office receipts showed that special effects action films gave tinsel town more monetary satisfaction. The movies, *Country,* showing farmers facing debt, *The River,* with farmers fighting floods, and *Places in the Heart*, about the Great Depression, all lost the money game to the likes of *Indiana Jones and the Temple of Doom, Beverly Hills Cop*, and *Ghostbusters*.

I lost out on a sweet deal because I refused to raise my ante from nine hundred thousand and change to a cool million. My assistant showed me an ad in the *Wall Street Journal* for the sale of a marina at the Chesapeake Bay. I inspected the property, figured out a development plan, and submitted a contract. The price was a little over a million clams, but during negotiations the million mark was cast in stone by the sellers. I couldn't climb the wall and fell flat on my face, forfeiting the deal to a competitor.

Another time I found a scenic little bayfront farm with a small farmhouse and a sandy beach and lots of privacy that I envisioned as a nice retreat for my family. It was the kind of place that everybody drools over, but few are able to find. I submitted a full price offer to the real estate agent and left the scene feeling comfortable about the deal, only to have him call me a day later and tell me he sold it to his boss. He said his boss made the owner an offer he could not refuse. The character traded the owner a piece of land in the deal and threw my contract out the window. I was furious and filed suit, believing there was a conflict of interest by the agent and some dirty dealing from the bottom of the deck. Still, I lost the suit and the deal.

It's hard to lose the good ones. You sometimes feel like your guts have been kicked out. But I've made it a practice to do the best I can with what I've got, and then move on. I never admit defeat. I only look back on events to profit from what I've lost or gained. I just keep going. And until I give up this game, I'm always there for another round, another deal, another life.

Mt. Jackson, VA
CHERNENKO DIES–GORBACHEV LEADS USSR – March,1985
Madonna

Mikhail Gorbachev, the youngest man to take charge in Moscow since Stalin, took the helm in Russia and immediately called for a "real and major reduction in arms stockpiles." Vice President Bush met with the new leader for an hour, handing him a letter from President Reagan urging that the two leaders meet in the near future. Gorbachev, not known as a militarist, became a hero of peace with his commitment to "detente"–the lessening of diplomatic and military tensions between the two nations.

Mount Jackson, in the Shenandoah Valley, was originally known as Mount Pleasant. But the town changed its name after the War of 1812 between the United States and Great Britain, this to honor Andrew Jackson, the hero of the Battle of New Orleans. This engagement was the last campaign of that war, a conflict in which 1500 British soldiers were mowed down at the sacrifice of a few entrenched American "sharpshooters." In 1985, the war on land prices was still ablaze in the Shenandoah Valley, and people were making a killing in waterfront property:

FARM FLOP!
Prices Nose-dive on Valuable Riverfront

The ad described a three-acre "Fish 'n Farm" ranchette on the legendary Shenandoah River that you could have picked up for a song–$7950. And just over the mountains, in West Virginia, the hills were alive with the sound of falling prices:

CHEAP HILLS!
Joins State Game Lands

Here was a valuable mountain homestead adjoining 8,000 acres of state hunting lands–wild country of black bear and migrating coyotes. Just whistle a happy tune and you could own two sprawling acres with more than a thousand trees–some too big to reach around–a talking creek, and a meadow where white-tailed deer were your neighbors every night. No restrictions. Build, camp, or bring in a mobile home. Hunt, shoot, hike or ride wilderness trails in your backyard to fish and swim in remote lake deep in the gamelands. In the spring of 1985 the whole show was yours for $3650, with $150 down and $50 a month.

Over the trackless past lie the lost days of our
tropic and desolate decisions.

In simple terminology, we look back at past decisions and revere the good ones, and we are generally somewhat remorseful about "what could have been." Let's take a look at a half-dozen past country property offers in early 1985, and then flash forward to 2003.

HUNGRY MAN CABIN - Joins State Gamelands - 2 ac. **$6950**

LANDSLIDE! 2 ac. just $4850. Foreclosure off I-66 - **$66 Mo.**

OLD HOUSE BY SIDE OF THE ROAD - W. VA - 2 ac. **$14,500**

HERMIT'S CABIN, STREAM, WATERFALL - 2 ac.W.VA - **$4400**

HAVE-IT-ALL FARM - 5 acres - open, wooded, stream - **$6500**

CHEAP COMMUTE - Forced Bank Sale - 20 ac. farm - **$19,950**

In April of 2003, the *Washington Post* sent a reporter into the countryside beyond the D.C. metropolitan area to investigate the changing migratory patterns of second-home buyers.

The reporter could hardly find a portion of an acre that reminded us of the above prices and offers. The article, in a three-page spread, said that land prices had "doubled and even tripled in the past couple of years" in a couple of nearby West Virginia counties west of Front Royal and Winchester, VA (both on the western edge of the D.C. metropolitan area). Prices of $3,000 to $5,000 per acre for some lots (20 acres) were said to be raising eyebrows.

The article quoted figures from a West Virginia University analysis of census data revealing that, at the turn of this century, the Mountain State had the second largest increase in "seasonal" housing in the nation. A new interstate highway–Corridor-H–linking central West Virginia ski resorts and industrial areas with the Shenandoah Valley is expected to shift prices on nearby country and mountain properties into overdrive.

By early 2003, the attractive geographical features and recreational opportunities in the mountains were beginning to rival those of the seashore. The stock market had dried up, and money was flowing into West Virginia land and second homes from a flood of primary-home refinancing. Low taxes, more land for the money, lack of overbearing restrictions, and a quest for privacy were cited as reasons to head for land in the hill country.

Flashback to 1985. I was crunching numbers trying to come up with a cabin offer that would put customers under roof in a second home for under $100 per month. In making decisions, I have found that, with rare exceptions, whatever we undertake we should finish, and that alterations can often disrupt or spoil the original fresh concept. For example, you may want a nice home. But you start out dwelling in a trailer; then, to save money, you attach it to a house. You then decide to build a room around the trailer to incorporate it into the home structure. You still have a trailer home. In order to have the nice home you desire, you must dismember the house and extract the trailer. Similarly, a nice deal could become a bad deal if something in the transaction goes sour. You must remove the problem.

I had purchased a tract of land for the "Cabin Crunch" shown below, and in my haste to meet advertising deadlines, I had ordered a model cabin to be built before closing. A survey showed that I was not getting the amount of land called for in the contract, so I requested the required adjustment in price.

The seller, having observed that we had constructed a shell cabin on the land, decided he would not reduce the price, no doubt believing that I would have to eat the loss or lose the cabin. I decided otherwise and ordered the cabin dismantled and moved. The seller, not wanting to lose the deal, promptly closed with the adjusted reduced price, and

I restored the cabin to its original position on the land. I had a choice: throw away the entire promotion by not closing on the land, or extract the source of contention by removing the cabin. Take time to deliberate, but move on when it's time to go. Here is selected copy from the promotion. Such prices are long gone, glimmering through the dreams that are no more.

CABIN CRUNCH
Nearby West VA mountains
Cabin on 2 acres $98 per mo.
$6950

"Best deal in the mountains. We put unemployed builders back to work on some of the best land we could find. In whitewater canoeing country, adjacent to 8,000-acre state hunting and fishing lands, with those famous Mountain State views."

"New 16X20' Sportsman shell cabin is stick-built from the ground up. Trouble-free, quality-crafted hideout has studs 16" on center. Blizzard-fighting exterior of pressure-treated white pine. Plus insulated windows that laugh at the cold. Fix up on weekends for fun and future profit. Check out the tax breaks. Help your children escape cares and troubles of city life. Don't they deserve a vacation place?"

Another successful cabin promotion was labeled:

YOUR HOME IN THE WOODS
from $6950 on 2 acres. Just $96 mo.

The ad showed a small log-sided cabin surrounded by trees and included this quote:

I packed my bags to search for gold
where the woods are deep and rivers cold.
Off to a cabin in a brand new land
and a brand new life to make a stand.

A feature of this promotion was a FREE CABIN, given away to a lucky visitor who attended the sale and registered for the drawing. The contest was widely advertised on the airwaves under a joint sponsorship with a Washington D.C. radio station.

Romney, W.Va.
REAL VERSUS "UNREAL" IN COLA WARS – April, 1985 –
Phil Collins

Coke drinkers began to panic when it was announced that Coca-Cola was changing its formula to create a "new" Coke. And while this change may have given the advertising community a jolt, the new formula had a negative effect on the public, and Coke profits went as flat as the taste. Taste, like truth, needs no spin.

The mythlogy of productive farmland disappearing because of urbanization has been proven false countless times, though the myth persists as a faith-based principle of radical, die-hard preservationists. In fact, simple economics is the root cause of farmland loss. Orchards were failing all over West Virginia in the mid-eighties. Farmers were drowning in debt, and many were bailing out. The forced preservation of failed farmland enterprises by rigid land control measures essentially compounds the financial plight of many farmers, denies them the opportunity to make money from dividing up their land, and often forces them into bankruptcy. Certainly, if the farmer can earn a living from his profession, he is not inclined to give it up.

Here is the desperate theme promoting one of my orchard dissolutions:

PANIC ON THE POTOMAC
Hard-luck Riverfront Bargains
Farms failing, Orchards freezing
People stealing rural land bargains every week
2-5 ac. on river from $69 per mo!

The introduction of preferential tax rates for farmers has proven to be the best remedy for encouraging agricultural enterprises. Another essential factor in the preservation of farms is the general economic health of the region where particular farms are located. A vibrant economy produces jobs, and the farmer can hopefully find employment nearby to supplement his income and to sustain operations when he is facing a period of agricultural losses. Farmland counties that do not have a strong commercial base for job creation, while imposing overly rigid controls on land ownership, inevitably face higher taxes and the loss of young people.

Here is another catchy headline used in liquidating failed orchard property:

> *Nearby Potomac Highlands*
> *Less than two hours Metro*
> # TWO-FOR-A-DOLLAR RANCH
> ## 2 AC. FOR A DOLLAR A DAY

The axis-of-evil economics that confronted us throughout the seventies and into the early eighties consisted of (1) inflation, (2) deflation, (3) high interest rates, and (4) soaring gas prices.

Economists dubbed the woeful situation as "stagflation," and they were at odds on how to grapple with price instability while inducing a healthy productivity recovery. Real estate prices were falling because of job losses, farm failures, and high interest rates that devastated the commercial sector and virtually halted new home construction.

You would be wise to watch for any signs of deflation in the real estate industry that could lead to a bursting of a bubble. Clearly, a steady climb in interest rates and a declining productivity rate would be a signal that prices had reached a market high. The country properties market is also somewhat vulnerable to drastic run-ups in gas prices; however, this oddity is often counterbalanced by terrorist threats and calamities in our cities, causing people to flee population centers at any price.

Deflation is, in essence, very bad news for hard-pressed sellers of country properties, because their real estate is effectively devalued, thus causing the sky to fall on this aspect of their investment portfolio. Financially secure buyers, picking up the pieces, can view deflation as manna from heaven, this aside from the fact that wages, profits, and business investment continue to wither away. Deflation can occur during recessions and depressions, and in such scenarios, real estate values can be impervious to interest rate cuts as a spur to economic recovery. If you observe the federal funds rate dropping below 1%, and the country is still in a recessionary mode, it is time to build liquidity and for overextended investors to run for cover. Interest rates to consumers could fall to 4 and 5% for mortgage loans; yet, in a prolonged recession or depression with mounting job losses, the real estate market could be flooded with distressed properties causing prices to nosedive. By the same token, low interest rates in a vibrant economy can lead to price stability and climbing real estate values. Moderate inflation in a healthy economy is generally good for the real estate market, since property values tend to rise with the inflation rate. High interest rates, falling prices, and a depressed economy, as I pointed out, are the ingredients for the monster economic headache of stagflation.

Toms Brook, VA
BANGLADESH REPORTS 10,000 LOST IN STORM – May, 1985 – Madonna

High waves and flooding caused by a fierce cyclone hit an island off the coast of Bangladesh, leaving the sea littered with floating bodies. The tragedy killed up to 10,000 people and left up to 250,000 homeless. Officials said the amount of lives and property lost in the storm was the worst in Bangladesh history.

River of the Valley Story

No storm had ever hit the coastline of the United States with such devastation as the one in Bangladesh, and I had experienced several gale-force storms in the Chesapeake Bay area. Fortunately, I was on land during these tempests and not at sea. I had been in the Bay area a few weeks before the following incident, where I had lost out on the purchase of a marina and proposed development, this when I refused to hit the million mark on my offer. So I was ready to outbid the Devil for a waterfront peninsula on the Shenandoah River when it came up for auction. As often happens at country property auctions, adjoiners are frequently the strongest opposing bidders, and they are usually primed to pay more than top dollar for land that joins their property.

The bidding in this case went out of sight to the highest price ever paid for a farm along the river at the time–in the lofty six figures–and I won the bid, later selling part of the farm to my opponent bidder, who did not depend on agriculture for a living. Farm profits had crashed, and I used the theme of declining farmland prices in my subsequent promotion.

I stressed the fact that most people are too busy waiting for bargains to spot a real steal.

Anybody who could read the papers knew about troubled farms. But I advised the reader that when the marketplace had discounted all the bad news, prices were already climbing. By 2003, the price for a few acres on this part of the river had quadrupled.

Sometimes a deal sounds too good to be true. So, to validate the offer, I closed the ad with a summary of facts:

Important Facts

If you build, you will be using your own well or cistern for water and a private in-ground sewage disposal system. Drinking water is available at reasonable depths. Untreated water may be pumped from the river. Roads are gravel-surfaced. Some are state-maintained. Others are private.

You pay $150 per year for road upkeep. Yearly taxes on 3 acres are about $75 at current rates. Electricity and telephone are ready when you are. You get a general warranty deed. You do not have to pay off the mortgage for the land to be yours. Land values, and the profitable resale of your property, are affected by changing economic conditions and interest rate factors. Therefore, no projected future value of this property can legitimately be given.

Cheapeake Bay, VA
DIVERS RECOVERING MILLIONS IN TREASURE – July, 1985
– Sting

In 1622, a hurricane swept through the Florida Keys, sinking the Spanish galleon Atocha. For 363 years, stacks of silver bars and thousands of gold, silver, and copper coins lay buried in the silt and mud of the ocean floor. For 16 years, the Fisher family had searched for this hidden treasure, losing two of their own in diving expeditions. In hauling buried treasure up from the deep, it could appear that the virtue of the effort lays more in the *struggle* for riches than in the prize itself. Put your mind to finding opportunity and it will seek you out.

As I remarked earlier, I had lost a bayfront opportunity and was hell bent to find another. When the break came to me I seized it immediately, polished it into six waterfront farms and transferred a veritable land treasure to six lucky buyers. Here was the offer:

Unheard of
BAYFRONT OPPORTUNITY
Valuable waterfront up for grabs on Chesapeake Bay and Intracoastal Waterway. Charted to the Atlantic Ocean.
5-6 ac. farms on the Potomac River and Chesapeake Bay off Intracoastal Waterway from $25,000. Retire like a millionaire on the sunny shores of the Chesapeake Bay. Now is the time to plan for those days when you are slowing down . . .When your children are grown . . . and when you'll want a milder climate and fun-filled days beside the sea.

The half-page ad showed a photo of a lonely sandy beach, with rolling surf and a single piece of driftwood in the foreground. I wanted to convey a sense of untrampled beachfront and the absence of crowds.

I broke a larger farm into five smaller farms, giving each of them a specific name and a board fence entrance: Blue Crab Cove, Shipwreck Reef, Surfside Meadows, Bayfront Farm, and Broadwaters by the Bay. Prices ranged from $25,000 to $49,500 and were based on the amount of beachfront and acreage, and the type of terrain.

To repeat a fact revealed earlier in this book, the Chesapeake Bay is the world's largest estuary. It's a small ocean, with 6,000 miles of shoreline. If you own land on the water, only the size of your boat keeps the world from your beach. Five or six acres on such a beach would be a very valuable asset. But the waterfront location notwithstanding, those were troubled times, in 1985, for farmland. And beachside opportunities, though rare, still existed. But few people knew about them.

I'll return to what I have often said: that when everyone knows about a troubled Miami Beach or Ocean City, the time for rapid appreciation in price is usually past. Most people are too busy waiting for a bottom in the market to recognize a ground floor opportunity in country and waterfront properties. Your primary motivation may be to tie up prime waterfront at a bargain price. Even more important is the quality of your destination point. How many people want to go there? Does it suit your lifestyle? What does it have to offer? To gain perspective, I likened owning a small waterfront farm near Reedville in 1985 to buying acreage on Hilton Head Island in 1965, 20 years before. Few people can now afford a waterfront lot (much less acreage) on that resort island.

In 1985, a bayfront farm at Reedville, VA, was affordable. But not today. The trick is to find a uniquely located resort or town yet to explode as a destination point. Buy waterfront in such an area before the crowd. If you can afford acreage, rather than a lot, so much the better. When you own five acres on the Bay, you own an estate, or compound, such as the rich own on Cape Cod, or at Hyannis Port. Reedville, though not a playground for the rich, is a quaint fishing village on the southeast tip of the Northern Neck of Virginia, where the mighty Potomac River enters the Chesapeake Bay. In 1911-12, the town was proclaimed the richest town per capita in the country.

In 1985, Reedville was still boasting of being the "Number One Fishing Port in the U.S."

Many grand Victorian homes reflect the village's prosperous past. Many old homes have been restored. When I sold these farms, an underutilized sewage treatment plant was in place and ready for those who followed and who settled for homes and cottages off the beach. Thousands of people flock to Reedvile every year for superb sailing, power boating, and deep sea fishing.

The village also serves as an embarkation point for cruise ships to Tangier and Smith Islands in the Chesapeake Bay.

Tangier Island, with about 600 closely knit inhabitants, is an historic fishing community on low-lying land constantly threatened by a marauding sea and totally dependent for its survival on boat delivery of supplies, medical attention, and tourism from the mainland. The island has few cars, and transportation essentials are largely met with bicycles and golf carts. A regularly scheduled mail boat offers access to and from the mainland town of Crisfield, Maryland. Tour boats set out from the Virginia side of the Bay from May through September. Television and church activities appear to occupy most of the spare time of the islanders, whose income is mostly derived from crabbing. I still own a small waterfront peninsula in that region and very much enjoy my visits to the Northern Neck.

Fredericksburg, VA
BUSH OBSERVES END OF WORLD WAR II – August, 1985 – Whitney Houston

Speaking from the deck of the carrier Enterprise, Vice President Bush announced that the United States was ready to adopt a strong military posture to deter sudden attacks and aggression against this country. He urged Americans not to close their eyes to evil and said that our unwillingness to prepare could imperil our future. His remarks were made in noting the fortieth anniversary of the end of World War II.

In addition, 1985 marked the end of a prolonged downward spiral in land prices. Investors with foresight who purchased land in those days around Fredericksburg, Virginia framed their own small fortunes. Due to widespread farm failures, the nation was awash in agricultural land. Despite this surplus, land within 50 miles of most major cities was rising in value due to housing pressures. At the time, the National Association of Homebuilders reported that the cost of developed lots accounted for 25% of the price on a new, detached home.

Investors and speculators were actively driving up prices on outlying farmland, this to fuel the demand for housing. The same is true today. Local land-use laws continue to stymie developers, jacking up costs on finished lots. As time progresses, the consumer's hope for that idyllic place in the country can seem like a star on a tremulous sea. Many with this dream will be forced into clustered housing and new planned communities. In one promotion around Fredericksburg, VA, I tried to make consumers aware of these facts. Here is a headline from a *Washington Post* display ad:

The current land glut and how you can profit from 10-acre estates just 45 miles from 495

Pockets of enormous value existed at the time, if the consumer knew where to look for land. This was because many investors and speculators were waiting for the new tax laws to be enacted. Will tax shelters be removed on farmland and second homes? Such uncertainty had created a temporary window of opportunity for buyers of country property. With prices on some land at a standstill, those who bought land from me during this promotion picked up 10 to 20 acres at a fraction of their worth today.

10-acre commutable estates
north of Fredericksburg from $12,950 to $19,950
with access to Rappahannock River

Area transportation officials were predicting an emerging megalopolis extending along I-95 from Washington D.C. to Richmond, Virginia. This meant crowded conditions and higher land prices were in the cards. Since I was offering 10-acre estates just off I-95 on the D.C. side of Fredericksburg, wise consumers and investors were buying in the path of progress.

Could anyone find 10 acres that cheap in Fairfax County? In Loudoun County? Or in Fauquier County? (A few of the fastest-growing population centers in the U.S.–all located outside of the nation's capital.) Sorry. The smart crowd got there first. To fully understand the value of the offer, consider this fact. The Homer Hoyt Institute, a D.C. land research firm, reported in 1985 that the average cost of a finished residential lot had reached $23,732 in 1980. (The cost of a well and septic system on country properties are usually offset by user fees and hookup charges for public sewer and water on finished lots.)

An unusual feature of this offer was the giveaway of a FREE TELEPHONE to all who called for an appointment to inspect the property. Of course, consumers were also invited to view the property on their own without an appointment. By 2003, some of these properties had increased in value by five or six times their original purchase prices.

This opportunity for consumers was fought tooth and nail by entrenched political forces who claimed sovereignty over the destiny of land use within the county, and who would preserve the countryside as common ground for the so-called masses to *observe*, and the elite to enjoy.

One group posted sentries at the project to prevent landowners from using an old right-of-way to the river, this under the guise of "saving the river." A few local big-wigs protested the "loss of farmland" when, in reality, the land was mostly forest. Some elected or appointed officials denounced the project as a malignant assault on "smart growth" and attempted unsuccessfully to defeat the development's approval by abridging their own development regulations. One hot head vested in a "preservation cult" called me up and told me to stop running ads saying there was too much farmland when we were–in the heat of his thoughts–burning crops and cooking up a food shortage by developing land purchased from farmers.

Front Royal, VA
U.S. IS A DEBTOR NATION–1st TIME SINCE 1914 – Sept., 1985
– Dire Straits

Commerce Department figures showed the U.S. was $30 billion behind in its current accounts with its foreign trading partners, this wiping out a $30 billion surplus the year before.

The deficit is a compilation of trade in goods and services, and the shortfall threatened a run on the dollar due to an imbalance in dividends and interest payments doled out to foreigners. Essentially, the nation was awash in debt, though the amount was minuscule in perspective to deficits yet to come. Few investors realized at the time that the land market had bottomed out. Except for a brief period in late 1985, some banks had left their vaults open. Consider this offer.

HOW TO ROB A BANK
Legally!
Front Royal, VA . Foreclosure property. Walk in and steal 10 lots on D.C. side of town–2 on river, 3 back lots (1/4 to 8 ac.) 1/4 mi. frontage on Shenandoah River. Old boat house w/water and septic system. Ideal for canoe livery, family retreat, or fishing camp. Just $18,950. Long-term bank financing with almost nothing down.

B.K. HAYNES REAL ESTATE

Less than 20 years later, a single camping lot on the river would be selling for the entire purchase price of the ten lots–and some lucky investor ended up with an unprecedented ¼ mile of riverfront for a song.

West Virginia
FLOOD OF CENTURY HITS W. VA AND VA – Nov., 1985 –
Stevie Wonder

I was staying at a motel in Romney, W. VA while working on a liquidation project when a local cabin builder knocked on my door and said I had better get out of town fast if I wanted to beat the flood waters on the Cacapon River. I packed up in a hurry and hit the road for Capon Bridge, crossing the river just before the flood waters washed over the pavement on the bridge. My destination was Richmond, Virginia where I had another land sale campaign in progress.

By the time I reached Front Royal, the Shenandoah River was over its banks, and the Potomac River near Washington was next in line. A stationary front hovered over the region, dumping up to 10 times as much water into the rivers and their tributaries than the beds could hold.

Near Front Royal, the South Fork of the Shenandoah River emerged into the front yard of one of the area's most historic sites, once part of a larger farm that I developed along the river. This ad is printed in its entirety to show you what you could have been purchased for $179,500, property that had probably tripled in value less than 20 years later.

UNIQUE WATERFRONT ESTATE
Cut $40,000. Front Royal, VA - only 1 hour out

Poca Bella farm was built in 1822 for the founder of the first bank in Virginia. A past garden week feature, it has been nominated to the National Register of Historic Places. Decorated for Christmas, it is a scene from Currier & Ives and an impressive entertainment home through all four seasons. Evidence of prehistoric Indian settlements have been discovered along its river banks. Completely restored main house of brick and frame has electric heat, wide-pine floors, AC, 2-4 BR, 2 ½ BA. 15' X 17' LR w/ fireplace, Florida room w/ Anderson windows and spectacular views of river, Blue Ridge, and Skyline Drive. Large eat-in kit., w/ enclosed fireplace, walk-in pantry, compactor, DW, disposal, microwave oven, double-door refrigerator/ freezer and breakfast bar. Lower level has washer/dryer, sink, sep. heat, pvt. entrance for main and guests. 900 ft. on popular Shenandoah. Ideal farm to raise show horses. 10-acre grounds include caretaker's trailer, machine shed, silo, feeding shed, box stalls, and split-rail fencing. 2 wells and river pumping system, Was $225,000. Now $179,500. Owners moving, have other interests. 95% financing possible. B.K HAYNES REAL ESTATE

In Richmond, the James River was about to assault the low-lying part of town. Back in West Virginia, entire communities had been wiped out. Trailers, homes, and cabins floated down the rivers like flotsam. Hundreds of people were killed, and bloated livestock carcasses were strewn along the river banks. Upper reaches of the Potomac swept into towns, invading main streets and even entering bank vaults, drenching currency and depositing mud on vital records.

West Virginia
THOUSANDS FLEE ATOMIC MISHAP IN RUSSIA – April, 1986
– Kiss

> Danger levels man and brute, and
> all are fellows in their need
>
> *–Byron*

Russia fell to her knees and asked West Germany and Sweden to help fight a fire in a nuclear reactor core at Chernobyl in the Ukraine. Hours after the disaster, monitoring stations in Sweden, Finland and Denmark reported abnormally high radioactivity levels. The Soviets broadcasted the incident–believed to be the worst in the history of nuclear power. Scores of people were said to be dead and injured in the catastrophe that caused the immediate evacuation and resettlement of 15,000 residents and the anticipated abandonment of the city of Pripyat.

Security in this nuclear age can be likened to the mother of danger and the grandmother of destruction, while adventure belongs to the essence of civilization. The marriage of danger and adventure have always been lures to those with nothing else to lose. So, in the spring of 1986, I used this theme in a successful campaign to attract low-end land buyers into the scenic Potomac Highlands of West Virginia, this where they could establish themselves on a two-acre plot of land for as little as $75 down and $25 per month.

The region reeks with charisma, adventure, and carries an element of danger. I called this particular development the "Badlands." It is located near a desolate wilderness area named Dolly Sods–a region that resembles northern Canada, where adventurers can challenge perilous whitewater rivers and man-killing rock climbs at Seneca Rocks, or explore the savage Smoke Holes –legendary hideout of Indians and moonshiners.

Fierce storms rip through the 3,000-ft. elevation region hurling small boats from Mount Storm Lake as if they were matchboxes. And the thunder from Black Water Falls in the fabled Canaan Valley, the highest valley east of the Rockies, can sometimes be heard from miles around. The region, encompassing a primitive national forest inhabited by bear and wildcat, is often isolated from normal civilization by Sierra-sized snow drifts. Why would anyone want to settle in such an environment? Cheap land? Adventure? Opportunity? I was swamped with respondents to the following ad, an abbreviated version of the actual two-column newspaper ad that included prices, terms, and the color and adventure I have just described.

SETTLERS WANTED

For cheap 2-10 acre ranches in West Virginia "Badlands." Open and wooded with spectacular views. Some border a mountain lake and bush airstrip. Others have raging streams. Largely unrestricted. Camp or build. Opportunity to claim land at depression-level prices. Cheap because region is devastated by rampant floods and failing farms. Values are real. Not a gimmick to sell land. People stealing bargains every week. Lower prices doubtful in future. Approx. 147 miles west in Allegheny Mountains, once barriers to the settlement of the West. A 2 ½ to 3 hour trip. Unfinished roads. High creeks and mud likely. Bargain of a lifetime to first who come. Deposit back if dissatisfied before closing.

B.K. HAYNES REAL ESTATE

Middletown, VA
TERRORISM IS TOPIC OF TOKYO SUMMIT – May, 1986 –
Madonna

U.S. Secretary of State George Shultz said, in reference to the Libyan leader, Colonel Muammar Khadafy, "You've had it, pal." In April, U.S. planes had bombed several Libyan military bases as punishment for Libya's international "reign of terror." A statement signed by leaders of the U.S., Britain, France, Canada, Italy, Japan, and West Germany at the economic summit meeting labeled international terrorism as a scourge that "must be fought relentlessly and without compromise."

Since 1984, following a business conference in Maui, Hawaii, I had become acquainted with a well-meaning spiritualist couple and had planned to travel with my wife on a metaphysical group trip to India, the seventh largest country in the world, and home to about one of every seven people on earth. Official figures in the late sixties showed that overcrowded India had an average of eight times as many people per square mile as did the United States, and that most lived in farm villages averaging 500 people. The city of Calcutta reportedly had the country's largest population density of about 75,000 persons per square mile. Most marriages in India are arranged by the family, and the culture considers nuptials as relationships between families rather than individuals.

I had been married for 27 years, and my wife had always been a close companion throughout my travels. Now her illness had weakened her to the point where she could not make the trip. Suddenly I was beset with a strange feeling that part of me was going away. It was not like losing a limb, because that is of a physical nature; the feeling came to me in a spiritual sense.

In deeply religious terms it would be like mankind is one spiritual body. When one part of that body dies, or is about to die, an emotional feeling takes hold when we feel the separation taking place; yet, though the physical form passes on, the unseen power of love, presumably the cement of Heaven, can continue to unite us, and death cannot forever divide us. My first thought was to find someone to take her place. But that turned out to be an impractical possibility, so I went on the trip alone. But, needless to say, the pleasures of travel don't seem gratifying without a companion.

As it turned out, the trip would have been much too arduous for a person in ill health.

Still searching for a cure to my wife's illness, I delved into eastern metaphysical thought and, in the process, I began an almost fruitless study of comparative religions.

India is still overwhelmingly a country of Hindus (85%), with a Moslem minority of about 10%. From New Delhi, we ventured into the Himalayas on a train packed with soldiers making their way to the contentious Indian frontier with Pakistan, a segmented country consisting mostly of Moslems. In Darjeeling, I caught a glimpse of Mount Everest before it became enveloped in clouds. In Calcutta, amidst the squalor, poverty, and people sleeping in the streets, I was not surprised to see Communist slogans painted on the walls of buildings.

I left the group one morning, wading into a swarm of bicycles, carts, and animals in search of Mother Teresa's hospice for the poor. A turbaned Sikh cab driver knew where it was and led me through narrow twisting streets, where buildings covered almost every square foot of land, and then to a cluster of low-slung dwellings where I found an American girl in a *sari* cuddling an impoverished Indian child. I left a monetary donation and returned to our hotel, only to be scolded by the spiritualist tour leaders for venturing out on my own. I suspected my basic Christian beliefs had something to do with the reprimand, since any coherent spiritual infrastructure within the realm of metaphysics appears now to be nonexistent.

In the Himalayas, many in the group sought out a ritual of meditation at a Buddhist monastery almost as if they were addicts assembling for a game of bridge. This is not to demonize or marginalize the meditative process. It's just that meditation has not been a spiritual exercise that I have cultivated. However, I have found God's favor to be at the ends of my prayers.

In one village hostel by the Ganges River *(though I never prayed for better accommodations)* we stayed in a lodge with bathroom facilities that, in terms of the western world, would be far more appropriate to those in the corner of an Iraqi prison cell. Squatting was another exercise that I was never fond of.

In the late sixties, it was estimated that India ranked fifth among the nations of the world in farmland. Seven out of every 10 adult Indians were farmers, two-thirds of whom owned their own land. The average size of farms was said to be less than five acres, while the average-sized American farm at the time was about 350 acres. Most of these small farms were subsidized by the government, and the farmers were barely able to live off of their crops. The vast majority of these farmers–men and women–were destined to die in debt, and they seldom had enough to eat.

India's strong religious heritage has produced much enlightenment, conflict, and confusion among the peoples of the world. Gurus from the sub-continent have often promulgated their message of universal love, peace, and societal harmony to cultural icons in the western world, such as the Beatles and other movie, theatrical, literary, and success-motivational personalities, who have in turn become disciples, twisters, and promoters of Eastern metaphysical thought in various, heightened degrees. One source of this diverse spiritual knowledge is the Theosophical Society, an organization formed in the 1920's by a cabal of controversial spiritualists to counterbalance the organized Christian church as the predominant religious force in western culture.

The group is based near the coastal city of Madras in the Deccan, a huge plateau in India that forms most of the southern peninsula of that country. The region consists of farmland and forests and is separated from the northern plains by mountain ranges. In simple terms, what this spiritualistic group has done is to amalgamate the world's religions into a hodge-podge of unstructured beliefs without any liturgical foundation and in a convoluted form that belies the Holy Trinity and lays waste to the concept of vicarious redemption through Christ.

Jesus, to the Theosophical way of thinking, was a mere, though acceptable, prophet. Theosophists believe there is no son of God, that the Bible is a fairy tale. Something called the Great White Brotherhood is supposedly in control of our destinies. And there exists on the higher planes of the universe an exalted group of "Masters" to whom we must pray and beg for guidance through endless reincarnations. In other words, fellow Christians, throw out your beliefs and start all over again with your spiritual orientation. For committed Christians, it all sounds like a quick path to the Devil and an attempted hijacking of the soul.

Consider this: If a political or religious force found it possible to annihilate the Bible, and with it, all of its influences, the base spiritual system of the entire moral world would be destroyed. Why then would a moral person want to bet his or her life on those who would darken the light of faith and undermine the credibility of the Bible as the living word of God?

West Virginia
U.S. CELEBRATES CENTENNIAL OF STATUE OF LIBERTY –
July 4, 1986 – Billy Ocean

The day after a spectacular fireworks celebration in New York Harbor, President Reagan had lunch with French President Franscois Mitterand to commemorate this country's independence and to discuss arms control. France, of course, had delivered to the U.S. our revered bronze Statue of Liberty 100 years earlier that has become a beacon for immigrants and oppressed people seeking freedom and opportunity on our shores. Aside from our conflict with France over its deceitful behavior during the war with Iraq, the two countries have much in common.

For example, China, France and the U.S. are the largest apple-producing countries in the world. In the U.S., the apple crop is worth close to $300 million a year. Yet despite the fact that the apple is the most valuable of all the fruits grown on trees, it can be a money-losing crop when subjected to bad weather conditions, such as prolonged drought and premature frost. That was the case in the mid-nineteen-eighties throughout parts of northern West Virginia and Virginia, when hundreds of orchards went on the block.

The Birth of the "Fruit Ranch"

The largest and most valuable apple in the world is actually an island. In 1616, the British and French were at war over the Spice Islands in the East Indies. At the conclusion of the war, and in return for a concession of another prized island noted for its spices, the Dutch yielded control of a barren off-shore piece of real estate to England. That island, now known as the "Big Apple," is Manhattan.

In 1986, a large and prominent apple orchard operation in West Virginia, about two hours west of Washington D.C., had gone under and was sold at auction. I purchased a section of the orchard that I felt would make a nice project and proceeded with a development plan. The concept I had in mind was a small affordable orchard that almost anyone could own and develop into a place to live. No need to plant trees and wait for them to bear fruit. This was largely an operating orchard with a productive crop in good years. If the owners did not want to harvest the apples, they could get together and retain an experienced orchardist to keep up the trees in return for the bulk of the crop.

California in West Virginia
FRUIT RANCHES FOR SALE
$3950 - $8950 for 3 to 5 acres. *None higher.*

One of the first geniuses of mail order was a man named John Harvey Kellogg who, in the 1890's, invented Corn Flakes as a health food. Incredibly, he successfully advertised that people should not order his product, because the cereal was in short supply, and he did not have enough to meet the demand. In one of my orchard promotions, I used a reverse twist on this concept by promoting the idea that the consumer could own a product that promised immediate satisfaction and infinite gratification. Here is part of the winning ad:

HAVE YOUR SITE AND EAT IT

Looking for some cool high ground? Now you can own the sky and get nutritious fruits for the rest of your life. Highest known fruit orchard in nearby W. VA. 6 acres of valuable productive apple trees at close to 2,000 feet elevation. **$8950. 90% fin.** See 50 miles into W. VA., MD., PA., and Virginia. . .

West Virginia
ICELAND ARMS CONTROL SUMMIT FAILS – October, 1986 – Janet Jackson

President Reagan and Soviet President Gorbachev packed up their bags and left Reykjavik, Iceland, each blaming the other for a breakdown in talks over the U.S. initiative to deploy a missile system in space called the Strategic Defense Initiative. Gorbachev said "only a madman" could go forward with arms control if such a system is built and deployed. The Soviets wanted a 10-year moratorium on "Star Wars" testing. Reagan believed that U.S. development and implementation of S.D.I. was the best way to resolve the issue of arms control.

In 1880, Irish tenant farmers took up arms against a British estate manager in County Mayo, Ireland. Their grievance was over his unwillingness to reduce rents during a disastrous harvest and his use of constables to evict them when they protested. The estate manager was subsequently shunned by local residents and suppliers to the extent that he fled the country in disgrace. His name was Charles *Boycott*. This tactic of disencouragement and disengagement used by the Irish tenant farmers spread throughout the world and became known as "boycotting."

In the fall of 1986, quite to the contrary of alienating the populace, I was interested in encouraging renters, investors, and hard-pressed consumers to participate in land ownership through the underpriced opportunities then emerging in nearby West Virginia. The favorable circumstances at the time could be likened to the old adage of "Go west, young man" to seek your fortune. Here is one of my advertise-

ments for a new breed of adventuresome settlers and homesteaders to
occupy a large orchard property that had fallen upon hard times:

HOMESTEADERS WANTED

To settle and improve distressed properties in the scenic Potomac Highlands. Drafty, rundown buildings in foggy mountain hollows. Some
buried in dark woods at the end of rough roads. Occasional hazardous
journey over wild creeks and fierce rivers. Bridges sometimes out.
Constant threat of unwanted wild creatures. Possible feelings of isolation. Hard-scrabble dwellings wrinkled and wrecked by time and
neglect, now abandoned to bats and tormenting winds. Considerable
repair work necessary to reclaim. Area ravaged by recent floods and
failing farms. Personal satisfaction, a new life, and possible future
profits to the first who come.

The ad described a small orchard village with a patched-up two-
story house with barn, migrant workers' cinderblock dorm with bath
house, a 2-story, 3-bay metal and cinderblock garage with attached 4-
vehicle shed, a massive 3-story packing shed with loading docks, plus
an assembly yard and a small fishing pond, together with seven acres
of land traversed by a gurgling mountain stream. The village was supplied with gas, oil, and diesel pumps, water lines from a spring, and
dusk-to-dawn lights. Some lucky buck stole the whole village for
$39,500.

Another homesteader settled in a 31-acre lost valley retreat back in
the boondocks accessible only by a jeep trail. The forested land, with
a beat-up house, was composed of valuable hardwood trees, primitive
rock formations, deer-infested meadows, and a year-round stream. The
pioneer buyer staked this claim for a mere $595 per acre.

One adventurer, tired of city life, settled on a 17-acre "Hermit's
Hideout" that was difficult to reach through a primeval forest, where
the sale of the big trees would have more than paid for the place. The
tract included a ghostly run-down house, storage building, spring, and
pond. He paid just $8950 for this discovery.

If you were out looking for country properties and you came upon
this depressed enterprise, you would have discovered a failed orchard
with rotted apples littered on the ground to be feasted upon by creatures of the wild, decrepit faded buildings fallen into disrepair, an overgrown forest thick with thorny vines, and rutted roads winding through

a foggy mountain hollow, the scene inviting your shiny new car to get stuck and painted with mud. Hardly a hospitable environment for city folks. Yet when broken down into homesteads, the orchard was actually a diamond in the rough and a treasure trove of bargains for new buyers.

GUARDING YOUR TREASURE
I'll give thrice as much land,
to any deserving friend;
But in the way of a bargain, mark me
I'll (quibble) on the ninth part of a hair
– *Shakespeare*

When subdividing country property, I am occasionally confronted with hard-nosed customers who seem to "know it all." They know that whatever price I have placed on the property is too high. They know everything that is wrong with the land.

They are wise to every sales pitch ever delivered and can knock it out of the park with one swing of aggressive rhetoric. They'll say, "The land is 'too steep' or 'that land's too flat.' 'This is too wooded,'" they'll exclaim, while snidely remarking that the next property you show them is "for billy goats." One of the cynical comments that makes me cringe is "You'll need a helicopter to get in here." You could be standing on a hilltop with the "know-it-all" customer and have to contend with the threat of floods. You say, "no way" and they cite the story of Noah and the Ark.

Dominance and belligerence is often the game of the "know it alls." You take them in the woods, and they complain about the trees blocking their view. You show them a beautiful open field, and they complain about having to mow the grass. A quiet country road is too dusty.

A paved road has too many cars. The sound of a distant freight train is annoying. You take them back in the boondocks for their precious seclusion, and they say, "What kind of a rip-off is this? I don't see any other houses around here. You couldn't pay me to live this far out in the sticks."

Yes sir, some people know a bargain when they see it. While it is understandable that the absolutely perfect piece of property does not exist, and that specific complaints about a property's deficiencies are legitimate, the constant harping on the inadequacies of the offer by prospective buyers can lead to conflict and misunderstanding and can be just as offensive as high-pressure salesmanship. As a general rule, many buyers engage in aggressive behavior because of intent. They want to belittle the offer to get a concession on price. A required tactic of this approach is to take control of the presentation. I have found that when you lose control over the presentation you are in danger of depleting your treasure because you may have the tendency to cut your price beyond your wishes. This does not mean you cannot be conciliatory. You simply must be aware of how you are being manipulated.

The hard-nosed character comes armed with arguments and information he has gleaned from previous encounters with sellers and their agents. Some of these verbal skirmishes have produced perceived benefits for this character through emotional antics such as intimidation.

He has discovered that, by finding flaws in properties and weaknesses in your presentation, he can dominate the discussion to achieve his ends. For example, if I am advertising a piece of country property as a "bargain," Mr. "Know-it All" will take the position that the establishment of worth on the property is merely my questionable judgment and not his own, and he will sniff at my facts and make repeated reference to the property's drawbacks and attempt to trounce the property's value by quoting some talking head's alarm about an impending real estate crash.

If I were an inexperienced salesperson with limited knowledge, the "know-it-all" could conceivably flatten me by taking over the presentation, this to discredit me and beat the offer down into an outrageous attempt to mislead him and pick his pocket.

It is obviously a good and practical idea for consumers to shop for bargains, though some offers may be morally suspect because one person's gain is theoretically another's loss. Morality aside, when selling country properties I try not to directly oppose the belligerent buyer in a confrontational way. The tendency would be for me to get defensive, and the end result would not be worth the effort. Sometimes I just have to accept the fact that there is no middle ground and take a powder. Temperament can be likened to a thermometer that reflects upon your character.

It is often in vain that we attempt to control our tempers. But no one likes to be around a hot-headed person who is constantly losing his cool.

While in graduate school studying communications at American University, I was on stage auditioning for a play when a hot-headed "know-it-all" director tried to beat my brains out with an unremitting assault of insults, but I wouldn't break. I was young then and possessed of a strong will and strength. Had I been prone to violence and unable to keep my cool, I would probably have leaped from the stage and knocked him off of his arrogant perch. Later in life, while studying alternative religions, an intemperate spiritual guru tried unsuccessfully to mesmerize me out of my body in a prolonged meditative ritual. The arduous episode produced nothing but a pound of sweat out of his body while leaving me physically calm and my mind still intact.

In rare cases I will encounter the benevolent "know-it-all" whose attitude may be arrogant and full of fiery bluster but whose friendly demeanor occasionally breaks through like sunshine on a cloudy day, thus allowing the blending of two strong wills. In such cases, I'm more likely to stick around and try to work out a deal.

Building Castles in the Air

West Virginia
THIN PROFITS FADE FROM INSIDER TRADING–Nov., 1986 – Bon Jovi

Investors seeking high yields from junk bonds saw their gilded castles come crashing down to earth in the midst of the greatest stock market boom in history. Ivan Boesky, the "Spiderman" of Wall Street, who wove a web of deceit by using illegal inside information to trade in stocks and securities, was hammered to the wall with 100 million dollars in penalties and barred for life from the U.S. securities industry. High-flying Boesky asked for redemption and agreed to squeal on other Wall Street figures involved in the corrupt scheme. Billions of dollars in profits vanished overnight in the scandal that took unsuspecting investors to the cleaners. High-yielding, high-risk junk bonds are usually sold to the public to raise money for corporate takeovers.

In one of my distressed-orchard promotions for a partnership, I developed a campaign to build chalets so far up in the air that cabin owners could view the four states of West Virginia, Virginia, Maryland, and Pennsylvania. I used a newspaper ad to display a castle-like chalet on a peak, with the world spread out below. A happy family waved from the deck. Here is the ad:

UNCOMMON CABIN AND TAX SHELTER
from $17,760
Shelter income with interest write-off on second home

Afraid of heights? Then you'd better forget this unusual Alpine Chalet lost in the heavens overlooking four states and the Potomac River. New 560 ft. shell home is built strong as a castle to withstand howling winds (and stray spears). Unique vacation lodge is constructed to last well into the 21st century, with studs 16" on center like in the finest homes. Crash-proof sliding glass doors will hold against low-lying aircraft (maybe a seagull). Complete with (1) insulated windows (2) termite shields (3) blizzard-fighting white pine siding (4) rock-solid deck for entertaining friends and (5) sleeping loft. High altitude home is set on solid foundation (not piers). Out-of-the-ordinary mini- chateau is guarded by ranks of apple trees. Interior room studding is provided at no extra charge. Ready now for your choice of paneling. Roomy uncommon cabin is guaranteed to give you class (at least it will make you look rich). Also for vacationers, deep thinkers, creative people, wilderness lovers, outdoorsmen, and investors, all of whom should be handy with tools if you're going to finish it yourself. Close to Canaan Valley, Wisp Ski Area, and state hunting lands. With quick access to the Potomac River (by hang glider). Plus get tax breaks under new reform. **B.K. HAYNES REAL ESTATE**

Fredericksburg, VA
LOSS OF FAMILY FARMS HIGHEST IN 50 YEARS – Jan., 1987
– Duran Duran

"No Pay" Dirt

Thomas Jefferson once said that the small independent farmer was the backbone of the country. Unfortunately for nostalgia buffs, the eternal landscape of the past has given way to practical economics. As I pointed out earlier in this book, most small farmers, as a rule, simply cannot make ends meet in this day and age while contending with falling prices for their products. To continue farming, most farmers must hold down second jobs.

Economy of scale in the industry has increasingly assigned the production of much of our food supplies to huge agricultural operations. Even the liberal and controversial government subsidies have not prevented the loss of small farms. These farms are rapidly being transferred to other segments of the population who, aside from hobby farming, will use them in diverse ways and forms such as homesites, vacation places, retirement abodes, hunting lands, developments, and investment opportunities. Here is how the wooded portion of a farm was reconfigured in 1987 for the segment of our population then moving to the countryside.

Attention: Commuters!

YOUR *Affordable* ESTATE
near LAKE ANNA

7 to 19 acre estates on state paved roads
without the expensive paved road price

from **$14,950** to $39,950

These estates are just eight miles from a 13,000-acre inland ocean with over 200 miles of shoreline for power boating, yachting, fishing, swimming, scuba diving, sailing, and waterskiing. And they're just 27 miles from Fredericksburg for a quick commute to D.C. All were sold with driveways and board fence entrances.

A study by the Metropolitan Washington Council of Governments concluded in 1987 that households on the fringe of Washington D.C. would probably double by the year 2000. The D.C. metropolitan area extended at the time to the Pennsylvania border in the north, south and east to the Chesapeake Bay, and west to the Appalachian Trail. By the year 2003, the D.C. metropolitan area had been pushed farther north and west to the Virginia and West Virginia line. A 50-mile commute in 1987 had stretched to a 75-mile commute. People are fed up with drug pressures on their children, crime in the streets, high taxes, outrageous home costs, and crowded living conditions. Look at this pitch for bargains a few smart commuters hit for a profitable home run in the winter of 1987:

CRAZY TO SELL 10 AC. ESTATES
NEAR D.C. FOR UNDER $20,000?

8 to 10 acre wooded estates $14,950 to $19,950

During the late fifties and into the sixties, well-known D.C.-area communities such as Frederick, Maryland, and Fredericksburg, Middleburg, and Leesburg, all in Virginia, were considered by many city dwellers as "out in the boonies." In 1987 you might have found 10 acres in "them thar parts" for around $35-75K. And local growth curbs and rapid settlement beyond the suburbs was slowly creating a high-priced noose to further strangle the ambitions of those seeking an affordable place in the country. Some developers thought I was crazy to sell nearby acreage so cheap. But it was the cheapest form of advertising. So I just kept on selling cheap land.

Winchester, VA
JAPANESE BUYING HEAPS OF U.S REAL ESTATE –March,1987
– Bon Jovi

Tora! Tora! Tora! was the signal that launched the Japanese attack on Pearl Harbor and thrust the U.S. into World War II. The battle cry meant "Climb the Mountain." No such blatant signal had been detected for a new assault on U.S. territory by the Japanese that began in the mid-eighties. Behind the storm clouds of March 1987, it became evident that aggressive investors from Japan had quietly established a significant beachhead in Hawaii by gobbling up nine of the 14 hotels on Waikiki Beach in Honolulu.

In New York, it was reported that one Japanese operative had paid $1,000 per square foot for the Tiffany Building in New York. Further investigation revealed that, because of a devalued dollar and high real estate prices in Japan, tons of excess Japanese capital had been dropped on construction projects throughout the United States, and there was talk of an inevitable new war with the "Land of the Rising Sun." The world's richest man was a real estate baron from Japan who was then worth $21 billion.

John Jacob Astor, once the richest man in the United States, signed closing papers on a lot he had sold near Wall Street at the bargain price of $8,000. The buyer, running numbers in his head, figured he could dump the lot in a few years and maybe pick up a profit of $4,000. Suddenly rich, the buyer spread his wings in front of Astor by remarking as much to the country's richest man. The financier sent the buyer into a tailspin with his retort, "Yes, but by the time your lot is worth $12,000, I will have turned your $8,000 into $80,000 by buying and selling 80 lots on Canal Street." But even high-flyers in real estate can come crashing down to earth. Bubbles can occur. And they always burst.

Ben Hecht was a U.S. playwright, novelist, and scriptwriter who achieved great wealth from the Florida real estate game in the 1920's.

He correctly predicted a bubble and suddenly became very fat. Friends remarked that he had gained weight. But it wasn't from overindulging himself with fine cuisine that he appeared excessively rotund. He saw the frenzy for Florida land as out of control, with prices and projected profits ballooning to unsupportable heights. Fearing the banks would go under, he carried his winnings on his person as ballast, lest he and his profit expectations come crashing to the ground. Sure enough the real estate bubble burst; yet Hecht sailed on to prosperity.

The year 1987 was a good time to buy land, because the next real estate crash was a few years distant. A bankruptcy attorney had called me to discuss an opening bid on an upcoming auction of a failed 5,000-acre recreational community with a considerable amount of undeveloped land.

I was invited to open the bidding and to bid what the trustee required to satisfy creditors and to cover the related fees. I would be obligated to buy at this price. Beyond this amount, I was on my own against any competitive bidders. Following is a fictional scene from a typical country properties auction, complete with the usual characters. I had attended so many auctions that fiction had became reality, and I could easily place myself in this scene.

In April of 1987, a real estate broker, Jasper Rakes, was lingering in front of the courthouse steps smoking his pipe, observing, listening. Pete Hammersmith, a local defense lawyer, was with him, and the two men were concerned about the auction about to begin, for they were partners in various developments, and they had grand plans to steal this land.

Rich Hawkins, the auctioneer, told the crowd, "We're ready to start this sale," and the buzzing faded into silence while he continued in his high-pitched voice. "First of all I'll explain the terms to you, and then you can ask questions."

People moved in closer to the auctioneer, and he pulled up the collar of his blue windbreaker, for it had started to rain, and the wind was whipping the crowd. Umbrellas began to blossom in the chilly air.

Someone from the crowd brought an umbrella to the auctioneer. He thanked the kind patron and continued reading a paper through his glasses . . . "and then, after answering questions, we will offer the real estate."

Two builder-types–baseball caps, smart leather jackets, pocket protectors with pens–moved in closer. One asked the other, "What do ya think it'll bring?"

"Three, four hundred thousand maybe. Can't get to most of it." Their hands clutched their umbrellas, and they huddled in a circle of inquisitive people close to the auctioneer while he answered questions.

A courthouse lawyer sort, dark suit, London Fog, stocky, with graying hair and glasses, worked his way to the front of the crowd next to Rakes and Hammersmith. The defense attorney, Hammersmith, ushered him under his umbrella, "Hey, good to see ya!."

The nimble Hammersmith was younger and flashier on his feet than the stocky man who, as county prosecutor and counsel to the board of supervisors, had often been his adversary in the courtroom.

The two men shook hands and the prosecutor talked to them about the developer who had gone under. "He was in way over his head. Interest rates killed him."

Jasper Rakes was fumbling with his pipe that had gone out, and without looking counsel in the eye, he posed the question, "What do ya think it'll bring?"

The prosecutor told them, "It better bring close to a half mil. Rascal took the bank for a ride."

Rakes, holding the umbrella in one hand, his pipe in the other, searched for words.

The real estate business had been lean and mean, and the corners of his eyes were stamped with crow's feet and his temples were frosted with a worrisome gray. "I told Bill to let it go, that the planning commission was gonna hold him up. He said it was his baby, that he could get the votes.

"He said the Board would go with him no matter what they did."

The prosecutor whipped him with a stern frown. "There's too many lots bein' cut up around here now, and I'm gonna try'n see that it's stopped. Bill didn't have a snowball's chance in hell with the Board. They'd shoot him down three to two no matter what he did."

The crowd huddled beneath their umbrellas, arms crossed, stomping their feet, anxious to get on with the show.

The auctioneer called out for everyone to listen, because the rain had picked up and it was difficult to hear. "Now, the property is bein' sold by the gross and not by the acre, 5,000 acres more or less. It comes with the platted lots shown on the handouts, but they come under the new county ordinance. So check with the folks at the courthouse. Now, this sale calls for cash within 30 days of a successful bid. Clear title will be given on a special warranty deed. I have an opening bid of $600,000. Who will give $650,000?"

As it turned out, I was the only bidder, probably because people were psyched on a half-million as top price, and no one knew what to do with the land, most of which was mountainous terrain. But at a price of a little over $100 an acre, I did not feel at risk. By the time the bubble had burst in 1990, I had, in round numbers, turned $600,000 and 5,000 acres into $3,000,000 and close to 100 parcels. In America, anybody can become wealthy. It's just the risk you take.

Stafford County, VA
URBAN GARBAGE SAILS BACK HOME – May, 1987 –
U2

Cities were becoming increasingly crowded, and the disposal of urban refuse had reached a crisis stage. One garbage barge set out to sea from New York on a 6,000-mile, 60-day odyssey to six states and three countries in search of a dumping site. All refused the Big Apple's trash, so the stinking barge returned to New York Harbor fully loaded. Landfills in Virginia for fetid New York waste became a controversial source of revenue for financially strapped rural counties.

Counties closer to the D.C. metropolitan area faced a much greater crisis than what to do with their refuse, and that was finding breathing room for its inhabitants. The Urban Land Institute reported that the region would have to accommodate 2.6 million more people by 2007. Prices on residential land had risen twice as fast as inflation over the previous 60 months. And in some high-growth areas, land values for housing had soared by more than 200% since 1980. If you had been looking for country property around Washington D.C. in 1987, and you had responded to the following appeal, you would have profited enormously had you bought land at one of my projects near Fredericksburg, Virginia.

The Urban Land Crisis and how you can profit from 10-acre estates just 42 miles from 495

Highest population growth in U.S. predicted for
D.C. Metropolitan area.

10-13 ac. of nearby country land could cost you $50,000 by 1990.

10-13 acre commutable estates from $18,950 to $29,950

The Stafford County Story

Stafford County, Virginia, had the second-highest growth rate in the state for 1986. And the Washington D.C. megalopolis was spreading at a record pace. Land purchased in the county is just minutes from the proposed new outer beltway, though, by 2004, this commuter relief system was never constructed due to pressure from no-growth advocates. Despite this fact, Stafford County leaped ahead to become one of the top ten growth counties in the country by the turn of the century. Many land investors, aware of this trend, or just plain lucky, increased their stack of chips by betting on growth.

Speculators Profit First

What do the speculators know that you don't know? It's not that they are smarter than you. It's just that you may be too busy making a living, while they're out making money. Here is what land speculators knew at the time. Stafford County had statistically become part of the D.C. metro area.

A commuter rail line from Fredericksburg to D.C was in the works. High-speed commuter ferry service on the Potomac River from Stafford County to D.C. was under study to bypass traffic congestion on I-95. These facts, and the proposed new outer beltway, had created a "countryfied" neighborhood extending 50 miles in all directions around the perimeter of Washington D.C.

Proposals for two gas pipelines were being spread through Stafford County to service thousands of homes, not to mention wildfire business and economic activity. Land prices were skyrocketing as urbanization of the Washington D.C.-to-Fredericksburg corridor was being pushed to record levels. Land speculators and investors make it a rule to follow the roads. They watched like hawks as highway corridors to regional population centers were transformed from two to four lanes.

News of new airport improvements to accommodate jet planes and larger aircraft was a signal to players that more industry was on the way, this to help pay for impending growth.

Winning the Game

On the face of Donald Trump's real estate game, TRUMP, the tycoon declares, "It's not whether you win or lose, it's whether you win!" To win is to act fast in the face of opportunity.

In the real estate game, to lose is to wait until new antigrowth measures strangle opportunity and profits. Experts in 1987 were predicting that the value of single-family homes would rise 55% within the next four years. Prices more than doubled during that period, this despite the crash of 1990 that saw tycoons like Trump knocked for a loop and vacant commercial structures left half finished, while others wasted away on the books of demolished lenders.

The run-up in land prices from 1987 to 1990, coupled with a surging regional population, left residential land buyers with a very strong hand. Area Realtors reported a severe shortage of affordable 10-acre parcels within striking distance of the D.C. beltway. Unlike stocks, and due to a political curtailment of buildable homesites, there was no way for residential land values to nosedive in the D.C. metropolitan area. My own base selling price for land offers in Stafford County increased by 50% in the period 1995-97, and every offer was quickly sold out.

Kilmarnock, VA
U.S.S.R. PUSHES FOR STRONG GROWTH – June, 1987 –
Whitney Houston

In a bold move to turn the Soviet Union into a world economic player, President Gorbachev told the Communist Party Central Committee that radical structural reforms were needed. Sacred cows for workers, like price subsidies and central economic controls, were recommended for the slaughterhouse. He encouraged preferential treatment for small businesses.

And an aggressive new road building campaign was encouraged as part of a package that included massive improvements in transportation, communication, tourism facilities, and sports activities. No mention was made of increased military spending.

The Tidewater, Virginia cities of Newport News, Hampton, and Portsmouth are home to ten military installations, including the Norfolk Naval Shipyard, and this megalopolis harbors the world's largest shipyard, Newport News Shipbuilding. Since 1986, defense spending in the U.S. had been on the rise. This initiative was leading to more jobs, more houses. Government figures showed a booming housing market in the Northern Neck of Virginia.

Total home starts had jumped an astounding 45% in the period 1995-96. Homebuilding was growing exponentially from the Tidewater cities, where immense military expenditures were targeted. And it seemed like most people wanted to get a place on or near the water while they could still afford it. New four-lane highways were under construction from Tidewater, Richmond, and the Washington D.C. area, all aimed toward the Chesapeake Bay.

My partner in Richmond contacted me about some waterfront property for sale just outside of the lovely town of Kilmarnock, Virginia. The Kilmarnock/Irvington area is right at the Bay. It's a swinging center for fun-seekers and retirees. Local planners in 1987 had pegged it as the third most popular town in the state for residents aged 65 and older.

As I pointed out earlier, in Kilmarnock, you get quick access to golf courses, tennis courts, the Tides Inn Resort, Bay cruises, salt air, fresh seafood, a fully staffed hospital, fashionable shops, gourmet restaurants, live entertainment–all just a few miles from the 40-mile-wide Chesapeake Bay. Since 1987, hotels and shopping centers have been added to the list of community amenities.

My research showed the Kilmarnock area on the Northern Neck to be the hotspot in Virginia for leisurely living by the sea.

Population density in the region during the eighties was a planner's dream–an estimated one person for every ten acres. Dwelling units had shot up 22% in 1986, establishing a strong growth pattern. And the local comprehensive plan expected the majority of new homes to be built in the Kilmarnock/Irvington area–exactly where we were offering "Waterman's Homesites" at greatly reduced prices. I pointed out to consumers that this offer was unlikely to be repeated due to planned restrictions against further growth.

To dramatize the offer, I placed a double-spread ad in the major Tidewater papers showing a wide-angle shot of the Bay and a full layout of a waterfront estate, complete with home, dock, barn, stables, pool, tennis court, garden, orchard, playfields, pasture, and woods.

The ad included photos of main street Kilmarnock, a local marina, and a nearby golf course.

The 200-Mile-Long Chesapeake Bay

3 AC. HOMESITE OPPORTUNITY AT KILMARNOCK–FUN CENTER OF THE BOOMING CHESAPEAKE BAY

Just 44 miles from York River Bridge–Commute to Newport News-Hampton

3 AC. WATERMAN'S HOMESITES
FROM $89 MO. $6950-$8950

3 AC. WATERSIDE ESTATES
CHARTED TO ATLANTIC OCEAN
$14,950-$29,950

Most of the homesites fronted on Indian Creek, on a highway, or along a 2,000-foot grass airstrip for light planes. I parked my Supercub on the strip to highlight the fact that landowners and their guests could arrive by air, motorized vehicle, or boat. These valuable tracts are only a mile from town and yielded considerable profits and enjoyment to those fortunate seekers of country properties who acted on the opportunity.

While it is true that wise investments in country properties can be a profitable pursuit, consideration must be given to the prudent disposal of accumulated wealth and the potential hazards of excessive speculation. At the conclusion of America's Revolutionary War, the Superintendent of Finance, Robert Morris, paid demobilized soldiers out of his own pocket, only to be thrown into debtor's prison in later years after failed efforts in land speculation. The flip side of the coin found John D. Rockefelller donating to charity at the age of 16, and when he died at the age of 82 in 1937 he had given away more than 500 million dollars. Death comes to the young it is said, but as we age the path to eternity becomes a journey in time worthy of our best efforts to improve our lives and to advance the lives of others. A study by sociologist Philip R. Kunz of Brigham Young University revealed that nearly half of us die within three months of our last birthday. One explanation for this fact is that the period following our birthday is anticlimactic, and that, especially if we are ill, we are depressed and can lose the will to live.

In the spring of 1987, my wife of 28 years, born in March, was taken ill with a malignant lung ailment, and though I shepherded her through an odyssey of hospital stays, the search for a cure and possible implant was nowhere to be found. She was not particularly inclined toward basic Christianity, so the spiritual aspects of the transition from this life to the next was somewhat difficult for her. She had seen a hypnotist on television and asked me to send for him. I called the man, and he came to Johns Hopkins Hospital in Baltimore, Md., and did what he could for her, but our ridiculous hopes were routed. I still remember the cold-shoulder looks I got from a local priest who was visiting the terminally ill at the hospital. Within a year, God's finger touched her, and she slept.

Richmond, VA
THATCHER WINS FOR 3rd TIME IN A ROW – June, 1987 –
Whitney Houston

British Prime Minister Margaret Thatcher clearly upstaged the Labor Party by nailing down her leading role for the third straight time. And a record number of voters applauded her efforts by giving the Conservatives a 100-seat majority in the House of Commons. Thatcher stood on her performance of expanding the middle class in England. During her reign, millions were able to buy homes and become stockholders. In response to socialist criticism that her policies had widened the gap between rich and poor, Thatcher remarked that, "Capitalism only works by spreading to more of the population what used to be the privileges of a few."

In dramatic contrast to her efforts to break down class consciousness and spread the wealth of her nation, figures from India during that era showed 34% of all rural families and 44% of all urban families living in one-room homes. In the largest cities of the subcontinent, the figure averaged 67%, and in Calcutta the figure soared to 79%, with the number of homeless living on the streets uncounted. By the 1980's, total population on earth was increasing by 150 million every two years; whereas in the days of Julius Caesar the entire population of the world was 150 million.

In the United States, the politics of a population explosion took on new dimensions as more and more people looked to the countryside for relief from urban congestion. Socialist-oriented politicos mandated more open space for the people, whom they would prefer to ghetto in clustered villages. Village statesmen, with profound looks of alarm at a shifting population base, talked of growth controls to restrict land ownership.

It took two hundred years to form this free nation where opportunities to own land were boundless; a few hours of political collusion in some rural areas were enough to lay this concept in dust.

I was spread thin, developing and selling country properties simultaneously in at least six counties in two states. Low interest rates had returned to the economy, causing a rush by the populace to buy new homes. Lot prices in desirable locations near the cities were soaring.

In Richmond, Virginia, Goochland County had become the west end suburbs, having increased in population 16.4% during the previous decade. And still more growth. This from the proposed widening of Broad Street from I-64 to the Goochland line, and the expansion of two parkways. The push for land as an investment was accelerated by the inflated dollar.

As incredible as it may now seem to Richmond residents, we were selling estate-sized land parcels in this region at what can appear to be prehistoric prices:

The West End Land Crisis and how you can profit from 8 to 18-acre estates at the James River just 29 miles out.
8 to14-acres $8950 to $16,950
16 to 18-acre Riverfront Farms
$24,500 to $39,500

Regardless of the amount of land they own, most people take pride in their homes; although Yogi Berra, when complimented on his beautiful new home, replied "It's nothing but rooms." In a display of royal humility, Queen Victoria, on one of her frequent visits from Buckingham Palace to the magnificent London home of her hostess, once remarked, "I have come from my house to your palace."

The opportunity to create an historic showplace home is often a motivating factor for buyers seeking country properties. Whether built from bricks and mortar, stone, wooden planks, or logs, the past will always speak to you in historic structures, though some may stay clear of old homes, fearing the beat of a devil's drum or the appearance of questionable apparitions. For those lovers of historic homes who missed them, look at these bargains, glimmering through the dreams of things that might have been:

Att: Fix-up Investors
BAY GHOST

Kilmarnock, VA - Ghostly waterman's farmhouse, stone's throw from access to sheltered cove off Chesapeake Bay. Authentic run-down relic to fix up weekends and vacations for fun and profit. 2-story, 7-room restorable frame ruin of early Americana. Massive shade trees have seen the Civil War. A sea captain's home? A plantation great house? Tired old home battered by Bay winds. Broken windows open to bats and waterfowl. Original wide-plank flooring. Fireplace in all rooms. Six-acre farmstead has three old barns, bold stream, magnificent shaded pond site and well. Borders state road for over 600 ft. Also joins 1800 ft. grass airstrip. One mile from town. Commute to Tidewater. Fix up, sell for $100,000. Steal this weekend for $27,500. Sold "as is."

B.K. HAYNES CORPORATION

When buying and selling country properties like these, particularly those with old homes and "fixer-uppers," the term "as is" is often used in the sales contract. The term means exactly what it says, notwithstanding deficiencies uncovered in home inspections. You may insert a provision for a home inspection in the purchase contract, but this contingency does not constitute an option to withdraw from the contract on the basis of faults found in the home prior to closing.

Homes sold "as is" are often sold below market value due to the costs and uncertainties of repairs, restoration, and remodeling. This factor aside, many historic homes are sold at a premium regardless of their condition. The critical factor for investors in old homes is the motivation of the seller to dispose of the property. If listed at a fair market price, approximately 60% of prospective buyers will visit the home. Overpriced listings can decrease showing percentages to as low as 15 percent of prospects. If priced under market, sellers can expect 80 to 90 percent of prospective buyers to visit the property.

A compelling reason to place realistic prices on properties is the simple fact that 90% of overpriced real estate ends up being sold below market value because of compromises made by sellers to outrageous low-ball offers. When priced at fair market or appraised value, offers are generally within the strike zone.

If you do strike it rich with an old country home, be sure to check the health permit for its current validation and for the number of bedrooms allowed. Over time, improvements and additions to the structure may have created more bedrooms than are legally permitted. This may not pose an immediate problem; however, if the permit has expired and needs to be renewed, an inspection by health department officials could invalidate the existing permit, this due to possible regulatory changes mandating stricter control standards, and an expensive new sewage disposal system may have to be installed.

Petersburg, W. VA
SHOOT-OUTS ON CALIFORNIA FREEWAYS – July, 1987 –
Bob Seger

Angry motorists, fed up with traffic jams on the Los Angeles freeways, began turning their frustration into violence. Since June of 1987, two more motorists had been shot to death and four injured in nine road-rage incidents. Police psychologists pinned the blame on Hollywood action movies, self-centered attitudes, and the breakdown of family values. They cautioned motorists to avoid confrontations.

Troubled times were expected as we approached the year 2000. Many people sought an escape from the cities to an environment where they could be isolated by mountains. Almost all of them wanted to be on a body of water. In 1987, I had located some land on the South Branch of the Potomac River where buyers could pick up two-acre waterfront ranchettes with mountain views and central water for as little as $8950. The fast-moving river offered fishing, canoeing, rafting, and swimming. Pilots could fly into a major airport in nearby Petersburg.

Small acreage parcels on navigable rivers at the time were in short supply and were selling at much higher prices than my new offer. Frontage on the Potomac was extra scarce. I decided to play up the Potomac River as a premium place on which to locate. People the world over know the name. Most associate this river with Washington D.C. and Mount Vernon, the home of George Washington. Most people have to be rich to own land on the lower Potomac. They may have scenic views of the river. But in many cases, their waterfront is unusable because of high banks or marshy terrain.

This offer provided consumers with land that was all usable, though their homes and cabins would have to be elevated, as on most beaches, this because of possible floods and sudden water surges. I stressed the importance of location, location, location when buying land. When you marry *waterfront* to the *location* factor you always have a winning combination. Twenty years before, I had sold land on the Potomac near Harpers Ferry, West Virginia, prior to this historic town's emergence as a focal point for Washington and Baltimore-area commuters.

By 2004, a major interstate, Corridor-H, would link the Petersburg-Moorefield area of West Virginia with the northern Shenandoah Valley, a region that, along with Harpers Ferry, has become part of the D.C. metropolitan area. The Potomac River around Petersburg, though not a playground for the rich, is the gateway to some of West Virginia's most scenic natural attractions.

Petersburg is located in the pathway of progress. The region is sure to be a destination point for vacationers around the world. And those who bought land on the Potomac in that region are well-rewarded. Here is the headline for that promotion:

Unusual opportunity to grab
POTOMAC RIVERFRONT
Out goes scarce waterfront upriver from dangerous
"Trough" in the nearby "Badlands" of West Virginia

Charlestown, W. VA
MARKET CRASH WORSE THAN 1929 – October 20, 1987 –
Michael Jackson

Panic hit Wall Street as the Dow collapsed by 508 points into a bloody river of diluted shares, losing 22.6 percent of its value and almost doubling the percentage crash of October 28, 1929. The chairman of the New York Stock Exchange compared the decline to a nuclear disaster, remarking, "It's the nearest thing to a meltdown that I ever want to see." Many economists feared the onset of a deep recession; other analysts cited safeguards in the economic system established after the collapse in 1929, and the emergence of global economic forces, as sufficient shields against another "Great Depression."

The plunge set off a worldwide search for villains. Large-scale budget and trade deficits were the logical scapegoats. Other usual suspects were the declining dollar, rising interest rates, and troubles in the Persian Gulf. Wall Street trading practices were also called into question.

Five hundred billion dollars had been stolen from investors' portfolios. Job losses loomed on the horizon. Workers' retirement plans were placed on indefinite hold. Production lines slowed to a crawl. A scattering of optimistic investors, attempting to capitalize on the unprecedented losses, pumped the market back up by 100 points, but it was too little and too late to save the day.

By nightfall, the minds of small investors were filled with images of stock-and-bond-trading operatives hanging in effigy on Wall Street.

In the Washington D.C. area, largely insulated from a financial crisis by the overflowing coffers and largesse of the federal bureaucracy, business proceeded as usual. Aside from the decline in the value of some personal portfolios, jobs were secure, the production of government was on the upswing, and the number of households in the region was expected to double by the year 2000. Loudoun and Jefferson counties, near booming Dulles Airport, had become the new D.C. suburbs. Land values within 50 miles of Dulles were skyrocketing. Smart investors saw the purchase of land parcels in this region as a much better bet than the stock market. People had to have homes, and land for homes was cheaper farther out.

Real estate speculators also knew that existing home prices were rising at a faster rate than the returns on an average stock portfolio, this promising much greater yields on their investments.

The National Association of Homebuilders predicted the cost of 10 acres west of Dulles could reach $100,000 by 1990. As it turned out, this figure was too low. And by 2003, the cost of ten acres within 50 miles of Dulles was closer to $200,000.

A West Virginia auctioneer, who had recently relocated to Richmond, Virginia, and from whom I had previously purchased land, sent me information on a farm that his company was preparing to sell, rather than auction off. I looked at the property near Charles Town, West Virginia, liked what I saw, and quickly bought the farm for development into country estates.

My offer was underpriced and affordable, with the land providing plenty of riding room for horses, lots of shade trees, streams, and lush pasture.

Plus the estates are close to the race track at Charles Town–a magnet for horse people. But you didn't have to have horses to hitch up to one of these bargains. You could hold for investment. Or you could simply pack up and move to estate country where you could build your dream home. You would not be cursed with any housing developments or industry as close neighbors. As a horse farm or investment, the property made a lot of sense. Here's how I characterized the offer in a classified ad:

Smart investors and commuters have
HORSE CENTS

Charles Town, W. VA–Cheap horse country estate you can steal this weekend for pennies on the dollar. 13 acre po' boy's ranch only 35 miles from the Dulles-Leesburg growth area. Plenty of riding room, shade trees, and lush pasture. Quick access to race track. Walk to stocked fishing stream. Perc tested for your new home. Great investment. Highest growth district in county. Farm across road just sold for $3300 per ac. Just $18,950 for 13 acre horse ranch. Owner financing available with little down.

Call B.K. HAYNES CORPORATION

A quarter-page ad in the *Washington Post* presented the following headline copy:

The exploding D.C. suburbs and how you can profit from 10 to 17-acre estates just 35 mi. from booming Dulles area

Highest population growth in U.S. predicted for Metro Area.
10 acres west of Dulles could cost you $100,000 by 1990
10 to 17-acre Horse Country Estates $18,950 to $39,950

This promotion also presented the concept of a "Two-State Ranch" in *Post* classified ads, since the farm was sprawled across the Virginia-West

Virginia line. Almost simultaneously with this campaign, I launched an orchard liquidation sale that offered views of four states and dealt with failing apple crops in the nearby West Virginia Highlands.

Growing crops on hardscrabble mountain land spurs an interesting anecdote. Thomas Carlyle, the British historian born in the Scottish highlands, was walking with Ralph Waldo Emerson in Scotland's scenic mountains. Emerson, believing the terrain to be worthless for food production, remarked, "What kind of crops can possibly grow up here?" Carlyle, remarking on the heartiness and stoutness of the Scottish people, replied, "We grow *men.*" The well-known adversity and difficulty of growing up in the mountains has become legend, personified in the stolid and austere figure of the "mountain man."

One of the most amazing and courageous men to be grown in West Virginia was the late Randolph Ewers, an acclaimed orchardist and Christian missionary who sold me his operation and moved to Jamaica to establish an outreach for the poor. His work has done a world of good for mankind, and he has become a saint for many Jamaican youth, modeling his life on Christ. Christianity, of course, is a doctrine of good will toward mankind and universal sacrifice. In abandoning his worldly possessions and giving of himself to the betterment of others, he exemplified the Christian belief that God seeks after man, as opposed to other religions that place an emphasis on man seeking after God. Randolph's first flock of sheep were the seasonal fruit pickers who traveled each fall from Jamaica to harvest the crops from his orchards.

Difficult times began with the 1984 crop. West Virginia orchardists were hit hard by a devastating early frost. Auction sellouts and liquidations followed in 1985. And the drought of 1987 was the crowning blow. Disaster had followed calamity. Randolph Ewers, struck down in the darkest storm by the brightest thunderbolt, gave up one of the most unique and unusual orchards in the world to follow Christ. Views from High Mountain Orchards outside of Romney, West Virginia are so spectacular they can be considered one of the wonders of the world.

How many people can boast that they own land overlooking four states? Plus you can see the Potomac River from much of the orchard.

The apple is the oldest fruit known to mankind, dating from Adam and Eve in the Garden of Eden. It is also the most valuable of fruits that grow on trees. Apple trees that are properly cared for will produce crops for 30 years or more. An acre of orchard averages 36 to 44 trees, with a 500-bushel or more per-acre harvest possible in good years. Not only are apples delicious to eat, they are also helpful to your digestion. Apples can make you feel better by providing your body with important minerals, such as phosphorous, calcium, iron, and potassium.

For some reason–we'll never know why–nature chose to flatten the top of a beautiful mountain in the magical Potomac River Valley for the growing of fruit. It's incredible.

The mountain forms a great, ever-changing wall on the western horizon above the Potomac River. Sometimes you're basking in sunshine, while scanning a cottony sea of clouds; yet the skies appear dark to those below. Moisture-laden winds hit the mountain, providing precious rain, but often leaving a shortfall in the valley.

This unique mountaintop produces its own Red Delicious and Golden Delicious apples. So tasteful and succulent are these varieties that the best were reserved by Randolph Ewers for seasonal gift-giving. Countless bushels of Rome Beauty, Jonathan, Stayman, York Imperial, Grimes Golden, and McIntosh have also been harvested from the orchards. In selling off sections of the orchard to new buyers, I commented, "Imagine owning valuable land that can actually yield you cash and food dividends year after year. And you're guaranteed to see friendly deer in your fields. They LOVE apples."

Randolph worked with me during the liquidation sale to advise consumers on orchard management. They could do it themselves or have a professional orchardist handle their crop.

And tax deductions are available for most agricultural activities. All of the subdivided parcels were "perc'd" for home and cabin construction. Several model cabins were built on the mountain to kick off the promotion. The location is up so high that you can actually see birds fly below you. And as part of my sales pitch, I stated that "You may feel closer to God than when you're in church." Some things in this world cannot be duplicated. And I literally took consumers to great heights to prove it. **"Including a bushel of free apples when you call for an appointment."**

Here are key elements of a *Washington Post* display ad showing a wide-angle photo of the landscape in West Virginia, Virginia, Pennsylvania, Maryland and the Eastern Seaboard. To stress historical significance, a photo was included in the ad showing orchard workers harvesting apples in 1924:

The plight of hard times and migrant workers brings to mind the saga of the Joad family in Steinbeck's novel about the Great Depression, *The Grapes of Wrath*. While disposing of High Mountain Orchards, I was asked to liquidate an adjacent orchard property, then in the first stages of development. Here is an incredible offer from that promotion:

Richmond, VA
INVESTORS FLEE COLLAPSING STOCK MARKET– Oct. 1987 – Prince

In the U.S., stocks were in free fall. World markets were unsettled. Young Wall Street bucks with BMWs and decks of credit cards awoke from the miser's dream to the realization that greed is bad. The troubled steel and concrete canyons that housed their passions became prisons of their very souls. Many fled in disgrace to re-establish their characters through other fields of endeavor in the cities; others abandoned their white-collar careers and searched for simpler lives in small towns and in the countryside. The nightmare crash jolted cadres of traders to go back and "follow your dream." Countless opportunities opened up beyond Wall Street for those who sought them out. Investors, too, turned away from trading stocks. Thousands began investing in real estate.

Prior to the crash, I had put the finishing touches on a riverfront promotion outside of Richmond, Virginia. When I received news of the disaster I had to adjust a few lines of copy in my ad to address the stock market issue and to further validate my claim that riverfront property was one of the best investments around. The Commonwealth of Virginia had designated parts of the nearby Rivanna and James Rivers as "Scenic Rivers." This means that if you own land along certain protected sections of these close-in rivers, you actually own a valuable natural resource.

And carefully chosen scenic riverfront property–close enough for you to live on the water and commute to Richmond–could offer more profit potential than any other investment.

Figures from the Richmond MLS showed housing sales doubling for the first six months of 1987 over the same period in 1986. Richmond was growing so fast in the West End that Henrico County was spilling over into Goochland. A flood of newcomers was about to swamp the designated growth areas, this aided and abetted by sweeping new road improvements to facilitate traffic and the construction of a new highway to the West End. Real estate speculators looked in their crystal balls and saw people packed like sardines in homes and apartments. They also saw skyrocketing land prices. Just over the horizon from this frenzy of activity, my partner and I were about to give away the store on riverfront property.

The Rivanna is not an ordinary river. It was once referred to as "Mr. Jefferson's River" because of Thomas Jefferson's personal interest in its use and development. In the past, the river has served as a power source for numerous mills. Riverboats, bound for Richmond, carried cargo down the Rivanna and into the James. Now the river is again clean and free-flowing. And with its scenic designation many people feel that the Rivanna is as beautiful as the James. Game and fish populations are bountiful along the Rivanna. And land on navigable water such as this is very valuable, especially where the Rivanna enters the James. But in 1987, farmers were facing an ocean of troubles, forcing them to sell their land. This dire situation for farmers opened rare navigable waterfront opportunities for country property seekers and investors. But few people knew about them at the time.

As more and more people searched for affordable land on the river near Richmond, new laws were in process to control future growth. Subdivisions were mushrooming so fast in Goochland that new regulations were rushed through to tighten control. Those who waited to buy riverfront found their dream of investing in that small ranch on the river vanishing, like the value of stocks, before their eyes. Inflation, too, was further eating up their dollars.

Waterfront buyers who acted on this offer were deeded 10 acres in a beautiful pastoral setting, with rolling fields, towering woods, and frontage along a delightfully scenic river in which they could swim, fish, and canoe. The canoe trip from their shoreline to the James River at Columbia, the first capital of Virginia, is about a mile. Going to "The Rivah" is big in Richmond. So these fortunate buyers would never have to worry about getting there, because they could live where they play.

This was a true ground-floor opportunity for landowners and investors alike. When it was gone, it was truly gone. You'll never see so much waterfront for so little money again.

Unusual opportunity to grab
SCENIC RIVERFRONT
Out goes scarce waterfront where the scenic Rivanna enters
the James just 30 miles out
Breakthrough prices on 10-ac. Ranches
Commute to Richmond $8950 to $18,950
10-acre off-water ranches $6950 to $14,950

Looking back on 1987 I find it hard to believe I was juggling so many projects over two states while still frantically seeking a cure for my wife's terminal illness. As I previously discussed, in the spring I had purchased 5,000 acres at a foreclosure sale for about $600,000

and change. This was a failed recreational and residential development near Winchester, Virginia. Due to tax and regulatory entrapments,
I did not take title to the developed lots, seeking only to liquidate the
undeveloped mountain land in large sections. The concept I had in
mind was to make the offer so attractive that the consumer would have
to "qualify" for ownership. Here is the print promotion word for word.
A photo of the Great North Mountain Range was shown within an
oval frame.

---

*An announcement of unusual importance for
wilderness lovers, environmentalists, hunters,
investors, mountain climbers and adventurers*

DO YOU QUALIFY FOR $399 PER AC. LAND 1 HOUR WEST OF LEESBURG?

For over 20 years we have been offering you bargain-priced land. Now,
for the first time, we are able to offer you affordable land so far below market
price that we must ask you to qualify for ownership on a first come, first
served basis.

New "Land Grants"

These are big sections–not lots–of the nearby Great North Mountain Range,
which was part of early land grants, dating to 1649. Recently, this historic
mountain range was freed for sale by the bankruptcy court. Now new "land
grants" can be made to qualified buyers for the first time in hundreds of
years.

Each section is 50 to 150 acres or more. You can actually own your own
mountain if you qualify. Basic road access, a health department approved
site for a sewage disposal system, and a free serviceable 4-wheel-drive vehicle for hauling in supplies will be provided with each section of land.

How to Qualify

You must agree to preserve your land in its natural state. This means no
commercial timbering, adverse usage, or engagement in any activities which
may pollute the air and ground water. You must agree to no residential construction and no further subdivision for two years (subdivided parcels must
be at least 20 acres). You must agree to a restriction of only one family per
subdivided lot. You must agree to noise abatement rules governing off-road
vehicles.

You must adhere to certain practices for the prevention of soil and erosion
when constructing roads and driveways. You must agree to pay your prorata

share of monies for road and trail upkeep. You must agree that any dwelling constructed in your wilderness section must have health department approval. You must agree to grant easements for electric and telephone lines. And finally, you must agree to a prorata assessment, if necessary, for the spraying of your timber against the Gypsy Moth. Financed purchases are subject to credit approval. Camping is permitted. Mineral rights do not convey.

Vanishing Wilderness

Wildfire growth in the Dulles Airport area, and the proposed new outer beltway, have effectively brought the D.C. Metro area to within 45 miles of the Great North Mountain Range. But your section will still provide a nearby habitat for deer, bear, eagles, hawks, and even an occasional wildcat. If you qualify, you are essentially a pioneer. In the 1990's there will be a conscious need for nearby wilderness and open space. People need homes now. But only a fortunate few will have the foresight and required qualifications to own their own wilderness.

Your Own Mountain

This limited offer of the Great North Mountain Range covers a portion of over 5,000 acres, extending approximately 15 miles on the mountain crest, partially along the Virginia-West Virginia border. Numerous streams are found winding down through almost virgin forest.

Your section may include a famous natural attraction such as *Pinnacle Rock, Fall Ridge, or Devil's Backbone.* The *Blue Trail* of the *Potomac and Appalachian Trail* traverses the mountain crest, from which you can view the expanded D.C. Metro area. You can watch your leaves turn in the fall and see your forest fill up with snow. Elevations rise to 2500 feet above sea level.

If you qualify for ownership, your section will be given your family name, if that is your desire. Donations of wilderness land to non-profit foundations can qualify for tax deductions. See your accountant or tax advisor.

Low Prices to All

The price per acre is low in accordance with our policy. We believe it is better to sell a large amount of land at a reasonably small margin of profit than to sell small lots at a large margin of profit. When qualifying for this offer, there is no discrimination against you as to race, color, religion, sex, age, or national origin.

We believe everyone should be able to share in the American dream of land ownership.

50 to 150 acre sections range from just $399 to $599 per acre. We are able to sell this land at a low price because we have found new ways to give you greater value without an increase in our own costs. We did not set out to sell land at such-and-such a figure. We decided on the most land we could provide, given the terrain features. Then we found ways to offer it at a low price.

Unlike your other material possessions, your 50 to 100-acre section can extend past your lifetime and will provide–potentially an hour or less from your home–a substantial nearby heritage in this great land. Recognizing the obvious investment potential of this close-in land, and to avoid excessive speculation, you must close on your section before you resell. Long-term bank financing has been arranged with as little as 10% down. A credit check is required.

How to Inspect

Call for an appointment to determine basic qualifications for ownership. Then follow directions to our main office complex in Front Royal, Virginia. There you can view aerial photographs, topographical maps, plats, slides, color photos, and video tape of the Great North Mountain Range.

You may then take a self-guided tour of the general area. Or a sales agent can accompany you. If you qualify for ownership, you can then reserve your land section. There is no restriction on the number of sections you can reserve. Prices of each section are based mainly on terrain features and the amount of acreage you acquire.

At closing you will receive a special warranty deed and certified survey. A serviceable 4-wheel drive vehicle (or $2,000 price reduction) will also be included for early purchase.

Basic access roads and trails, and approved sewage disposal site designations are underway and will be completed in 1989. Title insurance is required. You may use your section immediately after settlement; however roads, trails, and approved sewage disposal sites may be unfinished.

Upon closing, you will also be entitled to a free airplane tour of your section. Flights will originate from the Front Royal, VA and Winchester, VA airports. All sales are subject to the approval of Frederick County, Virginia officials concerned with the planning, zoning, and subdivision of land.

B.K. HAYNES CORPORATION
"Nearby Land Bargains Since 1966"

Article in the Fauquier Democrat

Opportunities Abound in Rural Real Estate
By Bob Naylor
Democrat Special Writer

When it comes to buying and selling rural real estate, Bradley K. (B.K.) Haynes wrote the book on the subject. The book is called, *HOW YOU CAN GROW RICH THROUGH RURAL LAND–Starting from Scratch.*

So when B.K. started advertising "An announcement of unusual importance for wilderness lovers, environmentalists, hunters, investors, mountain climbers, and adventurers," I took notice. If B.K. Haynes is involved, there *has* to be a story.

The man is an American original, though the bush hat and outback outfit he had on when I was ushered into his office in Front Royal not long ago was more the style of Crocodile Dundee, the Australian original. This may be fitting, because it was in the Australian Outback in the early 1970's that B.K. began writing an adventure novel that was to distract him from the hurlyburly of land huckstering into an extended hiatus of writing, teaching, and publishing. It was at the midpoint of a trip around the world that B.K. cut loose from business ties in the U.S. to begin unfolding this incredible tale of "self-destruction," a tale he entitled *The IdealESTATE MAN.*

B.K. Haynes is not one to sit and wait for things to happen. When his agent in New York failed to move the book as fast as he wanted, he formed his own publishing company, Greatland Publishing Company in Front Royal and published it himself. By this time, he had begun teaching a real estate course at Lord Fairfax Community College. His forte had always been taking pieces of rural land that others had failed to sell and making them move. So Greatland Publishing Company came out in 1979 with *HOW YOU CAN GROW RICH THROUGH RURAL LAND–Starting from Scratch*–the textbook around which he has marketed a correspondence course on making money in real estate.

After more than a decade-long struggle to survive, a resort development called Shawneeland on the east slope of the Great North Mountains west of Winchester finally went irrevocably belly-up in 1986. It had been a dream spawned in the second home boom of the late sixties, the era of B.K. Haynes' first incarnation as a real estate man. Refreshed by his sojourn in publishing and academia, B.K. had been lured back into real estate by the decline in rural land values–to B.K. this spelled opportunity–and he snapped up 5,000 acres of yet-undeveloped Shawneeland holdings at an auction price he could not resist.

The terrain is so rugged and so thickly wooded that it cost B.K. more than $100,000 just to survey it and divide it into these 100-acre land sections. He also hired a soils scientist to come in and find one location on each tract that would percolate (accommodate a septic system). And now he is putting in a road that makes the tracts accessible by four-wheel drive vehicles. In fact, for a while he was offering to give away a "serviceable four-wheel drive vehicle" with the purchase of each section. He says most people opted for a $2,000 discount on the price of the land instead.

"We started selling during the winter, off-site, using aerial maps and various related information," says B.K. "We couldn't begin construction of the road until this spring." During those winter months, he says, "Many people hiked in there and committed on sections even before we had finished surveying."

As of May 20, the B.K. Haynes Corporation had closed, or had sales contracts on, all but three of the first thirty-six 100-acre tracts surveyed. They are now about to offer comparable tracts on the remaining 2,000 acres B.K. picked up at the Shawneeland bankruptcy auction.

The difference between this and other developments is that, other than subdividing the mountainside into 100-acre tracts, locating perc sites, and cutting in a road of sorts, B.K. Haynes Corporation is not doing any developing. "This is rugged, wild mountain land," says B.K. "And we are not about to change that."

"We have some pretty restrictive covenants on this," B.K.. says, "because we intend to preserve the wilderness concept. We don't want people cutting off the timber or subdividing into small lots. We want to preserve the tranquility, the pristine atmosphere we have up there."

I had to postpone bouncing up what is now a very rugged jeep trail (the road work is not slated for completion until fall) until they finished spraying for gypsy moths, something B.K. has done because "we knew that unless we did, our buyers could lose their trees."

There is an adjoining section of flatter land at the base of the mountain that B.K. Haynes has subdivided into residential lots that have been sold for $999 per acre, but even these have been 20 to 32-acre tracts, with the same covenants applying that B.K. has written for the 100-acre wilderness sections. This was wilderness he is selling at prices ranging from $399 to $599 per acre for 100-acre tracts, each running up to the crest of the Great North Mountains, which is also the West Virginia line.

B.K. says there has been no previous habitation on this wilderness land, and I could see no evidence that there has been. When the tanneries flourished in the Shenandoah Valley in the 19th century, some of the original timber on these slopes may have been cut to satisfy that industry's insatiable appetite for charcoal. But the trees that stand there are fully mature and untouched, except for the narrow swath we negotiated in B.K.'s four-wheeler. I have to believe this is "pristine" wilderness.

He says buyers, most of whom are from Arlington, Fairfax, and Loudoun counties in Virginia, have been mainly professionals–engineers, scientists, attorneys, federal government employees. And he says in almost every case, the attraction has been owning and preserving a piece of what America has, but will not have much longer. There are deer and bear and wildcats up on that mountain, and maybe it looks about the way it did when John Lederer first explored the valley of the Shenandoah in the summer of 1670.

I looked back at the mountain as we drove away toward Middletown. I could not help thinking about those attention-grabbing 10-second spots we've been seeing on TV lately: "Is B.K. Haynes crazy?"

He surely is different, and I surely do like the way that mountain looks.

Winchester, VA
AMERICAN CENTURY FALLS TO JAPAN – Spring, 1988 –
George Michael

By 1988 the dollar had lost 50% of its value against the Japanese yen, and the U.S. trade deficit had risen to crisis proportions, half of it with Japan. The trade imbalance made the U.S. the world's largest debtor and Japan the top global creditor. Japanese investors, feasting on the weak dollar, swarmed into U.S. real estate like bees over honey.

At Great North Mountain, with a road network yet to be constructed into the wilderness area, we were flying prospective buyers over the various wilderness sections in a helicopter; other buyers were hiking in to claim their sections based on preliminary survey markers.

In late March, I received a call that my wife, who was in intensive care at Johns Hopkins hospital in Baltimore, was about to pass on. I asked the helicopter pilot if he could take me immediately to Johns Hopkins and get permission to land. He didn't think he could pull it off, so I had him drop me off at my farm where I asked my neighbor, a commercial pilot, to fly me to Baltimore, where I would rent a car. This done, I proceeded immediately to the hospital. My wife had requested that life support be removed. She was asleep, this after heavy injections of morphine. My son and other relatives were there. We prayed over her. And then she was gone.

Back home on the farm, I realized that I had made no plans for her death. I hurriedly tried to make up for lost time by calling a funeral home. My wife had told me she wanted to be cremated. But what about the service? I had not been to my church for years. I called the minister, a saintly woman, but she was in the hospital. Her husband, also a minister, suggested that he might be able to organize a memorial service, and he gave me some instructions. A few days later, the church was filled with friends and relatives. And he conducted a beautiful and memorable service. Still, my lack of planning was evident. I didn't know what to do after the ritual.

My sister-in-law suggested that the bereaved go back to the farm. Then what? I knew that I was to scatter her remains over the farm. My neighbor and I then went up in my Supercub. He took the controls, while I scattered her ashes in the wind. By then, my sister-in-law had come up with a plan. We would go back to her home in West VA for refreshments and a slightly delayed wake.

With regard to Great North Mountain, the development of 5,000 acres takes a lot of planning and engineering. I decided to proceed with a development plan at the southern end of the region and move north in phases. A primary obstacle to this strategy was the lack of access over suitable terrain. So I had purchased an adjoining farm, built an access road, and developed the farm into 20+ acre sections, this while donating 15 miles of trails to the Potomac and Appalachian Trail Club. Old mountain farms usually have haunted farmhouses and timeworn outbuildings, and this farm had its own reminder of days gone by.

At the turn of the 20th century, the following place would be worth close to $200,000 more than it sold for, even if you simply left it rest in the shadow of time.

Attention: Investors and history buffs

GRAY GHOST

Mountain Falls, VA–Ghostly remnants of a mountain civilization gone with the wind. Crumbling manor house and slave kitchen marked by rock chimney tombstone. Skeletons of outbuildings and farm wagons strewn in fields. Yard guarded by shadowy oak trees. Massive barn of yesteryear conceals small fortune in antique siding and oak beams. Enough valuable logs to build a large cabin. Rickety, wind-whipped garage. Two dying chicken houses. Lively spring. Pond site. Apple trees. Peaceful 20-acre farm buried in pretty valley framed by high mountains. Scene right out of the movies. Mostly productive fields and farmland. Largely fenced for horses and cattle. Park-like woods contain some trees too big to reach around. Perked 3 BR homesite. Subdivision permitted. Win-win investment. Private, one-of-a-kind estate site at end of state road. Ideal for your new home. Access to trails into the Great North Mountain Range. Only minutes from town. Super bargain at just $39,900 this weekend. 10% down. Owner financing possible.

B.K. HAYNES CORPORATION

Fredericksburg, VA
SANITY RESTORED TO NUCLEAR ARMS – May, 1988 –
Aerosmith

A new U.S.-Soviet arms agreement called for the elimination of land-based short-range and medium-range missiles installed in Europe by either country. European critics, remarking on the nuclear weapons buildup by the superpowers, labled the race for superiority as "crazy."

In the sixties, you may have thought it crazy that people would be commuting 50 miles or so and then racing back home before dark to spend time with their families.

The 1980 census showed a clear dispersal by urban dwellers away from the cities, with 1.5 million Americans traveling 100 or more miles each day between their homes and workplaces. People would become fed up with drug pressures on their children, crime in the streets, high taxes, exorbitant home costs, and living in a sardine can.

The area within 30 miles of I-95 around Fredericksburg has one of the highest growth rates in Virginia. In 1988, a commuter rail line was in the planning stage. And 1987 figures from the Virginia Association of Realtors showed that 75% of all listed residential property in adjoining Orange County was sold or under contract. This was a phenomenal 66% jump in the recorded sale of lots and acreage from the year before. Orange County, like the areas around Fairfax and Fredericksburg, had become a suburb of Washington. Land speculators, reaching farther and farther into the countryside and gobbling up buildable land, were crazy like foxes.

The economy looked so good in the spring of 1988 that it made an impending collapse almost inevitable. You can usually tell a market top from the crop of television commercials at a given time. Samples: (1) A farmer on his shiny new tractor in waving fields of grain, smiling over his bountiful harvest; (2) A couple sitting in front of the hearth, the woman perusing travel magazines while the man is happily tapping away at his P.C. investing online; (3) A rotund businessman on a golf course gabbing on a cell phone about his rising portfolio. In prosperous times we must be prepared to pay the tax of misfortune. The gloomy turn of the century and doomsday for the economy was less than two years away.

I came across an attractive piece of land at the time with considerable state road frontage, and I was able to pass on these small ranches to consumers at very enticing prices. Considering what these parcels would sell for today, you could very well have thought I was off my rocker to sell them so cheaply. Here's how I pitched the offer in a classified ad:

Hey, Investors!
Crazy to sell 2-22 acres near Fredericksburg from under $7,000?

First offer. Seller goes bananas. Peels price below market value for quick sale. Just 25 min. from I-95. Estate-quality fields and park-like woods with babbling shady brook and state road frontage. Perc tested. Area of nice homes. High growth region. 8 mi. Lake Anna. Crazy man's prices. $6950-$29,950. Bring ad for $200 discount. Looney terms: 2 ac. $6950. $200 deposit, $575 at closing; $69.50 mo. 180 mos., 13.50% apr w/ 5 yr. balloon. Lower rate with more down.

Urbanna, Virginia
BUSH AND QUAYLE NOMINATED – August, 1988 –
Guns 'n' Roses

Late-night comedians had a field day with the name of this duo when George Bush, the Vice President of the United States, and Dan Quayle, an Indiana senator, were chosen to lead the Republican ticket in the upcoming elections. "Sounds like the Republicans are declaring open season on themselves," remarked one pundit. Of course, the pairing was not as crazy as it sounded, since the Republicans won the White House.

On Virginia's historic Northern Neck, I kept the "Crazy" theme alive with the introduction of a once-in-a-lifetime "Golden Pond" offer that had come my way. But first a true story about a pond. A landowner named Childs discovered that someone had abandoned 10 domestic geese on his pond. He dutifully notified federal officials, who told him that if the geese had eaten any snails, he faced a fine of $50,000 per snail, making them, potentially, the most expensive geese in existence. Soon thereafter, a wildlife agent and a highway patrolman arrived at the pond with a shotgun. They planned to shoot the geese and remove their stomachs to find out how many snails had been eaten.

When a reporter showed up and threatened to expose the nasty episode in pictures and in print, the enforcers backed off, claiming it would be bad PR to show protectors of wildlife shooting innocent geese to save some snails. So the feds settled for making the geese vomit. No dead snails were found, and the geese were removed to a wildlife preserve.

The geese were given safe haven, but Mr. Childs claimed he was out $2.5 million because he could not use his property as he wished, since it was inhabited by the "endangered" snails.

The noble Nature Conservancy, in league with government landgrabbers, offered to pay half price for 300 acres of his property. Childs objected to the intimidation and strong-arm tactics and filed suit through the Mountain States Legal Foundation, claiming the government had illegally taken his property without compensation. The generation of such lawsuits is the fruit of government environmental madness.

Crazy to sell 25 to 34 acres on 100 acre lake off Chesapeake Bay from under $50,000?

Looking at this offer today it appears that somebody was indeed insane to give away the store like this. Here you had luxury waterfront estates selling at ordinary waterfront lot prices. The gimmick, if you would call it that, was that I was selling country property cheaply and quickly as an inexpensive form of advertising.

I had been going like gangbusters with these liquidation sales, and country property was flying off the shelf as fast as I could get it on the market. Record resale prices were being reported by purchasers of our previous waterfront offers. I wanted to keep up the momentum. The property was sold to me as the result of an estate settlement and was located in an established lakefront community– a clean, fiercely protected "Golden Pond" that dates from the 1700's.

I was not stretching the point when I told buyers that money could not buy priceless heritage. Historic properties are often passed down through generations and never appear on the market. This issue aside, the opportunity to live like Thoreau, in harmony with nature on a

"Walden Pond," was a tried and true selling point. Here the buyers could build a home under tall hardwood trees that had never seen a woodsman's axe. They would have enough land to create their own environment, molding green fields into playgrounds and gardens.

A display ad showed a photo of a lonely dock on a broad mirrored lake. Readers could see themselves and their families and friends boating, fishing, swimming from their own private dock.

I reminded them that they could enjoy all four seasons on this beautiful lake. And in the fall they could watch the skies for their neighbors–flocks of wild ducks and geese.

The six lakefront estates were given individual names: Waterwood, 31 acres $49,950; Stillwater, 24 acres, $55,000; Port Leisure, 27 acres, $59,950; Golden Point, 26 acres, $69,950; Duck Cove, 34 acres, $65,000; and Walden's Landing, 25 acres, with home, barn, outbuildings, $89,900. Resubdivision of the parcels was permitted if in accordance with county subdivision and zoning regulations.

It is worth remembering that nothing we have or possess in this world is truly ours, but is given by God to benefit ourselves and others. I was happy to transfer these unusual properties to new owners at a fair price, and I'm sure they have been well used and enjoyed by others and that the financial rewards of ownership have been satisfactory to all concerned.

Maui, Hawaii
AUTHOR TO DIE FOR WRITING BOOK – February. 1989 –
Paula Abdul

In a perversion of the doctrine that we may as well tolerate all religions, since God Himself tolerates all, Iran's Ayatollah Khomeini sentenced an Indian-born writer to death for questioning the truth of Islam. Salman Rushdie's novel, *The Satanic Verses,* was declared blasphemous by the ruling cleric of Iran, and a one million-dollar bounty was placed on Rushdie's head–three million if the author's killer was Iranian.

Following the death of my wife, I settled on the fool's paradise of travel and religious study. Much of my time was spent in Hawaii on the island of Maui. I had purchased a home there, had developed some friendships, and was engaged in metaphysical studies based on Far Eastern religious and mystical thought. Though I had neglected regular church attendance, I had never abandoned Christianity; but I was seeking to understand the human transition from this world to the next beyond Christian dogma. If any new truths came to me from this experience, it was that the belief in Christ as the son of God, the resurrection, the process of prayer, and the concepts of vicarious atonement and redeeming grace are all personally valid and supportive of my value system.

This whole process of self-reflection came about when practicing secular concentrated thought (as opposed to prayer) to solve problems and to achieve goals in life. While it is indeed true that we are each responsible for our thoughts and actions, it is sometimes difficult to sort out their validity. For example, many bleeding-heart humanitarians, practicing an unstructured spiritualistic view of the world, can find themselves experiencing the pain of every human being to their own emotional detriment and personal loss of joy in life. An open mind for the righteous person can be an undisciplined mind into which inaccurate or harmful thoughts can intrude, with this leading to incorrect and emotionally injurious actions; hence the need for a somewhat structured and validated spiritual belief system.

The well-adjusted person in this world must contend with balancing four main components of his or her life: (1) physical–body, material things; (2) mental–accurate and healthy thought processes; (3) social–friends, relationships; (4) spiritual–church, belief in God. When any of these components gets out of balance (too little or too much emphasis) we feel displeasure and discontent. For example, a rich man without friends or spiritual beliefs can be emotionally unbalanced, and these deficiencies will likely show in his thoughts and actions. An overzealously religious person can easily antagonize many of those around him, and his mental processes will subsequently be thrown off balance. He may even suffer physically, since the mind has an element of control over our health. And social butterflies, caught up in the whirlwind of prestige and pretense, may neglect their spiritual lives and personal finances to the point where the physical and mental worlds are thrown asunder.

An unbalanced life is often strewn with failure, leading to bitterness and cruel behavior.

Success in life, purged of vanity, egotism, and self-complacency, can lead to humility, tolerance, and kindness in the human psyche. Of course there is no immunity from failure and misfortune, even for saints. The story is told of St. Guy of Anderlecht who, in the eleventh century, invested his savings in a speculative business venture, the proceeds from which he would give to the poor.

When the ship carrying the goods for the venture sank while leaving the harbor, Guy heaped blame upon himself for market speculation, believing he should have relied on God to provide.

In recent times, a well-respected Christian author, educator, and humanitarian lost hundreds of thousands in gambling activities. Although he is a prominent speaker on morals and virtuous behavior, the revelation of his addiction to slot machines and casinos amounted to a fall from grace. Taking this misfortune as a sign from God, he gave up his penchant for gambling, which many Christians consider to be a vice. And Pete Rose, at the zenith of his baseball career after eclipsing Ty Cobb's record for base hits, found himself bounced from the game and purged from the waiting list for the Baseball Hall of Fame for unethical betting. Familiar vices, like gambling, are apparently not pardonable for us all and are set out in life to plague us with questionable thought and action.

How does one determine the validity of his thoughts and actions? Once you suspect that your troubled thought processes and the resultant actions are subject to doubt, you must identify the source of your discontent. What is disturbing you? Next, analyze your assumptions. Obviously you must determine what dysfunctional behavior pattern brought to you to the crossroads of right or wrong, good or bad. Many Christians ask for divine guidance through positive thought and prayer in the name of Jesus Christ, and a solution to their errant thoughts and actions is soon at hand. A much more arduous route is through the worldly pursuit of pop-psychology self-help techniques, support groups, and professional therapy. Here you will find yourself following one road after another until you finally are pointed, through trial and error, in the right direction toward a solution. Or, if you are strong-willed, you may eventually defeat your negative thoughts and build up enough self-confidence to trust yourself in making the right decision to alleviate your emotional problem, be it job loss, divorce, broken friendship, ill health, or death of a loved one.

Cumberland County, VA
MASSACRE IN CHINA STEMS DEMOCRACY – May, 1989 –
Bon Jovi

Hundreds of student protesters, demanding pro-democracy reforms in China, planted themselves on a hunger strike in Beijing's 100-acre Tiananmen Square as China's President Deng Xiao-Ping planned to welcome Soviet President Gorbechev. By June, the uprising had gained millions of supporters. The Chinese army responded with a bloody tank assault, crushing tents, mowing down human barricades and killing hundreds, perhaps thousands, of demonstrators. The West responded briefly with sanctions, but Deng did little more than release a few prisoners. He had observed the seeds of democracy sprouting in the Soviet Union and denounced the upheaval as a conspiracy to overthrow the government in China at the turn of the century.

It seems that, as the human species sprouts into the next decade or century, some sort of discord or controversy occurs. When Luther Burbank published his seed catalogue at the beginning of the twentieth century, he was accused of blasphemy and denounced by many churches as trying to change nature and interfere with natural laws of creation. His cross-breeding of plants was considered the Devil's work and interference with God's seeding of the earth.

In a 1989 Richmond, Virginia country property promotion, I had decided to offer 200 fast-growing hybrid poplar or pine seedlings to every buyer of a farmstead, this as an inducement for quick response. Those who planted the seedlings and cared for them no doubt have enjoyed the poetry of God's earth through the economic downturns, wars, and social upheavals of the early nineties and those dismal events occurring at the beginning of the twenty-first century.

Commute to your own affordable farmstead just 30 minutes from Chesterfield

The Richmond, Virginia Board of Realtors reported that the scarcity of affordable nearby land would soon force homebuyers to pay up to twice as much for a new home than was the case in 1986. Frustrated consumers were having to move farther west into Cumberland County because they could not afford the five-figure land costs in Chesterfield and Powhatan.

County planners reported that development in Chesterfield was eating up five square miles of land each year with no end in sight. By the year 2000, county population was expected to double. And the Richmond metropolitan area was expected to encompass the towns of Amelia, Goochland, and Powhatan.

Realtors were reporting newcomers flooding into Richmond at a record pace. Houses were being jammed closer and closer together as nearby land prices headed for the roof, this while inflation was burning up the consumer's money. Talk of an impending financial panic was widespread. Food costs were soaring. The issue of pesticides in food was causing alarm. The urge for a nearby survival farmstead, where the consumer could raise organic food, was a viable promotional theme to entice city people into the countryside.

Wildfire growth in Chesterfield, Goochland, and Powhatan counties had placed Cumberland County on the edge of the "Golden Crescent." This is where 90% of the state's population growth had occurred since 1980. It was the new frontier of the Richmond suburbs.

A new transportation bypass was about to whip through Chesterfield like a noose, further strangling consumers' hopes for affordable nearby acreage. The timing for this offer could not have been better for the country property seeker.

2 to 10 Acre Farmsteads Commutable to Richmond $3995 to $9995.
Most on state roads and ready for home construction

Another characterization of this offer was aimed at consumers with moderate income:

Att: Small Investors, Retirees, and Back-to-the Land people

PO' FOLKS FARMS!

all with pasture, woods, stream, and state road
2 to 10 ACRES from **$50** per month

Here are a few creative advertising headlines from the summer of 1989:

UNWANTED HOME
Seller bought home in Hawaii. Must sacrifice 2 BR home on Little Cacapon River. 4 acres . . . $29,500

GOD'S CREATION
Can be subdivided into 5 lots. But it would be a shame. 25-acre unspoiled stretch of nearby riverfront. Run-down 4 room cabin
$52,500

FARM CASHOUT
Seller packed up and moved to Florida. Needs quick cash. 122-acre farm I hour Dulles Airport . . . $1500 per acre.

Richmond, Virginia
HUNDREDS KILLED IN SAN FRANCISCO QUAKE – Oct. 1989
– Madonna

A killer earthquake erupted along the San Andreas fault during a Tuesday evening rush hour creating tremors from San Francisco north to Sacramento and south to Los Angeles.

The quake claimed the lives of an estimated 270 people and injured up to 3,000. Many buildings–supposedly earthquake-proof–were reduced to rubble, and part of the Oakland Bay Bridge collapsed on itself. President Bush toured the devastation in San Francisco while declaring seven California counties disaster areas.

I was in a Los Angeles hotel at the time, on a return trip to Virginia from a Hawaiian vacation. Originally I was scheduled to stop over in San Francisco, but the strings of fate pulled me to Los Angeles on that day. Earlier in the year I was on my way to the Bahamas. Knowing that my partner, Billy Clark, was in Key West, Florida, I detoured to Hemingway's favorite watering hole to hand over a deal to Clark for final negotiations. A few days earlier I had signed a contract for a prime piece of development property on the James River west of Richmond. After dropping off a copy of the contract, I then drove to back to Miami for a flight to Nassau, only to have the plane pulled back before takeoff due to a mechanical malfunction.

The book of fate is evidently hidden from all of God's creatures.

The Jamestown Story

In April 1607, three ships sailed up the James River from the Chesapeake Bay to establish the first permanent English settlement in America. Located on swampy marginal ground at Jamestown below Richmond, Virginia, the colonists were in constant trouble, suffering through Indian attacks, disease, starvation, and–after the departure of Captain John Smith–lack of strong leadership. Smith had returned to England to recover from wounds incurred in an accident. According to legend, Pocahontas, the daughter of a mighty Indian chief, had saved Smith's life in a previous incident. In 1614, the marriage of Pocahontas to John Rolfe, one of the colonists, was said to have brought eight years of peace between the settlers and the Indians.

By 1619, Jamestown had a population of about 1,000, mostly men. The London Company, a private enterprise then backing the settlement for purposes of monetary gain and Christian evangelism, sent a contingent of young ladies to mate with the young men of the colony so that the town could expand. Shipments of Negro slaves soon followed to help the community prosper. In 1622, the Indian attacks resumed, leaving 350 settlers dead. Another 500 colonists, mostly in outlying settlements, were killed in an Indian attack in 1644. In 1676, during a rebellion, the town was ravaged by fire. Another fire in 1699 wiped out the town, and the colonists chose to move the capital of Virginia to Williamsburg. Most of the settlement has since been washed away by currents in the James River.

Mini-Plantations on the James River
$24,500 to $59,500
seven to twenty-four acres

If you had the coins, you might pay a million dollars or more for a home on a small lot overlooking the James River outside of Richmond, or a great deal more for a home along the Potomac near Washington D.C. Here was a truly amazing offer.

Why the high price on riverfront outside of our major cities? Limited supply. Big demand. They're obviously not making any more land along the James. And the scarcity is getting worse. Much of the upper

James cannot be developed because of flood plains, railroad tracks, and canal systems along the riverbank. South of Richmond you'll find the old-monied plantations gobbling up most of the riverfront.

Until we presented this riverfront offer in the fall of 1989, no reasonable amount of money–either old or new–could buy you a "mini-plantation" on the James near Richmond. This was a conceptual approach to offering estate-sized waterfront acreage at an affordable price. You can search the newspapers, scout the Realtors' offices, plead with landowners; still you won't find affordable acreage on the James close to Richmond. And if you happen to inherit land on the James, you'll unload your stocks and bonds, sell your gold and silver, and mortgage your home, if necessary, to keep the property in your family. The early settlers viewed the James River as their waterway link to England.

The Killing Waters

This is the same area of rich riverfront that hostile Indians killed settlers for at Jamestown and beyond. The same waterfront region that flowed red with blood when the British moved upriver from Richmond in 1781 to destroy American military stores. The same river where, in 1850, travelers could make the 33-hour journey by riverboat from Richmond to Lynchburg, VA, for five silver dollars.

Early settlers watched this bustling river traffic from the same hills overlooking the James where a small number of fortunate contemporary land buyers would be building their new homes. The James is the Old South–a river of Cavaliers, tobacco fields, and fish-trapping Indians. A river sacked by Union General Sheridan in 1865, leaving the old James River plantations in smoking ruins. Now visitors come from all over the world to see the restored historic sites along the James.

America for Sale

Of all the great and historic rivers of the world, the James–like the Thames in England–manages to remain within the confines of a single state, or country. And the rivers share a common heritage of gracious living. It is this unique connection with the culture of Old England that makes property on the James attractive to foreign investors. Such an historic opportunity was available then. But not today. *Business Week* magazine reported in 1989 that a staggering 64% of Americans were alarmed over foreign investors outbidding Americans for valuable U.S. real estate.

Live Like the Rich

With the completion of a new western bypass to I-64, the true Richmond area had been extended about 20 miles upriver. These mini-plantations are located about 29 miles from the Richmond bypass–about as close upriver to the bypass as Leesburg is to D.C. And Washington-area buyers would find this select property only 2 ½ hours away. A display ad in the *Washington Post* encouraged readers to tie up this valuable waterfront for investment or retirement.

It's a shrinking world. The Richmond area was growing so fast in 1989 that 70% of Richmond residents were classified by the Census Bureau as newcomers. And the trend has continued into the twenty-first century. At the time, and when viewed from the D.C. area, finding any land on the James River, commutable to Richmond, could be like getting rich by investing in land on the Potomac near Leesburg in 1959, the year I graduated penniless from college with zero knowledge of real estate values. In 1989, only the rich could afford such property. The same is true today.

Why the Windfall Prices?

This was a farm liquidation. Three investors owned the land. They wanted a hard, high-dollar price. But much of the riverfront was floodable and as worthless as Confederate money for homesites. We offered to take the good land at a higher price and leave them the bad. They liked the win-win situation. With all waterfront to offer, we were able to slash development costs and pass the savings on to consumers. To keep prices low we elected not to pave the roads, leaving that to the estate owners. And the land was not manicured. But fine estates were created along the river, just as early settlers had done with their land on the James.

A mini-plantation on the James–close enough for folks to live and retire on the water and commute to Richmond and Charlottesville–offered more profit potential and stability than any other investment at the time. As more and more people searched for affordable crime-free havens on the water, new laws were passed to control growth and to "protect" the environment.

The Chesapeake Bay Clean-up Act is one of these laws. Its intent was noble. But politicians and radical environmentalists have seized the Act as a tool to "control" growth. And each day it continues to drive up the cost of owning riverfront property as obscure tentacles of the Act reach further and further afield into the countryside, encompassing far-flung water courses that may have some microscopic impact on the Chesapeake Bay estuary.

Paper Money

Those who knew about this opportunity and passed it up may have seen their dream of investing in that little plantation on the river vanish in a hurricane of inflated paper money and deflated stock values. The dollar at the time was being devalued, and paper profits from stocks were falling like the leaves of autumn. After the 1987 crash, disenchanted investors led the rush to grab every parcel we had for sale on the nearby Rivanna River.

Life on the River

These mini-plantations are about 30 miles from Charlottesville and the University of Virginia. This is the land of Jefferson and Madison. And like George Washington, our first president, these fortunate land buyers have the plantation owner's advantages of a breezy hilltop building site overlooking the great and beautiful James. They can look down on rich and productive bottom land, where they can raise cash crops and livestock. And horses can graze under trees along the river bank. Wild ducks and geese are constant visitors. The land slopes from a private road to the water's edge. You can drive or walk to the river. River enthusiasts never have to worry about trespassing on private property when they go fishing or boating because they, their families, and friends can fish from their own riverbanks and set out on canoe voyages from their own dock.

True Ground Floor

When you hear about most ground-floor opportunities, you'd better bite the coin that's offered. But not in this case. Like our first-minted 100% pure silver dollars, this was the first and only offer of this valuable James riverfront. When it was gone, it was gone with the proverbial wind.

Free Bag of Silver

The Morgan silver dollar is rich in history like the James. It is one of the most sought-after coins in the world. Jesse James and Cole Younger killed for it. Gamblers used it to settle their debts in frontier saloons and riverboats of the Old South. Black Bart ordered strongboxes full of it thrown down to him at gunpoint from Wells Fargo stagecoaches.

So spellbinding are these rare coins that the world's worst misers and hoarders bury them in secret caches rather than use them in trade. I tried for months to locate a few bags of these amazing coins. Then a rare-coin collector told me where I could ransom a small supply to dramatize this historic offer.

While they lasted, I gave away, with the deed to each mini-plantation, a free 20-coin bag of these century-old masterpieces that may have passed through the hands of thieves, scoundrels, and cutthroats far more terrifying than the outlaws described above. Plus, when consumers called for appointments I reserved in their names a free 100-year-old Morgan silver dollar from my limited supply. There was no catch. And if they brought the ad, I gave them a $500 discount.

Richmond, Virginia
GERMANY UNITED AS BERLIN WALL CRUMBLES – Nov.1989
– Billy Joel

Thousands of East Germans streamed across the border into West Germany as a relic of the Cold War, the Berlin Wall, was given last rites by a reformed Stalinist government. Massive protests and a continued exodus from communist rule had crushed the 8-foot-high barrier to a united Germany and buried the political career of East German leader Erich Honecker, who had predicted that the wall would last for 100 years. Protesters expressed their anger by picking the wall apart piece by piece, taking some to sell as souvenirs, while hundreds of other dissenters danced for hours on top of the barrier.

In the U.S., the first signs of a crumbling economy were at hand, and many banks began building barriers to potential foreclosures and defaults by tightening credit standards. We had sold out a recent farmstead project west of Richmond and were awaiting approval on a stack of loan applications. Nervous banking officials, their fingers wet and poised before the winds of impending calamity, decided that good credit was not good enough. Never mind that I was personally endorsed on all the loans. Theoretically I could go down the tubes. And if there is one smell that bankers cannot tolerate it is the stench of a dying developer.

In times of tight money, the nostrils of bankers become as laser-guided as those of a bloodhound. Most of the loans were thrown out, this as obscure loan officials at our primary bank ran for cover. This community bank, one that I had helped to build over the years through tons of consumer and corporate loans, had merged with an out-of-state group and had become somewhat immune to the needs of its valued customers. I later pulled out all of my accounts. The bank's insensitive and arbitrary action marginalized our profits by forcing me into a secondary campaign to sell most of the parcels all over again.

PART SIX

The Nineties

With an aging population, it is not surprising that the booming rural counties in the U.S. are mostly in warm-weather regions with retirement communities, golf resorts, beaches, and casinos. And counties oriented toward golf and outdoor recreation such as Washington County in southwest Utah are actually surpassing traditional "retirement" counties in population gains.

The vast majority of "recreational" counties throughout the country appear to be gaining population in record numbers. Dare County, for example, on the Outer Banks of North Carolina, is experiencing phenomenal growth to the point where people flock to the beach year-round.

Less dramatic growth is occurring in rural "manufacturing" counties where jobs are likely to be plentiful. In Arizona, residents in Prescott commute 100 miles to Phoenix. In Virginia, a 70-mile commute has become commonplace. In Washington state, most of the non-metropolitan counties are growing faster than they did in the eighties, this as commuters search for a better quality of life. Even the "poverty" counties are fair game for commuter homesteads. The 1990 census showed 73% of these poorer counties experiencing growth as we entered the nineties.

West Virginia
BUSH DUMPS PROMISE NOT TO RAISE TAXES – June, 1990 –
Madonna

President Bush, attempting to narrow government deficits, made a
U-turn on his "Read my lips. No new taxes" campaign statement by
calling for new "tax revenue increases."

In concert with the proposed tax hikes, housing prices had started to
fall. After factoring in inflation, home values had dropped by about
20% in some regions of the country, and this precipitous decline would
continue for the next two years, dampening the price of land.

This gloomy scenario followed the usual trend of economic downturns, where lower home prices generally lag behind job losses. Hard-
pressed consumers usually sell their primary homes only as a last resort, or lose them to foreclosure when their finances hit bottom.

Price run-ups in real estate can move in cycles, ranging from five
years to a full decade.

In 1990, when I sold my second home on Maui in Hawaii, the uptrend
in real estate prices–largely due to huge Japanese investment activity–
was coming to an end. A general home price decline then swept over
the Hawaiian Islands that lasted about ten years.

On the West Coast, cities like San Francisco and San Jose saw home
values fall by almost 40% during the period 1989 to 1995. With interest rates at comparatively high levels, and no particular incentive to
refinance, there was no safety net to catch the impending collapse of
the real estate market. Investors and speculators had bid up prices to
unrealistic levels that were unsustainable in the economic turmoil that
loomed on the horizon.

Flipping homes for profit was becoming a con game for suckers at
the tail end of a Ponzi scheme. In the long term, of course, real estate
generally recovers and can yield significant profits. But for those who
buy homes and raw land on margin at the top of the market and who
are financially ill-equipped to ride out inevitable crashes, the future
can be very dim.

Selling land in a financial hurricane is a difficult task calling for
imaginative advertising and promotional themes. This is because the
consumer base has run for cover and must be coaxed back into the
market through irresistible offers. The closest you can get to "FREE"
the better.

Here is a headline I used to sell some land for a farmer and orchardist who needed money:

DO YOU QUALIFY FOR $7.44 PER AC. LAND IN NEARBY WEST VIRGINIA?

The consumer may not have been able to own a section of the Spring-
field Public Hunting and Fishing Area. But if his land joined the 800-
acre preserve, he would have use of a game-filled forest large enough
for a king. The sales promotion was launched as a "program" to provide fee simple ownership of two to ten acres of land, plus the use of
an adjoining 800-acre section and deeded access to the South Branch
of the Potomac River. The total land cost was about $7.44 per acre
when factoring in the use of the adjoining 800 acres.

How to Qualify

Financial worth was considered secondary. Dedication to preserving and protecting the environment was more important than the manner in which the consumer was to pay for the land.

There was to be no clear-cutting of timber, no dumping or storage
of junk cars, and no polluting of groundwater. The consumer was expected to abide by all state and federal game laws, including the safe
use of firearms and the obtaining of required permits and licenses for
hunting and fishing. Homes were required to have at least 480 square
feet of living space. Mobile homes were permitted. And finally, the
consumer was called upon to pay $100 per year for maintenance of
common roadways and river access areas. Camping was allowed. All
mineral rights conveyed.

Almost Free Prices

When qualifying for this "program" there was no discrimination
against race, creed, color, religion, sex, national origin, age, or handi-
cap. The owner, a local orchardist, was portrayed as a compassionate
person who cared for the earth and the environment and who wanted
to share the dream of home and land ownership with equally caring
people. Prices for the two to seven acre parcels ranged from $3995 to
$6995.

Tough Times

This offer was not meant to sell country club-type lots. The "program" was designed to make affordable land available to those of modest means who would be willing to preserve and protect the earth. West Virginia is not a rich state. And times were tough. So some farmers and orchardists needed to sell off part of their land to survive. They lived close to the earth and loved their land. It was logical that these landowners would sell to those consumers who shared their concern for the environment.

Hard Facts

The land is mostly wooded. Some parcels have streams. Many enjoy attractive views of the mountains. Some new homes had been constructed in the area. Electric and telephone service was available, and well water was obtainable at reasonable depths. The owner guaranteed that all tracts would meet health department requirements for in-ground sewage disposal. Most of the roads were dirt and gravel-based. Some tracts front on paved roads. The town of Romney, with shopping areas and a hospital, is about 20 minutes away.

Planning the Trip

To encourage the consumer to leave his home, where he was under constant economic assault, and venture out into the countryside to look at land, I attempted to make the trip comfortable and totally without the threat of salesmanship. The ad described how a former orchardist and his wife would meet with those readers who had accepted the basic qualifications of ownership. When the prospect arrived, he would be given a plat, price list, and a bag of delicious West Virginia apples from the owner's orchards. When the prospects had viewed the available parcels and agreed with the protective covenants, they could then leave a refundable deposit and sign an "ownership agreement."

Terms of Ownership

Buyers received a general warranty deed at closing. Title insurance and up to 90% financing were available. Payments on the lowest-priced properties amounted to pocket change a day. If the consumers were short of funds, and if their credit was good, I advised them to talk to the orchardist about owner financing. The orchardist felt that good neighbors might as well pay him as to pay the bank. No professional salespeople were used in this promotion so that overhead could be kept at rock bottom. In many cases, some of our fees were returned to us in the form of interest-bearing notes. Interest rates on raw land at the time ranged from 12 to 13% apr.

Shenandoah Valley, VA
S&L CRISIS ROCKS BUSH ADMINISTRATION – July, 1990 – Mariah Carey

Federal regulators predicted a massive government bailout of 500 billion dollars over the ensuing 40 years to correct excesses in lending practices and to implement reforms in the beleaguered savings and loan industry, where–due to high interest rates paid to depositors–reckless speculation in junk bonds and questionable real estate ventures had occurred. The government would soon withdraw its guarantees (up to $100,000 on passbook savings) and render S&Ls relatively impotent as mortgage lenders, eventually reducing their home financing portfolios to a mere 12% of outstanding loans in the U.S. Neil Bush, the President's son, was caught up in the scandal because of his alleged conflict of interest with main borrowers while serving on the board of directors at a Colorado-based S&L.

Banks were experiencing record-level charge-offs on bad mortgage loans, and a glut of real estate would soon be thrust upon the market. Here is how I played the land game as this trend became apparent:

The real estate glut and how you can profit from 3 ac. riverfront estates commutable to D.C.
Most people are too busy waiting for bargains to spot a real steal

---

Despite the glut of homes and building lots, local riverfront homesites had skyrocketed due to high demand and scarcity of supply. And the price of waterfront homesites can easily dwarf the construction cost of a home on water because of new environmental laws, such as the Save the Bay Act and the Wetlands Preservation Act. Activist pressure to preserve and protect our rivers further restricts the number of potential homesites on water.

Builders' Loss, Your Gain

I had purchased a riverfront peninsula at auction and, having sold most of the parcels, was at the tail end of the promotion. But now the money spigot had been turned off by the feds.

The economy was heading south, and builders were, well, out fishing. There was a severe slowdown in home construction. So the remaining riverfront estates–all with central sewer–were being offered at prices almost anyone could afford. Prices were so low that the average consumer could live on the water and commute along I-66 to the heart of D.C. And the below-market prices could be verified by checking with local Realtors for comparables.

The Profit Takers

As guidance from the past has proven, investors and speculators would continue to drive up prices on nearby riverfront to fuel the demand for waterfront homesites. But most investors and finicky consumers would be too busy searching for "bargains" and the "right land" to spot a real steal. By mid-1990, everybody knew about a troubled housing market. But when the market had discounted all the bad news, prices on buildable nearby riverfront acreage were already climbing. How much more would they pay if they had waited five years? Ten years? Prices had doubled in five; tripled in ten.

Location, Location, Location

Growth usually follows new highways, sewer lines, and mass transit, as do successful real estate speculators. In the D.C. area, this trend was evident by a surging population in suburban Maryland and Virginia counties. Figures from the Virginia Employment Commission in 1989 showed job opportunities being snapped up in urban fringe areas. And commuter rail lines were transforming outlying communities like Manassas and Fredericksburg into D.C. suburbs. These facts, and a proposed outer beltway, have created a D.C. bedroom community in the northern Shenandoah Valley, extending 80 miles or more west of the city. That's why people are fleeing in record numbers to the exurban Virginia counties of Frederick, Warren, and Shenandoah, all in the upper Shenandoah Valley near the junction of I-66 and I-81, both major transportation corridors.

More Location

This riverfront offer was located just 3 ½ miles off of I-81. Land buyers could have their choice of two nearby universities–James Madison U. in Harrisonburg, and Shenandoah U. in Winchester, plus Lord Fairfax Community College in Middletown. They would also have access to three convenient shopping malls, two regional airports, three hospitals, gourmet restaurants, three live theater groups, numerous country clubs and golf courses, and two nearby ski areas.

The Power of the River

For country property seekers, the feature of locating on navigable water is generally at the top of their list, if they can find it. What attracts people to rivers? Maybe, like our first president, George Washington, who was rumored to have thrown a silver dollar across the Potomac, people want to build a home overlooking an ever-moving landscape. Maybe they see themselves relaxing in a hammock beside their own rapids or deep clear pools of water. No doubt the happiness of their children and grandchildren are of major concerns as they see their family fishing, boating, swimming and engaged in playful activity. And, of course, there is an element of prestige in owning waterfront property, particularly if you can acquire it at an enviable price.

Others Pay More

Alert investors knew that prices on waterfront property were relatively unaffected by the nosedive in prices for building lots. There is only a limited amount of buildable riverfront, coastline, and beachfront. When it's gone, it's gone. In this case, it took over 235 years for this historic property to become available to new owners. My company aside, new buyers enjoyed the unique distinction of being only the third land holders in the history of this country to own this unusual riverfront. History has proved that good waterfront seldom changes hands and always goes up in price. Three-acre riverfront estates were offered with central sewer in 1990 at prices ranging from $18,950 to $27,950. By the turn of the century, prices had reached the $50-60,000 price range, if you could find someone who wanted to sell.

Unlike the housing sector, which is propped up by lending policies that are largely subsidized and often overly aggressive, the market for waterfront properties is "real" and driven by scarcity, limited supply and consistent demand. As such, waterfront is not subject to inflated and deflated price swings, making it relatively immune from economic vagaries and consequently presenting a more stabilized short or long-term investment for country property seekers who do their homework.

Front Royal, VA
IRAQI FORCES INVADE KUWAIT – August, 1990 –
Jon Bon Jovi

Saddam Hussein, the Iraqi dictator, unleashed an overwhelming force of tanks, aircraft and troops on the tiny oil-rich kingdom of Kuwait in the Persian Gulf, crushing the feeble Kuwaiti defense line and taking over a country that, when merged with Iraq, would control 40% of the world's oil reserves.

The United Nations imposed an embargo on Iraq, and the U.S. and other world leaders condemned the invasion. President Bush subsequently dispatched troops and warships to the region, this while the United Nations Security Council debated the eventual use of force to carry out the embargo against Iraq. Saddam Hussein threatened to turn Kuwait into a graveyard if any outside powers intervened.

I had purchased a second riverfront farm at auction back in June and was wrapping up a sales campaign when the imminent Gulf War sent almost all of my contracts to the graveyard, this as insecure buyers cancelled their deals in a panic over the threat of the U.S. engaging the third-largest army in the world. Again, my promotional theme was based on the potential profits to be gleaned from the economic downturn. The lesson here is to not let the media take control over your life. Unfounded fear, in this case, made folly of an otherwise sound investment for consumers, and cost these panicky investors literally thousands of dollars in virtually guaranteed profits.

The real estate glut and how you can profit from 20 to 40 ac. estates commutable to the D.C. Metro Area from $69,500
20-acre Riverfront Plantations 45 minutes from Reston
40-acre Secluded Estates 39 miles from Middleburg

Usually you would have to be very rich to own a forty-acre estate west of Middleburg, Virginia, where land sells for $50,000 an acre; or a 20-acre mini-plantation on the main branch of the Shenandoah River just 7 miles off of I-66, near Fauquier County, Virginia, where fifty-acre parcels, in the early nineties, could fetch three quarters of a million dollars.

In the summer of 1990, all it took was a real estate crisis to move you into an affordable nearby estate–some of which were over twice as large as the White House grounds. Despite the area's glut of homes and building lots, local land prices continued to skyrocket due to high demand and scarcity of supply. Land development restrictions in some counties near D.C. have become so tight that $500,000 homes on 10 acres are considered modest dwellings, and 50-acre parcels are mandated for home construction in some rural areas that have become sanctified fiefdoms for the super-rich elite.

The Profit Takers

Investors and speculators in land who had foreseen the real estate crash, and who had kept their powder dry with a degree of liquidity, were out in force in 1990. They were driven by one simple fact: we will never run out of houses, but buildable land is getting scarce. In other words, homes, as a commodity, will always be subject to price gyrations; while the scarcity of buildable land, due primarily to political maneuvering, places a floor under the market, this despite sporadic and temporary surpluses of building lots in economic downturns.

The home market is, to a certain degree, a false market, with values created by highly competitive lenders and through the cavalier free-spending operations of Fannie Mae and Freddie Mac, with their relatively risk-free government-guaranteed loans.

Home prices tend to rise over the years. They may level off for periods of time, and even decline, as they did in 1990. But there is less volatility in the land market than in homes, because land is an unrecoverable resource. Theoretically, you cannot make more of it, albeit you can create more lots. However, as I have pointed out, the creation of building lots is becoming increasingly more difficult and expensive due to political and environmental pressures. It seems the longer you wait, the more you will pay for the land you want. But in a soft real estate market there are fewer players, and pockets of enormous opportunity exist if you know where to look.

As the recession of 1990 rolled in, all of my previous offers in Frederick, Warren, and Stafford Counties had been sold out, and resale prices were yielding quick profits to those who had essentially "flipped" their land.

The Fairfaxing Factor

One question I asked consumers was this: Will nearby Frederick and Warren counties mean Fairfax-sized profits for the smart investor? Fairfax County, of course, is now so convenient to the center of D.C. that many area newcomers consider it part of the city. These two relatively close-in counties, which are adjacent to Clarke, Loudoun, and Fauquier, have become the new D.C. suburbs. Wildfire growth in the Dulles Airport area, the construction of I-66, and the proposed new outer beltway have effectively dragged the D.C. metro area westward to the doorstep of Frederick and Warren counties.

The Dulles Blitz

The coming outer beltway could very well blast through the Dulles area, where Xerox has built a new city near Leesburg. Thousands of homes have been built west of Dulles, with many thousands more on the way. A commuter rail line is now operating from Manassas–about 40 minutes from Warren County, in which this offer was located. Other satellite communities were proposed for adjacent Loudoun County, many of which have since been constructed. And the new Dulles Toll Road, as expected, spurred extraordinary growth in western Loudoun, causing the imposition of obscene growth restrictions by local reactionary politicians.

Moreover, the D.C. Metropolitan Area Council of Governments expects an increase of 1.3 million new jobs in the area by the year 2010. These facts were available to those who responded to the 20 to 40-acre offer and to the purchasers who have significantly profited by acting on the opportunity when it was presented.

Quality of Life

Explosive growth can bring real and imagined problems: Groundwater contamination, waste disposal, pollution, erosion, high-rise buildings, people stacked on top of each other like sardines. But when you're sitting in the middle of 20 or 40 acres of your own estate-quality land, you realize how lucky you really are. Others know that, too. That's why people spend hundreds of thousands of dollars for ten acres near

Middleburg, Warrenton, and Leesburg outside of Washington D.C. For those who took advantage of this offer, it was like buying a small farm near Leesburg in the 1950's. That's how some smart investors got rich. And if you were into horses, you were right at home. Whether it was a 20-acre plantation on the river, or a secluded 40-acre estate, this offer would have given you plenty of riding room, big trees, and lush pasture. Plus, the setting provided all the adventure and pleasure of owning land on a great river.

Large, flat-bottomed barges, filled with agricultural bounty of the Shenandoah Valley, once plowed this famous waterway on their way to the Potomac at Harpers Ferry, where, in 1859, the abolitionist, John Brown, was captured by Colonel Robert E. Lee, this after the outlaw and 18 of his followers attempted to raid the U.S. Arsenal and encourage slaves to rebel. Brown was later convicted on charges of treason and hanged.

An Uncertain Economy?

Some of those who waited for the economy to turn around saw their dream of investing in that secluded 40-acre estate or 20-acre riverfront plantation near Middleburg vanish in a hurricane of inflated paper money, and they could not thereafter afford to buy similar property, this as their financial strength was dashed by rising land prices and falling stock values. Forty-acre commutable country estates sold at prices ranging from $69,500 to $79,500. Twenty-acre commutable riverfront plantations on the main branch Shenandoah went from $89,500 to $139,500 in 1990. The availability of such parcels today is almost unheard of.

Missed Opportunities

When we were children at the seashore, we filled our little hands with sand and let the grains fall–seemingly one by one–back upon the beach until all were gone. And in the stream of life, the golden moments rush by, but we see only the sand. Heaven help us. The angels come to comfort us, and we know them only when they're gone. In troubled times we often spend our moments nourishing our sorrows and fail to take swift advantage of the hour. Look at two other opportunities you may have missed on two of the nation's most famous rivers.

Moorefield, W. VA
SUPERPOWERS SHOW UNITY AGAINST IRAQ – Sept., 1990 –
George Michael

President Bush and Soviet leader Mikhail Gorbachev met in Helsinki, Finland and agreed to stand firm against Iraq's occupation of Kuwait and its seizure of "human shield" hostages.

The Soviets later took a tough stand in the U.N. by voting to add an air embargo to the existing naval blockade of Iraq and suggesting that they would be willing to send troops under a UN umbrella. Iraq showed no sign of backing down, and the U.S. continued to form a coalition.

The impending war ravaged the real estate market and my widespread operations began to fall apart. In Moorefield, I had won a sealed bid for an unusual tract of land on the South Branch of the Potomac that joined an 18-hole golf course. This was to be an upscale development with central water lines. Customers, as it turned out, were hard to find. And although this was a successful and profitable project in the long term it was not until 1992 that we were sold out.

HOMESITE OPPORTUNITY ON SOUTH POTOMAC NEXT TO GOLF COURSE

3 to 7 acre Riverfront Homesites from $12,950 to $29,950

All with access to central water and golf course.

Golf initiation fee included in price.

I was spread thin in my operations from the Chesapeake Bay to the West Virginia mountains, loaded up with land and staff and rapidly running out of cash. With sales in a downspin, overhead was eating me alive. Ever the optimist, I figured that when the war was over, things would turn around, and I would get back on track. Foolishly, I refused to downsize my company at the time, not wanting to throw people out of work. A fool at forty is a fool indeed.

A fool in his fifties is really stupid. It was not long before I was down to about $30,000 in cash reserves, and although I was up to date on mortgage payments, the lender on my farm, sensing trouble in River City, sent me a subtle letter of concern that read like a requiem for a developer.

I punched them back with an indignant letter that told them to back off–this since I was not behind in my payments–and that the real estate market would come roaring back like a lion.

Here are some headlines from those *cold* pre-war days:

DEFAULTED LAND–Little Farm on the River $95 DN.

ALMOST FREE LAND at Potomac River. Bring $95

BARN ALONE WORTH ASKING PRICE OF RANCH

WANT TO STEAL SOME NEARBY LAND? $95 DOWN

BROKER NEEDS CASH. RIVERFRONT ESTATE $25K
HOT WATERFRONT PICKS IN A *COLD* MARKET
BAYFRONT UP FOR GRABS - CHARTED TO ATLANTIC

Chesapeake Bay
JUNK BOND KING JAILED – November, 1990 –
Mariah Carey

Michael Milken, the Drexel Burnham whiz kid and creator of the "junk bond" financing scheme used in corporate takeovers, was sent to the slammer for 10 years, with three years on probation. Milken, who took down a $550 million paycheck in 1987, was also more than bled dry of a year's work by a $600 million fine for securities violations and helping to file false income tax returns. Meanwhile, in the Bay area, developers were getting slammed hard by the imminent war, and many were bleeding badly.

Bay Blood Bath

Bay area developers bleeding. Losing millions to war fears and recession. Their loss, your gain. Steal valuable waterfront at 50 cents on the dollar. Pick up homesites on a paved road for a song. Samples: Bay woods with stream. Walk to sandy beach and dock, $6950. Seven acre compound on harbor overlooking Bay. Seagulls and salt air, $39,950. Five acre estate on lake, navigable river, and state road, $29,500. Two acres of big woods on Little Wicomico River off Bay for $19,950. Unheard of terms: 5% down, 6% interest. Not a gimmick to sell land. Values are real. People stealing bargains every week. Some waterfront up triple in value since our sales in 1980 recession. Hurry! Prices have bottomed. Smart investors buy when blood is flowing in the Bay. Call for latest Hotsheet. B.K. HAYNES REAL ESTATE.

Front Royal, VA
IRAQ LAUNCHES SCUDS AT ISRAEL & SAUDIS – Jan., 1991 –
Janet Jackson

In response to an intensive allied air assault, Iraq hit back with SCUD missiles, sending them into populated areas of Israel and Saudi Arabia.

The Soviet-built missiles were considered primitive and inaccurate when compared with modern military standards; however, the fearful psychological effect on the masses of people in targeted cities was considered significant.

Allied military commanders expressed concern that the Iraqis would arm the missiles with chemical or biological warheads, posing the risk of drawing Israel into the war.

In the D.C. area, a developer had risked his bankroll on a ski slope venture in the Blue Ridge Mountains within commuting distance of the city. Some nationally known political personalities had second homes in an adjoining upscale development. This was a high-risk gamble due to weather uncertainties and the lack of adequate snowfall to sustain profitable operations over time. Nevertheless, the slopes faced north and provided, at 1.5 miles in length, the most expansive run in Virginia. I was hired by some local developers to promote the sale of homesites in the subdivision adjoining the ski area. This looked like the perfect fit for a "first home" ski community, where you could ski after your work in D.C. Several promotional themes popped up in my mind:

SKI WHERE YOU LIVE
SKI D.C.
DON'T JUST BUY A HOME–BUY A LIFESTYLE

I had bumper stickers made up, redesigned billboards, and contributed significantly to the stock price of the *Washington Post* through some hefty advertising. Unfortunately for the ski area, and for my bottom line, the weather during the winter of 1991 and 1992 was unusually warm, and the venture failed. Then, after dealing with hundreds of customers and making sparse sales, I folded my tent and moved on to those proverbial greener pastures; though, at the time, the real estate landscape seemed denuded of color.

Middletown, Virginia
KUWAIT FREE AFTER 100-HOUR WAR – February, 1991 –
Whitney Houston

Desert Storm was over, and the Kuwaiti people were liberated after almost seven months of Iraqi occupation. U.S. casualty figures amounted to 141 dead and 472 wounded. The allies estimated that 150,000 Iraqis were killed in battle. Tens of thousands more surrendered or were captured by allied troops. Kuwait was left in ruins. Behind the few moments of joy there was widespread anger among the people whose country had been looted of its wealth and artifacts by Iraqi soldiers and officials. Electric power had been cut. Hospital facilities were severely wrecked. And oil wells were flaming torches spewing flames and blotting out the sun with black smoke.

The recession and war had lingered ominously on the horizon for more than a year, and the future seemed dark indeed. Still not willing to bite the bullet by downsizing and throwing my people out of work, I decided to sell off some five-acre building lots from my farm to raise operating capital. My son and I had started a commercial brokerage business when he had graduated from college in 1988, and this operation, too, was foundering in a dead sea of dried up business and cash. I had already gone off salary and borrowed my limit to meet the relentless and recurring payroll, and I had never seen cash disappear so fast.

If there is a lesson to this lack of good business judgment on my part, it is that wisdom appears to come to no one by chance. Most likely we earn it. A soft heart in business affairs can be potentially more injurious to the giver than if he or she were to follow sound and proven business practices when dealing with people. Emotion and misplaced compassion are strangers to the marketplace, making the soft-hearted ever more the victims of ourselves and dupes of the insensitive around us.

The Freeloader

A classic example of this type of personality is the person looking for a free appraisal. Unwilling to pay someone to appraise his property, he will appear before the experienced real estate broker with the following proposition: I have this land out there, but I don't know what it is worth. I would like you to go look at it and tell me what you think. The broker asks what value the county has placed on the land for tax purposes. The Freeloader responds that he does not know, or that he thinks the land is undervalued. The broker is thinking, *What's in this for me?*

The Freeloader says he might give a listing to the broker if the price is right; although the Freeloader has no intention of paying a commission for the sale of his land, much less coughing up for an appraisal. To stop this nonsense, I have had to impose a fee for such potentially fruitless chats and consultations, with the understanding that the fee is deductible from the commission in the event of a sale. Imagine, if you will, the audacity of a person trying to pull this stunt with an attorney or doctor when seeking advice. "Tell me what I did wrong, and I might let you represent me;" or "Tell me what's wrong with me, and I may let you operate?" No charge, of course. In business and human relations, there is the element of value to everyone's time.

The Con Man

The unrepentant con man earns wisdom by moving on to the next con, each one hopefully more progressively slick and sophisticated than the one before. In real estate, this character is all over the map. I have mentioned the antics of other con artists in this book, but one hustler who comes to mind was operating in my orbit during this lean period of slow sales and scarce cash.

The mind, unguarded against evil, and weakened by unresolved problems, can be the gateway for misery, trifling thoughts, and the machinations of scoundrels. My mind, particularly after my wife had died in 1988, was not as guarded as I would have liked, and I had left its welcome mat out for a diversity of goblins through my unstructured spiritual studies.

The guy walks in with a deal for our commercial business that I wanted to get off of dead center, and the proposition seemingly makes sense at the time. I suggest a meeting with my accountant and my lawyer at an upscale local restaurant, where the guy is to pitch the deal to the guardians of my purse. Right away the ominous overtones of the deal are foreshadowed when the lawyer gets sick and excuses himself before the presentation. I let the incident pass and eventually fork over $25,000 to buy into the deal. When he next appears, his clunker coach has been transformed into a shiny new station wagon. He uses well-rehearsed theatrical gestures, such as raising his voice when things go wrong, or, if asked to account for possible malfeasance, calling for prayer to seek guidance.

I ask him to negotiate a deal, and he tongue-whips the client with fast talk and high pressure, losing the client and the deal. I arrange an out-of-town trip where he is to make a presentation, and he checks into the room I have reserved for myself and blows the presentation by bullshitting the group we are trying to influence. I try to brief him on solving a problem in the Chesapeake Bay area, only to discover than he "Don't Know Much About Real Estate."

His commercial deal is dead in the water, and he ends up being nothing but trouble. So I tell him to get lost and stay out of my life. He suggests we pray about it. Go figure. The deceiver dies a thousand deaths, the honest man but one.

I think I reached the lowest point in my real estate career when I found myself out hustling cheap lots in the mountains in the spring of 1991. The Gulf War was over, and Alan Greenspan was defending the nation against inflation by maintaining a barrier of high interest rates. Corporate downsizing was in full force, this compounding the unemployment problem by throwing an army of white-collar workers out on the street to hunt for jobs. And job hunters are in no mood or financial shape to buy real estate. Few people at the time doubted that this was a real recession.

After a trip to Richmond, where I had an epiphany of sorts, I returned with a plan to downsize the company and restore some degree of order to the cash flow problem. I released most of my staff and salespeople, dissolved the commercial component of the business and discontinued outside consulting services. At home one morning, I turned my life over to Christ and gained a measure of inner peace. Afterwards I resumed church attendance and enrolled in a Bible study class. To build liquidity, I got busy selling the lots from my farm that I had subdivided for just such an emergency. Here is one of the ads:

HORSES?

Middletown, VA–10 acres of rolling pasture and scattered trees. Small stream. Pond site. Beautiful mountain views. Just off I-66. 2 miles from college and historic Belle Grove Plantation. Surveyed as 2 lots. $69,500. Or 5 acres $39,500. 90% financing. Owner/broker.

Winchester, VA
GORBACHEV SURVIVES KREMLIN COUP – August, 1991 –
Good Vibrations

A bungled coup by hardline military and KGB leaders to take over the Soviet government quickly unraveled as President Mikhail Gorbachev was released after being held under house arrest for 60 hours in the Crimea. Boris Yeltsin was hailed as a hero for organizing resistance to the coup, sending forces to free Gorbachev and beating back an assault on the Russian parliament building when it was attacked by coup supporters in tanks and armored vehicles.

Yeltsin refused to enter into talks with Gorbachev, closed down all communist party premises, and suspended communist newspapers, such as *Pravda*, for supporting the coup.

Many top Soviet military officers and KGB leaders fell in behind Yeltsin, as did most of the Russian people. Gorbachev went before the Russian parliament to publicly thank Yeltsin; and though Gorbachev survived the coup, his power was greatly diminished.

After essentially closing down operations of B.K. Haynes Corporation, I managed to survive by going back into sales. One of my partners had left for Florida to ride out the downturn.

We owned an old farm that I managed to get subdivided and subsequently sold. Here are a couple of the ads:

---

1 hour out
GRAY GHOST
21 Acres

One of the earliest log cabins built in frontier Virginia. Discovered under a shroud of board siding on farm near Winchester. Grim treasure has hand-hewn logs, wide plank flooring, massive stone fireplace, well water. Restorable 4 room antique guarded by ghostly trees of yesteryear. Old outbuildings gasp for life beside old farm road. Park-like woods of Christmas trees to fill up with snow. Estate-quality fields. Small stream. Mountain views. Perc'd. 15 min. university, jet airport, and 3-state medical center. $69,950. 90% financing. Owner/broker.

Giveaway Getaway

33 acres. 1 hour out. Road's end. No neighbors in sight. Big trees and hidden meadows. Wildlife paradise. Deer, turkey, grouse, quail. Low density area. Hunt, keep horses. Stream in woods. Perc'd. Share road upkeep. Get lost close to town. 15 min. Winchester. 39 mi. west of Middleburg, VA. A giveaway at $39,500. 10% down. Owner/broker.

Las Vegas, Nevada
PAM AM MAKES LAST FLIGHT – December, 1991 –
Michael Jackson

The deep recession and airline deregulation reached into the hostile skies over Miami, Florida and brought down Pan American Airways, the 64-year-old pioneer of commercial aviation, making it the third airline to crash in 1991 due to financial problems.

I decided to forget my money woes that winter and, in early December, I flew in the friendly skies of United to Hawaii for the 50th anniversary of the Japanese attack on Pearl Harbor. Before I left, I received my designation as an Accredited Land Consultant (ALC) from the Realtors Land Institute, later serving as president of the Virginia Chapter and regional vice president of the national organization.

Though I am not hung up on professional titles, I felt it worthwhile to complete the work required for this designation. And while I'm not even a moderate "joiner"–choosing to being loner of sorts–I do belong to one other business organization, of which I am a lifetime member, and one that I find admirable and nurturing for the entrepreneurial mind. That is the CEO CLUBS, INC. in New York, organized and headed by Joe Mancuso.

Webster's New World Dictionary describes an entrepreneur as "a person who organizes and manages a business undertaking, assuming the risk for the sake of profit." The technological boom of the eighties and nineties has certainly produced a fair share of new entrepreneurs.

But looking back a century at the year 1800, you could say there were proportionally more entrepreneurs relative to the population in this country than there are today. That's because 85% of the labor force worked in agriculture, many managing their own small farms.

This number fell to 52.0% in 1870, 25.2% in 1920, 4.2% in 1970, and 2.1% in 2000.

By the late twenties, farmers, as entrepreneurs, were becoming America's field hands, constituting nearly a third of the population, but enjoying less than 10% of the nation's income pie. Prosperity in the twenties did not offset the loss of overseas markets following the end of World War I, and farmers continued to produce food to preserve their meager incomes. By 1929, the era of farm subsidies was launched by Congress to stabilize prices on farm commodities and to hopefully end farmers' distress.

At the end of 1991, I flew back to Hawaii for an extended Christmas vacation and enrolled in a computer course. You might say I learned how to operate a computer in paradise.

Front Royal, VA
AUTO GIANTS SKID TO RECORD LOSSES – February, 1992 –
George Michael/Elton John

Job cuts loomed on the horizon for Ford and General Motors as the world's mightiest car titans struggled with a mountain of debt piled up by the recession. General Motors reported a record loss of $8.5 billion in North America, offset by a $4 billion overseas profit while Ford staggered under its biggest yearly losses in history–$2.3 billion in North America and $970 million overseas.

Seems like almost everybody was short of the green grease in those days. Here are a few of my advertising snippets from 1992:

CITY GIRL GIVES UP INHERITANCE
Daughter inherits country property but needs money. Sacrificing parent's dream homesite off of Rt. 340...

BROKER GIVES UP LAND 30 CENTS ON THE DOLLAR
Sacrifice to pay taxes. Over 3 times as much land for the money...

LUNCH MONEY BUYS PEACH FARM
Orchardist hits hard times. Gives you a sweet little farm for sandwich money a day...

Shades of the Great Depression. Some economists and historians saw the deadly plague of deflation and underconsumption again sweeping across the country. This pernicious economic ailment can be diagnosed as the inability of a large number of the American people to buy goods produced by a rapidly expanded and efficient industrial plant. Agriculture, coal mining, textiles, and railroads were all perennially doomed to a slow death following the Great Depression of 1929. Who would be targeted this time?

To acquaint you with the root cause and monetary imbalances of those dark days, consider these facts from the *PENGUIN ENCYCLO-PEDIA OF AMERICAN HISTORY*: In 1929, the richest fifth of the population pocketed 54.4 percent of the nation's loot. Only 2.3 percent of American families had incomes exceeding ten grand a year. Most of America was in the poorhouse. A staggering 71 percent of families were struggling to make ends meet, with money dribbling in per year at the cost of a rich man's gold watch–$2500. The richest *families* in the country–those with incomes over $100,000–controlled most of the wealth; yet their aggregate amounted to just 14,000 *families,* these representing a mere 0.1 percent of the total population. Their combined annual income equaled the amount of money received each year by the bottom 42 percent of American *families*.

Between 1929 and 1933, 12 to 15 million people were thrown out of work, this number leveling off to 10 million unemployed in 1939, at the onset of World War II. Deadly deflation was rampant, with price declines on consumer products of 18% and prices of farm products falling as much as 50%. Some 124,000 businesses and 9,000 banks failed. Encampments of the poor and homeless, called "Hoovervilles," sprouted up on vacant lots and city dumps across the nation. Dispossessed farm families took to the roads in old jalopies and beat-up trucks loaded down with the worldly possessions of a civilization devastated by drought and overproduction, and gone with the winds that whisked away the topsoil, leaving vast parts of the west in a swirling dust bowl.

Many of the rich, when they caught wind of a coming revolution howling through the concrete canyons of the cities, boarded steamships bound for Europe. The poor, too dispirited and frightened to openly revolt, hunkered down in shanties, under bridges, in cardboard shacks, still believing in the promises of democracy and the fairness of a nation that rewarded hard work and encouraged free enterprise.

"Prosperity is just around the corner" was a rallying call of the Hoover administration as the government freely dispensed federal aid to banks and railroads, this while denying unemployment benefits to the poor because it would "destroy their spirit of self-reliance."

West Virginia
WORLD POPULATION DOUBLES SINCE '52 – March, 1992 –
Vanessa Williams

Figures from the Census Bureau reveal that, in just 40 years–from 1952 to 1992–Planet Earth had become home to twice as many people. The Bureau estimated more than 280 million Americans would inhabit the U.S. by the year 2000. A "World Profile" from the Bureau estimated that, by 2020, the universal population explosion was expected to mushroom to 8.2 billion humans, all crammed onto a planet that still is unable to adequately feed its inhabitants.

The most vulnerable region on earth? Africa. The dark continent, with the world's highest infant mortality rate, was literally starving to death.

For West Virginia, a state often plagued with poverty, the population explosion was like the visible horizon. It simply went away. Young people were retreating to other states looking for jobs. The Mountain State's economy, once driven by coal mines, a black energy source now in disrepute, needed a cleansing tonic. It began with legislation to clean up the environment to attract more tourists. Strict new environmental laws were passed. Clean industry was encouraged to locate within the state. Influential lawmakers in Congress flooded the state with federally funded improvements. Roads and highways seemed to be built with blank checks.

All of this financial and bureaucratic tinsel did little for the besieged orchardists who were suffering from a triple whammy of a prolonged drought, premature freezing, and falling crop prices. City people from Washington D.C. and Baltimore, under siege by forces of the recession, sought relief beyond their congested existence, but within their limited means. Like butterflies emerging from their cocoons, these reborn homesteaders and country folk began fluttering back to the land looking for their roots and new opportunity. Having a considerable amount of distressed land to sell, I was happy to oblige:

Middletown, VA
ANDREW RIPS THROUGH FLORIDA–15 DEAD – August, 1992 – Madonna

After the costliest natural disaster in American history, thousands of people were left homeless and 15 were dead, this in the wake of Hurricane Andrew. An estimated damage toll of $200 billion was expected. Torrential rains from the hurricane reached into Virginia, almost washing out a dam that I had constructed for a lake on my farm. The lake was saved, but I lost the land around it; not to Andrew, however. The recession was far more devastating. To raise operating capital, I was forced to sell off all the waterfront lots I had developed as an emergency reserve, this in case I was faced with hard times.

LAKEFRONT OPPORTUNITY
NEAR MIDDLETOWN, VIRGINIA

First offer of prime waterfront from a private farm to be sold at below auction prices. If you've been looking for affordable land near Middletown, this could be your window of opportunity to steal a place in the country on a quiet lake and in a sought-after location that will provide a lifetime of pleasure for you and your family. Five acres on the lake from $27,500. Call Owner.

Having called upon my last bastion of reserves, I felt like the Union General, Nathanial Banks, whose infantry was chased out of Middletown 130 years earlier by the Confederate General Stonewall Jackson during the Civil War.

Front Royal, VA
CLINTON DEFEATS BUSH – November, 1992 –
Guns 'n' Roses

Bill Clinton, the first "baby-boomer" president, rode into town on a horse called "New Democrat," hoping to spur his party to the middle of the political track on socioeconomic and fiscal issues. In national elections, I had usually voted for Republicans. This time I voted for a baby-boomer Democrat.

The "baby-boom" cohort represents that segment of the population born between 1946 to 1964, during which the birthrate averaged 24.2 per 1,000 population, peaking in 1957 at 25.3%.

When I got my broker's license, a large number of this generation was old enough to be sent to fight and die in the rice fields and jungles of Vietnam. By 1992, as the recession was ending, the first contingent of "boomers" –those born in the period 1946-1950–were in their forties, established in their career fields, and contemplating retirement. Many turned their thoughts to the countryside. They saw themselves settling down in the country beyond the hustle and bustle of the cities, most likely on a body of water with a view.

The economy was improving, and like a swell moving far out to sea, this new wave of country property seekers would soon become a tsunami as the nineties came crashing into the twenty-first century.

Every person has his or her appointed day or lucky moment in time. Some people recognize opportunity when they see it and seize the moment; others get bogged down in the swamps of delay. Many of these early boomers took the right current and it served them well.

A RIVER RUNS THROUGH IT

Middleburg, VA area–Fly fisherman's paradise. 23.6 ac., including part of island in Shenandoah River. Rapids and deep water. 1900 ft. riverfront. Quick commute. Old woods. Pasture. Mountain views. Storage bldg. Across from large estates. Mostly fenced. Perc'd for 2 homes. $139,500. B.K. HAYNES REAL ESTATE

COMMUTER RIVERFRONT FARM NEAR MIDDLEBURG, VA $75,000

Closest riverfront on Shenandoah you can buy. World-shaking discovery of Paleo-Indian civilization dating to 9500-8000 B.C. Many buried tools and artifacts. Rapids and deep water. Fly fishing, canoeing. Pasture, huge trees. 20 acres of estate-quality land in horse country. Paved state road. Mountain views. B.K. HAYNES R.E.

Front Royal, VA
WORLD TRADE CENTER BOMBED – February, 1993 –
Duran Duran

As the nation was emerging from a devastating recession, the precursor of a more sinister enemy–terrorism–struck the Twin Towers in lower Manhattan. Five people were killed and hundreds suffered from smoke inhalation in the worst terrorist attack in U.S. history. Until this bombing, the United States had considered itself immune from terrorist strikes. Now our attention turned to the many buildings within our cities that would be potential targets. This uneasiness and fear struck like a dagger at the souls of city dwellers. Baby boomers, already psyched up on retirement and watching their bleeding financial portfolios slowly improve, added safety to their concerns and accelerated their search for that idyllic little place in the country. Fear is the mother of safety and the father of foresight. And many bargains were waiting to be snapped up.

LOST HORIZON FOUND
Just $697 per acre
Not a misprint. Estate settlement. 228 ac. mountain fortress joining
Shenandoah Nat'l Park. Own your own valley. Wildlife kingdom.
Stream, waterfall, paved road, valuable timber . . .

Whose woods are these beside this pretty pond?
Middletown, VA–Commute to D.C. Selling off part of farm. 5 ac.
deep woods with 500 ft. on lovely pond. 10 min. from college and
I-66. Adj. to airstrip. Horses welcome. $39,500 . . .

Economic studies had shown that the next land boom would begin
during 1993-1995, beyond the existing suburbs of major cities. As baby
boomers reached retirement age, most would locate in this new "Heartland" to be near family, friends, and city culture. By the spring of
1993, the deep-rooted recession gave way to sprouts of the new land
boom, and real estate values began to rise. Nothing could stop the
coming spending wave in "edge city" country property by baby
boomers approaching retirement age. Many boomers and second-home
seekers in search of outdoor recreation, lower prices, less density, more
land and value for the money, drew a line, say, 1 ½ to 2 ½ hours out,
and hit the road. In the Washington-Baltimore area, the hills of nearby
West Virginia seemed to fit the bill.

CANOE AND GOLF RANCHES
on Potomac River from $8950
Moorefield, W.VA–Only available riverfront homesites next to the
area's only golf course. 2½ - 5 acre ranchettes with central water
and golf course access. . .

STARTER RANCH w/CABIN
or HOME from $150 per month
Romney, W.VA–Can pay for itself in vacation savings, low-cost
retirement living, and potential rental income. 2-20 ac. of land
including new cabin with kitchen, bath from $19,990. . .

MOVIE RANCH

Nearby, W.VA–Right out of western movie. 20 ac. rangeland over-looking glimmering lake and peach orchard. Mountains on horizon. Huge packing shed can hold cattle herd or fleet of trucks. Run-down block garage and hired hands mess hall. Giant shade trees. $39,900. . .

LITTLE HOME ON THE LITTLE CACAPON AT TINY $49,900!

Little 4-acre ranch on the river. Newly remodeled 2 BR ranch-style frame home just 28 miles from Winchester, VA. New porch and deck. Half basement. 360 ft. on mountain river. Garden area. Fields for horses. Move in now or rent out . . .

CABIN AT END OF THE WORLD

Augusta, W. VA - Almost finished 2 BR vacation home lost in 11 acre forest at road's end. Story-book hidden valley laced with streams. Partly furnished. Sleep to sound of falling brook. Shoot deer from deck. $39,900.

Sometimes I get the feeling that the environmentalists think the world will come to an end if we don't save every single species of life on this planet. For the first time in the 20-year history of the Endangered Species Act, the U.S. Fish and Wildlife Service extended federal protection to a fly–you know, that endearing species that supports the fly-swatter industry, spoils cookouts, and spreads disease.

A February 1994 article in the *Richmond Times Dispatch* reported that an inch-long fly species in California was resting peacefully now that the government and entrenched hard-core environmentalists had decided that *no less a divine order than the ecosystem itself* is the hidden wind beneath the insect's fragile wings.

One local California mayor, in whose economically depressed habitat the pampered fly was given free reign, may still be unsure about the merits of fly worship. He was heard grumbling that the government and fellow-traveling environmentalists had gone too far. Now, through this window of insect reprieve, came the flies, and out went his city's plans for a local enterprise zone, with state-guaranteed tax breaks and other incentives designed to encourage business growth.

I was writing newsletters when this constituency for the preservation of flies was being established. And I thought at the time that, if this nonsense was carried to its illogical extremity, many of those people dealing with country properties could be out of work, this because vast amounts of land could be designated as off-limits for human habitation. Environmental groups were reported to be humming with happiness and buzzing about with joyful news that the fly, just like the hummingbird, could then continue its good-natured aerial missions. Builders, business leaders, and landowners were grousing that job-creating development projects and private property rights were being sacrificed for the folly of a fly's last stand.

Presumably, landowners who swat or spray one of these noble insects found on their land, and who do so with the intent to kill, harm, or harass, could receive up to $200,000 in fines and a year in the slammer. Read all about it in the Endangered Species Act. This doesn't mean that the insect has to be all that unpleasant to landowners. If a swarm of the endangered flies has preempted a homesite where you, God forbid, had intended to build a home for your human family, you can appeal to the government for relief. The authorities will–at your expense, of course–put you on indefinite hold. Yes . . . of course. That's only natural. Thankfully, some of this ridiculous legislation was modified, removed or unenforced by the subsequent administration.

What Went Wrong With the Endangered Species Act?

A *Wall Street Journal* editorial in December of 1993 had this to say: "When President Richard Nixon signed the Endangered Species Act into law in 1973, it was primarily intended to protect threatened bears, eagles, and wolves. Court rulings and bureaucrats have expanded its scope to include nearly everything bigger than a microbe, including many varieties of beetles and rats. The list of endangered species in 1992 exceeded 800 in number. Another 4,000 species were nominees for the list. At that rate, there would soon be only one species that will have no protection at all: the Human Property Owner."

Most of What I Know About Land-Use Abuse I Learned Out West

I made my pile in the East, but I like to go out west from time to time to see what's going on. After all, we know only what we have lived, and poor fools like me would have had no tutor without experience. I had landed in Jackson Hole, Wyoming on the mid-nineties when I picked up a newspaper and was welcomed to the New West by *shocking* news. God's country had once again given way to selfishness and greed.

An article in the *Wall Street Journal* reported on man's growing inhospitality to man, as evidenced by disturbing contemporary trends. It seems a sizable herd of nouveau riche city slickers wanted to set up their own private western fiefdom among long-standing communities of good 'ole boys. The nervy interlopers were fencing off access roads into the mountains, forcing locals out of their pick-ups and into multi-hour trail rides and hikes to reach their wilderness destinations.

This Land is My Land

You know how it goes. Rich guy with bucks flees California or New York and settles in the Old West. This scene has been played again and again for more than a hundred years in the U.S. and for thousands of years in human history. When a man owns land, the land owns the man. A man's life is defined by the boundaries of his land and his ability to control ingress and egress over his own piece of Mother Earth.

Rich "come-heres" padlock roads and build fences that obstruct paths and trails that the "people" have used for generations. Local landowners react by further blocking public access to the wild lands. This madness is compounded by growing violence in the cities and relatively easy access to guns. Suspicion, fear, and greed feed upon themselves. No one is to be trusted.

The Odd Couple

The *WSJ* article alluded to a strange alliance between conservationists and private property rights fundamentalists–like preachers going to bed with poachers in an unholy liaison.

A regional spokesman for The Wilderness Society was quoted as saying, "It's not so bad to have some public lands that are more difficult to get to than others." This comment begs an interesting question.

Why would conservationists want to deny the public legitimate access to the very public lands they hold so dear? The simple fact is that many die-hard conservationists and environmentalists love the *illusion* of reality, rather than reality itself. They have become, in their own minds, one with their ideals. And their ideals mask a self-serving desire to have the great outdoors for their hale and hearty selves. The public be damned. And the conservationist elite must be served. While acknowledging the noble concepts of resource conservation and practical environmental safeguards for the public good, these "earth first" movements appear to have been co-opted by extremist elements.

The *true conservationist* and the *real environmentalist* are contradictions in terms within modern western society, because earth-protection issues are relative, politically influenced, and subject to wide degrees of interpretation and concern by the public at large. Radical devotees of fundamentalism in these arenas have arguably become pulpiteers of a false religion–earth and creature worship–and this is basically a discredited and primitive spiritual doctrine of belief.

Advocates of fundamental environmental and conservation thought would find it better to have public lands untrampled by the public than to have the public trample public lands. So it is in this illusion, under the influence of radicals, that the government concocts ridiculous land use policies and supports the illogical schemes of idealistic environmentalist groups who would make habitats for flies a higher priority than habitats for humanity–the latter being a useful concept developed by their own kind, yet given only lip service when their false ideals are threatened by mankind's necessity for living space and economic security.

Slickers in Saddles

A city slicker, newly settled in Wyoming, bought a ranch in Big Sky country and established his ownership with barbed-wire fences, cabled roads, and "Keep Out" signs. Soon he found four of his cattle shot and a letter tacked to a fence post, threatening, "If you keep being a horse's ass about it, you'll probably lose." One day the slaughtered cattle were potential investment tax credits, and then they were dog meat. Inhospitality, the note would suggest, does not pay. This is not to say that the killings were justified, but only to make the point that it is not the size of the cattle herd, but the cheerfulness of the neighbors that makes a successful ranch.

There Goes the Neighborhood

A Las Vegas investor bought an Idaho ranch and sealed off the roads to a trout-filled lake located in public lands, this forcing outdoorsmen to hike 10 hours if they wanted to fish. Then he bought a vacant lot beside a neighboring cafe and put up boulders to prevent customers from parking there. Riled-up townfolks spray-painted a trashy version of his name on the boulder and blatantly camped out on his land in protest.

Guerrilla Warfare

Some of the newcomers in the West began fighting back with guerrilla tactics. One West Coast developer laid a spike board across the road on his Idaho ranch, blocking access to hunting territory. Along came a 66-year-old man in a pick-up truck. Psssssst. . .two tires go flat, and the old-timer had to hoof it back to town. "That's a hell of a thing," he groused, "setting a trap for your fellow man." He was then forced to drive 35 miles on back roads to hunt on public lands.

Lifestyles of the Rich and Famous

By 1994, the stock market, suddenly electrified by the tech boom and infusions of junk bonds into corporate mergers, began nurturing a new crop of millionaires and a smattering of billionaires. Wealthy homesteaders found their way to their "Last Frontier" in the Big Sky country of Idaho and Montana.

One tycoon closed off a road to a scenic hunting domain in Montana called "Cowboy Heaven." He said he wanted to protect local elk herds. Apparently elk and moose are so abundant in the region that they are clearly visible from small planes flying over the range. The area is so remote that one man armed with a cable and padlock can be a momentary monarch. An angry group, called the Public Lands Access Association, persuaded a state judge to open the trail. But locals don't always win.

Reportedly, Ted Turner, who owns a nearby spread the size of a small country, told public access agitators to take a hike. He advised them to hit the public roads or to work like hell and make $22 million to buy the place. Singer-songwriter Carole King bought a ranch along the Salmon River in Idaho. Seeking seclusion, she closed off an 11-mile loop road that runs for all but one mile on federal land. Neighbors griped. The county sued. Still, the state Supreme Court upheld the road closing.

The High and the Mighty

One wealthy outsider real estate magnate pulled in his stepbrother, the governor of a southern state, to exercise some political muscle for a road closing. The wealthy man's governor wrote a palsy-walsy letter to the Idaho governor asking him to lighten up on his boy. The Idaho governor wrote back advising his political colleague, in unflattering terms, to kiss off and stop meddling in his state.

Still, some local landowners, watching the town hardware store owner scoot about in his Range Rover, acquired through record sales of locks and cables, are throwing in with the enemy.

One son of a homesteader, out riding the range, found himself fenced in, this after his buddy-buddy ranchers locked gates up and down a 15-mile-long valley.

At the time, locks and gates were being shot up by gunfire throughout the Big Sky country of Montana and Idaho. And the aforementioned local hardware store owner had expanded his ranch through cash proceeds from record sales of guns.

Tax Traps in Farms and Country Property

Money is a necessity. But so is dirt. Piling it up is one thing. Keeping it from washing away in taxes is another. But there are few shortcuts around the IRS. Let's say you sell your home for $225,000, realizing a gain of $112,447. You then roll your profits into a small Texas ranch. On your tax return, you report a gain on your home sale of only, say, $18,936, claiming the balance of your gain ($93,511) was rolled into a new home. You figure correctly that the *ranching* part of the new property cannot be called *residential* for rollover purposes.

Based on previous rulings, the IRS may figure that your new ranch property was worth, say, $124,500, and you could agree. But you say you overpaid for the place by $60,500, and you attach that figure to the residential value of the ranch home, inflating its actual worth and reducing your tax exposure. Most of the gain from the sale of the old house could therefore be rolled into the ranch home.

Should the IRS disagree with this apportionment of value, they could come up with their own appraisal and allocate, say, only 40% of the ranch's value to the home. In this example, where the actual ranch cost for tax purposes would be $135,000 ($225,000 x 60%) leaving you a taxable gain of $135,000, higher than your previous reported gain of $112,447, not only would your "overpayment for the ranch" argument be thrown out, but you also would be hit with taxes on all of the $135,000 gain (as opposed to your reported $18,936 gain) plus a probable penalty for underpayment of taxes. It pays to have your transactions backed up with certified appraisals.

Middletown, VA
EAST COST BLIZZARD LEAVES 182 DEAD – March, 1993 –
Snow

Transportation came to a halt all along the east coast on March 16, 1993 as the worst U.S. blizzard on record battered the region with snow and piercing cold winds. The fierce late-winter storm left cars buried in snowdrifts throughout the Carolinas, Virginia, and northward into Maine. Few planes were able to get off of the ground. And in some cities cars, truck, buses, and trains were unable to move for several days.

Front Royal, VA
RECORD FLOODS HIT MIDWEST – August, 1993 –
Janet Jackson

The great Mississippi was over its banks, and the upper part of "Ole Man River" was unnavigable, this as the worst recorded floods in U.S. history swept away levees and sandbag walls. At least 50 people had died, while 38,000 people were forced from their homes. And 20 million acres of prime farmland had been converted into an interstate swamp. The estimated economic cost to the nation was 12 billion dollars.

Near Front Royal, Virginia, the Shenandoah was over its banks; but many homesites were well above the flood plain and out of danger. The North and South branches of the Shenandoah meet at Front Royal to form the main branch of the river. You must cross two bridges as you enter Front Royal from the north. Near the northern bridge is an historic spot where Colonel John Mosby, the ubiquitous Confederate "Gray Ghost," and his rangers, hung three Union soldiers in retaliation for a similar execution of three of Mosby's men by Union forces.

Downriver from this historic site, and the bridge over which the Confederate troops retreated during the Battle of Front Royal, was this twenty-acre farm bargain that offered plenty of room to avoid having to retreat from the threat of floods.

CHEAP 'N CLOSE 20 AC. ESTATE ON THE SHENANDOAH $89,900

Only 19 miles from Middleburg in horse country. River runs through it. Old woods and lush pasture. Ideal for estate-quality home or small vacation-retirement cottage close to the city. No restrictions. Fly fishing, canoeing, farming, horseback riding . . .

B.K. HAYNES LAND BROKERS

Middletown, VA
YELTSIN CRUSHES RUSSIAN REBELLION – October, 1993 – Mariah Carey

Hand-to-hand fighting raged inside the parliament building in Moscow as hard-line communist delegates and their sympathizers battled Soviet army soldiers during a day-long attempted coup. Black smoke poured from the shattered windows of the besieged Soviet White House as tank shells pounded the building, this while army commandos took it over floor by floor. When the battle was over, hundreds of delegates, who had erected barricades inside the building, emerged under the guns of soldiers. President Yeltsin declared victory over a potential defeat of his government and a prolonged extension of the Cold War as the rebels were packed onto buses and sent off to prison.

In October of 1864, 129 years prior to this victory over defeat, Union forces in the American Civil War scored a decisive win from a certain loss during the Battle of Cedar Creek in Virginia's Shenandoah Valley. Four Confederate divisions, then under the command of General Jubal Early, hit the Union army at Cedar Creek in a night surprise attack that appeared to be a victory. General Sheridan, the Union general, then headquartered in nearby Winchester, heard the thunder of distant guns and quickly galloped toward the battlefield, rallying his dispirited troops along the way. By morning, the Confederate divisions were in retreat, and Sheridan proceeded to carry out General Grant's order to turn the Shenandoah Valley into "a barren waste. . . so that the crows flying over it for the balance of the season will have to carry their provender with them."

My farm is located within 3 miles of the Cedar Creek Battlefield, and I was fighting my own war in the fall of 1993, turning a financial defeat into a victory by selling off a part of it:

Out goes my farm manager's house:

MIDDLETOWN FARM ADJACENT TO AIRSTRIP. SACRIFICE $139,500

Hard-to-part-with, close-in farm near Cedar Creek Battlefield. 19 beautiful acres, with rambling 2-story frame farm house sheltered by shade trees. Home is in excellent condition. Hardwood floors, carpeting, 4 BR, extra large BA, central air, ceiling fans, oil heat, family room, DR., LR, bright kit., utility room, laundry room, attic, fenced grounds, stable, shop, 2 ponds, woods, pasture, mountain views. Use of 2800 ft. airstrip. Close to I-66, I-81, schools, college, university, jet airport, river, hospital center, shopping malls, and G.W. Nat'l Forest. . .

Out goes my housekeeper's cottage:

CHEAP, CLOSE FIX-UP FARM ON SMALL LAKE $139,500

Sacrifice to cut debt load. Quick commute on I-66. 3 BR, 2 BA cabin-style home with walk-out basement apt. for in-laws, guests, or rental income. Could use a little paint and sprucing up. Elec. Heat, AC, deck, fireplace. Half pasture and half woods. Borders 1/4-mile-long lake to fish, boat, swim. Apple trees, grape arbor, garden plot. Keep horses, livestock. Partly fenced. Near everything. Selling cheap. Bank gets all proceeds. 95% financing possible. . .

How Ya Gonna Keep 'Em Down on the Farm?

A 1994 report from the Agriculture Department says things are changing in the U.S. farm industry, with more of the nation's farmers relying on outside income to survive. Farming households were receiving up to 80% of their of their average 1992 income from wages, salaries, and businesses outside of their farm operation. Even those

farmers running the largest commercial operations–defined as requiring substantial amounts of the farmer's time, and yielding at least
$250,000 in gross sales–received one-third of their household income
from outside sources.

The report, based on preliminary estimates of farm operators' incomes, said the average farmer took home $40,068 in 1992. Only one-
quarter of farm families in 1992 operated a "commercial farm" with
sales over $50,000. Viable noncommercial farms–those that earned
between $50,000 and $100,000–still accounted for more than half of
the nation's farms.

These households, many of them specializing in livestock production, lost an average of $817 in 1992 from farming and received about
80% of their income off the farm, according to the USDA report. But
22% of the farm households had incomes below the poverty line of
$15,000 or less. These marginal farms lost an average of $7,334 in
1992.

Front Royal, VA
NATO FIGHTER ATTACK OVER BOSNIA – February, 1994 –
Celine Dion

U.S. F-16 fighters led the first NATO offensive in its 45-year history. The American jets, firing heat-seeking missiles, pounced on four
Bosnian Serb aircraft that had ignored warnings to leave the NATO
no-fly zone and sent them crashing to earth. And in Virginia, the bucolic countryside was under attack by a mouse. . . Mickey, that is.

The Disney organization had optioned a huge swath of land on the
playing fields of the rich and influential, this for the establishment of
a proposed historical theme park. Suddenly the sky was falling. Polo-
playing movie stars fell out of their orbit. Historians of note and editorial elitists sniffed at this historical travesty, considering the concept a
trifling of fact by panderers of fiction.

Preservationists were ballistic with rage that a real world of mansions and fox hunters would be upstaged by a fantasy land of castles
and animated creatures.

Environmental radicals signed up for the fight when they heard the
cry "Remember Orlando." Money chests were thrown open in the vaults
of the lords and off they went on their high horses to attack the mouse.

Disney Haters

A riddle, circulated by Disney supporters in this land-use controversy, went like this:

What has six eyes, six legs, flies in thundering packs over fences in silly red costumes chasing bushy-tailed mammals to the cacophony of horns and barking dogs, yet fears noise and crowds? . .

Give up?. . . Why, it's a Disney-hating fox hunter.

Opponents of the theme park were out for blood. Only this time it was not the carcass of the lowly fox they wanted strewn across the landscape. It was the very hide of happiness itself–Disneyland–that must be sacrificed to keep wages low, outsiders out, and to protect the old-money lifestyle. Certainly no one would object to a castle on every farm. . . possibly a well-placed palace. . . but this thing! A whiny protest group planned a wine and cheese fete to stick hate pins in the Disney Doll–Disney's America–an historical theme park planned for a 1998 debut near Haymarket, Virginia in Prince William County. The issue was so contentious that it inspired a couple of Disney fables.

A Disney Myth

King Grinch, of Richmont, constructed a huge labyrinth beneath his castle. It was a dark and complex maze of corridors and false trails *(environmental roadblocks, legal suits, political intrigue, etc.)* An enemy of the King, tossed into the labyrinth, would be hopelessly lost. Even worse, King Grinch had imprisoned the Enviromonster–a shallow beast of half hysteria and half lies–in the heart of his underground dungeon.

Prince Disney, a young ruler from another land, *(Disney's America)* was scheduled to be sacrificed to the Enviromonster *(environmental correctness)*. He was imprisoned in a cell *(federal bureaucracy and the court system)* ready to be led to the labyrinth and abandoned to his cruel fate *(rejection of the theme park)*. But Virginia, the beautiful estranged daughter of King Grinch *(state government)* fell in love with the dashing Disney *(commercial enterprise, tourism, tax revenue)*. She vowed to save him from the dreadful plot. At midnight, she crept to the cell of Prince Disney and gave him a magic ball of thread *(state support)*. Assuring him that guidance and protection were now his, she helped him to escape from his cell.

Prince Disney slipped through the darkness to the entrance of the labyrinth. He tossed the magic ball of thread to the ground *(public opinion),* then followed along as it rolled its way down the dark passages *(phony environmental issues)* and around sharp bends *(no-growth legal maneuvers).* Finally, the young hero came face to face with the roaring Enviromonster. They battled, and soon, the monster was no more, because his once fierce substance had become that of hysteria and lies. Prince Disney followed the magic thread *(state support)* back through the labyrinth to his lover and to freedom and happiness for the people of their land, now called Virginia.

The Rest of the Story . . .

The Disney proposal, which promised $1.5 billion in new revenue over 30 years, along with 3,000 or more jobs, had the overwhelming backing of elected county and state officials, including Governor Wilder and Governor-elect George Allen, who was later elected to the U.S. Senate. Anti-Disney crusaders vowed to buy up all the newspapers, and all of the radio and television stations, if necessary, to save Virginia from her foolish love affair with Prince Disney and to return her to the fiefdom of King Grinch of Richmont.

In Dudgeon over Disney

(A *Richmond Times-Dispatch* editorial)

If there is one thing the opponents of Disney's America don't know how to do, it's how to lose gracefully. Having lost the fight in the executive and legislative branches, the anti-Disneyists now want to slug it out in the courts. The group Protect has filed lawsuits challenging nearly every aspect of Virginia's courtship and marriage to Disney, and is pressing for an annulment.

Protect members claim that sweetening the pot to attract Disney was an abuse of government power–a claim reminiscent of outraged children declaring, "That's not fair!" after being outmaneuvered in a game. The group is swinging bludgeons–such as the wetlands provisions–and dredging others from antiquity. They accuse Governor Allen of stifling Disney's opponents in violation of the Civil Rights Act of 1871.

When protestors have to dig out 123-year-old statutes to make a case in the here and now, perhaps they would do better to imitate the philosophical grace of media mogul Barry Diller after being bested in similar negotiations. "They won. We lost. Next?"

With regard to government power, I can only say that power is useless in a democracy unless channeled into something useful and productive for the people. No doubt the strategic objectives of the enviro movement point to a looming battle for the government and the people, this where a form of eco-environmental terrorism sweeps across the nation on the economic front, led by a cadre of radical enviros attacking free enterprise in a multitude of deadly and deceptive forms.

Another wag added this twist to the Disney story:

The Grinch and the Mouse–A Disney Fable

The Grinch of Richmont, a stack of poison pens in front of him, sat in the great room of his Whose Who-ville palace and weighed the sacrifice of an upstart mouse for the chance of keeping his rural fiefdom free of the earth's human rabble, who were followers of the garish mouse, Disney.

He was not a professional killer by any means, though, in the past, he had erased a number of presumptuous vassals from his fields and forests by zoning them into backwater ghettos. As an important protector of the Who's Who-ville fiefdom–inhabited by the rich and famous who were holding a hundred million in donations to his head like a loaded gun–it was the Grinch's duty to kill the mouse and send his riffraff followers packing back to their ticky-tacky homes and townhouse clusters.

So a mouse gets accidentally knocked off. Mice die all the time. Except if the King wants them to live. Then he will call them endangered. So why worry about it? Didn't the King find the sport of kings endangered and order a race track for Who's Who-ville? Anyway, who would dare compare a mouse with a horse. You could burn every mouse in the kingdom of Enviroland and it wouldn't be as great as saving a single fly from the rump of a horse. So why cry over a mouse? The important thing is to keep on living like lords.

Life and Death in Who's Who-ville

Those land developers who follow the mouse are no better than–even lower than mice. They peddle a man a quarter acre of dirt and rocks for twenty times what it's worth and burn him on the interest to satisfy a banker's greed. Yeah, it's time for that Disney Mouse character to die.

We got no land or jobs open around here for dirty developers, either. All full up, see. Not even a situation to muck our stables.

The demise of the mouse would pay off his obligations to his rich and famous friends; what's more, it would show the King of Enviroland that he could kill the mouse without spending more than a hundred million bucks. Piece of cake.

The Grinch held council with his supporters in his Who's Who-ville palace. Some were concerned about the mouse and the impact of the rodent and his men on their high-strung horses. How can we conduct civilized races and fox hunts in the shadow of a stupid roller coaster?

Who would be caught dead on such a field? Others bellowed about the environmental impact of possible human rabble on the local fox population. The opponents of the mouse groused, groaned, and whined until, finally, the palace itself seemed to rumble and shift from its foundation with the quake of a fearsome shout, "This could be the end of civilization as we know it!" When polled by the Grinch, the council confirmed what he already knew– the mouse must die.

Fear and Loathing in Who's Who-ville

Funny thing about that mouse, said the besieged residents of Who's Who-ville. One day he's on the Grinch's hit list, and the next day he and his groveling horde are dragging back those plans for that disgusting Mickey Mouse history park. What went wrong? My God. . . a hundred million dollars . . . down the tubes. I thought we owned all the newspapers around here. And we've got pals in the media. . . television. . . and the important dailies. . . the *Washington Post*. . . the *New York Crimes*. The big papers saw the dreadfulness of it all. All were slipped poison pens by the Grinch. And what happened to those wimpy politicians we bought? Caving in under all that rabble-rousing. Leaving us to the mercy of that dirty mouse.

The filthy-rich residents of Who's Who-ville felt like the sky was disgorging human dung on their manicured fields. They saw those Disney mouse lovers, a loud-mouthed crowd of low-lifers and commoners, marching into that scum governor's ball, celebrating the impending invasion of Who's Who-ville and its charming rural lands by a wicked mouse and his rabble army. . . a loutish band–laughing and drinking with an earth killer. Fat chance of a Disney Mouse lover getting into Earth Heaven, wherever that is.

The hard-pressed and deep-pocketed residents of Who's Who-ville groused long and hard about the repulsive blemish on their culture.

The Grinch was armed with a hundred million bucks to kill the rodent. But the revolting creature still crawls on their hallowed earth. The Grinch would be called to account for his bungling.

Dirty Tricks in Who's Who-ville

The Grinch unpacked his sack of alibis and dirty tricks. He rattled on that the political setback was part of his plan. A blessing in disguise, really. He didn't really plan to snuff out the mouse. That could backfire on the residents of Who's Who-ville. He boasted that the disruptive Disney rodent would soon be mousetrapped by Friends-of-the King United (FOKU). Everyone in Who's Who-ville would be clean– the Grinch safely in his palace contemplating the King's royal race track, a much more refined endeavor than a sinister FOKU mission. The hideous peoples' park would collapse under the weight of certain clean-air requirements that Heaven alone could meet. The soil would be salted with artifacts of the Civil War. Historians on the payroll could create new battlefields, never before revealed. He said the Tierra Club is considering making the mouse a test case for the enforcement of certain preservation and environmental statutes.

The Grinch will enlist the muscle of several Nimby (Not in my backyard) gangs, and if the mouse so much as blinks at Who's Who-ville he, and they, and the FOKU group will bushwhack the interloper. "If the mouse is still alive," said the Grinch, "we'll drown him in water pollution problems." He winked and grinned as the told them, "Water is a scarce commodity around Who's Who-ville." He added, "And if he's still breathing, we'll hang his rotten hide up in court 'til he's finished. One way on another, we'll nail him."

A Tough Life in Who's Who-ville

And so it goes. The poor little rich people of Whose Who-ville, the FOKU crew, and the Nimby gangs, all busied themselves with wicked plots to kill the mouse or to have his hide hung up to dry on a cross outside an urban ghetto. "Not in my backyard," went the cry. They met secretly with their entrenched pals high up in the government of Enviroland and in academia, where elitist and anti-entrepreneurial notions were encouraged in the name of civility. They whined that the state made a big mistake in setting out green cheese for the mouse. . . that the people elected the wrong governor. They must find ways to go over his head. . . perhaps chop it off. God knows, you can't have fat people in shorts pushing strollers with screaming babies and chewing cotton candy in the streets. The beautiful people of Who's Who-ville are owed a few favors. It's been a tough life.

Postscript:

Despite the fact that the voice of the people was heard loud and clear on the Disney issue, when the concept was granted approval by the peoples' elected representatives, the fat cat self-interest financing, and the whining and carping by Disney haters won the day. Disney eventually folded its tent and retreated to Hollywood, scrapping the idea for a history theme park in Virginia. Here is an organization with very deep pockets. You can imagine the economic ruin some well-funded self-interest groups can do to the small landowner who may not share the narrow vision of elitists on what he should do with his land, and who most likely has scarce money with which to fight to save his property rights.

Bonfire of the Vanities

After months of pandering to the landed gentry by attacking Disney's America through their articles and commentary, the *Washington Post* finally allowed a writer to lift the curtain on the ridiculous charade of some rich and famous area residents pretending to protect rural land for the benefit of all the people when, in fact, their reported actions revealed to Disney supporters and neutral observers alike a somewhat selfish desire to keep the whole outdoors for themselves.

The article reported on a wine-and-cheese soiree of high-profile TV talking heads precisely balanced with literati and political figures by their host—a millionaire network newsman and ex-badboy of White House reporters. After loosening up on TV biggies like Bosnia and Whitewater, the chardonnay beamed up the level of their banter to a heavyweight discussion on what's *really* wrong with the world—such as the menacing Disney theme park, soon to be hovering over them like a grotesque space-age city in their backyard. One Republican operative, married to a Democrat political hustler, allegedly fretted over the threat to their country lifestyle of sneakered *little* people in shorts pushing stollers and making noise.

Life in Who's Who-ville

According to the *Post* article, many of the vaunted hunt country vanities, charred by the Disney bonfire, were contributors to the theme park's main enemy, a regional environmental group. Supporters of this well-endowed rural preservation society's crusade against the infidel Disney mouse included high-powered publishers, an ambassador, a billionaire or two, multiple millionaires, super-rich sports figures, famous tabloid faces, Hollywood fox hunters, a smattering of royalist wannabes, a few TV bigwigs, and a U.S. senator.

The High Price of Serenity

One neighborhood horsewoman, allegedly offended by the Disney horror, remarked how expensive it had become to find peace and quiet in the region. Her neighbor across the road–a billionaire–agreed wholeheartedly. Both tithed generously, and with great sincerity, to the rural preservation society in its effort to crush Disney and to make quick history of the people's theme park. Singing in the chorus of this contemporary soap opera of the oppressed rich and famous were (appropriately) an heiress, a snobbish TV host, the daughter of a former presidential hopeful, and the widow of an influential media giant.

Hollywood Turns Horsey

Into this sorrowful scenario rides a famous Hollywood actor and his aspiring wife who want to fit into this esteemed culture of thoroughbred people and beautiful horses. So the star shells out a few mil and buys his way in. "Can you imagine?" a friend says. "He spends millions of dollars to get away from people and here's Disney moving in." It's a crying shame.

The star went on "Entertainment Tonight" and complained that the Disney chairman would not want a theme park in his backyard. The aging star's agent told him to cool it. The star was way out of line–negotiating with Disney for some coming films and shooting his mouth off about the Mouse. He was advised that he could find himself riding into Hollywood on the back of an ass.

In her scathing book, *Treason,* on liberal "treachery" in the U.S., Ann Coulter tells the story of what happens when Hollywood "do-gooders" get up on their high horses. It seems back in the eighties, congressional committee members ushered in a parade of Tinseltown tear-jerkers before the TV cameras to plead for every cause imaginable that would attract scads of cash–diseases of all kinds, childhood trauma and obesity, alar on apples, cruelty to circus elephants, and the plight of the besieged farmer. Coulter observed that in the House Committee on Agriculture, not a single farmer testified on troubled farms and the alleged problems of farmers.

She goes on to say that a coalition of millionaire actresses, however, had evidently felt the farmers' pain. Jane Fonda, Jessica Lange, and Sissy Spacek, all well ensconced in their palaces and estates, indeed were familiar with the injustices of contemporary farm life because they had suffered through the ordeal in fairy-tale land. So they were invited to testify.

Life Trials of the Rich and Famous

The *Post* article quoted a horsewoman's remark that, "Everyone's brokenhearted. We just don't want the tourists, fast-food joints, and third-class motels. It scares everybody." Presumably *everybody* is anybody who is *somebody* in the ethereal hunt country world. Another media somebody complained about the potential dreadful delays of getting out to Who's Who-ville on weekends to "veg." One environmental tagalong accused the Virginia governor of "genuflecting to the Mouse." And, of course, the biggest shocker at the soiree was the manner and method of Disney's dastardly and brutal assault on their sacred turf–comparable, it would seem from the caterwauling, to the Japanese sneak attack on Pearl Harbor. Real estate is simply not purchased in such a clandestine manner. It shocks the senses.

He Who Has ears. . .

The wine helped the conversation to regain its ideological base, and God was invited into the discussion. Remarking on the then-recent death of the Disney president in a freak helicopter accident, the horsewoman wondered, "Maybe it's God's way of saying it shouldn't be built here."

But even if God didn't say it, it really doesn't matter. They'll muddle through the crisis without him. Nevertheless, solid evidence of a higher power's payback time was contained in the scroll of the environmental society's television and radio ad campaign. The divinely inspired theme: "I-66, Disney's Parking Lot" was printed out, ceremoniously blessed with Perrier water (straight from our treacherous ally in the Iraq War), and plastered on the bumpers of the region's de riguer assault vehicles–Jaguars and Range Rovers.

All of God's Creatures

A prayerful quip was heard in a hunt country social assembly hour: "Can't we find a snail darter somewhere?" Indeed, the environmental society was already calling in favors from entrenched powers in the Clinton administration. Money is no problem. We got tons of it in Who's Who-ville. Hang 'em up on Clean Air. Hit 'em with impact studies. Find a Spotted Owl. Whatever it takes. Just bounce the Mouse.

The *Post* article said the environmental society's chairman, a former ambassador, accused Disney of spreading rubbish about his fine group being elitish; yet he certainly knew where people stood in this world. We got a lot of *little* people on our side, went his retort to a reporter on the phone, who committed the shameful faux pax of calling him by his first name. "Look here: The Mouse's chairman made $210 million last year," he groused. "That would make a fox hunter look like a pauper." Sure he was riled up about Disney. Who wouldn't be?

But something more pernicious than Disney was stuck in his craw. Then, his bit of undigested beef moved on, and maintaining his sense of breeding and protocol, he harrumphed and dismissed the reporter with the humility of a newly minted duke. "I know it sounds stuffy, but I rather don't appreciate being addressed by my first name by someone I've never met in person." Perhaps *elitish* is not the work for snobbish behavior. Try *phony*.

During the controversy, the historical elite sent two of their ivory tower hit men to Capitol Hill to whine for federal justice over the proposed theme park. Sitting gloomy-eyed and stern-faced in a packed senate hearing room, the historians moaned and groaned about the Mouse's threat to "hallowed ground" a distant 25 miles way. The whole sorry charade of federal meddling in a local land use issue, using the phony "sacred lands" dodge, begs the question of how the matter found its way to the sanctimonious chambers of congress in the first place.

The Enviro Elite

There's a musty odor in the clubby sanctums of the environmental and preservation movement, where landed gentry, ivory-tower historians, and radical environmentalists all meet to protect their privileged turf and to play God with other people's lives. The stench is the scent of money—mostly old stuff burning holes in the pockets of sedentary idealistic supporters of government land grabs—and with all due respect for moderates in these movements–also the smell of hustled lucre on the hands of the environmental S.S. from counting war chests of new bills sweated out of the public through slick direct mail appeals.

Don't for a moment think I am overstating my case against the hard-liners in these movements, for I have experienced their vitriol and blatant arrogance face to face in real estate transactions. Their shake-down and intimidation tactics make the Mafia look like schoolyard bullies. And the treachery and deception used to gain their ends have few equals beyond the widespread infiltration of the U.S. government by the Soviet spy network in the forties and fifties.

In my view, the radicals controlling these movements, and their militant supporters, pose a grave threat to private property rights and to individual freedom in this country. Dealing with these people makes President Reagan's admonition, "Trust, but verify" when dealing with Soviet deceit, sound like the height of naivete.

This intrusive shadow government, operating like a pedigreed se-cret society, looms from the palatial estates of the rich and famous to the halls of officialdom, having reached obscene levels of question-able conduct in the Clinton administration, this with the populist-talk-ing ex-president literally owing his political soul to environmental and preservation tyrants.

Outright Lies

One prominent preservationist leaped to trivialize the nation's in-ventory of historic real estate by casting the Disney concern in apoca-lyptic terms as the "single most important historic preservation issue in America today." Slapping his tainted wisdom in the face of local and state officials, he proceeded to advise the people's elected offi-cials on what was good and what was bad for the simple folks in their jurisdictions. Ignoring demographic growth patterns already in place, he said a city of 250,000 would be spawned within 20 years, and he blamed it on Disney.

Then he railed on about a busy Virginia shopping area called Tyson's Corner, as if commercial real estate threatened the soul of historic preservation, alluding to shopping malls as the creation of demented minds. No doubt quaint little village shops and cobblestone streets would be more to his liking.

Congressional Busybodies

The subcommittee chairman, a Civil War zealot, and a charter member of the shadow government of elitist enviros and preservationists, claimed it was his duty to butt in because the area contained some historical sites. He said he didn't like McDonalds and Holiday Inn, as if these enterprises had no positive significance in the nations's past, nor any future relevance. He lectured those in attendance on the alleged evils of commercial sprawl, as if the Prince William County zoning officials were a loose band of irresponsible dolts.

A Virginia senator, with mixed feelings about Disney, was forced by political reality to say enough is enough. "This is a state's rights issue," he said. "I can't find any basis for any action by the Senate or House in this case. *Were we to do so, we'd set a precedent which would have unlimited impact in other areas of this country."* A subcommittee member from Colorado–and a legislator of Native American descent–then spoke up. "The U.S. Senate has no business refereeing every Mickey Mouse dispute around the country." This viewpoint was echoed by some western and southern senators.

Well-Connected "Bananas"

"Build Absolutely Nothing Anywhere Near Anything" became the replacement cheer for the enviro NIMBYS and their assault chant, "Not in My Backyard." Virginia Governor Allen, setting the tone for the hearings, said, "History is not just for professional historians and professors. And its not just for smug, self-appointed arbiters of culture and Hollywood movie stars. It is for all our citizens, or it should be. And if this project will help stimulate a new generation to take an interest in history, as I believe it will, then we ought to be applauding the effort. We would not be here today if opposition to this park had not become a crusade for some well-connected folks who don't want it located within 30 miles of their neighborhood."

Reportedly, a "smug" Hollywood star, feeling duped by Disney (after buying a 400-acre estate, just eight miles from the proposed theme park) and offended by Allen's remarks, stuck out his tongue and mumbled "So's your old man." One stuffy historian in attendance characterized the pro-Disney arguments as the mindless babble of the uneducated and the uninformed. The hearing ended with no congressional action against Disney.

The Night The Lights Went Out in Virginia

Well, the mob finally got the Mouse. The uppity P.R. firm of Armpit, and Footsmeller, mercenary flacks for the Plutocratic Enviro Council–armed with a king's mint for expenses and payoffs–managed to pat the fannies of enough fat cats, landed gentry wannabes, ivory-tower historians, preservationist zealots, and environmental radicals to raise enough stink to run the sensitive Disney Mouse out of Haymarket, Virginia, and–as some correctly predicted–clean out of the state.

Not in My Backyard

While recognizing the inconvenience of growth on society as a whole, the foul odor of self-serving NIMBYS was liberally fanned by such hypocritic dailies as the busybody *New York Crimes*, an assortment of snooty wine-and-cheese columnists, and a devil's alliance of smug political operatives from both parties. All sanctified the Prince William turf as belonging to *all* the people. *Just keep out if you don't have deep pockets or refuse to make hay and muck stables.*

The preservationist argument, if carried to its ridiculous conclusion–since Virginia itself was a battlefield–would make most of the privately owned land in the state off-limits to development, my own farm included. The stench was too much for the Mouse.

Mouse Droppings

Disney, facing a looming financial hemorrhage from worldwide business setbacks, and suffering a recent loss of key management personnel in a helicopter crash, made a corporate business decision in California to throw the Disney America fight in return for a plutocrat mob payoff. *Keep off our turf and you won't get your image killed.* Some say Disney's cross-pollenation of cultural values had already smashed its famous name. Others say a sizable chunk of cash changed hands.

The truth lies in a sad tale of landed gentry intrigue and dishonor in the horse country of Virginia. Disney should hire a screenwriter to make a movie of the farce. Here's the story of a tough Golden Boy boxer who throws a fight for the promise, by an elitist mob, of a finer shirt and a softer image. The trouble is he took a lot of good and honest supporters down with him.

Disney backers across Virginia may never forgive the NIMBY mob for stealing their economic future as they saw it. Certainly the biggest loser was Prince William County, whose tax structure at the time was the highest in the state and whose economic relief during that difficult period was dashed on the rocks of lost enterprise.

When Prince William lost Disney, the flag in Haymarket was flown at half mast as a protest against the political meddling in local affairs by arrogant elitist outsiders as far away as the gilded canyons of Manhattan and the privileged estates of Long Island. Presumably, the local people did not know what was good for them.

One local delegate to the Virginia Assembly summed up the case against the gang of plutocrats when he remarked on the Disney dive, "It was. . . the opposition of one or two vocal groups of narrow focus. Those who are looking for employment might do as well to contact the organizations that hounded Disney out of Prince William. Perhaps those organizations have ideas on where people can find jobs."

The *Richmond Times-Dispatch* called it like this :"The landed gentry of Northern Virginia's hunt country, combined with environmental purists, were able to drive Disney out of Haymarket–effectively depriving their working-class neighbors in Prince William of jobs and taxes the county badly needed. . . Within hours of Disney's withdrawal from Haymarket, the governors of Maryland and West Virginia had come a-courtin' (could Maryland offer a site oh, say, five miles from Antietam)? And why shouldn't they? Disney's America was expected to provide 19,000 new jobs. By 2007, the park would have generated $47 million in annual tax revenue–money that could have gone for higher education, environmental cleanup, prison construction, or hundreds of other needs. Perhaps those who drove Disney out of the Commonwealth will be charitable enough– compassionate enough–to make up the difference."

On the Playing Fields of the Lords

While the vast majority of county officials take an objective view of land-use issues and try to be fair, others act like wild boars when you attempt to divide up the county turf. The phony self-righteousness of some lordly officials in playing games with private property rights is one of the great charades in local government. No one in public service is immune from the lust of dominion. Power-hungry elected, appointed, and salaried officials often like to point out alleged wrong-doing because it somehow gives them the bubbly feeling that they are above wrongness.

For example, the fact that a local planning commission can be wrong, and that right cannot be a simplistic drug that makes the self-righteous feel good, was brought home in a meeting in 1994 when property owners in an elitist Virginia county deep-sixed a poisoned county plan to kill growth. It seems that the antigrowth powers-that-be in the county were conniving to protect their privileged playing fields and "quality of life" by a no-development decree, designating 25% of the county as "environmentally sensitive"–an obvious and time-worn euphemism for "keep out."

Shove it Down Their Throats

One angry property owner was quoted as yelping to planners at a public meeting, "You're trying to shove this down my throat and I'm not going to (take it anymore)." Politically connected insiders in the county may have found it esthetically and socially profitable to embrace the view that the whole western part of the county was a divinely gifted land of milk and honey for the self-styled culturally correct, and the last line of defense against those "intruders" from the eastern crime-ridden cities. But property owners in the affected area didn't seem to share such elitist illusions.

Barbarians at the Gates

The so called "Scenic Land Area Plan" would have effectively prohibited anybody from buying newly developed country property and building a home in the region and would have preserved the landscape in that area as a private buffer zone for the environmentally hard-pressed "Who's-Who" residents protected by the extensive "Scenic Land" moat. It would be absolutely dreadful for proletarian roof lines to suddenly appear in the King's countryside to spoil the privileged pristine views from horsey manicured estates.

Clubby Correctness

Of course, the whole process, in county government eyes, was politically civilized, with "proper" hearings, the usual discreet collusive incorporation of the scheme in the county comprehensive plan, and clubby winks and pats on the back among political bigshots, idealistic planners, and fellow-traveling conservationists–everything had to he absolutely correct, you understand.

Alien, Bastard Children

One angry resident exclaimed, "You make all of these rules about how high we have to build our homes, how we are to put up our lights, and it's not fair. If you're going to do it here, do it in the entire county. Don't make us feel like alien, bastard children." One portion of the plan specified that houses in the "control zone" be painted unobtrusive colors that blend in with the landscape, and that outdoor lights not be visible beyond the property lines so as to protect the "view shed" of hunt country homeowners.

Beautyburg

Presumably, if the foul experiment had succeeded, the merry vassals, Tory wannabes, assorted courtiers, and roaming peasants in Beautyburg would have been privileged to visually feast upon an exquisite manicured landscape dotted with stark-red brick homes with dark-green shutters, all neatly nestled amidst rolling fields laced with rambling stone fences as far as the eye could see. And at Christmas in this fairy tale land, the homes would have just the correct amount of joyous and subdued lighting–a more fitting scene for the Christ Child than the rubbish of clutttered, garish frame homes lit up like neon marquees. Santa, of course, would no doubt find it more convenient to deliver gifts down the elaborate stone and brick chimneys provided by the wealthy than be subjected to the ordeal of forcing his jolly belly through the soot-clogged flues in the likes of a footman's hovel or a stableman's shack.

Doublespeak

You may wonder what goes on behind the closed doors of some county officials and their closet colleagues in government officialdom. In the midst of angry forays from private property owners, whose rights were being callously and blatantly served up as sacrifices to the gods of the environment, planners in Beautyburg prayed that the chosen people would be saved from "contamination of ground and surface water"–as if the state health department was staffed with incompetent airheads who dispense sewage system construction permits like lottery tickets.

Patron Games

Patronizing backers of the failed land grab seemed to have viewed the county as a private Monopoly board, with a collusive clique of politicians and planners having all the cards for passing "Go." The scheme, if it had passed, would have allowed almost nobody to build absolutely nothing near anything, presumably *for the property owner's own good,* this in 25% of the county. Stay away from streams and slopes. Increase your property line setbacks by 60%. Double the size of any lot we allow you to create. Give up your timber rights on mountain slopes.

Conservation Bullies

To gain public support in strong-arming property owners into accepting this tainted scheme, the land grabbers offered a side deal to an organized trail group–all perfectly legal, of course. The county would snitch to the trail organization if anybody tried to build a home, develop land, or harvest timber near the trail or its buffer zones. The trail group could then raise all kinds of legal hell with the property owner and shoot up a barrage of PR flak, this with the objective of forcing the errant landowner into a "settlement," while the county looked the other way. This is just one more example of how radicals in the environmental and conservation movements use less than ethical tactics in playing hardball with land owners, often with tacit government support at all levels.

In 1994, The *Washington Post* profiled David Lucas and his efforts on behalf of landowners concerned with private property rights. Lucas, some may remember, won a Supreme Court victory against South Carolina when the state tried to prevent him from building on his oceanfront lots. Lucas, a Charleston developer, has been lobbying congress and speaking out around the country as point man for the Council on Private Property Rights, a national legal action and lobbying group that he formed. The anti-regulation/private property rights movement has rallied around Lucas since his 1991 court victory. The movement is sweeping through state legislatures and is gaining ground in congress.

Lucas follows a simple credo: "If the government wants to put my land into a national park, or zone it a conservation area, fine. Pay me for it. The fifth amendment of the constitution requires exactly that . . . there's a growing backlash. I'm just the tip of the iceberg.

"The environmentalists now realize that people are tired of being pushed around by their laws and regulations."

The *Post* article said that, in 1994, 32 state legislatures were considering private property rights bills that would either require bureaucrats to assess how pending regulations would affect property values, or to compensate landowners if a regulation caused the value of affected property to fall by 50%.

Dr. Richard R. Stroup, professor of economics at Montana State University, writes in his book, *Eco-nomics,* "if the government had to compensate people for regulations that reduce the value of their property, more intelligent decisions would be made." He predicts that "If we give environmentalists the Alaska National Wildlife Refuge, you can bet your last dollar that there would be oil drilling. Why? Because it would cost them (the environmentalists) something to keep the oil in the ground." Remarking on the hypocrisy of the enviro movement, he cites the case of the Audubon Society and its ownership of the Rainey Preserve in Louisiana, a wildlife refuge.

Dr. Stroup says the strident enviro group has been drilling for oil on their land for over half a century, this to maintain their flow of revenue aimed at stopping other people from benefiting from the free and profitable use of their property.

The Greening of America

My success in the land business could seem somewhat remarkable, considering the fact that I'm usually playing against a stacked deck of increased regulations, gyrations in the economy, and exposure to financial setbacks. In the late sixties, thousands of ordinary people from all walks of life could literally walk in off the street and become land developers. In those days, the ease with which you could put land on the market spawned a virtual army of land hustlers. Each subsequent decade brought economic downturns and other calamities that tended to thin the ranks of land developers. Blips of prosperity and good times have since acted to bring shysters, neophyte developers, and speculators into the fold, albeit at a much slower pace each year than before.

Some will hustle land for a while; others will drift away to varied fields of endeavor; still others will venture on into the thickets of the real estate profession, to trade away the earth and its human monuments.

The simple fact is that there is enough blame to go around for the excesses in the transfer and development of country property in America. Every involved segment–real estate dealers, developers, government officials, environmentalists, conservationists, all have dirt on their hands. All of us, myself included, are fighting an unending war in a wilderness of faults and follies trying to dodge bullets that could finish us and our agendas. For every unfair regulation comes the revelation of scandal in government. Each act of self-interest by lobbyists brings the tax of shame and discredit on their hidden bags of faults. And for every alleged atrocity to the landscape there is the commensurate lynching of a developer.

In the well-documented book about the Ford Motor Company, *Wheels for the World,* by Douglas Brinkley, the author states that, "In the first eight years of the twentieth century, 502 car manufacturing firms were launched in the United States alone. And 302 of them either folded or shifted to another line of business." In the land development business I have noticed that, by the end of the century, almost all of the amateurs had left the field. Though sufficiently rewarding if you know the ropes, land development has become a very complicated and potentially risky business process, requiring market savvy, a sharp mind, unbridled confidence, a gambler's guts, experienced and qualified advisors or associates, and healthy financial strength. All of these attributes, qualities, and talents can of course be obtained or developed over time. I had none of them when I started out.

Consider the cards being dealt by planners to landowners and developers in the following county in 1994 and how they are stacked. With all due respect to planning officials, it appears to many real estate professionals as if some brainwashed planners from academia fiddle too much with their grand schemes of quaint little villages in a monarchal English countryside, this while arbitrarily tossing private property rights into the fire with little more concern than the act of removing clutter from their desks.

Stick it to the Little People

It seems the ruling oligarchy within Perfect County wanted to ration landowners in agricultural areas to a division of just one lot per year and to scrap the exemption of 20-acre parcels from the "King's" rules and regulations– all in the best interests of the citizens, of course. The county rulers and their master planners may have wondered what the little people could possibly do with a trifling 20 acres anyway, besides put it to the mischief of building a home and creating a small farm. You might think that any legitimate player in a respectable county game of land-use power would be expected to hold at least a hundred acres or more.

Government of the Rulers, by the Rulers, for the Rulers

A quick glance at a "Survey on the Future Growth and Development in Perfect County," distributed by county planning officials, shows how the deck of land-use cards can be cunningly and unfairly stacked against uninformed citizens. The questionnaire deceitfully places the planners' most desired answer on the top (or bottom) of the deck as follows: (1) Out of 12 options on what people like about living in Perfect County, <u>Scenic beauty of farmland</u> was first. (2) Out of 10 options on the worst problems facing the county, <u>Rapid housing development</u> was first. (3) Out of five degrees of feeling in answer to a loaded statement that "limited" highway funds should be used to improve existing roads (read no-growth) rather than to widen or add new roads (read pro-growth), the option (SA) <u>Strongly Agree</u> was the first choice given to readers. (4) The <u>Strongly Agree</u> option was listed first and was the reply most desired by the planners in compiling their death wish for private property rights in the county. Readers were coaxed in this subtle manner to give the planners the answer they wanted on almost all of the statements regarding population growth and real estate development. Examples:

(a) When new housing is built, it should be located in and around existing communities, rather than in the farming or forest areas. First option: <u>Strongly Agree</u>.

(b) New housing in the county should be required to have public water and sewer facilities, rather than individual wells and septic fields. First option: <u>Strongly Agree</u>.

(c) Perfect County is growing too fast. First option: Strongly Agree.

(d) Farmland in Perfect County is being developed with houses at too rapid a rate. First option: Strongly Agree.

(e) Local historic sites and buildings should be legally protected from development or destruction. First option: Strongly Agree.

Planner's Wish List

Out of all 10 statements concerning Taxes for Public Facilities and Services, the option Strongly Agree was the first response offered to weary readers–many of whom had little understanding of the issues and most of whom did not realize that their responses were being led by the planners–as to the planners' wish list for spending taxpayers' money.

Realizing that they could be accused of stacking the deck in their favor, the planners slipped in a couple of emotional "off-the-wall" statements so their more sheepish readers would embrace the planners' biased assumptions with less enthusiasm than the option Strongly Agree.

Examples: (a) All landowners in the county should be free to build on their land whatever type of structure they want to build, whenever they want. (Obviously a no-brainer that leaves out the more important option of dividing up their land). (b) New intensive farming activities, such as poultry houses and dairies, should be required to be set further back from neighboring property lines. (Who dreams up these rhetorical statements?)

The "loaded" questionnaire is a slick weapon of choice used by academic-minded planners to influence an often naive citizenry into taking more regulatory steps toward the gallows where private property rights are strangled in the name of the "public good."

A Tidewater newspaper, reporting on the controversial subdivision measure, said that an angry crowd of protesters at a recent public hearing accused the county planning officials of trying to sneak the ordinance through by advertising the meeting when people were focused on the Christmas holidays. Most attendees were not able to see the actual proposal until arriving at the hearing. Those speaking against the ordinance said it was too restrictive and took away their rights as landowners. The public outcry gained the support of most of the commissioners and forced the planners to table the proposed changes until a final comprehensive plan could be adopted later in the year.

Wetlands and the Abuse of Power

A 1994 article in the Harrisonburg, VA *Daily News Record* relates the following story about the need to reform the Clean Water Act.

It seems that a 60-year-old Hungarian emigre filled in a drainage ditch behind his home and was sent to prison for three years and fined $200,000 for defying the Corps of Engineers by refusing to apply for a permit. When the Corps won a court order to have him restore the land to its original elevation, the emigre lost. The case went before the Supreme Court. A previous Supreme Court ruling upheld the authority of the Corps to control "wetlands" as the Corps defines them. Since 1/6/94, the Soil Conservation Service has been given the responsibility for resolving conflicts between the Corps and the Fish and Wildlife Service on the definition of "wetlands."

Navigating on Trickling Streams

The Clean Water Act rests upon the power delegated to Congress to regulate commerce between the states. Without that foundation, the enforcement of implementing regulations in specific cases is caught up in murky waters.

In the case involving the emigre, the government contended that the drainage ditch was a tributary of the distant Pennsylvania Canal, which was last used in interstate commerce a hundred years prior to the filling incident. Counsel for the emigre assailed the absurdity of the government's position by remarking, "The commerce clause may be elastic, but it's not Silly Putty."

If such far-fetched theories are given validity by the court system and the enforcement arms of government agencies, then private property rights are rapidly becoming history.

Fortunately the Bush administration at the turn of the century recognized the abuse of this regulation and took steps to focus it on reality.

(Upside) Down on the Farm

By March of 1994 it was evident that a turnaround in farm values was surfacing. First some background:

Farmland was generally a good investment in the sixties and seventies. The high interest rates in the eighties caused inflated farmland prices to crash, with some sellers losing as much as 60% on the previous value of their land. In the seventies, farmland prices soared for a number of reasons: (1) detente, (2) world-wide crop failures, (3) increased commodity prices resulting from domestic drought, (4) subsidized credit to farmers, (5) rising inflation, and (6) negative interest rates in those investments pegged to the dollar.

In the eighties, a whole generation of farmers had to look for work elsewhere.

Though farm income stabilized, farmland prices never recovered their previous highs. Then, in 1994, certain fundamentals were at work in the economy that would begin to make farmland glitter again to investors. *LandOwner* news letter, reporting on the USDA's 1994 Outlook Conference, listed the following spurs to higher farmland prices:

(1) *Federal Debt*–growing faster than the economy

(2) *U.S. balance of payments*–up from $96 billion in 1993 to an expected $124 billion in 1994. Because we buy more from other nations than we sell, foreigners had accumulated more than $1.3 trillion in claims against U.S. assets since 1983.

(3) *Inflated U.S. stock prices*–could tumble with higher interest rates and possible exhaustion of new stock buyers.

(4) *Loss of the dollar's buying power against other currencies*–down two-thirds against the yen since 1975. Ancient Rome took 200 years to debase its coinage this far.

(5) *Flight of U.S. investment capital*–$100 billion per year outflow to foreign businesses and to bonds, leading to: (a) restricted investment job growth in U.S.; (b) higher U.S. Treasury rates to attract foreign capital; (c) lower U.S. savings needed to finance federal, state, and local deficits. All are dollar killers.

(6) *More S&L and bank bailouts*–another $18 billion voted by Congress. Cost to the taxpayers was expected to reach $500 billion–this to avoid a 1930's-style panic run on financial institutions.

(7) *Recession and depression trends in major overseas economies–* Breakup of the Soviet Union. 15% jobless rate in Germany. Both factors meant more inflationary public spending and a worldwide focus on hard-asset investments such as farmland.

Looking at these factors, I began shifting some of my investments in country properties toward potentially productive farmland.

What to Watch For

Dr. Ravi Batra, author of *The Great Depression of 1990*, said in his 1987 book to watch for the first half of 1994 for a signal on what lies ahead in the economy. He said if the stock market failed to crash in the early 90's, and if the "Depression" fails to materialize, then the danger of an economic calamity (like 1930-39) will, for all practical purposes, have passed. Batra based his theories on the emergence, in 1990, of a 60-year economic downturn cycle, which he believed was inevitable as the rising and the setting of the sun. As we have observed, he was correct about the 1990 downturn, but he failed to predict the economic calm of the tech boom approaching behind the storm clouds of the early nineties. Calamity cycles in the twentieth century generally began every ten years or so, at the turn of each decade, with corrections and moderation occurring over time as the decade progressed.

The Economy and Farmland Values

Bond prices seem to rise as interest rates and commodity prices fall. As interest rates climb, the demand for commodities increases and the demand for bonds declines. Accordingly, land, being a commodity, generally rises in value as interest rates go up–the move reflecting a growing investor disinterest in paper money. The demand for credit (also a commodity) usually follows the move into land by rising along with upticks in interest rates. Of course, land values can rise excessively regardless of whether interest rates go up or down.

This market trend occurs when land product within a region is in short supply and in great demand. For example, the swell of "Baby Boomers" looking for retirement homesites can flood a market with buyers, this while local governments are restricting land product through excessive regulation. The level of interest rates would have little impact on such a market.

You would normally think that low mortgage rates would stimulate the demand for land, but the opposite appears to be true, with a few caveats. Land values and interest rates generally respond in tandem to changes in the economy, because both react primarily to commodity-driven forces, and movement into commodities from dollar-denominated investments signals a trend toward higher interest rates and the specter of renewed inflation.

This is why country property investors should keep a close watch on interest rate trends. Land values, as a rule, go up with rises in interest rates. But as with any rule there are exceptions. We must remember the "stagflation" scenario of the seventies when interest rates went through the roof, while real estate values came crashing down in a disastrous twin hurricane of inflation and recession.

Country property investors who picked up underpriced land in 1994 may have been faced with interest rates on raw land of about 8 to 9%, but when their investments were converted to cash in, say, 1999, the profits in many cases were enormous, this despite onerous capital gains taxes. Those who entered into like-kind, tax-deferred exchanges in depressed urban real estate also may have had significant profits to play with after the turn of the century, this since busts in commercial real estate generally lag downturns in usable land, such as farms and timber tracts, by a few years.

A word of caution: Land investments during upswings should be based less on what crops the land produces and more on (1) proximity to major cities, (2) potential for worthwhile and profitable development, and (3) environmental pluses, such as clean air, clean water, and attractive natural features and surroundings.

Environmental Pressures and the Price of Land

People throughout the world are not inclined to give up their liberty unless they are deluded by their leaders. In this regard, dictators and socialist-leaning governments have much in common. In a dictatorship, the people are treated like birds in a cage; whereas, under socialism, liberty is likely to be rationed to humans, while being freely dispensed to the birds. This is particularly true when overzealous forces have a grip on government leaders to the extent that morals are distorted and political agendas become entangled in the warped thinking of some special interest groups.

In the Clinton years, much of the nation's land was being sacrificed to the gods of the environment. In 1994, a Midwestern farmer wrote in the *Wall Street Journal* about the impact on farmland of misguided environmental concerns. His conclusions were: (1) there is a decreasing amount of land being farmed, and (2) there will be decreased production on the land remaining in use. It seems that limited government funding to repair levees in the Midwest had left some 480,000 acres vulnerable to future floods. Many farmers were signing up for the Wetlands Reserve Program, which effectively shifts vast amounts of farmland from cultivation to wetlands –this to the great joy of environmentalists.

The Wisdom of the Wise

The *WSJ* article said that federal authorities, acting to protect wetlands, fish, and wildlife, had stripped away from many California farmers considerable portions of their water rights, removing expansive amounts of land from production. Other farmers, enticed by higher fees for water rights from non-farm users, were raising fees to their fellow farmers. The Clinton appointee to the federal Bureau of Reclamation had allegedly turned his bad ear toward the thirsty farmers and was listening with sympathy in his good ear to the needful cries of the cities and to the shriek of environmental radicals demanding more land for "endangered" species, all of which had been promised preferential habitats by entrenched bureaucratic and political leaders (6.6 million acres for the desert turtle alone).

God's Instructors

In 1994, Congress was debating a controversial bill that would list in its sacred halls all biological resources on both public and private land. If passed, the bill would no doubt have resulted in the discovery of even more "endangered" species than the 5,000 or so already signed up for habitats. The bottom line is that millions of additional acres would have been withdrawn from productive use and offered up as sacrifices to the gods of the environment–much of the land effectively confiscated by our righteous government from private landowners (who no doubt thought they could get away with stealing an "endangered" species habitat).

Along with the abdication of man's dominion over the creatures of the earth, we were given witness to government officials denying to agriculture the benefits of pesticides, thereby transforming thousands of previously productive farms and ranches into unprofitable estates and tempting tax shelters for the wealthy.

The glaring irony of such misguided government policy is that the Interior Secretary was at the same time pushing the government to eventually double grazing fees on federal lands, because a comparatively few ranchers were allegedly getting rich.

Conclusions for Country Property Seekers

(1) *Wanton environmental regulations will continue to restrict the number of good farms coming on the market,* this as savvy consumers and investors sop up the good deals on usable land in the face of an inevitable erosion of the dollar's value in years to come.

(2) *Prices of productive farmland will continue to rise.* While the farmland price boom of the 70's was fueled by a big increase in farm exports, the export market for U.S. farmers faltered in the 80's as the Common Market, with large export subsidies, captured many of our customers. Now new trade agreements with the Europeans and Japanese provide more open markets for U.S. farm products.

(3) *Food prices will rise, stimulating the demand for small farmsteads.* Rising interest rates signal inflation and price hikes.

(4) *Land values will peak and could begin to decline when and if interest rates reach excessive levels of, say, 10%, in a sustained recessionary period or prolonged calamity, such as a major war.* This would be ideal time to have available cash to buy land and country property.

The Ruse of Enviro Paternalism

The Church of the Earth

If you are a Christian, imagine, if you will, this scenario during Sunday morning worship services at your mainline church. Following the Affirmation of Faith, you are encouraged to drop your Bible and pick up your Environmental Awareness Kit.

Your preacher or priest then leads you on the following guilt trip: "We use more than our share of the earth's resources. We are responsible for massive pollution of the earth, water, and sky. We thoughtlessly drop garbage around our homes, schools, places of work, and places of play. We squander resources on technologies of destruction. Bombs come before bread."

You and the congregation then chant as if a spell has been cast upon you: "We are killing the earth. We are killing the waters. We are killing the skies."

While some environmental zealots may feel such extreme tactics are justified in the name of awareness, others oppose the growing strain of modern political theology that attempts to link religion, statist politics, and extreme environmentalism. A *Confession of Environmental Sins* in your church liturgy? Before you say it couldn't happen, consider the fact that at least one radical environmental group has spent millions of dollars to infiltrate the nation's religious congregations with "Environmental Awareness Kits." Traditional church clerics are aware of the inherent danger to fundamental precepts of western religious thought if such rituals become sacramental within the Christian church.

The New Church Bible

One prominent Catholic priest, the Rev. Robert A. Sirico, remarked in 1994 that, for many people, environmentalism has become a religion in itself, with some extremists pushing for superimposure of a "God-like" view of nature into traditional teachings from the Bible.

Still, there is dissension within the church community. A revisionist Catholic priest and author has described the earth as a kind of Christ figure and deems as "Cristofascism" any theology that views Jesus as the only son of God. He is on record as urging Christians to move beyond theology based on sin and redemption toward a concept of "oneness" with nature–a form of earth worship. Many Christians see the devil's handiwork in this abstraction.

Earth Worship

Paganism, it seems, has slipped into the controversy over the years, with some environmental "wackos" allegedly worshipping the so-called

Mother Earth god, Gaia. In the nineties, the obsession reached down to the office of the V.P. of the U.S., with Al Gore devoting an entire chapter to "Environmentalism of the Spirit" in his book, *Earth in the Balance.*

And reportedly, at a U.N.-sponsored Earth Summit in Rio de Janeiro, a contingent from the mainline United Church of Christ altered the traditional hymn "Were You There When They Crucified My Lord"– substituting Earth for Lord.

Critics of environmental extremism say public officials, in advancing human justice and quality of life, should serve mankind first and not give priority to plants and animals. They argue that environmentalists are trivializing the significant and positive role of development and consumption in our society. The environment, they claim, is far cleaner where economies are free from excessive centralized government control.

The Eleventh Commandment

To many environmental zealots, it may not be too far beyond reason to push for an ad hoc Council of Environmental Clerics to alter the Ten Commandments by adding an eleventh,

"Thou shalt not litter or defile the earth." Of course, if the extremists wanted to keep the divine directives to an even ten, that would be all right, too. They won't be needing the second one–about not worshipping other gods.

And God Created Man

Father Sirico, the Catholic cleric, thinks the enviro-zealots have it all wrong. Many of them think the earth created man as a gift to itself. The book of Genesis says the earth was a gift to man. The Bible says that after God created man and woman in his image, he blessed them with the words: "Be fertile and multiply; fill the earth and subdue it. Have dominion over the fish of the seas, the birds of the air, and all the living things that move on the earth." (Genesis 1:28).

Of course, if some enviros believe that Genesis is a fairy tale, or that God misspoke, or left something out, they are obviously free to program the changes into their revisionist Earth Bible. Man has often tried to be his own god. You usually see it before a fall–it's called *ego.*

To Have Dominion Over the Earth

In the second chapter of Genesis, after the earth's creation, God is said to have created man to till the earth and to make more of what he had been given. Man was explicitly given dominion over the earth *and not the other way around.* Many sincere Christians believe that, because of mankind's fall in the Garden of Eden, the devil, in the form of a serpent, has continued to deceive humans into worshipping the world (earth).

Sirico says the idea that nature itself has an independent and metaphysical right to be untouched, preserved, and adored is not part of the Judeo-Christian understanding of faith.

The simple reason for this fundamental religious perception is that true believers know they face God, not Gaia, on judgment day.

Food for the Soul

This said, it should also be recognized that human knowledge is the parent of doubt. For few of us have true knowledge of the afterlife. That happens to be a matter of faith.

We advance in life step by step, learning as we go. Every addition to our knowledge gives us power. Those who cease to learn pay the price of further ignorance. We seek knowledge like we seek financial security and wealth. Each acquisition increases the thirst for more.

In observing the environmental movement in this country, I find they have one thing in common with tyranny. Both forms of narrow interest approach us from a hidden agenda to consolidate power before acting, this to the detriment if the majority. And I feel that knowledge gained by personal observation and experience is of far greater value than what I read in books or learn from academia, a world that is conditioned by its ritualistic learning processes and conferred degrees to perpetuate bias and myths.

Dark Secrets of the Enviro Movement

In 1994, I wrote a newsletter article on the threat of the environmental movement to the real estate industry. Michael S. Coffman (PhD Forest Service, U. Of Idaho; M.S. Biology, Northern Arizona U.; B.S. Forestry, NAU) is a widely respected environmental consultant who had left a lucrative practice and comfortable job to expose the duplicity behind the agenda of environmental leadership.

In his book, *Saviors of the Earth,* he reveals the existence of an insidious and encroaching iron web of environmental tyranny that threatens–if left unchecked–to eventually snuff out the abused remains of almost all private property rights in this country. Passionate protectors of the environment can appear to be friends, but it is the enemy we do not suspect who can be the most dangerous.

Nature Worship

Nature-worshipping government officials and their initiates in Congress, rampant during the Clinton administration, have a record of diverting staggering amounts of money into meaningless laws and regulations that the environmental lobbyists and self-proclaimed saviors of the earth hold sacred. Hundreds of thousands of jobs have since been lost or never created, causing immense suffering and dislocation for our citizens. Americans to this day are still going to prison because of trivial violations of environmental laws and regulations, getting, in some cases, more jail time than killers. This insanity was given an element of reason with the change in administrations at the turn of the century.

The private ownership of, and proper stewardship of, land in this country has little or nothing to do with the defilement of the environment. But, through our observation of the war between radical environmental forces and free enterprise, we learn to avoid participating in a sacrament with nature where our livelihoods, homes, and properties are at risk.

The Bill Ellen Story

This story has some age to it, but it exemplifies the extremism at work within the environmental movement. Oft repeated, it always makes environmentalists cringe, and they like to trivialize the issue as though it were an aberration, when, in reality, entrenched regulations have made matters even worse.

In 1987, William Ellen was hired by a hotshot Wall Street trader to create a 103-acre wildlife sanctuary within a 3,200-acre hunting and conservation preserve on Maryland's Eastern Shore. Ellen is an environmental moderate who loves wildlife and who had returned nearly 2,000 ducks, geese, and other creatures to the wild.

Team Player

From the start, Ellen–a tidal wetlands regulator for the Virginia Marine Resources Commission in the 1970's, and a marine and environmental consultant for 20 years–worked closely with Maryland's Department of Natural Resources (DNR) and the U.S. Army Corps of Engineers. He invited Soils Conservation Service (SCS) officials and 24 scientists to visit the project.

In February 1988, Ellen received a visit from Corps personnel, who told him he was spilling road construction dirt into alleged wetlands, which were dry most of the year. Though the spill was accidental, Ellen, attempting to comply with regulations, and on the advice of the Corps, purchased $120,000 worth of special equipment.

Cease and Desist

A year later, the Corps closed him down. He was accused of filling wetlands. If he wanted to proceed with the project, he was told, he would have to hire a consultant to delineate wetlands in the area. Again, he complied with the Corps' request, with one exception–he dumped two loads of dirt on a three-acre administrative management site that had been delineated as *uplands* by the SCS only a month before.

Crimes Against Nature

Corps personnel, spying the dirt piles, launched a criminal investigation of Ellen for crimes against nature under the Clean Water Act. Ellen was dragged into court and accused of filling wetlands in the areas where accidental spills had occurred (for which he had taken the corrective action suggested by the Corps) on a table-sized wetlands spot within the administrative management site that had been overlooked in Ellen's wetlands delineation ordered by the Corps.

Enviro Scapegoat

A Corps spokesman, in a TV interview, arrogantly boasted that nobody flaunts government regulations and gets away with it. Ellen was strung up to twist slowly in the wind–a stern warning for other scofflaws who would sin against the environment.

What Ellen didn't know at the time was that the Corps, the SCS, the EPA, and the Fish and Wildlife Service–without holding public hearings–had been meeting in secret to double the amount of land considered wetlands in the U.S. Under intense pressure from enviro groups, the government changed the definition of wetlands– a definition that would toss Ellen into a jail cell.

Dry Wetlands

Under the new definition, even dry land could be locked up under the wetlands rules.

If **two of the three** following criteria were met, anybody's land could be classified as wetlands–and consequently devalued–by government enforcers. (Tough luck if you had counted on selling your land to pay medical bills or to tide you through retirement.) (1) If the soil was classified as "hydric" (saturated by water for long periods), (2) if the soil had an 18" water table for as little as 7 days during growing season, or (3) if the soil showed the presence of hydrophilic (water-loving) plants, such as poison ivy and loblolly pine. Man-made agricultural ditches, pine forests, and 40% of drought-stricken California also qualify as wetlands under this definition.

Government Tyranny

That single pseudo-scientific decision by government bureaucrats– in effect their worst guess–instantly created 175,000 new acres of wetlands in Maryland–up from 84,000 under the old definition. Ellen's project, as it happened, fell under the new definition–*developed in secret without public hearings*–and he was found guilty by an urban jury and thrown into prison for six months.

The prosecution asked for a term of 27 to 33 months–this for dumping two loads of dirt on soil that was later found *not* hydric and on which there was no evidence of surface water.

The alarming truth of this story is that, if Bill Ellen, who was versed in environmental regulations, and who tried to work with the regulators, could run afoul of these obscure regulations, what hope does the typical American landowner have? Reformers of the Clean Water Act say the government could save hundreds of millions of dollars by having the wetlands provisions apply only to areas having a permanent surface water connection to "navigable waters", rather than maintaining bureaus of fed watchdogs to patrol every pond and mud puddle in the U.S. looking for scofflaws, when they could be on the alert for real terrorists.

The Rise of the Environmental S.S.

Dr. Coffman, and other professionals familiar with the inner workings of the environmental elite, have broken ranks with the movement's radical leaders because of the organization's hidden agenda. The environmental leaders in this country, largely in their secret and most intimate discussions, talk in messianic terms about their role as "earth saviors."

To accomplish this mission, these self-styled earthly redeemers believe the social and economic structure of America and the western world must be totally transformed. (Huge monuments to civilized progress in this world have been reduced to rubble, and thousands killed by zealot terrorists who are at odds with western thought and accomplishment.)

Dr. Coffman says that, based on the demands of the enviro elite, the magnitude of this transformation is the equivalent of what occurred under the collapse of the USSR in the 1990's.

A seemingly valid interpretation of the enviro leadership's hidden agenda is the destruction of America's social and economic structure to save the country in a form deemed *pure* by the new order.

The Black Shadow

Lurking behind the Sierra Club image of spacious skies and purple mountain majesties is a black shadow of intimidation that arrogantly demands from the government the taking and condemnation of quantum chunks of private-sector land–this to feed the enviro elite's crusade to mold man and nature into a perverted oneness with Mother Earth. Property rights, in this grand environmental scheme, must be obliterated for the common good of a new world order.

An example of these extremist tactics is found in a radical environmental book published by the Sierra Club, *The Dream of the Earth*: "We must be clear concerning the order of magnitude of the changes that are needed. We are not concerned here with some minor adaptations, but with the most serious transformation of human-earth relations that has taken place at least since the classical civilizations were founded."

The Green Machine

Al Gore, ex-U.S.Vice President, and favorite son of Mother Earth–an advocate of universal government control of the environment (at the expense of U.S. sovereignty)–spearheaded the frenzied recruitment of environmental radicals for top-kick slots in federal regulatory agencies when he and bad boy Clinton were romping around the White House.

The Clinton adminstration brought us close to a real shooting war between the forces of radical environmentalism and free enterprise. If there had been such a war, Dr. Coffman pointed to the following key personalities as usual suspects. All were forced to clean out their desks when Clinton left town. In retrospect, had there been a supply of environmental "Most Wanted" cards available at the time, some free enterprise warrior would no doubt have imbedded the faces of this cozy clique throughout the deck, this because of their governmental and political positions, and not necessarily with any reflection on their character.

Carol Browner–Head of EPA–Key advisor for Senator Gore. Past head of the Florida Department of Environmental Regulation. She did the background work on Gore's enviro book.

George Frampton–Assistant Secretary of the Interior for Fish and Wildlife Parks. Past president of the Wilderness Society and formerly the Chairman of the League of Conservation Voters (LCV). The LCV is a political action group for big national environmental organizations. A rallying cry, donated to LCV from Interior Secretary Babbitt, a former Chairman, intones, "We must identify our enemies and drive them into oblivion." (Landowners take note)

Alice Rivlin–Chairman of the Board of the Wilderness Society. Deputy Director, Office of Management and Budget.

Jim Baca–Board member for the Wilderness Society. Deputy Director for the Wilderness Society.

Brooks Yeager-of the National Audubon Society, Interior Secretary Babbitt's chief of staff.

Kathleen McGinty–Gore's top environmental advisor in the Senate. Head of the Council on Environmental Quality.

Bonnie Cohen–of the National Trust for Historic Preservation. Assistant Secretary for Policy, Management, and Budget.

John Leshy,–mining industry foe. Solicitor.

Dr. Coffman, author of *Saviors of the Earth*, reported on an infestation of former private sector enviro leaders who were embedded in the Clinton Administration in roles beyond these aforementioned key positions–a nest of envirocrats from the National Audubon Society, the Wilderness Society, and other national environmental organizations. All appeared to him to hold extremist viewpoints that favored further strangulation of private property rights for the prosaic "common good."

Dangerous Autocrats

To many land owners, George Frampton, when he headed up the U.S. Fish and Wildlife Service in the Clinton-Gore dreamscape, was one of the most dangerous men in America to the cause of private property rights. One example of his reckless environmental advocacy was his public call for the taking of 26 million acres of northern forest land in the northeast away from landowners to create a vast wilderness area for the benefit of nature–this at the expense of hundreds of thousands of jobs and lost land values. One critic, observing the Clinton-Gore stacking of the Interior Department with environmental radicals, remarked of Frampton, "Here's a pompous wannabe who is so arrogant he started issuing orders before he was even confirmed."

Creeping Fascism

The Park Service, as many people know–because of an investigation in the early nineties by the Inspector General–was found in bed with the Nature Conservancy and the Trust for Public Land. These noble enviros buy land at bargain prices and sell it to their sweetheart, the Park Service, at inflated prices. The Greenshirts were paying the asking price with taxpayer money and continuing to space out on their growing domain. Former Interior Secretary Manual Lujan tried to stop the mischief by proposing new policies, but Land Minister Babbitt squelched the corrective measures right after Clinton slinked into office with Gore on his coattails.

The Hidden Agenda

Former V.P. Gore, some critics believe, has crafted the guidelines for further environmental tyranny in his book, *Earth in the Balance*. In one chilling statement, Gore says "the environment must be the central organizing principle of civilization." Few landowners are fully aware of the enviro elite's hidden agenda, as summed up in those words.

Now I don't know Al Gore personally. I can't recall having seen the man in person. But I did vote for him in the 1992 elections. I'm sure he feels he is doing what he thinks is best for his country as he sees it. We just happen to be miles apart on our views about environmental policy. Unfortunately, in my view, Gore, if he were President, would be given free reign to force-feed his ideals down the throats of private landowners by shilling for the "enlightened" enviro leadership, this when compelled by political reality to make certain demands from a bully pulpit such as the White House. Examples: (1) *"Every law, regulation, treaty, tactic, strategy, and plan must be used to save the earth."* (2) *"Rhetoric and minor policy changes are merely forms of appeasement to avoid the gut-wrenching transformation that all Americans are expected to undergo."*

Anybody want to take a kamikaze leap into the volcano for mass environmental crimes against Gaia–the angry earth goddess?

Heroes or Charlatans?

With all due respect to the former Vice President and his idealism, critics, like myself, of Gore and his league of self-styled masters of the environment feel that the hard-core enviro standard-bearers in this country are galaxies away from their crafty image as modern-day heroes–that they are, in fact, masked fanatics, some of whom, behind their princely disguises, are actually self-serving charlatans drawing six-figure salaries, while milking the public of their hard-earned dollars through elaborate and hysterical media productions of pseudo-scientific environmental calamities, such as the alar scam and the exaggerated "loss-of-wetlands" issue.

Legitimate Issues

Most people will agree that a concerted assault must be ordered against the pollution of our streams, rivers, lakes, oceans, and aquifers. If acid rain, global warming, ozone depletion, and ecosystem destruction are verifiable environmental issues, then all of us would agree that strong action is needed to correct these abuses and to reverse their paths.

But Dr. Coffman and other knowledgable professionals, including well-known scientists, say the enviro leaders are creating pseudo-scientific calamities and that opponents' voices were effectively silenced during the Clinton years by an entrenched "Green Party" in the White House.

These voices are ignored today by closet "Green Party" members in Congress who seek world government regulation of the environment at the ultimate expense of private property rights in the United States.

Are You My Mother?

If Gore and the enviro elite have their way, we are in for a heavy dose of ecumenical spiritualism that embraces evolution and distorts the Judeo-Christian concept of God as we know Him from the Bible. In his book, *Earth in the Balance*, Gore, an alleged avowed Christian, burrows further into the bosom of Mother Earth by criticizing other Christians for not appreciating *"the long and intricate process by which evolution helped to shape the complex interrelationship of living and non-living things."*

Indeed, Gore's critics feel his spiritual mixmaster is concocting a devil's brew if we drink down the concept of mankind worshipping God through the Creator's alleged spirit in plants, insects, animals, and even rocks. Of particular concern to Christian believers such as Dr. Coffman is the apparent widespread conviction among the enviro leadership that Christianity is at the epicenter of environmental calamities because of its established dualism (separation) between man and nature. A fundamental Christian belief–discredited by environmental radicals–is that man, through God's will, has dominion over the earth, and further, that this power is to be exerted primarily for the benefit of *mankind*. Nowhere in the Bible is there any reference to earth worship.

New Enviro Religion

A principal enviro mandate for Christian guilt over an afflicted environment comes from a paper delivered by medieval historian Lynn White before the American Association for the Advancement of Science on December 26, 1966. In essence, the paper assaults Christianity for (1) the destruction of paganism through the one-God concept, and (2) its rejection of the animistic belief that everything in nature is alive and has a spirit.

The enviro hidden agenda is entrenched in the following remarks by White: *"More science and more technology are not going to get us out of the present ecologic crisis until we find a new religion. We shall continue to have a worsening ecologic crisis until we reject the Christian axiom that nature has no reason for existence save to serve man."*

Doublespeak

It is doubtful that Gore would subscribe to such apostasy. Nevertheless, throughout his book, Gore jumps in and out of the fire he is unwittingly building to burn down the fundamental precepts of western religious thought, this by trying to intellectualize some creation-evolution link, particularly when pandering to his obsession over the sacredness of a blessed Mother Earth.

Gore says: *"A growing number of anthropologists and archaeo-mythologists, such as. . . argue that the prevailing ideology of belief in prehistoric Europe and much of the world was based on the worship of a single earth goddess who was assumed to be the fount of all life and who radiated harmony among all living things.. . .it seems obvious that a better understanding of a religious heritage preceding our own by so many thousands of years could offer us insights into the nature of the human experience."* Anybody for a regression to paganism?

Heaven in the Balance

Understand that Gore is not denying the existence of God as we know Him through the Bible. He is simply attempting to steer man's intellect closer to the physical world. Can the return of paganistic worship of a pantheon of earth gods be far behind the dilution of the Judeo-Christian God into a primordial spirit that moves rocks, plants, and insects, and animates all creatures?

Gore questions whether God has given us the appropriate technology to enjoy dominion over the earth, suggesting that mankind is screwing things up and that he, Gore, and his league of enviro masters can make things right again.

Medicine Men

Gore, seeking support for a universal mega-force to patrol the environment, quotes liberally from ancient spiritualists, shamans, and Eastern mystical prophets:

"The earth is our mother, and we are her children."

"Let the cosmic powers be peaceful."

"Will you teach your children what we have taught our children–that the earth is our mother? What befalls the earth befalls all the sons of the earth."

The former V.P., pushing for a comprehensive body of universal environmental regulations through various pacts and treaties, makes but a single reference to Christ in his book, and he quotes only sparingly from scripture, alluding to the account of Noah's Ark as evidence to mankind that God wants us to save all living species on earth from extinction. Gore even suggests that the enviro agenda could be summarized in an eleventh commandment: *Thou shalt preserve biodiversity* (the perpetuation of all living things).

Biocentrism

The life-centered reasoning (*biocentrism*) of the enviro elite embraces the concept that God is in everything, hence a certain equality of all living things must exist. Therefore man has to stop being so selfish and listen to nature because nature knows best. And since nature's nature is to perpetuate itself (biodiversity), then mankind's current socio-economic structure, with its priorities of production and consumption, poses a distinct threat to the natural world.

Back to Nature

In his book, Gore lays it on the Christian Church for not understanding his environmentally correct philosophy: "*The philosophy of life we have inherited, which tells us we are separate from the earth (presumably a cut above other living things) obscures our understanding of our common destiny and renders us vulnerable to an ecological catastrophe.*"

Al Gore suggests that man's biblical concept of having dominion over the earth is an outmoded delusion, comparable to the once misguided belief in slavery. Many Christians will no doubt find it disconcerting to their faith in the Holy Trinity when Gore (who may find his idealism misinterpreted) calls for faith in a *holistic* spirit that bonds mankind to plants, insects, rocks, and animals.

Gore says, "...*we have tilted so far toward individual rights and so far away from any sense of obligation (to the earth) that it is difficult to muster an adequate defense of any vested rights in the community or in the nation.*" With all due respect, this remark appears to reflect the weak shadow of a man who, if he were president, would be expected to aggressively defend this country against terrorism in the twenty-first century.

What follows in Gore's idealistic book is a grandiose scheme for a "Global Marshall Plan" where we essentially cut production and consumption as an atonement for environmental crimes, and surrender many of our private property rights for the good of the good ol' globe. As a disillusioned Gore supporter, I hope that he has moderated his views since he wrote this book.

That particular morning may never break. Because, while history shows the darkness of earth-bound religions passing on, a person who writes well usually believes his or her work is history.

Environmental Sin

Some modern-day biblical scholars appear to look the other way when private property rights are illegally snatched without compensation by the government as a sacrifice to the environment. These are the alarmists who support the concept of "Environmental Sin"–a biblical revisionist theory concocted by liberal clerics to heap guilt on mankind for alleged environmental abuse, as expressed in such spongy remarks as "exploiting the earth and its resources" or "a dangerous pattern of behavior that will surely bring God's wrath upon the children and their children's children."

Collective Guilt

With deserved respect for moderates in the enviro movement, the notion of mankind's "shared guilt" for the environmental wrongs of some offenders among us is a slick scheme for extorting "Friends of Nature" monetary contributions and passing abusive regulations.

Nature's miseries abound, and they will continue to plague us, even in the "perfect" secular world envisioned by the enviro elite. In their hearts they know this is true. They also know that the public would rather have, in one gulp, all of the miseries nature owns than to endure collective guilt. So the enviro leaders and their spiritualistic prophets keep manufacturing calamities and reinterpreting the Bible to invoke God's wrath on mankind as a collective environmental abuser, this while gleefully opening envelopes stuffed with cash and fat checks.

Enviro Overkill

In her bestselling book, *Environmental Overkill,* Dr. Dixy Lee Ray exposed the real truth behind the headlines of ecological disaster and how our livelihoods and private property rights are being callously prosecuted into oblivion by lawyers and bureaucrats in Washington, although this trend may be moderating with the advent of the change in political leadership after the Clinton administration. Bureaucrats, being paternal in nature, always know what is good for us, and bad policy could linger like a plague.

The late Dr. Ray served as Governor of Washington State, Chair of the Atomic Energy Commission, Assistant Secretary of State in the U.S. Bureau of Oceans, and was a longtime member of the zoology faculty at the University of Washington.

Spotted Owl Scam

According to Dr. Ray, "The Northern Spotted Owl is being used, quite cynically, as an excuse to stop logging in old-growth forests, *not to save owls from extinction.*" She quotes an economist from Portland, Ore., as saying in *Newsweek* magazine, "Cumulatively, the environmental movement is interested in shutting down the timber industry." Period.

The cynicism of the enviro elite apparently knows no bounds. A resource analyst for the Sierra Club and Legal Defense Fund is quoted in Ray's book as saying, *"The Northern Spotted Owl is the wildlife species of choice to act as a surrogate for the old growth (forest) protection, and I've often thought that thank goodness the Spotted Owl evolved in the Northwest, or we would have had to genetically engineer it."*

This scam on the American public by the enviro leadership is criminal and outrageous. It's like chemically engineering mad cow disease in the U.S. to stop people from eating beef.

At the time of her comments, Dr. Ray said that the greatest concentration of nesting pairs of Northern Spotted Owls yet recorded inhabited not an old-growth forest, but a privately owned tree farm in eastern Washington state, where the oldest trees would then be about 50 years old. A wildlife biologist working in California reported, "we have not found any areas where we do *not* have owls."

Criminal Waste

In a quixotic crusade to force the Spotted Owl to become "endangered," the government spent $22.5 million in 1990 and 1991. One year after the owl listing, 75 mills closed because they no longer had a stable wood supply. Forty thousand jobs were lost.

By 1994, the rising cost of timber had added, conservatively, about $5,000 to the construction cost of a three-bedroom home, and given the rising cost of goods, that figure would no doubt have doubled by 2004. The land locked up by the government in 1994 had meant $96 million in lost timber revenues per pair of owls, and the Clinton administration was joyfully banking on another six years to perpetuate this madness. Unemployment in the timber counties of Washington state had reached 34.9%, and at the turn of the century, the timber industry in the United States was on the ropes, leaving building construction dependent upon large supplies of imported lumber.

Enviro Commissars

It would seem that many of the enviro bigwigs who moved into plush government offices to sustain this scam could care less about the unemployed timber workers and how they would house, clothe, and feed their families. These officials were the well-fed party-line enviro bigshots–then fat and happy in their cushy regulatory jobs as environmental ministers during the eighties.

In his 2003 book, *Tales From The Left Coast,* James Hirson, the columnist and cable news commentator with *NewsMax.com,* said annual salaries for environmental CEOs were more than $200,000. He told of one severance package being doled out to an executive of $750,000.

Since Gore and Clinton sponsored these extremists, it seems logical that both he and Clinton were aware of the Owl scam, but it would appear that they marched in lockstep with the radicals because of political expediency.

Environmental Gestapo

By 1994, the U.S.Fish and Wildlife Service had become, to some observers, the Gestapo of the Interior Department. Dr. Ray reported on some of their dubious tactics. Up until the early nineties, the FWS was using poison to get rid of four trash fish in Colorado–the squawfish, two types of chub, and a sucker. *These same fish were, in 1994, listed as endangered by the FWS.* And their recovery at the time was estimated to cost $650 million.

The FWS is charged with enforcing the farcical Endangered Species Act. Penalties are more severe for committing so-called "environmental crimes," even when committed unknowingly, than for the unlawful acts of burglary or aggravated assault.

Dr. Ray said the endangered species legislation is so loosely drawn that it can be interpreted as a requirement to save *all* species and *all* subspecies and *all* geographically defined populations at *any* cost.

Agency Out of Control

Figures from 1994 showed the protection costs for each listed "species" was $2.6 million per year. U.S. taxpayer money is being lavished on questionable species such as the Puerto Rican Cave Cockroach and the American Burying Beetle. These are examples of real pork in government spending programs, and the money is going to insects, not people.

During the Clinton administration, billions and billions of dollars were siphoned from the U.S. Treasury by environmental blackmailers operating from swank office suites in Washington.

Some of these environmental operatives continue to hold for ransom every living creature on earth. Commenting on this sorry state of affairs at the time, Dr. Ray remarked, "Given the recent history of congressional action, or lack of action, on environmental issues, neither the dismal state of the economy, nor the property rights and economic survival of America's citizens counts for anything when weighed against the well-heeled activists of the environmental movement."

Whose Land is This?

An editorial in the *Richmond Times-Dispatch* called for a drastic revision of the Endangered Species Act when it came up for reauthorization by Congress in 1994. The article said: "In the 20 years since it was signed into law, the ESA has cost Americans millions of dollars and thousands of jobs, and it has done incalculable damage to the sanctity of personal property rights.

"The National Wilderness Institute recently combed through 25,000 pages of the U.S. Fish and Wildlife Department's plans for recovering 388 endangered species and pegged the cost at *'a minimum of $884 million.'* In many cases, the expenses would be to 'recover' animals that have long since repopulated. The inviolate rule of bureaucracy is to never discontinue a means–even when the end has been met.

"Not surprisingly, environmental groups are attempting to stall any proposed amendments, even though reform would probably be in their best interest. Frustrated property owners are becoming a threat in themselves. After one North Carolina farmer was forced to stop using 1,000 acres of his land surrounding a red-cockaded woodpecker–a suspension that cost him $1.8 million–he clear-cut the entire area so the woodpecker couldn't settle in and jeopardize all his land. . . So far, radical environmentalists seem more concerned with protecting blunt-nosed leopard lizards that preventing the endangerment and sometime extinction of property rights."

Endangered Landowners

Government envirocrats have been so worked up over exaggerated and emotional issues such as the loss of wetlands and threats to ecosystems that they are overkilling private property owners with regulations. These enviro zealots were at work in 1994 extrapolating federal environmental rules to local political and zoning issues, such as Disney's America in rural Virginia.

After launching false pollution balloons, creating hysteria over nonexistent battlefields, and distributing misleading information on traffic and commerce, the extremists were frantically searching the area for a phony "endangered" species to kill the project–this against the will of state and local government and in opposition to the free-market transfer of real estate.

An obvious first step for the new envirocrats could easily have been to decree regulatory guidelines for private forests and farmland, establishing required ratios allowed by the new "Bureau of Private Lands" within the Interior Department. This regulatory nightmare to be followed, no doubt, by federal directives restricting the development of further private property through subdivision and lot creation.

Dr. Coffman, in this book, *Saviors of the Earth?*, says, "All American law dealing with property is rooted in common law, which, in turn, was handed down from the days of the Magna Charta. Common law is based on the premise that owners can use and develop their land *as long as that activity does not infringe upon the rights of other land owners.*"

Dr. Coffman and others view the myth of eco-catastrophe as a deliberate attempt by enviro leaders to create guilt and fear in the American people to achieve a hidden agenda aimed at the destruction of property rights and the indoctrination of Americans into a regressive new anti-Christian enviro religion.

The Sixties Revisited

The basic danger in mainlining spirituality into the arms of the enviro cause is the inevitable secularization of the Judeo-Christian God. Christian clerics who decry fundamental western biblical interpretations seem convinced that the salvation of the earth is to be found in ecumenical spiritualism (the unification of world spiritual concepts). This doctrine calls for enviro/religious initiates to embrace the spirit gods of all the earth's people and to worship them as a singular metaphysical body having dominion over the earth.

The Age of Aquarius

Although it is unlikely that even the most liberal of Christian clerics would espouse a new environmental religion, such a sect, if hatched, would no doubt have New Age genes. One Great White Father over all religions; a brotherhood of spiritual masters, the belief in reincarnation; a revisionist "Book of God," enviro sacraments in a so-called Church of the Earth; and the sanctification of a pantheon of sub-gods, who were once prophets on Mother Earth.

The fact that this approach corrodes the foundation of Christianity and undermines faith in the Holy Trinity appears to have eluded naive proponents of this blasphemous idea. Mystic thinking was once again brought to mainstream America in the second half of the twentieth century, this time by the counterculture of the sixties. Popular concepts of the youth in those days were communal living, food gathering, an obsession with nature, drug-induced spiritualism, free love, and a diminution of God from a position of exaltation to a primitive energy force moving in every living thing.

Back to the Future

Dr. Coffman questions the wisdom of idealists who would create a new enviro religion based on ancient Greek and Roman mythic god beliefs, and on Eastern mystical religions, most of which are more man-centered–and hence theoretically more harmful to the environment–than Christianity. Viewing the deforestation of Hindu India and Buddhist Nepal, and the concomitant poverty in those countries, he observed: *"If poverty is the probable result of (such belief systems) then environmental degradation is also a natural consequence. If so, rather than being an answer to saving the earth, these Eastern religions, glorified by many environmental leaders, merely provide another path to destruction."*

By 1994, the sixties generation had grown up. Some of them found nirvana inside the halls of the Clinton administration; others had become fanatical enviro leaders. The misguided actions of these extremists have led to widespread disruption in the free-market system of transferring country properties. A flood of environmental regulations has swept across the countryside of this nation, adversely affecting private-property owners and even threatening our security, this because of restraints placed on the military when using government land for maneuvers and weapons testing.

The simple fact is that the environmental zealots could care less about private property rights, unless it's their own land that is being bulldozed. The enviro movement has, in effect, created a scarcity of land available for market consumption, thus driving up the price of country real estate for consumers. The tendency of local officials is to blame greedy developers for creating "urban sprawl" when, in actuality, it appears to be largely the selfishness of privileged landowners pushing for more restrictive regulations and the misguided policies of environmental radicals that have forced people farther and farther from the center of the cities, this in their search for an affordable place in the country.

It was really scary watching Clinton lock up millions of acres for the public "good" and then, at the behest of his environmental commissars, declaring the land "off limits" for any real use by the general public. The last big country that deluded the people about the collective use of land is now economically impoverished and rethinking the wisdom of such policies. It was called the Soviet Union.

The Creation of "Edge Cities"

In his 1991 book, *Edge Cities,* Joel Garreau spotlighted Gainesville, Virginia, near Washington D.C. as an emerging "Edge City." The significance of having this designation pinned on that relatively rural area was that Gainesville, at the time, was destined for phenomenal growth, which has since occurred, this even before Disney targeted the region for its proposed history theme park.

As with most no-growth groups–ad hoc or well-organized–Disney opponents futilely attempted to halt established growth patterns through the expenditure of vast sums of money on contrary research and propaganda to "save" the bucolic countryside from the development of new homes, apartments, and commercial activity, all needed by people moving farther out from the city and the existing suburbs.

This obstructionist agenda mirrors a group of small-town merchants marching about holding up "Stop WalMart" signs. The objective of special interest groups in attempting to control major population shifts already in place is only possible by establishing isolated dams of political intrigue bolstered by huge amounts of old money and newly acquired wealth. And then, all you have accomplished on the perimeter of major cities is to divert the emerging channels of progress around these islands of privilege.

"No-growth" interest groups target millions of dollars at the cause of halting the "Edge City" trend (read urban sprawl). Pro-growth supporters say critics of this trend would be happy if we could rescind the settlement of the west, or if we could somehow force people to stay down on the farm or be confined to small villages. Demographic experts realize that macro-management of growth trends in a democratic nation is an exercise in futility, if not the outright tampering with our basic freedoms.

When Does an Edge Become a City?

The author Joel Garreau offers the following characterization: When the city has (1) *five million square feet or more of usable office space –the workplace of the information age;* (2) *600,000 feet or more of leasable office space;* (3) *more jobs than bedrooms;* (4) *a perception of being a singular place by the populace* and; (5) *a reputation of being nothing like "city" as recently as 30 years before.*

The Manassas-Haymarket-Gainesville Edge City

In 1994, this community network was already in the making. Readers of the book *Edge City* were advised to project their vision 10 years into the future where they would see a dynamic urban complex, anchored by both the area's respect for the past, through the preservation of the Manassas Civil War Battlefield, and the accommodation of future reality through state and local government support for growth.

This new Edge City extends 40 miles or so from downtown Washington, D.C., and has transformed the lower Shenandoah Valley into the city's new "western suburbs." This outlying region includes the town of Front Royal, where I have my offices, and the city of Winchester.

As predicted, a considerable number of vacation homes in the Shenandoah Valley have become primary dwellings of many people working in the Edge City of Manassas-Haymarket-Gainesville.

As of 2004, a frantic new wave of construction is now underway in the Potomac Highlands farther west.

Law of the Land

These events reach far beyond the demographer's crystal ball. In fact, they are imbedded in the human psyche: *When people move in, it's time to think about moving on, or time to buy more privacy.* To the extent that a county can effectively and willingly promote the idea of keeping people and commercial activity out, it will, in effect, buy more privacy, albeit at the cost of higher taxes for those who can afford to live there, while fostering a community of "haves" and "have nots." As I have said before, the adoption of no-growth exclusionary policies based on self-interest is like a populist president preaching "habitats for humanity" but not in my backyard. For elitist conservative snobs, this exclusionary viewpoint has the din of selfish cocktail chatter about "How are you gonna keep 'em down in the city once they've seen Beautyburg?"

For those moving beyond the cities, Garreau, the author, cites an inviolate law: "Only if life is perceived as pleasant and affordable by the real human beings living further in, will there be any hope of relieving pressure on the land further out." One concerned citizen wrote to a local Shenandoah Valley newspaper addressing the issues of "urban sprawl" and why people want to live in the country. This is what he had to say:

". . . they've been driven out of the cities by high taxes and high housing costs and rents, thanks to inefficient government, rent control, invidious development restrictions and pandering regulations and entitlements. They've been driven out by crime and incompetent bureaucrats.

"But more than anything else, they've been driven out by lousy public schools. Our nations's suburbs are populated by a vast middle class unwilling to see their children's futures ruined by incompetent and indifferent public schools, but unable to afford private-school tuition. If their employers haven't followed them out of the cities, they endure a punishing commute.

"Washington, D.C. is perhaps the best worst-case. The city payrolls have been grotesquely infiltrated with patronage jobholders who deliver, with legendary ineptness, the same level of service provided by half as many city workers elsewhere. They have rent controls and myriad restrictions on high-density development, and a thousand meddling special-interest groups.

"Taxes are onerous. Crime is awful. And they have what may be the most spectacularly failed public school system in the nation, which manages to spend about $14,000 per pupil per year.

"The only people left in D.C. are either wealthy enough to insulate themselves from the incompetence, or they can't afford to get out.

"What is to be done about sprawl? If sprawl is a symptom of failing cities, one fix would pretty much amount to confining people in cities they desperately want to escape from.

"The alternative–fixing the cities–is beyond the reach of anything we can do in the Valley.

"After healing cities, the next best fix is controlling the pattern of development locally to encourage density. If a way can be found to get the public schools to perform without onerous expense, that's half the battle. . . a revenue-sharing arrangement (with the county) would make sense, too.

"In the long run, the cities will become relatively attractive, and the pattern of population increase will reverse. Maybe the cities will get their act together; or maybe the sprawl will get so bad that the countryside will have been ruined, and the cities won't look so bad, after all.

"The message of these emerging Edge Cities is clear. Suburbia, as we have known it, is fading as a place apart. That's because the workplace of the middle and upper-middle class is moving closer to their homes."

Interest Rates and the Land Market

Jane Bryant Quinn, the financial columnist, says the real killer to business growth is high interest rates–and not jittery news events. The economy's savings–including the buildup of funds in banks–flows into securities when business is weak, because there is not a lot of demand for money. Prices for stocks and bonds go up, and interest rates go down.

Spending for Land

But when business catches fire, the demand for funds increases as consumers step up their spending and as businesses borrow to expand production. Consumers, of course, buy land and houses, and developers borrow money to create various land products, improved and unimproved. Rapid business growth, as economists like to put it, is the harbinger of inflation.

And the quick-fingered reaction of the Federal Reserve Board to the gluttonous shadow of consumer and business spending is to shoot at demand with exploding interest rates.

Why Invest in Land?

How do these rate hikes affect growth in the land industry? A key indicator to rising demand for land in some sectors is the increased flow of funds from stocks and bonds into other investments, such as productive farms and timberland. Aberrations to this theory can, of course, occur when gluts of agricultural and wood products appear on the world market, this causing distortions in commodities trading. Higher interest rates generally cause the value of bonds and many mutual funds to decline.

The Giant Sucking Sound

Investors in this scenario also seek safety in the higher interest rates paid by short-term treasuries and money-market funds. In turn, this investment tide sucks money from the stock market, hurting prices across the board. Lower stock prices, of course, dampen consumer confidence; so business expansion, through the sale of expensive products, such as homes and cars, is consequently moderated. The demand for building lots is measured by the health of the construction industry and is calibrated by consumer confidence levels, both of which are on the downside when interest rates are being stabilized by the Federal Reserve Board.

Inflation Come Home

In 1994, Quinn said that 40% of all bull markets in the twentieth century began in the second year of a president's term. History also shows that money habitually flows from depressed stocks and bonds into select land investments. A bigger boost to a more active land market would be a measurable dose of inflation in the economy, rather than the bitter pill of high interest rates.

How the Government Lied About Economic Growth in the Nineties

Most people look back on the nineties and see a rosy picture of spiraling growth, lavish lifestyles, full employment, a cadre of newly-minted millionaires, and new cars flying out of showrooms like loaves of bread from grocery stores before a blizzard. The truth is that growth really did not begin to take off until the mid-nineties. Land prices were still relatively low in 1994.

Business Week magazine investigated the "growth" issue at the time and found that bureaucrats had scandalously been misleading the American public through the release of "pulp fiction" statistics. For example, the true rate of inflation was at least a percentage point lower than the consumer price index (CPI). And the Fed, reacting to fairy tale inflation numbers, took positions resulting in higher mortgage interest rates, thereby threatening progress in the struggling real estate recovery.

Sucker Bet

The situation called to mind the wager made by Dr. Julian Simon, the renowned economist, with doomsday author and pseudo economist Paul Ehrlich. Simon bet that any basket of goods selected by Ehrlich would decrease in price from 1980 to 1990. Ehrlich took the challenge and called Simon a "Space Quacko Economist" and boasted that he would win, hands down.

At the decade's end, Ehrlich was forced to consume an entire humble pie in the presence of his contemporaries. He failed to account for the most important resource of all–progress brought about by human ingenuity and creativity, both having been given free reign during the technological revolution of the Reagan years.

Take From the Rich

President George Bush's failure to capitalize on this positive trend by taking a nosedive on the Robin Hood Tax Act of 1986 led to the following: (1) the decimation of the real estate industry at the turn of the decade, (2) the force-feeding of a deadly dose of recession to the American public, and (3) the eventual election of the dreamy socialist-oriented regime that succeeded his administration. In my opinion, one of the most harmful legacies of the Clinton administration was the unrestrained release on American citizens of bloodhound bureaucrats and enviro tyrants–this imperial posse charged with tracking down private-property owners who may have violated harsh environmental laws, and the quiet nod of these enforcers that sanctioned the seizure of private lands without compensation.

The Coast is There, the Valley is Here

A 1994 editorial in the Harrisonburg, VA *Daily News-Record* took exception to proposed regulations designating the Shenandoah Valley as a coastal zone of the Chesapeake Bay and a potential source of pollution to the Bay waters. "When was the last time you went to Virginia Beach to climb a mountain?" was the opening query in the article. "Obviously there are no mountains on the (Virginia) coast, and it is just as obvious that there are no salty waves lapping against the Valley's green foothills." The editorial said the Shenandoah Valley Soil and Erosion Control Conservation District is opposing the designation, listing nine separate reasons why the proposal is a bad idea.

Undue hardships imposed on farmers by the proposal include the taking of valuable bottomland out of production, and the required building and maintenance of livestock fences to create "buffer strips" along waterways–fences that would likely wash away during frequent flooding. The editorial concluded by saying: "The cleanup of the Chesapeake Bay is essential, as is the restoration of jobs that have been lost in coastal regions as the result of pollution. But the cleanup will be of little lasting value if, in the process of revitalizing the economy in the eastern portion of the state, we jeopardize the economic base supported by agriculture in the west."

No-growth advocates saw more in the Chesapeake Bay Act than was legitimately intended. They viewed the legislation as a broom to sweep out development activities from the mountains to the seashore, and they used the act like an arrow in their quiver of arguments against the division of non-productive farms, the creation of new residential areas, the development of resorts, and the expansion of commercial growth in outlying towns.

The Case Against Selling Easements on Your Land

I make it a practice not to sell easements in return for giving up my development rights. Unless you've got millions enough to keep your brains to yourself and your guests to a minimum, it may not be worth the few bucks tendered by the government for you to agree to never develop your land. I have sold land to government agencies and given public easements free of charge, but I refuse to voluntarily give up my development rights. **(See Land Trusts–*A Discussion*– Appendix V)**

Fine Print

In 1994, the government planned to add some 157,000 acres to the USDA's Wetlands Reserve programs. Some people took the money and removed wetlands areas from development, this while not realizing that the devil was lurking in the fine print.

A perpetual easement is *forever.* Once you've sold your land, its economic life becomes indentured to Satan's officialdom. Of course, this metaphor may be meaningless babble to some trust-funded enviros and landed gentry who cynically forswear the nasty business of making profits from land sales. *LandOwner* newsletter reported on saddened heirs of a farmer who was paid $1.95 an acre in the 60's to preserve "prairie potholes."

Thirty years later the heirs were struggling with the feds to clean out an improperly installed drainage ditch. It seems that heavy rains had left a township road flooded for months, as well as drowning out roughly 800 acres of farm fields, mostly native pasture. The Soil Conservation Service–reaching for security through inaction–warned the heirs that the ditch was part of the navigable water system of the U.S. and that nobody deposits fill along such waters and gets away with it. Enter the Corps of Engineers.

While on a merry-go-round of discussions with the SCS and the Corps, the Fish and Wildlife Service jumped on board, frisking the heirs for a permit (part of the land was covered by a wetlands easement).

Operation Overreach

Tough luck if the farmer failed to "record" these easements. The position of the Fish and Wildlife Service was that he, his heirs and assigns, would then forfeit their rights to maintain any water courses within the easement areas–this despite the fact that the easements were subject to any *existing* ditches, rights-of-way, and so on. Selling easements to a government agency can be like enmeshing you and your heirs in bureaucratic quicksand.

Critics say some agents–embracing the concept of expanding their agency's mission–will bluff if they think they can get away with it, such as the act of seizing authority over private lands when the agency feels landowners are not maintaining water courses exempted from government control under existing easements granted by landowners to the feds.

Front Royal, VA
O.J. SIMPSON SUSPECTED OF KILLINGS – June, 1994 –
Madonna

The saga of O.J. Simpson began in the late spring of 1994 and lasted until the winter of 1997, all the while boiling up public interest, this as the economy gained steam before surging ahead to record levels before the almost predictable calamity at the decade's end. Country property buyers may not have realized it at the time, but they were at the threshold of a major upswing in land values. Friends of the person who purchased the following property would later flip when he told them what he paid for it in 1994.

COMMUTER'S LOST HORIZON

Front Royal, VA–Only one hour west of Manassas. Just $897 per acre for a 228 ac. wild kingdom adjoining Shenandoah Nat'l Park. Actually own your own mountain valley. Walled off from the world by high forested ridgelines offering some of the most beautiful views in the Blue Ridge and Shenandoah Valley. Hidden valley traversed by wild stream in woods used as watering hole by deer and occasional bear. Pure spring water. Waterfalls. Escape to this mountain fortress and do your own thing. On paved road. Site of old manganese mine. Neglected for many years–silted-in dam, fallen trees, poachers, worthless junk to be buried, etc. Cheap because heirs need quick sale. Lots of timber. A wealth of firewood. Will consider selling half for $79,500.

B.K. HAYNES REAL ESTATE

In the summer of 1994, a cable operator to whom I had sold some valuable riverfront property came to see me about disposing of his land. It seems he was downsizing his operations due to the introduction of satellite transmission into consumer households, which would put a lid on the cable business. I had previously sold this historic site to a hippie group back in the seventies. The communal digs were once home base to a couple of budding Hollywood actresses in their halcyon barefoot days. This profitable opportunity and tax shelter was purchased by a retiree who remodeled the homes and turned the camp into a steadily booked rental property for vacationers and weekenders looking for relaxation in the mountains.

COMMUTER RIVERFRONT FIXER-UPPER COMPOUND

First offer. Nationally-unique 12-acre site has 1300 ft.on Shenandoah River with dock and 950 ft. on Rt. 340. Just 12 miles south of Front Royal. 3 old homes. All occupied. Millionaire's views of river and mountains from high bluffs. Home of historic Skymont Camp. Ruins of Olympic pool stocked with trophy-sized fish. Nat'l Park-quality features. Ideal for country inn. Live in stone house. Rent out the others. Swimming, fishing, boating. Hiking and riding in Shenandoah National Park. $119,500. Not a misprint. B.K. HAYNES LAND BROKERS

Front Royal, VA
SADDAM SETS OFF NEW GULF CRISIS – October, 1994 –
Elton John

In response to Saddam Hussein's stationing of two Republican Guard divisions near Kuwait's border, the U.S. began a rapid buildup of its air and ground forces in the Persian Gulf.

As expected, Iraq eased off on the deployment of 700 tanks and 60,000 soldiers in the region.

It is no good to confirm whatever you please about Saddam Hussein. Good is good. Evil is evil. Real is real. False is false. Accurate intelligence pays off.

Imagine yourself back in the fifties being tipped off to buying riverfront on the Potomac River near the two Washington D.C. satellite communities of Leesburg or Fredericksburg by an insider who knew that the D.C. suburbs were about to explode toward these cities. This was an accurate call and very profitable to those who were in a position to seize the moment. What is that land worth today? Fortunes were made by wise investors who bought low and sold high along the Potomac. Unlike the Persian Gulf, the invasion of the countryside outside of Washington D.C. by a burgeoning population could not be called off, and there would be no retreat.

A thousand-acre riverfront tract near my farm had failed to bring a satisfactory price to the lender in a foreclosure sale. Curious as to what the payoff figure would be, and confident of the development potential, I formed a partnership to privately bid on the property. We settled with the bank at a million-two and change and arranged financing through a large pension and profit-sharing plan.

Here is what I knew. Front Royal was then, and is now, part of the D.C. metro area. The historic town of Front Royal is just 35 miles from the new edge city of Manassas-Haymarket-Gainesville, where Disney's America was to locate. This emerging "city" could become the third-largest community in Virginia. And it backs up to Fairfax County, now with a swollen population greater in number than D.C.

Of course, no one can guarantee profits in any investment. But few, if any, have lost money on riverfront near D.C. after getting in before the river was "discovered." In 1994, the first wave of baby boomers were approaching fifty years of age and thinking about retirement. I knew that no finer waterfront was on the market at the time. And this was not hype. I had developed enormous amounts of land along all of the region's rivers. I could produce documented evidence of comparable sales to substantiate steadily rising prices and accurate appraisals of value. Scarcity of riverfront properties could be proven by the lack of such offers in local real estate publications.

I predicted at the time that in ten years anyone who had the financial ability to buy and who did not take advantage of my development offer would figuratively kick themselves.

Once-in-a-Lifetime
RIVERFRONT OPPORTUNITY
inside D.C. Metro area just off I-66 interchange
20 to 50 acre luxury estates ON THE RIVER
from $49,500 to $99,500
20-30 acres off the river from $29,500 to $49,500

True Ground Floor

My last ground-floor riverfront offer at Front Royal for primary homes had been in 1976, in anticipation of I-66 being completed. The offer was sold out in weeks. People who waited to actually see the highway before buying actually left significant profits for the first who bought.

For some of those who would hold their riverfront property for, say, 25-30 years before selling, the yield on this singular investment would soon prove to exceed the total amount of retirement benefits accrued to them over a lifetime in their place(s) of employment.

True ground-floor opportunities in real estate are rare for many consumers–usually occurring for many people only once in a lifetime, mostly through their first purchase of a home. Super deals on country properties come around every decade or so, generally following a recession or economic downturn. That's when inflationary puff has been deflated from real estate values. Deflation, of course, is not totally dependent upon inflation in the economy. Prices on land and homes could reach unsustainable levels in some areas when irrational or "panic" buying of homes and land leads to overpricing, and this can happen in prosperous times, regardless of movements in interest rates.

Emerging Edge City

In 1994, a ground-floor opportunity similar to the one in 1976 existed on the Shenandoah River at Front Royal. This scenic town along I-66 was, at the time, the "Leesburg" of the new edge city at Manassas-Haymarket-Gainesville. In fact, Front Royal is the next principal commercial exit on I-66 after Manassas. And these estates are just two to three miles from the second exit.

You couldn't actually "see" the emerging city in 1994, any more than you could see the coming outer beltway, or the extra lanes that were later constructed on I-66. But alert investors knew these improvements were on the way. Then, as now, the search for a better lifestyle continues to push people west. Transportation experts and savvy real estate investors know what's going on. That's why Disney was hooked on Haymarket. It would have been a critical I-66 exit in the path of growth.

Proof of Progress

By 1994, 20,000 housing units had been approved around Gainesville, with 2800 permitted on the site that Disney had grabbed. That's about one home per acre. Commercial development in and around Manassas continues to mushroom to support this massive concentration of homes and apartments, the bulk of which have already been constructed upon publication of this book. No-growth elitists view this progress with great revulsion as it were a public execution, this without planting a seed of thought on the matter of housing the nation's citizens.

Establishing Value

When I had nothing, I did not rail against the broad estates of the rich, nor did I envy them or covet what they had. But I remembered the imposing homes perched upon high bluffs above the river around Washington D.C. And contrary to the widespread myth about the street urchin rising from rags to riches by repeating to himself the mantra that "someday, I, too, will live in a castle," that aspiration for wealth barely scratched my mind. But in designing the layout for the display ad promotion, I had the graphic artist draw a huge mansion and insert it in a box above an aerial photo of the Shenandoah River, showing the Washington suburbs in the background.

The caption read: A typical $4,950,000 Estate on the Potomac. The seven-figure comparison with the meager $49,500 entry-level price for an estate on the Shenandoah was self-evident.

Following are a few classified ad snapshots of this promotion, which was quickly sold out, with some riverfront estates having more than doubled in value in five years, and re-selling at more than $200,000 within 10 years:

Close-in Fixer-Upper
30-Acre Farm on River

First offer. 3 mi. off of I-66. Historic run-down farmhouse, BA, Kit, 12 rooms, creaky barn, tractor shed, garage, garden, grazing land, mountain views. . . $129,500

Horse Farm Has Old
Barn, Pond, Hard Road

Front Royal, VA - 20 ac.fenced for horses. Sturdy 6-stall barn with elec. and corral. Dream homesite on knoll overlooking pond and mountains . . . $69,500

Commute to Riverfront
Land of the Eagles

First offer. Unique 20.4 ac. retirement or relocation site with 1,000 ft. on Shenandoah River. Mostly gentle pasture with homesite in woods. Mountain views . . . $89,900

Stephens City, VA
TERROR STRIKES AMERICA'S HEARTLAND – April, 1995 –
Madonna

The second strike against America by terrorists was not launched by Islamic militants. It was carried out by an American using a two-ton homemade bomb planted in a rental truck.

On the morning of April 19, 1995, Timothy McVeigh, a 27-year-old Gulf War veteran, parked the truck in front of the Murrah Federal Building in Oklahoma City and walked away.

Minutes later, the bomb exploded, leaving 167 dead, including nineteen children, and hundreds more wounded. The first significant terrorist strike had been against the World Trade Center in 1993 by Islamic militants, who also struck again in the devastating attack on the Twin Towers in September 2001.

The second strike was a wake-up call for Americans in the heartland who felt themselves immune from terrorist attacks. Many of them had never heard of the World Trade Center, and New York City was as far away as the moon. Now it was as if blood was on the planet, and a meteor could strike them dead at any moment. For thousands of fearful city dwellers, the gate to security appeared to be in the countryside.

The Purchase of Rural Land

Earlier in this book we discussed the purchase of country properties with fixer-upper homes, the home inspection process, and the elements of home construction. Over time I have developed a FEASIBILITY CHECKLIST with an accompanying QUALITY REFERENCE SHEET for the purchase of rural land that I have used to avoid marginal projects and to maximize profitable acquisitions. This information is discussed in the following pages. Complete details on this scoring system are printed in the **Appendix I** of this book for readers interested in the purchase of country properties for investment and development. A second scoring system, entitled *HOW TO BUY THE RIGHT LAND EVERY TIME,* is available in **Appendix II** for those readers primarily concerned about the safe acquisition of country property for personal use.

Once the acquisition price has been targeted, and aside from the usability factor, the three most critical features sought by purchasers of rural land are **water**, **roads**, and **views**. Is there water on the land? What kind of access will I have? Will I have a pretty view? Of course, my considerations may vary from those of the average country property seeker, since my primary motivation is investment. The profit factor, however, may be secondary in the mind of the typical consumer, who may just want to get away from it all. This said, I will proceed with a discussion of how I analyze the merits of country properties for potential investment and possible development.

As an investor and developer, the more usable waterfront and roadfront, the better.

The ideal ratio I have found for a development project is at least one mile of road or water frontage for each hundred acres of back land. Obviously, not many properties provide this ratio; a few will be better than the ideal; most offer less than I would desire.

Subdivesting for Profit

In my book, *HOW YOU CAN GROW RICH THROUGH RURAL LAND–Starting From Scratch,* I describe in detail the process of "Subdivesting," which can be defined as: *Making maximum profits from a minimum investment in the development and quick sale of rural land which, in turn, can be resold at a profit.*

You'll notice that I'm not talking about buying rural land and holding it with the expectation that I'll make money out of it somewhere down the line; although for the non-dealer in country properties, a wise investment held throughout the storm of time can rain down great profits. As a dealer in country properties, I get no special capital gains treatment when I turn over land. On a typical deal, I could have capital tied up in a down payment, mortgage payments, taxes, interest on money borrowed, closing fees, insurance charges, taxes, and miscellaneous costs–such as repairs to fences and buildings, and the maintenance of fields and roads. In the short term, and in the absence of subdividing the property, the return on investment–all factors considered–may not be high enough to justify the investment and risk of holding the property.

As a general rule, when acquiring rural land for purposes of *Subdivesting,* I buy only those properties that can be resold immediately at a profit without subdividing, and to buy these properties with a minimum outlay of my own capital. In following this rule, it is essential that I do not overpay for properties and that I carefully screen what I buy. I view this rule as an insurance policy against something going wrong with my subdivision plans, such as a sudden economic calamity, or newly enacted county ordinances and zoning changes. Even the most elaborately planned scheme for making windfall profits from rural land can be bottled up by elected or appointed officials who are out to control growth and land speculation. There have been cases where I may not have been able to sell newly acquired property as a whole *immediately* after purchase and turn a profit. It was critical in those situations that I subdivide the land to make the project work for me financially. These, of course, would be the high-ticket properties purchased for extensive development, or land with a study-period option to determine salibility before financially committing to the acquisition.

The definition of *Subdivesting* also calls for the *quick sale of subdivided land which, in turn, can be resold at a profit.* Does this always occur? Since 1965 when I first entered the field of real estate, it has been my experience that about 95% of all my transactions have produced profits for me and the consumer. But for one reason or another, you will always have somebody who loses money in a real estate transaction, myself included. People lose money through foreclosures, misunderstandings, premature sales, changing county regulations, tax sales, faulty judgment, new zoning laws, title errors, etc.

As I have pointed out, a great deal of money can be made through the wise acquisition of land and country properties and holding real estate for maximum profits. This is particularly true if you target the path of future growth, and when there is scarcity of certain land offers. Of course, the size of your investment bankroll would eventually limit the number of deals on your plate.

And to truly gain, it is important that your appetite for riches be moderate. My practice has usually been to turn properties over very quickly using the *Subdivesting* technique, a system that has generated extra profits to me through resale brokerage activities on many of my developed properties.

With regard to profits, I follow one all-important axiom: *Profits come at the front end*—when I first buy the property—*not when I sell it.* I usually have a plan in my mind for disposing of the property before I make an offer. With few exceptions, the plan comes to me immediately.

I know exactly how I want to obtain, develop, and sell any tract of land that I target for investment. The plan, in essence, is the substance of any financial reward. I don't view myself as a land speculator.

Finding Profitable Land Deals

My rating system for investors and developers gives an optimum 100 points for the theoretically best *Subdivesting* deal in the world. A rating of 50 would give the deal a 50/50 chance of producing profits, and I would automatically reject the deal. If I could, for example, realistically rate a proposed project at 75 or 80 points, it should be a winner for me. For beginning *Subdivestors,* I recommend rejection of any deal rated below 70 points, this because novice investors may not have the experience to accurately rate potential acquisitions. The rating system works whether or not you intend to subdivide the property. (You may want to turn to **Appendix I** if you wish to follow this discussion in detail.)

I developed the system to give me an edge over the other pros in the business, many of whom often operate as gamblers and speculators, paying twice as much to bring the product to market and squeezing the customer for his last dime. They do nicely with a loosely woven system patterned on their experience and expertise, which allows them a comfortable margin of error. I have no time to wail about my losses. To succeed, you must believe what you say. When I was a failure, I was like a seedling, not knowing if I would grow into a scrub, or sprout into the tallest tree. This scoring system has now been absorbed on the canvas of my mind. I no longer need to total up a score on paper. By teaching and practicing what I preach, I have learned.

The FEASIBILITY CHECKLIST is composed of three basic elements:

(1) Physical characteristics of the land

(2) Location, Location, Location

(3) Profit and risk factors

We have already discussed the desirability of long road and water frontage for investors. Other important questions to be considered are: Is there any marginal land, such as severe slopes, swamps, marshland, desert, etc.? Is the soil suitable for crops? Will the soil perc? (Is it porous enough and otherwise acceptable for the installation of conventional home sewage disposal systems?) How much of the land is immediately productive (for home construction, grazing, cropland, timber harvest, etc.)?

You've heard that the key to the successful purchase of real estate is *Location, Location, Location.*

This is certainly true; however, in rural real estate, the meaning of location can be interpreted in a different light. Many people are motivated to buy rural land and country properties because they are *away* from things, i.e. located where masses of people and transportation corridors will not disturb them. Rural locations are often sought out because of factors such as low price and a low cost of living.

Such concerns–privacy, price, or cost of living–do not, however, lessen the importance of *Location, Location, Location* when acquiring land for *Subdivesting*. By even the narrowest of interpretations, any land acquisition project usually begins with someone's concern with location. For what is the worth of a remote, inexpensive site in a low-cost-of-living area if no one wants to go there. In the past, the United States government literally paid people to settle in remote parts of Alaska, where the low-cost-of-living attraction of land acquisition would be calibrated by individual initiative.

In giving weight to government land boundary, I generally place primary emphasis on the amount of usable land open to public recreation that borders the proposed acquisition, this because of the following reason: *Land you can use is land you don't have to pay for.* As we continue this discussion and begin to move down the FEASIBILITY CHECK LIST, you'll see that the *profit and risk* factors are largely determined by what you purchase and where it is located. To enhance the objective analysis of a given project, I have compiled a QUALITY REFERENCE SHEET (See **Appendix I**) to be used in conjunction with the SCORING KEY included on the CHECK LIST.

The Story of Coal Mine Lake

Years ago, a couple of hotshot stock brokers called me up to look at some lakefront property in Pennsylvania that they had for sale. The low price sounded like they were overlooking diamonds in a coal mine because the tract had extensive lake frontage. I made arrangements to meet with them at the lake, which was located in a coal mining region. My assistant and I drove up to the county seat, a small town in the mountains, fully intending to submit a contract if the property checked out.

When we arrived at the lake, it was immediately evident that I would have to deal with a lot of steep land around the lake. Not an insurmountable problem with waterfront, but a potential marketing problem. I figured the lakefront buyers could create winding trails to the lakeshore and that the beautiful views of the lake would offset the negative element of having to walk to the shoreline. My first consideration was to rate the amount of *Usable Water Frontage*–almost two miles of waterfront for the 225 acres. I gave it 5 points, the top score.

Though there were old roads on the property, I would basically have to rebuild them; but since I would not have to start from scratch, I scored *Usable Road Frontage* at 2, only fair. Not being familiar with the soils and average well depth at this point, I also scored this factor as fair, giving it 2 points. *Views* were great. I went for 5. Access was from a state paved road, on which there was limited frontage. I noted that electricity and telephone service was available.

No problem with *Access and Utilities*. I scored this at 5. *Location* was about 2 1/2 hours from the Washington and Baltimore areas, and about 15 minutes from a local town. I figured this was good for lakefront property and worth 8 out of 10 points.

Development Costs (primarily road construction, survey, sales and promotion expenses, and overhead) were roughed out in my head. The property had two existing woods roads; the land had a recent boundary survey. Advertising would be a breeze (everybody wants a place at the lake). I could get a local agent to handle my steady flow of customers on a co-brokerage arrangement. If he generated the prospect and made the sale, I would pay him more. Road construction would be the backbreaker. Only 3 points for the bundle. The price was sweet–25 points. Terms: 10% down; my bank floats 90% of the deal. I'll go for 20 points on this one.

So what if I have to cough up 10%. Even a rosy "nothing down" deal can have its thorns. That's 45 out of 50 allotted points for the *Price and Terms* category.

Salability After Development was a salesman's dream come true, but this factor was somewhat clouded with the possibility of a few customers stumbling down the steep grade into the lake–3 points. *Ease of Entry*–or our ability to get into the project fast and begin sales–was directly affected by existing government regulations on subdivisions and zoning laws. Other factors would have been the weather, speed of survey and road construction, title problems, etc., none of which adversely affected us. Our initial investigation revealed that the subdivision ordinance would permit a division into smaller tracts if no lot was smaller than five acres. On the surface it appeared as if we could move fast–5 points. With 83 points out of a possible 100 going for us, I felt comfortable in proceeding with the project. Since I run these numbers in my mind, I do not keep records. But here is how the list would have looked in my files:

Feasibility Check List

PROJECT: Smith Tract

DEVELOPMENT NAME: Lakeside Forest

Scoring Key

TOP SCORE	Excellent	Good	Fair	Poor
5 points	5	3-4	1-2	0
10 points	9-10	7-8	5-6	0-4
50 points	45-50	35-40	25-30	0-20

	Top Score	Points
Price & Terms	50	45
Location	10	8
Usable Water Frontage and/or Govt. Land Boundary	5	5
Usable Road Frontage	5	2
*Soil Conditions and Average Well Depth	5	2
Views	5	5
Access & Utilities	5	5
Development Costs	5	3
Salability After Development	5	3
Ease of Entry	5	5
Total	100	83

Would an 83-point score mean you couldn't go wrong on a country property deal?

Not necessarily. What if, for example, you miscalculated or over-weighted the scoring in several critical categories? That mistake would bring down your margin of error. You could even lose on a project if your scoring is inaccurate or unrealistic. Let me give you an example; and this is out of an actual case study, taken from the project I have just cited to you.

I assumed, on the basis of walking over the property, that my customers would have no problem building homes on the property. But when we went to the county courthouse for further investigation, we discovered that there was an easement on the land for the possible underground excavation of coal deposits. In fact, there was reason to believe that there were tunnels or caverns beneath the surface which would affect the peace of mind of potential buyers when this fact was disclosed–a detraction that would possibly undercut the stability of any homes built in that vicinity. To further blacken the deal, we unearthed the fact that the sellers had just purchased the property and were flipping it, perhaps for reasons other than a quick profit.

These discoveries rendered the deal as bad news, devastating the CHECK LIST score and causing me to reject the deal for a multitude of reasons; though I could have kissed it goodbye on the issue of soils and well depth alone. I have also rejected high-scoring projects on the basis of latent discoveries of problems with rights-of-way, utilities, titles, financing, development costs, and ease of entry, any one of which, in my opinion, could have exposed me to an uncomfortable degree of risk.

Front Royal, VA
SOMBER JAPAN REMEMBERS THE A-BOMB – August, 1995 – Michael Jackson

On August 6, 1945, a silvery U.S. B-29 appeared in the skies over Hiroshima and dropped a four-ton atomic bomb that virtually incinerated the city. The blast razed most of the buildings, burned people to death as far as 2.5 miles away, and sparked a gruesome end to World War II. At the Hiroshima Peace Park, 60,000 people, including survivors of the bombing, stood silently for a moment of remembrance to mark a solemn 50th anniversary of the devastation.

Glancing back at the past, here are some country properties that I sold in the summer of 1995. All were destined to explode in value by more than twice their purchase price in less than 10 years.

40 AC. RIVER AND MOUNTAIN RANCH FOR HOME OR INVESTMENT $99,500

20 AC. CHEAP WOODS AT RIVER FOR PRICE OF A REGULAR LOT $39,500

WANT TO STEAL A BAYFRONT POINT FOR
0% DN, 3% INTEREST? $99,500

"RAPIDAN FARM" - HISTORIC RESTORED ESTATE
ON 30 ACRES $169,500

COMMUTE TO 33-ACRE RANCH
IN THE SHENANDOAH VALLEY–$69,500

34 AC. ESTATE ON RIVER NEAR MIDDLEBURG,
3800 SQ. FT. HOME $325K

Front Royal, VA
O.J. SIMPSON GETS "OUT OF JAIL FREE" CARD – Oct., 1995
– Mariah Carey

The "Trial of the Century" lasted nine months, and at the end, O.J. Simpson was given a ticket to ride by a jury of 10 women and 2 men who returned a "not guilty" verdict. Simpson, the ex-football and movie star, was apprehended and accused of murdering his wife, Nicole, and Ron Goldman, her acquaintance, this after leading police on a widely televised chase over the Los Angeles freeways.

The economy was starting to hum. Suburban Virginia, outside of Washington, D.C., was rapidly becoming an East Coast technology Mecca, and the chase for country properties shifted into high gear. Here are some of my "BEST FALL BUYS IN COUNTRY PROPERTY" from the fall of 1995:

100-ACRE FARM NEAR CULPEPER
AT COST OF SMALL HOME $149,500

BACK IN THE SADDLE AGAIN
ON 33-ACRE HORSE RANCH JUST $69,500

BIG SKY RANCH ON SHENANDOAH RIVER
NEAR I-66 – 21 ACRES $59,900

40 AC. HUNTING, FISHING RANCH
ON RIVER AT FRONT ROYAL $99,500

BEST ESTATE BUY IN SHENANDOAH VALLEY
21 AC. WITH POND $39,500

ROCKY GLEN FARM,
HISTORIC HOME, BARN, POND, 30 ACRES $159,500

Observing the heightened activity in country properties, I cautioned customers not to wait until 1996 to buy riverfront acreage unless they wanted to pay more than a hundred thousand dollars, and to snap up 20-30 acres of commutable land while the opportunity presented itself.

I predicted that prices would double within 10 years, and I still underestimated market forces.

I have seen some properties triple in value over a ten-year span. Here are a few samples of solid country property investments in 1995, all commutable:

ROCKLAND ESTATE JUST OFF I-66
20 ACRES ONLY $39,500

RAPIDAN FARM BELOW COST OF COTTAGE
30 AC. $57,500

10 ACRES FOR THE PRICE OF FIVE
AT RIVER–$29,500

Take a look at this beauty. Sold for $49,500 in December of 1995 and worth about $149,500 in 2003. I think I sold it too cheap the first time:

CHEAP CLOSE-IN LAND WITH PONDS

Warren, Clarke Co. line. Rockland area just off I-66. 20-acre estate for home, horses, cattle, farming. Rich pasture, woods. Joins horse trails over 300 acres. Neighborhood of fine homes and estates. Hot location. Melted price. $49,500. EZ terms to suit with little down.

B.K. HAYNES LAND BROKERS

Fauquier County, VA
SHEEP CLONED IN SCOTLAND – March, 1996 –
Celine Dion

A pair of cloned sheep were revealed to the public by the Roslin Institute in Edinburgh, Scotland. Scientists, remarking on the creation of a lamb without sexual involvement, said that the breakthrough would lead to the cloning of thousands of mammals, and possibly humans in the future. Bertrand Russell, the outspoken British philosopher and pacifist, once said that "Change is one thing, progress another. 'Change' is scientific, 'progress' is ethical; change is (unquestionable), whereas progress is a matter of controversy." It appears that this "change" in the natural birth process has been born into the realm of controversy.

In early 1996, I became involved in a controversial project that turned out to be a real loser. My partner and I had ponied up $25,000 as a down payment on a sod farm along the Rappahannock River. I figured I could clone the sod farm into 50-acre luxury riverfront estates. Unfortunately it did not work out that way. The land was, pure and simple, relatively flat farmland that did not inherently enjoy any estate-like features, this despite the fact that several estates would be on the river. During the initial study period allowed for in the contract, we literally went through dozens of customers without making a single sale, this before throwing in the towel, eating thousands of dollars in expenses, and forfeiting our deposit. Flat farmland is what it is–flat land. This type of terrain is more suitable for growing crops and creating housing developments, shopping centers and industrial sites than for upscale estates.

Once-in-a-Lifetime
RIVER FARM OPPORTUNITY
Unheard-of offer this close to any major world city
50-acre Fauquier Farms on the river from $129,500
Adjacent to the river from $99,500

Fredericksburg, VA
ENGLAND'S TONY BLAIR WINS IN LANDSLIDE – May, 1997
– Puff Daddy

After carefully studying the Clinton campaign strategy in the U.S., Tony Blair's New Labour Party totally overwhelmed the incumbent conservative Tories, this as the youngest prime minister in the 20th century took government control in Great Britain. The 43-year-old Blair led his party to a political victory that captured a clear majority in the House of Commons, while booting out Michael Portillo, the touted next Tory leader. Blair, of course, would become a favorite son of Bush supporters in the U.S. for the prime minister's strong and unrelenting stand against worldwide terrorism and his backing of the American-led wars in Afghanistan and Iraq.

Winning the Land Wars

What does it take to achieve success in any endeavor? The ingredients are a mixture of perseverance, talent, knowledge, skill, and imagination. In the development of country properties, a number of people can be called upon for contributions to this mixture. For field operations, I may need a surveyor and his crew, a road construction outfit, a soils scientist, and salespeople. An office staff may be required for administrative support. The objective, in this case, may be a large project with the planned production of developed lots. Governmental restraints and economic factors are often the overriding considerations when determining the profile of a given development.

For many years, and prior to the downsizing my company in the early nineties, I brought home significant profits from widespread operations and a relatively large staff. Several survey crews and multiple road construction outfits would be operating out of field offices in up to three states. I was in charge of the whole show, but my main contributions were in land acquisition, financing, and sales promotion. In almost all cases I had the development concept visualized before the land acquisition process was finalized.

In 1997, I was operating with one assistant and no salespeople. Rural counties were becoming increasingly more cautious about permitting the subdivision of land within their jurisdictions, particularly where new roads did not meet certain state specifications and where large numbers of new lots were being created. Many counties have effectively stopped growth through harsh subdivision and zoning ordinances and strict road-building requirements, this under a false rubric of "preserving the rural character of the landscape" or of "protecting the family farm." Anti-growth forces and land developers have always been at war.

A group of professional people came to see me about a 238-acre tract of land they wanted to sell along the Rappahannock River. They were originally from the Far East and had resettled in this country. After some discussion, we arrived at a selling price. I suggested a slightly higher sales figure if we developed the land. I would conceptualize and oversee the development for an additional fee beyond the brokerage commission. Their only additional expenses would be a survey and minor charges for cleanup from timber cutting that they had sanctioned. They were familiar with my past work and agreed to the deal.

Before suggesting the development of their property, I knew I could do six parcels of about 40 acres each on the existing road system and be in conformity with local subdivision and zoning ordinances. No large-scale disturbance of soils was envisioned to alarm government watchdogs. And no federal agency would have a meddlesome role in the development.

A development of six parcels could theoretically give me up to eleven combinations in which to sell the land, though all may not have been practical. My first attempt would be to sell it as a whole. My other options would be to market the tract in up to six sections or, say, in partitions of two, three, four, or even five. Following is a classified ad for the property as a whole.

I envisioned the land as evolving into a camp, this being the highest and best use for the property in that area.

UNIQUE 238-AC. RAPPAHANNOCK RIVER CAMP WITH RAPIDS & ROCK GARDENS

Fredericksburg, West–The last frontier. One-of-a-kind outpost above confluence of Rappahannock and Rapidan Rivers. Canoe outfitter's dream setting for wilderness adventures along river largely unchanged in 300 years. Secluded. At road's end. Old home now rented has 3 BR, 2 baths, historic outbuildings, plus separate apartment with bath. Ancient shade trees. River alive with Canadian geese. Forest filled with deer. Cleared land for playfields or future cultivation. Unspoiled scenery right out of the movies. Large pond to swim, boat, fish, Ideal for camp or retreat. $395,000. 95% financing possible.

Another advertising approach was put into play during the subdivision process. The ad contained photos of four features within the tract: (1) the home and apartment, (2) the Rappahannock River, (3) the beaver pond, and (4) the entrance road. I called the development PORT RAPIDS. Here were components of the ad:

THE LAST FRONTIER

Fredericksburg, West–One-of-a-kind bastion from civilization above the turbulent confluence of the Rapidan and Rappahannock Rivers. Rare site on the Rappahannock cannot be duplicated because of environmental regulations. Nestled along the wooded shores of fiercely protected white water inside the D.C. Metro Area. Enjoy the type of setting that costs millions out west.

Yours for the Price of a Home

A King's forest on the river for the price of a home. Peaceful and leafy refuge guarded by massive oaks at road's end. Every room is within earshot of rapids traversed by Indians and 17th century explorers. Spacious Hansel and Gretel home in the woods has three bedrooms, two baths. Now rented, it begs for the commuter with a restorer's touch. Cheap, close-in camp or estate includes historically-significant early American outbuildings and a separate fix-up apt. with bath.

River of No Return

Isolated site now serves as a port in the storm for canoeists challenging the sometimes thunderous river. As a private retreat or camp, the compound provides launching grounds for action-packed rafting adventures along rapid waters shared with skeins of migrating Canadian geese. The wild, rock-strewn river has remained largely unchanged for over 300 years. Some scenes are right out of the movies.

Lake in the Woods

A bonus attraction close to the home is quiet Beaver Pond, a small fishing, swimming, and boating lake surrounded by a tall pine and hardwood forest alive with deer, turkey, and rabbits. Numerous camp and cabin sites can be developed in the woods above the river and on the shores of the pristine lake. Some forest has been cleared for playfields or cultivation. The whole show is yours for just $395,000 with 95% financing possible.

As it turned out, most of the property was sold as a whole. All but 50 acres of backland forest went to a church group for use as a regional camp. This was the highest and best use for the property. The Beaver Pond with 50 acres was offered for sale at $79,900–an absolute steal; however, the church group contract for five of the parcels was accepted by the sellers before any other contract was written.

Front Royal, VA
CLINTON DENIES AFFAIR WITH LEWINSKI – January, 1998 – Spice Girls

Special Prosecutor Kenneth Starr, probing into President Clinton's alleged sexual harassment of Paula Jones, called on Monica Lewinski, a former White House intern, to corroborate Jones's claim. Lewinski was caught on tape bragging about having a sexual affair with Clinton and remarking about a suggested coverup by the president and his friend, attorney Vernon Jordan. The tape was secretly recorded by Linda Tripp, a co-worker of Lewinski, who was concerned about Clinton's sexual misconduct and Lewinski's exposure to scandal and personal harm. Clinton appeared on television and emphatically denied the allegations.

The scandal raged in the media for the entire year, coming to a fiery debate in the halls of Congress and ending with Clinton's impeachment by the House of Representatives.

I recall watching this real-life soap opera while recovering from a hip implant in early September. The year had been hectic. Business was good. But I had been in constant pain.

All of the cartilage in my right hip joint was gone. It was agonizing for me to cram myself into the cockpit of my Super Cub, and throwing my leg over the saddle on a horse was excruciating. When showing property, I carried a walking stick, using it almost like a cane. And in 1998, I had for sale some of the best values in country properties of my entire career to show to customers.

Cheap, Close River Camp

I had purchased a riverfront farm in late 1997 and offered 40 acres with ½ mile on the river for $179,900. Five years later, 20 acres of that parcel was worth the sales price.

Steal This Abandoned Farm

Some people came to my office and asked me to list an abandoned 65-acre farm just out of town. I advertised it for $124,500, and when it didn't sell right away, I bought the place and later subdivided the land for significant profits.

Cheap Fixer-Upper on the River

Another person visited me with some riverfront property for sale on the Shenandoah that had been hit by a flood. The house was still intact and in fix-up condition. I quickly sold it to a customer for $35,000 and resold it for him two years later to another buyer for $60,000.

Cheap Ranch on the Potomac River

A South Vietnamese customer was going back to his native land. I had sold him an 18-acre ranch with long frontage on the South Branch of the Potomac River in West Virginia. I listed his land and sold it to the state at a bargain price of $65,000 for use as a river access park.

Cheap North River Farm

A past customer was retiring and wanted me to list part of his farm in West Virginia. I ended up buying the 22 acres with home and outbuildings along the North River. I doubled my commission when I resold it for $125,000. Today people are begging for places like this.

Cheap Mountain Farm Joins National Park

A family was selling a 50-acre old mountain farm with a Gray Ghost house, but they didn't want to give a real estate broker an exclusive listing; and they would have preferred not to pay any commission. I took the place on an open listing and had to bat off customers like flies. I finally sold the place for $137,500, and the sellers soaked me for part of the commission.

Cabin on 56 acres Joins National Forest

I heard about a man who had a rustic cabin for sale on 56 acres that joined the national forest. I called him up and offered to sell it for him. He settled for a Realtor acquaintance listing it at a lower commission. When it didn't sell, I took the listing at my full commission and handed a fistful of future profits to a lucky buyer. It sold for just $79,900. In five years it would be worth more than twice that figure.

All of these properties had superficial problems that some finicky customers found insurmountable, and they let profits fall through their hands like grains of sand, this by failing to act when virtual treasures were staring them in the face. For example, the CHEAP, CLOSE RIVER CAMP had some flood plain area, as most riverfront does. The CHEAP ABANDONED FARM was choked with weeds covering up the treasure. The CHEAP FIXER-UPPER ON THE RIVER still held the threat of future floods, a rarity in these parts, and since flood insurance is available, any damage is usually covered. Some people claimed the CHEAP RANCH ON THE POTOMAC was too far, yet a new highway has made it close. Others said the CHEAP NORTH RIVER FARM was not far enough away from a paved road that most people would prefer to be on. Many turned up their noses at the CHEAP MOUNTAIN FARM JOINING THE NATIONAL PARK because it was too far off a paved road, when this feature gave them maximum privacy. And to reach the CABIN ON 56 ACRES JOINING THE NATIONAL FOREST you needed to ford a stream, a minor obstruction for most of the year.

Upon reflection, all of these arguments against buying at the time seem to be peevish obstacles when considering the money that could have been made by smart investors holding on to these properties while they soared in value. Whoever thinks they are going to find the perfect property thinks of what never was, nor is, nor ever shall be. Over the years, and after talking with thousands of customers, I have found that the search for perfection in country properties is absolute folly, a waste of time, and dangerous to your purse. It is far better to aim at sharpening your eye for value and a reasonable amount of use.

Front Royal, VA
DOW JONES BREAKS 10,000 POINT LIMIT – March, 1999 –
Britney Spears

For the first time in its 103-year history, the Dow Jones Industrial Average stock index closed above 10,000 points. Amid the joy of investors and stockbrokers, a few contrarians saw the milestone as a precursor of a market crash. Rumblings of the impending crash were felt by insiders in the dot coms and technology sectors who quietly began disposing of their stock booty at record high prices, sensing, no doubt, that people were investing in dreams. A bubble of dramatic proportions was forming, and a great fear of investors was that they could be left holding shares when it burst.

By 1999, it was clear to me that Internet marketing was the best and least expensive form of advertising for me and that an effective website was a requirement for success in real estate.

Sensing that consumers were being drawn in great numbers to the web in their search for properties and consumer products, I cut back most of my advertising in major metropolitan newspapers without a drop in sales and tied all of my print promotions to the web, this while saving untold thousands of dollars. Other industries had come to the same conclusion about the Internet. At the beginning of 1999, and into early 2000, Ford Motor Company–then setting on a comfort pillow filled with more than $20 billion in cash–launched three interactive web sites.

My major concern as the year progressed was when the other shoe would drop. At the end of every decade that I could recall, some calamity had occurred that caused financial panic, anxiety, and distress. Of course I didn't realize at the time that the calamity bubble would burst in the dot com and technology sector, this through investor madness and stock shenanigans.

The coming stock market collapse would soon spill over into manufacturing, cutting into Ford's $20-plus billion comfort cushion faster than the treads were flying off the Firestone tires on their Explorers. Having cut my overhead to the bone, I decided to concentrate on paying off debt and building liquidity to seize the opportunities in country properties yet to come.

Shenandoah Valley, VA
SMOKERS STRIKE IT RICH WITH CLASS ACTION – July,1999
– Ricky Martin

Thousands of sufferers from smoke-related diseases were expected to hit the five major tobacco companies for compensatory and punitive damage claims as the result of a successful class action suit brought in Florida. A Miami jury found the tobacco giants guilty of making a defective product and conspiring to conceal its addictive properties. The anticipated claims were said to be in the multibillion dollar range and threatened to drain the coffers of the industry.

Thousands of acres of tobacco fields were expected to lie fallow in years to come.

Acres of Diamonds

Smart land investors, with access to capital, can often find "acres of diamonds" in rural land by following a simple strategy: *Buy what others overlook, upgrade it, and help a buyer see a valuable use for it.* The amount of your bounty is based on your creative talents and your management and marketing abilities. A quick look at my Shenandoah Valley listings in 1999 reveals a number of profit-makers for the investor searching for diamonds in the rough.

BUY A FARM FOR COST OF HOME–22 ACRES

(Home needed minor fix-up work. Purchased for $100,000.
Sold quick for $130,000)

CHEAP, CLOSE CANOE ISLAND RETREAT–12 ACRES

(Land needed mowing, brush clearing. Selling price: $69,500.
Worth twice that in 5 years)

CHEAP LAND ON POTOMAC RIVER–2.5 ACRES

(Needed mowing, minor flood plain area. Sold for $11,500.
5-year resale: $25,000)

CHEAP, CLOSE, NEAR COMING OUTER LOOP–2.3 ACRES

(Needed mowing, holding for investment. Sales price $14,950.
5-year resale: $30-35,000)

CHEAP, CLOSE WOODS AT RIVER - 6 ACRES

(Needed minor clean-up, holding for investment. Sold for $27,500.
Worth in 5 years: $60,000)

BUY A HOME, GET A FARM AT RIVER–9 ACRES

(Needed minor fix-up, subdividing into 2 lots. Sold for $139,500. 2 lots
worth in 5 years: $280K)

10 ACRES FOR PRICE OF 5 ON RIVER

(Woods needed TLC, brush clearing. Sales price: $45,000.
Value in 5 years min. $100,000)

For the land investor willing to inject "sweat equity" into the right deal, here are a few tips that I use to maximize profits when buying and selling country properties:

1. Clean up the area to remove all clutter and junk.

2. Use a front-end loader or bulldozer as a cosmetic tool.

3. Tear down and remove useless buildings.

4. Develop a conservation plan on appropriate property with the assistance of the Soils Conservation Service (SCS) or Forest Service.

5. Check out "stale" listings and make low-ball offers for properties that have not moved, but which you feel you can turn around.

Lost City, W. VA
JUDGE DECLARES MICROSOFT A MONOPOLY–Nov., 1999 – Shania Twain

In an antitrust case brought by the federal government against the computer organization co-founded by Bill Gates, a U.S. judge said that the company had used its monopoly power to stifle innovation, reduce competition, and hurt consumers, this by linking its web browser to its Windows operating system. "Most harmful of all is the message that Microsoft's actions have conveyed to every enterprise with the potential to innovate in the computer industry."

Black Bear Recreation Region

Innovation in any field of endeavor is the ability to see things with a pair of fresh eyes.

Here is a classic example of innovative thinking in the country properties field. A former U.S. congressman had asked me to handle the sale of his hunting lodge in the mountains about two hours west of Washington D.C. The lodge had given the congressman many years of pleasure and had been an occasional den of weekend relaxation for such high-powered political figures as Vice President Dan Quayle and numerous Capitol Hill luminaries. The offering price for the lodge on 100 acres joining the G.W. National Forest was about three hundred thousand dollars. After a considerable amount of advertising and frequent showings, I was unable to come up with an acceptable contract. So I later decided to buy the place, develop it into lots, and create a recreation area for consumers interested in outdoor activities.

This concept would not fly unless I could obtain a right-of-way of a specific width from the state road, about a mile away. The primary

access road to the lodge ran through a subdivision, which would preclude me from granting additional property owners a similar right of
ingress and egress. A secondary route into the lodge grounds was over
a narrow road that did not have the specified width necessary for a
new subdivision. I saw that an adjoining parcel with a home was for
sale, and that if I built a short road through this ten acres I could mend
part of the problem. Beyond that move, I would have to convince an
adjacent landowner to sell me additional footage to come up with the
required width for subdivision approval. After a prolonged period of
negotiations, I was able to maneuver myself into a very profitable
project. Here are a few brief descriptions of the offers:

BLACK BEAR LODGE JOINS FOREST 8.5 AC.
$145,000

Custom-built mini-lodge with million acre backyard to hunt, hike,
ride. 3 floors, 3 BR, 3 BA, incl. Sep. apt, shop. 2,000 sq. ft., 2 decks.
Soaring views, 3-car pole garage or potential stable, storage barn,
lighted game-feeding station. Rental poss. 10 mi. to ski resort & golf.

"BASS POND" JOINS FOREST 11.8 AC.
$59,900

Almost ½ mi. on Nat'l Forest. Gentle woods, meadows. Stocked bass
pond. Road's end for privacy. For home, camp, trailer. Hunt, hike,
ride for days in boundless forest. Fish for breakfast in your own pond.
Ducks, geese, deer, wild turkey. 95% financing possible.

TROUT POND JOINS NAT'L FOREST 7+ ACRES
$35,000

A million acres of tax-free hunting land for price of 7 acres. Plus
stocked trout pond to fish for your supper. Trek, drive, through Forest
to golf, ski resort. Gushing stream, spring, great views. Woods, clearings. One-of-a-kind. For home, camp, trailer. 95% financing possible.

PART SEVEN

The New Century

Wardensville, W. VA
CUBAN BOY SEIZED BY U.S. AGENTS – April, 2000 –
'N Sync

A bitter standoff between Cuban exiles and the U.S. government ended at dawn on April 22 as armed agents broke into the Miami home of relatives harboring little Elian Gonzalez and seized the sobbing 6-year-old from a bedroom closet. The youngster was then flown to Andrews Air Force Base near Washington D.C., where he was reunited with his father, a Cuban national, for the child's relocation to Cuba. Furious exiles from the Castro regime, their eyes filled with pepper spray and tear gas, wept for the boy outside of the Miami home, as if the tot were a bird set free and now being returned to a cage.

The image of armed police seizing a frightened child was flashed across television screens around the world. Janet Reno, the attorney general, said to negotiators who were haggling over the boy's fate, "You are running out of time." And then she broke the impasse by issuing orders to take him by force.

Castro's revolution had divided many Cuban families, but the Elian Gonzalez feud contained the spark of potential armed conflict between two nations. On the other side of the world, in Afghanistan, Osama Bin Laden was busily training a small army of terrorists for war against the United States. Soon to be drawn into that war was a high-ranking military official and jet pilot for a small middle eastern kingdom, who had been assigned to a key diplomatic post in Washington D.C. He came to see me during the fall in response to an advertisement for some wilderness property that he found much too remote. I asked him why he had called me to look at wilderness land if he wanted more polished terrain. He said the confusion was in language interpretation. I did find him a 22-acre estate close to town and near my farm, which he and his family have visited many times.

The following summer he informed me that he was being reassigned to his country to advise the king–a staunch ally of this country–on certain urgent military matters, and he was ordered to leave immediately. I presume this was in expectation of an impending attack on the United States in one form or another. A few months later, the Twin Towers in New York had turned to rubble, thousands of innocent people were dead, and we were at war with terror.

Here is a description of this officer's land, now worth considerably more than he paid. I expect he will build a home here when he returns to this country, either for frequent visits or for a diplomatic post.

ROCKING HORSE FARM–22.8 ACRES
$129,900

Front Royal, VA–Hunt country-quality horse farm in D.C. Metro area at a fraction of hunt country prices. Ideally-shaped estate has commercial potential, with 783 ft. on main highway. Level to rolling pasture fields and scattered trees. Scenic views of Blue Ridge. Commute to D.C. on I-66. Unrestricted. Do your own thing. 90% financing avail.

Lost City, W. VA
BUSH ELECTED 43rd PRESIDENT OF U.S. – November, 2000 – Garth Brooks

After a contentious election between Democrats and Republicans, President-elect George Walker Bush began his reconciliation effort by stating that he was elected to represent all of the people and not just one party. Less than a year later the World Trade Center would lay in dust, and he would be called upon to lead a divided nation into the unrelenting war against terror.

West Virginia, a state usually crawling with Democrats, sent voters swarming to the polls, only this time for Bush. And as President Bush sought out "common ground" with his diverse constituency, thousands of land-seekers swarmed into the mountain state from nearby mid-Atlantic cities looking for "cheap ground," a commodity that had largely disappeared from the countryside near Washington D.C. and Baltimore, Maryland.

Take a look back at these bargains in late 2000:

BIG SKY FARM–40 ACRES $89,900

Nearby W. VA–Top quality horse farm at pony-sized price. Real "out-west" panorama of mountains stalking the horizon. Sparkling pond for horses, cattle. Beautiful rolling fields. Patches of woods. 1200 ft. paved road. Mostly fenced. 2 homes allowed. 40 min.Winchester. Sacrifice.

B.K. HAYNES LAND BROKERS

MOUNT LEVELS RANCH–20 ACRES $39,500

Nearby, W. VA–Small starter ranch. Half green pasture, half woods. 2,000 ft.on all-year creek and state road. Great views of Mt. Levels from homesite. Keep a garden, horses, cattle. Camp now, build later. Private, at road's end. Partly fenced. 95% financing possible. Hurry!

B.K. HAYNES LAND BROKERS

Finding Profitable Properties

Shakespeare said, "Heaven never helps the man who will not act." And I have always believed that once you act, you must try to finish what you start and do the best you can with what you have; then you should move on. The world will never be at a loss for people who will attempt to tear down, spoil, and alter what you have created. But for those who refuse to accept defeat, I believe it is then mandated that we should restore, reformulate or reassemble a new creation from the ruins, despoilment, or disfigurement of our work.

As an entrepreneur, starting without a grubstake, I have found that making my first million dollars was much harder than those millions to come. One simple reason for this fact of life is that money begets money. More opportunities are available to those with deep pockets than to those who must watch their pennies. This said, it should be understood that opportunities are boundless for those who seek them out. Whether you start out as I did with almost nothing, or with a war chest of cash, the world is only as big as your money boat. In theory, the bigger your boat, the faster you will go around.

In the year 2000, I had been playing the country properties game close to the vest, anticipating a crash. The century had slipped by without the ordained calamity. Lessons to be learned would come from the level of the next downturn, and not from precipitous action on my part to get into a deal. I spent the first half of the year finishing a screen play, paying down my debts and building liquidity. But my eye was still open for new opportunities.

How to Cut into the Land for Maximum Profits

I saw an ad for a 500-acre tract of land joining the national forest in West Virginia, so I called the listing agent and scheduled an appointment. He mentioned that he also had a 1,100-acre tract that I might be interested in–a parcel that I had bypassed because it was cut up by roads and a new highway corridor. I told him I would take another look at it. I rejected the first tract because of the steep terrain. When I asked him about the eleven-hundred acres he said he had two contracts ready for submission. The sellers were asking for a cool million. I reviewed the topographical map and figured it could be sold in sections without building any roads, so I asked the agent what it would take to buy the place. He said they were firm on the price, but would sell by the acre with about twenty grand down. We wrote up a contract. The seller reviewed the three offers and accepted mine at full price. I financed the transaction with a local bank using my $20,000 deposit and pledging the proceeds from a timber contract on the property as a down payment. Essentially this was a roughly two-percent-down land deal ($20,000 divided by a million). Let's take it step by step as sales and development evolved over a two-year period.

Step #1

The land joined the G.W. National Forest in one section and had a trout river running through it. Most of the property was in timber. Before closing on the property, I wrote a contract to sell off 368 acres to an adjoiner for $478,000, or $1300 per acre, leaving me with a theoretical 732 acres, but with me still holding the timber rights. This move cut my preliminary acquisition price down from around $909 per acre to about $713 per acre. ($1,000,000 minus $478,000 divided by 732 acres).

Step #2

Again, before my own closing, I signed a timber contract to sell off most of the timber that was more than 16 inches in diameter. This would bring in about $330,000. A survey showed I was losing approximately 146 acres. Since I had purchased the land by the acre, the shortage reduced my acquisition price by roughly $132,000 and downsized my original purchased acreage from 1,100 to 954 for a negotiated selling price of $873,000. After factoring in (1) the $478,000 sale to an adjoiner, and (2) the sale of timber for $330,000, my actual per-acre acquisition price for the remaining 586 acres was cut to $111 per acre ($65,000 balance due on land divided by 586 acres).

Step #3

My third move was to sell off 51 acres of non-usable riverfront along the main road to the West Virginia Department of Natural Resources for use as public access to the trout river and national forest. This property was mainly located in the frequent flood plain and composed of wetlands. It was a good deal for them, because the state was required by law to offset wetlands destroyed within the new highway corridor by acquiring wetlands elsewhere. State highway monies were therefore directed toward the public good. The "win-win" transaction was worth another $210,000, for total projected income of $1,018,000 ($478,000 + $330,000 + $210,000), and reducing my remaining acreage to 535 (954 acres minus 368 +51). Assuming these three transactions closed (as they did), the land would be paid for, leaving a theoretical $145,000 on the table, along with a free and clear 535 acres.

Step #4

So far I had picked up more than enough to offset my acquisition cost of $873,000, and I was in the profit picture. I then sold a prime

15-acre site along the river that I had reserved from any timber cutting to a couple who wanted to build a log home. The sale was for $70,000.

Step #5

A religious group was looking for a site on which to build a monastery. They needed extreme privacy and preferably a river on the property flowing to the east. I had such a site joining the national forest, but most of it was accessible only by fording the river. This inconvenience did not matter to them, because the congregation would build a bridge. After some negotiations, we arrived at a price of $3500 per acre for 126 acres of my best land. Price: $441,000.

Step #6

The religious group looked at the survey and decided they needed an additional seven acres to secure their perimeter. I sold them seven acres for about $20,000.

Step #7

Another tract, across the road from the river and the national forest, was sold off to a family for hunting and general recreational use. They paid $60,000 for the 24 acres, with a half-mile of road frontage.

Step #8

The religious group purchased the last tract on the south side of the river. This 73 acres borders the river and the national forest and now gives them a total of 206 acres. The price was $255,500, or $3500 per acre.

Summary

Let me recap the transactions to this point: (1) sale to adjoiner, $478,000, loss of 368 acres; (2) timber sale, $330,000, no loss of acreage; (3) sale to W. VA Dept. of Natural Resources, $210,000, loss of 52 acres; (4) sale to religious group $441,000, loss of 126 acres; (5) purchase of additional land by religious group, $20,000, loss of 7 acres; (6) private sale, $70,000, loss of 15 acres; (7) sale of 24 acres, $60,000; (8) third sale to religious group, $255,500, loss of 73 acres.

Total sales in the first eight stages had approached two million dollars by the year 2002. I paid close to nine hundred thousand for the land, so I had essentially burned the mortgage, and I was ahead by about a million dollars before expenses. I had sold 665 acres out of the

954-acre parcel, and I still had 289 acres left, free and clear of any liens, this as of the publication of my book in 2004. The remainder of the property was planned for eight-to-ten-acre lots, with projected gross land sales of more than a million, pushing total sales volume beyond the two-and-a-half-million mark. Development expenses–primarily survey and road costs–were relatively low. Property values continued to rise like the tide, and they were expected to skyrocket when (1) the new highway was completed, and (2) soon after the state's opening of public access points along the river. Realizing the fact that the area was soon to be crowned as a destination point for recreational activity in the mountains, I began a program of building affordable cabins in the region. This was another win-win project and a classic example of the *Subdivesting* technique at work.

Capon Bridge, W. VA
TERRORISTS ATTACK U.S. BY AIR – September 11, 2001 –
Jennifer Lopez

In a coordinated attack, terrorists, said to be Islamic radicals, flew two hijacked commercial airliners into the World Trade Center in New York, demolishing both towers. A third plane crashed into the Pentagon near Washington, setting off a massive explosion and devastating fire. Thousands of people were believed dead, with countless others maimed and wounded in the worst terrorist assault in U.S. history. A fourth hijacked airliner plunged into the Pennsylvania countryside in what was thought to be a failed attempt to destroy the White House and kill the president. All on board this doomed aircraft perished. President Bush vowed to exact punishment for an unprovoked strike that brought back the memory of the Japanese sneak attack on Pearl Harbor. World conditions had changed dramatically, and virtually every American's life would be forever altered in some way.

Earlier in the year, I had purchased a 650-acre tract of land from a Georgia developer for well over a million dollars. The land featured extensive frontage on the Cacapon River, a huge mansion in need of restoration, and several homes with various levels of fix-up possibilities. I concluded that one reason the property was unsold was that no one knew what to do with the run-down mansion, which stuck out like a sore thumb. I decided up front to bypass the mansion in my financial analysis because no comparable values existed. I would tag it with a nominal figure of a hundred grand with, say, twenty to twenty-five acres, crunch my numbers, and then move on.

The terrorist attack on the United States occurred about a week before the launch of a major promotional effort, and I was unsure about the level of consumer response. Either people would want to flee the cities in droves, or they would slap a clamp on their spending and stay put. As it turned out, they did both. Many city dwellers, driven by fear and other emotional concerns, opted to remove themselves from what they perceived to be "harm's way" by purchasing country property for immediate relocation to a safer environment. Others, watching images of buildings collapsing into fiery dust piles, simply channeled more of their investment funds into the perceived security of country real estate for later resettlement. Some stayed put, frozen with fear.

It was in this environment of uncertainty and fear that the following *Announcement of Unusual Importance* was delivered to readers in a quarter-page newspaper ad:

THE AFFORDABLE RIVERFRONT FARM
This may be your last opportunity to own a nearby farm, ranch, or retreat on the river

A spread large enough for you to feel you are not confined to a subdivision, but close enough to Winchester and the D.C.- Baltimore area for many commuters. The low price is attractive enough for investors and affordable for anyone making a good salary.

Changing World Conditions

Concerns about "urban sprawl" are creating an "affordability moat" around the cities, restricting ownership of large land parcels to the very affluent. Now we are faced with new and more ominous threats to our population centers. See how an affordable nearby farm can actually change your life.

World Class Riverfront

Your riverfront will compare in quality with the best you can find anywhere in the world. See for yourself. Choose a ranch of flat or gently rolling fields and tall woodland with refreshing mountain views. Or select a wooded high mountain retreat offering less accessible riverfront, but with astounding vistas. Located on the Cacapon river in nearby West Virginia, you can hunt, fish, canoe, kayak, with no fear of flooding to your homesite.

Life on Your River Farm

Ownership of this land is more a lifestyle than just a possession. Make of your land what you will. A horse ranch. A mountain retreat. A farm on the river to make you and your family self-sufficient. A heritage and safe haven for your children. Presidents have their famous farms, ranches and retreats. Now, in this democracy, you can establish your own.

Enduring Value and Investment

Waterfront is the heart of land valuation. In our 35 years of handling land transactions, waterfront property values have soared beyond any other type of real estate investment. There is no safer place for your money in troubled times than premium waterfront. This offer was 1/3 sold out in the first weekend.

Land Planning and Trails

Your farm was not created in a day by drawing lines on a plat. We sell land quickly. But we take a long time designing a ranch or farm. After all, future generations may inherit what you establish here, so we have to get it right. Some farms will even join a network of horse trails.

Why the Low Price?

We believe that it is better to sell a large amount of land at a low margin of profit than to sell a few tracts at a large margin of profit. As land brokers, we must allow for automatic and consistently higher resale values. We have no sales force, high overhead, and multiple levels of management to support. We decided on the type of waterfront offer we wanted to make and found a way to offer it at a low price. This is a preview sale, and some roads are under construction over a 650-acre region. You may look on your own, or we can help you if you are not prepared to drive through fields and woods.

The Trip to Fortune

You've driven by pricey farms and estates on the river and wished and wondered. The foresighted founders of these estates simply got there first and made wise decisions at the right time. In years to come, we will be reselling these riverfront farms at progressively higher prices. Opportunity, when taken at the flood, leads on to fortune. When omitted, life's voyage often ends in the shallows of misery and regret. First to come get first choice.

20 to 27-acre riverfront farms, ranches, retreats
$69,900 to $99,900
20-acre river access ranches $65,000 to $75,000
100% financing possible. Unheard-of low interest rates

B.K. HAYNES LAND BROKERS

Ultimately, I purchased more than a thousand acres of the developer's land and sold it out in four sections over a two-year period from 2001 to 2003 with little of my own money up front.

Usually I have sufficient contracts under my belt to cover all, or a good portion of, the amount I wish to borrow, this before I ever close on a property. And I use these contracts as collateral for mortgage loans. As I have stressed in this book, the technique I use is called *Subdivesting*. Again, this method is defined as follows:

"Making maximum profits from a minimum investment in the development and sale of subdivided land which, in turn, can be resold at a profit ."

Shenandoah Valley, VA
ATTACK, ATTACK, ATTACK – 2002-2003 –
Alan Jackson

Consumers were under assault on a multitude of fronts across the country, though these troublesome events had little effect on spending for country properties near Washington D.C.

Sniper attacks in the D.C.-to-Richmond, VA corridor chased consumers out of the stores and into the countryside looking for a safe haven. Frequent terror alerts, augmented by the SARS outbreak, accelerated this movement away from the cities. Travel plans were scrapped or put on hold, with money diverted into country real estate. And millions of dollars were switched from the stock market into nearby land when widespread fraudulent corporate activity became the main topic of the evening news.

In 2002, the pending war with Iraq and corresponding military build-up showered the mid-Atlantic region with jobs and money, stabilizing the local economy. Few were afraid of war.

We had trounced Saddam before. We could do it again. Spending on area homes and real estate continued unabated, reaching record levels as the year progressed, this as the worst winter storms since the mid-nineties hit the Shenandoah Valley and neighboring West Virginia, limiting the creation of land product. Torrential rains during the year brought building construction to a virtual halt. If you were looking for country properties in 2002, the shelves were getting bare.

The Creation of Country Property Listings

Most of the country properties I had for sale in 2002 and 2003 were of my own creation.

In addition to 2,000 acres of rural development property in West Virginia, I had purchased three farms in Virginia's Shenandoah Valley (two at auction) and was a partner in an airpark that straddled both states. Following are samples of the developed land product:

1. **Five to ten-acre farmettes on a fishing creek**
2. **22-acre fixer-upper farm with old home**
3. **Five-acre ranches on the Shenandoah River**
4. **40-acre horse ranch with home and barn joining Shenandoah National Park**
5. **20-acre farms on the Cacapon River**
6. **Fixer-upper homes on 15-25 acres**
7. **20-acre ranches with ponds**
8. **3.5-acre homesites on a paved road and grass airstrip**

These products were created to fulfill consumer needs, and all have appreciated significantly in value. Not surprisingly, they were quickly sold. No-growth advocates, if given free license, would have severely restricted these offerings.

Some of the most virulent "greenies," having obtained their own slices of the countryside, would call for a jihad against developers to restrict the further production of affordable country properties.

Dennis Miller, the comedian and political commentator put it this way:

"Remember–a developer is someone who wants to build a house in the woods.
An environmentalist is someone who already owns a house in the woods."

PART EIGHT

Anatomy of a No-Money-Down Land Deal

The concept of buying property with none of your own money and using other people's money is behind all great fortunes made in real estate. All over the country there are thousands of successful real estate investors who became rich after literally starting from scratch. Many of them began right here, in Virginia's Shenandoah Valley. This first decade of the twenty-first century promises that there will be more millionaires created in the United States than ever before. Inflation virtually assures this. But equally important is the fact that, during the first ten years of this century, most of our population will fall into the fifty to fifty-nine year-old age group.

Aging Baby-Boomers

Historically, this burgeoning crop of baby-boomers has been the most inclined toward opportunity. During the first decade of the millennium they will be in their peak earning years, most with a laser-guided eye focused on retirement. Their thrust for increased income will be intense. Competition for the coming fortunes in real estate will be keen. Make no mistake about this.

But if you can somehow gain an edge–stay out in front of the pack–you're bound to profit.

What follows is the type of analysis I try to apply to every deal. This type of evaluation gives me an edge in the country properties game.

The Birth of a Deal

Back in the fall of 1980, a salesman came to me with a deal he had found. He said the owner was willing to sell on terms. The price? About a thousand dollars an acre. He said the tract had a house on it. Somebody was renting it. The lease had just been signed, and it was good for a year. Right away I saw a red flag.

As a *Subdivestor*, I usually sell off the improvements first. This move gets my land cost down. It may also provide some operating capital. But how could I sell off the house in a hurry if somebody was living in it? I could be held up. I couldn't get in and out fast. That's not how I played the game. Still the price wasn't bad. I asked the salesman if he had a plat.

The salesman said he was working through another broker–a woman. She told him she thought the seller would be agreeable to almost any kind of terms. He said he hadn't walked the land. The tract was close to my office. He said I might be interested in the deal because of the terms. Well, could be, if I could get in for little or no money down, sell off the house, split the commission, pay this fee off in notes. . .

Wait a minute. I can't sell off the house right now. Somebody's living in it. Besides, I'll probably have to come up with a down payment because of the house. But maybe he'll be willing to keep the house on, say, five acres, and sell me the rest. Maybe for no money down–also at a reduced price because he's keeping the house. I could get into the deal for under market value. But would the lots sell?

Red Flags

I asked the salesman what he knew about the place. He said it joined the Shenandoah National Park. Sounds good. Any water? Roads? He said it bordered a good-sized stream. How much waterfront? He didn't know. No road frontage, he said. It has a right-of-way. How wide?

Again, he didn't know. Anything else? There is one thing, he said. I don't know how you'll feel about it, and, well, I don't know whether it will affect sales or not. But the property is down by the landfill.

Of course, you can't see it, he said. But there are signs pointing to it. The landfill? Isn't that like a county dump. Sure is, but now they have to cover it up every day. Still, it doesn't sound good at all, I thought. Who wants to buy land near a dump? But what if it doesn't look like a dump? What if it's not offensive at all? Maybe the tract's a sleeper. Nobody wants to buy it because it's near the landfill. That means the price is right. Same with terms. Another thing, if it's near the landfill, the soil must be golden. The county had to check it out pretty good. It's probably deep and well-drained.

Checking It Out

I decided to go look at it. The key might be in how the area looked to lot buyers. If it turned me off, it might do the same to my customers. On the way down to the property, I went over my FEASIBILITY CHECK LIST for investors and developers. (shown in **Appendix I** of this book)

Again, if you wish to refer to this Check List you will notice that it is broken down into three basic elements: (1) *Physical Characteristics of the Land*: how it lays, the soil quality, average well depth, natural features–such as streams, rivers, views, etc. (2) *Location, Location, Location:* How far are you from town, from a major city? How many people want to go there? Is it a major destination area, or off the beaten path? (3) *Profit and Risk Factors:* Is it a good buy for the money? What about terms? How much will it cost to develop and sell the subdivided lots? Would it be better to turn the property over as a whole, rather than to divide it? How hard is it to get local approvals? Will the lots be easy to sell? How can I get in and out fast and make a decent profit at low risk? First off, I knew I might have close to 70 points before I ever set eyes on the land.

Here's how I figured: *Price and Terms* on the Check List are worth a maximum of 50 points, roughly 25 points for each. If I could buy the land without the house, I might be able to drop the cost per acre to around $700. From what I had been told about the house, I figured it was probably worth about $35-$40,000 on, say, five acres. Once this figure is deducted from the asking price on the property, a per-acre land price can be determined. The asking price was $110,000 for approximately 110 acres. Deduct $35,000 from the total price, and you arrive at $75,000. Remember also that you must deduct five acres of ground from the proposed acquisition. I figured I would offer $75,000 if the property checked out. But, being a broker, I would also want a break on the commission. So my actual offer would be in the neighborhood of $70,000 for roughly a hundred acres. A survey may show more or less acreage.

Price and Terms

I would want into the deal for no money down. The owner could keep the house on five acres. If I could buy the land alone for about $700 per acre, the price would be about $300 below market value for good land in that area at that time. Even if a portion of it was not too good, the actual land cost might still come out below the mark, especially since the property enjoyed a long border on the national park. And if the terms were as dreamy as the salesman said, I could pick up a full 25 points. The *Price and Terms* element carries a maximum of 50 points when (1) the price and (2) the terms can each be characterized as excellent. I was banking on the land cost coming out under market value. Remember that market value is largely determined through sales of comparable property in a given area. So you must gain this information from personal observation, experience, appraisals, or through communication with local Realtors and brokers.

Scoring Location

I also expected to buy the property on dream terms. The **Quality Reference Sheet** shows that good land purchased below market value with no money down can qualify for 50 out of 100 maximum points. Let's say I might have 50 points on *Price and Terms*, and I'm shooting for a minimum of 70 points to justify a safe land investment. Figure the *Location* element as worth a maximum of 10 points. The property is less than 1 ½ hours from a major city, and is not too far from a good-sized town, Front Royal, VA. Now, since Front Royal is a major resort area, I had another plus for the *Location* element. So I might be able to pick up a full 10 points by scoring *Location* as excellent. That's 60 points.

Soils and Well Depth

What else did I know? Remember, I had assumed that the soil conditions in that area were excellent due to the landfill location. The *Soils and Well Depth* component of the **Check List** is worth a maximum of five points. So fifty for *Price and Terms*, 10 for *Location*, and five for *Soils and Well Depth* could give me a preliminary total of 65 points. Understand that preliminary scoring means little until you look at the property, regardless of any high score. As a general rule, water can be found within reasonable depths when drilling through good soil.

Water Frontage and Government Land Boundary

We met the owner of the property, and he showed me a preliminary drawing of the land. It was originally designed to be a subdivision. But the previous owner had gone bankrupt. By this time, I also had a topographical map, on which the salesman had sketched out what he thought were the boundaries. Using the map scale, I determined that there might be about a mile of stream frontage and border on the national park. If my calculations were right, this was an ideal ratio to the acreage involved. We are talking about approximately 100 acres. The *Usable Water Frontage/Government Land Boundary* component of the Checklist carries a maximum weight of five points. Using the **Quality Reference Sheet** as a guide, I added five points to the 65 already in hand.

What About Views, Access and Utilities?

The property was all wooded. There would be some views when the roads were constructed, but the property was not strong on views. I rated this component as "poor," hence a score of zero. I was still at 70 points. I turned to the *Access and Utilities* component on the **Check List.** It seemed to me that the property had a right-of-way. But how wide was it? Electricity and phone service were already in place on the property. I knew from experience that the county required a 50-foot right-of-way for new subdivisions.

Here was a potential problem. I asked the owner about it. He said he thought he had the required width. The county agreed to give him 50 feet when they put in the landfill. Still, I knew I would have to pin this down in writing before closing; otherwise, I was prepared to scratch the whole project. On this particular project, I was not interested in the deal if I could not divide the land into five-acre lots. Because the issue was clouded, I scored the *Access and Utilities* component at zero.

I was still holding a point score of 70; but I knew that my *Subdivesting* rules called for possible rejection of any project scoring a confirmed zero in *Access and Utilities, Soils Condition and Well Depth*, and *Ease of Entry.*

Development Costs

I saw potential problems with the survey, and I would have to construct a road. So I immediately honed in on a conservative rating of "fair" and a score of one. This brought my preliminary total score to 71, certainly ample for a *Subdivesting* project–if the score held to its current level. Let's see how I arrived at this single percentage point in *Development Costs.* I saw potential road-building problems because of the dense foliage. Timber would have to be cleared and disposed of. The construction men would have to move slowly. There was no recent survey on the place–only a subdivision drawing. Also, I would have to come up with a great advertising concept to sell these heavily wooded tracts. Most city people like some cleared land on their sites; only a few of the lots would have some clearings. This is the profile of a project that can be rated as only "fair" in *Development Costs.* In following the guidelines shown on the **Quality Reference Sheet**, I stayed on the low side and opted for a single percentage point in this category.

Salability after Development

I had a point score of 71 points, and if it held, I would have a winner. Right? Well, it depends. Maybe, if I don't have soils and right-of-way problems. Suppose these components are paper tigers. I still have the *Ease of Entry* factor. A zero entry in this category is also cause for possible rejection of the project. I will get to that next. But what about a zero in *Salability After Development* when you have a safe 71 points in hand? Can you really get a project off the ground and make it fly if you have potential sales problems?

Let's examine this proposition. Only rarely would I have a project that scored low on *Salability After Development* when I had a solid score of 71 or more points. But since this project was close to the county landfill, the potential problem did exist. Consider first, the salable features about the property. *Location* was basically in my favor, regardless of the landfill. The low *Price and* generous *Terms* on the subdivided lots would act to the consumer's benefit. And customers would be within 1½ hours of a major city and close to a good-sized town. Another strong point was the stream and park frontage on the property. These features are in short supply and big demand. An assumption must be made that any property with these features is immediately salable, this providing the land has acceptable location and terrain features.

Since none of the lots were within sight of the landfill, I assumed they could be sold easily. But assume the worst about those lots without stream or park boundary. What if I had to sacrifice them at cost because of objections over the landfill? What sales volume could I count on, considering only my immediately salable lots? Would I be exposed to abnormal financial risks?

A five-acre lot comprises 217,800 square feet. To arrive at this figure, you multiply the square footage in an acre by five (43,560 sq.ft.x 5). How much square footage can you comfortably allot to each lot along the stream and the park without creating lots that are too skinny to be salable at the price you need to get? From experience, I knew that a one-to-three ratio was ideal, and that a lot size allocating four feet in length to each foot of width was acceptable to customers.

Next question. How many linear feet in a mile? Answer: 5,280 ft. How much frontage can I allocate to each parcel along the park boundary without making the lots appear too skinny?

Remember that a five-acre lot is composed of 217,000 square feet of land. So the dimensions of the lot with, say, 200 ft. frontage would be approximately 200 X 1080 (216,000 sq. ft.). For five acres, this one-to-four ratio would make the lot look much too narrow, whereas a one-acre lot with dimensions of, say, 100 X 430, could be viewed by the customer as comparatively normal.

I opted for more frontage and a better-looking lot. What the consumer sees on paper is a replica of what he will find in the field. I figured an approximate three-to-one lot size of about 270 X 800 (216,000 sq.ft.) would be more appealing. Dividing 270 feet of frontage into 5,280 ft. (border on the park and stream) gave me, on paper, about 19 premium lots. Due to terrain features I knew this number was unrealistic, so I reduced the projected number of my best lots by 20%. I could count on, say, 17 premium lots.

What will I charge per lot? I compared this figure with the price per acre and the total price I would be paying for the property. The price per acre was $700, and the total price for the approximately 100 acres was $70,000. On the project cost sheet, the price per lot is determined after considering actual land costs, projected development expenses, estimated cost of borrowed money, and profit expectations. In this example, I was looking for sales figures in the arena of about two-to-two-and-a-half times my land cost, since I was buying the land for no money down,

I knew I would be able to generate a profit at relatively low risk. But there was still the unknown factor of the landfill and what impact it would have on consumer response. At this point, I was trying to determine if my immediately salable lots–those with stream and park frontage–would carry me through.

Again, my actual land cost was $700 per acre. I was looking to at least double that figure per acre in sales volume. To determine projected gross sales from the premium lots, I first multiplied $700 per acre times two-and-a-half to reach $1750, which I then multiplied by the proposed lot size (5 acres) $1750 X 5 = $8750 per lot, rounded off to $8950. Could I sell my best lots at that figure, this using my generous terms and discount for cash? I thought at the time that this was a reasonable expectation, even though I was unsure about the sales price on the less desirable lots. So far my analysis had revealed that I could expect gross sales of around $152,150 on my best lots ($8950 X 17). My mortgage obligation to the seller would be $70,000 plus interest. So when I subtracted the mortgage figure ($70,000) from the projected gross sales on my premium lots ($152,150), I ended up with a gross profit of $82,150, plus a small inventory of theoretically unsold lots. This figure does not reflect interest on the mortgage loan.

How many lots are left after the best lots are sold? I quickly saw there would be only three, if the plat turned out according to my lot plan. My 17 best lots ate up 85 out of approximately 100 acres (17 X 5 = 85), leaving me with an hypothetical inventory of three five-acre lots. Even if I dumped these lots at cost, say, $15,000, I would still end up with a gross profit of about $97,150 ($82,150 + $15,000), this assuming (1) that I moved fast on the sales campaign, as I usually did, and (2) that I sold all of the lots. Adding in $15,000 for the less desirable lots, the sales volume was increased to $167,150. ($152,150 + $15,000) How would I handle my mortgage obligation to the seller? Remember, the contract allowed me to transfer mortgage notes from my sales. Further conjecture suggested that sales from the project, given the times, would bring in only ten percent in cash, an abnormally low figure.

How would I pay my bills for road building, survey, advertising, sales commissions, and overhead? In those days, I would have expected to cover some of these expenses by selling or trading some of my mortgage notes. Though not particularly in vogue today, the concept of bartering notes for, say, part of the survey work and road construction was commonplace in previous hard times. As a general rule, these owner-financed notes were subject to a first lien (in this case, $70,000). However, on some projects, the first mortgage or deed of trust note, was satisfied at some point through the transfer of notes to the mortgagee (the person from whom I purchased the property) on the subdivided land. Cash sales were immediately released from the blanket lien though payment at closing to the mortgage holder of 70-75% of the cash proceeds from each cash sale.

But for purposes of this discussion, where I was determining potential risk, I assumed that all expense obligations beyond the mortgage had to be met with cash. A rough guideline, based on my past experience at the time, was that approximately 25% of sales revenue could be allocated to the aforementioned expenses, this on a low-overhead operation.

Worst-Case Scenario

This risk analysis showed that, *in a worst-case scenario*, approximately $42,000 of the projected total sales figures would have gone toward expenses ($167,150 in sales X .25). I may have collected a minimum of $16,700 in cash from sales (10% of $167,150). When I subtracted the $16,700 in cash from the $42,000 in projected expenses, I was faced with a cash shortfall of roughly $25,300. And in those days it was customary to sell mortgage notes at a discount to raise needed cash. This additional expense is considered part of the *cost of money*. Let's run the numbers to determine how much in notes you must sell to raise $25,000 in cash.

The cost of money in hard times can reach, say, 20%. This particular expense item factors into the analysis the specter of abnormally high interest rates. Essentially, this cost is an interest figure, meaning that a discounted note must yield the investor a 20% return on his money. Now, a yield rate is different from a discount rate See **Appendix VI**). During periods of tight money and high interest rates, it is usually the case that mortgage notes are discounted at a higher figure than the yield rate, this due to extra charges on the loan, such as points and processing fees. But let's stick with the yield rate and assume that the buyer of your notes is looking for a 20% return on his money. Assume further that your note package for sale is $38,000 and that monthly payments on the bundle total $456 over an average of 14 years, at approximately 11.5% annual percentage rate.

Your financial calculator shows that a note package of $38,000 with the given characteristics in this example might sell for approximately $25,000 to yield the buyer about 20% on his money. In my case, I may have figured that the same note package could possibly be discounted to a bank or cooperative lender by roughly 33%, this while yielding me approximately the same amount of cash. The bottom line is that I would incur an additional expense of $12,400 ($38,000 in notes, less $25,000 yield from the sale). My hypothetical gross profits of $97,150 would therefore have shrunk to $84,750 ($97,150 less $12,400), this in the form of interest-bearing mortgage notes. *Bear in mind the fact that this risk analysis was a worst-case scenario.* Eventual profits turned out to be much higher.

So now I've made a cursory analysis of the project using the **Feasibility Check List**.

This preliminary review of the fundamentals suggested that the project was a potential profit-maker. Reviewing my point score I saw that I had 71 points before scoring the elements of *Salability after Development* and *Ease of Entry*.

Referring to the **Quality Reference Sheet**, I returned to accurately score these two elements. First: *Salability After Development*. Based on experience, I knew that people want land with a stream. They also desire park frontage. Customers have told me this in the past. I've never had enough to go around. I've sold all the land I could get my hands on that had these features. Based on these facts, I scored *Salability After Development* at three points. This is on the low side of "good." Ordinarily I would have gone with a maximum of five in the category of "excellent," but I had three lots that might have to be dumped at cost, plus I was confronted with the deleterious aspect of the landfill. I now had 73 conservative points in hand.

What about the final element: *Ease of Entry*? Again, looking at the **Quality Reference Sheet**, I found that this element was only "fair." I would need approval of my Soils and Erosion Control plan before sales could begin. This was the only approval I would need; yet I felt I had to remain conservative in my analysis, chalking up only two points, for a grand total of 75. I then decided to submit a contract on the property. What were the crucial points I needed to cover in order to protect myself against undue risk? As a *Subdivestor*, I had learned never to ink my name to a contract without consulting my **Land Acquisition Check List** for investors and developers. (See **Appendix I**)

This list has many more considerations than a companion list for those who are buying country properties for personal use and without particular concern for development. (See **Appendix II**)

We can now run down this **INVESTOR-DEVELOPER LIST**, as it applies to this acquisition. (Also see pgs. 172-175)

Item #1: I had spotted the property on a topographical map. There seemed to be few troublesome terrain features, such as steep land and drainage gullies. My surveyor would have to plan carefully, so that each lot would have a building site and suitable terrain for a septic tank and drainfield.

Item #2: I was not positive about the soil. I thought it was alright; nevertheless, in the contract I would insist that the deal was off if soils tests did not meet with my approval. I could not take a chance that any of my lots would be rejected by local health authorities. I originally gave *Soils and Well Depth* a maximum of five points, assuming that this element would be excellent due to the requirement that landfills are to be located in areas with deep, well-drained soils. I also noted that there were numerous houses in the area, all of which were using drilled wells for water. The owner had told me that local wells seldom went below 250 feet, a reasonable depth. I also knew that ample watershed was provided by an abundance of forested land in the adjoining Shenandoah National Park. I could not afford to rely on assumptions.

Item #3: None of the land was floodable, or subject to any recurring natural disasters, such as hurricanes, earthquakes, or tidal waves. No rust on the blade of progress.

Item #4: Regarding easements and encroachments. I would have this checked out by a lawyer's title search. The deal would be off if the search revealed anything I could not live with.

Item #5: There were no apparent subdivision or zoning problems. I could develop five-acre lots without the approval of local governing bodies. I knew this to be true because I was familiar with the county subdivision ordinance. I would follow up by checking the zoning regulations for any provisions affecting lot configuration, setbacks lines, and road requirements.

Item #6. Were there any adverse influences that could lower property values? Obviously, the landfill was a possible sore point. The important issue is that I had taken this factor into consideration during my preliminary analysis. I would not want to be surprised by any negative influences after I had made a decision to wrap up the deal.

Item #7: Were utilities available? Yes. No problem here.

Item #8: Who maintains the road to the property? The owner had assured me that I would have a 50-foot right-of-way. If this was factual, I would maintain the road until I could turn it over to a property owners association. Each lot owner agrees when he buys the property to pay a fixed or adjusted amount each year into a road maintenance fund administered by the lot owners themselves, or by an appointed agent, who will charge a fee for handling the collection of fees and scheduling road work.

Item #9: Adverse possession claims are rare, but they can occur. I would make sure in the contract that I was buying the land with undisputed boundaries. If I ran into problems before or after survey, the seller must correct any adverse possession claim. If not, he must guarantee reimbursement for loss of land or legal expenses through an adjustment in the contract price. Any serious claim by an adjoining property owner that part of the land was in dispute had to be dealt with before closing. Adverse possession claims usually arise when encroaching fences and unauthorized use of other people's land continues without challenge for a specified number of years.

Item #10: How close is this land from a town or city? My property owners would want access to various services. I was okay here. The location was excellent.

Item #11: Of primary concern to me was the survey. My position was that the seller had to guarantee acreage within 10% of the deed description. Any loss of acreage would result in a downward adjustment of the price. In the early days, I usually did not address the matter of a survey turning up more acreage than I had bargained for. Today, most conventional contracts provide for price adjustments, either up or down, after the survey has been completed.

Item #12: What about title defects? Standard real estate contracts call for the seller to clear up any defects prior to closing, or settlement will be postponed for a reasonable amount of time. I could not afford to be held up for a prolonged period while serious title problems are rectified; hence I had an automatic escape clause. I also needed to have title insurance. Once I had sold off the lots, I did not want to be haunted years later by lawsuits from irate property owners.

Sure, a lawyer's title certificate is supposed to uncover all flaws in the title, but the lawyer who guarantees the title may not be financially able to offset a large volume of claims, or he may no longer be in business.

Item #13: I did not need any financing. This was a no-money-down deal. The seller had agreed to take mortgage notes from my lot sales as payment for the land, these to be delivered with my personal endorsement.

Item #14: No problem with mineral and water rights. In this case, I would get all subsurface rights, which I would subsequently pass on to my lot buyers.

Item #15: Taxes would be prorated at closing.

Item #16: Riparian rights usually refer to your right to enjoy the use of a river, pond, lake, or water course bordering your property. In this situation, I knew that the property line went to the middle of the stream. Affected lot owners would have unrestricted access to the stream.

Item #17: What about unknown tax assessments? A doubling of the assessed value of the land, to take place, say, soon after the purchase could have cost me money. If such assessments had been in the wind I would have wanted to know about these increased costs prior to closing.

Abnormally burdensome taxes can also dampen sales, since many people are stimulated to buy country properties by the abhorrence of high taxes in city and suburban locations.

Item #18: I was buying the property with no imposed restrictions. I felt comfortable here.

Item #19: This contract provision deals with specific performance. If the deal had checked out, I was prepared to go ahead with it. I did not want the seller trying to back out on some real or imagined technicality. The contract would be legally binding on the seller providing I lived up to my end. Of course, I had protected myself with sufficient loopholes in case the deal turned sour for some unforeseen reason.

Item #20: What about approvals? I did not want to be tied down by a specific amount of time in which to obtain approvals which could unnecessarily hold me up through roadblocks such as political prejudice, or the whims of inefficient and self-important officials. So I would purchase subject to obtaining any required approvals. Period. Today's contracts generally have specified time limits for hurdling regulatory barriers to development. Provisions for extensions could be imbedded in the contract.

Item #21: Does an "interest-only" provision at the beginning of a deal make sense? In this particular deal, I was getting in for no-money-down, and my first payment would be due in notes six months after closing. Even if I had to come up with a down payment, I would want to avoid any further cash burden in the near term. At the time, and for purposes of maintaining a degree of liquidity, I needed to pay all of my expenses out of sales. I did not want to dip into my own pile of chips unless it was absolutely necessary.

Item #22: No problem with releases (payment to seller for outsales from the parent tract). Everything was spelled out in the contract. For example, land purchased at $700 per acre could be released from the first mortgage at $125% of the purchase price per acre. In this case, a five-acre lot that sold at, say, $9,000 would yield the seller a mortgage note of $4,375 ($700 per acre X 125% = $875 X 5). Notes were generally delivered in packages using a system of debits and credits. Often the package totaled up to more than $875 per acre for the amount of acreage sold off in lots, and the extra amount was applied to future releases. In the early days, I did not usually ask for releases unless the purchaser was paying cash, or when I planned to sell notes to a third-party lender, such as a bank. Any required financial adjustment on release figures with the seller of the parent tract was made at the time the first mortgage was paid off.

Item #23: *Subordination* deals with the holder of the first mortgage allowing another lender to take first position in return for improving the property with, say, a home or office building. For example, if I had wanted to build a cabin on the land to use as a sales office, I could have borrowed money from a bank and used the building lot as collateral. The seller would either have insisted on release fees, or he could have *subordinated* (agreed to hold a second lien) feeling secure because of the increased value of the land created through the construction of a cabin.

Item #24: An exculpatory clause in the contract would have allowed me an out if I had suddenly found myself in financial difficulty. I may have just wanted to take a loss and run, rather than remaining on the hook for the balance of the agreed-upon mortgage. If the contract had contained an exculpatory clause, where it had been agreed that the land was the sole security for the debt, I could have walked away from the deal without worry.

Without this clause, a foreclosure could take place if I had failed to meet my mortgage obligations. Should such a sale fail to bring enough to cover the outstanding mortgage, plus foreclosure expenses, my feet could have been held to the fire for the balance. This type of clause, and the provision for subordination, would rarely, if ever, be used by me today. Both devices presume a level of financial insecurity and lack of confidence in the project's viability.

Item: #25: This provision is often overlooked by unsophisticated land investors and developers. On owner-financed deals, the reason you want all release payments from the first mortgage applied to the next payment due is that it helps cash flow. Whatever you can do to increase your flow of cash is usually beneficial to your operations, notwithstanding your sizable bankroll. Say I had a quarterly mortgage payment of $30,000 and that, during the preceding three months, I had paid to the mortgagee $29,000 to release lots from the blanket mortgage. Without a provision that all release fees would be applied to the next mortgage payment due, I would be drained of another $30,000 in cash, rather than $1,000. This $30,000 would give me greater flexibility and leverage in my operations. Third-party lenders, such as banks, will generally not allow this provision in their documents.

Item #26: Obviously you will not want to be penalized for prepaying your mortgage. In all the years I have been in business, I have never had a seller object to inserting this provision in the contract of sale. Most standard real estate contracts now include a paragraph that allows prepayment without penalty.

Item #27: Easements and encroachments could take up a significant portion of the land I have under consideration. Lets say a high-tension power line ran through the property (possible reason for rejection) gobbling up a 200-foot-wide swath extending for 1,000 feet. That's 200,000 square feet, or approximately five acres of land that I may be able to use, but on which I could not build. I often have the seller proportionally reduce his price for the amount of land containing such an easement. Obviously I do not want this argument to prevail on behalf of my lot buyers, although I have, in the past, adjusted the price for minor encroachments such as small cemeteries.

Where appropriate, I generally run lot lines to the center of roads, utility easements, ponds, and small man-made lakes. It hardly makes sense to haggle with lot buyers over unusable land set aside for easements, such as roads and common access areas within developments.

Of greater importance to me would be the tax consequences of creating easements while not assigning ownership, either to individual lot buyers or property owners associations. The tax assessor will catch up with the person or entity who retains ownership.

Item #28: A provision in the contract of purchase calling for the suspension of mortgage payments during unforeseen delays in the development process caused by governmental authorities can be helpful to me as a developer. However, such a stipulation is more appropriate when I am dealing in a buyer's market, where the seller is faced with few competitive buyers and has little leverage. Under normal economic conditions, the seller would likely balk at including this type of provision in a sales contract. Of course, banks and other third-party lenders would reject such a proviso out of hand.

Item #29: Are closing costs apportioned in accordance with legal standards? Obviously, neither buyer nor seller want to pay more closing costs than are customary. When confronted with an unconventional contract, I usually have an attorney review the document to ensure, among other things, that I am not hit with extraneous or questionable closing costs.

Item #30: In owner-financed deals, and if the seller agrees, I always want to name the trustee in the mortgage or deed of trust securing the property. A friendly face can expedite the release of lots from the blanket mortgage.

Though the type of acquisition we are examining here would be more likely in a buyer's market, the principles are valid to the extent you are able to use them. When investing in, and developing country properties, I try to use as many of these land acquisition provisions as I deem appropriate for the times and for the deal itself. Sloppy land acquisition practices can dampen profits and can even lead to losses. The landfill deal came out pretty much as I described, this for a few weeks of concentrated work.

The techniques and advice in this book are provided primarily for their narrative value. Due to the complexity and constantly changing nature of laws governing the transfer of real estate and related tax angles, readers are advised to consult with an attorney or appropriate financial advisor when confronted with legal questions or matters concerning taxable income on real estate transactions. Of particular concern to some real estate investors is whether or not they are considered "dealers" by the IRS. Full-time operatives are generally classified as dealers. As such, installment sales contracts held by sellers can be taxed as if the face amount of the notes has been received in full at closing.

Conclusion

Success in life is not granted to the first in line, nor is power given to those who seize it. Neither are the smartest among us assigned the best seats at the table; nor is wealth handed out to those of privilege or cunning. Time and chance find them all. When I advertise an "Opportunity" it does not have a value stamped on it. You are challenged to determine that for yourself.

Each opportunity, like every hour of every day, can be viewed with hope and expectation, or it can be discounted. You may be reading this book because you hope to learn from it, and for many readers there are the expectations of profit. Learning, for some of us, is better than having wealth, or owning a home or land. Of course, the futile pursuit of useless knowledge can be of little value to your success in life.

Take from this book the information you feel will be of help to you in your life's journey, bearing in mind the fact that, though we may aspire to wealth, it is not a measure of human character, nor is it a primary standard of estimating human worth.

What's ahead for the rest of the decade? Obviously the largest tidal wave of retirees in history is about to wash up on our shores, this accompanied by a massive transfer of wealth to a younger generation. Inflation will continue to eat up the value of our currency, this due to monetary policy, record deficits, and expenditures for the unrelenting war on terror. More and more people will be working from their homes, this as improved technology accelerates the outsourcing of labor. Job slots in manufacturing and in some white-collar sectors will fall to attrition as workers retire in record numbers.

Baby-boomers, born in 1945, will be 65 years old in 2010. Many may take early retirement in 2008. The economy will recover, and prosperity will flow across the nation as tax cuts take effect and new jobs are created. Crime will increase as the gap between "haves" and "have nots" grows wider. Unbridled immigration, sanctioned by political forces in both parties, will continue to swell our population, expanding the need for homes and land. And, if the past is any guide, some calamity will occur toward the end of the decade that could have unsettling and potentially disastrous repercussions. All of these projections point to a continuing exodus from the cities and considerable upside potential for sound investments in country properties.

APPENDIX I

Developer's-Investor's Land Acquisition Check List and Scoring System

Feasibility Check List (Sample)

Project _____

Development Name _____

TOP SCORE	Excellent	Good	Fair	Poor
5 points	5	3-4	1-2	0
10 points	9-10	7-8	5-6	0-4
50 points	45-50	35-40	25-30	0-20

	Top Score	Points
Price and Terms	......50......	40
Location	......10......	8
Usable Water Frontage and/or Government Land Boundary	........5......	4
Usable Road Frontage	........5......	0
*Soil Conditions and Average Well Depth	........5......	5
Views	........5......	4
*Access and Utilities	........5......	4
Development Costs	........5......	4
Salability after Development	........5......	4
*Ease of Entry (Development)	........5......	4
TOTAL	......100......	77

(margin note: 3 7 / 4 0 / 7 7)

*A zero in Soils, Access and Utilities, or Ease of Entry is possible cause for rejection of the project regardless of the total score since is is assumed that, without these elements, sales of subdivided parcels will never get off the ground. Your option is to go for selling the property as a whole. Your total point score will tell you whether such a move is feasible

Quality Reference Sheet

CHECK LIST ELEMENT	EXCELLENT	GOOD	FAIR	POOR
Usable Water Frontage and/or Govt. Land Boundary	One plus mile frontage per 100 acres.	One-half-plus mile frontage per 100 acres.	¼-plus mile frontage per 100 acres.	0 to ¼ mile frontage per 100 acres.
Usable Road Frontage	,, ,, ,,	,, ,, ,,	,, ,, ,,	,, ,, ,,
Soil Conditions and Average Well Depth	Well-drained. Well & septic allowed on 1 acre or less.	Moderate drainage. Well & septic OK on 3 or less acres.	Slow drainage. Well & septic OK on 5 plus acres.	Problem drainage. Unsuitable for small lot development.
Views	Appealing views everywhere.	Appealing views on about half.	Appealing views on about ¼ of property.	No appealing views.
Access and Utilities	Elec. & tel. service across prop. Beautiful access along state paved road. No esthetic drawbacks.	Elec. & tel. service to prop. line. No access problems from state-maintained road.	Elec. & tel. ready to come in. Right-of-way to prop. Some esthetic drawbacks.	No utilities available. Restricted or undefined right-of-way to property.
Location	1-1½ hours from major city. Adjoining or just outside town limits or at major resort area.	2-2½ hours from major city. Near small town or major resort area.	3-3½ hours from major city. Near hamlet or village.	4-5 hours from major city. Sparsely populated area.
Development Costs	Roads completed or roughed in on gentle terrain and/or survey completed showing lots & roads. Prop. will sell itself if advertised and shown by the average real estate agency.	Easy terrain for building roads. Boundary survey completed or easy to complete. Needs effective advertising & normal sales presentation.	Possible road building problems. No recent survey. Persuasive advertising and sales promotion needed.	Terrain unsuitable for building satisfactory roads. Only metes and bounds description available. High-pressure sales and marketing methods needed to move property.

Continued on next page

Quality Reference Sheet *(Continued)*

CHECK LIST ELEMENT	EXCELLENT	GOOD	FAIR	POOR
Price and Terms	Priced below market value. Dream terms.	Priced at or below market value. Reasonable terms.	Priced at market value. Lousy terms.	Overpriced. Lousy terms.
Salability after Development	People waiting in line to buy. Exactly what they are looking for.	People say this is what they want. You feel they will buy if shown by competent people.	Maybe you could talk people into buying if you or your agent were persuasive enough.	Strong-arm methods and high-pressure sales tactics needed to move property.
Ease of Entry	Sell right now. No approvals needed by anybody.	Sell right now. Minor approvals needed or questionable.	Approvals needed now from various agencies before sales can begin.	Questionable whether approvals can be obtained.

APPENDIX II
How to Buy the Right Land Every Time using the B.K. Haynes professional scoring system

Here is a time-tested and proven system for buying land that will steer you around potentially marginal property and help you to score a winner every time. The three basic tools of the system are (1) LAND PURCHASE CHECK LIST (2) QUALITY REFERENCE SHEET, and (3) SCORING KEY.

Land Purchase Check List

This list is composed of more than 20 elements of consideration, most of which you will want to reflect upon when buying land.

Quality Reference Sheet

On this sheet you will find the three basic components of concern to most land buyers: (1) PRICE AND TERMS, (2) UNIQUE APPEAL, and (3) LOCATION. If the price and terms are right, and if the land has the "right stuff" or UNIQUE APPEAL you are looking for, and if the LOCATION is super, you are only *part way* home to a good deal. Using my scoring system, these three components are worth a maximum of 65 total points out of a top score of 100.

You should realize, however, that even if you literally stole the land, and if it had 100% of the unique appeal you are looking for, and if the location is "perfect," you could still be thrown out at the plate, so to speak. To produce a winner, you have to touch all of the bases. The other bases, or components, in my **Land Acquisition Check List** are, in general, necessary concerns about certain physical characteristics of the land under consideration by purchasers of country property.

Most land buyers would like some WATERFRONT on the land. PO-TABLE WATER (for drinking) is important. Many buyers doggedly hold out for property that offers stunning VIEWS. Is most of the land USABLE? Are you confronted with steep slopes, desert, or wetlands? Will you be satisfied with the road ACCESS and degree and quality of UTILITY SERVICE? Access roads could be a positive or negative factor in your analysis. SOILS quality is usually critical to land buyers. Will the land "perc" for home construction? Is the land suitable for grazing and crop production? Does the land give you the PRIVACY you require? Do you need to UPGRADE, or physically improve, the land to enhance its visual appeal? What is the RESALE potential of the property?

Scoring Key

My system allows an optimum 100 points for the theoretically best land purchase you can make. As pointed out earlier, a rating of 60 would give you only a marginal chance of roping in a satisfying and profitable deal. You must build up more points to capture a true winner. If you could, for example, realistically rate a potential land purchase at 75 to 80 points, it should be a safe and possibly profitable deal for you. For first-time land buyers, however, I suggest rejection of any purchase you rate below 70 points, because you may not have the depth of experience to accurately score your potential acquisition.

Consumer-Investor Land Purchase Check List

ACCESS

Will you be located on a public road, or will you have a deeded right-of-way?

Lenders require legally recorded access. If the state, county, or municipality does not maintain the roads, then who is responsible for maintenance? If you are responsible for your own maintenance, then do you have a sufficient-sized and valid right-of-way in your deed to adequately maintain this and other private roads, and to allow for the movement of construction trucks during building activity and the installation of utilities? A 20-foot minimum width is usually required for maintenance of limited-use private access rights-of-way. Widths of 40-60-feet are generally acceptable for small to large subdivisions. Many states are now attempting to obtain 60-foot minimums on secondary roads.

SEWAGE DISPOSAL

Are you sure about the "perc"? Standard in-ground home sewage disposal systems are generally preferred by land buyers. And they are relatively trouble-free. Alternative systems, using such disposal devices as "sand filters," "mounds," "spray irrigation," "peat moss," and "aerobic" processes are more costly, but these systems are approved by many state health departments for installation in marginal soils. If you are buying raw land for home construction, you should purchase subject to your approval of a current health permit or your satisfaction with the results of a recent valid "perc" test. For limited use in some remote areas, your local health authority may approve the use of a low-cost composting (waterless) toilet system.

EASEMENTS

Are there any objectionable easements or encroachments on the land? Are they serious enough to cause you to reject the purchase of the property?

FLOODS

Is your building site exposed to potential flooding, earthquakes, sink-holes, underground caves, caverns, or mining shafts; and can the site be made relatively safe from undue exposure to other surface natural disasters, such as landslides, hurricanes, and tornadoes?

WELLS

What are the depths of existing wells in the area? Without a municipal water source or supply, you need to be concerned about well-drilling costs and the availability and potential volume of underground water to supply your requirements. Will you be satisfied with a cistern that collects rainwater and that can be filled up when needed by a water supply truck?

MINERAL RIGHTS

Who controls the mineral rights? Is this information spelled out in the contract and deed?

Many early reservations of mineral rights in the chain of title can turn out to be of little or no consequence in a fast-moving society. Consult with your attorney.

UTILITIES

Are electric and phone lines available? If not, how much will it cost to bring in service?

Can the required easements be obtained to run these lines? What will be the user costs?

Can you be content with using a generator and cell phone?

SURVEY

Is there a recent survey? If not, will the seller guarantee the acreage within, say, 5-10%, if you commission the survey? Will there be a price adjustment if the acreage called for in the deed is insufficient? If you pay for the survey, you will probably not want to pay more if you get more land although this windfall may be wishful thinking from the seller's point of view. If the survey costs are split, or if the seller pays, there will likely be a price adjustment up or down if the surveyed acreage differs from the deed description. Should you have questions about the property lines, you would be wise to request a recent survey to avoid conflicts with adjoining land owners.

ADVERSE POSSESSION

Can you see any evidence of adverse possession? (squatters, unauthorized use of the land and unapproved ingress and egress over a long period of time) Land ownership can be claimed against the real owner (you) through a claimant's reliance on the law of adverse possession, whereas, under color of title, the trespasser claims he has established actual, open, notorious, exclusive, and continuous possession for a statutory period. This situation can occur on remote or abandoned land, where absentee owners fail to correct unwarranted changes in boundary lines, or when they fail to assert their right of ownership.

RIPARIAN RIGHTS

Will you receive full riparian rights? Generally, this question asks: Will you–as the owner of property adjoining a watercourse, such as a lake, river, stream, or canal–enjoy unobstructed use of these waters?. Consult with your attorney.

DETRACTIONS

Are there any adverse influences present in, or planned for in your area of purchase that could affect your enjoyment of the land, or which may lead to a negative impact on land values?

Examples of this type of detraction are nearby landfills, large-scale hog and poultry operations, timber clear-cutting over a broad region, municipal sewage treatment plants, junkyards, industrial pollution, shooting ranges, rock quarries, etc.

ZONING

Is the property properly zoned for the use(s) you have in mind? Check the latest local zoning ordinance and confirm your findings with the proper county officials or a local attorney.

SUBDIVISION

Will you be able to subdivide the property according to your needs and expectations?

Check the latest local governmental subdivision ordinance and confirm your findings with the county administrator or planning officer, and consult with your attorney.

RESTRICTIONS

Are there any restrictions on the property? If you are buying land in a subdivision, you will generally be confronted with a set of "protective covenants" that spell out what you can and cannot do with the land, and what guidelines, if any, are set down for building construction.

If you are buying land that is not subject to a list of restrictions, check to see if the deed includes restrictions on your planned use of the land. For example, some sellers convey their land with a prohibition against using the property for the storage of unlicensed vehicles. In other cases, recreational vehicles and boats must be garaged, possibly adding costs to your construction plans. The deed may state that timber harvesting is prohibited, this when you had planned to clear some land for pasture. Other sellers have imbedded "scenic easements" in their deeds, restricting construction and further development.

ASSESSMENTS

Will you be confronted with any assessments, such as road maintenance fees?

When buying land in a subdivision, periodic assessments, or the legal mechanism for imposing same, are generally spelled out in the protective covenants and deed restrictions. Sometimes the adoption of measures for fee assessments on landowners is voted upon in regular meetings of property owners associations. Local governmental jurisdictions, such as sanitary districts, can also impose assessments on landowners who use private road systems.

LOCATION

How important is it for you to be close to a town or city? Shopping? Doctors? Schools? Police? Fire protection? Lack of proximity to these basic municipal services can cause discomfort to many buyers of country property and can depress land values in some rural areas.

SPECIFIC PERFORMANCE

Is there a provision in the contract preventing the seller from reneging? Do you have a loophole or two built into the contract so you can get out of the obligation if you want to?

If time and circumstance permit, consult with your attorney about your concerns, so appropriate language can be drafted.

TAXES

Will real estate taxes be prorated at closing? Generally, this is the rule.

TITLE

Are there any known defects on the title, such as obscure easements, right-of-way problems, or lack of proper signatures in the chain of title? If so, can they be cleared up before closing, along with any other uncovered flaws that may result in legal action down the line.

Can you obtain title insurance to protect you against those defects of most concern to you and your lender? If closing is extended, what effect will this delay have on your plans?

FINANCING

Is your financing lined up? Are the terms and conditions clearly spelled out, and are these provisions comfortable for you? If the owner is financing the sale, will you get an immediate deed? If you are buying on a land sales contract, or *contract for deed*, you will want the contract recorded in the local courthouse to prevent the seller, his heirs and assigns from (1) imposing further encumbrances on the property and/or (2) selling the property to other buyers, whether by intention, or inadvertently. Plus you'll need to be kept up to date on your real estate taxes.

Without a courthouse record of your ownership, you may not receive your tax bills, and your property could be sold, without your knowledge, for back taxes.

CLOSING COSTS

Are closing costs apportioned in accordance with legal standards? Most standard contracts used by Realtors contain specific information regarding this issue.

PREPAYMENT

Are you protected against any penalty for prepayment of your debt in the contract and loan documents? Refinancing may be critical to you, possibly because of any construction plans you may have, and in consideration of volatile interest rates.

How to Score a Potential Land Purchase

TOP SCORE	Excellent	Good	Fair	Poor
5 points	5	3-4	1-2	0
10 points	9-10	7-8	5-6	0-4
20 points	17-20	12-16	7-11	0-6
30 points	26-30	21-25	16-20	1-15

	Top Score	Points
Price and Terms	......30.......	*25*
Unique Appeal	......20.......	*16*
Location	......10.......	*7*
Waterfront	........5.......	*2*
Potable Water	........5.......	*4*
Usable Land	........5.......	*3*
Soil Conditions (see example #3)	........5.......	*4*
Privacy	........5.......	*3*
Access and Utilities	........5.......	*4*
Upgrade Costs	........5.......	*2*
Resale Potential	........5.......	*2*
TOTAL	.....100......	*72*

SCORING SAMPLES

EXAMPLE #1: After years of fruitless searching, you stumble onto the place of your dreams. It's perfect–in the middle of a national forest, with a trout stream running through it. You can steal it. And it's in the exact LOCATION you want. You quickly score 30 points for PRICE & TERMS, 20 points for UNIQUE APPEAL, and 10 points for LOCATION. More investigation tells you that the forest service will not let you have access for a cabin. Nor can you drill a well, cut any trees, or build a road. You score 5 points for PRIVACY, 0 points for the other components. Your score totals 65. A likely winner is actually a loser.

EXAMPLE #2: You're new to the area, so you don't know land values. You find a desirable piece of waterfront property that scores 40, without counting PRICE & TERMS. Further investigation shows that it will only appraise out at 60% of the asking price. Unless you can cut a deal on the price, you will arrive at a score of less than 70. A potential loser.

EXAMPLE #3: You strike a deal on a one-acre lot that you score at 85. You feel the lot is perfect for the mobile home you are going to buy. Come to find out the land area is too small to support any approved home sewage disposal system. Big score. Still a loser.

Quality Reference Sheet

SCORING KEY

TOP SCORE	Excellent	Good	Fair	Poor
5 points	5	3-4	1-2	0
10 points	9-10	7-8	5-6	0-4
20 points	17-20	12-16	7-11	0-6
30 points	26-30	21-25	16-20	1-15

CHECK LIST

COMPONENT	EXCELLENT	GOOD	FAIR	POOR
PRICE & TERMS (maximum 30 pts.)	Below market. Dream terms.	Below market. Good terms.	Market value. Lousy terms.	Overpriced. Terrible terms.
UNIQUE APPEAL (maximum 20 pts.)	Just what you are looking for. Hard to beat.	Not perfect, but good enough for another look.	Coach-class land. Could upgrade w/ vision, more work.	Real turn-off. Lousy setting. Forget it.
LOCATION (maximum 10 pts.)	Within 1 hr. of a major city and near your work; or at resort area.	Up to 1.5 hrs. to a major city, town, resort area Commutable.	1.5 to 2 hrs. from a major city, town, resort area, natural attractions.	Out in boondocks. Long way from home. Boring when you get there.
WATERFRONT (maximum 5 pts.)	All the features you want on river, creek, lake, pond, ocean, quarry.	2nd best on your wish list. Most of what you want. Nice setting.	Some water on site even if it is not navigable. You can try building a pond.	If water is there, it is underground. Area is bone dry. Pray for rain.
USABLE WATER (maximum 5 pts.)	Central water; or good well. Spring water available.	Easy to drill well. Lots of water at reasonable depths.	Well depths deeper than normal, but good flow possible.	Subsurface water not available at reasonable depths.
USABLE LAND (maximum 5 pts.)	All usable, and/or joins public/govt. forest, park, etc.	Most is usable & acceptable for use now and in future.	Want more usable ground, but other features override.	Too steep, too wet, too dry, too rough. But it's dirt cheap.
SOIL QUALITY (maximum 5 pts.)	Deep, well-drained. Good for in-ground septic, agriculture.	Good for regular septic. Marginal for profitable crops.	Some clay-like, wet, shallow. Marginal for crops and septic.	Clay, wet, shallow depth to rock. Bad for crops, septic.

VIEWS (maximum 5 pts.)	Appealing views. Just what you've Looking for.	Attractive views from homesite. Limited elsewhere.	Partial views from homesite. No views on balance of land.	No appealing or possible views at at any spot on land.
PRIVACY (maximum 5 pts.)	Perfect spot out of sight and sound of homes, traffic.	A neighbor or two in sight. Occasional traffic passing by.	Neighbors on large lots. Some density. On, near main road.	Neighbors on small lots. Traffic noise. High-density area.
ACCESS AND UTILITIES (maximum 5 pts.)	State or paved road. Elec., tel., cable all in or ready to go.	Good all-year road or right-of-way. All utilities available.	Passable road or right-of-way. Extra costs to run in lines.	Rough, tight access road. Utilities will be costly to install.
UPGRADE (maximum 5 pts.)	No improvements to site necessary. Ready to build.	Some landscaping and clearing needed before building.	Clearing, cleanup needed to fix-up total appearance.	Totally overgrown, marshy, cut over, hit by hurricane.
RESALE (Maximum 5 pts.)	Buyers waiting in line. Exactly what they are looking for.	People say this is what they want. Quick sale possible.	Might sell if time & tides are right. Persuasion needed.	Few, if any, features of interest to buyers Must sell at a loss.

Once you have successfully scored a property and are prepared to buy, remember these key elements of successful negotiating. (1) Verify what the seller tells you. (2) Carefully read all documents and preferably have them reviewed by an attorney or legal advisor before you buy. (3) Don't be afraid to ask for concessions. (4) Don't get angry if the seller refuses to budge. (5) Take a firm stand when you feel you are right. (6) Be prepared to compromise if you really want the property. (7) Don't appear too anxious to buy.

APPENDIX III
Environmental Laws Affecting Land Use in the U.S.

National Environmental Policy Act (NEPA)–Requires all federal agencies to prepare environmental impact statements before undertaking major activities. (January 1970)

Clean Air Act–Authorizes the EPA to set air quality standards for seven major pollutants and emission standards for motor vehicles and factories. Major concerns are urban smog, automobile exhaust, toxic air pollution, and acid rain. (1963, 1955, 1967, 1970, 1990)

Clean Water Act–Sets water quality standards for all U.S. navigable waters and limits discharges by polluters. Major concerns are sewage treatment and oil spills. Goal is to make water safe for fish, shellfish, wildlife, and public recreation. Permits for discharges are required by state agencies or the EPA. (1948, 1966, 1970, 1972, and 1987)

Resource Conservation and Recovery Act–Provides federal funds to encourage state and local governments to develop and implement solid waste disposal programs. Requires the EPA to develop regulations for "cradle to grave" handling of hazardous wastes (1976).

Superfund–Created by Congress to pay for cleanup of toxic waste sites abandoned by industry. (1980)

Pesticide Control Act–Gives the EPA authority to control, manufacture, distribute and use all pesticides. (1972)

Wilderness Act–Preserves certain wilderness areas from development by placing them in the wilderness system, or within the jurisdiction of national parks. (1964)

Alaska Lands Act–Removed most of the public lands in Alaska from possible development by designating more than 104 million acres as national parks, wildlife refuges, and wilderness areas. (1980, 2001)

Endangered Species Act–Gives the Fish and Wildlife Service responsibility for maintaining lists of endangered and threatened species, including the legal right to acquire their habitats. Prohibits any federal agency from taking actions that would jeopardize a listed species or its habitat. (1973)

APPENDIX IV
Foreign Investor Disclosure Information

It is important for investors and buyers and sellers of country properties to be familiar with the *Agricultural Foreign Investors Disclosure Act of 1978*, which may require aliens to make specific disclosures on certain types of real estate.

Under the Act, any foreign person who acquires or transfers any interest, other than a security interest, in agricultural land is to submit a completed ASCS - 153 form to the Secretary of Agriculture not later than 90 days after the date of acquisition or transfer. Forms are available from county ASCS offices to which the forms must be returned upon completion.

Any foreign person who holds, acquires, or transfers any interest in agricultural land, who the Secretary of Agriculture determines to have failed to submit this form, or who knowingly has submitted a report which is incomplete, misleading, or false, is subject to civil penalty not to exceed 25 percent of the fair market value of the land on the date of the assessment of the penalty.

The reports shall be analyzed by the U.S. Department of Agriculture agency staff to develop reports for the Secretary of Agriculture for issue to Congress and the Department of Agriculture in each state. The reports and the analysis shall be available for public inspection at the Department of Agriculture located in the District of Columbia.

The U.S. Department of Agriculture requires that this filing be made on any tract of more than one acre used in agricultural, forestry, or timber production; idle land must also be reported. Small plots, such as gardens, are normally excluded from this act; but if an alien produces more than one thousand dollars in gross agricultural value from any plot, this fact must be reported.

Further information and copies of any revisions in this act may be obtained through local ASCS offices.

APPENDIX V
Land Trusts–A Discussion

Essentially, a "land-trust" is a form of ownership in which title to real estate is held. After 1976, with the blessing of the U.S. Congress, conservation easements to protect open space became tax-deductible. A flood of abuse then followed.

Give to the Rich

Some developers have been known to donate scenic easements on golf courses for tax breaks, this while retaining the rights to build homes on land that was already planned as "open space." And countless landowners have reaped tax benefits from huge amounts of useless land that was impractical to develop with any degree of density; yet these same landowners reserved the rights to build within the easement areas. Many wealthy estate owners have in the past panhandled tax credits from the U.S. government for land that counties had already declared off-limits for development and on which the estate owner had never planned to build anyway. And some castle-building developers have set aside vast swaths of open space for rich patrons, this while collecting big bucks from Uncle Sam at tax time for creating "scenic easements" that were originally part of the price tag for the mansions they had built.

Pigs at the Trough

These abuses aside, diehard preservationists swear on their enviro bibles that conservation easements are God's gift to mankind. Citing arguable issues such as the protection of our allegedly threatened ecosystem, the controversial creation of national monuments, and the urgent need for expansion of our vast national parks and forests, the preservation lobby from all appearances evidently feels the more land we can lock up from practical human use, the better. The fact that some environmental groups have been pigging out at the trough on their land holdings by selling healthy portions to their privileged supporters at bargain prices has been conveniently hushed up.

A December 2003 article in the *Washington Post* spilled the beans on this piggishness and hypocritical behavior. Reportedly, the Nature Conservancy, the world's largest environmental group, had in past years been caught flipping "in-house" scenic-easement properties to Conservancy trustees and cronies at reduced prices. The buyers received cheap land, with permission to build, in return for coughing up cash donations that oiled the wheels of the Conservancy's tax dodge.

Coasting along on a boatload of land trusts, the group was heady with power during the Clinton years, this until 2003 when the Senate Finance Committee pulled them over for a wide-ranging inquiry regarding their shady easement practices.

Do as I Say

These "Saviors of the Earth" preach protection and often practice deception. Enforcement of these scenic easements is as shallow as a grave. The *Post* article chronicles the sorry episode of conservationists and affluent landowners pocketing fat tax savings and skirting the development restrictions if the land trust approves, this without a single audit by the IRS. The theoretical loss of value through the donation of these scenic easements is computed and deducted from the donor's income tax. The tax-shelter issue is further skewed by exaggerated appraisals of donated property to these land trusts–entities that, in effect, police themselves. Evidence showing the existence of these scenic easements can usually only be found by the public in courthouse records, though some data is available on scattered websites.

As a consequence, violations are rampant across the nation. Potentially billions of tax revenue have essentially gone down the drain.

Double Dipping

Imagine, if you will, a developer building a golf course and placing a scenic easement on the property that will, in effect, pay for the course through tax savings and still allow the construction of the same number of homes as originally planned. The property set aside for the easement is simply appraised at the market value of developed lots, which were never going to be developed anyway, this according to the developer's master plan. Pockets of this unused land, or planned open space, can be assembled for donation to a land trust as scenic easements, marked up to outrageous value levels, and, the inflated figures deducted from the developer's bottom line come tax time. Some preservationists wink at these shenanigans because many are involved in the same scam.

Wealthy estate owners are notorious for keeping out the "little people." They would never dream of cutting up their precious grounds. But they would not hestate one second to cut their taxes by claiming a plump deduction for meaningless scenic easements on land that the county had already prohibited from development into small lots. By appraising land at the value of fictitious developed lots, the wealthy estate owner can claim a humongous loss though the donation of a phony scenic easement to a land trust, thus creating a potential million-dollar tax break.

The Future is Now

I would advise landowners to steer clear of donating scenic easements to land trusts, for the simple reason that these easements could do more harm than good to your financial position. Land is always in transition. Why let conservationists influence your future? Another important consideration is that these easements are yet to be broadly challenged in court. With all due respect to those individuals and land trusts with altruistic motivations, the whole scenic-easement tax dodge should be thrown out and exposed for what it is. Most land developers have little in common with wealthy estate owners and conservationists beyond an unholy alliance to perpetuate this shameless scam on the American taxpayer.

APPENDIX VI
The Wealth-Building Process of Holding Your Own Notes

Most of my sales are financed by local banks and lending institutions; however there are some cases in which I may agree to owner financing. The major disadvantage of owner financing, using a deed of trust or mortgage on the property, is that the sale will be taxed by the IRS just as if you received the cash in full. In the event of default by the purchaser, a credit to your tax position can then be made by your accountant. This drawback of paying taxes on monies yet to be received is offset by the higher interest rate you will be charging to the buyer. If the transaction is a land sales contract and you are not considered a "dealer" by the IRS, you will only be taxed on income as it comes in, this because you will not be delivering the deed until the property is paid for. Contracts for deeds are not generally recommended by attorneys in many states due to stiff consumer protection laws that complicate the foreclosure process and generally do not provide fees for trustees to foreclose.

After you have sold a property, you will usually be scheduling the closing with an attorney or title company agent. I try to use the lawyer or firm handling my legal affairs in any particular region. At closing, your buyer signs a mortgage or deed of trust pledging the property as security for the balance owned after the down payment. The buyer(s) also signs a note or bond by which he agrees to pay the amount stated on the instrument. If you have sold him improved property, such as land with a home, cabin, or barn, he should be required to carry adequate fire and hazard insurance.

The note or bond states specifically how much is owed, the rate of interest, the amount and frequency of payments, and the rights and remedies of both parties in the event of default. After settlement, the attorney or settlement agent records the deed and mortgage or deed of trust in the official records of the county in which the property is located. The public is thereby notified that a lien against the property exists. You, as the seller, will receive the recording receipts along with copies of the settlement statement and the note or bond. In the case of a mortgage or deed of trust, or contract for deed, the instrument will be returned to the buyer at a later date by the county clerk or appointed official at the courthouse.

When the buyer has paid for the property, the seller, or his assigns, will be requested to mark the obligation, "paid in full," and this information is subsequently recorded for future reference. Sellers transferring land on a *contract for deed* should not fail to have the instrument recorded, since the danger and illegality of multiple sales of the same property could occur, thus opening up charges of fraud and court action against the seller.

Discounting Notes

Assuming you are holding a creditworthy note with a good record of payment and accumulated equity, and you wish to sell the note to a bank in order to raise cash, you will be suffering a loss, or **_discount_** from its future value. Generally you would use a financial calulator to figure the discount and yield rates; however, you can obtain the same figures using simple math and the tables in the booklet: *Truth in Lending - Regulation Z - Annual Percentage Rate Tables*, available from the Board of Governors of the Federal Reserve System and from Financial Publishing Company, 82 Brookline Ave. Boston, MA 02215.

Example: Your note has a **face value of $22,448.20**, and the annual interest rate is 9 percent simple. (Note history: You sold a lot for $25,000, receiving $1,000 down and a note for $24,000. Since then, through installment payments, $1,551.80 has been applied toward principal. The note, originally for 10 years, has nine years to run. Now you want to sell it.)

Question No. 1: **What is the finance charge per $100 of the loan?**

Answer: Go to Table A. Read across on the 108 payment line (9% yearly for the remaining life of note) to annual percentage rate: 9%. Finance charge per $100 of amount financed is **$46.26**.

Question No. 2: **What is the amount of remaining interest (finance charge) if the note goes to full term?**

Answer: Divide the face amount of the note by 100; then multiply the quotient by the above finance charge (<u>$22.449.00</u> x $46.26). Remaining interest on the note is $10,384.91.   100

Table A

FRB-202-M

ANNUAL PERCENTAGE RATE TABLE FOR MONTHLY PAYMENT PLANS
SEE INSTRUCTIONS FOR USE OF TABLES

NUMBER OF PAYMENTS	ANNUAL PERCENTAGE RATE							
	8.00%	8.25%	8.50%	8.75%	9.00%	9.25%	9.50%	9.75%
	(FINANCE CHARGE PER $100 OF AMOUNT FINANCED)							
101	37.74	39.03	40.34	41.65	42.97	44.29	45.63	46.96
102	38.14	39.46	40.78	42.10	43.44	44.78	46.13	47.48
103	38.55	39.88	41.21	42.56	43.91	45.26	46.63	48.00
104	38.96	40.30	41.65	43.01	44.38	45.75	47.13	48.51
105	39.37	40.73	42.09	43.47	44.85	46.23	47.63	49.03
106	39.78	41.15	42.53	43.92	45.32	46.72	48.13	49.55
107	40.19	41.58	42.97	44.38	45.79	47.21	48.64	50.07
108	40.60	42.01	43.42	44.84	46.26	47.70	49.14	50.59
109	41.01	42.43	43.86	45.29	46.74	48.19	49.65	51.11
110	41.43	42.86	44.30	45.75	47.21	48.68	50.15	51.64
111	41.84	43.29	44.75	46.21	47.69	49.17	50.66	52.16
112	42.25	43.72	45.19	46.67	48.17	49.66	51.17	52.69
113	42.67	44.15	45.64	47.14	48.64	50.16	51.68	53.21
114	43.09	44.58	46.09	47.60	49.12	50.65	52.19	53.74
115	43.50	45.01	46.53	48.06	49.60	51.15	52.70	54.27

Table B

FRB-204-M

ANNUAL PERCENTAGE RATE TABLE FOR MONTHLY PAYMENT PLANS
SEE INSTRUCTIONS FOR USE OF TABLES

NUMBER OF PAYMENTS	ANNUAL PERCENTAGE RATE							
	14.00%	14.25%	14.50%	14.75%	15.00%	15.25%	15.50%	15.75%
	(FINANCE CHARGE PER $100 OF AMOUNT FINANCED)							
101	70.75	72.21	73.67	75.14	76.62	78.10	79.59	81.08
102	71.55	73.03	74.51	76.00	77.49	78.99	80.50	82.01
103	72.35	73.85	75.35	76.85	78.37	79.89	81.41	82.94
104	73.16	74.67	76.19	77.71	79.25	80.78	82.33	83.88
105	73.97	75.50	77.03	78.58	80.13	81.68	83.25	84.81
106	74.78	76.33	77.88	79.44	81.01	82.58	84.17	85.75
107	75.59	77.16	78.73	80.31	81.90	83.49	85.09	86.70
108	76.40	77.99	79.58	81.18	82.78	84.39	86.01	87.64
109	77.22	78.82	80.43	82.05	83.67	85.30	86.94	88.59
110	78.04	79.66	81.29	82.92	84.56	86.21	87.87	89.54
111	78.86	80.50	82.14	83.80	85.46	87.13	88.80	90.49
112	79.68	81.34	83.00	84.67	86.36	88.04	89.74	91.44
113	80.50	82.18	83.86	85.55	87.25	88.96	90.67	92.40
114	81.33	83.02	84.73	86.44	88.15	89.88	91.61	93.35
115	82.15	83.87	85.59	87.32	89.06	90.80	92.55	94.31

Question No. 3: **What are the proceeds if the note goes to full term?**

Answer: Add total finance charge to face amount of note (balance owed) ($10,384.91 + $22,448.20) Total proceeds = **$32,833.11**

Question No. 4: **What are my proceeds at the banker's expected yield rate?**

Answer: Go to Table B. Read across on the 108 payment line (9 years remaining) to the banker's expected yield rate (15%). Finance charge per $100 of amount financed at 15% yield equals **$82.78**.

Convert the above figure to divisor by moving decimal two places left and adding the number "1" ($82.78 = 1.8278).

Divide the total proceeds of the note by divisor. $\underline{\$32,833.11} = \$17,963$
                                                    1.8278

Total proceeds from the sale of this $22,448.80 note at a 15% yield = **$17,963**

Question No. 5: **What is the percentage rate of discount on this note at an expected 15% yield rate?**

Answer: Divide your proceeds by face amount of the note $17.963.00 divided by $22,448.80 = 80%

The discount rate on your note if sold to bank or investor = **20%**

Present and Future Values

Let's assume you have established a retirement fund composed of $500,000 in interest-bearing notes, secured by first and second mortgages on country properties that averages a 7% annual percentage rate. How long will it take for you to double your money? Here is a quick way to come within range of your target number. Simply divide the annual percentage rate into 72. In this case, the apr is 7.00%. 72 divided by 7.00 = 10.29. Your retirement fund, if left intact, could exceed the million-dollar mark after approximately 10 years, this through the magic of compound interest. When approximating double-your-money numbers at interest rates of 10 or higher, the number 75 works better. Of course, you can use your financial calculator to give you more precise figures for specific time frames with various interest rates.

A useful calculator for real estate transactions is the Qualifier Plus 11x, available from Caluated Industries, Inc. 4840 Hytech Drive, Carson City, NV 89706, USA. Phone 1-775-885-4975 Fax: 1-775-

885-4949. E-mail: techsup@calculated.com. Website: www. calculated.com

For example, using the Real Estate Master Qualifier Plus 11x calculator you may want to determine the future value of a country home you are considering for purchase as an investment for a low-ball price of $175,000. What will it be worth in five years, this assuming a 10 percent yearly increase in value? Here are the steps you would take with the calculator in hand.

(1) Press "On/C" key to clear calculator. The display will read: 0.0 (2) Press the "Set" key to 1 payment per year by pressing 1, then Set; next press the "division" key. This step shows you are are calculating yearly and not monthly. **Display: 1.0**. Clear calclator. (3) Enter the figure, $175,000 (present value), and then press the L/A key (loan amount). **Display: $175,000**. (4) Press 5, and then Term, to enter the term of your investment in years: **Display: 5.0** (5) Press the number 10 to enter the yearly increase-in-value rate; then press the interest key: Int. **Display: 10.0**. (6) Press the FV key to determine the projected future value of the home at the end of 5 years. **Display: "run"**; then the number $281.839 will appear in the display box.

Assuming an actual yearly increase in value of 10 percent, this figure represents the projected worth of your $175,000 investment at the end of a five-year holding period. Your bottom-line profit figure, of course, would depend on your expenses and tax angles.

The Future Value of Income-Producing Notes

Using the financial calculator, you can determine the future value of a package of mortgage notes, this given an average interest-rate yield. For example, you may have a $650,000 note package that is yielding you more than $6,000 a month in payments on lots and homes you have sold. The interest rate on this package ranges from 7% to 9%, with the notes averaging 8% annual percentage rate, compounded monthly over an average period of, say, fifteen years. Some of these notes will balloon (come due) within this period, but you are prepared to refinance those notes at approximately the same interest rates. Other note-makers will find lower rates elsewhere and refinance their debts; nevertheless, you expect to replace these balloon and early-payoff notes with other first and second-trust notes on real estate that will bear interest averaging 8% apr. Your objectives are to build net worth and liquidity for future financial security. Tax angles aside, you are interested in estimating the the value of this package and monthly yield at the end of the next seven years, after which you feel you will be relatively debt-free.

1. Using the Qualifier Plus 11x calculator, turn it off and then back on **(On/C)**.

2. Press **12**, (12 months in a year) next **SET**; then press the **"division"** key and clear the calculator.

3. Enter loan amount, interest, term; then find the monthly payment: (LA) **$650.000** (INT) **8.0** (TERM) **15.0** (PMT) **$6,211.70**

4. To find the number of payments, press **(AMORT)**; "run" = **1-180** (180 pmts.)

5. To find the total amount of interest paid after 7 years, press 7 **(SET)** **(AMORT)**; "run" = **$439,405.00**.

6. Press 7 **(SET)** **(PER)** **(AMORT)** to find total principal paid = **$636,585.20**

7. Add the interest to the principal ($439,405.00 + $636,585.20).Total estimated value of the note package after 7 years = **$1.075.990.20**

APPENDIX VII
Real Estate Investment
Questions and Answers

1. How is real estate used as a tax shelter?

Answer: Mainly through depreciation. Depreciation on real estate used for commercial purposes is considered–along with such items as mortgage payments, taxes, repairs, and maintenance–an operational expense. However, because depreciation requires no cash outlay, as do the other expenses, many investors view the purchase of income producing real estate as the creation of a "tax shelter."

2. How does depreciation work to shelter my income?

Answer: While your property appreciates in value, you can claim a deduction for wear, tear, and obsolescence based on a straight-line depreciation schedule of 27.5 years (30 years for commercial property). Current tax law also allows up to a $100,000 deduction for the purchase of business equipment and heavy-duty vehicles. If you buy personal property to be used in your investment properties, such as appliances and furniture, these items may be depreciated over periods of 5-10 years. All of these deductions act to reduce your taxable income. On paper, your properties may be declining in value, while in actuality, their market value is usually climbing beyond the rate of inflation. History has shown this to be true.

3. Can raw land be depreciated?

Answer: No; however, commercial buildings on the land such as apartments, homes and shopping centers can qualify for depreciation. You can depreciate rental homes over 27.5 years and commercial property over 39 years on a straight-line basis. Equipment, trucks, and automobiles used in business are depreciated over shorter periods. A recent tax ruling allows a first-time 100 percent expense deduction for investments up to $100,000 in equipment and on many vehicles used for business purposes.

4. As a real estate investor, can I deduct the expenses of my car and home office?

Answer: Generally, these deductions are only available when you are using the office and car for your full-time employment. In real estate, this means that you must devote more than half of your time to your real estate activities; or if you spend a minimum of 750 working hours per year in the business of real estate you may qualify as a professional. It may be helpful for some investors to have a real estate license, but many unlicensed real estate investors prefer the freedom from regulation offered to those without a license, and they devote more than the minimum number of hours required by law, this while claiming their full bounty of tax deductions. Mortgage brokers and real estate attorneys are not eligible for these tax breaks.

5. Can a partner or manager take care of my real estate investments and still leave me with the same tax breaks?

Answer: Again, you must still devote at least 750 working hours or over 50 percent of your time to your real estate investment activities; however, if you are making the major decisions in buying, selling, improving, and renting the properties, you may delegate day-to-day business affairs to a partner or manager. The primary advantage to being a real estate professional is your ability to claim almost unlimited tax deductions to offset your ordinary income or salary. Nonprofessional investors are restricted to a loss deduction of $25,000 each year from their adjusted annual gross income of up to $100,000. Deductions above this figure can be accumulated, or "suspended," for use in later years, this on an aggregate basis. These losses cannot be used to offset specific property losses in prior years. The limited $25,000 deduction is phased out completely if your gross annual income exceeds $150,000.

6. How can I benefit from capital gains?

Answer: The net profit from the sale of a capital asset, such as real estate, is considered capital gains. In 2003, the tax rate on capital gains was reduced to from 20% to 15% on assets held for more than a year, this to encourage investment activity and to stimulate the economy. But the government retained the right to "recapture" 25% of your previous depreciation deductions, thus reducing your profits after calculating the 15% on your capital gains. Here's how this works. You buy a country fixer-upper for $150,000, and you have deducted $25,000 of depreciation during the years you owned the property. Now you have a sale for $300,000. You think you will enjoy a capital gain of $150,000 ($300,000 minus $150.000). But this profit figure is watered down further through the "recapture" by the tax man of 25% from the $25,000 in deductions you have claimed for depreciation on this property. You pay a 15% capital gains tax on the $150,000 ($22,500) plus the $6,250 "recapture" from your previous depreciation deductions. Your capital gain after taxes is therefore $121,250 ($150,000 minus $28,750). This "recapture" provision does not apply to allowable tax-deferred exchanges of investment real estate.

7. Can I buy land and put it in my IRA?

Answer: Yes. But you must have a qualified trustee to manage this type of asset. And you cannot technically buy real estate with IRA funds if the property will be used by you or related persons. The trustee or administrator of your IRA can take title to the land and manage the property for you. You can also buy raw land through your IRA, sell to a developer, and develop the land yourself, though all funding for improvements must come from your IRA, with any profits being returned to your IRA, where they would continue to enjoy tax-free growth. Expenses, improvements, and fees connected with rental properties purchased by your IRA must be funded from the IRA, with all income from such properties returning to your retirement account, after which this money could be channeled into other investments types such as stocks, bonds and precious metals.

These provisions are subject to change and professional interpretation. For detailed information on tax matters you should contact a knowledgeable tax advisor or accountant. The Internal Revenue Service also provides information on its website: (**www.irs.gov**).

504

APPENDIX VIII
Measurement Tables

Common Measure

Linear Measure
12 inches = 1 foot (ft.)
3 feet (ft.) = 1 yard (yd.)
36 inches = 1 yard
5½ yards = 1 rod
16½ feet = 1 rod or pole (p.)
320 rods = 1 mile (mi.)
5,280 feet = 1 mile
40 rods = 1 furlong (fur.)
3 miles = 1 statute league (l.)

Square Measure
144 square inches = 1 square foot
9 square feet = 1 square yard
30¼ square yards = 1 square rod
160 square rods or
4,840 sq. yards or
43,560 square feet = 1 acre
640 acres = 1 square mile

Surveyor's Chain Measure
7.92 inches = 1 link
100 links = 1 chain or 66 feet
100 links = 4 rods
10 chains = 1 furlong or 220 yards
80 chains = 1 statute mile

Surveyor's Square Measure
625 square links = 1 square pole
16 square poles = 1 square chain
10 square chains = 1 acre
640 acres = 1 square mile
36 square miles = 1 township

Metric System and Common Equivalents

Linear Measure
1 millimeter = 0.03937 inch

10 millimeters =	1 centimeter	= 0.3937 inch
10 centimeters =	1 decimeter	= 3.937 inches
10 decimeters =	1 meter	= 39.37 inches
10 meters =	1 decameter	= 393.7 inches
10 decameters =	1 hectometer	= 328.08 feet
10 hectometers =	1 kilometer	= 0.621 mile
10 kilometers =	1 myriameter	= 6.21 miles

Square Measure
1 square millimeter = 0.00155 square inch

100 sq. millimeters (mm.) =	1 sq. centimeter	= 0.15499 sq. inch
100 sq. centimeters (cm.) =	1 sq. decimeter	= 15.499 sq. inches
100 sq. decimeters =	1 sq. meter	= 1,549.9 sq. inches or 1.196 sq. yards
100 sq. meters (m.) =	1 sq. decameter	= 119.6 sq. yards
100 sq. decameters =	1 sq. hectometer	= 2.471 acres
100 sq. hectometers =	1 sq. kilometer	= 0.386 sq. mile or 247.1 acres

Land Measure

1 sq. meter =	1 centiare	= 1,549.9 sq. inches
100 centiares =	1 are	= 119.6 sq. yards
100 ares =	1 hectare	= 2.471 acres
100 hectares =	1 sq. kilometer	= 0.386 sq. mile or 247.1 acres

APPENDIX IX

Occasionally you may want to quickly estimate the amount of acreage in a particular tract of land. If you can draw the rough boundaries onto a map with a specified scale, you can often "guesstimate" the acreage involved.

IF IT LOOKS LIKE THIS:　　　　　*DO THIS:*

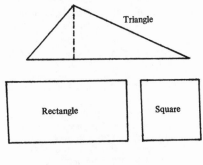

Multiply the base line (or length) by half of the height (which is determined by drawing a perpendicular line from the base line to the angle opposite this base).

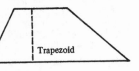

Multiply the length by the width.

Add the lengths of the two parallel sides; multiply this sum by one-half the height (the perpendicular distance between the two parallel sides).

Convert the area into two triangles (as shown). Figure the area of each triangle, then add the sums of each.

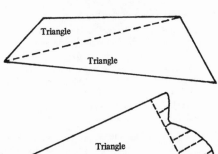

Draw a base line as close to the irregular boundary as possible, and then draw various lines from this base line, which are equidistant from each other, to the irregular boundary line. Take one-half the sum of the first and last line and add it to the sum of all the intermediate lines. Multiply this sum by the distance between the lines.

GLOSSARY

of Real Estate Terminology

For additional details on real estate terminology, including examples, graphs, tables, etc., refer to Dictionary of Real Estate Terms, Barron's Educational Series, Inc., 250 Wireless Boulevard, Hauppauge, N.Y., 11788.

ABANDONMENT: To surrender or vacate use of, or rights in, real property.

ABSOLUTE AUCTION: An auction in which there is no "floor," or minimum price, for the subject property. The property is sold to the highest bidder regardless of the amount of the bid.

ABSTRACT OF TITLE: A summarization or condensed history of conveyances, transfers, and relevant information pertaining to the title of a particular tract of land, including recorded encumbrances, liens, and other charges.

ACCELERATION CLAUSE: A clause or provision in a note, trust deed, mortgage, or land contract giving the lender the right to demand immediate and full payment when a particular covenant in the contract has been violated. Failure to meet installment and/or interest payments on time are cases in point.

ACCESS: The right to enter, approach, use, and leave a parcel of land, often over land belonging to others.

ACCRETION: The addition of soil to land due to gradual changes in a water course, excessive wind, and continuous waves.

ACCRUAL METHOD: A method of accounting that requires income to be recognized, for tax purposes, when it is earned, and expenses to be recognized when they are due. This differs from the cash method of accounting, which requires income to be recognized when it is received, and expenses to be recognized when they are actually paid out.

ACCUMULATED DEPRECIATION: An accounting term that refers to the amount of depreciation expense that, for tax purposes, has been claimed to date on real property, such as a building, or on personal property, such as equipment.

ACQUISITION COST: The entire costs, including purchase price, fees, etc., required to obtain property.

ACQUISITION LOAN: Money that is borrowed in order to purchase a property.

ACRE: A measure of land equaling 4,840 square yards, or 43,560 square feet.

ACT OF GOD: A natural, destructive occurrence, such as a hurricane, flood or earthquake.

ADDENDUM: An attachment, typically to a contract, that spells out certain provisions, such as definitions, requirements, fees, etc., that are not included in the main body of the agreement.

ADD-ON INTEREST: The amount of interest that is added to the principal of a loan, then used as a basis for repayment. *Example:* A 10-year loan of $100,000, at 4 percent per year add-on interest, is computed as $400 interest per year. This amount is added to the principal of the loan and $104,000 would generally be paid in equal monthly installments.

ADJACENT: In real estate, property that is next to, or nearby, a subject property, but not necessarily connected to it.

ADJOINING: In real estate, properties that are connected, as in sharing a border.

ADJUSTABLE-RATE MORTGAGE (ARM): A mortgage loan on which the interest rate can be changed, or adjusted, at specified intervals during the term of the loan.

ADJUSTED TAX BASIS: The original cost of property, either personal or real.

ADMINISTRATOR: A person appointed by the court to administer the estate of a deceased person who has left no will.

AD VALOREM TAX: A tax, commonly referred to as property tax, that is imposed by local and/or state governments as a percentage of the value of real and/or personal property.

ADVERSE LAND USE: Land use having an unfavorable effect on nearby property—for example, a junkyard in the midst of expensive country estates.

ADVERSE POSSESSION: A claim or right to land ownership against the real owner, wherein claimant, under color of title, establishes actual, open, notorious, exclusive, and continuous possession for a statutory period. This can occur on remote or abandoned properties where the absentee owners fail to correct unwarranted changes in boundary lines or to exercise their required right of ownership.

AFFIDAVIT: A written statement that is affirmed under oath before a judge, notary, or other official who is authorized by law to administer oaths in connection with legal documents.

AFFIRM: To confirm or ratify.

A-FRAME: A particular style of house with a frame that is shaped like an 'A.'

AFTER-TAX CASH FLOW: In real estate, cash remaining from income-producing property after accounting for taxes on the property's income. Generally, tax savings, derived from tax losses on the property, are added to the property's cash flow.

AFTER-TAX EQUITY YIELD: The rate of return on an investor's interest in real estate, after income taxes and financing costs.

AGENCY: The business of any person, firm, etc. empowered to act for another; specifically, in real estate, a fiduciary relationship between an agent/broker and the principal/owner wherein the former negotiates the sale, purchase, leasing, or exchanging of property. Agency can also exist in the relationship between a broker/principal and his salesman/agent.

AGENCY DISCLOSURE: In real estate, a written statement that explains which party the broker represents: the buyer, the seller, or both. The purpose of the statement, which is signed by the prospective buyer and/or seller, is to ensure that all parties to the transaction understand where the broker's loyalties lie.

AGENT: One who transacts business or manages affairs for, on behalf of, another.

AGREEMENT OF SALE: A written agreement or contract dealing with the transfer of real estate or personal property between buyer and seller in which the terms and conditions of sale are specified.

AIR RIGHTS: The right obtained by lease, sale or donation to use or occupy the space above a specified piece of property.

AMENITIES: Attractive or desirable features within a development which act to improve the quality and enjoyment of life, and which are generally considered improvement features to that property. Tennis courts, swimming pools, pleasing views, etc. are examples.

AMORTIZATION: Repayment of borrowed money on a systematic basis, wherein the principal sum of a note or mortgage is reduced over its life.

ANNUAL PERCENTAGE RATE: The true interest rate charged on a given loan, specifically meant to correct misunderstandings when interest has been "added on" at the front end of a transaction before computation of an amortization schedule. For example, a 6 percent interest rate is, in actuality, a 10.21 annual percentage rate using the "add on" form of computation. In effect, this is a 10.21 percent interest rate.

ANTICIPATION: A term used in real estate connoting the creation of value through future benefits. For example, the vacant lots in a subdivision will derive benefit from future homebuilding because such improvements will add value to unimproved lots. The opposite term is "regression."

APPRAISAL: An estimate of the value of a specified property. The estimate generally is calculated by a certified, independent appraiser for a fee.

APPRAISAL APPROACH: A method that is used to appraise, or estimate, the value of a property: cost approach, income approach, or market approach.

APPRAISAL REPORT: A written report, generally compiled by an certified, independent appraiser, as to the estimated value of a property. The report includes data and the rationale employed to calculate the estimate.

APPRECIATION: A rise in the value, worth, or price of a piece of property, usually caused by economic factors such as inflation.

APPROPRIATION: In real estate, the set-aside of land for public use, most often in accord with local, state, and/or federal requirements.

APPURTENANCE: In real estate, anything that has been added to or has become a part of a property and which is usually conveyed as an easement when the property is sold, leased, or bequeathed.

ARTESIAN WELL: A well that is drilled deep enough to reach groundwater that rises as the result of natural underground pressure.

AS IS: Generally refers to property that is presented and/or offered for sale without guarantees as to its condition, including encumbrances and defects.

ASSEMBLAGE: The combining of two or more parcels of land.

ASSESSED VALUE: The value placed on a property by local taxing authorities and used as a basis of taxation.

ASSESSMENT: An amount of tax, charge, or levy placed on a parcel of property, usually based on established rates.

ASSET: Something of value.

ASSIGNEE: A person to whom a claim, right, property, etc. is transferred. Also a person empowered to act for another.

ASSIGNMENT: A transfer of any claim, right, property, etc. from one person to another.

ASSIGNOR: A person making the transfer of any claim, right, property, etc.

ASSUMPTION OF MORTGAGE: The act of taking over or co-guaranteeing the obligations of another on a mortgage in which the new purchaser or grantee assumes liability for payment of a note secured by the mortgage or deed of trust.

AT-RISK RULES: Laws that limit the amount of tax losses (on real estate) that an investor can claim on his or her tax return. Essentially, deductions cannot exceed the amount of money the investor actually has at risk—that is, the amount that he or she actually stands to lose. (See your accountant or tax adviser.)

ATTACHMENT: A legal taking of property by court order, usually to satisfy a plaintiff or complainant seeking settlement of a debt.

ATTORNEY-IN-FACT: A person, not necessarily an attorney by trade, who is authorized to act for another by means of a power-of-attorney.

ATTORNEY'S OPINION OF TITLE: A written statement by an attorney, after examination of relevant public records, that, in his or her judgment, a title to a particular property is good.

ATTORNEY'S DISCLAIMER: A written form, signed by the purchaser of real estate, wherein it is acknowledged that the agreed-upon settlement attorney did not coerce, intimidate, or force the purchaser to select him as the closing attorney.

ATTRACTIVE NUISANCE: An appealing amenity that can be hazardous to trespassers who are lured by the feature, such as a swimming pool or a deep, swift-running stream.

AUCTION: The marketing and sale of property to the highest bidder; often used in connection with foreclosed real estate.

AVULSION: A change in the amount of land on adjacent parcels when a river or stream along a boundary line changes its course.

BACKFILL: The replacement of excavated earth, either into the hole from which the earth was removed, or against a building in order to strengthen the foundation.

BALANCE SHEET: A financial statement showing that assets are equal to liabilities plus equity.

BALLOON PAYMENT: Usually a lump sum payment of unamortized principal on a mortgage or trust deed which is greater than any preceding payment. A balloon mortgage may be amortized over 20 years, yet carry a "balloon" provision wherein the unamortized principal is due and payable at the end of a 10-year span. Often, refinancing at a higher interest rate then occurs.

BANKRUPTCY: A legal declaration, generally approved by a bankruptcy court, that a debtor is unable to pay his or her debts, and that either restructures or eliminates the debt.

BARGAIN AND SALE DEED: A deed in which the grantor either has, or has had, an interest in the property, but which affords no warranty to the receiver of the deed (grantee), such as in a simple transfer of title to a piece of real or personal property.

BASE LINE: A horizontal line measured with special accuracy to provide a base for survey by triangulation. Also an imaginary line through the initial point of a principal meridian, used to establish the location of township lines in the government survey system.

BASIS: Often referred to as *tax basis*. The amount that an owner has invested in a piece of property; essentially, the cost or purchase price of the property.

BEDROCK: Solid rock beneath the soil and superficial rock.

BEFORE-AND-AFTER RULE: The value of real estate before and after the taking of the property in an eminent domain procedure. The rule is designed to account for changes in the property's value as a result of the condemnation.

BENCHMARK: A fixed point that real estate surveyors use to either begin their surveys, or to measure the property's elevation.

BID: The amount a prospective buyer offers to pay for a particular piece of property.

BILATERAL CONTRACT: In real estate transactions, an agreement by which each party pledges performance, generally in accord with conditions that are set forth in the contract.

BILL OF SALE: A written statement certifying that the ownership of something has been transferred by sale. In real estate, the statement is used for the transfer of personal property associated with the transfer of real property.

BINDER: An acknowledgment or memorandum of earnest money deposited by a buyer to secure the right to purchase a specific property under certain terms agreed upon by both buyer and seller.

BLADED-IN ROAD: Initial stage of road construction in which a tractor with blade cuts out the road course.

BLANKET MORTGAGE: A mortgage covering more than one piece of real estate. This term is frequently used in the land development industry, where a single lien "blankets" all the subdivided lots in a particular development. As the lots are sold, releases can be made from the blanket mortgage.

BLIGHT: A condition in real estate in which neighborhoods and areas are in a state of decay or stunted growth, as with the slums of major cities.

BOARD OF REALTORS: A group of licensed real estate agents who are members of the local, state, and/or National Association of Realtors, and who generally determine real estate business guidelines in their particular localities.

BOND: A written obligation to pay specified sums, or to do or not do specified things. In real estate, a bond can be an interest-bearing security evidencing a long-term debt, such as a mortgage.

BOOK VALUE: A value typically shown on a company's books as the amount paid for an asset, less depreciation.

BOOT: The value of property and/or assets that are used to equalize the value of properties traded in Section 1031 (tax-deferred) exchanges. See EXCHANGES, TAX-DEFERRED; REALIZED GAIN; RECOGNIZED GAIN; REVERSE EXCHANGE.

BOTTOM LAND: Low land near a river, lake, or stream. See FLOOD PLAIN.

BREACH OF CONTRACT: A violation of the terms of an agreement. See DEFAULT.

BRIDGE LOAN: Financing given by a lender (mortgagee) to sustain a borrower between the termination of one loan and the origination of another loan. For instance, such financing might be obtained by a developer to pay off a construction loan while he or she arranges new financing for a permanent loan on a project.

BROKER: A licensed agent who generally acts on behalf of the buyer in a real estate transaction.

BROOM CLEAN: A condition by which property, typically a house or other building, is swept and cleared of debris before it is transferred to the buyer.

BUFFER STRIP: A strip of land located between two types of land use areas, such as a separation between residential and industrial. Often this parcel is unimproved except for landscaping, and its primary function is to lessen friction resulting from incompatible or inharmonious land uses.

BUILDER WARRANTY: A guarantee on the quality of construction offered by the developer or building contractor.

BUILDING CODE: An ordinance, enforced by local and state governments, and designed to regulate construction, maintenance, and alterations of structures within specific jurisdictions.

BUILDING LINE: This is also referred to as a setback line. The line marks the boundary beyond which no structure may extend and is fixed at a certain distance from the front, back, and sides of a particular lot, or at specific distances from streets or roads.

BUILDING PERMIT: A document issued within certain jurisdictions granting permission to build a structure on a specific site.

BUILDING RESTRICTIONS: Provisions established by local governments and/or homeowners associations that govern the size and appearance of a building. See BUILDING CODES.

BUILT-INS: Fixtures, such as appliances and equipment, that are considered part of the structure, rather than moveable.

BUNDLE OF RIGHTS THEORY: The theory, often prescribed or supported by state and local laws and regulations, that ownership of property carries certain implied rights, such as various uses of the property, quiet enjoyment, and the right to sell, bequeath, give away, or lease the property and/or such implied rights.

BUNGALOW: A small, one-story house that usually has an open or enclosed porch.

BUREAU OF LAND MANAGEMENT: A federal agency with general responsibility for public lands in the United States. Its principal function is to protect these lands from improper use and poor management.

BUY-BACK AGREEMENT: A provision in a sales contract by which the seller agrees to repurchase the property under specified conditions within a specified period of time.

BUYER'S MARKET: A real estate market condition, often created by economic downturns and/or oversupply, in which buyers have a wide choice of properties at favorable prices.

BUY-SELL AGREEMENT: A contract between or among partners or stockholders by which some partners agree, under certain conditions, to purchase the interest or shares of another partner—typically upon that partner's death or retirement.

BY-LAWS: A set of rules or regulations by which an organization conducts its business.

CANCELLATION CLAUSE: A contract provision that conveys the right to terminate the agreement under specified conditions.

CAP: In adjustable-rate mortgages, a limit that is placed on periodic adjustments to the loan interest rate.

CAPACITY OF PARTIES: A term that refers to the reasonable ability of certain persons to sign a valid contract. Typically, this precludes minors, the severely mentally disabled, et. al.

CAPITAL ASSETS: Certain assets, such as a primary residence or securities held for investment, that receive favorable tax treatment upon sale, as defined in Section 1221 of the Internal Revenue Code. Certain assets, such as inventory and property used in a trade or business, are excluded. (See your accountant or tax adviser.)

CAPITAL EXPENDITURE: A property improvement that has a useful life of more than one year. When calculating depreciation deductions, be mindful that improvements differ from repairs. (See your accountant or tax adviser.)

CAPITAL GAINS: Profits from the sale of capital investments such a stocks, real estate, etc. which are taxed at a lower rate than other income.

CAPITALIZATION: The process of determining the present value of property through the conversion or discounting of expected future income payments.

CAPITAL LOSS: Loss from the sale of a capital asset.

CAPITALIZATION RATE: In real estate investment, the rate of return that is used to calculate the value of a continuous stream of income. Essentially, the capitalization rate is composed of a reasonable return on investment (often determined by an appraiser), plus the amount that is allowed, or estimated, for depreciation. The value of the income stream is then determined by dividing annual investment income by the capitalization rate.

CAPITALIZED VALUE: The current, or lump-sum, value of a continuing stream of income.
Example: A country bed-and-breakfast inn generates annual income of $50,000. Assuming an 11 percent capitalization rate (considering the reliability of the estimated income stream), the *capitalized value* is $454,500 ($50,000 annual income divided by 11 percent, or 0.11).

CARRYING CHARGES: Taxes, interest, and other expenses associated with holding idle property or property that is under construction.

CARRYOVER BASIS: In a tax-deferred exchange, the adjusted basis that is transferred from the relinquished property to the property that is acquired.
Example: You are trading a $100,000 home for a similar property. Assuming there are no additional assets, or boot, involved in the transaction, your *carryover basis* in the property you acquire will be $100,000.

CASH FLOW: Cash remaining in a business after all operating expenses and debt services have been paid, but not including income taxes and deductions for depreciation.

CASH METHOD: An accounting method that recognizes income when it is actually received, versus when it is earned; and disbursements when they are actually made, versus when they due. See ACCRUAL METHOD.

CAVEAT EMPTOR: Latin term meaning "let the buyer beware," or "buy at your own risk."

CERTIFICATE OF DEPOSIT (CD): A banking certificate acknowledging the receipt of a specified sum of money in a special kind of time deposit drawing interest and requiring written notice for withdrawal.

CERTIFICATE OF OCCUPANCY: A certificate issued by a local government to a developer or builder indicating that the property in question is suitable for occupancy by the general public.

CERTIFICATE OF TITLE: An attorney's written opinion as to the validity and purity of ownership on a particular piece of real estate.

CERTIORARI (WRIT OF): A document issued by a higher court to a lower court, or to a board or official with some judicial power, requesting the record of a case for review. In real estate, this proceeding is often used by property owners protesting rises in tax assessments.

CESSPOOL: A cistern or deep hole in the ground to receive drainage or sewage. Cesspools, where found in use, are usually covered and are now widely outlawed throughout the United States.

CHAIN OF TITLE: A summary or history of a particular title to property showing out-conveyances, encumbrances, and other transactions and documents affecting the title as far back as records are available.

CHATTEL MORTGAGE: A mortgage against personal property as opposed to real property.

CIRCA: A Latin term that is used to describe an approximate time period of certain construction of particular buildings (e.g., circa, or ca., 1890).

CISTERN: A large receptacle or tank for storing rainwater. Usually the cistern is located underground and connected to drainpipes and guttering on buildings. Cisterns are widely used in areas where wells are impractical or too costly to drill.

CLOSING: Often used synonymously with the word "settlement" when referring to the formal conclusion of a real estate transaction. In surveying, the term can apply to the successful bringing together of boundary lines. In sales, the word can refer to the process of getting a prospect to sign, or "close," a contract.

CLOSING COSTS: Fees and expenses, such as discount points, title insurance, tax payments, sales commissions, special assessments, attorney's fees, costs of credit reports, recording fees, etc., paid by the buyer and the seller at a real estate closing.

CLOSING DATE: The date on which the seller delivers the deed, and the buyer pays for the property.

CLOSING STATEMENT: A document that accounts for all funds involved in a real estate transaction, and which must be delivered by the broker, closing attorney, or settlement agent to the buyer and the seller.

CLOUD ON TITLE: A condition revealed as the result of a title search that impairs the title to property in some way, usually minor. Court action or a quitclaim deed can often clear the defect.

CO-BROKER AGREEMENT: An agreement between real estate salespeople that they will share commissions on a particular sale.

COLLATERAL: Anything, such as stocks, bonds, or notes, that secures or guarantees the discharge of an obligation.

COMMISSION: An amount earned by a real estate agent or broker for his services in a real estate transaction.

COMMISSION SPLIT: The sharing of commissions between a sales agent and a sponsoring broker, or between the settlement agent and the listing agent.

COMMITMENT FEE: A charge to a prospective borrower by a lender for the lender's agreement to provide loan funds in the future. Usually, the fee is based on a percentage of the anticipated loan.

COMMITMENT LETTER: An official letter from a lender to a borrower stating the financing has been approved, and setting out the terms of the loan. Generally, a copy of the commitment letter must be supplied to the seller, and to the insurance company that is providing the homeowner's policy.

COMMON AREAS: Land set aside for all the property owners in a particular development to utilize and enjoy. Often this land is improved with recreational facilities such as pools, tennis courts, ponds, etc. In a condominium project, the common area may also refer to parking lots, playgrounds, and waterfront adjacent to or adjoining the buildings.

COMMON LAW: Initially developed in England, a presumptive body of law that has grown from legal customs and practices of a particular state. Common law generally is superseded by specific legislation.

COMMUNITY ASSOCIATION: An organization of property owners, such as a condominium or homeowners' association, that enforces covenants and oversees elements of common interest, such as common areas in townhouse or planned-unit developments.

COMMUNITY PROPERTY: In certain states, this term is used to describe property acquired by a husband and wife, or by both, during marriage and consequently owned by both. The term does not apply to property acquired separately by either spouse, say, through inheritance.

CO-MORTGAGOR: One who signs a mortgage contract with another party, and is thereby partially liable for repayment. The co-mortgagor generally retains a share of the property.

COMPOUND INTEREST: Interest received on (1) the principal amount of your investment and; (2) on the unreceived interest that has accumulated.
Example: Your $5000 CD may earn 4% interest the first year. In the second year, your interest earnings would be 4% of $5200 or 208.00. Each year's interest is received on previously earned interest yet to be distributed; thus the term *compound interest.* A financial calculator is useful in quickly determining your earnings over time.

CONDEMNATION: The act of declaring property legally appropriated for public use under the right of eminent domain. Quasi-governmental bodies can appropriate private property for the public good providing the owner is justly compensated.

CONSIDERATION: Anything of value, such as cash, property, or services, that is offered or given as an inducement to enter into a contract.

CONSTRUCTION LOAN: Usually, short-term financing arranged by builders until the structure is completed and a permanent, long-term loan can be obtained.

CONSTRUCTION LOAN DRAW: Funds drawn against the construction loan at designated stages of construction.

CONTINGENCY: Something whose occurrence depends on chance or uncertain conditions, such as the sale of a house contingent upon the purchaser first selling his own home.

CONTOUR MAP: A map that is drawn with contour lines to show the various elevations of a building or development site. Also known as a topographical map.

CONTRACT: An agreement between or among competent parties to perform, or not to perform, certain functions for consideration. In real estate, a valid contract is characterized by an offer, an acceptance, competent parties, consideration, legal purpose, documentation, a description of the property, and the signatures of the principals or of their attorney(s)-in-fact.

CONTRACT FOR DEED: *See* LAND CONTRACT.

CONTRACTOR: In real estate, one who contracts to supply goods and/or services in connection with property development.

CONVENTIONAL LOANS: Loans considered customary or ordinary, as opposed to mortgages guaranteed by government agencies. Usually, conventional loans are made by private institutions such as banks.

CONVEYANCE: The transfer of ownership of real property from one person to another by deed, mortgage, or lease.

COOPERATING BROKER: A broker who shares with another broker the handling of a transaction, usually sharing the commission.

CORPORATION: A legal entity, typically a business, that is registered with the secretary of state, and which is defined by certain characteristics, such as limited liability, perpetual life, and/or centralized management.

CO-SIGNER: One who signs a loan document along with the borrower so that the borrower may obtain the necessary financing. Generally, the co-signer is one whose credit and/or reputation is more solid than that of the borrower.

COST APPROACH: A method of property appraisal based on the depreciated replacement cost of improvements to the property, plus the value of the site.
Example: An appraiser determines that it would cost you $500,000 to reproduce your home in today's market. You are credited with $200,000 in depreciation over the years. The depreciated value of the improvements on the land is therefore $300,000. Adding $150,000 to the land value gives you *cost approach* value on the property of $450,000.

COST OF LIVING INDEX: The current price level of goods and services, related to a base year set by the state or federal government.

COST OF MONEY: Cost for loan funds or the amount of note discounts due to interest charges and the lender's required yield on invested capital.

CO-TENANCY: Any form of multiple ownership. *See* JOINT TENANCY

COUNTEROFFER: A substitute offering price made after the rejection of an initial offer to buy or sell property.

COUNTY BOARD OF SUPERVISORS: Elected officials within a county who act as a governing body.

COVENANTS: Clauses or agreements embodied in deeds and other instruments promising certain performances, nonperformances, and land uses by and on behalf of the grantor and his assigns.

CUL DE SAC: A street with only one outlet, usually with a turnaround at the dead end.

CURRENT YIELD: The ratio of annual investment income to investment cost. A $50,000 investment that earns $5,000 a year has a *current yield* of 10 percent.

CURTESY: The lawful right or interest that a husband has in the property of his deceased wife.

CUSTOM BUILDER: One who builds unique homes, or homes to suit a particular buyer's requirements.

DEALER: For tax purposes, one who buys and sells merchandise, real estate, or other products for his own account in the course of his own trade or business. Thus, any gain on the real estate sold by dealers is considered ordinary income, and not eligible for favorable (capital gains) tax treatment. *Example:* Johnson develops country property as his primary occupation, then sells the lots to his customers. Any profit from the sales is considered ordinary income.

DEBIT: In a closing statement, typically issued at settlement, any item that is charged to the buyer or the seller.

DEBT: An obligation to pay.

DEBT/EQUITY RATIO: Also known as the loan-to-value ratio, the relationship between the amount of the mortgage and the amount of equity (often, the down payment), the buyer brings to the transaction. For instance, a $200,000 mortgage with a $50,000 down payment might be expressed as a 4:1 *debt/ equity ratio.*

DEBT SERVICE: The total cost of repaying a loan; the sum of principal and interest required to amortize the obligation.

DEDICATION: To devote or give away land or property for public use, and the acceptance of this gift by authorized public officials.

DEED: A document under seal which, when delivered, transfers a present interest in property.

DEED BOOKS: Deeds and other real estate-related documents maintained by local governments as public records.

DEED IN LIEU OF FORECLOSURE: The returning of property to a mortgagee (lender) without undergoing the foreclosure process.

DEED OF RELEASE: A legal document by which a lender or lienholder cedes its limited rights to a piece of real estate back to the property's owner.

DEED OF TRUST: A legal instrument given by the borrower to a trustee to be held on behalf of a beneficiary as security for the fulfillment of an obligation, usually a loan for the purchase of real property.

DEED RESTRICTIONS: Restrictions written into the deed limiting the use of the property.

DEFAULT: Failure to fulfill an obligation, such as repayment of a real estate loan.

DEFEASANCE CLAUSE: A mortgage clause stating a condition that, when met, makes the investment valid. For example, upon payment of the mortgage, the mortgagee gains the right to redeem his property with no further obligation under the mortgage.

DEFECT IN TITLE: Any encumbrance, such as a lien, that would prevent a buyer of real estate from obtaining a clear title.

DEFICIENCY JUDGMENT: A judgment in favor of a mortgagee for the remainder of a debt not completely cleared by foreclosure and sale of the mortgaged property.

DEMAND LOAN: A loan, the full payment of which might be required by the lender at any time.

DEMOGRAPHIC: Relating to the statistical science dealing with the distribution, density, vital statistics, etc. of populations.

DENSITY: In land use, the concentration of development on a cluster of parcels, or in a subdivision.

DEPLETION: The gradual using up or destruction of capital assets, especially natural resources.

DEPRECIATION: A decrease in the value of property through wear, deterioration, or obsolescence, and the allowance made for this in bookkeeping, accounting, etc., to amortize or write off the cost of the property over its estimated useful life.

DISCLOSURE STATEMENT: A legally required statement in which sellers of a property, in certain circumstances, must reveal specified information to potential buyers.

DISCOUNT: When an obligation, such as a mortgage, is sold, the difference between the face amount of the loan, and the amount received in the sale.

DISCOUNTED CASH FLOW: A calculation by which estimated investment income is converted to a rate of return on the initial investment. See NET PRESENT VALUE.

DISCOUNTING NOTES: To sell notes receivable at less than their present values, with the reductions largely covering interest for the purchaser.

DISCOUNT POINTS: Also called a loan fee when the lender charges for his services in making the loan. Generally these fees are based on a percentage of the loan amount and are meant to compensate the lender for the discount at which he must sell the loan on the secondary market. Discount points are not to be confused with interest points, a separate item.

DISCOUNT RATE: The percentage charge paid by banks that are members of the Federal Reserve System when borrowing from the Reserve's fund.

DISINTERMEDIATION: An outflowing of funds from thrift institutions generally precipitated by higher interest rates and yields that depositors can earn from other investments, such as stocks, bonds, precious metals, etc.

DISTRESSED PROPERTY: Real estate that has been, or will be, foreclosed upon because of insufficient income production.

DOWER: The part of a man's property that his widow inherits for life.

DOWNZONING: The act of rezoning property for a less intensive use than is currently allowed by law or regulation.

DRAGNET CLAUSE: A clause in a mortgage that pledges several properties, instead of just one property, as collateral for the loan. A default on one property might trigger a foreclosure on a second property, even if pay-

ments on the second property are current—providing the mortgage on the second property contains the *dragnet clause.*

DRAIN FIELDS: The area receiving drainage from a septic system.

DRIVE-BY APPRAISAL: A property appraisal that is based solely on a review of the exterior of a building, without the usual inspection of the interior.

DUAL AGENCY: A situation in which an agent represents more than one party—for instance, both the buyer and the seller—in a real estate transaction.

DUE DILIGENCE: A study, usually accompanying the purchase of property or a business, that reflects a reasonable effort to determine and provide accurate and complete information about the property, such as financial strength, marketability, development history, etc.

DUE-ON-SALE CLAUSE: A provision in a mortgage that states the loan is due upon the sale of the property.

EARNEST MONEY: A nominal amount preferred by the buyer to show "good faith" that he will go through with the transaction, and which can be forfeited if he backs out. Later it can be considered as part of the down payment.

EASEMENT: A right or privilege that a person or entity might have in another's land, such as a right-of-way, or a grant to a utility company.

EASEMENT BY PRESCRIPTION: The use by one person or entity of another's property by right or privilege that eventually can become a permanent right under certain conditions, which are generally set by law or regulation.

ECONOMIC OBSOLESCENCE: The loss of a property's value resulting from external factors, such as the construction of a landfill near the property.

EGRESS: The act or right of going out of, or leaving, a property.

EMBLEMENT: A right associated with growing and/or harvesting crops on one's own, or another's, land.

EMINENT DOMAIN: The right of a government or quasi-governmental agency to take, or to authorize the taking of, private property for public use, with just compensation usually given to the owner.

EMPTY NESTERS: A market segment of older homeowners whose children have grown and left the household.

ENCROACHMENT: The act of advancing beyond the proper, original, or customary limits, as when a building or part of a building intrudes upon a neighboring property line or public sidewalk.

ENCUMBRANCE: A lien, charge, or claim attached to the real or personal property of another and which has the effect of lessening or limiting value.

ENDORSEMENT: A form denoting a change, as of coverage or beneficiary, written on or added to an insurance policy or a commitment for title insurance; also, the act of a payee signing his or her name on the back of a check or note, authorizing the instrument to be cashed or paid.

ENTITY: A legal form by which property is owned, or by which a business is constructed.

ENTREPRENEUR: A person who organizes and manages a business undertaking, assuming the risk for the sake of profit.

ENVIRONMENTAL AUDIT: An investigation of a property to determine real or potential hazards.

ENVIRONMENTAL IMPACT STUDY: A formal statement or official account of the impact that a particular land use will have on the local environment. Such studies may be required by governing bodies concerned with the effects of development on the natural or fabricated environment.

ENVIRONMENTAL PROTECTION AGENCY (EPA): A federal government agency whose purpose is to create and enforce regulations to safeguard the environment against water, ground, and air pollution.

EQUAL CREDIT OPPORTUNITY ACT: Federal law that prohibits lending institutions from discriminating against loan applicants on the basis of age, race, religion, gender, national origin, or receipt of public assistance.

EQUITY: In real estate, equity can be taken to mean an owner's invested interest in a particular property over and above the liens against it.

EQUITY OF REDEMPTION: A mortgagee's right to redeem or recover his property prior to a foreclosure sale by paying the debt. This right can also extend for a specified period after the sale.

EQUITY PARTICIPATION: Also called a kicker, this term is usually applied to a transaction in which the lender, in addition to a fixed rate of interest, retains a share in the profits of the borrower's project. Brokers and syndicators also utilize this transaction in lieu of, or in addition to, their customary fees.

EQUITY YIELD RATE: The rate of return on principal, or the equity portion of an investment before taxes, but after payment on debt.

EROSION: The gradual wearing away or disintegration of land area through processes of nature, as by water or winds.

ESCALATOR CLAUSE: A clause in a contract providing for increases or decreases in certain items to cover unpredictable changes such as adjustments in tax rates or operating costs.

ESCAPE CLAUSE: A provision of a contract that allows one or more of the parties to the agreement to cancel or back out of the contract under specified conditions.

ESCHEAT: The reverting of property to the government when there are no legal heirs, and when there is no will disposing of the property to others.

ESCROW: A written agreement (as a bond or deed), or funds, deposited to the care of a third party and not delivered or put into effect until certain conditions are fulfilled.

ESTATE: The degree, nature, extent, and quality of interest or ownership that one has in land or other property. The term can also mean a person's possessions.

ESTOPPEL CERTIFICATE: A certificate that, when signed and delivered to another person, legally prevents that person from making an affirmation or denial contrary to facts that had been set forth earlier.

EXCHANGE, TAX-DEFERRED: A transaction in which, under Section 1031 of the Internal Revenue Code, real property used in a trade or a business or held as an investment can be exchanged tax free for another similar property. See BOOT, REALIZED GAIN, RECOGNIZED GAIN, STARKER, REVERSE EXCHANGE.

EXCLUSIONARY ZONING: A type of zoning, illegal in most jurisdictions, that would directly or indirectly prohibit the incursion of certain kinds of real estate development, such as low–and moderate–income housing, or housing for the elderly.

EXCLUSIVE AGENCY LISTING: An agreement between a property owner and a particular real estate broker that gives that broker and his agents the exclusive right to sell certain property for a specified period of time, but which reserves the owner's right to sell the property himself without paying a commission.

EXCLUSIVE RIGHT TO SELL LISTING: A listing agreement between a broker and a property owner that gives the agency exclusive rights to sell a specified property and guaranteeing a commission to the brokerage house if the property is sold by anyone else during the term of the agreement.

EXCULPATORY CLAUSE: The clause or provision in a contract, financial instrument, or agreement that frees a debtor from personal liability if he defaults. For example, a mortgage clause might release a mortgagor in default from further obligation and provide that the property is sole security for the debt.

FACE VALUE: The dollar amount of an instrument as shown on the "face" of the instrument, such as a check, bond, note, etc.

FAIR MARKET VALUE: An estimation of price that a given property would bring if sold on the open market, allowing for a reasonable period of time to locate and familiarize a buyer with the property's full use, value, and potential.

FANNIE MAE (FNMA): A shortened name for the Federal National Mortgage Association. This is a private corporation, sponsored by the federal government, and designed to supplement private mortgage market operations by purchasing and selling conventional loans, as well as loans made by the Federal Housing Association (FHA) and the Bureau of Veterans Affairs (VA).

FARM CREDIT AGENCY: A federal government agency that makes mortgage loans at below-market rates to farmers, and to those who provide services to farmers and ranchers. The loans are secured in part by stock the borrowers purchase in a local land bank agency or organization.

FARMERS HOME ADMINISTRATION (FmHA): A division of the U.S. Department of Agriculture that provides and oversees assistance programs to buyers of homes in rural areas and small towns.

FARMSTEAD: The land and buildings of a farm, or a rural tract of land that suggests farm use.

FEASIBILITY STUDY: A critical examination and investigation of a proposed plan of a project to determine whether the undertaking is capable of being managed, utilized, or dealt with successfully. Specific attention is directed toward an analysis of attainable income, probable expenses, and suitability of design and function.

FEDERAL DEPOSIT INSURANCE CORPORATION (FDIC): A quasi-governmental agency that insures depositor accounts of up to $100,000 in member banks and savings and loan associations, and, as such, regulates those institutions as to debt ratio, capitalization rate, etc., requiring them to maintain a "safe and sound" condition.

FEDERAL FAIR HOUSING LAW: A federal law that prohibits those who sell or rent houses from discriminating on the basis of age, race, gender, creed, national origin, religion, or disability.

FEDERAL HOME LOAN MORTGAGE CORPORATION (FHLMC): Also known as "Freddie Mac," a private corporation, sponsored and overseen by the federal government, that buys mortgages from lending institutions (primarily savings and loan associations), and re-sells the loans to investors in order to sustain a high level of mortgage money available to the nation's home buyers.

FEDERAL HOUSING ADMINISTRATION (FHA): A division of the U.S. Department of Housing and Urban Development which administers loan programs and guarantees loans to qualified buyers, generally requiring minimal down payments.

FEDERAL RESERVE SYSTEM (FRS): A centralized banking system in the United States under a board of governors with supervisory powers over twelve federal reserve banks, each a central bank for its respective district, and about 6,000 member banks. The system was established in 1913 to develop a currency that would fluctuate with business demands, and to regulate the member banks of each district.

FEE SIMPLE: An arrangement by which an owner of real property is entitled to use and dispose of the property unconditionally, and to bequeath the property to heirs whom he alone designates.

FEE SIMPLE DEFEASIBLE: An arrangement by which ownership of real property, and/or the duration of ownership, is dependent on certain conditions, such as how the property is used.

FIDELITY BOND: A bond that is purchased by an employer to cover employees who routinely handle funds or valuable property.

FIDUCIARY: Of, or having to do with, or involving a confidence or trust, as in a broker/client relationship.

FINDER'S FEE: Money that is paid to those, excluding brokers, who locate suitable property or prospective buyers for another person.

FIRST MORTGAGE: A mortgage that has priority over all other liens on a property, and that must be paid before all other debts against the property are satisfied.

FIXED EXPENSES: In real estate, expenses, such as taxes and utilities, that must be paid continuously, regardless of external factors.

FIXED-PAYMENT MORTGAGE: A loan, secured by real property, that calls for periodic payments of principal and interest, the amounts of which remain the same over the term of the loan.

FIXED-RATE MORTGAGE: A loan, secured by real property, carrying an interest rate that remains the same over the term of the loan.

FIXING-UP EXPENSES: Expenses such as repairs and upgrading, incurred for the purpose of preparing a property for sale.

FIXTURES: Any of the fittings or furnishings of real property that are attached, annexed, or installed in the building and ordinarily considered legally a part of it. Examples are furnaces, wall-to-wall carpeting, plumbing fixtures, and hot-water heaters.

FLAT-FEE BROKER: A licensed broker who charges a fixed fee, rather than a commission, for the provision of his or her services in the sale of real property.

FLOOD PLAIN: A plain along a river or tributary, formed from sediment deposited by floods.

FORECLOSURE: The legal process and forced sale of property by a mortgagee or other lien creditor to deprive a mortgagor in default from redeeming the mortgage through resumption of regular payments.

FORFEITURE: The act of relinquishing or losing money and/or other valuable consideration through failure to comply with specified conditions in a contract, option agreement, or other legal document.

FRAUD: The use of deception in a transaction, generally resulting in financial loss to a customer or investor.

FREEHOLD: An estate in land held for life or with the right to pass it on through inheritance.

FREELANCE: A person who is not under contract for regular employment, but who sells his services to any buyer. Examples are writers, artists, consultants, actors, et. al.

FRONT FOOT: A standard unit of measurement that is used to determine the total frontage of a piece of real property.

FRONT MONEY: The amount of money that is necessary to launch a development project.

FROSTLINE: The point beneath the soil beyond which frost cannot penetrate. In building construction, footings that do not exceed this depth are in danger of movement.

FSBO: For Sale By Owner, indicating a property sale that is being handled by the owner, without the aid of a real estate agent.

FULLY AMORTIZED LOAN: A loan, typically a mortgage, whose designated payments of principal and interest are sufficient to retire the debt.

GAP FINANCING: Loan money advanced to cover a borrower's temporary needs until permanent financing can be arranged. For example, the developer of a shopping center might be required to achieve a certain occupancy level before his lender will grant a permanent loan. Gap financing is often a solution to the developer's interim needs.

GATED COMMUNITY: A private, fenced housing development, often equipped with a security guard who is posted at the front gate.

GENERAL CONTRACTOR: One who constructs buildings or who makes improvements for landowners and developers.

GENERAL PARTNER: A partner whose liability in a business or an investment is not limited.

GENERAL WARRANTY DEED: A deed carrying the seller's warranty that title is good in fee, that it is free and clear of all liens and encumbrances, and giving the grantor's assurance that he will defend the title against all claims.

GENTRIFICATION: The upgrade or rehabilitation of a neighborhood, often resulting in the displacement of storefront businesses and/or lower-income residents due to increases in home prices and rental rates.

GEOGRAPHIC INFORMATION SYSTEMS (GIS): A computer program that generates an overlay map, generally used to pinpoint land characteristics and/or demographic information of a certain geographic area.

GIFT DEED: A deed that is given by a property owner to another party for no material consideration.

GOOD FAITH: Refers to the concepts of honesty and trust; in real estate, a pledge, often backed by cash or assets, that a transaction will be completed.

GOVERNMENT RECTANGULAR SURVEY: A survey method, often employed by local government planning agencies, that divides a sector of land into 24 square-mile sections, which are further broken down into townships and individual sections.

GRACE PERIOD: A fixed period of time, after the due date of a payment, during which a debtor may still make payment without being considered in default.

GRADE: The ground level at the foundation of a building.

GRANDFATHER CLAUSE: When a law is changed, a provision in the new law that allows those who were operating under the requirements of the old law to continue their activities.

GRANT: In real estate, the conveyance, or transfer, of a deed by one party to another.

GRANTEE: A person or party to whom a grant is given, as a deed to real property.

GRAVITY FLOW: The supplying of a substance (such as water) by force of gravity alone. In rural areas, a well or spring may be so positioned above the dwelling that a free flow is established, thus eliminating the need for a pump.

GROSS INCOME MULTIPLIER (GIM): A figure or ratio computed by dividing the annual gross income for a rental property into the sales price. This figure, when multiplied by gross income, can also be useful in estimating market value on unsold rental properties.

HALF BATH: A partial bathroom in a residence—one that contains a sink and a toilet, but no bathtub or shower; often referred to as a powder room.

HARD MONEY: A term describing cash down payments and payments on the principal portion of a loan (as opposed to interest). This money has the effect of improving the payor's equity or ownership position and is generally not tax deductible.

HAZARD INSURANCE: An insurance policy, often required by lenders as a condition to approving a mortgage, that protects against property damage caused by certain natural occurrences, such as fires or storms.

HEALTH PERMIT: Written authorization from the local or regional health department to proceed with the installation of a septic system or other method of sewage disposal within specified design limits, and on an approved site adjacent to a dwelling or other building.

HECTARE: A land measurement equivalent to about 2.5 acres.

HEIR: One who inherits property or assets.

HEIRS AND ASSIGNS: A term, generally contained in a provision of a deed or a will, that grants certain unconditional rights (fee simple) in an estate.

HIGHEST AND BEST USE: A land use that will legally, possibly, and probably produce the best net return or give the greatest value to a parcel of real property over a specific period of time, while preserving its utility and present element of risk.

HOLDBACK: A portion of a loan that is not remitted to the borrower until certain conditions are met. For example, part of a construction loan might be held back until 50 percent of the project is complete.

HOLD HARMLESS CLAUSE: A contract provision by which Party 'A' agrees to protect Party 'B' from claims against the contract. Party 'A' thereby assumes all the risk, and Party 'B' is held *harmless*.

HOLDING COMPANY: A person or company that owns or controls another company, or other companies. For example, a bank and an associated investment company might be owned or controlled by a single *holding company*.

HOLDING PERIOD: The time period during which one owns property, typically for investment purposes.

HOME EQUITY LOAN: A loan, typically in the form of a second mortgage, that is drawn from one's equity in a principal residence. The funds, which can be tax deductible, often are used for nonresidential purposes, such as debt consolidation, or a college education.

HOME IMPROVEMENT LOAN: Essentially a second mortgage on a residence, the proceeds of which are used to remodel the home or to make major repairs.

HOME INSPECTOR: A licensed professional who checks a home for structural and mechanical defects, usually just prior to the sale of the home.

HOMEOWNERS' ASSOCIATION: See COMMUNITY ASSOCIATION

HOMEOWNERS' INSURANCE: An insurance policy designed to protect homeowners from theft, liability, and certain natural disasters.

HOMEOWNERS' WARRANTY PROGRAM: A private insurance program, generally funded by homebuilders, that protects buyers of newly constructed homes against built-in mechanical or structural defects.

HOMESTEAD EXEMPTION: A law exempting a homestead (real estate occupied by an owner as a house) from seizure or forced sale to meet general debts, excluding mortgages and tax liens. In certain states the law has been expanded to include exemption from some or all property taxes.

HOUSING CODE: An ordinance, promulgated by local governments, that establishes sanitation and structural standards for residences.

HUD: An agency of the federal government known officially as the Department of Housing and Urban Development. The Office of Interstate Land Sales Registration (OILSR) is a division of HUD.

IMPOUNDS: Funds or payments taken from a mortgagor and held by a lender or fiduciary for purposes of paying property taxes, assessments and insurance. This money can be withheld from mortgage payments to further protect the mortgagee against adverse claims and increased risk resulting from nonpayment of taxes or insurance.

IMPROVED LAND: Land on which construction or development work has been initiated or completed. The term can apply to land improved by roads, sewage and water lines, houses, shell cabins, and other buildings or outbuildings.

IMPROVEMENTS: Changes or additions to land or real property, such as sewers, fences, roads, etc., to make the property more valuable.

INCHOATE: Unfinished, not complete, as in certain dower rights that were not spelled out before the death of a spouse.

INCOME APPROACH: A method of real estate appraisal that bases the market value of a property on the property's expected income. According to the *income approach*, the market value of the property is the expected annual income divided by the capitalization rate.
Example: A shopping center is expected to produce $200,000 net operating income per year for the owners. By studying comparable properties, an appraiser determines that a reasonable capitalization rate for the shopping center is 8 percent. Thus, the market value of the property is $2.5 million ($200,000 net operating income divided by 8 percent, or 0.08.)

INCOME STREAM: The amount of money generated continually by a business or an investment.

INDEPENDENT CONTRACTOR: A self-employed person who sells his or her services for a set or negotiated fee

INFLATION: A general increase in the price of goods and services, often resulting in the loss in the purchasing power of money. Changes in the price of goods and services are measured by the consumer price index, which is monitored and published by the U.S. Bureau of Labor Statistics.

INFRASTRUCTURE: The basic framework and structural systems of a town or subdivision, including utilities and sewage disposal.

INGRESS: The right or permission to enter a given property; also, access to enter.

INHERITANCE TAX: A tax imposed by some states on the value of property an heir receives from a decedent.

INJUNCTION: A writ or order from a court prohibiting a person or group from carrying out a given action, or ordering a given action to be taken.

INSIDE LOT: In a development or subdivision, a lot that is landlocked, or surrounded by other lots.

INSTALLMENT NOTE: A debt instrument providing for payments at regular times over a specified period.

INSTITUTIONAL LENDERS: Financial organizations, such as banks and insurance companies, that make or invest in loans on behalf of their depositors or customers; earnings from those loans generally increase the pool of funds available for additional loans.

INTANGIBLE ASSETS: Nonphysical property that has measurable value, such as goodwill, mineral rights, partnership interests, or customer lists.

INTEREST: An amount, generally set by market variables, that a lender adds to a loan as compensation for the use of that lender's money.

INTEREST DEDUCTIONS: Certain types of interest, such as mortgage, investment, or business interest, that are tax deductible under circumstances specified by the Internal Revenue Code. (See your accountant or tax adviser.)

INTEREST-ONLY LOAN: A loan on which the borrower pays only the interest portion at regular intervals until the loan term expires, at which time the entire loan becomes fully due and payable.

INTEREST RATE: The portion, or percentage, of a loan that a lender charges the borrower for the use of the funds; also, the rate of return, or yield, on an investment.

INTERIM FINANCING: A temporary loan, usually for construction, that is to be repaid from the proceeds of a permanent loan.

INTERNAL REVENUE CODE: A federal law, overseen and enforced by the Internal Revenue Service, that specifies how income and assets are to be taxed, and what shelters and deductions are available.

INTERNATIONAL REAL ESTATE FEDERATION: A worldwide organization devoted to encouraging, sustaining, and protecting private property rights and ownership.

INTERSTATE LAND SALES ACT: A federal law requiring certain disclosures and advertising procedures for the sale of land to buyers in other states.

INTESTATE: A person's legal status when he has died without leaving a will or last testament.

INVENTORY: Property that is held for sale, or materials that are used in the manufacture of goods held for sale. For builders and developers, projects under construction and vacant lots are considered inventory. *Note:* Profits from the sale of inventory do not qualify for favorable capital gains tax treatment.

INVOLUNTARY LIEN: A lien, such as taxes, a special assessment, or a judgment, imposed upon a property without the owner's consent.

IRREVOCABLE: Cannot be canceled or revoked, as an *irrevocable* trust.

JOINT AND SEVERAL LIABILITY: In reference to multiple borrowers of a single loan, or multiple investors of a single property: a status by which all the borrowers or investors are responsible for repayment of the loan or claims against the property, not just his or her prorated share.

JOINT TENANCY: One of several forms of tenure in which two or more persons hold in concurrent ownership the same estate in realty or personalty and agree that upon the death of one joint tenant the full title to the estate remains in the surviving joint tenant(s) and finally in the last survivor.

JOINT VENTURE: An undertaking, such as an investment or property development, to which two or more persons or organizations agree to share the benefits and risks.

JUDGMENT LIEN: A lien on property resulting from a court decree in favor of a creditor.

JUNIOR MORTGAGE: A mortgage whose claim(s) against a property can be paid only after the claims of a prior, or senior, mortgage have been satisfied.

KICKBACK: A giving back of part of the money received as payment, commission, etc.

LABOR AND MATERIAL RELEASE: A written statement given to a developer by laborers and materialmen who agree to waive their rights under any mechanic's liens.

LAND BROKER: One who sells land and country properties.

LAND COST: The cost of land after deducting the estimated or real value of any buildings, appurtenances, and improvements; also, the cost of raw land, including recording fees, escrow costs, related interest, and property taxes prior to construction.

LAND DEVELOPMENT LOAN: A loan given to a developer to cover specified costs connected with land improvements. The loan is generally secured by a mortgage.

LAND LEASE: A lease that applies only to the portion of a property that is land, excluding any structure the lessee might build on the land.

LAND LOAN: A loan granted to the purchaser of raw land and secured by the property. Generally, this loan is paid off or subordinated by a construction loan.

LANDLOCKED: The condition of a piece of property whereby the property is surrounded by other parcels, with the only access to public thoroughfares being through adjacent properties.

LANDMARK: A fixed object used by surveyors to mark the boundary mark of a tract of land.

LAND SALES CONTRACT: A contract for the purchase of land on an installment basis, with the title remaining in the seller's possession until the purchase price of the land has been paid and the terms of the contract fulfilled.

LANDSCAPE ARCHITECT: A real estate development professional who specializes in the design of vegetation, infrastructure, and other site improvements.

LEACH FIELD: The ground area surrounding a septic system into which liquid waste passes before dissipating into the soil. Where drainage is not rapid, a series of ditches is dug to accept fluid through a fill of sand and stone.

LEASEHOLD: The interest that a tenant possesses in a property on which he or she is paying rent, and which the tenant might use as security to obtain a loan.

LEASE WITH OPTION TO PURCHASE: A lease that gives a tenant the right, though not the obligation, to eventually purchase the property at a specified price, typically in the form of a balloon payment at the expiration of the lease term.

LEGAL DESCRIPTION: The written legal representation of property that enables it to be located on approved recorded maps and government surveys.

LESSEE: Also referred to as a tenant, a person to whom property is rented under a lease.

LESSOR: Also referred to as a landlord, the person who rents property to another under a lease.

LETTER OF CREDIT: An arrangement, in the form of a signed document, by which a bank agrees to lend the strength of its own credit in support of a person's quest to purchase property from another private party.

LETTER OF INTENT: A letter from one party to another, that expresses a desire to enter into a contract with no obligation to do so.

LEVERAGE: A means of obtaining a potentially greater rate of return on capital investment through the use of borrowed funds. When purchasing real property, greater leverage is obtained when there is a low down payment relative to loan amount.

LEVY: An action taken to impose a charge or collect a debt.

LIABILITY: A debt, or exposure to loss.

LIABILITY INSURANCE: An insurance policy that protects a property owner from actions or lawsuits filed by persons who claim they were damaged or injured while perusing the owner's property.

LICENSED APPRAISER: An appraiser who has obtained a license for having met a particular state's requirements. *Note*: Licensure is a lesser credential than certification.

LIEN: A claim on the property of another for the payment of a just debt.

LIFE ESTATE: An estate of interest in property held only during or measured by the term of the life of a specified person.

LIKE-KIND PROPERTY: A term largely used to describe property that can be exchanged or traded to gain exemption from capital gains taxation. Like-kind property can include all real estate, except that owned by a dealer.

LIMITED PARTNERSHIP: An association of two or more persons in a business enterprise in which some partners' contributions and liabilities are limited.

LINE OF CREDIT: An arrangement whereby a borrower has access to a certain amount of funds at a financial institution, without the need to file a loan application each time the borrower draws from the funds.

LINK: One division (1/100) of a surveyor's chain, equal to 66/100 ft.

LINKAGE: A bondage between two or more land uses that spurs the movement of goods or people between them.

LINK FINANCING: Additional financing often obtained by borrowers when lenders require compensation balances in checking accounts. For example, if a bank insists on a compensation balance of $20,000 before granting a loan of $100,000, then the borrower might need link financing of $20,000 in order to obtain the loan.

LIQUIDATE: Generally, to dissolve a business by paying off all of its debt, and/or by selling its remaining assets for cash.

LIQUIDATED DAMAGES: A contract provision whereby one party agrees to pay a specified amount to the other party if the contract is breached (broken).

LIQUIDATION VALUE: The amount a property would currently bring if sold, less fees and transactions costs.

LIQUIDITY: The quality or state of possessing liquid assets; also, the ease and readiness with which assets can be converted to cash relative to the value of the investment.

LIS PENDENS: Notice that a suit is pending, and that, under law, a court located where the notice has been recorded will hear the case.

LISTING: An agreement, usually in writing, between a real estate broker and a client for the sale, lease, or rental of property. Authority is defined in the type of listing agreement, such as an exclusive right to sell or an exclusive agency. A listing can also authorize a broker to buy, lease, or locate property for a client.

LITTORAL: Refers to the portion of a property that contains the shore, or part of the shore, of a large body of water, such as an ocean or one of the Great Lakes.

LOAN COMMITMENT: The written promise from a lender to a borrower to grant a loan of a specified amount over a certain period at an agreed-upon interest rate. Often there is a charge by the lender for this commitment.

LOAN FEE: Often called points, this fee is a charge by the lender for making the loan and is generally used to compensate the lender for rising money costs. Generally, this charge is based on a percentage of the loan.

LOAN PACKAGE: The assembled documents, such as income verification, appraisals, etc., that relate to, and/or are required for, a loan application.

LOAN TO FACILITATE: In a general sense, this is a loan given a purchaser to facilitate the purchase of repossessed property held by the lender. A lending institution—not in the business of buying and selling property—will often grant very favorable terms to prospective buyers.

LOAN-TO-VALUE RATIO (LVR): The proportion of a mortgage loan relative to the appraised value of the property. For example, if a property is appraised at $80,000, and a loan of $60,000 is approved, then the LVR is 75 percent ($60,000/$80,000).

LOCK-IN PERIOD: A length of time during which prepayment on a note is not allowed by the lender. During this period, a borrower is prohibited from selling or otherwise transferring the property secured by the note.

LONG-TERM CAPITAL GAIN: For income tax purposes, the profit from a capital asset that is held long enough by the seller to qualify the gain for favorable tax treatment.

LOT: A distinct plot of ground.

LOT LINE: A property's boundary line, as defined by a survey.

M.A.I.: A designation used by appraisers who are members of the American Institute of Appraisers of the National Association of Real Estate Boards.

MAINTENANCE FEE: An assessment, typically levied annually by a homeowners' association, to fund the upkeep of common elements in a townhouse or condominium development.

MANAGEMENT FEE: A fee assessed by a professional manager who oversees property on a landlord's behalf; generally charged to the landlord as a percentage of rental income.

MANUFACTURED HOME: Typically, a home constructed in two or more sections, and transported to a homesite for installation.

MARGINAL LAND: Land of questionable use and/or value.

MARGINAL TAX BRACKET: A percentage of income, on a graduated scale, that a taxpayer is assessed, depending on the amount of his or her income. For example, a taxpayer's *marginal tax bracket* might increase from 28 percent to 36 percent as his or her income rises.

MARGIN OF SECURITY: The lender's margin between the amount he has loaned and the appraised value of the property.

MARITAL DEDUCTION: The amount, currently unlimited, that the first spouse to die may pass, by will, to the surviving spouse, free of federal estate tax.

MARKET ANALYSIS: A study designed to predict changes in the types and amounts of real estate facilities needed within a given community or area. For example, a market analysis for a condominium development would include information on the number of existing units, the demand for condominiums (present and future), and pricing factors.

MARKET PRICE: The amount received by a seller for his property regardless of outside pressures and influences.

MARKETABILITY STUDY: An analysis of how well a particular type of real estate will sell in the general market.

MARKETABLE TITLE: A title, free and clear of all liens and encumbrances, that can be readily transferred.

MARKET AREA: A geographic region from which a developer can expect the primary demand for his or her particular real estate product.

MARKET COMPARISON APPROACH: A method of appraisal by which the sale price of a particular property is determined by analyzing the prices of similar properties ("comparables") that have been sold within a specific geographic area surrounding the property in question, and within a specific time frame.
Example: The property in question is a residence of 2,150 square feet, with four bedrooms and three baths. Two similar properties within the specified geographic area have been sold recently. One home, of 2,000 square feet, with four bedrooms, but only two-and-a-half baths, sold for $175,000. The other, of 2,150 square feet, with five bedrooms and three baths, sold for $183,000. For the property in question, the appraiser makes adjustments for the additional bathroom space, less bedroom space, as well as room size, etc., and values the home at $179,000.

MARKET INDICATORS: Data that show leasing, sales, and development or construction activity within a certain market area; data might include the number of building permits issued, and the rise and fall of lease and/or rental rates.

MARKET VALUE: A theoretical calculation that combines the highest price a buyer would be willing to pay for, and the lowest price at which a seller would be willing to sell, a particular piece of real estate.

MATERIAL PARTICIPATION: For income tax purposes, a term that refers to the level of an owner's or investor's participation, or involvement, in the operation of his or her trade, business, or rental property, and that determines the type and amount of business deductions the owner or investor may claim on his or her return. (See your tax adviser for the ways in which material participation may apply to farmers and/or limited partners.)

MATURITY: The due date of a loan.

MARSHLAND: A tract of soft, wet land usually treeless and characterized by grasses and cattails.

MASTER PLAN: A basic comprehensive plan for dealing with the effects on a community of social and economic change. Incorporated in the plan are ways and means of adjusting to changing situations.

MECHANIC'S LIEN: A legal encumbrance against a property, generally filed by trades-people who have not been paid for their work in making improvements to the property. The lien(s) must be satisfied before the owner/builder/developer can obtain clear title to the property.

METES AND BOUNDS: A method of legally describing the boundaries of land by direction and distances.

METROPOLITAN STATISTICAL AREA (MSA): A county or region having a population of at least 50,000, which serves as a study area for the purpose of compiling demographic data.

MINERAL RIGHTS: The legal right or title to all or to specified minerals in a given tract; also, the right to explore for and extract such minerals or to receive a royalty for them.

MINGLING OF FUNDS (often referred to as "co-mingling"): The illegal mixing of a client's money with personal funds. In real estate, this can occur when a broker deposits, or transfers to his own account from escrow, any or all funds entrusted to him by his clients. Lawyers, too, are in a position to mingle funds.

MINIMUM LOT AREA: The smallest lot allowed by local ordinance in a subdivision.

MISREPRESENTATION: An untrue statement or presentment, not necessarily intentional, which gives a prospective customer or investor a false or skewed impression of the product or investment opportunity, and which renders the presenter liable for damages, regardless of intent.

MOBILE HOME: A large trailer outfitted as a home meant to be parked more or less permanently at a location.

MODIFIED ACCELERATED COST RECOVERY SYSTEM (MACRS): One of several methods of depreciation for the purpose of calculating income tax deductions. (See your accountant or tax adviser.)

MODULAR HOUSING: *See* MANUFACTURED HOME.

MOISTURE BARRIER: A layer of natural or synthetic material, such as plastic or industrial paper, that is used in the construction of building exteriors to prevent moisture from penetrating base wood or insulation.

MONUMENT: *See* LANDMARK.

MORATORIUM: A time period during which certain activity, such as the building or development of certain types of real estate, is not permitted; generally imposed by local governmental authorities, such as zoning commissions.

MORTGAGE: The pledge of real property to a creditor as security for a debt or obligation.

MORTGAGE BANKER: A person or firm in the business of making mortgage loans, frequently with the intent of selling the loans to institutional lenders, but often receiving the right to service the mortgages for a fee.

MORTGAGE BROKER: A firm or individual acting as a middleman between the borrower and lender and who receives a fee for his services.

MORTGAGE COMMITMENT: *See* LOAN COMMITMENT.

MORTGAGEE: The person or party to whom a mortgage is given; the lender.

MORTGAGE GUARANTEE INSURANCE CO. (MGIC): A private organization that insures payment of mortgage obligations in the event of default or foreclosure; generally funded by the borrower in the form of mortgage insurance, the premiums of which are usually part of the monthly mortgage payment.

MORTGAGE INSURANCE: Insurance obtained by or on behalf of the lender to protect him against financial loss in the event of default.

MORTGAGE POOL: A package of loans, of similar terms and interest rates, which is sold to investors on the secondary market in order to sustain the nationwide flow of mortgage funds.

MORTGAGE RELIEF: An action that frees a borrower from mortgage debt, most often through the assumption of, or the taking over of, the mortgage by another party, or by retiring the debt. *Note:* Mortgage relief received as part of a Section 1031 tax-deferred exchange might be subject to immediate capital gains tax. See your tax adviser.

MORTGAGOR: The person or party giving the mortgage; the borrower

MULTIPLE LISTING: A written agreement (usually an exclusive right to sell), between a real estate broker and client, which has been placed in a pool of listings maintained by an organization to which the listing broker belongs.

MULTIPLIER: A factor that multiplies a specified financial element of a property, thereby determining the property's immediate sale value.

Example: A market study has determined that a reasonable gross rent *multiplier* is a factor of ten. Thus, a country getaway that rents for $1,200 a year has a current sale value of $120,000 ($1,200 multiplied by 10.)

MUTUAL SAVINGS BANKS: State-chartered banks that are owned by their depositors, and operated for the depositors' benefit; generally, the banks' primary product is home mortgages.

NATIONAL ASSOCIATION OF HOMEBUILDERS (NAHB): A trade association that provides information and research services to a nationwide membership of homebuilders, and that lobbies before Congress on behalf of the homebuilding industry.

NATIONAL ASSOCIATION OF REALTORS (NAR): A trade association, composed of a nationwide membership of Realtors, that promulgates standards for, and lobbies on behalf of, the real estate industry.

NATIONAL PARK OR FOREST: An area of special scenic, historic, scientific, or recreational importance set aside and maintained by a national government. As a rule, hunting and the harvesting of timber is not allowed in national parks, but can be permitted in national forests.

NATIONAL SOCIETY OF REAL ESTATE APPRAISERS: A trade organization through which appraisers receive national certification, and other professional designations.

NEGATIVE CASH FLOW: A financial situation in income-producing properties when outgo exceeds income.

NEGOTIABLE INSTRUMENT: A written promise to pay money; generally transferable.

NET INCOME: The amount of income remaining after taxes and expenses.

NET OPERATING INCOME: The amount of income remaining after operating expenses, but before income taxes and debt service.

NET PRESENT VALUE: The current value of the return that one can reasonably expect on a proposed investment; essentially, a calculation by which an investor can determine today whether a future return will be adequate.

NET LEASE: A lease under which the tenant assumes only partial responsibility for direct expenses such as taxes, insurance, and maintenance. Under a "net-net lease," these additional expenses are customarily paid by the lessee. A "net-net-net lease," also known as a triple-net lease, implies that all expenses connected with the rental property are paid by the lessee.

NET LISTING: An agreement between a seller and his broker/agent that the agent may keep as his commission all monies obtained for the seller over and above the agreed-upon asking price.

NET WORTH: The excess of assets over liabilities.

NET YIELD: The return on investment after expenses.

NO BID: An action by which the Bureau of Veterans Affairs, in the case of a defaulted VA loan, pays the lender the amount of the guarantee instead of taking possession of the property in a foreclosure.

NONCONFORMING LOAN: Generally, a mortgage loan that is too large to be purchased by the secondary market agencies (FNMA or FHLMC), and thus carries an interest rate that is higher than the rate for conforming loans.

NONCONFORMING USE: A particular use of property that is prohibited by local ordinance, but is allowed to continue because the use existed before the restriction was enacted.

NONRECOURSE NOTE: A note, signed by the debtor, by which the debtor carries no personal responsibility in the event of default. When the note is secured by real estate, the property becomes the sole security for the debt. See EXCULPATORY CLAUSE.

NOTARY PUBLIC: One who is authorized by the state to affirm, by official seal, certain legal documents, such as deeds, contracts, and affidavits.

NOTE: A written promise to pay a certain sum of money to a certain person or bearer on demand or on a specified date. Also called a promissory note, the instrument can provide for installment payments, and it customarily calls for a specified rate of interest.

NOTE PROCEEDS: A term primarily taken to mean the sum of money left over after a note is discounted.

NOTICE OF COMPLETION: Notification to the builder that construction is compete. This notice is recorded, and any mechanic's liens must be filed within a prescribed period thereafter, generally 30 to 60 days.

NOTICE OF DEFAULT: Recorded notification that a default has occurred in a mortgage or deed of trust. See FORECLOSURE.

NOTICE OF NONRESPONSIBILITY: Notification by an owner that he is not responsible for any debts owed to contractors and materialmen and that his property is thereby relieved of any mechanic's liens. If all other legal conditions are met, the property owner posts this notice on his property and records it in the county where his land is located.

NOTICE TO QUIT: An eviction notice given by a landlord or his agent.

NUISANCE: A land use that is not compatible with the uses of surrounding properties. Examples are private landfills, factories that emit noxious fumes, or businesses that produce inordinate traffic congestion.

NULL AND VOID: A contract, or a provision of a contract, that cannot be enforced because it does not conform with established law, regardless of prior agreement of the parties to the contract.

OBSOLESCENCE: Loss of value and usefulness due to economic and functional change, but not attributed to deterioration.

OFFSITE COSTS: Those raw land improvement costs not directly related to building construction; specifically, roads, curbs, gutters, sidewalks, etc. In the sales and marketing of improved or unimproved lots, the term can be applied to those costs not incurred on or at the development itself.

OILSR (OFFICE OF INTERSTATE LAND SALES REGISTRATION): A division of the U.S. Department of Housing and Urban Development (HUD).

OIL AND GAS LEASE. An agreement that assigns a right to explore for, extract, and retain royalties from, oil and gas on a particular property. See MINERAL RIGHTS

ONSITE COSTS: Generally meant to include those costs directly related to the construction of a building or buildings on raw land. In the development and sale of improved or unimproved lots, these costs can mean any and all expenses incurred on or at the development site.

OPEN-END LOAN: A secured loan that provides for the borrower to obtain additional sums of money at various times, thus allowing a continuous source of credit.

OPEN-END MORTGAGE: A mortgage or trust deed under which the borrower can increase or renew his debt at various times, with the property standing as security against the outstanding obligation.

OPEN HOUSING: A condition, required by federal and most state laws, by which housing may be sold or rented regardless of a prospective customer's race, creed, color, gender, or ethnic origin.

OPEN LISTING: An agreement between a real estate broker and a client giving the broker a nonexclusive right to sell the listed property. Any number of open listings may be given out, but only the procuring broker is entitled to a commission.

OPEN SPACE: Often referred to as green space, a specified amount of land within a real estate project that is left undeveloped as an attraction to owners and prospective buyers.

OPERATING EXPENSES: Certain costs, such as property taxes, maintenance, and management fees, associated with maintaining property; such expenses do not include debt, depreciation, or income taxes.

O.P.M.: An acronym for "other people's money."

OPTION: The right, acquired for a consideration, to buy, sell, or lease something at a fixed price; also, the right to sign or renew a contract within a specified time.

OPTION LISTING: A listing agreement in which the broker reserves an option to buy the property.

ORAL CONTRACT: An unwritten agreement; in real estate, unenforceable in most states.

ORDINANCE: A local governmental statute or regulation, such as a zoning ordinance.

ORDINARY INCOME: Personal income subject to federal taxation at the regular rate; examples are salaries, professional fees, commissions, rents, royalties, interest, wages, and dividends not considered capital gains.

ORDINARY LOSS: For tax purposes, a loss that is deductible against ordinary income, such as wages and dividends.

OVERRIDE: A fee, typically a percentage of a sales commission, that often is paid to the supervisor or manager of the person who earned the commission.

OWNERSHIP FORM: A legal entity through which real estate or a business is owned, the structure of which has significant effect on taxation, liability, rights of survivorship, etc. Examples include corporation, partnership, and variations of tenancy.

PACKAGING: The arranging for or actual performance of certain activities required to get a development off the ground. A packager will arrange for, coordinate, or handle such diverse activities as market research, land evaluation and acquisition, project design and concept, architecture, engineering, zoning, and securing financing.

PAPER PROFIT: Assuming that a particular property is not for sale, an increase in the value of the property that would be realized, if the property were sold.

PARTIAL RELEASE: A provision in a mortgage contract, which can be amended to the contract at any time during the term of the loan, that releases part of the property from its use as collateral for the loan.

PARTITION: The legal process of dividing property and giving separate title to those who previously had joint or common title.

PARTNERSHIP: An agreement between or among persons or entities to make an investment or to form a business together. Partners share varying degrees of liability; income and deductions flow through the partnership to each partner's individual tax return.

PASSIVE ACTIVITY INCOME: Income that is generated from a trade or business in which the owner or investor does not have a level of involvement that is set by law (see MATERIAL PARTICIPATION); also, any rental income. (See your accountant or tax adviser.)

PASSIVE INVESTOR: Often referred to as a silent partner, one who invests money in a business or real estate enterprise, but who takes no management role.

PATENT: Title to public land granted by the U.S. government to an individual or group.

PERCENTAGE LEASE: A lease by which rent is based on the amount of business conducted by the lessee. The lease is usually structured to allow for a minimum rental fee against a percentage of gross business.

PERCOLATION (PERK) TEST: A test of soil conditions, sanctioned or performed by local health authorities, to determine if the ground will readily accept and dissipate the liquid wastes from a septic system. Holes are dug at various spots and filled with water. If the rate of absorption is satisfactory, the test is generally considered positive.

PERFORMANCE BOND: Insurance, generally required by a client, that a contractor performs as agreed under the terms of his contract. Municipal authorities usually require such a bond before contracting for public construction.

PERSONAL PROPERTY: Any property that is not considered real estate, or "real" property.

PLANNING COMMISSION: A group of people, generally appointed by elected officials, who are responsible under state or local law for the preparation and adoption of measures dealing with the orderly development of land within the commission's jurisdiction. The ultimate objective of this group is a comprehensive, long-term growth plan that will be sanctioned by local elected officials, as representatives of the public will.

PLAT: A map or plan (usually a survey) of a piece of land showing divisions (into lots), property lines, easements,. etc., and entered into the public records, as for a subdivision.

POINTS: A term describing a loan fee. Each point represents one percent of the loan amount. *See* DISCOUNT POINTS

POPULATION DENSITY: A term relating to the average number of permanent residents within a given area, such as per square mile.

POTABLE WATER: Water that is fit to drink.

POWER OF ATTORNEY: A written statement authorizing another person to act on one's behalf. The person using this statement is customarily called an "attorney-in-fact."

PRELIMINARY PLAT: A tentative map of a subdivision submitted by a developer to local elected and planning officials for study and approval. Often the planning officials must approve the plat before it can be submitted to local governing officials, such as a county board of supervisors. The submission of a final plat follows this first approval.

PREMIUM: In land development, a reward or prize often given to prospective buyers for visiting and touring a project.

PREPAYMENT CLAUSE: A provision in a loan contract that allows the borrower to prepay on the debt under certain conditions. If this clause is described as a "prepayment privilege," then there is no penalty for early payments. Should the contract contain a "prepayment penalty," the borrower must pay a fee (usually expressed as a percentage of the debt) for the right to prepay.

PRESCRIPTION: The acquisition of the title or right to something through its continued use or possession over a long period, as with a prescriptive right-of-way.

PRESERVATION DISTRICT: A historic, scenic, or particularly sensitive environmental area set aside by local ordinance or state regulation in order to restrict development within the district, and to minimize changes to the aesthetics of buildings and sites within the area.

PRIMARY FINANCING: A loan on real property secured by a first mortgage or deed of trust.

PRIMARY METROPOLITAN STATISTICAL AREA (PMSA): A sizable area or community that is linked to other communities of similar size within a larger metropolitan area.

PRIMARY MORTGAGE MARKET: A collective term referring to banks, savings and loan associations, and other lending institutions that originate mortgage loans directly to home buyers.

PRIME RATE: The interest rate charged by commercial banks to their prime, or most valued, borrowers.

PRINCIPAL: A person who employs another to act as his agent; also, the capital amount of a loan or investment.

PRINCIPAL AND INTEREST PAYMENT (P&I): The combined periodic (monthly) payment on a mortgage, composed of the amount of interest charged by the lender, and the principal, which is the portion of the payment that actually reduces the amount of debt outstanding.

PRINCIPAL BROKER: The licensed broker in charge of a brokerage firm.

PRINCIPAL, INTEREST, TAXES, AND INSURANCE PAYMENT (PITI): Typically, the total periodic (monthly) payment on a mortgage, composed of the amount of interest charged by the lender; the principal, which is the portion of the payment that amortizes, or pays down, the debt; property taxes, which are paid in advance and escrowed on an annualized basis; and mortgage insurance, which can be required by the lender, depending on the creditworthiness of the borrower, and/or the size of down payment the borrower provides.

PRINCIPAL RESIDENCE: The home in which one lives most of the time. Compare with a vacation property or "second" home, where one might live for only a few weeks or months during the year.

PROCURING CAUSE OF SALE: Where two or more brokers have shown the same property to a buyer, and they both have valid listing agreements, the first broker is generally considered to be the procuring cause of sale, though the commission may be split between them.

PRO FORMA STATEMENT: A financial statement prepared by a broker or lender to show projected results, such as the performance of a proposed loan contract, or the cash flow anticipated from a real estate development.

PROMISSORY NOTE: *See* NOTE.

PROPERTY REPORT: Data and analysis required by the federal government (specifically, the Interstate Land Sale Act) for the sale of large subdivisions containing lots that are sold across state lines. For exemptions, check with the Office of Land Sale Registration (OILSR) at the U.S. Department of Housing and Urban Development, 451 Seventh St. SW, Washington, D.C., 20410.

PROPERTY TAX: A tax, generally imposed by state and/or local governments, based on the market value of privately owned real or personal property.

PROPRIETORSHIP: Also referred to as "sole proprietorship," the ownership of a business or income-producing real estate by one person under a form, or structure, in which all of the owner's personal assets are at risk, unless otherwise protected by law.

PRO RATA: The distribution of income or gain, typically to owners or investors, that is based on the portion of the business or investment that each partner or investor owns.

PRORATED EXPENSES: Those expenses such as property taxes and interest that are divided among buyer and seller and based on the actual closing date of the sale.

PROXY: A person who represents, or votes on behalf of, another, as in a meeting of a company's shareholders.

PUBLIC HOUSING: Government-owned housing made available to persons of low income at no or minimal cost.

PUBLIC LANDS: Government-owned property that is set aside for conservation and/or public enjoyment.

PUBLIC REPORT: A report issued by a state agency concerned with subdivision control.

Before the sale of lots can commence, some states require designated agencies to check the subdivision's compliance with existing law, and to report any shortcomings. A report to the public is issued when this authority is assured that the developer has installed promised improvements and facilities, or that he has made satisfactory financial arrangements for their completion. An additional concern is that property owners are protected, or made aware of their positions with respect to potential default or bankruptcy on the part of the developer.

PUBLIC SALE: An auction of property to the general public.

PUD: Planned unit development.

PURCHASE MONEY MORTGAGE: Essentially this is a mortgage or trust deed given by the purchaser to the seller to secure the full purchase price of the property. In the event of default, the seller can, in some states, seek a deficiency judgment against the purchaser if the property does not bring the amount owed at a foreclosure sale.

QUIET TITLE: A court action used to clear an impaired title or to establish title.

QUITCLAIM DEED: A deed or other legal paper in which a person relinquishes to another a claim or title to some property or right without guaranteeing or warranting such title.

RADON: A potentially cancer-causing gas, forming naturally in the air, that can be trapped inside homes and other buildings, and can pollute interior air and water. Many local jurisdictions require periodic radon tests; foundation-to-rooftop ventilation is recommended.

RAW LAND: Generally, land that has not been improved by any structure or other work such as roads, sewers, etc.

REAL ESTATE: Land, including any buildings and improvements on it and its natural assets such as minerals, water, etc.

REAL ESTATE INVESTMENT TRUST (REIT): A method of holding real estate in trust form, by which investors can enjoy limited liability similar to a corporation. Once it has met Internal Revenue requirements, a REIT has the ability to pass profits to its investors, free of corporate taxes. A minimum number of shareholders must participate in its formation, and most of its capital must be invested in real estate loans and properties, with a substantial part of its income earned from such real estate investments.

REAL ESTATE OWNED (REO): Property a lending institution acquires through foreclosure and holds in its own portfolio—thus, the term *owned* (by the lender).

REAL ESTATE SETTLEMENT PROCEDURES ACT (RESPA): A federal law that governs mortgage lenders' activities and procedures when considering applicants for federally backed loans to finance the purchase of homes with one to four dwelling units. *Note:* Lenders generally provide RESPA information to borrowers shortly after loan applications are filed.

REALIZED GAIN: In a Section 1031 tax-deferred exchange, a profit that might be earned by either or all parties to the exchange, but is not necessarily taxed. *See* BOOT.

REAL PROPERTY: The interests, benefits, and rights that one has in the ownership of real estate, as opposed to personal property. It is the package of rights that confers ownership.

REALTOR: A real estate broker, salesperson, appraiser, etc., who is a member of the National Association of Real Estate Boards.

REASSESSMENT: A procedure employed periodically by local government authorities to review and update property values within a particular jurisdiction for property tax purposes.

REBATE: A return of part of an amount paid (as for goods and services) that serves as a reduction or discount.

RECESSION: A general economic slowdown, often accompanied by low interest rates, which, ironically, tend to boost the real estate industry.

RECIPROCITY: In real estate, an agreement between or among states that one state will honor real estate licenses earned in the other state(s).

RECOGNIZED GAIN: In a Section 1031 tax-deferred exchange, the portion of profit, or *gain*, that is taxable

RECONVEYANCE: The release of specific property from the lien on a mortgage or deed of trust through a deed granted by the mortgagee or trustee of a deed of trust.

RECORDING FEE: A fee charged by counties for entering legal instruments or documents, such as a mortgage or deed, into the public records.

RECOURSE NOTE: A note, signed by the debtor, that carries personal responsibility

beyond the repossession of security or collateral in the event of default. *See* NONRECOURSE NOTE.

RECOVERY FUND: A central pool of money, funded by licensed real estate brokers and overseen by the local real estate commission, that is available to customers who are unable to collect damages from brokers for wrongdoing during a particular real estate transaction..

RECREATIONAL PROPERTY: In land development, a term used to describe property used primarily for camping and secondary-home construction; also, any parcel of real estate mainly utilized by the owner on weekends and vacations.

REDEMPTION: *See* EQUITY OF REDEMPTION.

REDLINING: A practice, banned by federal law, by which lenders designate certain sections of communities in which they will not make mortgage loans. Redlining causes real estate devaluation and was once was common in areas of high minority populations.

REFERRAL: In real estate sales, a potential buyer who is directed by an existing-property owner to a sales agent.

REFORMATION: The act of correcting mistakes and defects in a deed or document.

REFUNDABLE UTILITY CONTRACT: A written agreement between a developer and a utility company in which the utility company promises to reimburse the developer for the installation of utility extensions such as water, gas, and electric lines. Costs are generally returned from revenues received from the new users.

REGRESSION: In real estate, a term or principle alluding to the decrease in value of certain homes in a particular neighborhood caused by the expected construction or condition of inferior dwellings in that same area. Thus, regression connotes diminished value through anticipated disadvantages, such as a planned low-cost housing development in an area of high-priced homes.

REGULATION Z: A federal regulation that requires lenders to disclose to borrowers, in detail, the terms of the loan, including a precise accounting of the portion of the loan that is principal, the portion that is interest, and the loan's annual percentage rate (APR).

REGULATORY TAKING: Generally refers to the desultory effects on property of gov-

530

ernment regulations, such as highly restrictive zoning ordinances that might have a chilling effect on an area's economic development.

REHABILITATION TAX CREDIT: A federal tax credit that is available to builders and developers for refurbishing historically significant properties according to local and/or regional restoration guidelines; a lesser credit is available for the restoration of buildings constructed after 1936. (See your tax adviser.)

RELEASE CLAUSE: A provision in a deed that allows for divisions or lots to be released from the blanket lien upon payment to the lienholder of a specified amount.

RELICTION: The gradual receding of waters, leaving dry land.

REMAINDER: An estate of expectancy but not in possession, as when land is conveyed by the same deed to one person during his lifetime, and at his death to another and his heirs.

REMAINDERMAN: The person who inherits the remainder estate.

REMEDIATION: The cleanup of contaminated property.

REPLACEMENT COST: The cost of constructing a building to replace, and that performs the same function of, a previous structure; typically considered when a previous structure has been destroyed by fire or other natural cause.

REPRODUCTION COST: The cost of reproducing, or duplicating, a previous structure.

RESALE PRICE: The projected price that certain real estate will bring if sold at the end of a certain period of time.

RESERVE PRICE: A minimum sale price, or bid, for a property at auction.

RESCISSION: To revoke, repeal, or cancel, as with a contract to purchase real estate.

RESTRICTIVE COVENANT: A provision in a deed that limits the use and occupancy of real property. Any such provision is binding on subsequent owners of the property.

RETENTIONS: Money held back, either by contractors or by persons receiving services, from billings or invoices during the construction phase to ensure satisfactory completion of the work.

REVENUE STAMPS: Stamps that are affixed to deeds or other real estate documents indicating that the transfer tax has been paid.

REVERSE ANNUITY MORTGAGE: A type of mortgage by which a lender essentially takes back the equity a borrower has built up in a residence, then remits a monthly income to the borrower based on that equity; often used by elderly persons who have paid off, or substantially paid down, the mortgages on their homes.

REVERSE EXCHANGE: A transaction in which a participant in a Section 1031 tax-deferred exchange receives property from a third party before he (the Section 1031 participant) surrenders his own property in the tax-deferred exchange. (For income tax consequences, see your tax adviser.)

REVERSION: The right of succession, future possession, or enjoyment, as the return of an estate to the grantor and his heirs by operation of law after the period of grant is over.

REVOCATION: The act of canceling a legally sanctioned power or authority, as in revoking a power of attorney.

RIGHT OF FIRST REFUSAL: The opportunity offered to a favored party (customer, client, et. al.) to purchase a property or service, or to enter a contract, before the property or contract is offered to other prospective clients or investors.

RIGHT-OF-WAY: The right, established by common or statutory law, of ingress and/or egress over another's property; also, a strip of land set aside for utility easements, railroads, and public roads.

RIPARIAN RIGHTS: Generally, the right of a property owner to use water that is on, under, or adjacent to his or her land. These rights can be limited based on potential pollution of the water in question, or on the possibility of nuisance to other qualified users. In the western United States, these rights generally are referred to as USUFRUCTUARY RIGHTS.

ROAD GRADE: The degree of rise and descent of a road surface.

ROD: A linear unit of measurement equal to 16-1/2 feet.

ROLLOVER LOAN: A type of mortgage in which the interest rate on the loan is short term—that is, less than the term of the loan—while the principal is set for a longer term. At the end of the shorter term, the loan may be extended, or rolled over, at the current market interest rate (which might be higher than the initial rate on the loan).

RULE OF 72: The approximate time it takes for the principal of an investment to double at compound interest, based on a factor of 72. *Example:* $100,000 in interest-bearing notes earning 8 percent compound interest will double to $200,000 in about nine years (72 divided by 8 percent equals 9 years.)

RUN WITH THE LAND: A right or restriction that applies to all current and future owners of a property; that is, the right or restriction does not expire, as does a deed, when the property is sold or transferred.

SALE-LEASEBACK: The sale of property and subsequent leasing back to the seller by the purchaser.

SALVAGE VALUE: The estimated value of an asset at the end of its useful life. *Note:* Salvage value, generally determined by an appraiser, must be subtracted from the amount that is applied to depreciation deductions. (See your accountant or tax adviser.)

SCENIC EASEMENT: An easement sold or granted by a property owner to a governmental authority or nonprofit organization wherein the owner restricts the use of all or part of his property in favor of preserving the scenic and natural beauty. Generally, the owner agrees not to sell to development interests or to develop his property in a way that would conflict with the true intent of the easement.

SECONDARY FINANCING: A real estate loan that is subordinate to the first mortgage or deed of trust. *See* JUNIOR MORTGAGE.

SECTION 1031: *See* EXCHANGE, TAX-DEFERRED.

SECTION 1034: The section of the Internal Revenue Code that applies to the sale of personal residences. (See your accountant or tax adviser.)

SECTION 1221: The section of the Internal Revenue Code that defines a capital asset, essentially by specifying what types of assets are excluded, such as mortgages, inventory, raw land, etc. (See your tax adviser.)

SECTION 1231: The section of the Internal Revenue Code that defines assets used in a trade or business, such as vehicles, machinery, etc., and that defines the tax treatment of such assets when they are sold. In many cases, profits from the sale of such assets are taxed at favorable capital gains rates, while losses can be deducted against ordinary income, such as wages. (See your tax adviser.)

SECTION 1245: The section of the Internal Revenue Code that specifies how depreciation already claimed on personal property is accounted for when the property is sold. (Generally, such depreciation deductions are recaptured, or added back to the value of the property, thus reducing the amount of profit that is eligible for favorable capital gains tax treatment. See your accountant or tax adviser.)

SECTION 1250: The section of the Internal Revenue Code that applies to gains from the sale of real estate on which accelerated depreciation, as opposed to general depreciation, had been claimed. (See your accountant or tax adviser.)

SECTION OF LAND: A 640-acre parcel of land comprising one square mile.

SECURED PARTY: Any party possessing secured evidence of debt. Thus, a mortgagee could be considered a secured party, as could a conditional seller or a pledgee.

SECURITIZATION: The process of packaging, or "bundling," assets, such as mortgages, for sale as securities to investors in the capital markets.

SECURITY INTEREST: A specified interest, such as a real estate lien, when such real estate serves as collateral for a loan. *Note*: Lenders generally have a *security interest* in mortgaged property,

SEIZIN: Legal possession, especially of a freehold estate.

SELF-AMORTIZING MORTGAGE: A mortgage that is paid off by regular principal and interest installments as provided in the loan contract.

SELLER FINANCING: Refers to the financing of a property by the seller of the property, generally offered and/or employed when a prospective buyer cannot obtain conventional financing from a bank; also offered when the buyer assumes, or takes over, the seller's mortgage payments, but cannot supply the difference between the outstanding debt and the sale price of the property.

SEPTIC SYSTEM: In-ground sewage disposal system consisting of a buried concrete tank to collect solid wastes and attached by piping to a concrete distribution box from which liquid waste is funneled through pipes into excavated drain fields, where the absorption of liquid waste occurs. Perforated pipe, surrounded by gravel and connected to solid piping from the distribution box and septic tank, is laid in trenches of specific depth, length, width, and number, this mainly dependent on the size of the building(s) being serviced by the system. When full, the tank is pumped out by a service truck.

SETBACK LINES: The prescribed distance that a building must be set back in relation to the perimeter of the property.

SHERIFF'S DEED: A deed given to a purchaser who buys at a court-ordered foreclosure sale to satisfy a judgment. At best, the grantee receives only such title as the mortgagor had at the time he originally made the obligation.

SHORT-TERM CAPITAL GAIN: Profit on the sale of a capital asset that was held for less than one year; such profit generally does not qualify for favorable capital gains tax rates and is taxed as ordinary income. (See your tax adviser.)

SIGNATURE CAPITAL: Money invested in a business venture for which the only collateral was a written promise to repay the loan.

SIMPLE INTEREST: Interest that is charged only once, against the principal of the loan; that amount is then divided into equal monthly installments for the purpose of retiring the debt. Compare with compound interest, which is added each month to the amount of debt outstanding.
Example: You accept a second deed of trust on a lot of $1,000 paying 10% simple interest over 3 years. Using the following formula you will gain $300 on simple interest: Interest = principal x rate x time

SITE: Generally, a parcel of land suitable for building that fronts on a road and has access to utilities.

SITE ASSESSMENT (ENVIRONMENTAL): An evaluation of a property for the presence of hazardous waste; generally conducted just before the property is sold. *Note:* Responsibility for hazardous waste on the property transfers to the buyer, though there is some legal recourse if the buyer can demonstrate that he or she conducted a proper evaluation—even though such evaluation might not have detected the hazardous substance.

SITE PLAN: A document, generally filed by a builder or developer with local planning and zoning authorities, that specifies how a piece of property is to be improved.

SOFT MONEY: Prepaid interest, forfeitable option money, and the interest portion of an installment debt; generally, any money that does not improve the equity position of the payor.

SOIL MAP: A map describing the soils within a given area, with specific emphasis on their suitability for crops, building construction, and sewage disposal.

SPEC HOUSE: A single-family home that is built on "spec," or "speculation," in anticipation of a buyer coming to the fore.

SPECIAL ASSESSMENT: A charge against real property by a public or quasi-public authority to cover the proportionate share of improvements such as streets and sewer lines. These fees can be imposed by law or covenant.

SPECIAL USE PROPERTY: A property, such as a church or a theater, that has limited use, as well as limited sale value.

SPECIFIC PERFORMANCE: The exact performance of a contract, or a court order enjoining such performance.

SPOT ZONING: The rezoning of a parcel or an area for a use that is radically different from, or incompatible with, the uses of the surrounding properties.

SQUATTERS RIGHTS: As provided by law, the right of one person to use another's property, such rights being established if the property owner fails to take action against the squatter within a specified period of time.

STAGNANT WATER: Water that has become foul from lack of movement.

STANDBY COMMITMENT: A promise from a lender to make a temporary loan to a borrower if he cannot obtain an immediate permanent loan or other satisfactory financing. There is a charge for the commitment, usually based on a percentage of the loan.

STAR ROUTE: Postal route between one city or town and another over which mail is transported in bulk by a private carrier under contract.

START-UP COSTS: Those costs—usually nonrecurring—connected with getting a project underway.

STATUTE OF LIMITATIONS: A statute limiting the period within which a specific legal action may be taken. Title to real estate by adverse possession is gained under this statute.

STATUTORY DEDICATION: The process by which a builder, developer, and/or owner of a subdivision cedes part of the property for the purpose of constructing and/or installing roads, utility connections, etc.

STEPPED-UP BASIS: Additional basis, or equity, in a property that is gained by certain holders of the property under certain circumstances, such as inheritance.

STRAIGHT-LINE DEPRECIATION: For tax purposes, equal yearly reductions in the book value of a property.

SUBAGENCY: A relationship between or among brokers by which one agent sells a property that is listed with another agent. This arrangement generally results in the agents sharing the sales commission.

SUBDIVIDER: One who divides a tract of land into smaller parcels, which that person then sells.

SUBDIVISION: A piece of land divided into smaller parcels for sale.

SUBJECT TO MORTGAGE: A term used to describe the assumption of a title to real estate without any obligation to the holder of the promissory note. In the event of foreclosure, the grantee loses only that amount he has paid in. The original maker of the note is held responsible for the balance due on the mortgage.

SUBLEASE: A lease granted by a lessee to another person for all or part of the property.

SUBMERSIBLE PUMP: An electrically operated pump installed near the bottom of a well for purposes of pumping water to ground level, often into a pressure tank from which the flow is controlled and regulated.

SUBORDINATION: The act of relinquishing a prior position on a mortgage or deed of trust, often in return for compensation or other favors. For example, the holder of a first mortgage may agree to take second position in a refinancing if he can retain a certain favorable rate of interest.

SUBROGATION: The substitution of one creditor for another, along with a transference of the claims and rights of the old creditor.

SULFUR WATER: In some areas of the country, well water may produce an odor and taste resembling sulfur. Though there is generally no health hazard, this condition can usually be corrected through the use of a filter.

SUMP PUMP: A pump used to remove collected liquid from a pit, trench, or cellar.

SUPERFUND: Common reference to the Comprehensive Environmental Response, Compensation and Liability Act of 1980, which is the nation's principal law requiring the cleanup of hazardous waste and pollutants. Superfund requires polluted properties to be cleaned up by any and all prior owners, transporters, and users of the property; or that such prior users contribute cleanup costs to the Superfund, in which case the federal government will clear the property.

SURVEY: To determine the location, form, or boundaries of a tract of land by measuring the lines and angles in accordance with the principles of geometry and trigonometry.

SURFACE RIGHTS: The right to use and modify the surface area of a property.

SURVIVORSHIP: The status by which a joint tenant, or tenants, retain ownership rights to property following the death of another joint tenant, thereby protecting the surviving tenants from claims to the property by heirs of the deceased.

SYNDICATION: A grouping of individuals or corporations to carry out a business venture requiring capital investment, as with a real estate project.

TAKE-OUT LOAN: A permanent loan or mortgage given to finance a structure upon completion of certain improvements. Loan proceeds are used primarily to pay off the construction loan.

TAX BASE: The total value of property, income, and/or assets that are subject to taxation. In real estate, the assessed value of all taxable property, less exemptions.

TAX DEED: The deed to a property foreclosed on because of unpaid taxes.

TAX ESCALATOR: A provision in a lease whereby a tenant agrees to pay higher rent based on rising tax rates.

TAX LOSS CARRYOVER: The amount of tax loss allowed to be carried forward or backwards for a specific number of years. The loss can be taken as a deduction against other taxable income and is computed by deducting interest paid and depreciation taken from net operating income. To gain this tax advantage, the deductions must, of course, exceed net operating income.

TAX MAP: A map, typically on file in the local assessor's office, showing location, dimensions, and other attributes of property subject to taxation.

TAX SALE: A forced sale of real estate by local taxing authorities to cover delinquent taxes.

TENANCY BY THE ENTIRETY: The principle that husband and wife are legally regarded as one person on matters of real estate ownership. Both must consent to any disposition of the property, and the property passes to the survivor upon the death of either one.

TENANCY IN COMMON: Ownership of real property by two or more persons, each of whom has an undivided interest in the property, but none of whom has rights of survivorship.

TENANT FARMER: A person who farms another's land, usually for a share of the crops; also, an individual who rents land from another for the use of the land, with payment being made in cash, services, or crops.

TENDER: Specific performance under a contract; or an offer to perform an obligation combined with actual performance, or evidence of one's ability to perform the obligation.

TESTATE: Having made and left a legally valid will.

TESTATOR: A person who has made a will, especially one who has died leaving a valid will.

TIME VALUE OF MONEY: The concept that money in hand is worth more now than it will be worth in the future, assuming the gradual loss of the money's earning power.

TITLE: Evidence of ownership rights.

TITLE INSURANCE: A policy, issued by a title insurance company, that offers protection against financial loss due to defects in the title to real property which were unknown or undiscovered at the time of purchase.

TITLE SEARCH: A search through public records, laws, and court decisions to obtain the current facts about the title to specific real estate.

TOPOGRAPHIC MAP: A map showing the surface features of a region.

TRANSACTION COSTS: Costs associated with buying and selling real estate. Such costs include, but are not limited to, appraisal and recording fees, mortgage points, and sales commissions.

TREASURY BILL: A short-term obligation of the U.S. Treasury, usually maturing in 91 days, bearing no interest and sold periodically on the open market at a discount.

TRUST ACCOUNT: A segregated bank account in which a broker must deposit all funds collected from his or her clients.

TRUSTEE: A person or institution holding and administering property under a trust.

TRUSTOR: One who grants property to a trustee.

TURNKEY PROJECT: A development project produced, start to finish, by a single contractor, from initial land purchase to final construction. At completion of the project, keys to the buildings are turned over to the buyer.

UNDERLYING MORTGAGE: The first-mortgage portion of a wraparound mortgage, which provides additional loan funds for the purchase of property.

UNDERWRITER: One who assumes risk; an insurer. In real estate, an officer in a lending institution assigned to approve or deny a loan application based on the level of risk associated with the property and the borrower.

UNEARNED INCREMENT: An increase in the value of real estate due to influences beyond any effort of the owner. Increases in population or inflationary pressures could stir a rise in value.

UNENCUMBERED PROPERTY: Real estate with free and clear title.

UNIFORM SETTLEMENT STATEMENT: A document containing specified information pertaining to the settlement, or closing; required by the Real Estate Settlement Procedures Act for federally backed mortgages, such FHA and VA loans. The statement must be presented to both the buyer and the seller, and must be prepared by whomever presides at the closing.

UNILATERAL CONTRACT: An obligation pledged by one party contingent upon the performance of another party, without actually requiring the second party to perform.

UNRECORDED DEED: A document that transfers title from one party to another, as in a sale of real estate, without public notice of the transaction. *Note:* A properly recorded deed protects the buyer from the possibility of fraudulent transactions, such as a sale of the same property to another buyer, without the first buyer's knowledge.

USUFRUCTUARY RIGHTS: Rights to use another's property, or to access amenities located on another's property, such as a river, that is designated for public use.

VA LOAN: A home mortgage issued by a conventional lender, but the payment of which is substantially guaranteed by the U.S. Bureau of Veterans Affairs. Such loans, generally limited to military veterans, typically carry minimal down payments.

U.S. SOIL AND CONSERVATION SERVICE: An agency of the U.S. Department of Agriculture. Its main purpose is to assist farmers and ranchers in land use and to help prevent soil erosion and flood loss. Other functions include soil surveys, and the development of technical plans for individual farms, including the lending of specialized equipment to carry out conservation practices. The agency also assists ind advises local authorities charged with enforcing soil and erosion control legislation.

USURY: The act or practice of lending money at excessive or unlawfully high interest rates.

VALUABLE CONSIDERATION: Promised payment of goods and/or services in return for certain performance, or as an inducement to enter a contract. The promisor of such consideration is liable for claims.

VALUE IN USE: The worth of a property as it is currently used. Such value may differ from the property's market value.

VICARIOUS LIABILITY: The responsibility of one person for the actions of another.

VOLUNTARY LIEN: A lien placed on property with the owner's approval, or as a result of a consenting act by the owner.

WAREHOUSING: An activity largely used by mortgage bankers whereby mortgages or trust deed notes are held in inventory for future sale. To finance this inventory, the "warehouse" borrows short term and repays from the proceeds of periodic sales.

WARRANTY DEED: A deed to real estate in which the grantor gives his formal assurance that he is, in fact, the legal owner. He further guarantees that he will defend the title against all adverse claims.

WATER RIGHTS: Rights granted by a property owner to another for the use of a water facility not on the grantees's land. Such uses could include livestock watering, fishing, boating, and swimming privileges, or the actual piping of water from the grantor to the grantee.

WATER TABLE: The level below which the ground is saturated with water. Often a high water table can hamper building construction and can preclude the installation of a septic system. Drilled wells are also influenced by the water level in given areas.

WORKING CAPITAL: The difference between current assets and current liabilities.

WORKOUT: An agreement between a borrower and a lender to restructure a loan in order to avoid default or bankruptcy.

WRAPAROUND MORTGAGE OR TRUST DEED: A financing technique used when additional financing is obtained that overlaps any existing obligations. The new mortgage is junior to the prior loans and is secured by a debt that includes all loans combined. *Example:* The owner of a land development has existing loans totaling $1 million secured by all the remaining lots in his development. A lender advances him an additional $250,000 and takes a "wraparound" mortgage on the entire project. In the process, the lender assumes the responsibility of paying off the prior loans. The new mortgage is for $1,250,000.

YIELD: The percentage rate of return expected or earned on an investment.

ZONING ORDINANCE: See ORDINANCE.

ZONING VARIANCE: Official permission to bypass existing zoning laws, in many cases because strict enforcement would cause undue hardship on the applicant.

INDEX